D0899842

Selected Writings of
Edward Sapir

Selected Writings of
Edward Sapir
in Language, Culture and Personality

EDITED BY DAVID G. MANDELBAUM

1958

Berkeley and Los Angeles

UNIVERSITY OF CALIFORNIA PRESS

University of California Press
Berkeley and Los Angeles, California
Cambridge University Press
London, England
Copyright, 1949, by
The Regents of the University of California
Third Printing, 1958
Manufactured in the United States of America

408.1
Sab

42013
October, 1961

EDITOR'S INTRODUCTION

E DWARD SAPIR was one of those rare men among scientists and scholars who are spoken of by their colleagues in terms of genius. The papers selected for this volume give only part of the reason for that judgment, for there was an uncommon quality of the man himself which attracted and stimulated—inspired may not be too strong a word—many of those who knew him.

His talents were manifest in many fields, in none more brilliantly and effectively than in linguistics. He had a truly phenomenal knowledge of languages; linguists have commented that his command of the facts, of specific linguistic phenomena, was unsurpassed among linguistic scientists. Sapir began his linguistic studies in the field of Germanics while he was still an undergraduate. Early in his graduate work he undertook the recording and analysis of an American Indian language, Takelma, and throughout his professional career he carried on intensive work within the various families of American Indian languages. When a speaker of the West African language Jabo (Gweabo) was found working in a Chicago bowling alley, Sapir availed himself of the opportunity to extend his linguistic knowledge of the African field. In later years, his interests turned again to problems in the Indo-European group and he found time to continue work on languages of the Sinitic and Semitic stocks as well.

In all his work on these diverse tongues, Sapir showed a sure grasp of the basic form and the interlocking elements of the structure of each language. The Sanskrit scholar, Franklin Edgerton, has put it thus: "He seemed able to meet every one of us on our own grounds, to see the minutiae of many provinces as with a magnifying glass, and at the same time effortlessly to survey the whole terrain."[1] And his ability to view the whole scope of language extended beyond the sheerly formal aspects of speech. Formal linguistic descriptions and analyses were, for Sapir, only the beginning of the linguist's task. For he understood

---

[1] The references in this introduction, except where otherwise noted, are to obituary notices written by the following authors and listed in order of reference: Franklin Edgerton in *Year Book of the American Philosophical Society* (1939), pp. 460–464; Franz Boas in *International Journal of American Linguistics*, 10: 58–63; Morris Swadesh in *Language*, 15 (1940): 132–135; Ruth Benedict in *American Anthropologist*, 41 (1939): 465–477; Diamond Jenness in *Transactions of the Royal Society of Canada*, 33 (1939): 151–153; E. A. Hooton in *Proceedings of the American Academy of Arts and Sciences*, 74: 157–159; Leslie Spier in *Science*, 89 (1939): 237–238; Louis Hjelmslev in *Acta Linguistica*, 1 (1939), 76–77; Leslie Spier in *Man*, 39 (1939): 92–93.

linguistics as a social science, and every language as one aspect of a whole culture. In his writing and teaching he stressed the importance of dealing with the phenomena of language in the culture context, of studying speech in its social setting.

Sapir's field work among American Indian tribes was done primarily to collect data for linguistic study, but it also furnished material for papers which dealt with the tribal cultures. In ethnology as in linguistics, Sapir had a way of illuminating an array of factual data with felicitous theoretical insights. Some of his earlier writings in American Indian ethnology, particularly the *Time Perspective in Aboriginal American Culture*, have become classics in that they are read by most students professionally interested in anthropology.

As he developed his thinking concerning the processes of culture growth, Sapir came increasingly to deal with fundamental problems of culture theory. In a number of the papers written in his mature years, his insight into cultures generally is brought to bear on the problems of our culture. His examining of the outer facets and inner forces of contemporary life was accompanied by two developing interests: one had to do with semantics, particularly the semantics of English; the other, with the interplay between culture and personality. His writings in the latter field especially have had important influence.

The same sensitivity to nuances of language and custom, the same feeling for form which made Sapir so gifted a scholar, enabled him to write poetry. The extensive list of his published poems which appears at the end of this volume is but one indication of Sapir as an artist, for his aesthetic gifts shone through all his writing and his teaching. A linguist once remarked that, for him, Sapir's analysis of the Navaho word for corn was an artistic masterpiece. And in less recondite fields as well, Sapir's works have savored of aesthetic as well as intellectual accomplishments.

At one period, mainly during his years at Ottawa, he was a frequent contributor of musical and literary criticism to such journals as *The Dial*, *The Nation*, and *The Musical Quarterly*. An able pianist himself, and one who had tried his hand at musical composition, he was able to write about a work of music with an understanding which encompassed the variant meanings for composer, for performer, and for listener.

His literary criticism is marked by a rare depth and discernment. His acumen clove clean to the heart of a piece of writing, nor would he be distracted by new phrasings or unfamiliar trappings. Thus he was one of the first to herald the influence which the poetry of Gerald Manley Hopkins was to have. His critiques of scientific writing are no less keen, and are equally appreciative of fresh approaches. Sapir's reviews of some of the early psychoanalytic writings may still serve to sum up the anthropologist's appraisal of the Freudian concepts.

His own scientific contributions, in every field of his endeavor, are marked by a freshness and an originality that bespeak the intellectual vigor and intuition that he possessed. And he was capable of documenting his intuitive insights with a broad control of factual data. Not all were so documented, for the flashes of his vision sometimes extended beyond the frontiers of fully controlled data. Hence some of his writing is programmatic and pioneering rather than definitive. But always, even in his slighter papers, there is cognizance of basic form and fundamental meanings, and not infrequently a reader has felt that Sapir has opened whole new vistas of knowledge for him.

It may be too soon to assess the real impress of Sapir's work on the course of linguistics and anthropology, but a number of his fellow scholars have attested the influence of his ideas. Just two such comments may be cited. One is by his teacher, Franz Boas, who noted that the strictures of the phonetic method and the general adoption of phonemic principles in the study of primitive languages are largely due to him. And treating of another field, Clyde Kluckhohn says that the tough insights which Sapir drew from psychiatry not only forced a basic reconstruction of anthropological postulates but led to new types of specifically pointed field work.[2] Not a few of his colleagues and students are still following through the research leads which Sapir first indicated to them.

Sapir was born in Lauenburg, Germany, on January 26, 1884. When he was five years old his parents migrated to the United States, where his father, Jacob Sapir, carried on his profession of cantor. Edward Sapir's abilities found early recognition, for he won scholarships at Horace Mann School and then a four-year Pulitzer fellowship to Columbia College, where he was graduated in 1904. He went on to do gradute work at Columbia and took a Master's degree in Germanics. About this time he came to know Franz Boas and, as Morris Swadesh has written, came away from a conference with Boas impressed that he had everything to learn about language. For every generalization he had before believed was certain and exceptionless, Boas could summon indubitable contrary examples from American Indian languages he knew. Sapir was stirred by the prospect of studying living languages through the recording and analysis of the dialects of native speakers. Hence at the end of

[2] In *One Hundred Years of American Psychiatry*, J. K. Hall, gen. ed. (New York, 1944), p. 601.

his first year of graduate work he went to the state of Washington to study the language of the Wishram Indians. In the following year he journeyed to Oregon to work on the Takelma language, the grammar of which he presented as his doctoral dissertation. His first papers, published while he was in his early twenties, are no apprentice fumblings, but models of clarity and keen analysis.

For a year, 1907–1908, he was research associate in the Department of Anthropology at the University of California, and worked on the language of the Yana Indians. His stay in Berkeley remained a favorite memory, a period of concentrated achievement and pleasant associations. He then went to the University of Pennsylvania for two years, first as fellow and then as instructor. In 1909 he was awarded the Ph.D. by Columbia. The Museum of the University of Pennsylvania sponsored his field trips to the Ute Indians, and arranged to have a Paiute student, Tony Tillohash, from the Indian school at Carlisle, work with Sapir in Philadelphia as linguistic informant. Although the Paiute materials did not receive full publication until 1930, papers based on them appeared earlier and formed significant advances in the comparative American Indian linguistics.

In 1910 he went to Ottawa as chief of the newly created Division of Anthropology in the Geological Survey of the Canadian National Museum. In the same year he married Florence Delson, and his three children of this marriage, Michael, Helen, and Philip, were born in Ottawa. Sapir's fifteen years in Canada were somewhat dulled by isolation from the men of science and scholarship with whom he had most in common, but they did provide ample opportunity for field work with Indian tribes. It was during this period that he did his major work with the Nootka of Vancouver Island; he began his long study of the Athapascan languages with the Sarcee of Alberta; Tlingit, Kutchin, and Ingalik were some of the other languages of the Indians of Canada that he recorded. In addition to his intensive work with Canadian Indians, he found energy for several diverse projects. With the secretary of the Chinese legation in Ottawa he worked out a study of Chinese humor and folklore. He translated and transcribed many French-Canadian folk songs, some of which were published in a volume with the collaboration of Marius Barbeau. He gave a course on English literature before a local Ottawa society. Music and literature were his chief relaxation; the greater part of his poetry and musical studies was done during this period.

When a call to the University of Chicago came in 1925, he was glad to accept. His wife had died shortly before, after a long illness, and he had become restless in Ottawa. And the post at Chicago at last gave ample scope for the exercise of his talents. Ruth Benedict has written that the position at Chicago was one he was uniquely qualified to adorn. He attracted graduate students in linguistics whom he could train in the rigorous methods he had developed. And students in ethnology were drawn to him as well. His field work was continued with trips to the Hupa and Navaho. He was in great demand to speak to groups of all kinds outside the university. Within two years of his arrival he was promoted to the rank of Professor of Anthropology and General Linguistics. Honors and recognition came in quick succession, and it has been said that at this period Sapir was easily one of the most influential figures in American anthropology.

Sapir's six years at Chicago were happy ones. He married Jean McClenaghan in 1926 and their first son, Paul, was born there. Their second son, David, was born in New Haven, where Sapir had accepted a Sterling Professorship in Anthropology and Linguistics at Yale.

The call to Yale in 1931 was a most attractive one. The terms of the appointment were so favorable that Sapir was able at once to set up one of the great centers of anthropological and linguistic work in the country. In 1932–1933 he gathered a unique seminar of foreign students holding scholarships from the Rockefeller Foundation to study the impact of culture on personality.

His years at Yale were strenuous ones. Administrative duties and scientific responsibilities made demands on him while his adventurous mind was ranging ever farther into new fields and deeper into those with which he was long familiar. A series of heart attacks in 1937 and 1938 brought him under a doctor's regimen of quiet and a slower pace, but his intellectual enthusiasms would not be contained by the restraint which his physical condition demanded. He died of the ailment on February 4, 1939.

It is no difficult task to give the measure of the man in terms of his official honors. His position at Yale, the honorary Doctor of Science degree which Columbia University awarded him in 1929, his membership in the National Academy of Sciences, his election to the office of president of the American Anthropological Association and of the Linguistic Society of America—these and his other titles bear witness that high academic distinctions were bestowed on Edward Sapir.

It is more difficult to indicate what Sapir meant to those who knew him and were his students. Listening to him could be a lucid adventure in the field of ideas; one came forth exhilarated, more than oneself. Diamond Jenness, Sapir's successor at Ottawa, relates how he once saw Sapir enter a hall filled with tumultuous children, ". . . and with only three scraps of paper, one white, one yellow, one black, hold them spellbound for an hour while he discoursed, simply and clearly as only a great scholar can, on human races and their differences."

With his contemporaries, as Earnest Hooton has noted, he tended to be shy. But as soon as he felt the social atmosphere to be congenial he unfolded all his unusual personal charm and became a most brilliant and fascinating companion.

His students found in Sapir a sympathetic mentor and the kindliest of men. With him they could stand high and see the subjects of their study from the panoramic view and in an integrated, synthesizing manner. For their particular scientific problems, he was ever willing to give generously of his guidance. If one of us was able to present a striking new idea or fresh and valid evidence to revise an old concept, he was always ready, even eager, to take it up and carry it forward. He had no vested intellectual interests.

Sapir had a staunch belief in human rights which led him to resent oppression and discrimination wherever they occurred. His attitude was not only the observant and analytic one of the anthropologist whose training admits him to a place in the press box of the human arena; for, in his latter years especially, he felt that a place at the observation post does not exclude one from a share in the action on the field. He became increasingly interested in Jewish affairs, lending his support to the Yiddish Scientific Institute and participating in the program of the Conference for Jewish Relations.

In conversation he would occasionally tell how profoundly Judaism had affected his life. During childhood he had rebelled against it. The interminable regulations, the blinding restrictions of orthodoxy seemed unnecessary, intolerable. But as he grew older he came more and more to appreciate the grand plan that lay beneath the irksome details. Toward the end of his life he turned to the ethnological and linguistic study of the Talmud, and in it he found both the delight of the pursuit of scholarship and invigoration of spirit.

Only small bits of his extensive studies in Semitics were ever published. Indeed, the swift inclosing of his illness and death deprived science and scholarship of the results of a number of studies which he had carried far along. Among his papers there was left a large collection of notes on Tocharian, an Indo-European language once spoken in central Asia. Jenness notes that for many years Sapir had collected materials for a study which might indicate a possible relationship between ancient Sinitic forms and old forms of the American Indian languages which he grouped under the name Na-Dene. A magnificent collection of ethnological materials concerning the Nootka, Yana, and Hupa is mentioned by Leslie Spier. One of Sapir's major projects left uncompleted was a book which had been tentatively titled *The Psychology of Culture*, an outline for which had been submitted to his publisher. It is fortunate that some of Sapir's associates have worked with and published parts of his notes, as Harry Hoijer has done with the Navaho linguistic materials, Morris Swadesh with the Nootka texts, and Leslie Spier with the Yana ethnological observations. Still more are to be utilized for further publications.

For all the mass of unpublished studies which Sapir left, the list of his publications is no inconsiderable one. But it is, with a single exception, in the form of monographs and articles. His one general book, *Language*, was published in 1921, and Jenness tells that it was dictated in the space of two months from a few hastily jotted notes. In after years Sapir would comment that if he were to do it over, the book would contain new ideas and some of its concepts would be revised and presented in quite a different way. Such, in fact, was Sapir's attitude toward all his work. As his thinking developed, and new information or new principles required the revision of some of his earlier postulates, he saw no reason why his earlier efforts should not be modified to attune with advances in knowledge. Nonetheless the book remains a notable contribution to linguistic science. Thus the Danish linguist Louis Hjelmslev has written that, when he first read the work, it was to him a revelation and a confirmation of his own vague anticipations of establishing a comparative general linguistics that would supersede the previous kind of approach.

The present volume is intended to present, in accessible form, those of Sapir's writings which carry the gist of his thought. No passages from *Language* have been included since that book is more readily available than are most of the sources in which the journal articles originally appeared. The phonetic orthography of the linguistic papers has been reproduced as it appeared in the original version of each article. The editor is most grateful to the many colleagues and former students of Edward Sapir who were consulted and who aided in the selection of these papers, but the responsibility for the selection is the editor's alone. Special thanks are due to Mrs. Jean Sapir, who gave the editor full leeway in the preparation of this volume, and to Philip Sapir, who aided in many ways. The general bibliography was originally prepared by Leslie Spier, and the poetry bibliography was compiled by Philip Sapir; both have been slightly revised and brought up to date by Mrs. Mary Anne Whipple, who also has been most helpful in the preparation of the manuscript.

On the opening page of each article and excerpt included in this volume there is notation of the original publisher of the piece. All appear with the permission of the original publishers; our thanks are extended to these publishers for their permissions.

A few months before Sapir's death, plans were made by his students to present him a volume of studies written in his honor. Knowing that he was seriously ill, the group decided to tell him of the plans. He responded with characteristic modesty, disclaiming any right to special honor, but expressing his pleasure and the pride he felt in his students. The volume appeared in 1941 under the title of *Language, Culture, and Personality: Essays in Memory of Edward Sapir*, and was edited by Leslie Spier, A. Irving Hallowell, and Stanley S. Newman. Those essays are an indication of the continuing vitality of Sapir's influence. An eminent psychiatrist once remarked that Sapir was an intoxicating man. That he was. And the stimulus of his life and work will continue to enliven many of his students and associates for a long time to come.

Leslie Spier has aptly noted that no life can be long enough to accomplish the program Sapir set for himself, but we can only regret that his proved so brief. Yet for all the untimely end to his career, Edward Sapir made much of his times, his talents, his opportunities; so much, indeed, that many will subscribe to Earnest Hooton's characterization of Sapir as one whose rare fineness of personality and breadth and depth of understanding shed luster upon the very title "anthropologist."

DAVID G. MANDELBAUM

CONTENTS

PART TWO: CULTURE

The General View

American Indians

Literature and Music

PART THREE: THE INTERPLAY OF CULTURE AND PERSONALITY

Contents

BIBLIOGRAPHY

Part One
LANGUAGE

THE NATURE OF LANGUAGE

EDITOR'S PREFACE

T HE PAPER *which opens this section on the nature of language was written as an article for the* Encyclopedia of the Social Sciences. *Its scope encompasses the whole field of language, as did Sapir's earlier book* Language, *although the article is necessarily much more concise and tautly written. The basic contributions of the book, such as the concept of linguistic drift and the outline for a structural classification of languages, are included. But this article also deals with some of the ideas and interests which Sapir had developed in the twelve years between the publication of the book in 1921 and the appearance of the encyclopedia article in 1933. Thus there is use of the term "phoneme" in the discussion of speech sounds, there is consideration of the psychological aspects of language, and there is concern with the matter of an international language.*

Two papers which have contributed significantly to the development of the phonemic approach in linguistics follow next, "Sound Patterns in Language" (1925) and "The Psychological Reality of Phonemes" (1933). Both stress the importance of a configurational or field approach to understanding the elements of language, and underscore the fallacy of purely mechanistic or atomistic analyses of linguistic phenomena. The first paragraph of the former paper states that the author's purpose is "to indicate that the sounds and sound processes of speech cannot properly be understood in such simple, mechanical terms." And the same paper ends with the note that the discussion is an illustration of the necessity of "getting behind the sense data of any type of expression in order to grasp the intuitively felt and communicated forms which alone give significance to such expression."

The latter, and later, of these two papers similarly begins with the theme that no entity in human experience can be defined adequately as the mechanical sum or product of its physical properties. Sapir's demonstration in this paper utilizes examples from the phonemic systems of Southern Paiute, Sarcee, Nootka, and English. This article was first published in a French translation; the present version is from Sapir's original manuscript.

The next paper, "A Study in Phonetic Symbolism" (1929), also deals with the sounds of speech, but does so by means of experiment, and indicates the "tendency of symbolisms to constellate in accordance with an unconscious or intuitive logic which is not necessarily based on experience

[3]

with the stimuli in their normal, functional aspect." For all his rejection of conventional behaviorism, Sapir was able to use experimental methods to advantage. Although, in Sapir's published work, this is almost the sole example of his interest in this type of linguistic experiment, in his courses on the psychology of language he continued to utilize experimental techniques.

The more usual, historical, approach to the data of language is exemplified in the 1931 paper on the concept of phonetic law. Using case materials from Indo-European, Algonkian, and Athapascan, Sapir demonstrates the regularity of change within a language at a particular period of its development and the consistency and conservatism of these patterned regularities within the languages of a single stock. This phenomenon had long been noted and its operations formulated by the philologists, especially by those working with Indo-European languages. Sapir's noteworthy article, "Philology," published in 1926 in one of the supplementary volumes of the thirteenth edition of the Encyclopedia Britannica, is not included in the present collection, but may be referred to for an amplification of many of the points made in this article on phonetic law. Bloomfield and Sapir were among those who broadened the use of the concept by applying it to the languages of nonliterate peoples and deepened its implications by using it within a reference frame which includes all phases and functions of language.

The brief paper "Dialect" (1931) is also mainly in the historical vein. And, as in much of Sapir's work, the formal and historical considerations are related to the symbolic and social-psychological aspects of the problem.

The relations of language to other phases of human life are dealt with in the earliest paper included in this section, "Language and Environment" (1912). Many of the points made in it have now become part of the common parlance of anthropology and linguistics, e.g., the reflection of the interests of a culture in the vocabulary of its language, but it was here and in other of his papers that many of the observations now generally accepted were first made and documented. As Sapir said of an argument made by the eighteenth-century linguist Herder: "This to us is very axiomatic, but we should not forget that it was necessary for Herder to demonstrate it." The paper on Herder's Ursprung der Sprache, published in 1907 and one of the very first of Sapir's writings, contains yet another passage that is not inapplicable to Sapir himself, in which he makes note of the "great service Herder accomplished in merely shifting the point of view. That alone was of inestimable service."

The encyclopedia article "Communication" (1931) is one evidence of the manner in which Sapir contributed to a broadening of the perspective *of linguistics. It has to do principally with the relation between language and society, with the functions of speech as societal bond. The concluding sentence of this paper touches upon a problem to which Sapir devoted considerable attention for a time. He writes: "In the long run it seems almost unavoidable that the civilized world will adopt some one language of intercommunication, say English or Esperanto, which can be set aside for denotive purposes pure and simple."*

The criteria for an efficient and satisfactory international language are set forth in "The Function of an International Auxiliary Language" (1931). This paper received especially wide attention since it was reprinted as part of a booklet entitled International Communication: A Symposium on the Language Problem *(1931). To this article Professor C. K. Ogden wrote a rejoinder, "Debabelization: A Reply to Prof. Sapir,"* Psyche, *11 (1931): 16–25. Sapir's own view of partisan espousal of any particular international language form is indicated by the comment in his article that "intelligent men should not allow themselves to become international language doctrinaires. They should do all they can to keep the problem experimental, welcoming criticism at every point and trusting to the gradual emergence of a modern language that is a fit medium for the modern spirit."*

In order to provide the basic data necessary for a competent handling of the problems involved in an international language, Sapir conducted some research under the sponsorship of the International Auxiliary Language Association. Three papers appeared as a result of this work: Totality, *in 1930;* The Expression of the Ending-Point Relation in English, French, and German *(done in collaboration with Morris Swadesh and edited by Alice V. Morris), in 1932; and the paper included in this volume, "Grading," which was posthumously published in 1944. In his prefatory note to* Totality *Sapir noted that it was intended as the first installment of a general work on language which was to be entitled* Foundations of Language, Logical and Psychological: An Approach to the International Language Problem *and was to be done with William E. Collinson and Mrs. Alice V. Morris. Various circumstances intervened to halt the work not long after it was begun, so that the outline of the projected work as given in the prefatory note to* Totality *could be realized only in small part. The outline lists fifteen sections of the* Foundations of Language. *The monograph on the ending-point relation comes under the fourth section, "Fundamental Relational Notions and Their Linguistic Expression." The other two published papers relate to the seventh section, on "Quantity." This section is outlined in more detail than the others. "Grading" appears as the fourth of eight topics under the heading, "Notions*

Applied to Quantification," and "Totality" as the third of seven under the rubric "Types of Quantification."

Although Sapir was not able to carry forward this type of research himself in his later years, he continued to be most interested in the development of semantics. Thus his comment in "Grading" that "it seems best to offer this fragmentary contribution to semantics in the hope that others may be induced to explore the sadly neglected field of the congruities and noncongruities of logical and psychological meaning with linguistic form."

The paper next following, "The Grammarian and His Language" (1924), bears the marks of having been written for the first volume of the old American Mercury *under the editorship of H. L. Mencken. And though its style is quite different from that of "Grading," in which a difficult subject is treated in an austerely technical manner, it includes some cogent and important remarks concerning the relation of language to modes of thought. In the last paragraph Sapir tells something of the aesthetic rewards to be found in the technical pursuit of linguistics. "To a certain type of mind linguistics has also that profoundly serene and satisfying quality which inheres in mathematics and in music and which may be described as the creation out of simple elements of a self-contained universe of forms."*

The relations of linguistics to the other social sciences and the scientific responsibilities of the linguist are discussed in the final paper of this section, "The Status of Linguistics as a Science" (1929). It stresses the strategic importance of linguistics for the methodology of social science. It sounds a theme which pervaded Sapir's teaching, the importance of extending linguistic knowledge and research beyond any narrowly defined, parochial concern with formal pattern alone.

LANGUAGE*

THE GIFT of speech and a well ordered language are characteristic of every known group of human beings. No tribe has ever been found which is without language, and all statements to the contrary may be dismissed as mere folklore. There seems to be no warrant whatever for the statement which is sometimes made that there are certain people whose vocabulary is so limited that they cannot get on without the supplementary use of gesture so that intelligible communication between members of such a group becomes impossible in the dark. The truth of the matter is that language is an essentially perfect means of expression and communication among every known people. Of all aspects of culture, it is a fair guess that language was the first to receive a highly developed form and that its essential perfection is a prerequisite to the development of culture as a whole.

There are such general characteristics which apply to all languages, living or extinct, written or unwritten. In the first place, language is primarily a system of phonetic symbols for the expression of communicable thought and feeling. In other words, the symbols of language are differentiated products of the vocal behavior which is associated with the larynx of the higher mammals. As a mere matter of theory, it is conceivable that something like a linguistic structure could have been evolved out of gesture or other forms of bodily behavior. The fact that at an advanced stage in the history of the human race writing emerged in close imitation of the pattern of spoken language proved that language as a purely instrumental and logical device is not dependent on the use of articulate sound. Nevertheless, the actual history of man and a wealth of anthropological evidence indicate with overwhelming certainty that phonetic language takes precedence over all other kinds of communicative symbolism, all of which are, by comparison, either substitutive, like writing, or excessively supplementary, like the gesture accompanying speech. The speech apparatus which is used in the articulation of language is the same for all known peoples. It consists of the larynx, with its delicately adjustable glottal chords, the nose, the tongue, the hard and soft palate, the teeth, and the lips. While the original impulses leading to speech may be thought of as localized in the larynx, the finer phonetic articulations are chiefly due to the muscular activity of the tongue, an organ whose primary function has, of course, nothing whatever to do with sound production but which, in

* *Encyclopaedia of the Social Sciences* (New York, Macmillan, 1933), 9: 155–169.

actual speech behavior, is indispensable for the development of emotionally expressive sound into what we call language. It is so indispensable, in fact, that one of the most common terms for "language" or "speech" is "tongue." Language is thus not a simple biological function even as regards the simple matter of sound production, for primary laryngeal patterns of behavior have had to be completely overhauled by the interference of lingual, labial, and nasal modifications before a "speech organ" was ready for work. Perhaps it is because this "speech organ" is a diffused and secondary network of physiological activities which do not correspond to the primary functions of the organs involved that language has been enabled to free itself from direct bodily expressiveness.

Not only are all languages phonetic in character; they are also "phonemic." Between the articulation of the voice into the phonetic sequence, which is immediately audible as a mere sensation, and the complicated patterning of phonetic sequences into such symbolically significant entities as words, phrases, and sentences there is a very interesting process of phonetic selection and generalization which is easily overlooked but which is crucial for the development of the specifically symbolic aspect of language. Language is not merely articulated sound; its significant structure is dependent upon the unconscious selection of a fixed number of "phonetic stations" or sound units. These are in actual behavior individually modifiable; but the essential point is that through the unconscious selection of sounds as phonemes, definite psychological barriers are erected between various phonetic stations, so that speech ceases to be an expressive flow of sound and becomes a symbolic composition with limited materials or units. The analogy with musical theory seems quite fair. Even the most resplendent and dynamic symphony is built up of tangibly distinct musical entities or notes which, in the physical world, flow into each other in an indefinite continuum but which, in the world of aesthetic composition and appreciation, are definitely bounded off against each other, so that they may enter into an intricate mathematics of significant relationships. The phonemes of a language are, in principle, distinct systems peculiar to the given language, and its words must be made up, in unconscious theory if not always in actualized behavior, of these phonemes. Languages differ very widely in their phonemic structure. But whatever the details of these structures may be, the important fact remains that there is no known language which has not a perfectly definite phonemic system. The difference between a sound and a phoneme can be illustrated by a simple example in English. If the word "matter" is pronounced in a slovenly fashion as in the phrase "What's the matter?" the *t* sound, not being pronounced with the proper amount of energy required to bring out its physical characteristics, tends to slip into a *d*. Nevertheless, this phonetic *d* will not be felt as a functional *d* but as a variety of *t* of a particular type of expressiveness. Obviously the functional relation between the proper *t* sound of such a word as "matter" and its *d* variant is quite other than the relation of the *t* of such a word as "town" and the *d* of "down." In every known language it is possible to distinguish merely phonetic variations, whether expressive or not, from symbolically functional ones of a phonemic order.

In all known languages, phonemes are built up into distinct and arbitrary sequences which are at once recognized by speakers as meaningful symbols of reference. In English, for instance, the sequence *g* plus *o* in the word "go" is an unanalyzable unit and the meaning attaching to the symbol cannot be derived by relating to each other values which might be imputed to the *g* and to the *o* independently. In other words, while the mechanical functional units of language are phonemes, the true units of language as symbolism are conventional groupings of such phonemes. The size of these units and the laws of their mechanical structure vary widely in their different languages and their limiting conditions may be said to constitute the phonemic mechanics, or "phonology," of a particular language. But the fundamental theory of sound symbolism remains the same everywhere. The formal behavior of the irreducible symbol also varies within wide limits in the languages of the world. Such a unit may be either a complete word, as in the English example already given, or a significant element like the suffix *ness* of "goodness." Between the meaningful and unanalyzable word or word element and the integrated meaning of continuous discourse lies the whole complicated field of the formal procedures which are intuitively employed by the speakers of a language in order to build up aesthetically and functionally satisfying symbol sequences out of the theoretically isolable units. These procedures constitute grammar, which may be defined as the sum total of formal economies intuitively recognized by the speakers of a language. There seem to be no types of cultural patterns which vary more surprisingly and with a greater exuberance of detail than the morphologies of the known languages. In spite of endless differences of detail, however, it may justly be said that all grammars have the same degree of fixity. One language may be more complex or difficult grammatically than another, but there is no meaning whatever in the statement which is sometimes made that one language is more grammatical, or form bound, than another. Our rationalizations of the structure of our own language lead to a self-consciousness of speech and of academic discipline which are of course interesting psychological and social phenomena in themselves but have very little to do with the question of form in language.

Besides these general formal characteristics language has certain psychological qualities which make it peculiarly important for the student of social science. In the first place, language is felt to be a perfect symbolic system, in a perfectly homogeneous medium, for the handling of all references and meanings that a given culture is capable of, whether these be in the form of actual communications or in that of such ideal substitutes of communication as thinking. The content of every culture is expressible in its language and there are no linguistic materials whether as to content or form which are not felt to symbolize actual meanings, whatever may be the attitude of those who belong to other cultures. New cultural experiences frequently make it necessary to enlarge the resources of a language, but such enlargement is never an arbitrary addition to the materials and forms already present; it is merely a further application of principles already in use and in many cases little more than a metaphorical extension of old terms and meanings. It is highly important to realize that once the form of a language is established it can discover meanings for its speakers which are not simply traceable to the given quality of experience itself but must be explained to a large extent as the projection of potential meanings into the raw material of experience. If a man who has never seen more than a single elephant in the course of his life, nevertheless speaks without the slightest hesitation of ten elephants or a million elephants or a herd of elephants or of elephants walking two by two or three by three or of generations of elephants, it is obvious that language has the power to analyze experience into theoretically dissociable elements and to create that world of the potential intergrading with the actual which enables human beings to transcend the immediately given in their individual experiences and to join in a larger common understanding. This common understanding constitutes culture, which cannot be adequately defined by a description of those more colorful patterns of behavior in society which lie open to observation. Language is heuristic, not merely in the simple sense which this example suggests, but in the much more far-reaching sense that its forms predetermine for us certain modes of observation and interpretation. This means of course that as our scientific experience grows we must learn to fight the implications of language. "The grass waves in the wind" is shown by its linguistic form to be a member of the same relational class of experiences as "The man works in the house." As an interim solution of the problem of expressing the experience referred to in this sentence it is clear that the language has proved useful, for it has made significant use of certain symbols of conceptual relation, such as agency and location. If we feel the sentence to be poetic or metaphorical, it is largely because other more complex types of experience with their appropriate symbolisms of reference enable us to reinterpret the situation and to say, for instance, "The grass is waved by the wind" or "The wind causes the grass to wave." The point is that no matter how sophisticated our modes of interpretation become, we never really get beyond the projection and continuous transfer of relations suggested by the forms of our speech. After all, to say "Friction causes such and such a result" is not very different from saying "The grass waves in the wind." Language is at one and the same time helping and retarding us in our exploration of experience, and the details of these processes of help and hindrance are deposited in the subtler meanings of different cultures.

A further psychological characteristic of language is the fact that while it may be looked upon as a symbolic system which reports or refers to or otherwise substitutes for direct experience, it does not as a matter of actual behavior stand apart from or run parallel to direct experience but completely interpenetrates with it. This is indicated by the widespread feeling, particularly among primitive people, of that virtual identity or close correspondence of word and thing which leads to the magic of spells. On our own level it is generally difficult to make a complete divorce between objective reality and our linguistic symbols of reference to it; and things, qualities, and events are on the whole felt to be what they are called. For the normal person every experience, real or potential, is saturated with verbalism. This explains why so many lovers of nature, for instance, do not feel that they are truly in touch with it until they have mastered the names of a great many flowers and trees, as though the primary world of reality were a verbal one and as though one could not get close to nature unless one first mastered the terminology which somehow magically expresses it. It is this constant interplay between language and experience which removes language from the cold status of such purely and simply symbolic systems as mathematical symbolism or flag signaling. This interpenetration is not only an intimate associative fact; it is also a contextual one. It is important to realize that language may not only refer to experience or even mold, interpret, and discover experience, but that it also substitutes for it in the sense that in those sequences of interpersonal behavior which form the greater part of our daily lives speech and action supplement each other and do each other's work in a web of unbroken pattern. If one says to me "Lend me a dollar," I may hand over the money without a word or I may give it with an accompanying "Here it is" or I may say "I haven't got it" or "I'll give it to you tomorrow." Each of these responses is structurally equivalent, if one thinks of the larger behavior pattern. It is clear that if language is in its analyzed form a symbolic system of reference, it is far from being merely that if we consider the psychological part that it plays in continuous behavior. The reason for this almost unique position of intimacy which language holds among all known symbolisms is probably the fact that it is learned in the earliest years of childhood.

It is because it is learned early and piecemeal, in constant association with the color and the requirements of actual contexts, that language, in spite of its quasi-mathematical form, is rarely a purely referential organization. It tends to be so only in scientific discourse, and even there it may be seriously doubted whether the ideal of pure reference is ever attained by language. Ordinary speech is directly expressive and the purely formal pattern of sounds, words, grammatical forms, phrases and sentences are always to be thought of as compounded by intended or unintended symbolisms of expression, if they are to be understood fully from the standpoint of behavior. The choice of words in a particular context may convey the opposite of what they mean on the surface. The same external message is differently interpreted according to whether the speaker has this or that psychological status in his personal relations, or whether such primary expressions as those of affection or anger or fear may inform the spoken words with a significance which completely transcends their normal value. On the whole, however, there is no danger that the expressive character of language will be overlooked. It is too obvious a fact to call for much emphasis. What is often overlooked and is, as a matter of fact, not altogether easy to understand is that the quasi-mathematical patterns, as we have called them, of the grammarian's language, unreal as these are in a contextual sense, have, nevertheless, a tremendous intuitive vitality; and that these patterns, never divorced in experience from the expressive ones, are nevertheless easily separated from them by the normal individual. The fact that almost any word or phrase can be made to take on an infinite variety of meanings seems to indicate that in all language behavior there are intertwined, in enormously complex patterns, isolable patterns of two distinct orders. These may be roughly defined as patterns of reference and patterns of expression.

That language is a perfect symbolism of experience, that in the actual context of behavior it cannot be divorced from action and that it is the carrier of an infinitely nuanced expressiveness are universally valid psychological facts. There is a fourth general psychological peculiarity which applies more particularly to the languages of sophisticated peoples. This is the fact that the referential form systems which are actualized in language behavior do not need speech in its literal sense in order to preserve their substantial integrity. The history of writing is in essence the long attempt to develop an independent symbolism on the basis of graphic representation, followed by the slow and begrudging realization that spoken language is a more powerful symbolism than any graphic one can possibly be and that true progress in the art of writing lay in the virtual abandonment of the principle with which it originally started. Effective systems of writing, whether alphabetic or not, are more or less exact transfers of speech. The original language system may maintain itself in other and remoter transfers, one of the best examples of these being the Morse telegraph code. It is a very interesting fact that the principle of linguistic transfer is not entirely absent even among the unlettered peoples of the world. Some at least of the drum signal and horn signal systems of the West African natives are in principle transfers of the organizations of speech, often in minute phonetic detail.

Many attempts have been made to unravel the origin of language, but most of these are hardly more than exercises of the speculative imagination. Linguists as a whole have lost interest in the problem, and this for two reasons. In the first place, it has come to be realized that we have no truly primitive languages in a psychological sense, that modern researches in archaeology have indefinitely extended the time of man's cultural past and that it is therefore vain to go much beyond the perspective opened up by the study of actual languages. In the second place, our knowledge of psychology, particularly of the symbolic processes in general, is not felt to be sound enough or far-reaching enough to help materially with the problem of the emergence of speech. It is probable that the origin of language is not a problem that can be solved out of the resources of linguistics alone but that it is essentially a particular case of a much wider problem of the genesis of symbolic behavior and of the specialization of such behavior in the laryngeal region, which may be presumed to have had only expressive functions to begin with. Perhaps a close study of the behavior of very young children under controlled conditions may provide some valuable hints, but it seems dangerous to reason from such experiments to the behavior of pre-cultural man. It is more likely that the kinds of studies which are now in progress of the behavior of the higher apes will help to give us some idea of the genesis of speech.

The most popular earlier theories were the interjectional and onomatopoetic theories. The former derived speech from involuntary cries of an expressive nature, while the latter maintained that the words of actual language are conventionalized forms of imitation of the sounds of nature. Both of these theories suffer from two fatal defects. While it is true that both interjectional and onomatopoetic elements are found in most languages, they are always relatively unimportant and tend to contrast somewhat with the more normal materials of language. The very fact that they are constantly being formed anew seems to indicate that they belong rather to the directly expressive layer of speech which intercrosses with the main level of referential symbolism. The second difficulty is even more serious. The essential problem of the origin of speech is not to attempt to discover the kinds of vocal elements which constitute the historical nucleus of language. It is rather to point out how vocal articulations of any sort could become dissociated from their original expressive value. About all that can be said at present is that while speech as a finished organization is a distinctly human achievement, its roots probably lie in the power of the higher apes to solve specific problems by abstracting general forms or schemata from the details of given situations; that the habit of interpreting certain selected elements in a situation as signs of a desired total one gradually led in early man to a dim feeling for symbolism; and that, in the long run and for reasons which can hardly be guessed at, the elements of experience which were most often interpreted in a symbolic sense came to be the largely useless or supplementary vocal behavior that must have often attended significant action. According to this point of view language is not so much directly developed out of vocal expression as it is an actualization in terms of vocal expression of the tendency to master reality, not by direct and *ad hoc* handling of this element but by the reduction of experience to familiar form. Vocal expression is only superficially the same as language. The tendency to derive speech from emotional expression has not led to anything tangible in the way of scientific theory and the attempt must now be made to see in language the slowly evolved product of a peculiar technique or tendency which may be called the symbolic one, and to see the relatively meaningless or incomplete part as a sign of the whole. Language, then, is what it is essentially, not because of its admirable expressive power but in spite of it. Speech as behavior is a wonderfully complex blend of two pattern systems, the symbolic and the expressive, neither of which could have developed to its present perfection without the interference of the other.

It is difficult to see adequately the functions of language, because it is so deeply rooted in the whole of human behavior that it may be suspected that there is little in the functional side of our conscious behavior in which language does not play its part. The primary function of language is generally said to be communication. There can be no quarrel with this so long as it is distinctly understood that there may be effective communication without overt speech and that language is highly relevant to situations which are not obviously of a communicative sort. To say that thought, which is hardly possible in any sustained sense without the symbolic organization brought by language, is that form of communication in which the speaker and the person addressed are identified in one person is not far from begging the question. The autistic speech of children seems to show that the purely communicative aspect of language has been exaggerated. It is best to admit that language is primarily a vocal actualization of the tendency to see realities symbolically, that it is precisely this quality which renders it a fit instrument for communication and that it is in the actual give and take of social intercourse that it has been complicated and refined into the form in which it is known today. Besides the very general function which language fulfills in the spheres of thought, communication, and expression which are implicit in its very nature, there may be pointed out a number of special derivatives of these which are of particular interest to students of society.

Language is a great force of socialization, probably the greatest that exists. By this is meant not merely the obvious fact that significant social intercourse is hardly possible without language but that the mere fact of a common speech serves as a peculiarly potent symbol of the social solidarity of those who speak the language. The psychological significance of this goes far beyond the association of particular languages with nationalities, political entities, or smaller local groups. In between the recognized dialect or language as a whole and the individualized speech of a given individual lies a kind of linguistic unit which is not often discussed by the linguist but which is of the greatest importance to social psychology. This is the subform of a language which is current among a group of people who are held together by ties of common interest. Such a group may be a family, the undergraduates of a college, a labor union, the underworld in a large city, the members of a club, a group of four or five friends who hold together through life in spite of differences of professional interest, and untold thousands of other kinds of groups. Each of these tends to develop peculiarities of speech which have the symbolic function of somehow distinguishing the group from the larger group into which its members might be too completely absorbed. The complete absence of linguistic indices of such small groups is obscurely felt as a defect or sign of emotional poverty. Within the confines of a particular family, for instance, the name "Georgy," having once been mispronounced "Doody" in childhood, may take on the latter form forever after; and this unofficial pronunciation of a familiar name as applied to a particular person becomes a very important symbol indeed of the solidarity of a particular family and of the continuance of the sentiment that keeps its members together. A stranger cannot lightly take on the privilege of saying "Doody" if the members of the family feel that he is not entitled to go beyond the degree of familiarity symbolized by the use of "Georgy" or "George." Again, no one is entitled to say "trig" or "math" who has not gone through such familiar and painful experiences as a high school or undergraduate student. The use of such words at once declares the speaker a member of an unorganized but psychologically real group. A self-made mathematician has hardly the right to use the word "math" in referring to his own interests because the student overtones of the word do not properly apply to him. The extraordinary importance of minute linguistic differences for the symbolization of psychologically real as contrasted with politically or sociologically official groups is intuitively felt by most people. "He talks like us" is equivalent to saying "He is one of us."

There is another important sense in which language is a socializer beyond its literal use as a means of communication. This is in the establishment of rapport between the members of a physical group, such as a house party. It is not what is said that matters so much as that something is said. Particularly where cultural understandings of an intimate sort are somewhat lacking among the members of a physical group it is felt to be important that the lack be made good by a constant supply of small talk. This caressing or reassuring quality of speech in general, even where no one has anything of moment to communicate, reminds us how much more language is than a mere technique of communication. Nothing better shows how completely the life of man as an animal made over by culture is dominated by the verbal substitutes for the physical world.

The use of language in cultural accumulation and historical transmission is obvious and important. This applies not only to sophisticated levels but to primitive ones as well. A great deal of the cultural stock in trade of a primitive society is presented in a more or less well defined linguistic form. Proverbs, medicine formulae, standardized prayers, folk tales, standardized speeches, song texts, genealogies are some of the more overt forms which language takes as a culture-preserving instrument. The pragmatic ideal of education, which aims to reduce the influence of standardized lore to a minimum and to get the individual to educate himself through as direct a contact as possible with the realities of his environment, is certainly not realized among the primitives, who are often as word-bound as the humanistic tradition itself. Few cultures perhaps have gone to the length of the classical Chinese culture or of the rabbinical Jewish culture in making the word do duty for the thing or the personal experience as the ultimate unit of reality. Modern civilization as a whole, with its schools, its libraries, and its endless stores of knowledge, opinion, and sentiment stored up in verbalized form, would be unthinkable without language made eternal as document. On the whole, we probably tend to exaggerate the differences between "high" and "low" cultures or saturated and emergent cultures in the matter of traditionally conserved verbal authority. The enormous differences that seem to exist are rather differences in the outward form and content of the cultures themselves than in the psychological relation which obtains between the individual and his culture.

In spite of the fact that language acts as a socializing and uniformizing force, it is at the same time the most potent single known factor for the growth of individuality. The fundamental quality of one's voice, the phonetic patterns of speech, the speed and relative smoothness of articulation, the length and build of the sentences, the character and range of the vocabulary, the scholastic consistency of the words used, the readiness with which words respond to the requirements of the social environment, in particular the suitability of one's language to the language habits of the persons addressed—all these are so many complex indicators of the personality. "Actions speak louder than words" may be an excellent maxim from the pragmatic point of view but betrays little insight into the nature of speech. The language habits of people are by no means irrelevant as unconscious indicators of the more important traits of their personalities, and the folk is psychologically wiser than the adage in paying a great deal of attention, willingly or not, to the psychological significance of a man's language. The normal person is never convinced by the mere content of speech but is very sensitive to many of the implications of language behavior, however feebly (if at all) these may have been consciously analyzed.

All in all, it is not too much to say that one of the really important functions of language is to be constantly declaring to society the psychological place held by all of its members.

Besides this more general type of personality expression or fulfillment there is to be kept in mind the important role which language plays as a substitutive means of expression for those individuals who have a greater than normal difficulty in adjusting to the environment in terms of primary action patterns. Even in the most primitive cultures the strategic word is likely to be more powerful than the direct blow. It is unwise to speak too blithely of "mere" words, for to do so may be to imperil the value and perhaps the very existence of civilization and personality.

The languages of the world may be classified either structurally or genetically. An adequate structural analysis is an intricate matter and no classification seems to have been suggested which does justice to the bewildering variety of known forms. It is useful to recognize three distinct criteria of classification: the relative degree of synthesis or elaboration of the words of the language; the degree to which the various parts of a word are welded together; and the extent to which the fundamental relational concepts of the language are directly expressed as such. As regards synthesis, languages range all the way from the isolating type, in which the single word is essentially unanalyzable, to the type represented by many American Indian languages in which the single word is functionally often the equivalent of a sentence with many concrete references that would, in most languages, require the use of a number of words. Four stages of synthesis may be conveniently recognized: the isolating type, the weakly synthetic type, the fully synthetic type, and the polysynthetic type. The classical example of the first type is Chinese, which does not allow the words of the language to be modified by internal changes or the addition of prefixed or suffixed elements to express such concepts as those of number, tense, mode, case relation, and the like. This seems to be one of the more uncommon types of language and is best represented by a number of languages in eastern Asia. Besides Chinese itself, Siamese, Burmese, modern Tibetan, Annamite, and Khmer, or Cambodian, may be given as examples. The older view, which regarded such languages as representing a peculiarly primitive stage in the evolution of language, may now be dismissed as antiquated. All evidence points to the contrary hypothesis that such languages are the logically extreme analytic developments of more synthetic languages which because of processes of phonetic disintegration have had to reëxpress by analytical means combinations of ideas originally expressed within the framework of the single word. The weakly synthetic type of language is best represented by the most familiar modern languages of Europe, such as English, French, Spanish, Italian, German, Dutch, and Danish. Such languages modify words to some extent but have only a moderate formal elaboration of the word. The plural formations of English and French, for instance, are relatively simple and the tense and modal systems of all the languages of this type tend to use analytic methods as supplementary to the older synthetic one. The third group of languages is represented by such languages as Arabic and the earlier Indo-European languages, like Sanskrit, Latin, and Greek. These are all languages of great formal complexity, in which classificatory ideas, such as sex gender, number, case relations, tense, and mood, are expressed with considerable nicety and in a great variety of ways. Because of the rich formal implications of the single word the sentence tends not to be so highly energized and ordered as in the first mentioned types. Lastly, the polysynthetic languages add to the formal complexity of the treatment of fundamental relational ideas the power to arrange a number of logically distinct, concrete ideas into an ordered whole within the confines of a single word. Eskimo and Algonquin are classical examples of this type.

From the standpoint of the mechanical cohesiveness with which the elements of words are united languages may be conveniently grouped into four types. The first of these, in which there is no such process of combination, is the isolating type already referred to. To the second group of languages belong all those in which the word can be adequately analyzed into a mechanical sum of elements, each of which has its more or less clearly established meaning and each of which is regularly used in all other words into which the associated notion enters. These are the so-called agglutinative languages. The majority of languages seem to use the agglutinative technique, which has the great advantage of combining logical analysis with economy of means. The Altaic languages, of which Turkish is a good example, and the Bantu languages of Africa are agglutinative in form.

In the third type, the so-called inflective languages, the degree of union between the radical element or stem of the word and the modifying prefixes or suffixes is greater than in the agglutinative languages, so that it becomes difficult in many cases to isolate the stem and set it off against the accreted elements. More important than this, however, is the fact that there is more or less of a one-to-one correspondence between the linguistic element and the notion referred to than in the agglutinative languages. In Latin, for instance, the notion of plurality is expressed in a great variety of ways which seem to have little phonetic connection with each other. For example, the final vowel or diphthong of *equi* (horses), *dona* (gifts), *mensae* (tables), and the final vowel and consonant of *hostes* (enemies) are functionally equivalent elements the distribution of which is dependent on purely formal and historical factors which have no logical relevance. Furthermore in the verb the notion of plurality is quite differently expressed, as in the last two consonants of *amant* (they love). It used to be fashionable to contrast in a favorable sense the "chemical" qualities of such inflective languages as Latin and Greek with the soberly mechanical quality of such languages as Turkish. But these evaluations may now be dismissed as antiquated and subjective. They were obviously due to the fact that scholars who wrote in English, French, and German were not above rationalizing the linguistic structures with which they were most familiar into a position of ideal advantage.

As an offshoot of the inflective languages may be considered a fourth group, those in which the processes of welding, due to the operation of complex phonetic laws, have gone so far as to result in the creation of patterns of internal change of the nuclear elements of speech. Such familiar English examples as the words "sing," "sang," "sung," "song" will serve to give some idea of the nature of these structures, which may be termed "symbolistic." The kinds of internal change which may be recognized are changes in vocalic quality, changes in consonants, changes in quantity, various types of reduplication or repetition, changes in stress accent, and, as in Chinese and many African languages, changes in pitch. The classical example of this type of language is Arabic, in which, as in the other Semitic languages, nuclear meanings are expressed by sequences or consonants, which have, however, to be connected by significant vowels whose sequence patterns establish fixed functions independent of the meanings conveyed by the consonantal framework.

Elaboration and technique of word analysis are perhaps of less logical and psychological significance than the selection and treatment of fundamental relational concepts for grammatical treatment. It would be very difficult, however, to devise a satisfactory conceptual classification of languages because of the extraordinary diversity of the concepts and classifications of ideas which are illustrated in linguistic form. In the Indo-European and Semitic languages, for instance, noun classification on the basis of gender is a vital principle of structure; but in most of the other languages of the world this principle is absent, although other methods of noun classification are found. Again, tense or case relations may be formally important in one language, for example, Latin, but of relatively little grammatical importance in another, although the logical references implied by such forms must naturally somehow be taken care of in the economy of the language as, for instance, by the use of specific words within the framework of the sentence. Perhaps the most fundamental conceptual basis of classification is that of the expression of fundamental syntactic relations as such versus their expression in necessary combination with notions of a concrete order. In Latin, for example, the notion of the subject of a predicate is never purely expressed in a formal sense, because there is no distinctive symbol for this relation. It is impossible to render it without at the same time defining the number and gender of the subject of the sentence. There are languages, however, in which syntactic relations are expressed purely, without admixture of implications of a nonrelational sort. We may speak therefore of pure relational languages as contrasted with mixed relational languages. Most of the languages with which we are familiar belong to the latter category. It goes without saying that such a conceptual classification has no direct relation to the other two types of classification which we have mentioned.

The genetic classification of languages is one which attempts to arrange the languages of the world in groups and subgroups in accordance with the main lines of historical connection, which can be worked out either on the basis of documentary evidence or of a careful comparison of the languages studied. Because of the far-reaching effect of slow phonetic changes and of other causes languages which were originally nothing but dialects of the same form of speech have diverged so widely that it is not apparent that they are but specialized developments of a single prototype. An enormous amount of work has been done in the genetic classification and subclassification of the languages of the world, but very many problems still await research and solution. At the present time it is known definitely that there are certain very large linguistic groups, or families, as they are often called, the members of which may, roughly speaking, be looked upon as lineally descended from languages which can be theoretically reconstructed in their main phonetic and structural outlines. It is obvious, however, that languages may so diverge as to leave little trace of their original relationship. It is therefore very dangerous to assume that languages are not, at last analysis, divergent members of a single genetic group merely because the evidence is negative. The only contrast that is legitimate is between languages known to be historically related and languages not known to be so related. Languages known to be related cannot be legitimately contrasted with languages known not to be related.

Because of the fact that languages have differentiated at different rates and because of the important effects of cultural diffusion, which have brought it about that strategically placed languages, such as Arabic, Latin, and English, have spread over large parts of the earth at the expense of others, very varied conditions are found to prevail in regard to the distribution of linguistic families. In Europe, for instance, there are only two linguistic families of importance represented today, the Indo-European languages and the Ugro-Finnic languages, of which Finnish and Hungarian are examples. The Basque dialects of southern France and northern Spain are the survivors of another and apparently isolated group. On the other hand, in aboriginal America the linguistic differentiation is extreme and a surprisingly large number of essentially unrelated linguistic families must be recognized. Some of the families occupy very small areas, while others, such as the Algonquin and the Athabaskan languages of North America, are spread over a large territory. The technique of establishing linguistic families and of working out the precise relationship of the languages included in these families is too difficult to be gone into here. It suffices to say that random word comparisons are of little importance. Experience shows that very precise phonetic relations can be worked out between the languages of a group and that, on the whole, fundamental morphological features tend to preserve themselves over exceedingly long periods of time. Thus modern Lithuanian is in structure, vocabulary and, to a large extent, even phonemic pattern very much the kind of a language which must be assumed as the prototype for the Indo-European languages as a whole.

In spite of the fact that structural classifications are, in theory, unrelated to genetic ones and in spite of the fact that languages can be shown to have influenced each other, not only in phonetics and vocabulary but also to an appreciable extent in structure, it is not often found that the languages of a genetic group exhibit utterly irreconcilable structures. Thus even English, which is one of the least conservative of Indo-European languages, has many far-reaching points of structure in common with as remote a language as Sanskrit in contrast, say, to Basque or Finnish. Again, different as are Assyrian, modern Arabic, and the Semitic languages of Abyssinia, they exhibit numerous points of resemblance in phonetics, vocabulary, and structure which set them off at once from, say, Turkish or the Negro languages of the Nile headwaters.

The complete rationale of linguistic change, involving as it does many of the most complex processes of psychology and sociology, has not yet been satisfactorily worked out, but there are a number of general processes that emerge with sufficient clarity. For practical purposes, inherent changes may be distinguished from changes due to contact with other linguistic communities. There can be no hard line of division between these two groups of changes because every individual's language is a distinct psychological entity in itself, so that all inherent changes are likely, at last analysis, to be peculiarly remote or subtle forms of change due to contact. The distinction, however, has great practical value, all the more so as there is a tendency among anthropologists and sociologists to operate far too hastily with wholesale linguistic changes due to external ethnic and cultural influences. The enormous amount of study that has been lavished on the history of particular languages and groups of languages shows very clearly that the most powerful differentiating factors are not outside influences, as ordinarily understood, but rather the very slow but powerful unconscious changes in certain directions which seem to be implicit in the phonemic systems and morphologies of the languages themselves. These "drifts" are powerfully conditioned by unconscious formal feelings and are made necessary by the inability of human beings to actualize ideal patterns in a permanently set fashion.

Linguistic changes may be analyzed into phonetic changes, changes in form, and changes in vocabulary. Of these the phonetic changes seem to be the most important and the most removed from direct observation. The factors which lead to these phonetic changes are probably exceedingly complex and no doubt include the operation of obscure symbolisms which define the relation of various age groups to each other. Not all phonetic changes, however, can be explained in terms of social symbolism. It seems that many of them are due to the operation of unconscious economies in actualizing sounds or combinations of sounds. The most impressive thing about internal phonetic change is its high degree of regularity. It is this regularity, whatever its ultimate cause, that is more responsible than any other single factor for the enviable degree of exactness which linguistics has attained as a historical discipline. Changes in grammatical form often follow in the wake of destructive phonetic changes. In many cases it can be seen how irregularities produced by the disintegrating effect of phonetic change are ironed out by the analogical spread of more regular forms. The cumulative effect of these corrective changes is quite sensibly to modify the structure of the language in many details and sometimes even in its fundamental features. Changes in vocabulary are due to a great variety of causes, most of which are of a cultural rather than of a strictly linguistic nature. The too frequent use of a word, for instance, may reduce it to a commonplace term, so that it needs to be replaced by a new word. On the other hand, changes of attitude may make certain words with their traditional overtones of meaning unacceptable to the younger generation, so that they tend to become obsolete. Probably the most important single source of changes in vocabulary is the creation of new words on analogies which have spread from a few specific words.

Of the linguistic changes due to the more obvious types of contact the one which seems to have played the most important part in the history of language is the "borrowing" of words across linguistic frontiers. This borrowing naturally goes hand in hand with cultural diffusion. An analysis of the provenience of the words of a given language is frequently an important index of the direction of cultural influence. Our English vocabulary, for instance, is very richly stratified in a cultural sense. The various layers of early Latin, mediaeval French, humanistic Latin and Greek, and modern French borrowings constitute a fairly accurate gauge of the time, extent, and nature of the various foreign cultural influences which have helped to mold the English civilization. The notable lack of German loan words in English until a very recent period, as contrasted with the large number of Italian words which were adopted at the time of the Renaissance and later, is again a historically significant fact. By the diffusion of culturally important words, such as those referring to art, literature, the church, military affairs, sport, and business, important transnational vocabularies have grown up which do something to combat the isolating effect of the large number of languages which are still spoken in the modern world. Such borrowings have taken place in all directions, but the number of truly important source languages is surprisingly small. Among the more important of them are Chinese, which has saturated the vocabularies of Korean, Japanese, and Annamite; Sanskrit, whose influence on the cultural vocabulary of central Asia, India, and Indo-China, has been enormous; Arabic, Greek, Latin, and French. English, Spanish, and Italian have also been of great importance as agencies of cultural transmission, but their influence seems less far-reaching than that of the languages mentioned above. The cultural influence of a language is not always in direct proportion to its intrinsic literary interest or to the cultural place which its speakers have held in the history of the world. For example, while Hebrew is the carrier of a peculiarly significant culture, actually it has not had as important an influence on other languages of Asia as Aramaic, a sister language of the Semitic stock.

The phonetic influence exerted by a foreign language may be very considerable, and there is a great deal of evidence to show that dialectic peculiarities have often originated as a result of the unconscious transfer of phonetic habits from the language in which one was brought up to that which has been adopted later in life. Apart, however, from such complete changes in speech is the remarkable fact that distinctive phonetic features tend to be distributed over wide areas regardless of the vocabularies and structures of the languages involved. One of the most striking examples of this type of distribution is found among the Indian languages of the Pacific coast of California, Oregon, Washington, British Columbia, and southern Alaska. Here are a large number of absolutely distinct languages belonging to a number of genetically unrelated stocks, so far as we are able to tell, which nevertheless have many important and distinctive phonetic features in common. An analogous fact is the distribution of certain peculiar phonetic features in both the Slavic languages and the Ugro-Finnic languages, which are unrelated to them. Such processes of phonetic diffusion must be due to the influence exerted by bilingual speakers, who act as unconscious agents for the spread of phonetic habits over wide areas. Primitive man is not isolated, and bilingualism is probably as important a factor in the contact of primitive groups as it is on more sophisticated levels.

Opinions differ as to the importance of the purely morphological influence exerted by one language on another in contrast with the more external type of phonetic and lexical influence. Undoubtedly such influences must be taken into account, but so far they have not been shown to operate on any great scale. In spite of the centuries of contact, for instance, between Semitic and Indo-European languages we know of no language which is definitely a blend of the structures of these two stocks. Similarly, while Japanese is flooded with Chinese loan words, there seems to be no structural influence of Chinese on Japanese.

A type of influence which is neither exactly one of vocabulary nor of linguistic form, in the ordinary sense of the word, and to which insufficient attention has so far been called, is that of meaning pattern. It is a remarkable fact of modern European culture, for instance, that while the actual terms used for certain ideas may vary enormously from language to language, the range of significance of these equivalent terms tends to be very similar, so that to a large extent the vocabulary of one language tends to be a psychological and cultural translation of the vocabulary of another. A simple example of this sort would be the translation of such terms as "Your Excellency" to equivalent but etymologically unrelated terms in Russian. Another instance of this kind would be the interesting parallelism in nomenclature between the kinship terms of affinity in English, French, and German. Such terms as "mother-in-law," "belle-mère," and "Schwiegermutter" are not, strictly speaking, equivalent either as to etymology or literal meaning but they are patterned in exactly the same manner. Thus "mother-in-law" and "father-in-law" are parallel in nomenclature to "belle-mère" and "beau-père" and to "Schwiegermutter" and "Schwiegervater." These terms clearly illustrate the diffusion of a lexical pattern which in turn probably expresses a growing feeling of the sentimental equivalent of blood relatives and relatives by marriage.

The importance of language as a whole for the definition, expression, and transmission of culture is undoubted. The relevance of linguistic details, in both content and form, for the profounder understanding of culture is also clear. It does not follow, however, that there is a simple correspondence between the form of a language and the form of the culture of those who speak it. The tendency to see linguistic categories as directly expressive of overt cultural outlines, which seems to have come into fashion among certain sociologists and anthropologists, should be resisted as in no way warranted by the actual facts. There is no general correlation between cultural type and linguistic structure. So far as can be seen, isolating or agglutinative or inflective types of speech are possible on any level of civilization. Nor does the presence or absence of grammatical gender, for example, seem to have any relevance for our understanding of the social organization or religion or folklore of the associated peoples. If there were any such parallelism as has sometimes been maintained, it would be quite impossible to understand the rapidity with which culture diffuses in spite of profound linguistic differences between the borrowing and giving communities.

The cultural significance of linguistic form, in other words, lies on a much more submerged level than on the overt one of definite cultural pattern. It is only very rarely, as a matter of fact, that it can be pointed out how a cultural trait has had some influence on the fundamental structure of a language. To a certain extent this lack of correspondence may be due to the fact that linguistic changes do not proceed at the same rate as most cultural changes, which are on the whole far more rapid. Short of yielding to another language which takes its place, linguistic organization, largely because it is unconscious, tends to maintain itself indefinitely and does not allow its fundamental formal categories to be seriously influenced by changing cultural needs. If the forms of culture and language were, then, in complete correspondence with each other, the nature of the processes making for linguistic and cultural changes respectively would soon bring about a lack of necessary correspondence. This is exactly what is found as a mere matter of descriptive fact. Logically it is indefensible that the masculine, feminine, and neuter genders of German and Russian should be allowed to continue their sway in the modern world; but any intellectualist attempt to weed out these unnecessary genders would obviously be fruitless, for the normal speaker does not actually feel the clash which the logician requires.

It is another matter when we pass from general form to the detailed content of a language. Vocabulary is a very sensitive index of the culture of a people and changes of the meaning, loss of old words, the creation and borrowing of new ones are all dependent on the history of culture itself. Languages differ widely in the nature of their vocabularies. Distinctions which seem inevitable to us may be utterly ignored in languages which reflect an entirely different type of culture, while these in turn insist on distinctions which are all but unintelligible to us.

Such differences of vocabulary go far beyond the names of cultural objects such as arrow point, coat of armor, or gunboat. They apply just as well to the mental world. It would be difficult in some languages, for instance, to express the distinction which we feel between "to kill" and "to murder," for the simple reason that the underlying legal philosophy which determines our use of these words does not seem natural to all societies. Abstract terms, which are so necessary to our thinking, may be infrequent in a language whose speakers formulate their behavior on more pragmatic lines. On the other hand, the question of presence or absence of abstract nouns may be bound up with the fundamental form of the language; and there exist a large number of primitive languages whose structure allows of the very ready creation and use of abstract nouns of quality or action.

There are many language patterns of a special sort which are of interest to the social scientist. One of these is the tendency to create tabus for certain words or names. A very widespread custom, for instance, among primitive peoples is the tabu which is placed not only on the use of the name of a person recently deceased but of any word that is etymologically connected in the feeling of the speakers with such a name. This means that ideas have often to be expressed by circumlocutions, or that terms must be borrowed from neighboring dialects. Sometimes certain names or words are too holy to be pronounced except under very special conditions, and curious patterns of behavior develop which are designed to prevent one from making use of such interdicted terms. An example of this is the Jewish custom of pronouncing the Hebrew name for God, not as Yahwe or Jehovah but as Adonai, "My Lord." Such customs seem strange to us but equally strange to many primitive communities would be our extraordinary reluctance to pronounce obscene words under normal social conditions.

Another class of special linguistic phenomena is the use of esoteric language devices, such as passwords or technical terminologies for ceremonial attitudes or practices. Among the Eskimo, for instance, the medicine man has a peculiar vocabulary which is not understood by those who are not members of his guild. Special dialectic forms or otherwise peculiar linguistic patterns are common among primitive peoples for the texts of songs. Sometimes, as in Melanesia, such song texts are due to the influence of neighboring dialects. This is strangely analogous to the practice among ourselves of singing songs in Italian, French, or German rather than in English, and it is likely that the historical processes which have led to the parallel custom are of a similar nature. Thieves' jargon and secret languages of children may also be mentioned. These lead over into special sign and gesture languages, many of which are based directly on spoken or written speech; they seem to exist on many levels of culture. The sign language of the Plains Indians of North America arose in response to the need for some medium of communication between tribes speaking mutually unintelligible languages. Within the Christian church we may note the elaboration of gesture languages by orders of monks vowed to silence.

Not only a language or a terminology but the mere external form in which it is written may become important as a symbol of sentimental or social distinction. Thus Croatian and Serbian are essentially the same language but they are presented in very different outward forms, the former being written in Latin characters, the latter in the Cyrillic character of the Greek Orthodox church. This external difference, associated with a difference in religion, has of course the important function of preventing people who speak closely related languages or dialects but who wish for reasons of sentiment not to confound themselves in a larger unity from becoming too keenly aware of how much they actually resemble each other.

The relation of language to nationalism and internationalism presents a number of interesting sociological problems. Anthropology makes a rigid distinction between ethnic units based on race, on culture, and on language. It points out that these do not need to coincide in the least—that they do not, as a matter of fact, often coincide in reality. But with the increased emphasis on nationalism in modern times, the question of the symbolic meaning of race and language has taken on a new significance and, whatever the scientist may say, the layman is ever inclined to see culture, language, and race as but different facets of a single social unity which he tends in turn to identify with such political entities as England or France or Germany. To point out, as the anthropologist easily can, that cultural distributions and nationalities override language and race groups, does not end the matter for the sociologist, because he feels that the concept of nation or nationality must be integrally imaged in behavior by the nonanalytical person as carrying with it the connotation, real or supposed, of both race and language. From this standpoint it really makes little difference whether history and anthropology support the popular identification of nationality, language, and race. The important thing to hold on to is that a particular language tends to become the fitting expression of a self-conscious nationality and that such a group will construct for itself, in spite of all that the physical anthropologist can do, a race to which is to be attributed the mystic power of creating a language and a culture as twin expressions of its psychic peculiarities.

So far as language and race are concerned, it is true that the major races of man have tended in the past to be set off against each other by important differences of language. There is less point to this, however, than might be imagined, because the linguistic differentiations within any given race are just as far-reaching as those which can be pointed out across racial lines, yet they do not at all correspond to subracial units. Even the major races are not always clearly sundered by language. This is notably the case with the Malayo-Polynesian languages, which are spoken by peoples as racially distinct as the Malays, the Polynesians, and the Negroes of Melanesia. Not one of the great languages of modern man follows racial lines. French, for example, is spoken by a highly mixed population which is largely Nordic in the north, Alpine in the center, and Mediterranean in the south, each of these subraces being liberally represented in the rest of Europe.

While language differences have always been important symbols of cultural difference, it is only in comparatively recent times, with the exaggerated development of the ideal of the sovereign nation and with the resulting eagerness to discover linguistic symbols for this ideal of sovereignty, that language differences have taken on an implication of antagonism. In ancient Rome and all through mediaeval Europe there were plenty of cultural differences running side by side with linguistic ones, and the political status of Roman citizen or the fact of adherence to the Roman Catholic church was of vastly greater significance as a symbol of the individual's place in the world than the language or dialect he happened to speak. It is probably altogether incorrect to maintain that language differences are responsible for national antagonisms. It would seem to be much more reasonable to suppose that a political and national unit, once definitely formed, uses a prevailing language as a symbol of its identity, whence gradually emerges the peculiarly modern feeling that every language should properly be the expression of a distinctive nationality.

In earlier times there seems to have been little systematic attempt to impose the language of a conquering people on the subject people, although it happened frequently as a result of the processes implicit in the spread of culture that such a conqueror's language was gradually taken over by the dispossessed population. Witness the spread of the Romance languages and of the modern Arabic dialects. On the other hand, it seems to have happened about as frequently that the conquering group was culturally and linguistically absorbed and that their own language disappeared without necessary danger to their privileged status. Thus foreign dynasties in China have always submitted to the superior culture of the Chinese and have taken on their language. In the same way the Moslem Moguls of India, while true to their religion, made one of the Hindu vernaculars the basis of the great literary language of Moslem India, Hindustani. Definitely repressive attitudes toward the languages and dialects of subject peoples seem to be distinctive only of European political policy in comparatively recent times. The attempt of czarist Russia to stamp out Polish by forbidding its teaching in the schools and the similarly repressive policy of contemporary Italy in its attempt to wipe out German from the territory recently acquired from Austria are illuminating examples of the heightened emphasis on language as a symbol of political allegiance in the modern world.

To match these repressive measures, we have the oft repeated attempt of minority groups to erect their language into the status of a fully accredited medium of cultural and literary expression. Many of these restored or semimanufactured languages have come in on the wave of resistance to political or cultural hostility. Such are the Gaelic of Ireland, the Lithuanian of a recently created republic, and the Hebrew of the Zionists. Other such languages have come in more peacefully because of a sentimental interest in local culture. Such are the modern Provençal of southern France, the Plattdeutsch of northern Germany, Frisian, and the Norwegian *landsmaal*. It is very doubtful whether these persistent attempts to make true culture languages of local dialects that have long ceased to be of primary literary importance can succeed in the long run. The failure of modern Provençal to hold its own and the very dubious success of Gaelic make it seem probable that, following the recent tendency to resurrect minor languages, there will come a renewed leveling of speech more suitably expressing the internationalism which is slowly emerging.

The logical necessity of an international language in modern times is in strange contrast to the indifference and even opposition with which most people consider its possibility. The attempts so far made to solve this problem, of which Esperanto has probably had the greatest measure of practical success, have not affected more than a very small proportion of the people whose international interest and needs might have led to a desire for a simple and uniform means of international expression, at least for certain purposes. It is in the less important countries of Europe, such as Czechoslovakia, that Esperanto has been moderately successful, and for obvious reasons.

The opposition to an international language has little logic or psychology in its favor. The supposed artificiality of such a language as Esperanto or any of the equivalent languages that have been proposed is absurdly exaggerated, for in sober truth there is practically nothing in these languages that is not taken from the common stock of words and forms which have gradually developed in Europe. Such an international language could, of course, have only the status of a secondary form of speech for distinctly limited purposes. Thus considered, the learning of a constructed international language offers no further psychological problem than the learning of any other language which is acquired after childhood through the medium of books and with the conscious application of grammatical rules. The lack of interest in the international language problem in spite of the manifest need for one is an excellent example of how little logic or intellectual necessity has to do with the acquirement of language habits. Even the acquiring of the barest smattering of a foreign language is imaginatively equivalent to some measure of identification with a people or a culture. The purely instrumental value of such knowledge is frequently nil.

Any consciously constructed international language has to deal with the great difficulty of not being felt to represent a distinctive people or culture. Hence the learning of it is of very little symbolic significance for the average person, who remains blind to the fact that such a language, easy and regular as it inevitably must be, would solve many of his educational and practical difficulties at a single blow. The future alone will tell whether the logical advantages and theoretical necessity of an international language can overcome the largely symbolic opposition which it has to meet. In any event it is at least conceivable that one of the great national languages of modern times, such as English or Spanish or Russian, may in due course find itself in the position of a *de facto* international language without any conscious attempt having been made to put it there.

SOUND PATTERNS IN LANGUAGE*

THERE USED TO BE and to some extent still is a feeling among linguists that the psychology of a language is more particularly concerned with its grammatical features, but that its sounds and its phonetic processes belong to a grosser physiological substratum. Thus, we sometimes hear it said that such phonetic processes as the palatalizing of a vowel by a following *i* or other front vowel ("umlaut") or the series of shifts in the manner of articulating the old Indo-European stopped consonants which have become celebrated under the name of "Grimm's Law" are merely mechanical processes, consummated by the organs of speech and by the nerves that control them as a set of shifts in relatively simple sensorimotor habits. It is my purpose in this paper, as briefly as may be, to indicate that the sounds and sound processes of speech cannot be properly understood in such simple, mechanical terms.

Perhaps the best way to pose the problem of the psychology of speech sounds is to compare an actual speech sound with an identical or similar one not used in a linguistic context. It will become evident almost at once that it is a great fallacy to think of the articulation of a speech sound as a motor habit that is merely intended to bring about a directly significant result. A good example of superficially similar sounds is the *wh* of such a word as *when*, as generally pronounced in America (i.e., voiceless *w* or, perhaps more accurately analyzed, aspiration plus voiceless *w* plus voiced *w*-glide), and the sound made in blowing out a candle, with which it has often been compared. We are not at the present moment greatly interested in whether these two articulations are really identical or, at the least, very similar. Let us assume that a typically pronounced *wh* is identical with the sound that results from the expulsion of breath through pursed lips when a candle is blown out. We shall assume identity of both articulation and quality of perception. Does this identity amount to a psychological identity of the two processes? Obviously not. It is worth pointing out, in what may seem pedantic detail, wherein they differ.

1. The candle-blowing sound is a physical by-product of a directly functional act, the extinguishing of the candle by means of a peculiar method of producing a current of air. So far as normal human interest is concerned, this sound serves merely as a sign of the blowing out, or attempted blowing out, itself. We can abbreviate our record of the facts a little and say that the production of the

* *Language*, 1 (1925): 37–51.

candle-blowing sound is a directly functional act. On the other hand, the articulation of the *wh*-sound in such a word as *when* has no direct functional value; it is merely a link in the construction of a symbol, the articulated or perceived word *when*, which in turn assumes a function, symbolic at that, only when it is experienced in certain linguistic contexts, such as the saying or hearing of a sentence like *When are you coming?* In brief, the candle-blowing *wh* means business; the speech sound *wh* is stored-up play which can eventually fall in line in a game that merely refers to business. Still more briefly, the former is practice; the latter, art.

2. Each act of blowing out a candle is functionally equivalent, more or less, to every other such act; hence the candle-blowing *wh* is, in the first instance, a sign for an act of single function. The speech sound *wh* has no singleness, or rather primary singleness, of reference. It is a counter in a considerable variety of functional symbols, e.g., *when, whiskey, wheel*. A series of candle-blowing sounds has a natural functional and contextual coherence. A series of *wh*-sounds as employed in actual speech has no such coherence; e.g., the series *wh*(en), *wh*(iskey), *wh*(eel) is non-significant.

3. Every typical human reaction has a certain range of variation and, properly speaking, no such reaction can be understood except as a series of variants distributed about a norm or type. Now the candle-blowing *wh* and the speech sound *wh* are norms or types of entirely distinct series of variants.

First, as to acoustic quality. Owing to the fact that the blowing out of a candle is a purely functional act, its variability is limited by the function alone. But, obviously, it is possible to blow out a candle in a great number of ways. One may purse the lips greatly or only a little; the lower lip, or the upper lip, or neither may protrude; the articulation may be quite impure and accompanied by synchronous articulations, such as a *x*-like (velar spirant) or *sh*-like sound. None of these and other variations reaches over into a class of reactions that differs at all materially from the typical candle-blowing *wh*. The variation of *wh* as speech sound is very much more restricted. A *when* pronounced, for instance, with a *wh* in which the lower lip protruded or with a *wh* that was contaminated with a *sh*-sound would be felt as distinctly "off color." It could be tolerated only as a joke or a personal speech defect. But the variability of *wh* in language is not only less wide than in candle-blowing, it is also different in tendency. The latter sound varies chiefly along the line of exact place (or places) of articulation, the former chiefly along the line of voicing. Psychologically *wh* of *when* and similar words is related to the *w* of *well* and similar words. There is a strong tendency to minimize the aspiration and to voice the labial. The gamut of variations, therefore, runs roughly from hW (I use W for voiceless w) to w. Needless to say, there is no tendency to voicing in the candle-blowing *wh*, for such a tendency would contradict the very purpose of the reaction, which is to release a strong and unhampered current of air.

Second, as to intensity. It is clear that in this respect the two series of variations differ markedly. The normal intensity of the candle-blowing sound is greater than that of the linguistic *wh;* this intensity, moreover, is very much more variable, depending as it does on the muscular tone of the blower, the size of the flame to be extinguished, and other factors. All in all, it is clear that the resemblance of the two *wh*-sounds is really due to an intercrossing of two absolutely independent series, as of two independent lines in space that have one point in common.

4. The speech sound *wh* has a large number of associations with other sounds in symbolically significant sound-groups, e.g., *wh-e-n*, *wh-i-s-k-ey*, *wh-ee-l*. The candle-blowing sound has no sound associations with which it habitually coheres.

5. We now come to the most essential point of difference. The speech sound *wh* is one of a definitely limited number of sounds (e.g., *wh*, *s*, *t*, *l*, *i*, and so on) which, while differing qualitatively from one another rather more than does *wh* from its candle-blowing equivalent, nevertheless belong together in a definite system of symbolically utilizable counters. Each member of this system is not only characterized by a distinctive and slightly variable articulation and a corresponding acoustic image, but also—*and this is crucial*—by a psychological aloofness from all the other members of the system. The relational gaps between the sounds of a language are just as necessary to the psychological definition of these sounds as the articulations and acoustic images which are customarily used to define them. A sound that is not unconsciously felt as "placed"[1] with reference to other sounds is no more a true element of speech than a lifting of the foot is a dance step unless it can be "placed" with reference to other movements that help to define the dance. Needless to say, the candle-blowing sound forms no part of any such system of sounds. It is not spaced off from nor related to other sounds—say the sound of humming and the sound of clearing one's throat—which form with it a set of mutually necessary indices.

It should be sufficiently clear from this one example—and there are of course plenty of analogous ones, such as *m* versus the sound of humming or an indefinite series of timbre-varying groans versus a set of vowels—how little the notion of speech sound is explicable in simple sensorimotor terms and how truly a complex psychology of association and pattern is implicit in the utterance of the simplest consonant or vowel. It follows at once that the psychology of phonetic processes is unintelligible unless the general patterning of speech sounds is recognized. This patterning has two phases. We have been at particular pains to see that the sounds used by a language form a self-contained system which makes it impossible to identify any of them with a non-linguistic sound produced by the "organs of speech," no matter how great is the articulatory and acoustic resemblance between the two. In view of the utterly distinct psychological backgrounds of the two classes of sound production it may even be seriously doubted whether the innervation of speech-sound articulation is ever actually the same type of physiological fact as the innervation of "identical" articulations that have no linguistic context. But it is not enough to pattern off all speech sounds as such against other sounds produced by the "organs of speech." There is a second phase of sound patterning which is more elusive and of correspondingly greater significance for the linguist. This is the inner con-

[1] This word has, of course, nothing to do here with "place of articulation." One may feel, for instance, that sound A is to sound B as sound X is to sound Y without having the remotest idea how and where any of them is produced.

figuration of the sound system of a language, the intuitive "placing" of the sounds with reference to one another. To this we must now turn.

Mechanical and other detached methods of studying the phonetic elements of speech are, of course, of considerable value, but they have sometimes the undesirable effect of obscuring the essential facts of speech-sound psychology. Too often an undue importance is attached to minute sound discriminations as such; and too often phoneticians do not realize that it is not enough to know that a certain sound occurs in a language, but that one must ascertain if the sound is a typical form or one of the points in its sound pattern, or is merely a variant of such a form. There are two types of variation that tend to obscure the distinctiveness of the different points in the phonetic pattern of a language. One of these is individual variation. It is true that no two individuals have precisely the same pronunciation of a language, but it is equally true that they aim to make the same sound discriminations, so that, if the qualitative differences of the sounds that make up A's pattern from those that make up B's are perceptible to a minute analysis, the relations that obtain between the elements in the two patterns are the same. In other words, the patterns are the same pattern. A's s, for instance, may differ quite markedly from B's s, but if each individual keeps his s equally distinct from such points in the pattern as th (of *think*) and sh and if there is a one-to-one correspondence between the distribution of A's s and that of B's, then the difference of pronunciation is of little or no interest for the phonetic psychology of the language. We may go a step further. Let us symbolize A's and B's pronunciations of s, th, and sh as follows:

$$\text{A: } th \qquad s \qquad sh$$
$$\text{B: } th_1 \quad s_1 \qquad sh_1$$

This diagram is intended to convey the fact that B's s is a lisped s which is not identical with his interdental th, but stands nearer objectively to this sound than to A's s; similarly, B's sh is acoustically somewhat closer to A's s than to his sh. Obviously we cannot discover B's phonetic pattern by identifying his sounds with their nearest analogues in A's pronunciation, i.e., setting $th_1 = th$, $s_1 =$ variant of th, $sh_1 = s$. If we do this, as we are quite likely to do if we are obsessed, like so many linguists, by the desire to apply an absolute and universal phonetic system to all languages, we get the following pattern analysis:

$$\text{A: } th \qquad s \qquad sh$$
$$\text{B: } th_1 \ s_1 \qquad sh_1 \qquad —$$

which is as psychologically perverse as it is "objectively" accurate. Of course the true pattern analysis is:

A: *th*   *s*   *sh*
B: *th₁* *s₁* *sh₁*

for the objective relations between sounds are only a first approximation to the psychological relations which constitute the true phonetic pattern. The size of the objective differences *th—s*, *s—sh*, *th₁—s₁*, *s₁—sh₁*, *th—s₁*, *s₁—s*, *s—sh₁*, and *sh₁—sh* does not correspond to the psychological "spacing" of the phonemes *th*, *s*, and *sh* in the phonetic pattern which is common to A and B.

The second type of variation is common to all normal speakers of the language and is dependent on the phonetic conditions in which the fundamental sound ("point of the pattern") occurs. In most languages, what is felt by the speakers to be the "same" sound has perceptibly different forms as these conditions vary. Thus, in (American) English there is a perceptible difference in the length of the vowel *a* of *bad* and *bat*, the *a*-vowel illustrated by these words being long or half-long before voiced consonants and all continuants, whether voiced or unvoiced, but short before voiceless stops. In fact, the vocalic alternation of *bad* and *bat* is quantitatively parallel to such alternations as *bead* and *beat*, *fade* and *fate*. The alternations are governed by mechanical considerations that have only a subsidiary relevance for the phonetic pattern. They take care of themselves, as it were, and it is not always easy to convince natives of their objective reality, however sensitive they may be to violations of the unconscious rule in the speech of foreigners. It is very necessary to understand that it is not because the objective difference is too slight to be readily perceptible that such variations as the quantitative alternations in *bad* and *bat*, *bead* and *beat*, *fade* and *fate* stand outside of the proper phonetic pattern of the language (e.g., are not psychologically parallel to such qualitative-quantitative alternations as *bid* and *bead*, *fed* and *fade*, or to such quantitative alternations as German *Schlaf* and *schlaff*, Latin *āra* and *ārā*), but that the objective difference is felt to be slight precisely because it corresponds to nothing significant in the inner structure of the phonetic pattern. In matters of this kind, objective estimates of similarity or difference, based either on specific linguistic habits or on a generalized phonetic system, are utterly fallacious. As a matter of fact, the mechanical English vocalic relation *bad*: *bat* would in many languages be quite marked enough to indicate a relation of distinct points of the pattern, while the English pattern relation *-t*: *-d*, which seems so self-evidently real to us, has in not a few other languages either no reality at all or only a mechanical, conditional one. In Upper Chinook, for instance, $t{:}d$ exists objectively but not psychologically; one says, e.g., *inat* 'across,' but *inad* before words beginning with a vowel, and the two forms of the final consonant are undoubtedly felt to be the "same" sound in exactly the same sense in which the English vowels of *bad* and *bat* are felt by us to be identical phonetic elements. The Upper Chinook *d* exists only as a mechanical variant of *t;* hence this alternation is not the same psychologically as the Sanskrit sandhi variation *-t: -d.*

Individual variations and such conditional variations as we have discussed once cleared out of the way, we arrive at the genuine pattern of speech sounds. After what we have said, it almost goes without saying that two languages, A and B, may have identical sounds but utterly distinct phonetic patterns; or they may have mutually incompatible phonetic systems, from the articulatory and acoustic standpoint, but identical or similar patterns. The following schematic examples and subjoined comments will make this clear. Sounds which do not properly belong to the pattern or, rather, are variants within points of the pattern are put in parentheses. Long vowels are designated as $a{\cdot}$; η is *ng* of *sing;* θ and δ are voiceless and voiced interdental spirants; x and γ are voiceless and voiced guttural spirants; ' is glottal stop; ' denotes aspirated release; ϵ and o are open *e* and *o.*

A:	a		(ϵ)	(e)	i	u	(o)	(o)
	$(a{\cdot})$		$(\epsilon{\cdot})$	$(e{\cdot})$	$i{\cdot}$	$u{\cdot}$	$(o{\cdot})$	$(\mathit{o}{\cdot})$
	'		h	w	y	l	m n	(η)
	p		t	k				
	p'		t'	k'				
	(b)		(d)	(g)				
	f	θ	s	x				
	(v)	(δ)	(z)	(γ)				
but B:	a		ϵ	e	i	u	o	o
	$(a{\cdot})$		$(\epsilon{\cdot})$	$(e{\cdot})$	$(i{\cdot})$	$(u{\cdot})$	$(o{\cdot})$	$(\mathit{o}{\cdot})$
	$(')$		h	(w)	(y)	(l)	m n	η
	p		t	k				
	(p')		(t')	(k')				
	b		d	g				
	(f)	(θ)	s	(x)				
	v	δ	z	γ				

We will assume for A and B certain conditional variants which are all of types that may be abundantly illustrated from actual languages. For A:

1. ϵ occurs only as palatalized form of *a* when following *y* or *i*. In many Indian languages, e.g., *yε* = *ya*.

2. *e* is dropped from *i*-position when this vowel is final. Cf. such mechanical alternations as Eskimo *-e: -i-t*.

3. *o* is dropped from *u*-position when this vowel is final. Cf. 2.

4. *ɔ* occurs only as labialized form of *a* after *w* or *u*. Cf. 1. (In Yahi, e.g., *wɔwi* 'house' is objectively correct, but psychologically wrong. It can easily be shown that this word is really *wawi* and "feels" like a rhyme to such phonetic groups as *lawi* and *bawi;* short *ɔ* in an open syllable is an anomaly, but *ɔ·* is typical for all Yana dialects, including Yahi.)

5. *η* is merely *n* assimilated to following *k*, as in Indo-European.

6. *b, d, g, v, z, δ, γ* are voiced forms of *p, t, k, f, s, θ, x* respectively when these consonants occur between vowels before the accent (cf. Upper Chinook *wa'pul* 'night': *wabu'lmax* 'nights'). As the voiced consonants can arise in no other way, they are not felt by the speakers of A as specifically distinct from the voiceless consonants. They feel sharply the difference between *p* and *p'*, as do Chinese, Takelma, Yana, and a host of other languages, but are not aware of the alternation *p:b*.

And for B:

1. Long vowels can arise only when the syllable is open and stressed. Such alternations as *ma·'la*: *u·'-mala* are not felt as involving any but stress differences. In A, *ma·la* and *mala* are as distinct as Latin "apples" and "bad" (fem.).

2. ' is not an organic consonant, but, as in North German, an attack of initial vowels, hence '*a-* is felt to be merely *a-*. In A, however, as in Semitic, Nootka, Kwakiutl, Haida, and a great many other languages, such initials as '*a-* are felt to be equivalent to such consonant + vowel groups as *ma-* or *sa-*. Here is a type of pattern difference which even experienced linguists do not always succeed in making clear.

3. *w* and *y* are merely semi-vocalic developments of *u* and *i*. Cf. French *oui* and *hier*. In A, *w* and *y* are organically distinct consonants. Here again linguists often blindly follow the phonetic feeling of their own language instead of clearly ascertaining the behavior of the language investigated. The difference, e.g., between *aua* and *awa* is a real one for some languages, a phantom for others.

4. *l* arises merely as dissimilated variant of *n*.

5. *p', t', k'* are merely *p, t, k* with breath release, characteristic of B at the end of a word, e.g., *ap-a: ap'*. This sort of alternation is common in aboriginal America. It is the reverse of the English habit: *tame* with aspirated *t* (*t'e·ᶦm*) but *hate* with unaspirated, or very weakly aspirated, release (*he'ᶦt*).

6. *f, θ*, and *x* similarly arise from the unvoicing of final *v, δ* and *γ*; e.g., *av-a*: *af. z* and *s* also alternate in this way, but there is a true *s* besides. From the point of view of B, *s* in such phonemes as *sa* and *asa* is an utterly distinct sound, or rather point in the phonetic pattern, from the objectively identical *as* which alternates with *az-a*.[2]

---

[2] If B ever develops an orthography, it is likely to fall into the habit of writing *az* for the pronounced *as* in cases of type *az-a: as*, but *as* in cases of type *as-a: as*. Philologists not convinced of the reality of phonetic patterns as here conceived will then be able to "prove" from internal evidence that the change of etymological *v, z, δ, γ* to *-f, -s, -θ, -x* did not take place until after the language was reduced

The true or intuitively felt phonetic systems (patterns) of A and B, therefore, are:

A: *a*   *i*   *u*
      a·   *i·*   *u·*

	ʔ			*h*		*w*	*y*		*l*		*m*	*n*
	p	*t*		*k*								
	p'	*t'*		*k'*								
	f	*θ*		*x*	*s*							

B: *a* *ε*   *e*   *i*   *u*   *o* *ɔ*

                     h   *m* *n* *ŋ*

	p	*t*		*k*
	b	*d*		*g*
		s		
	v	*δ*	*z*	*γ*

which show the two languages to be very much more different phonetically than they at first seemed to be.

The converse case is worth plotting too. C and D are languages which have hardly any sounds in common but their patterns show a remarkable one-to-one correspondence. Thus:

C: *a*   *ε*   *i*   *u*
      a· *ε·*

     h   *w*   *y*   *l*   *m*   *n*

	p	*t*		*k*	*q* (velar k)
	b	*d*		*g*	*g* (velar g)
	f	*s*		*x*	*x̣* (velar x)

---

to writing, because otherwise it would be "impossible" to explain why -*s* should be written -*z* when there was a sign for *s* ready to hand and why signs should not have come into use for *f*, *θ*, and *x*. As soon as one realizes, however, that "ideal sounds," which are constructed from one's intuitive feeling of the significant relations between the objective sounds, are more "real" to a naïve speaker than the objective sounds themselves, such internal evidence loses much of its force. The example of *s* in B was purposely chosen to illustrate an interesting phenomenon, the crossing in a single objective phoneme of a true element of the phonetic pattern with a secondary form of another such element. In B, e.g., objective *s* is a pool of cases of "true *s*" and "pseudo-*s*." Many interesting and subtle examples could be given of psychological difference where there is objective identity, or similarity so close as to be interpreted by the recorder as identity. In Sarcee, an Athabaskan language with significant pitch differences, there is a true middle tone and a pseudo-middle tone which results from the lowering of a high tone to the middle position because of certain mechanical rules of tone sandhi. I doubt very much if the intuitive psychology of these two middle tones is the same. There are, of course, analogous traps for the unwary in Chinese. Had not the Chinese kindly formalized for us their intuitive feeling about the essential tone analysis of their language, it is exceedingly doubtful if our Occidental ears and kymographs would have succeeded in discovering the exact patterning of Chinese tone.

D: $ä$ e i $ü$
       $ä\cdot$ $e\cdot$

       h v j^3 r m η ✕

       $p^‘$ $t^‘$ $k^‘$ $q^‘$
       β^4 δ γ γ (velar γ)
       f $š$ $\underset{\sim}{x}^5$ $ḥ$ (laryngeal h)

Languages C and D have far less superficial similarity in their sound systems than have A and B, but it is obvious at a glance that their patterns are built on very much more similar lines. If we allowed ourselves to speculate genetically, we might suspect, on general principles, that the phonetic similarities between A and B, which we will suppose to be contiguous languages, are due to historical contact, but that the deeper pattern resemblance between C and D is an index of genetic relationship. It goes without saying that in the complex world of actual linguistic history we do not often find the phonetic facts working out along such neatly schematic lines, but it seemed expedient to schematize here so that the pattern concept might emerge with greater clarity.

An examination of the patterns of C and D shows that there is still a crucial point that we have touched on only by implication. We must now make this clear. We have arranged the sounds of C and D in such a way as to suggest an equivalence of "orientation" of any one sound of one system with some sound of the other. In comparing the systems of A and B we did not commit ourselves to specific equivalences. We did not wish to imply, for instance, that A's *s* was or was not "oriented" in the same way as B's, did or did not occupy the same relative place in A's pattern as in B's. But here we do wish to imply not merely that, e.g., C's *p* corresponds to D's *p‘* or C's *h* to D's *h*, which one would be inclined to grant on general phonetic grounds, but also that, e.g., C's *w* corresponds to D's *v* while C's *b* corresponds to D's *β*. On general principles such pattern alignments as the latter are unexpected, to say the least, for bilabial *β* resembles *w* rather more than dentolabial *v* does. Why, then, not allow *β* to occupy the position we have assigned to *v*? Again, why should D's *j* be supposed to correspond to C's *y* when it is merely the voiced form of *š*? Should it not rather be placed under *š* precisely as, in C's system, *b* is placed under *p*? Naturally, there is no reason why the intuitive pattern alignment of sounds in a given language should not be identical with their natural phonetic arrangement and, one need hardly say, it is almost universally true that, e.g., the vowels

[3] As in French *jour*.
[4] Bilabial *v*, as in Spanish.
[5] As in German *ich*.

form both a natural and a pattern group as against the consonants, that such stopped sounds as *p, t, k* form both a natural and a pattern group as opposed to the equally coherent group *b, d, g* (provided, of course, the language possesses these two series of stopped consonants). And yet it is most important to emphasize the fact, strange but indubitable, that a pattern alignment does not need to correspond exactly to the more obvious phonetic one. It is most certainly true that, however likely it is that at last analysis patternings of sounds are based on natural classifications, the pattern feeling, once established, may come to have linguistic reality over and above, though perhaps never entirely at variance with, such classifications. We are not here concerned with the historical reasons for such phonetic vagaries. The fact is that, even from a purely descriptive standpoint, it is not nonsense to say that, e.g., the *s* or *w* of one linguistic pattern is not necessarily the same thing as the *s* or *w* of another.

It is time to escape from a possible charge of phonetic metaphysics and to face the question, "How can a sound be assigned a 'place' in a phonetic pattern over and above its natural classification on organic and acoustic grounds?" The answer is simple. "A 'place' is intuitively found for a sound (which is here thought of as a true 'point in the pattern,' not a mere conditional variant) in such a system because of a general feeling of its phonetic relationship resulting from all the specific phonetic relationships (such as parallelism, contrast, combination, imperviousness to combination, and so on) to all other sounds." These relationships may, or may not, involve morphological processes (e.g., the fact that in English we have morphological alternations like *wife: wives, sheath: to sheathe, breath: to breathe, mouse: to mouse* helps to give the sounds *f, θ, s* an intuitive pattern relation to their voiced correlates *v, δ, z* which is specifically different from the theoretically analogous relation *p, t, k: b, d, g;* in English, *f* is nearer to *v* than *p* is to *b*, but in German this is certainly not true).

An example or two of English sound-patterning will help us to fix our thoughts. *P, t,* and *k* belong together in a coherent set because, among other reasons: (1) they may occur initially, medially, or finally; (2) they may be preceded by *s* in all positions (e.g., *spoon: cusp, star: hoist; scum: ask*); (3) they may be followed by *r* initially and medially; (4) each has a voiced correspondent (*b, d, g*); (6) unlike such sounds as *f* and *θ*, they cannot alternate significantly with their voiced correspondents; (7) they have no tendency to be closely associated, either phonetically or morphologically, with corresponding spirants (*p:f* and *t:θ* are not intuitively correct for English; contrast Old Irish and Hebrew

$t:\theta$, $k:x$, which were intuitively felt relations—Old Irish and Hebrew θ and x were absolutely different types of sounds, psychologically, from English θ and German x). These are merely a few of the relations which help to give p, t, k their pattern place in English.

A second example is η of *sing*. In spite of what phoneticians tell us about this sound ($b:m$ as $d:n$ as $g:\eta$), no naïve English-speaking person can be made to feel in his bones that it belongs to a single series with m and n. Psychologically it cannot be grouped with them because, unlike them, it is not a freely movable consonant (there are no words beginning with η). It still *feels* like ηg, however little it sounds like it. The relation $ant:and = sink:sing$ is psychologically as well as historically correct. Orthography is by no means solely responsible for the *"ng* feeling"* of η. Cases like -ηg- in *finger* and *anger* do not disprove the reality of this feeling, for there is in English a pattern equivalence of -ηg-:-η and -nd-:-nd. What cases like *singer* with -η- indicate is not so much a pattern difference -ηg-:-η-, which is not to be construed as analogous to -nd-:-n- (e.g., *window:winnow*), as an analogical treatment of medial elements in terms of their final form (*singer:sing* like *cutter: cut*).[6]

To return to our phonetic patterns for C and D, we can now better understand why it is possible to consider a sibilant like j as less closely related in pattern to its voiceless form $š$ than to such a set of voiced continuants as v, r, m, η. We might find, for instance, that $š$ never alternates with j, but that there are cases of $š:\delta$ analogous to cases of $f:\beta$ and $x:\gamma$; that *ava*, *aja*, *ara* alternate with *au*, *ai*, *ar*; that combinations like -$a\beta d$, -$a\delta g$, -$a\gamma d$ are possible, but that combinations of type -ajd and -avd are unthinkable; that v- and j- are possible initials, like r-, m-, and η-, but that β-, δ-, γ-, γ- are not allowed. The product of such and possibly other sound relations would induce a feeling that j belongs with v, r, m, η; that it is related to i; and that it has nothing to do with such spirants as $š$ and δ. In other words, it "feels" like the y of many other languages, and, as y itself is absent in D, we can go so far as to say that j occupies a "place in the pattern" that belongs to y elsewhere.

[6] Incidentally, if our theory is correct, such a form as *singer* betrays an unconscious analysis into a word of absolute significance *sing* and a semi-independent agentive element -*er*, which is appended not to a stem, an abstracted radical element, but to a true word. Hence *sing*: *singer* is not psychologically analogous to such Latin forms as *can-*:*can-tor*. It would almost seem that the English insistence on the absoluteness of its significant words tended at the same time to give many of its derivative suffixes a secondary, revitalized reality. -*er*, for instance, might almost be construed as a "word" which occurs only as the second element of a compound, cf. -*man* in words like *longshoreman*. As Prof. L. Bloomfield points out to me, the agentive -*er* contrasts with the comparative -*er*, which allows the adjective to keep its radical form in -ηg- (e.g., *long* with -η:*longer* with -ηg-).

In this paper I do not wish to go into the complex and tangled problems of the nature and generality of sound changes in language. All that I wish to point out here is that it is obviously not immaterial to understand how a sound patterns if we are to understand its history. Of course, it is true that mechanical sound changes may bring about serious readjustments of phonetic pattern and may even create new configurations within the pattern (in modern Central Tibetan, e.g., we have *b-*, *d-*, *g-*: *B'*, *D'*, *G'*,[7] while in classical Tibetan we have, as correspondents, *mb-*, *nd-*, *ŋg*: *b-*, *d-*, *g-*; *mb-*, *ŋg-* are here to be morphologically analyzed as nasal prefix + *b-*, *d-*, *g-*). But it is equally true that the pattern feeling acts as a hindrance of, or stimulus to, certain sound changes and that it is not permissible to look for universally valid sound changes under like articulatory conditions. Certain typical mechanical tendencies there are (e.g., *nb* > *mb* or *-az* > *-as* or *tya* > *tša*), but a complete theory of sound change has to take constant account of the orientation of sounds in our sense. Let one example do for many. We do not in English feel that *θ* is to be found in the neighborhood, as it were, of *s*, but that it is very close to *δ*. In Spanish, *θ* is not far from *s*, but is not at all close to *δ*.[8] Is it not therefore more than an accident that nowhere in Germanic does *θ* become *s* or proceed from *s*, while in certain Spanish dialects, as so frequently elsewhere, *θ* passes into *s* (in Athabaskan *θ* often proceeds from *s*)? In English *θ* tends to be vulgarized to *t* as *δ* tends to be vulgarized to *d*, never to *s;* similarly, Old Norse *θ* has become *t* in Swedish and Danish. Such facts are impressive. They cannot be explained on simple mechanical principles.

Phonetic patterning helps also to explain why people find it difficult to pronounce certain foreign sounds which they possess in their own language. Thus, a Nootka Indian in pronouncing English words with *ŋ* or *l* invariably substitutes *n* for each of these sounds. Yet he is able to pronounce both *ŋ* and *l*. He does not use these sounds in prose discourse, but *ŋ* is very common in the chants and *l* is often substituted for *n* in songs. His feeling for the stylistic character of *ŋ* and for the *n-l* equivalence prevents him from "hearing" English *ŋ* and *l* correctly. Here again we see that a speech sound is not merely an articulation or an acoustic image, but material for symbolic expression in an appropriate linguistic context. Very instructive is our attitude towards the English sounds *j*, *ŋ*, and *ts*. All three of these sounds are familiar to us (e.g.,

---

[7] *B*, *D*, *G* represent intermediate stops, "tonlose Medien." In this series they are followed by aspiration.

[8] The slight objective differences between English and Spanish *θ* and *δ* are of course not great enough to force a different patterning. Such a view would be putting the cart before the horse.

azure, sing, hats). None occurs initially. For all that, the attempt to pronounce them initially in foreign words is not reacted to in the same way. ŋa- and *tsa*- are naïvely felt to be incredible, not so *ja*-, which is easily acquired without replacement by *dja*- or *ša*-. Why is this? ŋa- is incredible because there is no *mba*-, *nda*-, *ŋ(g)a*- series in English. *tsa*- is incredible because there is no *psa*-, *tsa*-, *ksa*-, series in English; *-ts* is always morphologically analyzable into *-t* + *-s*, hence no feeling develops for *ts* as a simple phoneme despite the fact that its phonetic parallel *tš* (*ch* of *church*) is found in all positions.[9] But *ja*- is not difficult, say in learning French, because its articulation and perception have been mastered by implication in the daily use of our phonetic pattern. This is obvious from a glance at the formula:

$$-j- \qquad -z- \qquad -\delta- \qquad -v-$$
$$\text{—} \qquad z- \qquad \delta- \qquad v-$$

which is buttressed by:

$$-š- \qquad -s- \qquad -\theta- \qquad f-$$
$$š- \qquad s- \qquad \theta- \qquad -f-$$

Is it not evident that English speaker's pattern has all but taught him *j*- before he himself has ever used or heard an actual *j*-?

There are those who are so convinced of the adequacy of purely objective methods of studying speech sounds that they do not hesitate to insert phonetic graphs into the body of their descriptive grammars. This is to confuse linguistic structure with a particular method of studying linguistic phenomena. If it is justifiable in a grammatical work to describe the vocalic system of a language in terms of kymograph records,[10] it is also proper to insert anecdotes into the morphology to show how certain modes or cases happened to come in handy. And a painter might as well be allowed to transfer to his canvas his unrevised palette! The whole aim and spirit of this paper has been to show that phonetic phenomena are not physical phenomena *per se*, however necessary in the preliminary stages of inductive linguistic research it may be to get at the phonetic facts by way of their physical embodiment. The present discussion is really a special illustration of the necessity of getting behind the sense data of any type of expression in order to grasp the intuitively felt and communicated forms which alone give significance to such expression.

[9] Obviously we need not expect *-ts* and *-tš* to develop analogously even if *s* and *š* do.

[10] Needless to say, such records are in place in studies explicitly devoted to **ex**perimental phonetics.

THE PSYCHOLOGICAL REALITY OF PHONEMES*

THE CONCEPT of the "phoneme" (a functionally significant unit in the rigidly defined pattern or configuration of sounds peculiar to a language), as distinct from that of the "sound" or "phonetic element" as such (an objectively definable entity in the articu ated and perceived totality of speech), is becoming more and more familiar to linguists. The difficulty that many still seem to feel in distinguishing between the two must eventually disappear as the realization grows that no entity in human experience can be adequately defined as the mechanical sum or product of its physical properties. These physical properties are needed of course to give us the signal, as it were, for the identification of the given entity as a functionally significant point in a complex system of relatednesses; but for any given context it is notorious how many of these physical properties are, or may be, overlooked as irrelevant, how one particular property, possessing for the moment or by social understanding an unusual sign value, may have a determinedness in the definition of the entity that is out of all proportion to its "physical weight."

As soon, however, as we admit that all significant entities in experience are thus revised from the physically given by passing through the filter of the functionally or relatedly meaningful, as soon as we see that we can never set up a scale of added or changed meanings that is simply congruent to the scale of physical increments, we implicitly make a distinction, whether we know it or not, between the phoneme and the sound in that particular framework of experience which is known as language (actualized as speech). To say that a given phoneme is not sufficiently defined in articulatory or acoustic terms but needs to be fitted into the total system of sound relations peculiar to the language is, at bottom, no more mysterious than to say that a club is not defined for us when it is said to be made of wood and to have such and such a shape and such and such dimensions. We must understand why a roughly similar object, not so different to the eye, is no club at all, and why a third object, of very different color and much longer and heavier than the first, is for all that very much of a club.

Some linguists seem to feel that the phoneme is a useful enough concept in an abstract linguistic discussion—in the theoretical presentation of the form of a language or in the comparison of related languages—but that it has small relevance for the actualities of speech. This point of

* Published originally in French under the title "La Réalité psychologique des phonèmes," *Journal de Psychologie Normale et Pathologique*, 30 (1933): 247–265.

view seems the reverse of realistic to the present writer. Just as it takes a physicist or philosopher to define an object in terms of such abstract concepts as mass, volume, chemical structure, and location, so it takes very much of a linguistic abstractionist, a phonetician pure and simple, to reduce articulate speech to simple physical processes. To the physicist, the three wooden objects are equally distinct from each other, "clubs" are romantic intrusions into the austere continuities of nature. But the naïve human being is much surer of his clubs and poles than of unnamed objects to be hereinafter defined in physical terms. So, in speech, precise phonetic stations can be abstracted only by patient observation and frequently at the expense of a direct flouting of one's phonetic (one should say "phonemic") intuitions. In the physical world the naïve speaker and hearer actualize and are sensitive to sounds, but what they feel themselves to be pronouncing and hearing are "phonemes." They order the fundamental elements of linguistic experience into functionally and aesthetically determinate shapes, each of which is carved out by its exclusive laws of relationship within the complex total of all possible sound relationships. To the naïve speaker and hearer, sounds (i.e., phonemes) do not differ as five-inch or six-inch entities differ, but as clubs and poles differ. If the phonetician discovers in the flow of actual speech something that is neither "club" nor "pole," he, as phonetician, has the right to set up a "halfway between club and pole" entity. Functionally, however, such an entity is a fiction, and the naïve speaker or hearer is not only driven by its relational behavior to classify it as a "club" or a "pole," but actually hears and feels it to be such.

If the phonemic attitude is more basic, psychologically speaking, than the more strictly phonetic one, it should be possible to detect it in the unguarded speech judgments of naïve speakers who have a complete control of their language in a practical sense but have no rationalized or consciously systematic knowledge of it. "Errors" of analysis, or what the sophisticated onlooker is liable to consider such, may be expected to occur which have the characteristic of being phonetically unsound or inconsistent but which at the same time register a feeling for what is phonemically accurate. Such "errors," generally overlooked by the practical field linguist, may constitute valuable evidence for the dynamic reality of the phonemic structure of the language.

In the course of many years of experience in the recording and analysis of unwritten languages, American Indian and African, I have come to the practical realization that what the naïve speaker hears is not phonetic elements but phonemes. The problem reaches the stage of a practical test when one wishes to teach an intelligent native, say one who can read and write English reasonably well and has some intellectual curiosity besides, how to write his own language. The difficulty of such a task varies, of course, with the intelligence of the native and the intrinsic difficulty of his language, but it varies also with the "phonemic intuitiveness" of the teacher. Many well-meaning linguists have had disappointing experiences in this regard with quite intelligent natives without ever suspecting that the trouble lay, not with the native, but with themselves. It is exceedingly difficult, if not impossible, to teach a native to take account of purely mechanical phonetic variations which have no phonemic reality for him. The teacher who comes prepared with a gamut of absolute phonetic possibilities and who unconsciously, in spite of all his training, tends to project the phonemic valuations of his own language into what he hears and records of the exotic one may easily befuddle a native. The native realizes when what he is taught "clicks" with what his phonological intuitions have already taught him; but he is made uncomfortable when purely phonetic distinctions are pointed out to him which seem real enough when he focuses his attention on them but which are always fading out of his consciousness because their objective reality is not confirmed by these intuitions.

I have selected for brief discussion five examples of phonemic versus phonetic hearing and writing out of many which have come to me in the course of my experience with natives and students. In each of these, it will be observed, we have clear evidence of the unconscious reinterpretation of objective facts because of a disturbing phonological preparedness not precisely adjusted to these facts.

I. When working on the Southern Paiute language of southwestern Utah and northwestern Arizona I spent a little time in trying to teach my native interpreter, a young man of average intelligence, how to write his language phonetically. Southern Paiute is an unusually involved language from the phonological standpoint and, as my point of view at that time stressed phonetic accuracy rather than phonemic adequacy, I doubt if I could have succeeded in teaching him well enough to satisfy my standard even if I had devoted far more time to the effort than I did. As an example of a comparatively simple word I selected *pá·βaʻ* "at the water" (voiceless labial stop; stressed long *a*; voiced bilabial spirant; unstressed short *a*; final aspiration). I instructed Tony to divide the word into its syllables and to discover by careful hearing what sounds entered into the composition of each of the syllables, and in what order, then to attempt to write down the proper symbol for each of the discovered phonetic elements. To my astonishment Tony then syllabified: *pa·*, pause, *paʻ*. I say "astonishment" because I at once recognized the paradox that

Tony was not "hearing" in terms of the actual sounds (the voiced bilabial β was objectively very different from the initial stop) but in terms of an etymological reconstruction: *pa·*: "water" plus postposition *-pa‘* "at." The slight pause which intervened after the stem was enough to divert Tony from the phonetically proper form of the postposition to a theoretically real but actually nonexistent form.

To understand Tony's behavior, which was not in the least due to mere carelessness nor to a tendency of the speakers of this language "to confuse sounds," to quote the time-worn shibboleth, we must have recourse to the phonology of Southern Paiute. The treatment of the stopped consonants may be summarized in the following table:

| | Initial | Postvocalic | | | |
| | | 1. Spirantized | 2. Nasalized | 3. Geminated | |
				a. After voiced vowel	b. After unvoiced vowel
Labial	*p*	*β*	*mp*	*p·*	*p*
Dental	*t*	*r*	*nt*	*t·*	*t*
Guttural	*k*	*γ*	*ηk*	*k·*	*k*
Labialized guttural	*kw*	*γw*	*ηkw*	*k·w*	*kw*

The postvocalic forms of the stops of types 1, 2, and 3*a* are further modified before an unvoiced vowel, the voiced spirants becoming unvoiced spirants (*θ, R, χ, χW*),[1] and the nasalized and geminated stops becoming aspirated (*mp‘, p·‘; nt‘, t·‘; ηk‘, k·‘; ηkW, k·W*). It is impossible here to give a systematic idea of the phonologic processes which bring about the sound interchanges within a given articulatory series, but it is important to know that the spirantized, nasalized, and geminated stops can occur only in postvocalic position and that they are largely determined by the nature of the element (stem or suffix) which precedes them and which may be said to have an inherently spirantizing, nasalizing, or geminating force. The stem *pa·-* is a spirantizing stem, and the spirantizing of a theoretical *-pa‘* "at" to *-βa‘* is parallel to the spirantizing of *pɔ·-* "trail" to *-βɔ·-* in such a compound as *pa·-βɔ·-*, "water-trail." In other words, the language is so patterned that examples of type *pɔ·-: -βɔ·-* lead to the proportion **pa‘: -βa‘*[2] and, while **pa‘* "at" does not actually exist as an independent element but must always be actualized in one of the three possible postvocalic forms, its theoretical existence suddenly comes

---

[1] *W* represents voiceless *w*.

[2] This theoretical **pa‘*, occurring only as *-βa‘, -mpa‘, -p·a‘* in postvocalic position, is not to be confused with secondary *-pa‘* (type 3*b*) < *-p·a‘* (type 3*a*).

to the light of day when the problem of slowly syllabifying a word is presented to a native speaker for the first time. It then appears that the -βaʻ of speech behavior, as a self-contained syllabic entity without immediately preceding syllable, is actually felt as a phonologic *pa'*, from which it differs in two important phonetic respects (voiced, not voiceless, consonant; spirant, not stop).

All this has an important bearing on the construction of a maximally correct orthography of Southern Paiute, if by "maximally correct" we mean, not most adequate phonetically, but most true to the sound patterning of the language. As it happens, there is reason to believe from both internal and comparative evidence that the spirantized form of a consonant is its normal or primary form after a vowel and that the nasalized and geminated forms are due to the emergence of old nasal and other consonants that had disappeared in the obsolete form of the preceding element.[3] It follows that the postvocalic -β- is more closely related functionally to a simple initial *p-* than is the postvocalic -*p-* (after unvoiced vowel), which must always be interpreted as a secondary form of -*p·*-. These relations are summarized in the following table of theoretical nonfinal forms.

Phonetic Orthography	Phonologic Orthography
1. pa-	pa-
2. paβa-	papa-
3. paθA-[4]	papa-
4. pap·a-	pap·a-
5. pApa-	pap·a-
6. pap·A-	pap·a-

The phonetic orthography is more complex and, in a sense, more adequate, but it goes against the grain of the language in one important respect, for it identifies the second *p* in type 5 with the initial *p*, which is phonologically unsound. The phonologic orthography, on the other hand, is useless for one who has not mastered the phonology of the language, as it leads, or seems to lead, to incorrect pronunciations which would have the cumulative effect of making the language, so read, entirely unintelligible to a native. To a slightly schooled native, however, there can be no serious ambiguity, for the phonetic forms result from the phonologic only by the application of absolutely mechanical phonetic laws of spiran-

---

[3] The analogy to French liaison and, still more, to the three types of consonantal treatment in Old Irish (spirantized or "aspirated," nasalized or "eclipsed," and geminated) is obvious.

[4] *A* represents voiceless *a*.

tizing, alternating stresses, and unvoicing. It is not necessary to deal with these laws here[5] but we can indicate their operation by the following table of theoretical final forms:

PHONETIC ORTHOGRAPHY	PHONOLOGIC ORTHOGRAPHY
1. *páθA*	*papa*
2. *paβá'*	*papa·*
3. *pá·φA*	*pa·pa*
4. *pá·βa'* "*water-at*"	*pa·pa·*
5. *páp·A*	*pap·a*
6. *pApá'*	*pap·a·*
7. *pá·p·A*	*pa·p·a*
8. *pá·p·a'*	*pa·p·a·*
9. *maβáφA*	*mapapa*
10. *maβáβa'*	*mapapa·*
11. *maβá·θA*	*mapa·pa*
12. *maβá·βa'*	*mapa·pa·*
13. *maβáp·A*	*mapap·a*
14. *maβáp·a'*	*mapap·a·*
15. *maβá·p·A*	*mapa·p·a*
16. *maβáApa'*	*mapa·p·a·*
17. *MApáφA*[6]	*map·apa*
18. *MApáβa'*	*map·apa·*
19. *MApá·φA*	*map·a·pa*
20. *MApá·βa'*	*map·a·pa·*
21. *MApáp·A*	*map·ap·a*
22. *MApáp·a'*	*map·ap·a·*
23. *MApá·p·A*	*map·a·p·a*
24. *MApáApa'*	*map·a·p·a·*

Obviously, in such a language as this, spirants, whether voiced or voiceless, and voiceless vowels are not phonemes but are merely phonetic reflexes of stopped consonants and voiced vowels under fixed dynamic conditions. Long consonants and long vowels are sub-phonemes. The former are the resultants of simple phonemes (stopped consonants) and the operation of certain phonologic (and morphologic) latencies in given syllables, present or formerly present. The latter are phonologically resolvable into short vowel plus short vowel, i.e., into two syllables of unit length (moras), of which the second begins with a zero consonant.

Southern Paiute, then, is a language in which an unusually simple

[5] They are described in detail in E. Sapir, *The Southern Paiute Language*, Proceedings of the American Academy of Arts and Sciences, 65 (1930).
[6] *M* is voiceless *m*.

phonemic structure is actualized by a more than ordinarily complex phonetic one. Tony's "error" unconsciously registered this contrast.

II. When working on Sarcee, an Athabaskan language of Alberta, Canada, I was concerned with the problem of deciding whether certain words that seemed homonymous were actually so or differed in some subtle phonetic respect that was not immediately obvious. One such homonymous, or apparently homonymous, pair of words was *dìnì*[7] "this one" and *dìnì* "it makes a sound." In the early stage of our work I asked my interpreter, John Whitney, whether the two words sounded alike to him and he answered without hesitation that they were quite different. This statement, however, did not prove that he was objectively correct, as it is possible for perfectly homonymous words to give the speaker the illusion of phonetic difference because of the different contexts in which they appear or because of the different positions they occupy in their respective form systems.[8] When I asked him what the difference was, he found it difficult to say, and the more often he pronounced the words over to himself the more confused he became as to their phonetic difference. Yet all the time he seemed perfectly sure that there was a difference. At various moments I thought I could catch a slight phonetic difference, for instance, (1) that the *-nì* of "this one" was on a slightly lower tone than the *-nì* of "it makes a sound"; (2) that there was a slight stress on the *dì-* of "this one" (analysis: stem *dì-* "this" plus suffix *-nì* "person") and a similarly slight stress on the *-nì* of "it makes a sound" (analysis: prefix *dì-* plus verb stem *-nì*); (3) that the *-nì* of "this one" ended in a pure vowel with little or no breath release, while the *-nì* of "it makes a sound" had a more audible breath release, was properly *-nì'*. These suggestions were considered and halfheartedly accepted at various times by John, but it was easy to see that he was not intuitively convinced. The one tangible suggestion that he himself made was obviously incorrect, namely, that the *-nì* of "it makes a sound" ended in a "t."

[7] The grave accent represents a low tone, the acute accent a high one. Sarcee is a tone language.

[8] Thus, in English, the word *led* (e.g., "I *led* him away") is felt as having a vowel which has been deflected from the vowel of *lead* (e.g., "I *lead* him away") and is therefore not psychologically homonymous with the word for a metal, *lead*, in which the vowel is felt to be primary, not deflected (cf. further. "the *leading* of the windowpane," "the *leaded* glass," "the different *leads* now recognized by chemists"). The homonymy of *led* and *lead* (metal) is therefore of a different psychological order from the homonymy of *yard* ("He plays in my yard") and *yard* ("I want a *yard* of silk"), for the last two words enter into roughly parallel form systems (e.g., "Their *yards* were too small to play in": "I want two *yards* of silk"; "*yard* upon *yard* of railroad tracks": "*yard* upon *yard* of lovely fabrics"). It is probably easier for the naïve speaker, who does not know how to spell either *led* or *lead* (metal), to convince himself that there is a phonetic difference between these two words than between the two words *yard*.

John claimed that he "felt a *t*" in the syllable, yet when he tested it over and over to himself, he had to admit that he could neither hear a "*t*" nor feel his tongue articulating one. We had to give up the problem, and I silently concluded that there simply was no phonetic difference between the words and that John was trying to convince himself there was one merely because they were so different in grammatical form and function that he felt there ought to be a difference.

I did not then know enough about Sarcee phonology to understand the mysterious "*t*" theory. Later on it developed that there are phonologically distinct types of final vowels in Sarcee: smooth or simple vowels; and vowels with a consonantal latency, i.e., vowels originally followed by a consonant which disappears in the absolute form of the word but which reappears when the word has a suffix beginning with a vowel or which makes its former presence felt in other sandhi phenomena. One of these disappearing consonants is -*t'*, of which -' may be considered a weakened form. Now it happens that all final vowels are pronounced with a breath release in the absolute form of the word and that there is no objective difference between this secondary -', which may be symbolized as -('), phonologically zero, and the etymologically organic -', which may affect certain following consonants of suffixed elements or, in some cases, pass over to one of certain other consonants, such as *t'*. The -*ní* of "this one," phonetically -*ní'* in absolute form, is phonologically simple -*ní*; the -*ní* of "it makes a sound," phonetically -*ní'* in absolute form, can be phonologically represented as -*ni'* (-*nít'-*). We can best understand the facts if we test the nature of these two syllables by seeing how they behave if immediately followed by suffixed relative -*í* "the one who . . . " and inferential -*la*[9] "it turns out that."

		plus -*í*	plus -*la*
dìní	"this one"	*dìná·*ᵃ[10]	*dìníla*
dìní	"it makes a sound"	*dìnít'í*	*dìníla*[11]

We see at once that *dìní* "this one" behaves like a word ending in a smooth vowel (witness contraction of *í* + *í* to an over-long vowel and

---

[9] The lack of a tone mark indicates that this syllable is pronounced on the middle tone.

[10] *a·*ᵃ is an over-long *a*, consisting of a long *a·* followed by a weak rearticulated *a*. Syllables of this type result in Sarcee from contraction of old final vowels with following suffixed vowels. The change in quality from -*í* to -*á·*ᵃ is due to historical factors. -*ní* "person" is an old ˣ-*né* (with pepet vowel), relative -*í* is old *-*é̜*; two pepet vowels contract to long open *-é̜·é̜*; as Athabaskan ε becomes Sarcee *a*, this older *-é̜·é̜* passes into Sarcee -*á·*ᵃ.

[11] *ł* is voiceless spirantal *l*, as in Welsh *ll*.

unaffected *l* of *-la*), while *dìnì* "it makes a sound" acts as though the final vowel had a voiceless consonantal latency, which registers partly as -ʻ (-ʻ-*la* passing, as always, to *-la*), partly as *-tʻ-*.

It is clear that, while John was phonetically amateurish, he was phonologically subtle and accurate. His response amounted to an index of the feeling that *dìnì* "this one" = *dìnì*, that *dìnì* "it makes a sound" = *dìnìʻ*, and that this *-nìʻ* = *-nìtʻ*. John's certainty of difference in the face of objective identity is quite parallel to the feeling that the average Englishman would have that such words as *sawed* and *soared* are not phonetically identical. It is true that both *sawed* and *soared* can be phonetically represented as *sɔ·d*,[12] but the *-ing* forms of the two verbs (*sawing*, *soaring*), phonetically *sɔ·-iŋ* and *sɔ·r-iŋ*, and such sentence sandhi forms as "Saw on, my boy!" and "Soar into the sky!" combine to produce the feeling that the *sɔ·d* of *sawed* = *sɔ·-d* but that the *sɔ·d* of *soared* = *sɔ·r-d*. In the one case zero = zero, in the other case zero = *r*. Among educated but linguistically untrained people who discuss such matters differences of orthography are always held responsible for these differences of feeling. This is undoubtedly a fallacy, at least for the great mass of people, and puts the cart before the horse. Were English not a written language, the configuratively determined phonologic difference between such doublets as *sawed* and *soared* would still be "heard," as a collective illusion, as a true phonetic difference.

III. The most successful American Indian pupil that I have had in practical phonetics is Alex Thomas, who writes his native language, Nootka,[13] with the utmost fluency and with admirable accuracy. Alex's orthography, as is natural, is phonologic in spirit throughout and it is largely from a study of his texts that I have learned to estimate at its true value the psychological difference between a sound and a phoneme. Anyone who knows the phonetic mechanics of Nootka can easily actualize his orthography. Thus, *ḥi*,[14] phonologically parallel to *si* or *ni*, is actually pronounced *ḥɛ*, with a vowel which is much nearer to the *e* of English *met* than to that of *sit*. This is due to the peculiar nature of the laryngeal consonants, which favor an *a*-timbre and cause the following vowels *i* and *u* to drop to *ɛ* and *ɔ* respectively. The orthographies *ḥi* and *ḥu* are entirely unambiguous because there can be no phonologically distinct syllables of type *ḥɛ* and *ḥɔ*.

Another mechanical peculiarity of Nootka is the lengthening of consonants after a short vowel when followed by a vowel. This purely

---

[12] These remarks apply to British, not to normal American, usage.
[13] This is spoken on the west coast of Vancouver Island, B. C.
[14] *ḥ* is a voiceless laryngeal spirant, almost identical with the Arabic *ḥā*.

mechanical length has no morphological or phonological significance and is ignored in Alex's orthography. His *hisi·k* and *ḥisa·* are, then, to be normally pronounced *his·i·k'* and *ḥɛs·a·*. It sometimes happens, however, that a long consonant, particularly *s·* and *š·*, arises from the meeting of two morphologically distinct consonants (e.g., *s* + *s* > *s·* or *š* + *š* > *š·*. or, less frequently, *š* + *s* or *s* + *š* > *s·*). In such cases the long consonant is not felt to be a mechanical lengthening of the simple consonant but as a cluster of two identical consonants, and so we find Alex writing, for example, *tsi·qšit'lassatlni*[15] "we went there only to speak," to be analyzed into *tsi·qšitł-'as-sa-('a)tł-ni*. The *s* of *-'as* "to go in order to" and the *s* of *-sa* "just, only" keep their phonologic independence and the normal intervocalic *-s·-* of *-'as·atł* is interpreted as *-ss-*. Similarly, *kwis-sila* "to do differently," to be analyzed into *kwis-sila*. It does not seem, however, that there is an actual phonetic difference between the *-s-* (phonologically *-s-*) of such words as *tlasatł* "the stick takes an upright position on the beach" (= *tla-satł*), pronounced *tlas·atł*, and the *-s·-* of *-'assatł* above. Here again we have objectively identical phonetic phenomena which receive different phonologic interpretations.

IV. In the earlier system of orthography, which Alex was taught, the glottalized stops and affricatives were treated differently from the glottalized nasals and semivowels. The former were symbolized as *p!*, *t!*, *k!*, *k!w*, *q!*, *q!w*, *ts!*, *tc!* (= *tṣ̌*), and *L!* (= *ił̣*); the latter as *'m*, *'n*, *'y*, and *'w*. The reason for this was traditional. The glottalized stops and affricatives, as a distinctive type of consonants, had been early recognized by Dr. F. Boas in many American Indian languages and described as "fortes," that is, as stops and affricatives "pronounced with increased stress of articulation." The type *'m*, *'n*, *'l*, *'y*, and *'w* was not recognized by Dr. Boas until much later, first in Kwakiutl, and described as consisting of nasal, voiced lateral, or semivowel immediately preceded by a glottal closure. The orthography for these consonants (later discovered in Tsimshian, Nootka, Haida, and a number of other languages, but not as widely distributed as the so-called "fortes") suggested their manner of formation, but the orthography for the glottalized stops and affricatives was purely conventional and did not in any way analyze their formation except to suggest that more energy was needed for their pronunciation.[16] As a pure matter of phonetics, while the Nootka glottalized

---

[15] I have slightly modified Alex's orthography to correspond to my present orthography, but these changes are merely mechanical substitutions, such as *tl* for L, and in no way affect the argument. *q* is velar *k* (Arabic ḳ), *tl* is a lateral affricative, *tł* its glottalized form.

[16] This, incidentally, is not necessarily true. In some languages the glottalized stops and affricatives seem to be somewhat more energetic in articulation than the corresponding unglottalized consonants, in others there is no noticeable

stops and affricatives are roughly parallel in formation with the glottal-ized sonantic consonants, they are not and cannot be entirely so. In a glottalized *p*, for instance, our present *ṗ* and former *p!*, there is a syn-chronous closure of lips and glottal cords, a closed air chamber is thus produced between the two, there is a sudden release of the lip closure, a moment of pause, and then the release of the glottal closure. It is the release of the lip (or other oral) closure in advance of the glottal closure that gives consonants of this type their superficial "click-like" char-acter.[17] On the other hand, in a glottalized *m*, our *'m*, while the lip closure and glottal closure are synchronous as before,[18] the glottal closure must be released at the point of initial sonancy of the *m*. Roughly speaking, therefore, *ṗ* may be analyzed into *p* + ', while *'m* may be analyzed into ' + *m*. Such an orthographic difference as *p!* versus *'m*, therefore, which I had inherited from the Americanist tradition, was not unjustified on purely phonetic grounds.

We now come to the intuitive phonologic test whether *ṗ* and *'m* are consonants of the same type or not. Alex learned to write consonants of type *ṗ* and *ṫs* very readily (our earlier *p!* and *ts!*), e.g., *ṗapi·* "ear" (earlier *p!ap!ī*), *ṫsa'ak* "stream" (earlier *ts!a'ak*). To my surprise Alex volunteered *m!* in such words as *'ma·mi·qsu* "the older [brother or sister]," which he wrote *m!ām!īqsu*. In other words, we had valuable evidence here for the phonologic reality of a glottalized class of conso-nants which included both type *ṗ* (with prior release of oral closure) and type *'m* (with prior release of glottal closure). A phonologically consistent orthography would require *ṗ* and *ṁ* (or *p!* and *m!*). Once more, a naïve native's phonetic "ignorance" proved phonologically more accurate than the scientist's "knowledge." The phonologic justification for Alex's

difference so far as "stress of articulation" is concerned. In the Athabaskan languages that I have heard (Sarcee, Kutchin, Hupa, Navaho) the aspirated voiceless stops and affricatives (of type *t'*, *k'*, *ts'*) are far more "fortis" in char-acter than the corresponding glottalized consonants (e.g., *t̉*, *k̉*, *ts̉*). There is no necessary correlation between laryngeal type of articulation (voiced, voice-less, glottalized; or any of these with aspiration) and force of articulation (fortis, lenis). So far as Nootka is concerned, it did not seem to me that the glottalized stops and affricatives (Boas' "fortes") were significantly different in emphasis from the ordinary stops and affricatives. In such languages as recognize a phono-logical difference of emphatic and nonemphatic and, at the same time, possess glottalized consonants, there is no reason why the glottalized consonants may not appear in both emphatic and nonemphatic form. As Prince Trubetzkoy has shown, some of the North Caucasic languages, as a matter of fact, possess both emphatic and nonemphatic glottalized stops and affricatives.

[17] These consonants are apparently identical with the "ejectives" of Daniel Jones. There is another, apparently less common, type of glottalized stop or affricative in which the oral and glottal releases are synchronous.

[18] The pronunciation of *'m*, *'n*, *'w*, and *'y* as a simple sequence of glottal stop (') plus *m*, *n*, *w*, and *y* is rejected by the Nootka ear as incorrect.

"error" is not difficult. Consonants of type $\dot{p}$ are entirely analogous to consonants of type 'm for the following reasons.

1. Each occurs at the beginning of a syllable and, since no word can begin with a cluster of consonants, both $\dot{p}$ and 'm are felt by Nootka speakers to be unanalyzable phonologic units. In other words, the glottal stop can no more easily be abstracted from 'm than from $\dot{p}$. Similarly, the affricatives and glottalized affricatives are phonologically unanalyzable units.

2. All consonants can occur at the end of a syllable except glottalized stops and affricatives, glottalized sonantic consonants ('m, 'n, 'y, 'w), semivowels (y, w), nasals (m, n),[19] the glottal stop ('), and h. This rule throws consonants of type 'm more definitely together with consonants of type $\dot{p}$.

3. Many suffixes which begin with a vowel have the effect of "hardening"[20] the preceding consonant, in other words, of glottally affecting it. Under the influence of this "hardening" process p, t, k become $\dot{p}$, $\dot{t}$, $\dot{k}$, while m and n become 'm and 'n. For example, just as the suffixes '$-a'a$[21] ('$-a\cdot'a$) "on the rocks" and '$-aḥs$ "in a receptacle" change the stem $wi\cdot nap$- "to stay, dwell" to $wi\cdot na\dot{p}$- (e.g., $wi\cdot na\dot{p}a'a$ "so stay on the rocks") and wik- "to be not" to wik'- (e.g., $wiḳaḥs$ "to be not in a receptacle, a canoe is empty"), so $t' łum$- (alternating with $t'łup$-) "to be hot" becomes $t'łu'm$- (alternating with $t'łu\dot{p}$-)(e.g., $łu'ma\cdot'a$ "to be hot on the rocks" and $iłu'maḥs$ "to be hot in a receptacle, there is hot water"; compare $iłu\dot{p}i\cdot tš̌ḥ$ "summer, hot season" = parallel $łup$- + '$-i\cdot tch$ "season") and kan- "to kneel" (e.g., $kanił$ "to kneel in the house") becomes $ka'n$- (e.g., $ka'naḥs$ "to kneel in a canoe"). As there seem to be no stems ending in h or ', the group 'm, 'n, 'w, 'y[22] is left over as functionally related to the group m, n, w, y in the same sense as the group exemplified by $\dot{p}$ is related to the group exemplified by p. Morphology, in other words, convincingly supports the phonologic proportion $p:\dot{p} = m:'m$. It is maintained that it was this underlying phonologic configuration that made Alex hear 'm as sufficiently similar to $\dot{p}$ to justify its being written in an analogous fashion. In other languages, with different phonologic and morphologic understandings, such a parallelism of orthography might not be justified at all and the phonetic differences that actually

---

[19] m and n may be followed by a murmured vowel of i-timbre which is a reduced form of a, u, or i. Syllables or half-syllables of type m^i or n^i are preceded by i, an assimilated product of a, u or i; in^i and im^i result therefore, in part, from sequences of type ama, umi, anu. Simple $-em$ or $-an$ become $-ap$, $-at$.

[20] A term borrowed from Boas' equivalent Kwakiutl phenomenon.

[21] The symbol ' indicates the "hardening" effect of a suffix.

[22] The phonologic details involving 'w and 'y and their relation to w and y and other consonants are too intricate for a summary statement in this place.

obtain between 'm and $\acute{p}$ would have a significantly different psychologic weighting.

V. In a course in practical phonetics which I have been giving for a number of years I have so often remarked the following illusion of hearing on the part of students that there seems no way of avoiding a general phonologic theory to explain it. I find that, after the students have been taught to recognize the glottal stop as a phonetic unit, many of them tend to hear it after a word ending in an accented short vowel of clear timbre (e.g., *a*, *ε*, *e*, *i*). This illusion does not seem to apply so often to words ending in a long vowel or an obscure vowel of relatively undefined quality (ə) or an unaccented vowel. Thus, a dictated nonsense word like *smε* or *pilá* would occasionally be misheard and written as *smε'* and *pilá'* but there seems far less tendency to hear a final glottal stop in words like *pila or pilá·*. What is the reason for this singular type of "overhearing?" Is it enough to say that students who have learned a new sound like to play with it and that their preparedness for it tends to make them project its usage into the stream of acoustic stimuli to which they are asked to attend? No doubt such a general explanation is a correct dynamic formula so far as it goes but it is not precise enough for a phonologist because it does not take sufficient account of the limitations of the illusion.

It must be remembered that the language of my students is English. We may therefore suspect that the illusion of a final glottal stop is due to some feature in the phonologic structure of English. But English has no glottal stop. How, then, can English phonology explain the overhearing of a consonant which is alien to its genius to begin with? Nevertheless, I believe that the students who projected a final glottal stop into the dictated words were handling an exotic phonetic element, the glottal stop, according to a firmly established but quite unconscious phonologic pattern. It requires both the learning process, with its consequent alert preparedness to recognize what has been learned, and English phonology to explain the illusion. If we study the kinds of syllables in English which may normally constitute an accented monosyllabic word or an accented (or secondarily accented) final syllable of a word, we find that they may be classified into three types:

A. Words ending in a long vowel or diphthong, e.g., *sea, flow, shoe, review, apply.*
B. Words ending in a long vowel or diphthong plus one or more consonants, e.g., *ball, cease, dream, alcove, amount.*
C. Words ending in a short vowel plus one or more consonants, e.g., *back, fill, come, remit, object.*

The theoretically possible fourth class:

D. Words ending in a short vowel, e.g, French *fait, ami;* Russian *xărăšɔ'*

does not exist in English. English-speaking people tend to pronounce
words of type D in a "drawling" fashion which transfers them to type A
(e.g., *ami·* for *ami*). Observe that the apparently inconsistent possibility
of a nonfinal accented syllable ending in a short vowel (e.g., *fiddle, butter,
double, pheasant*) is justified by the English theory of syllabification,
which feels the point of the syllabic division to lie in the following consonant (*d, t, b, z,* in the examples cited), so that the accented syllables of
these words really belong phonologically to type C, not to type D. Intervocalic consonants like the *d* of *fiddle* or *z* of *pheasant,* in spite of the fact
that they are not phonetically long, are phonologically "flanking" or two-
faced, in that they at one and the same time complete one syllable and
begin another. Should the point of syllabic division shift back of the
consonant, the preceding vowel at once lengthens in spite of its "short"
quality (type A), and we thus get dialectic American pronunciations of
words like *fiddle* and *pheasant* in which the accented vowel keeps its
original quality but has been lengthened to the unit length of "long
vowels" of type *feeble, reason,* and *ladle.*

We are now prepared to understand the illusion we started with. Such
words as *smɛ* and *pilá* are unconsciously tested as possible members of
class A or class C. Two illusions are possible, if the hearer is to be a victim
of his phonologic system. Inasmuch as a final accented short vowel is an
unfamiliar entity, it can be "legitimized" either by projecting length into
it (misheard *smɛ·* and *pilá·* fall into class A) or by projecting a final
consonant after it (class C). We shall call this imaginary consonant *"x"*
and write *smɛx* and *pildx.* Now the fact that one has added the glottal
stop to his kit of consonantal tools leads often to the temptation to solve
the phonologic problem symbolized as *smɛx* and *pildx* in terms of the
glottal stop and to hear *smɛ'* and *pilá'.* The glottal stop is the most unreal
or zerolike of consonants to an English or American ear and is admirably
fitted, once its existence has been discovered, to serve as the projected
actualization of a phonologically required final consonant of minimum
sonority. The illusion of the final glottal stop is essentially the illusion of
a generalized final consonant (*"x"*) needed to classify the dictated words
into a known category (type C). Or, to speak more analytically, English
phonology creates the groundwork (*-x*) of the synthetic illusion, while the
learning process colors it to the shape of *-'*. The error of hearing a glottal
stop where there is none, in words of type D, is fundamentally a more
sophisticated form of the same error as hearing a dictated final glottal

stop as *p* or *t* or *k*, which occurs frequently in an earlier stage of the acquiring of a phonetic technique.

The danger of hearing a glottal stop when the dictated word ends in a long vowel or diphthong is of course rendered very unlikely by the fact that such words conform to a common English pattern (type A). The reason why the error does not so easily occur in hearing dictated words ending in an unaccented short vowel (e.g., *o·nɛ, sú·li*) is that such words, too, conform to an English pattern, though the range of the qualities allowed a vowel in this position is not as great as when the vowel is covered by a following consonant (e.g., *idea, very, follow*).

A STUDY IN PHONETIC SYMBOLISM*

THE SYMBOLISM of language is, or may be, twofold. By far the greater portion of its recognized content and structure is symbolic in a purely referential sense; in other words, the meaningful combinations of vowels and consonants (words, significant parts of words, and word groupings) derive their functional significance from the arbitrary associations between them and their meanings established by various societies in the course of an uncontrollably long period of historical development. That these associations are essentially arbitrary or conventional may be seen at once by considering such a proportion as

> phonetic entity 'boy': idea (or reference) 'boy'
> = phonetic entity 'man': idea (or reference) 'man.'

In passing from the notion of 'boy' to that of 'man' we experience a definite feeling of relationship between the two notions, that of increase in size and age. But the purely phonetic relationship of 'boy' : 'man' takes no account of this. So far as the referential symbolism of language is concerned, the words 'boy' and 'man' are discrete, incomparable phonetic entities, the sound-group b-o-y having no more to do with the sound-group m-a-n, in a possible scale of evaluated phonetic variants, than any randomly selected pair of sound-groups, say 'run' and 'bad,' have to do with each other.

This completely dissociated type of symbolism is of course familiar; it is of the very essence of linguistic form. But there are other types of linguistic expression that suggest a more fundamental, a psychologically primary, sort of symbolism.[1] As examples may be given the interrogative tone in such a spoken sentence as "You say he's dead?" in comparison with the simple declarative tone of the corresponding "You say he's dead"; further, the emphatically diminutive *ee* of *teeny* as contrasted with the normal *i* of *tiny*. In both of these examples the phonetic difference is undoubtedly felt as somehow directly expressive of the difference of meaning in a sense in which the contrast between say 'boy' and 'man' is not. We may call this type of symbolism 'expressive' as contrasted with the merely 'referential' symbolism which was first spoken of. It

* *Journal of Experimental Psychology*, 12 (1929): 225–239. Publication of the Behavior Research Fund, the Institute for Juvenile Research, Chicago (Herman M. Adler, Director), Ser. B, No. 132. For valuable suggestions in the preparation of this paper I am indebted to Professor H. A. Carr, University of Chicago.
[1] For the two symbolic layers in speech, as in all expression, see Edward Sapir, "Language as a Form of Human Behavior," *English Journal*, 16 (1927): 421–433.

goes without saying that in actual speech referential and expressive
symbolisms are pooled in a single expressive stream, the socialization of
the tendency to expressive symbolism being far less extreme, in the great
majority of languages, than of the tendency to fix references as such.

We may legitimately ask if there are, in the speech of a considerable
percentage of normal individuals, certain preferential tendencies to expressive symbolism not only in the field of speech dynamics (stress, pitch,
and varying quantities), but also in the field of phonetic material as
ordinarily understood. Can it be shown, in other words, that symbolisms
tend to work themselves out in vocalic and consonantal contrasts and
scales in spite of the arbitrary allocations of these same vowels and consonants in the strictly socialized field of reference? The present paper is
a preliminary report of certain aspects of a study, still in progress, intended to probe into any such latent symbolisms as may be thought to
exist. The field of inquiry is vast and difficult to chart and I cannot hope
to have guarded against all the possible fallacies of interpretation. For
the present I have limited myself to the meaning contrast 'large' : 'small'
as offering the most likely chance of arriving at relatively tangible
results.

The main object of the study is to ascertain if there tends to be a feeling of the symbolic magnitude value of certain differences in vowels and
consonants, regardless of the particular associations due to the presence
of these vowels and consonants in meaningful words in the language of
the speaker. The results so far obtained seem to go far in demonstrating
the reality of such feelings, whatever may be their cause. It has also
become very clear that individuals differ a good deal in the matter of
sensitiveness to the symbolic suggestiveness of special sound contrasts.

A number of distinct schedules have been devised and applied in the
research. In the early stages of the work the various types of sound difference were studied independently. For instance, the contrast between the
vowel *a* and the vowel *i* (the phonetic or continental values are intended)
was illustrated in every one of sixty pairs of stimulus words, the subject
being requested to indicate in each case which of the two in themselves
meaningless words meant the larger and which the smaller variety of an
arbitrarily selected meaning. For example, the meaningless words *mal*
and *mil* were pronounced in that order and given the arbitrary meaning
'table.' The subject decided whether *mal* seemed to symbolize a large or
a small table as contrasted with the word *mil*.

In the first experiments schedules of sixty stimulus word-pairs were used,
each of which was divided into two sections. The first thirty word-pairs involved
only such sounds as the subject, an English-speaking person, would be familiar

with, the second set of thirty word-pairs, while still illustrating the same phonetic contrast as the first thirty, say that of *a* to *i*, also involved sounds that the subject was not familiar with. Each of the two sets of thirty was further subdivided into functional groups: nouns, verbs with reference to large or small subject of verb, adjectives with reference to large or small things, verbs with reference to large or small object of verb, and verbs with reference to intense or normal degree of activity. It is important to note that the words were so selected as to avoid associations with meaningful words and it was the special purpose of the second set of thirty word-pairs to remove the subject still further from the intercurrent influence of meaningful linguistic associations.

If the results obtained from a considerable number of individuals can be relied upon as symptomatic, the influence of accidental, meaningful linguistic associations is less than might have been supposed, for the percentage of responses in favor of one of the two vowels as symbolizing the large object tended to be little less if at all, in the second set of word-pairs than in the first. For example, Subj. IK found that of the first thirty word-pairs illustrating a contrast between the vowels *a* and *i* twenty-two examples of *a* "naturally" carried with them the connotation "large," five examples of *i* carried this connotation, and three word-pairs were responded to indifferently. The effective score in favor of *a* as the vowel inherently symbolizing a large rather than a small reference was 22/27 or 81 per cent. In the second set of thirty word-pairs illustrating the same vocalic contrast, 21 of the words involving the vowel *a* were said to connote the large reference, 5 with the vowel *i* connoted the small reference, and 4 were indifferent. Here the effective score in favor of the symbolic value of the vowel *a* as large by contrast with *i* is 21/26 or, again, 81 per cent. In the case of the vowel contrast *a* to *e* (with the short value of the French *e*, as in *été*) IK's effective score in favor of the *a* vowel as connoting the larger reference was 24/29 or 83 per cent for the first 30 word-pairs, 73 per cent for the second 30 word-pairs.

The essential points that seemed to appear from these first experiments with individuals were: (1) that vocalic and consonantal contrasts tended with many, indeed with most, individuals to have a definite symbolic feeling-significance that seemed to have little relation to the associative values of actual words; (2) that it made surprisingly little difference whether the phonetic contrast was contained in a phonetically "possible" or a phonetically "impossible" context; and (3) that the certainty of the symbolic distinction tended to vary with the nature of the phonetic contrast. The last point, which is important, will be discussed later on in this report.

These earlier experiments with individuals, though revealing, were felt as the work proceeded to be deficient in one important respect, namely, that the simple nature of the vocalic or consonantal contrast in a set of word-pairs might be expected to lead to a too ready systematization of responses on the part of the subject. In other words, the average subject could not help noticing after responding to a few stimuli that a certain consistency in the responses would naturally be expected, and that if the vowel *a*, for example, as contrasted with *e* or *i*, is felt satisfactorily to symbolize the larger of two objects, all other examples of word-pairs illustrating the same vocalic contrast should be dealt with in the same manner. The primary purpose of the experiment, however, was to elicit spontaneous feelings of symbolic contrast, unrevised by any judgment as to consistency of response. For this reason a further and, it is believed, much more efficient experiment was devised consisting of 100 word-pairs involving every type of phonetic contrast that was investigated. These hundred word-pairs were not arranged in any logical order, nor was the order of the contrasted phonetic elements in any particular entry necessarily the same as in another entry involving the same contrast. In the table that was finally adopted the first word-pair illustrated the contrast between *a* and *i*, the second the contrast between *e* and *a*, the third the contrast between *z* and *s*, and so on through the list. The contrast between *a* and *i* was illustrated not only in Entry 1 but also in Entries 41, 81, and 87. In this way, it was hoped, systematization on the part of the subject was necessarily hindered, if not entirely blocked, and the responses actually obtained may be looked upon as normally spontaneous feeling judgments following in the wake of an initial suggestion as to preferred class of symbolic response (*i.e.*, variations in magnitude).

For this second experiment 500 subjects were employed, most of them students of the University of Chicago High School. The subjects were eventually analyzed into the following groups; 6 cases of 11-year-old children, 30 of 12 years, 86 of 13 years, 94 of 14 years, 124 of 15 years, 81 of 16 years, 33 of 17 years, 10 of 18 years, 21 University of Chicago students, 8 adults who were not students, and 7 Chinese. The subjects were provided with forms in which there were blank spaces for each of the entries, and they were carefully instructed to check off the first of the two stimulus words announced by the investigator as to whether it symbolized the larger or the smaller reference. If the response was indifferent, no check was to be entered in either the large or the small column. Very little difficulty was experienced in explaining the conditions of the experiment, which seemed to be enjoyed by the great majority of the subjects as a rather interesting game. It is believed that the results obtained are as reliable as material of this kind can be, every precaution having been taken to arrange conditions favoring simple and unambiguous responses and only the investigator himself pronouncing the stimulus words, in order that all confusion due to slight variations of pronunciation might be avoided.

The phonetic contrasts may be classified on phonetic and acoustic grounds into five main groups. There are also two minor groups which are of lesser interest. In the first group the contrasting vowels belong to the series *a*, *ä*, *ɛ*, *e*, *i*. The pronunciation of these vowels, as of all other vowels, was *quantitatively uniform in a given pair* in order that the independent symbolic suggestiveness of quantity differences as such be ruled out of consideration where quality alone was being studied. The phonetic values of these vowels were respectively those of *a* of German *Mann* (*a*), *a* of English *hat* (*ä*), *e* of English *met* (*ε*), *e* of French *été* (*e*), *i* of French *fini* (*i*). It will be observed that the phonetic contrast is gradually lessened within the scale as one moves from *a* to *i*. Thus, *a* to *i* affords the greatest objective contrast, *ä* to *i* or *a* to *e* a lesser contrast, *ε* to *i* or *a* to *ε* a still lesser one, and *a* to *ä* or *ä* to *ε* or *ε* to *e* or *e* to *i* a minimal contrast. In other words, on purely objective phonetic grounds, one might imagine that the responses would tend to be further removed from a purely random or 50–50 distribution the greater the contrast between the vowels. It was therefore of great interest to determine not only whether there were preferred symbolisms, but also whether the varying percentages of response bore a fairly close relation to objective differences in the sounds themselves as determined on phonetic and acoustic grounds.

The second group of word-pairs illustrates the contrast between vowels on the scale *a, ɔ, o, u*, *i.e.*, a scale with progressive lip-rounding. The third group illustrates contrasts between rounded back vowels (*u, o, ɔ*) and unrounded front vowels (*i, e, ε, ä*). In the fourth group of word-pairs there was illustrated the contrast between voiced and voiceless consonants, *e.g.*, between *z* and *s*, *v* and *f*, *b* and *p*. The fifth group illustrates the contrast between stopped consonants and spirants or fricatives, *e.g.*, between *f* and *p*, *x* (*ch* of German *Bach*) and *k*.

It would be quite impossible to report on all the details of the experiment in this place. I shall content myself with giving two selected tables. The first shows the distribution of responses for the word-pairs illustrating the contrast between *a* and *i*, classified according to the groups of subjects (11–18 yrs, university students, adults, and Chinese).

It will be observed that the percentage of responses in favor of *a* vs. *i* ranges all the way from about 75 per cent to about 96 per cent. For the largest group of subjects, the 124 fifteen-year-olds, the percentage is as high as 83, while the small number of 11-year-olds reach the figure 87.5. It is obvious that, regardless of infinite differences of an individual nature as to the general symbolic value of this phonetic contrast or as to its specific value in particular cases, English-speaking society does, for some reason or other, feel that of these two vowels, *a*, by and large, is possessed of a greater potential magnitude symbolism than the contrasted vowel *i*. The same feeling seems to be illustrated by the small number of Chinese cases. Furthermore, within the English-speaking community there seems little reason to believe that there is a significant growth in the firmness of the symbolic feeling after the age of 11. The case of the eight adults is not really significant because they consisted of high school teachers of English who answered the forms at the same time as their classes. They would naturally have a more self-conscious attitude toward the problem of sound symbolism than individuals selected at random. In other words, however these symbolisms are fixed, it is probable that they are so fixed at a rather early age and that familiarity with literature is not likely to count as a heavy factor in the situation. These general considerations are borne out by all the other findings, and it is of particular interest to note that the Chinese evidence is nearly always in the same general direction as that of the English-speaking subjects. Further work needs to be done on responses of this kind from younger children

TABLE I

PERCENTAGE OF RESPONSES SHOWING PREFERENCE FOR *a* VS. *i* TO SYMBOLIZE 'LARGE'

ENTRY NO.	OBSERVED										
	6	30	86	94	124	81	33	10	21	8	7
	Age										
	11	12	13	14	15	16	17	18	Univ.	Adults	Chin.
1......	83.3	86.7	90.6	92.3	83.1	84.0	78.8	80.0	85.0	100.0	100.0
41......	100.0	70.0	82.7	78.0	76.4	71.6	69.7	50.0	95.2	100.0	85.7
81......	83.3	93.3	74.7	72.2	81.8	80.0	77.4	100.0	70.0	85.7	85.7
87......	83.3	83.3	84.1	86.0	91.8	86.1	72.7	80.0	90.0	100.0	42.9
Ave.....	87.5	83.3	83.0	82.1	83.3	80.4	74.6½	77.5	85.0½	96.4	78.6

and from other groups of foreigners before the age and language factors can be properly evaluated or dismissed as irrelevant.

The second table is an attempt to show the differential symbolic value of the vocalic contrasts in the *a* to *i* series. Four age-groups (13–16), involving 385 subjects, are represented in this table. It was found in comparing the responses to the different vocalic pairs that they tended to arrange themselves roughly into four distinct groups (A, B, C, D). In the first group, typically illustrated by the contrast between *a* and *i* and *ä* and *i*, the percentage of a response in favor of the vowel nearer *a* of the scale ranged from 80 per cent upward. The second group of responses was found to be somewhat set off from the preceding one by a marked decrease in the percentage of responses favoring the vowel toward *a* of the scale. This group is typically illustrated by the contrast between *a* and ε, the percentage in favor of the 'larger' vowel running from about 73 per cent to 78 per cent. The third group, illustrated by the typical

TABLE II

CONFIGURATED DISTRIBUTION OF "*a:i*" RESPONSES IN AGES 13–16

	AGE 13 (86 CASES)	AGE 14 (94 CASES)	AGE 15 (124 CASES)	AGE 16 (81 CASES)
Group A	a:ε (2 steps) 86.0 ä:i (3 " ") 84.7 a:i (4 " ") 83.0 ε:i (2 " ") 82.0	a:i (4 steps) 82.1 ä:i (3 " ") 80.3	a:i (4 steps) 83.3 ä:i (3 " ") 80.0	ä:i (3 steps) 87.0 ε:i (2 " ") 81.8 a:i (4 " ") 80.4
Group B	ä:ε (1 step) 76.4 *a:e (3 steps) 75.3	ε:i (2 steps) 78.2 a:ε (2 " ") 76.9 ä:ε (1 " ") 74.9 *a:e (3 " ") 73.1	ε:i (2 steps) 76.8 a:ε (2 " ") 72.8	a:ε (2 steps) 75.7 ä:ε (1 " ") 74.8
Group C	ε:i (1 step) 67.8 a:ä (1 " ") 62.5	ε:i (1 step) 67.5 ε:e (1 " ") 60.3	ε:i (1 " ") 72.7 a:e (1 step) 69.5 *a:e (3 steps) 68.6	*a:e (3 steps) 70.7 ε:i (1 " ") 70.2
Group D	ε:e (1 step) 53.6	a:ä (1 step) 56.5	a:ä (1 step) 59.0 ε:e (1 " ") 58.3	ε:e (1 step) 60.4 a:ä (1 " ") 58.7

contrast *e* to *i*, ranges from about 60 per cent to 70 per cent. The last group, that of minimal psychological contrast in the *a* to *i* set, runs below 60 per cent in favor of the vowel toward *a* of the scale.

The table has been arranged chiefly from the point of view of the internal 'hiatus' between the percentages of response within each age-group. It is noteworthy that the 'configurated distribution' of the responses runs fairly parallel in the four age groups both as to the stepwise discriminations which seem to be felt by many of the subjects and as to the actual order of the specific vocalic contrasts when evaluated by means of percentages in favor of the vowel toward *a* of the scale. Naturally, the reality and normal limits of these stepwise discriminations need to be tested by a careful examination of the individual records, supplemented by further experiments.

On the whole, it will be observed that the symbolic discriminations run encouragingly parallel to the objective ones based on phonetic considerations. This may mean that the chances of the responses being to a high degree determined by actual word associations of the language of the subject are slim, the meanings of words not being distributed, so far as known, according to any principle of sound values as such; and, further, that we are really dealing with a measurably independent psychological factor that for want of a better term may be called 'phonetic symbolism.'

One vocalic contrast, however, falls out of the expected picture. This is the *a* to *e* set, which is starred in the table. Though the *a* vowel is judged prevailingly 'large' as contrasted with *e*, there seems to be present some factor of hesitation which lessens the value of the contrast. If we go by objective distances between vowels, the *a* to *e* contrast, being a '3-step' one, should have fallen into Group A, instead of which it actually either comes last in Group B or falls even as low as Group C. I believe that a very interesting and sufficient reason can be given for this curious fact. The short vowel *e*, as in French *été*, is not native to the English language. Subjects hearing the vowel *e*, when pronounced in the proximity of *a*, which is acoustically far removed from it, would tend not to hear what was actually pronounced, but to project the characteristic long '*e*-vowel' familiar to us in such words as *raise* or *lake*. In other words, the qualitative symbolism would tend to receive a revision in the opposite sense because of an intercurrent quantitative symbolism. This example is suggestive as illustrating the importance of the linguistic factor vs. the merely phonetic one, though not in the sense in which the term 'linguistic factor' is ordinarily understood. What skews the picture here is probably not the associative power of particular English words but the *phonetic configuration* of English as such.[2] That even this configuration, however, is of limited importance in interpreting the experiment is shown by the fact that in word-pairs illustrating the contrast *e* to *i*, *ε* to *e*, the acoustic nearness of the two vowels prevents the unconsciously imputed quantitative interference from making itself felt in the symbolic response.

These and many other similar results need interpretation. One's first temptation is to look about for some peculiarity of English speech, some distribution of sounds in actual words, that would make the results we have secured intelligible. A simple associational explanation, however, is not likely to prove tenable. The weighting of the responses is altogether too much in accordance with an absolute phonetic scale to make it possible in the long run to avoid at least some use of 'natural' or 'expressive,' as contrasted with socially fixed verbal, symbolism as an explanation. It is difficult to resist the conclusion that in some way a significant proportion of normal people feel that, other things being equal, a word with the vowel *a* is likely to symbolize something larger than a similar word with the vowel *i*, or *e*, or *ε*, or *ä*. To put it roughly, certain vowels and certain consonants 'sound bigger' than others. It would be an important check to amass a large number of randomly distributed meaningful words, to classify into the two groups of 'large' and 'small' those which could be so classified without serious difficulty, and to see if in sets in which equal numbers of phonetically contrasted words are found the meaning classes were or were not correlated with the sound classes and to see further, if they are so correlated, if the distributions are of the same nature as those studied in the experiments.

The reason for this unconscious symbolism, the factor of linguistic interference being set aside for the present, may be acoustic or kinesthetic or a combination of both. It is possible that the inherent 'volume' of certain vowels is greater than that of others and that this factor alone is sufficient to explain the results of the experiment. On the other hand, it should be noted that one may unconsciously feel that the tongue position for one vowel is symbolically 'large' as contrasted with the tongue position for another. In the case of *i* the tongue is high up toward the roof of the mouth and articulates pretty well forward. In other words, the vibrating column of air is passing through a narrow resonance chamber. In the case of *a* the tongue is very considerably lowered in comparison, and also retracted. In other words, the vibrating column of air is now passing through a much wider resonance chamber. This kinesthetic ex-

---

[2] For the significance in language of 'sound patterns' or 'phonetic configurations' as distinct from sounds as such, see Edward Sapir, "Sound Patterns in Language," *Language*, 1 (1925) 37–51. [This article is reprinted in this volume, pp. 33–45.]

planation is just as simple as the acoustic one and really means no more than that a spatially extended gesture is symbolic of a larger reference than a spatially restricted gesture. In discussing some of the results with the children themselves, who seemed very much interested in the rationale of the experiment, the impression was gained that the subjects differed somewhat in the psychological basis of the symbolism, some being apparently swayed entirely by the acoustic factor, others by the acoustic factor only or mainly insofar as it was itself supported by the kinesthetic factor.

The tabulated results, of which we have given a brief sample, have the disadvantage of drowning out significant individual variations. For a preliminary report such a method of presentation is at least suggestive; but it would be important to know to what extent individuals differ significantly in their ability to feel symbolism in sound contrasts. The schedules need to be gone over from the point of view of working out individual indices of 'symbolic sensitiveness' to sounds.

Meanwhile a third experiment, intended to bring out individual idiosyncrasies, was carried out with a number of selected subjects, chiefly adults. The results were interesting.

In this experiment an artificial 'word' was taken as a starting point and assigned an arbitrary meaning by either the investigator or the subject. The subject was asked to hold on to this arbitrary meaning and to try to establish as firm an association as possible between the imaginary word and its given meaning. Some phonetic element in the word, a vowel or a consonant, was then changed and the subject asked to say what difference of meaning seemed naturally to result. The answer was to be spontaneous, unintellectualized. The process was kept on for as long a period as seemed worth while, the saturation point of meaningful and interested responses being reached very soon in some cases, very late in others. In the case of certain individuals more than 50 distinct 'words' were found to build up a constellated system in which the meanings were rather obviously the results of certain intuitively felt symbolic relations between the varied sounds. In the case of other individuals actual word associations tended to creep in, but on the whole there was surprisingly little evidence of this factor. The subjects were found to differ a great deal in their ability to hold on without effort to a constellation once formed and to fit new meanings into it consistently with the symbolisms expressed in previous responses. Some would give identically the same response for a stimulus word that had been—so it was claimed—forgotten as such. In its imaginary, constellated context it evoked a consistent response. Others lost their moorings very rapidly. It is hoped to discuss these interesting variations of sensitivity to sound symbolism, *i.e.*, to the potential meaningfulness of relations in sound sets, in the final report of these investigations.

In the present purely preliminary report we can do little more than give a few examples of the responses of two of the subjects, KP and JS.

The word *mīla* was arbitrarily defined as 'brook' by the subject KP. Fifty-three responses were obtained from her, starting with this nucleus. The following excerpts from the material will be illuminating.

1. *mīla*: "Brook."
2. *mila*: "Smaller brook."
3. *mēla*: "Larger brook; nearer a river; swifter; no longer thought of as part of the meadow landscape."
4. *mɛla*: "Larger, not so flowing; large lake like Lake Superior."
5. *mɛla*: "Little lake for fishing."
6. *mela*: "Smaller brook than *mīla*, larger than *mila*."
7. *māla*: "Larger than brook. Perhaps water running through a ravine; mixed up with the scene."
8. *mīna*: "Water trickling down in a ravine through the rocks scattered on the side."
9. *mēna*: "A little larger but still diminutive. Water travels through a gravel pit."
10. *mɛna*: "Deep, narrow, swiftly moving stream rushing through a cut in the rocks."

. . . .

14. *mīni*: "Tiny but swift stream spurting out of the rocks like a jet of water."

. . . .

18. *mūla*: "Fairly large, rather rambling brook at night."
19. *mōla*: "Ocean at night."
20. *mɔla*: "Ocean in the daytime."
21. *māla*: "Bright ocean."

. . . .

2[1]. *mila*: (21st response after 2): "A little brook." (The jump back to the earlier response was made at once, without hesitation.)

. . . .

14[1]. *mīni*: (15th response after 14): "Spurt of water from the rocks, small but swift."

. . . .

48. *wīla*: "Can be wet, but water is more like dew on wet grass after rain. Belongs to the same set."
49. *wēla*: "Wet trees after a rain. No feeling of a body of water. General dampness, a 'larger' feeling than *wīla*."

Not all subjects by any means were as responsive as KP; but a surprising number showed a very definite tendency toward the constellating of sound symbolisms. A few responses from JS, based on the same stimulus word, will be interesting for purposes of comparison. The meaning 'brook' was assigned by the investigator and accepted as satisfactory by the subject.

1. *mīla*: "Brook."
2. *mēla*: "Seems to sort of broaden out. Brook got much calmer."
3. *mila*: "Got to chattering again; smaller brook; stones visible, which make the noise."[1]

4. *mɛla*: "Brook gets stagnant with rushes growing in it. The rushes hold the water back so it forms pools. The flow is in the middle; relatively stagnant at the edges."

5. *mäla*: "Almost like a lake. An uninteresting lake."

6. *mɑ̄la*: "More color in it. May have been shallow before; now has greater depth of color, greener shadows; still a lake."

7. *mɛla*: "Pools taken out at the side from 4. Regains a little of its chattering. Sort of tiny. Less cheerful and chirpy than 3. No great difference as to size between 7 and 3. Merely has a deeper note."

6^{1}. *mɑ̄la* (4th response after 6): "Nice broad pool with all nice colors in it. Shadows and water rich green, as of tree shadow in pool."

1^{1}. *mīla* (11th response after 1): "Rather nice chattering brook."

17. *mīlɛ*: "A little splash of water. Tiny stream hit a rock and spattered out in all directions."

18. *mīli*: "Water has gone. A bit of rather dense woods with lots of moisture. Water not evident, but obviously somewhere. You don't see water but you know it is there. Rather soggy to walk around."

6^{2}. *mɑ̄la* (23d response after 6^{1}, with much material in between that was definitely removed from suggestions of 6): "Quick sweep of water view over a lake. Not just a pond. A few islands, but they look like dots. The sun is setting. There are nice black shadows this side of the island. The scenery is darkest where I am. I am interested in the distant brightness."

A comparison of these excerpts from the two schedules shows certain interesting resemblances and differences. Both subjects constellate their responses; but KP does so more rigidly, 'geometrically,' as it were. With JS the underlying 'geometry' of response is enriched by imaginative overtones. Incidentally, it will be observed by the attentive reader, a considerable number of the responses here quoted from the third series of experiments check some of the magnitude symbolisms independently obtained from the first and second. This is true of most of the schedules in this set and is significant because neither magnitude variations nor any other class of variations in the responses had been suggested.

It is believed that studies of this type are of value in showing the tendency of symbolisms to constellate in accordance with an unconscious or intuitive logic which is not necessarily based on experience with the stimuli in their normal, functional aspect. In the realm of articulate sounds, to take a specific type of perceptive field, it is believed that the experiments here referred to give cumulative evidence for the belief that unsocialized symbolisms tend to work themselves out rather definitely, and that the influence of specific, functional language factors need not be invoked to explain these symbolisms.

THE CONCEPT OF PHONETIC LAW AS TESTED IN PRIMITIVE LANGUAGES BY LEONARD BLOOMFIELD*

A LARGE PART of the scientific study of language consists in the formulation and application of phonetic laws.[1] These phonetic laws are by no means comparable to the laws of physics or chemistry or any other of the natural sciences. They are merely general statements of series of changes characteristic of a given language at a particular time. Thus, a phonetic law applying to a particular sound in the history of English applies only to that sound within a given period of time and by no means commits itself to the development of the same sound at another period in the history of English, nor has it anything to say about the treatment of the same sound in other languages. Experience has shown that the sound system of any language tends to vary slightly from time to time. These shifts in pronunciation, however, have been found to work according to regular laws of formulas. Thus, the *f* of the English word *father* can be shown by comparison with such related languages as Latin, Greek, and Sanskrit to go back to an original *p*. The change of *p* in the original Indo-European word for "father," reflected in the Latin *pater* and the Greek *patēr*, is not, however, an isolated phenomenon but is paralleled by a great many other examples of the same process. Thus, *foot* corresponds to Greek *pous*, genitive *podos; five* corresponds to Greek *pente; full* corresponds to Latin *plēnus; and for* is closely related to Latin *prō*. A comparison of English with certain other languages, such as German, Swedish, Danish, Old Icelandic, and Gothic, proves that these languages share with English the use of the consonant *f* where other languages of the same family which are less closely related to English than these have a *p*.

Inasmuch as such languages as Latin, Greek, Sanskrit, and Slavic differ among themselves about as much as any one of them differs from the Germanic group to which English belongs, it is a fair assumption that their concordance is an archaic feature and not a parallel

* Stuart A. Rice, ed., *Methods in Social Science: A Case Book* (Chicago, University of Chicago Press, 1931), pp. 297–306. For Bloomfield's studies, see "A Set of Postulates for the Science of Language," *Language*, 2 (1926): 153–164; "On the Sound-System of Central Algonquian," *ibid.*, 1 (1925): 130–156; "A Note on Linguistic Change," *ibid.*, 4 (1928): 99–100; and see also Edward Sapir, MS materials on Athabaskan languages.

[1] [In preparing this analysis, Professor Sapir was invited to discuss his own work at length because of its similarity to the work of Bloomfield.—Stuart A. Rice, Ed.]

development, and that the *f* of English and its more closely related languages is a secondary sound derived from an original *p*. This inference is put in the form of a phonetic law, which reads: "Indo-European *p* becomes Germanic *f*." The change cannot be dated, but obviously belongs to at least the period immediately preceding the earliest contact of the Germanic tribes with the Romans, for in all the Germanic words and names that have come down to us from the classic authors this change is already manifest. It is important to realize that two distinct historic facts may be inferred from such evidence as we have given, which is naturally but a small part of the total evidence available. In the first place, the change of *p* to *f* is regular. In other words, we do not find that in one correspondence *f* is related to *p* while in another correspondence *f* seems to parallel *w* or *b* or some other sound. In the second place, the general consensus of the Indo-European languages indicates that the change has been from *p* to *f* and not from *f* to *p*. Incidentally, this is in accord with general linguistic experience, for stopped consonants more often become spirants (continuous "rubbed" consonants) than the reverse.

Such phonetic laws have been worked out in great number for many Indo-European and Semitic languages. There are obviously many other historical factors that contribute their share to the phenomena of change in language, but phonetic law is justly considered by the linguist by far the most important single factor that he has to deal with. Inasmuch as all sound change in language tends to be regular, the linguist is not satisfied with random resemblances in languages that are suspected of being related but insists on working out as best he can the phonetic formulas which tie up related words. Until such formulas are discovered, there may be some evidence for considering distinct languages related— for example, the general form of their grammar may seem to provide such evidence—but the final demonstration can never be said to be given until comparable words can be shown to be but reflexes of one and the same prototype by the operation of dialectic phonetic laws.

Is there any reason to believe that the process of regular phonetic change is any less applicable to the languages of primitive peoples than to the languages of the more civilized nations? This question must be answered in the negative. Rapidly accumulating evidence shows that this process is just as easily and abundantly illustrated in the languages of the American Indian or of the Negro tribes as in Latin or Greek or English. If these laws are more difficult to discover in primitive languages, this is not due to any special characteristic which these languages possess but merely to the inadequate technique of some who have tried to study them.

An excellent test case of phonetic law in a group of primitive languages is afforded by the Algonkian linguistic stock of North America. This stock includes a large number of distinct languages which are, however, obviously related in both grammar and vocabulary. Bloomfield has taken four of the more important of the languages that belong to the central division of the stock and has worked out a complete system of vocalic and consonantal phonetic laws. We have selected in Table I five of these phonetic laws in order to give an idea of the nature of the correspondences.

Table I shows how five different consonantal combinations in which the second element is *k* were respectively developed in Fox, Ojibwa, Plains Cree, and Menomini. The Primitive Central Algonkian prototype (PCA) is, of course, a theoretical reconstruction on the basis of the actual dialectic forms.

TABLE I

PCA	Fox	Ojibwa	Plains Cree	Menomini
1. tck.	hk	ck	sk	tsk
2. ck.	ck	ck	sk	sk
3. xk.	hk	hk	sk	hk
4. hk.	hk	hk	hk	hk
5. nk.	g	ng	hk	hk

Observe that this table does not say that a particular *k* combination of one dialect corresponds uniquely to a particular *k* combination of another dialect, but merely that certain definite dialectic correspondences are found which lead to such reconstructive inferences as are symbolized in the first column of the table. Thus, the Plains Cree *sk* does not always correspond to the Fox *hk* but may just as well correspond to the Fox *ck*.[2] The Cree *sk* that corresponds to the Fox *hk*, however, is obviously not the same original sound as the Cree *sk* which corresponds to the Fox *ck*, as is indicated by the fact that in Menomini the former corresponds partly to *tsk*, partly to *hk*, while the latter regularly corresponds to *sk*. None of the four dialects exactly reflects the old phonetic pattern, which must be constructed from series of dialectic correspondences.

The methodology of this table is precisely the same as the methodology which is used in Indo-European linguistics. The modern German *ei* of *mein* corresponds to the diphthong *i* of English *mine*, but it does

[2] *C* indicates the sound of *sh* in *ship*; *tc* indicates the sound of *ch* in *chip*; *x* indicates the sound of German *ch* in *ach*.

not follow that every modern German *ei* corresponds to the English diphthong. As a matter of fact, a large number of German words with *ei* have English correspondents in *o*, as in *home*. Thus, while *mine* corresponds to German *mein*, *thine* to German *dein*, and *wine* to German *Wein*, the English *home* corresponds to German *Heim*, *soap* to German *Seife*, and *loaf* (of bread) to German *Laib*. We have to conclude that the modern German *ei* represents two historically distinct sounds. In this particular case we have the documentary evidence with which to check up a necessary or, at least, a highly plausible inference. The type illustrated by English *mine* :: German *mein* corresponds to Old High German *ī* and Anglo-Saxon *ī*, while the type illustrated by English *home* :: German *Heim* corresponds to Old High German *ei* and Anglo-Saxon *ā*. We can briefly summarize all the relevant facts by saying that Early Germanic *ī* has become a diphthong in Modern English and a practically identical diphthong in modern German, while an Early Germanic sound which we may reconstruct as *ai* (cf. Gothic *ai* in such words as *haims*, "home") has developed to *ā* in Anglo-Saxon, whence modern English *ō*, and *ei* in Old High German, whence the diphthong in modern German. The important thing to observe about the English and the German examples is that even in the absence of historical evidence it would have been possible to infer the existence in Early Germanic of two distinct sounds from the nature of the correspondences in English and German.

Table II gives examples of actual words illustrating the five phonetic laws in question. The examples given are not isolated examples but are, for the most part, representative of whole classes. The true generality of the phonetic laws illustrated in Table I goes even farther than there indicated, as is shown by the set of correspondences in Table III. It will be observed that in this table *p* takes the place, for the most part, of *k* of Table II.

Bloomfield found, however, that there was one Algonkian stem evidently involving a *k* combination which did not correspond to any of the five series given above. This is the stem for "red" illustrated in Table IV.

For this series of correspondences Bloomfield has constructed a sixth phonetic law, which is expressed in Table V. It should be understood that the symbol *ç* is not a phonetic symbol in the ordinary sense of the word. It is merely a formula or tag which is intended to hold down a place, as it were, in a pattern. It may represent a sound similar to the *ch* of the German *ich*, or it may represent some other sound or combination of sounds. Its chief purpose is to warn us that the *ck* or *hk* of the Central Algonkian dialects is not to be historically equated with other examples of *ck* or *hk* in these dialects.

The justification for setting up a special phonetic law on the basis of one set of correspondences is given by Bloomfield himself. He says,

TABLE II

PCA	Fox	Ojibwa	Plains Cree	Menomini
1. **-alakatckw-* "palate"	. . . .	*-inagacku-*	*-ayakask*	*-inākatsku-*
*ketckyäwa "he is old"	*kehkyäwa*	. . . .	. . . .	*kotskīw*
2. **ickutäwi* "fire"	*ackutäwi*	*ickudä*	*iskutäw*	*iskōtäw*
3. **maxkesini* "moccasin"	*mahkasähi* (dim. form)	*mahkizin*	*maskisin*	*mahkäsin*
4. **nōhkuma*	*nohkuma* "my mother-in-law"	*nōhkumis*	*nōhkum*	*nōhkumeh*
*nohkumehsa "my grand-mother"	*nohkumesa* "my grand-mother"			
5. **tankeckawäwa* "he kicks him"	*tageckawäwa*	*tangickawād*	*tahkiskawäw*	*tahkäskawew*

TABLE III

PCA	Fox	Ojibwa	Plains Cree	Menomini
1. tcp.	ʔ	hp	ʔ	tsp
2. cp.	hp	cp	sp	sp
3. xp.	hp	hp	sp	hp
4. hp.	hp	hp	hp	hp
5. mp.	p	mb	hp	hp

"Since there appeared to be no point of contact for analogic substitution of *hk* for *ck*, or vice versa, in any of the languages, and since borrowing of the stem for *red* seemed unlikely, it was necessary to suppose that the parent speech had in this stem for *red* a different phonetic unit."

Sometimes one is in a position to check up a phonetic reconstruction such as is implied in the use of the symbol *çk*. A related dialect may turn up in which the theoretical phonetic prototype is represented by

a distinctive sound or sound combination. As a matter of fact, exactly
this proved to be the case for Central Algonkian. Some time after
Bloomfield set up the sixth phonetic law, he had the opportunity to
study the Swampy Cree dialect of Manitoba. Interestingly enough,
this Cree dialect had the consonant combination *htk* in forms based on
the stem for "red," e.g., *mihtkusiw*, "he is red"; and in no other stem
did this combination of sounds occur. In other words, the added evidence obtained from this dialect entirely justified the isolation for Primitive Central Algonkian of a particular phonetic-sound group, symbolized
by *çk*. The setting-up of phonetic law No. 6 was, by implication, a
theoretically possible prediction of a distinct and discoverable phonetic
pattern. The prediction was based essentially on the assumption of the
regularity of sound changes in language.

TABLE IV

PCA	Fox	Ojibwa	Plains Cree	Menomini
5. *meçkusiwa* "he is red"	*meckusiwa*	*mickuzi*	*mihkusiw*	(*mehkōn*)

TABLE V

PCA	Fox	Ojibwa	Plains Cree	Menomini
6. çk	ck	ck	hk	hk

Bloomfield's experience with the Central Algonkian dialects is entirely parallel to my own with the Athabaskan languages. These constitute an important linguistic stock which is irregularly distributed
in North America. The northern group occupies a vast territory stretching all the way from near the west coast of Hudson Bay west into the
interior of Alaska. To it belong such languages as Anvik (in Alaska),
Carrier (in British Columbia), Chipewyan, Hare, Loucheux, Kutchin,
Beaver, and Sarcee. We shall take Chipewyan and Sarcee as representatives of this group. The geographically isolated Pacific division of Athabaskan consists of a number of languages in southwestern Oregon and
northwestern California. We shall take Hupa as representative. The
southern division of Athabaskan is in New Mexico and Arizona and
adjoining regions, and is represented by Navaho, Apache, and Lipan.
We shall take Navaho as representative of the group. In spite of the
tremendous geographical distances that separate the Athabaskan lan-

guages from each other, it is perfectly possible to set up definite phonetic laws which connect them according to consistent phonetic patterns. Navaho, Hupa, and Chipewyan are spoken by Indians who belong to entirely distinct culture horizons, yet the languages themselves are as easily derivable from a common source on the basis of regular phonetic law as are German, Dutch, and Swedish.

Table VI shows the distribution in Hupa, Chipewyan, Navaho, and Sarcee of three initial consonantal sets, each of which consists of five consonants. In other words, the table summarizes the developments of

TABLE VI

Ath.	Hupa	Chipewyan	Navaho	Sarcee
I. 1. s..........	s	ϑ	s	s
2. z..........	s	δ	z	z
3. dz..........	dz	dδ	dz	dz
4. ts..........	ts	tϑ	ts	ts
5. ts..........	ts'	tϑ'	ts'	ts'
II. 1. c..........	W	s	c	s
2. j..........	W	z	j	z
3. dj..........	dj	dz	dj	dz
4. tc..........	tcw	ts	tc	ts
5. tc'........	tc'	ts'	tc'	ts'
III. 1. x..........	W	c	s	c
2. y..........	y	y	y	y
3. gy..........	gy	dj	dz	dj
4. ky..........	ky	tc	ts	tc
5. ky'........	ky'	tc'	ts'	tc'

fifteen originally distinct Athabaskan initial consonants in four selected dialects. Each of the entries must be considered as a summary statement applying to a whole class of examples.[3]

The table merits study because of its many implications. It will be observed that no one dialect exactly reproduces the reconstructed Athabaskan forms given in the first column. Series I is preserved intact in Navaho and Sarcee and very nearly so in Hupa, but has been shifted to another series in Chipewyan. Series II is preserved intact in Navaho,

[3] The apostrophe symbolizes a peculiar type of consonantal articulation, characterized by simultaneous closure of the glottis and point of contact in the mouth, with glottal release preceding oral release. *J* is the French *j* of *jour*; *dj* is the *j* of English *just*; *x* is the *ch* of German *ich*; *W* is approximately the *wh* of English *what*; *ϑ* is the *th* of English *thick*; *δ* is the *th* of English *then*.

but has been shifted in Sarcee to identity with the series that corresponds to original I, while Hupa has introduced several peculiar dialectic developments and Chipewyan has shifted it to the original form of I. Series III is nowhere kept entirely intact but nearly so in Hupa, while in Chipewyan and in Sarcee it has moved to the original form of Series II, in Navaho to a form which is identical with the original and the Navaho form of Series I. It is clear from the table that a Sarcee *s* is ambiguous as to origin, for it may go back either to Athabaskan *s* or Athabaskan *c*. On the other hand, a Sarcee *s* which is supported by either Navaho or Hupa *s* must be the representative of an original Athabaskan *s*. Sarcee *tc* is, in the main, unambiguous as to origin, for it corresponds to the original Athabaskan *ky*. It is curious and instructive to note that, of the four languages given in the table, Hupa and Chipewyan are the two that most nearly correspond as to *pattern* but never as to actual *sound* except in the one instance of *y* (III, 2).

TABLE VII

ATH.	HUPA	CHIPEWYAN†	NAVAHO†	SARCEE†
*kyan............. "rain"	....	tcq	n-l-tsq "there's a rainfall"	tcq

† q represents nasalized *a* as in French *an*. Sarcee *ǫ* is a peculiar *a* with velar resonance, regularly developed from Athabaskan *a*.

Let us take a practical example of prediction on the basis of the table· If we have a Sarcee form with *tc*, a corresponding Navaho form with *ts*, and a Chipewyan form with *tc*, what ought to be the Hupa correspondent? According to the table it ought to be *ky*.

Table VII shows the distribution in three dialects of the Athabaskan sound *ky* (III, 4) in the word for "rain." When I first constructed the Athabaskan prototype I assumed an initial *ky*, in spite of the absence of the test form in Hupa, on the basis of the dialectic correspondences. Neither an original *ts* nor *tc* could be assumed in spite of the fact that these sounds were actually illustrated in known dialects, whereas *ky* was not. The Hupa column had to remain empty because the cognate word, if still preserved, was not available in the material that had been recorded by P. E. Goddard.

In the summer of 1927, however, I carried on independent researches on Hupa and secured the form *kyaŋ-kyoh*,[4] meaning "hailstorm." The

4 ŋ is the *ng* of English *sing*.

second element of the compound means "big" and the first is obviously the missing Hupa term corresponding to the old Athabaskan word for "rain." In other words, an old compound meaning "rain-big" has taken on the special meaning of "hailstorm" in Hupa. The Hupa form of the old word for "rain" is exactly what it should be according to the correspondences that had been worked out, and the reconstruction of the primitive Athabaskan form on the basis of the existing forms was therefore justified by the event.

Table VIII gives the chief dialectic forms that were available for the reconstruction of the Athabaskan word for "rain." Observe that not one of these has the original sound *ky* which must be assumed as the initial

TABLE VIII
DIALECTIC FORMS FOR "RAIN"

Anvik (Alaska)	*tcɔN**
Carrier (B.C.)	*tcan*
Chipewyan	*tcq*
Hare	*tcǫ*
Loucheux	*tcien*
Kutchin	*tscin*
Beaver	*tcǫ*
Sarcee	*tcą*
Navaho	*n-ł-tsq*

*ɔ represents open *o*, as in German *voll;* ǫ is nasalized *o*. *N* is voiceless *n*.

of the word. This is due to the fact that the old Athabaskan *ky* and related sounds shifted in most dialects to sibilants but were preserved in Hupa and a small number of other dialects, some of which are spoken at a great remove from Hupa. In other words, in working out linguistic reconstructions we must be guided not merely by the overt statistical evidence but by the way in which the available material is patterned.

For those interested in a summary statement of the concepts and assumptions involved in the foregoing, the following quotations from Bloomfield's "A Set of Postulates for the Science of Language" may prove of interest:

Def.—A minimum same of vocal feature is a *phoneme* or *distinctive sound.*

Assumption.—The number of different phonemes in a language is a small sub-multiple of the number of forms.

Assumption.—Every form is made up wholly of phonemes. . . . Such a thing as a "small difference of sound" does not exist in a language.

Assumption.—The number of orders of phonemes in the morphemes (i.e., "minimum forms") and words of a language is a sub-multiple of the number of possible orders.

Assumption.—Every language changes at a rate which leaves contemporary persons free to communicate without disturbance.

Assumption.—Among persons, linguistic change is uniform in ratio with the amount of communication between them.

Assumption.—Phonemes or classes of phonemes may gradually change.

Def.—Such change is *sound-change.*

Assumption.—Sound-change may affect phonemes or classes of phonemes in the environment of certain other phonemes or classes of phonemes.

Def.—This change is *conditioned sound-change.*

At the end of "A Note on Sound-Change," in which the Swampy Cree forms in *htk* are discussed, Bloomfield remarks:

> The postulate of sound-change without exceptions will probably always remain a mere assumption, since the other types of linguistic change (analogic change, borrowing) are bound to affect all our data. As an assumption, however, this postulate yields, as a matter of mere routine, predictions which otherwise would be impossible. In other words, the statement that *phonemes change* (sound-changes have no exceptions) is a tested hypothesis: in so far as one may speak of such a thing, it is a proved truth.

It may be pointed out in conclusion that the value to social science of such comparative study of languages as is illustrated in the present paper is that it emphasizes the extraordinary persistence in certain cases of complex *patterns* of cultural behavior regardless of the extreme variability of the content of such patterns. It is in virtue of pattern conservatism that it is often possible to foretell the exact form of a specific cultural phenomenon.[5]

[5] [This analysis was first written in December, 1928, and revised by the analyst in February, 1929.—Stuart A. Rice, ED.]

DIALECT*

THE TERM "dialect" has a connotation in technical linguistic usage which is somewhat different from its ordinary meaning. To the linguist there is no real difference between a "dialect" and a "language" which can be shown to be related, however remotely, to another language. By preference the term is restricted to a form of speech which does not differ sufficiently from another form of speech to be unintelligible to the speakers of the latter. Thus, Great Russian and White Russian are said to be dialects of the same language. Similarly, Alsatian, Swabian, and Swiss German are dialects or groups of dialects of a common folk speech. Literal mutual intelligibility, however, is not a criterion of great interest to the linguist, who is more concerned with the fact and order of historical relationships in speech. To him Venetian and Sicilian are equally dialects of Italian, although as far as mutual intelligibility is concerned these two might as well be called independent languages. Russian, Polish, Czech, Bulgarian, and Serbian, conventionally considered independent languages because of their national affiliations, are no less truly dialects of a common Slavic speech or linguistic prototype than Venetian and Sicilian are dialects of a supposedly common Italian language. If two obviously related forms of speech are spoken at the same time, the linguist does not say that one of them is a dialect of the other but that both are sister dialects of some common prototype, known or inferred. When they diverge so far as not only to be mutually unintelligible but no longer to be too obviously related to each other, the term "language" is more freely used than "dialect," but in principle there is no difference between the two. Thus, in a sense, all Romance languages, all Celtic languages, all Germanic languages, all Slavic languages, and all Indo-Aryan vernaculars are merely dialect groups of a common Aryan or Indo-European language.

A group of dialects is merely the socialized form of the universal tendency to individual variation in speech. These variations affect the phonetic form of the language, its formal characteristics, vocabulary, and such prosodic features as intonation and stress. No known language, unless it be artificially preserved for liturgical or other nonpopular uses, has ever been known to resist the tendency to split up into dialects, any one of which may, in the long run, assume the status of an independent language. From dialects formed by inherent differen-

* *Encyclopaedia of the Social Sciences* (New York, Macmillan, 1931), 5: 123–126.

tiation one may distinguish dialects which owe their origin to speech transfers. A community which takes on a language that is different from the one to which it has originally been accustomed will unconsciously carry over into the adopted language peculiarities of its own form of speech which are pronounced enough to give its use of the foreign language a dialectic tinge. Many linguists attach much importance to the influence of superseded languages in the formation of dialects. Thus some of the distinctive peculiarities of both Celtic and Germanic are supposed to be due to the retention of phonetic peculiarities of pre-Aryan languages.

In less technical or frankly popular usage the term "dialect" has somewhat different connotations. Human speech is supposed to be differentiated and standardized in a number of approved forms known as "languages," and each of these in turn has a number of subvarieties of lesser value known as "dialects." A dialect is looked upon as a departure from the standard norm, in many cases even as a corruption of it. Historically, this view is unsound, because the vast majority of so-called dialects are merely the regular, differentiated development of earlier forms of speech which antedate the recognized languages. Popular confusion on the subject is chiefly due to the fact that the question of language has become secondarily identified with that of nationality in the larger cultural and ethnic group which, in course of time, absorbs the local tradition. The language of such a nationality is generally based on a local dialect and spreads at the expense of other dialects which were originally of as great prestige as the culturally more powerful one.

Of the large number of dialects spoken in Germany, German Switzerland, and Austria, for example, very few, if any, can be considered as modified forms of the culturally accepted *Hochdeutsch* of literature, the pulpit, the stage, and cultural activity generally. The dialects of the German-speaking folk go back unbrokenly to the Old High German of early medieval times, a German which was even then richly differentiated into dialects. The present standardized German of the schools arose comparatively late in the history of German speech as a result of the fixing of one of the Upper Saxon dialects as the recognized medium of official communication within the German-speaking dominions. Luther's Bible helped considerably in the diffusion of this form of German as the recognized standard. It has taken a long time, however, for *Hochdeutsch* to take on a recognized phonetic form and to be looked upon as a well standardized form of oral communication, and to this day a large proportion of Germans, including the educated ranks, are bilingual in the sense that they use the standardized German for formal purposes but employ the local dialect for more familiar uses.

The history of German is paralleled more or less by the history of all the other national languages of Europe and of other parts of the world. As a result of cultural reasons of one kind or another a local dialect gets accepted as the favored or desirable form of speech within a linguistic community that is cut up into a large number of dialects. This approved local dialect becomes the symbol of cultural values and spreads at the expense of other local forms of speech. The standardized form of speech becomes more and more set in its vocabulary, form, and eventually pronunciation. The speakers of local dialects begin to be ashamed of their peculiar forms of speech because these have not the prestige value of the standardized language; and finally the illusion is created of a primary language, belonging to the large area which is the territory of a nation or nationality, and of the many local forms of speech as uncultured or degenerated variants of the primary norm. As is well known, these variations from the standard norm are sometimes much more archaic, historically speaking, than the norm from which they are supposed to depart.

Local dialects are, in a sense, minority languages, but the term "minority language" should be reserved for a completely distinct form of speech that is used by a minority nationality living within the political framework of a nation. An example of such a minority language would be the Basque of southwestern France and northern Spain or the Breton of Brittany. These languages are not dialects of French and Spanish but historically distinct languages that have come to occupy culturally secondary positions.

There is naturally no hard and fast line between a dialect and a local variation of a minor nature such as New England English as contrasted with middle western English. In the older dialects the connection with the standardized speech is quite secondary, whereas in such local variations as New England versus middle western American speech standard English, however loosely defined, is present in the minds of all as the natural background for these variations, which are thus psychologically, if not altogether historically, variations from the primary or standard norm. It would be possible for the speaker of a local Swiss dialect or of Yorkshire English to build up a nationalistic gospel around his local dialect in opposition to the accepted speech of the cultured group, but the attempt to do this for middle western English in America would have something intrinsically absurd about it because of the feeling that this form of English is, at best, but a belated departure from an earlier norm. As usual in social phenomena, however, it is the symbolism of attitude that counts in these matters rather than the objective facts of history.

Ever since the formation of the great national languages of Europe toward the end of the medieval period there have been many social and political influences at work to imperil the status of the local dialects. As the power of the sovereign grew, the language of the court gained in prestige and tended to diffuse through all the ramifications of the official world. Meanwhile, although the Roman Catholic and Greek churches, with their sacred liturgical languages, were little interested in the question of folk versus standardized speech, the Protestant sects, with their concern for a more direct relation between God and His worshippers, naturally emphasized the dignity of folk speech and lent their aid to the diffusion of a selected form of folk speech over a larger area. The influence of such documents as Luther's Bible and King James's Authorized Version in the standardization of English and German has often been referred to. In more recent days, the increase of popular education and the growing demand for ready intelligibility in the business world have given a tremendous impetus to the spread of standardized forms of speech.

In spite of all these standardizing influences, however, local dialects, particularly in Europe, have persisted with a vitality that is little short of amazing. Obviously the question of the conservatism of dialect is not altogether a negative matter of the inertia of speech and of the failure of overriding cultural influences to permeate into all corners of a given territory. It is, to a very significant degree, a positive matter of the resistance of the local dialects to something which is vaguely felt as hostile. This is easily understood if we look upon languages and dialects not as intrinsically good or bad forms of speech but as symbols of social attitudes. Before the growth of modern industrialism culture tended to be intensely local in character in spite of the uniformizing influences of government, religion, education, and business. The culture that gradually seeped in from the great urban centers was felt as something alien and superficial in spite of the prestige that unavoidably attached to it. The home speech was associated with kinship ties and with the earliest emotional experiences of the individual. Hence the learning of a standardized language could hardly seem natural except in the few centers in which the higher culture seemed properly at home, and even in these there generally developed a hiatus between the standardized language of the cultured classes and the folk speech of the local residents. Hence cockney is as far removed psychologically from standard British English as is a peasant dialect of Yorkshire or Devon. On the continent of Europe, particularly in Germany and Italy, the culture represented by, say, standardized German or standardized Italian was, until very recent days, an exceedingly thin psychological structure, and its official speech could hardly take on the task of adequately symbolizing the highly differentiated folk cultures of German-speaking and Italian-speaking regions.

The Age of Enlightenment in the eighteenth century was, on the whole, hostile to the persistence of dialects, but the Romantic movement which followed it gave to folk speech a glamour which has probably had something to do with the idealization of localized languages as symbols of national solidarity and territorial integrity. Few writers of the seventeenth or eighteenth centuries would have taken seriously the use of dialect in literature. It was only later that Lowland Scotch could be romantically restored in the lyrics of Robert Burns, that Fritz Reuter could strive to establish a Low German (*Plattdeutsch*) literary language, and that Mistral could attempt to revive the long lost glory of Provençal. One may suspect that this renewed emphasis on linguistic differences is but a passing phase in the history of modern man. Be that as it may, it has had much to do with the emergence of new nationalisms in recent time. It is doubtful if such countries as Lithuania, Esthonia, and Czechoslovakia could have so easily proved their right to exist if it had not come to be felt that just as every nationality needs its language, so every unattached language needs its nationality and territorial independence to fulfill its inherent mission. Perhaps the best example of what might be called linguistic romanticism is the attempt of the Irish nationalists to renew the vitality of Gaelic, a form of speech which has never been standardized for literary, let alone folk, purposes and which is profoundly alien to the majority of the more articulate of Irish nationalists.

No doubt the respect for local forms of speech has received assistance from scientific linguistics and its tendency to view all languages and dialects as of equal historical importance. It is very doubtful, however, if linguistic localism can win out in the long run. The modern mind is increasingly realistic and pragmatic in the world of action and conceptualistic or normative in the world of thought. Both of these attitudes are intrinsically hostile to linguistic localism of any sort, and necessarily therefore to dialectic conservatism. Compulsory education, compulsory military service, modern means of communication, and urbanization are some of the more obvious factors in the spread of these attitudes, which, so far as language is concerned, may be defined by the thesis that words should either lead to unambiguous action among the members of as large a group as is held together culturally or, in the domain of thought, should aim to attach themselves to concepts which are less and less purely local in their application. In the long run therefore it seems fairly safe to hazard the guess that such movements as the Gaelic revival in Ireland and the attempt to save as many minority languages and dialects from cultural extinction as possible will come to be looked upon as little more than eddies in the more powerful stream of standardization of speech that set in at the close of the medieval period. The modern problem is more complex than the classical or medieval problem because the modern mind insists on having the process of standardization take the form of a democratic rather than an aristocratic process.

A word may be added in regard to the social psychology of dialectic forms of speech. In the main, markedly dialectic peculiarities have been looked upon as symbols of inferiority of status, but if local sentiment is strongly marked and if the significance of the local group for the larger life of the nation as a whole allows, a local dialect may become the symbol of a kind of inverted pride. We thus have the singular spectacle of Lowland Scotch as an approved and beautiful linguistic instrument and of cockney as an undesirable ugly one. These judgments are extrinsic facts of language themselves but they are none the less decisive in the world of cultural symbolisms.

If an individual is brought up in a community that has its characteristic dialect and if he becomes identified later in life with another community which has a second mode of speech, some very interesting personality problems arise which involve the status symbolism or affectional symbolism of these differing forms of speech. Individuals who vacillate somewhat in their conception of their own role in society may often be detected unconsciously betraying this feeling of insecurity in a vacillating pronunciation or intonation or choice of words. When, under the influence of an emotional crisis, such individuals are thrown back upon their earliest emotional experiences—"regress," in short—they are likely to relapse into early dialectic habits of speech. It is suggested that the question of the relation of the individual to the various dialects and languages to which he has been subjected from time to time is of far more than anecdotal interest, that it constitutes, as a matter of fact, a very important approach to the problem of personality subjected to the strains of cultural change.

LANGUAGE AND ENVIRONMENT*

THERE is a strong tendency to ascribe many elements of human culture to the influence of the environment in which the sharers of that
culture are placed, some even taking the extreme position of reducing
practically all manifestations of human life and thought to environmental influences. I shall not attempt to argue for or against the importance of the influence had by forces of environment on traits of
culture, nor shall I attempt to show in how far the influence of environment is crossed by that of other factors. To explain any one trait of
human culture as due solely to the force of physical environment,
however, seems to me to rest on a fallacy. Properly speaking, environment can act directly only on an individual, and in those cases where
we find that a purely environmental influence is responsible for a communal trait, this common trait must be interpreted as a summation of
distinct processes of environmental influences on individuals. Such,
however, is obviously not the typical form in which we find the forces
of environment at work on human groups. In these it is enough that a
single individual may react directly to his environment and bring the
rest of the group to share consciously or unconsciously in the influence
exerted upon him. Whether even a single individual can be truthfully
said to be capable of environmental influence uncombined with influences of another character is doubtful, but we may at least assume the
possibility. The important point remains that in actual society even the
simplest environmental influence is either supported or transformed by
social forces. Hence any attempt to consider even the simplest element
of culture as due solely to the influence of environment must be termed
misleading. The social forces which thus transform the purely environmental influences may themselves be looked upon as environmental in
character in so far as a given individual is placed in, and therefore
reacts to, a set of social factors. On the other hand, the social forces
may be looked upon, somewhat metaphorically, as parallel in their
influence to those of heredity in so far as they are handed down from
generation to generation. That these traditional social forces are themselves subject to environmental, among other, changes, illustrates the
complexity of the problem of cultural origins and development. On the
whole one does better to employ the term "environment" only when
reference is had to such influences, chiefly physical in character, as lie

* *American Anthropologist*, n.s., 14 (1912): 226–242. Read before the American
Anthropological Association. Washington, D. C., December 28, 1911.

outside the will of man. Yet in speaking of language, which may be considered a complex of symbols reflecting the whole physical and social background in which a group of men is placed, it is advantageous to comprise within the term environment both physical and social factors. Under physical environment are comprised geographical characters, such as the topography of the country (whether coast, valley, plain, plateau, or mountain), climate, and amount of rainfall, and what may be called the economic basis of human life, under which term are comprised the fauna, flora, and mineral resources of the region. Under social environment are comprised the various forces of society that mold the life and thought of each individual. Among the more important of these social forces are religion, ethical standards, form of political organization, and art.

According to this classification of environmental influences, we may expect to find two sets of environmental factors reflected in language, assuming for the moment that language is materially influenced by the environmental background of its speakers. Properly speaking, of course, the physical environment is reflected in language only in so far as it has been influenced by social factors. The mere existence, for instance, of a certain type of animal in the physical environment of a people does not suffice to give rise to a linguistic symbol referring to it. It is necessary that the animal be known by the members of the group in common and that they have some interest, however slight, in it before the language of the community is called upon to make reference to this particular element of the physical environment. In other words, so far as language is concerned, all environmental influence reduces at last analysis to the influence of social environment. Nevertheless it is practical to keep apart such social influences as proceed more or less directly from the physical environment, and those that can not be easily connected with it. Language may be influenced in one of three ways: in regard to its subject matter or content, i.e., in regard to the vocabulary; in regard to its phonetic system, i.e., the system of sounds with which it operates in the building of words; and in regard to its grammatical form, i.e., in regard to the formal processes and the logical or psychological classifications made use of in speech. Morphology, or the formal structure of words, and syntax, or the methods employed in combining words into larger units or sentences, are the two main aspects of grammatical form.

It is the vocabulary of a language that most clearly reflects the physical and social environment of its speakers. The complete vocabulary of a language may indeed be looked upon as a complex inventory of all the ideas, interests, and occupations that take up the attention of the community, and were such a complete thesaurus of the language of a given tribe at our disposal, we might to a large extent infer the character of the physical environment and the characteristics of the culture of the people making use of it. It is not difficult to find examples of languages whose vocabulary thus bears the stamp of the physical environment in which the speakers are placed. This is particularly true of the languages of primitive peoples, for among these culture has not attained such a degree of complexity as to imply practically universal interests. From this point of view the vocabulary of primitive languages may be compared to the vocabularies of particular sections of the population of civilized peoples. The characteristic vocabulary of a coast tribe, such as the Nootka Indians, with its precise terms for many species of marine animals, vertebrate and invertebrate, might be compared to the vocabulary of such European fisher-folk as the Basques of southwestern France and northern Spain. In contrast to such coast peoples may be mentioned the inhabitants of a desert plateau, like the Southern Paiute of Arizona, Nevada, and Utah. In the vocabulary of this tribe we find adequate provision made for many topographical features that would in some cases seem almost too precise to be of practical value. Some of the topographical terms of this language that have been collected are: divide, ledge, sand flat, semicircular valley, circular valley or hollow, spot of level ground in mountains surrounded by ridges, plain valley surrounded by mountains, plain, desert, knoll, plateau, canyon without water, canyon with creek, wash or gutter, gulch, slope of mountain or canyon wall receiving sunlight, shaded slope of mountain or canyon wall, rolling country intersected by several small hill-ridges, and many others.

In the case of the specialized vocabularies of both Nootka and Southern Paiute, it is important to note that it is not merely the fauna or topographical features of the country as such that are reflected, but rather the interest of the people in such environmental features. Were the Nootka Indians dependent for their food supply primarily on land hunting and vegetable products, despite their proximity to the sea, there is little doubt that their vocabulary would not be as thoroughly saturated as it is with sea lore. Similarly it is quite evident from the presence in Paiute of such topographical terms as have been listed, that accurate reference to topography is a necessary thing to dwellers in an inhospitable semi-arid region; so purely practical a need as definitely locating a spring might well require reference to several features of topographical detail. How far the interest in the physical environment rather than its mere presence affects the character of a vocabulary may be made apparent by a converse case in English. One who is not a botanist, or is not particularly interested for purposes of folk medicine or otherwise in plant lore, would not know how to refer to numberless plants that make up part of his environment except merely as "weeds," whereas an Indian tribe very largely dependent for its food supply on wild roots, seeds of wild plants, and other vegetable products, might have precise terms for each and every one of these nondescript weeds. In many cases distinct terms would even be in use for various conditions of a single plant species, distinct reference being made as to whether it is raw or cooked, or of this or that color, or in this or that stage of growth. In this way special vocabularies having reference to acorns or camass might be collected from various tribes of California or Oregon. Another instructive example of how largely interest determines the character of a vocabulary is afforded by the terms in several Indian languages for sun and moon. While we find it necessary to distinguish sun and moon, not a few tribes content themselves with a single word for both, the exact reference being left to the context. If we complain that so vague a term fails to do justice to an essential natural difference, the Indian might well retaliate by pointing to the *omnium gatherum* character of our term "weed" as contrasted with his own more precise plant vocabulary. Everything naturally depends on the point of view as determined by interest. Bearing this in mind, it becomes evident that the presence or absence of general terms is to a large extent dependent on the negative or positive character of the interest in the elements of environment involved. The more necessary a particular culture finds it to make distinctions within a given range of phenomena, the less likely the existence of a general term covering the range. On the other hand, the more indifferent culturally are the elements, the more likely that they will all be embraced in a single term of general application. The case may be summarized, if example can summarize, by saying that to the layman every animal form that is neither human being, quadruped, fish, nor bird, is a bug or worm. To this same type of layman the concept and corresponding word "mammal" would, for a converse reason, be quite unfamiliar.

There is an obvious difference between words that are merely words, incapable of further analysis, and such words as are so evidently secondary in formation as to yield analysis to even superficial reflection. A lion is merely a lion, but a mountain-lion suggests something more than the animal referred to. Where a transparent descriptive term is in use for a simple concept, it seems fair in most cases to conclude that the knowledge of the environmental element referred to is comparatively recent, or at any rate that the present naming has taken place at a comparatively recent time. The destructive agencies of phonetic change would in the long run wear down originally descriptive terms to mere labels or unanalyzable words pure and simple. I speak of this matter here because the transparent or untransparent character of a vocabulary may lead us to infer, if somewhat vaguely, the length of time that a group of people has been familiar with a particular concept. People who speak of lions have evidently been familiar with that animal for many generations. Those who speak of mountain lions would seem to date their knowledge of these from yesterday. The case is even clearer when we turn to a consideration of place-names. Only the student of language history is able to analyze such names as Essex, Norfolk, and Sutton into their component elements as East Saxon, North Folk, and South Town, while to the lay consciousness these names are etymological units as purely as are "butter" and "cheese." The contrast between a country inhabited by an historically homogeneous group for a long time, full of etymologically obscure place-names, and a newly settled country with its Newtowns, Wildwoods, and Mill Creeks, is apparent. Naturally much depends on the grammatical character of the language itself; such highly synthetic forms of speech as are many American Indian languages seem to lose hold of the descriptive character of their terms less readily than does English, for instance.

We have just seen that the careful study of a vocabulary leads to inferences as to the physical and social environment of those who use the vocabulary; furthermore, that the relatively transparent or untransparent character of the vocabulary itself may lead us to infer as to the degree of familiarity that has been obtained with various elements of this environment. Several students, notably Schrader, in dealing with Indo-Germanic material, have attempted to make a still more ambitious use of the study of vocabularies of related languages. By selecting such words as are held in common by all, or at least several, of a group of genetically related languages, attempts have been made to gather some idea of the vocabulary of the hypothetical language of which the forms of speech investigated are later varieties, and in this way to get some idea of the range of concepts possessed by the speakers of the reconstructed language. We are here dealing with a kind of linguistic archeology. Undoubtedly many students of Indo-Germanic linguistics have gone altogether too far in their attempts to reconstruct culture from comparative linguistic evidence, but the value of evidence obtained in this way can not be summarily denied, even granted that words may linger on long after their original significance has changed. The only pity is that in comparing languages that have diverged very considerably from each other, and the reconstructed prototype of which must therefore point to a remote past, too little material bearing on the most interesting phases of culture can generally be obtained. We do not need extended linguistic comparison to convince us that at a remote period in the past people had hands and fathers, though it would be interesting to discover whether they knew of the use of salt, for instance. Naturally the possibility of secondary borrowing of a word apparently held in common must always be borne in mind. Yet, on the whole, adequate knowledge of the phonology and morphology of the languages concerned will generally enable a careful analyst to keep apart the native from the borrowed elements. There has been too little comparative linguistic work done in America as yet to enable one to point to any considerable body of tangible results of cultural interest derived from such study, yet there is little doubt that with more intensive study such results will be forthcoming in greater degree. Surely a thoroughgoing study of Algonkin, Siouan, and Athabascan vocabularies from this point of view will eventually yield much of interest. As a passing example of significance, I shall merely point out that Nahua *oco-tl*, "Pinus tenuifolia," and Southern Paiute *oγó-mp'ᵛ*, "fir," point to a Uto-Aztekan stem *oko-* that has reference to some variety of pine or fir.

If the characteristic physical environment of a people is to a large extent reflected in its language, this is true to an even greater extent of its social environment. A large number, if not most, of the elements that make up a physical environment are found universally distributed in time and place, so that there are natural limits set to the variability of lexical materials in so far as they give expression to concepts derived from the physical world. A culture, however, develops in numberless ways and may reach any degree of complexity. Hence we need not be surprised to find that the vocabularies of peoples that differ widely in character or degree of culture share this wide difference. There is a difference between the rich, conceptually ramified vocabulary of a language like English or French and that of any typical primitive group, corresponding in large measure to that which obtains between the complex culture of the English-speaking or French-speaking peoples of Europe and America with its vast array of specialized interests, and the relatively simple undifferentiated culture of the primitive group. Such variability of vocabulary, as reflecting social environment, obtains in time as well as place; in other words, the stock of culture concepts and therefore also the corresponding vocabulary become constantly enriched and ramified with the increase within a group of cultural complexity. That a vocabulary should thus to a great degree reflect cultural complexity is practically self-evident, for a vocabulary, that is, the subject matter of a language, aims at any given time to serve as a set of symbols referring to the culture background of the group. If by complexity of language is meant the range of interests implied in its vocabulary, it goes without saying that there is a constant correlation between complexity of language and culture. If, however, as is more usual, linguistic complexity be used to refer to degree of morphologic and syntactic development, it is by no means true that such a correlation exists. In fact, one might almost make a case for an inverse correlation and maintain that morphologic development tends to decrease with increase of cultural complexity. Examples of this tendency are so easy to find that it is hardly worth our while going into the matter here. It need merely be pointed out that the history of English and French shows a constant loss in elaborateness of grammatical structure from their earliest recorded forms to the present. On the other hand, too much must not be made of this. The existence of numerous relatively simple forms of speech among primitive peoples discourages the idea of any tangible correlation between degree or form of culture and form of speech.

Is there, then, no element of language but its mere concrete subject matter or vocabulary that can be shown to have any relation to the physical and social environment of the speakers? It has sometimes been claimed that the general character of the phonetic system of a language is more or less dependent on physical environment, that such communities as dwell in mountainous regions or under other conditions tending to make the struggle for existence a difficult one develop acoustically harsh forms of speech, while such as are better favored by nature make use of relatively softer phonetic systems. Such a theory is as easily disproved as it seems plausible. It is no doubt true that examples may be adduced of harsh phonetic systems in use among mountaineers, as for instance those of various languages spoken in the Caucasus; nor is it difficult to find instances of acoustically pleasant forms of speech in use among groups that are subjected to a favorable physical environment. It is just as easy, however, to adduce instances to the contrary of both of these. The aboriginal inhabitants of the Northwest Coast of America found subsistence relatively easy in a country abounding in many forms of edible marine life; nor can they be said to have been subjected to rigorous climatic conditions; yet in phonetic harshness their languages rival those of the Caucasus. On the other hand, perhaps no people has ever been subjected to a more forbidding physical environment than the Eskimos, yet the Eskimo language not only impresses one as possessed of a relatively agreeable phonetic system when compared with the languages of the Northwest Coast, but may even perhaps be thought to compare favorably with American Indian languages generally. There are many cases, to be sure, of distinct languages with comparable phonetic systems spoken over a continuous territory of fairly uniform physical characteristics, yet in all such cases it can readily be shown that we are dealing not with the direct influence of the environment itself, but with psychological factors of a much subtler character, comparable perhaps to such as operate in the diffusion of cultural elements. Thus the phonetic systems of Tlingit, Haida, Tsimshian, Kwakiutl, and Salish are not similar because belonging to languages whose speakers are placed in about the same set of environmental conditions, but merely because these speakers are geographically contiguous to each other and hence capable of exerting mutual psychological influence.

Leaving these general considerations on the lack of correlation between physical environment and a phonetic system as a whole we may point to several striking instances, on the one hand, of phonetic resemblances between languages spoken by groups living in widely different environments and belonging to widely different cultural strata, on the other hand, of no less striking phonetic differences that obtain between languages spoken in adjoining regions of identical or similar environment and sharing in the same culture. These examples will serve to emphasize the point already made. The use of pitch accent as a significant element of speech is found in Chinese and neighboring languages of southeastern Asia, Ewe and other languages of western Africa, Hottentot in South Africa, Swedish, Tewa in New Mexico, and Takelma in southwestern Oregon. In this set of instances we have illustrated practically the whole gamut of environmental and cultural conditions. Nasalized vowels occur not only in French and Portuguese, but also in Ewe, Iroquois, and Siouan. "Fortis" consonants, i.e., stop consonants pronounced with simultaneous closure and subsequent release of glottal cords, are found not only in many languages of America west of the Rockies, but also in Siouan, and in Georgian and other languages of the Caucasus. Glottal stops as significant elements of speech are found not only plentifully illustrated in many, perhaps most, American Indian languages, but also in Danish and in Lettish, one of the Letto-Slavic languages of Western Russia. So highly peculiar sounds as the hoarse ḥâ and strangulated-sounding ʿain of Arabic are found in almost identical form in Nootka. And so on indefinitely. On the other hand, while the English and French may, on the whole, be said to be closely related culturally, there are very striking differences in the phonetic systems made use of by each. Turning to aboriginal America, we find that two such closely related groups of tribes, from a cultural standpoint, as the Iroquois and neighboring eastern Algonkins speak widely different languages, both phonetically and morphologically. The Yurok, Karok, and Hupa, all three occupying a small territory in northwestern California, form a most intimate cultural unit. Yet here again we find that the phonetic differences between the languages spoken by these tribes are great, and so on indefinitely again. There seems nothing for it, then, but to postulate an absolute lack of correlation between physical and social environment and phonetic systems, either in their general acoustic aspect or in regard to the distribution of particular phonetic elements.

One feels inclined to attribute a lack of correlation between phonetic system and environment to the comparatively accidental character of a phonetic system in itself; or, to express it somewhat more clearly, to the fact that phonetic systems may be thought to have a quasi-mechanical growth, at no stage subject to conscious reflection and hence not likely in any way to be dependent on environmental conditions, or, if so, only in a remotely indirect manner. Linguistic morphology, on the other hand, as giving evidence of certain definite modes of thought prevalent among the speakers of the language, may be thought to stand in some sort of relation to the stock of concepts forming the mental stock in trade, as it were, of the group. As this stock of concepts, however, is necessarily determined by the physical and social environment, it follows that some sort of correlation between these environments and grammatical structure might be looked for. And yet the negative evidence is as strong in this case as in the parallel one just disposed of. We may consider the subject matter of morphology as made up of certain logical or psychological categories of thought that receive grammatical treatment and of formal methods of expressing these. The distinct character of these two groups of morphological phenomena may be illustrated by pointing out that neighboring languages may influence, or at any rate resemble, each other in the one set without necessary corresponding influence or resemblance in the other. Thus, the device of reduplication is widespread in American Indian languages, yet the concepts expressed by this method vary widely. Here we deal with a widespread formal device as such. Conversely, the notion of inferential activity, this is, of action, knowledge of which is based on inference rather than personal authority is also found widely expressed in American languages, but by means ofs everal distinct formal processes. Here we deal with a widespread grammatically utilized category of thought as such.

Now, in rummaging through many languages one finds numerous instances both of striking similarities in the formal processes of morphology and of striking similarities or identities of concepts receiving grammatical treatment, similarities and identities that seem to run in no kind of correspondence to environmental factors. The presence of vocalic changes in verb or noun stems in Indo-Germanic languages, Semitic, Takelma, and Yana may be given as an example of the former. A further example is the presence of the infixation of grammatical elements in the body of a noun or verb stem in Malayan, Mon-Khmer, and Siouan. It will be noticed that despite the very characteristic types of formal processes that I have employed for illustrative purposes they crop up in markedly distinct environments. A striking example, on the other hand, of a category of thought of grammatical significance found irregularly distributed and covering a wide range of environments, is grammatical gender based on sex. This we find illustrated in Indo-Germanic, Semitic, Hottentot of South Africa, and Chinook of the lower Columbia. Other striking examples are the existence of syntactic cases, primarily subjective and objective, in Indo-Germanic, Semitic, and Ute; and the distinction between exclusive and inclusive duality or plurality of the first person found in Kwakiutl, Shoshonean, Iroquois, Hottentot, and Melanesian.

The complementary evidence for such lack of correlation as we have been speaking of is afforded by instances of morphologic differences found in neighboring languages in use among peoples subjected to practically the same set of environmental influences, physical and social. A few pertinent examples will suffice. The Chinook and Salish tribes of the lower Columbia and west coast of Washington form a cultural unit set in a homogeneous physical environment, yet far-reaching morphologic differences obtain between the languages of the two groups of tribes. The Salish languages make a superabundant use of reduplication for various grammatical purposes, whereas in Chinook reduplication, though occurring in a limited sense, has no grammatical significance. On the other hand, the system of sex gender rigidly carried out in the noun and verb system of Chinook is shared by the Coast Salish dialects only in so far as prenominal articles are found to express distinctions of gender, while the interior Salish languages lack even this feature entirely. Perhaps an even more striking instance of radical morphological dissimilarity in neighboring languages of a single culture area is afforded by Yana and Maidu, spoken in north central California. Maidu makes use of a large number of grammatical prefixes and employs reduplication for grammatical purposes to at least some extent. Yana knows nothing of either prefixes or reduplication. On the other hand, Maidu lacks such characteristic Yana features as the difference in form between the men's and women's language, and the employment of several hundreds of grammatical suffixes, some of them expressing such concrete verbal force as to warrant their being interpreted rather as verb stems in secondary position than as suffixes proper. To turn to the Old World, we find that Hungarian differs from the neighboring Indo-Germanic languages in its lack of sex gender and in its employment of the principle of vocalic harmony, a feature which, though primarily phonetic in character, nevertheless has an important grammatical bearing.

In some respects the establishment of failure of phonetic and morphologic characteristics of a language to stand in any sort of relation to the environment in which it is spoken seems disappointing. Can it be, after all, that the formal groundwork of a language is no indication whatsoever of the cultural complex that it expresses in its subject matter? If we look more sharply, we shall find in certain cases that at least some elements that go to make up a cultural complex are embodied in grammatical form. This is true particularly of synthetic languages operating with a large number of prefixes or suffixes of relatively concrete significance. The use in Kwakiutl and Nootka, for instance, of local suffixes defining activities as taking place on the beach, rocks, or sea, in cases where in most languages it would be far more idiomatic to omit all such reference, evidently points to the nature of the physical environment and economic interests connected therewith among these Indians. Similarly, when we find that such ideas as those of buying, giving a feast of some kind of food, giving a potlatch for some person, and asking for a particular gift at a girl's puberty ceremony, are expressed in Nootka by means of grammatical suffixes, we are led to infer that each of these acts is a highly typical one in the life of the tribe, and hence constitute important elements in its culture. This type of correlation may be further exemplified by the use in Kwakiutl, Nootka, and Salish of distinct series of numerals for various classes of objects, a feature which is pushed to its greatest length, perhaps, in Tsimshian. This grammatical peculiarity at least suggests definite methods of counting, and would seem to emphasize the concept of property, which we know to be so highly developed among the West Coast Indians. Adopting such comparatively obvious examples as our cue, one might go on indefinitely and seize upon any grammatical peculiarity with a view to interpreting it in terms of culture or physical environment. Thus, one might infer a different social attitude toward woman in those cases where sex gender is made grammatical use of. It needs but this last potential example to show to what flights of fancy this mode of argumentation would lead one. If we examine the more legitimate instances of cultural-grammatical correlation, we shall find that it is not, after all, the grammatical form as such with which we operate, but merely the content of that form; in other words, the correlation turns out to be, at last analysis, merely one of environment and vocabulary, with which we have already become familiar. The main interest morphologically in Nootka suffixes of the class illustrated lies in the fact that certain elements used to verbify nouns are suffixed to noun stems. This is a psychological fact which can not well be correlated with any fact of culture or physical environment that we know of. The particular manner in which a noun is verbified, or the degree of concreteness of meaning conveyed by the suffix, are matters of relative indifference to a linguist.

We seem, then, perhaps reluctantly, forced to admit that, apart from the reflection of environment in the vocabulary of a language, there is nothing in the language itself that can be shown to be directly associated with environment. One wonders why, if such be the case, so large a number of distinct phonetic systems and types of linguistic morphology are found in various parts of the world. Perhaps the whole problem of the relation between culture and environment generally, on the one hand, and language, on the other, may be furthered somewhat by a consideration simply of the rate of change or development of both. Linguistic features are necessarily less capable of rising into the consciousness of the speakers than traits of culture. Without here attempting to go into an analysis of this psychological difference between the two sets of phenomena, it would seem to follow that changes in culture are the result, to at least a considerable extent, of conscious processes or of processes more easily made conscious, whereas those of language are to be explained, if explained at all, as due to the more minute action of psychological factors beyond the control of will or reflection. If this be true, and there seems every reason to believe that it is, we must conclude that cultural change and linguistic change do not move along parallel lines and hence do not tend to stand in a close causal relation. This point of view makes it quite legitimate to grant, if necessary, the existence at some primitive stage in the past of a more definite association between environment and linguistic form than can now be posited anywhere, for the different character and rate of change in linguistic and cultural phenomena, conditioned by the very nature of those phenomena, would in the long run very materially disturb and ultimately entirely eliminate such an association.

We may conceive, somewhat schematically, the development of culture and language to have taken place as follows: A primitive group, among whom even the beginnings of culture and language are as yet hardly in evidence, may nevertheless be supposed to behave in accordance with a fairly definite group psychology, determined, we will suppose, partly by race mind, partly by physical environment. On the basis of this group psychology, whatever tendencies it may possess, a language and a culture will slowly develop. As both of these are directly determined, to begin with, by fundamental factors of race and physical environment, they will parallel each other somewhat closely, so that the forms of cultural activity will be reflected in the grammatical system of the language. In other words, not only will the words themselves of a language serve as symbols of detached cultural elements, as is true of languages at all periods of development, but we may suppose the grammatical categories and processes themselves to symbolize corresponding types of thought and activity of cultural significance. To some extent culture and language may then be conceived of as in a constant state of interaction and definite association for a considerable lapse of time. This state of correlation, however, can not continue indefinitely. With gradual change of group psychology and physical environment more or less profound changes must be effected in the form and content of both language and culture. Language and culture, however, are obviously not the direct expression of racial psychology and physical environment, but depend for their existence and continuance primarily on the forces of tradition. Hence, despite necessary modifications in either with the lapse of time, a conservative tendency will always make itself felt as a check to those tendencies that make for change. And here we come to the crux of the matter. Cultural elements, as more definitely serving the immediate needs of society and entering more clearly into consciousness, will not only change more rapidly than those of language, but the form itself of culture, giving each element its relative significance, will be continually shaping itself anew. Linguistic elements, on the other hand, while they may and do readily change in themselves, do not so easily lend themselves to regroupings, owing to the subconscious character of grammatical classification. A grammatical system as such tends to persist indefinitely. In other words, the conservative tendency makes itself felt more profoundly in the formal groundwork of language than in that of culture. One necessary consequence of this is that the forms of language will in course of time cease to symbolize those of culture, and this is our main thesis. Another consequence is that the forms of language may be thought to more accurately reflect those of a remotely past stage of culture than the present ones of culture itself. It is not claimed that a stage is ever reached at which language and culture stand in no sort of relation to each other, but simply that the relative rates of change of the two differ so materially as to make it practically impossible to detect the relationship.

Though the forms of language may not change as rapidly as those of culture, it is doubtless true that an unusual rate of cultural change is accompanied by a corresponding accelerated rate of change in language. If this point of view be pushed to its legitimate conclusion, we must be led to believe that rapidly increasing complexity of culture necessitates correspondingly, though not equally rapid, changes in linguistic form and content. This view is the direct opposite of the one generally held with respect to the greater conservatism of language in civilized communities than among primitive peoples. To be sure, the tendency to rapid linguistic change with increasingly rapid complexity of culture may be checked by one of the most important elements of an advanced culture itself, namely, the use of a secondary set of language symbols necessarily possessing greater conservatism than the primarily spoken set of symbols and exerting a conservative influence on the latter. I refer to the use of writing. In spite of this, however, it seems to me that the apparent paradox that we have arrived at contains a liberal element of truth. I am not inclined to consider it an accident that the rapid development of culture in western Europe during the last 2000 years has been synchronous with what seems to be unusually rapid changes in language. Though it is impossible to prove the matter definitely, I am inclined to doubt whether many languages of primitive peoples have undergone as rapid modification in a corresponding period of time as has the English language.

We have no time at our disposal to go more fully into this purely hypothetical explanation of our failure to bring environment and language into causal relation, but a metaphor may help us to grasp it. Two men start on a journey on condition that each shift for himself, depending on his own resources, yet traveling in the same general direction. For a considerable time the two men, both as yet unwearied, will keep pretty well together. In course of time, however, the varying degrees of physical strength, resourcefulness, ability to orient oneself, and many other factors, will begin to manifest themselves. The actual course traveled by each in reference to the other and to the course originally planned will diverge more and more, while the absolute distance between the two will also tend to become greater and greater. And so with many sets of historic sequences which, at one time causally associated, tend in course of time to diverge.

COMMUNICATION*

I<small>T IS OBVIOUS</small> that for the building up of society, its units and subdivisions, and the understandings which prevail between its members some processes of communication are needed. While we often speak of society as though it were a static structure defined by tradition, it is, in the more intimate sense, nothing of the kind, but a highly intricate network of partial or complete understandings between the members of organizational units of every degree of size and complexity, ranging from a pair of lovers or a family to a league of nations or that ever increasing portion of humanity which can be reached by the press through all its transnational ramifications. It is only apparently a static sum of social institutions; actually it is being reanimated or creatively reaffirmed from day to day by particular acts of a communicative nature which obtain among individuals participating in it. Thus the Republican party cannot be said to exist as such, but only to the extent that its tradition is being constantly added to and upheld by such simple acts of communication as that John Doe votes the Republican ticket, thereby communicating a certain kind of message, or that a half-dozen individuals meet at a certain time and place, formally or informally, in order to communicate ideas to each other and eventually to decide what points of national interest, real or supposed, are to be allowed to come up many months later for discussion in a gathering of members of the party. The Republican party as a historic entity is merely abstracted from thousands upon thousands of such single acts of communication, which have in common certain persistent features of reference. If we extend this example into every conceivable field in which communication has a place, we soon realize that every cultural pattern and every single act of social behavior involve communication in either an explicit or an implicit sense.

One may conveniently distinguish between certain fundamental techniques, or primary processes, which are communicative in character, and certain secondary techniques which facilitate the process of communication. The distinction is perhaps of no great psychological importance but has a very real historical and sociological significance, inasmuch as the fundamental processes are common to all mankind, while the secondary techniques emerge only at relatively sophisticated levels of civilization. Among the primary communicative processes of society may be mentioned: language; gesture, in its widest sense; the

* *Encyclopaedia of the Social Sciences* (New York, Macmillan, 1931), 4: 78–81.

imitation of overt behavior; and a large and ill-defined group of implicit processes which grow out of overt behavior and which may be rather vaguely referred to as "social suggestion."

Language is the most explicit type of communicative behavior that we know of. It need not here be defined beyond pointing out that it consists in every case known to us of an absolutely complete referential apparatus of phonetic symbols which have the property of locating every known social referent, including all the recognized data of perception which the society that it serves carries in its tradition. Language is the communicative process par excellence in every known society, and it is exceedingly important to observe that whatever may be the shortcomings of a primitive society judged from the vantage point of civilization, its language inevitably forms as sure, complete, and potentially creative an apparatus of referential symbolism as the most sophisticated language that we know of. What this means for a theory of communication is that the mechanics of significant understanding between human beings are as sure and complex and rich in overtones in one society as in another, primitive or sophisticated.

Gesture includes much more than the manipulation of the hands and other visible and movable parts of the organism. Intonations of the voice may register attitudes and feelings quite as significantly as the clenched fist, the wave of the hand, the shrugging of the shoulders, or the lifting of the eyebrows. The field of gesture interplays constantly with that of language proper, but there are many facts of a psychological and historical order which show that there are subtle yet firm lines of demarcation between them. Thus, to give but one example, the consistent message delivered by language symbolism in the narrow sense, whether by speech or by writing, may flatly contradict the message communicated by the synchronous system of gestures, consisting of movements of the hands and head, intonations of the voice, and breathing symbolisms. The former system may be entirely conscious, the latter entirely unconscious. Linguistic, as opposed to gesture, communication tends to be the official and socially accredited one; hence one may intuitively interpret the relatively unconscious symbolisms of gesture as psychologically more significant in a given context than the words actually used. In such cases as these we have a conflict between explicit and implicit communications in the growth of the individual's social experience.

The primary condition for the consolidation of society is the imitation of overt behavior. Such imitation, while not communicative in intent, has always the retroactive value of a communication, for in the process of falling in with the ways of society one in effect acquiesces in the meanings that inhere in these ways. When one learns to go to church, for instance, because other members of the community set the pace for this kind of activity, it is as though a communication had been received and acted upon. It is the function of language to articulate and rationalize the full content of these informal communications in the growth of the individual's social experience.

Even less directly communicative in character than overt behavior and its imitation is "social suggestion" as the sum total of new acts and new meanings that are implicitly made possible by these types of social behavior. Thus, the particular method of revolting against the habit of church going in a given society, while contradictory, on the surface, of the conventional meanings of that society, may nevertheless receive all its social significance from hundreds of existing prior communications that belong to the culture of the group as a whole. The importance of the unformulated and unverbalized communications of society is so great that one who is not intuitively familiar with them is likely to be baffled by the significance of certain kinds of behavior, even if he is thoroughly aware of their external forms and of the verbal symbols that accompany them. It is largely the function of the artist to make articulate these more subtle intentions of society.

Communicative processes do not merely apply to society as such; they are indefinitely varied as to form and meaning for the various types of personal relationship into which society resolves itself. Thus a fixed type of conduct or a linguistic symbol has by no means necessarily the same communicative significance within the confines of the family, among the members of an economic group, and in the nation at large. Generally speaking, the smaller the circle and the more complex the understandings already arrived at within it, the more economical can the act of communication afford to become. A single word passed between members of an intimate group, in spite of its apparent vagueness and ambiguity, may constitute a far more precise communication than volumes of carefully prepared correspondence interchanged between two governments.

There seem to be three main classes of techniques which have for their object the facilitation of the primary communicative processes of society. These may be referred to as: language transfers; symbolisms arising from special technical situations; and the creation of physical conditions favorable for the communicative act. Of language transfers the best known example is writing. The Morse telegraph code is another example. These and many other communicative techniques have this in common, that while they are overtly not at all like each other, their organization is based on the primary symbolic organization which has arisen in the domain of speech. Psychologically, therefore, they extend the communicative character of speech to situations in which for one reason or another speech is not possible.

In the more special class of communicative symbolism one cannot make a word-to-word translation, as it were, back to speech but can only paraphrase in speech the intent of the communication. Here belong such symbolic systems as wigwagging, the use of railroad lights, bugle calls in the army, and smoke signals. It is interesting to observe that, while they are late in developing in the history of society, they are very much less complex in structure than language itself. They are of value partly in helping out a situation where neither language nor some form of language transfer can be applied, partly where it is desired to encourage the automatic nature of the desired response. Thus, because language is extraordinarily rich in meaning, it sometimes becomes a little annoying or even dangerous to rely upon it where only a simple this or that, or yes or no, is expected to be the response.

The importance of extending the physical conditions allowing for communication is obvious. The railroad, the telegraph, the telephone, the radio, and the airplane are among the best examples. It is to be noted that such instruments as the railroad and the radio are not communicative in character as such; they become so only because they facilitate the presentation of types of stimuli which act as symbols of communication or which contain implications of communicative significance. Thus, a telephone is of no use unless the party at the other end understands the language of the person calling up. Again, the fact that a railroad runs me to a certain point is of no real communicative importance unless there are fixed bonds of interest which connect me with the inhabitants of the place. The failure to bear in mind these obvious points has tended to make some writers exaggerate the importance of the spread in modern times of such inventions as the railroad and the telephone.

The history of civilization has been marked by a progressive increase in the radius of communication. In a typically primitive society communication is reserved for the members of the tribe and, at best, a small number of surrounding tribes with whom relations are intermittent rather than continuous and who act as a kind of buffer between the significant psychological world—the world of one's own tribal culture—and the great unknown or unreal that lies beyond. Today, in our own civilization, the appearance of a new fashion in Paris is linked by a series of rapid and necessary events with the appearance of the same fashion in such distant places as Berlin, London, New York, San Francisco, and Yokohama. The underlying reason for this remarkable change in the radius and rapidity of communication is the gradual diffusion of cultural traits, in other words, of meaningful cultural reactions. Among the various types of cultural diffusion that of language itself is of paramount importance. Secondary technical devices making for ease of communication are also, of course, of prime importance.

The multiplication of far-reaching techniques of communication has two important results. In the first place, it increases the sheer radius of communication, so that for certain purposes the whole civilized world is made the psychological equivalent of a primitive tribe. In the second place, it lessens the importance of mere geographical contiguity. Owing to the technical nature of these sophisticated communicative devices, parts of the world that are geographically remote may, in terms of behavior, be actually much closer to each other than adjoining regions, which, from the historical standpoint, are supposed to share a larger body of common understandings. This means, of course, a tendency to remap the world both sociologically and psychologically. Even now it is possible to say that the scattered "scientific world" is a social unity which has no clearcut geographical location. Further, the world of urban understanding in America contrasts rather sharply with the rural world. The weakening of the geographical factor in social organization must in the long run profoundly modify our attitude toward the meaning of personal relations and of social classes and even of nationalities.

The increasing ease of communication is purchased at a price, for it is becoming increasingly difficult to keep an intended communication within the desired bounds. A humble example of this new problem is the inadvisability of making certain kinds of statement on the telephone. Another example is the insidious cheapening of literary and artistic values due to the foreseen and economically advantageous "widening of the appeal." All effects which demand a certain intimacy of understanding tend to become difficult and are therefore avoided. It is a question whether the obvious increase of overt communication is not constantly being corrected, as it were, by the creation of new obstacles to communication. The fear of being too easily understood may, in many cases, be more aptly defined as the fear of being understood by too many—so many, indeed, as to endanger the psychological reality of the image of the enlarged self confronting the not-self.

On the whole, however, it is rather the obstacles to communication that are felt as annoying or ominous. The most important of these obstacles in the modern world is undoubtedly the great diversity of languages. The enormous amount of energy put into the task of translation implies a passionate desire to make as light of the language difficulty as possible. In the long run it seems almost unavoidable that the civilized world will adopt some one language of intercommunication, say English or Esperanto, which can be set aside for denotive purposes pure and simple.

THE FUNCTION OF AN INTERNATIONAL
AUXILIARY LANGUAGE*

As to the theoretical desirability of an international auxiliary language there can be little difference of opinion. As to just what factors in the solution of the problem should be allowed to weigh most heavily there is room for every possible difference of opinion, and so it is not surprising that interlinguists are far from having reached complete agreement as to either method or content. So far as the advocates of a constructed international language are concerned, it is rather to be wondered at how much in common their proposals actually have, both in vocabulary and in general spirit of procedure. The crucial differences of opinion lie not so much between one constructed language and another as between the idea of a constructed language and that of an already well-established national one, whether in its traditional, authorized form or in some simplified form of it. It is not uncommon to hear it said by those who stand somewhat outside the international language question that some such regular system as Esperanto is theoretically desirable but that it is of little use to work for it because English is already *de facto* the international language of modern times— if not altogether at the moment, then in the immediate future—that English is simple enough and regular enough to satisfy all practical requirements, and that the precise form of it as an international language may well be left to historical and psychological factors that one need not worry about in advance. This point of view has a certain pleasing plausibility about it but, like so many things that seem plausible and effortless, it may none the less embody a number of fallacies.

It is the purpose of this paper to try to clarify the fundamental question of what is to be expected of an international auxiliary language, and whether the explicit and tacit requirements can be better satisfied by a constructed language or by a national language, including some simplified version of it. I believe that much of the difficulty in the international language question lies precisely in lack of clarity as to these fundamental functions.

There are two considerations, often intermingled in practice, which arouse the thought of an international language. The first is the purely practical problem of facilitating the growing need for international

* *Psyche,* 11 (1931): 4–15. Also published in H. N. Shenton, E. Sapir, and O. Jesperson, *International Communication: A Symposium on the Language Problem* (London, 1931), pp. 65–94.

[110]

communication in its most elementary sense. A firm, for instance, that does business in many countries of the world is driven to spend an enormous amount of time, labour, and money in providing for translation services. From a purely technological point of view, all this is sheer waste, and while one accepts the necessity of going to all the linguistic trouble that the expansion of trade demands, one does so with something like a shrug of the shoulder. One speaks of a 'necessary evil.' Again, at an international scientific meeting one is invariably dissappointed to find that the primary difficulty of communicating with foreign scientists because of differences of language habits makes it not so easy to exchange ideas of moment as one had fantasied might be the case before setting sail. Here again one speaks of a 'necessary evil,' and comforts oneself with the reflection that if the scientific ideas which it was not too easy to follow at the meeting are of moment they will, sooner or later, be presented in cold print, so that nothing is essentially lost. One can always congratulate oneself on having had an interesting time and on having made some charming personal contacts. Such examples can, of course, be multiplied *ad infinitum.* Too much is not made, as a rule, of any specific difficulty in linguistic communication, but the cumulative effect of these difficulties is stupendous in magnitude. Sooner or later one chafes and begins to wonder whether the evil is as 'necessary' as tradition would have it. Impatience translates itself into a desire to have something immediate done about it all, and, as is generally the case with impatience, resolves itself in the easiest way that lies ready to hand. Why not push English, for instance, which is already spoken over a larger area than any other language of modern times, and which shows every sign of spreading in the world of commerce and travel? The consideration which gives rise to reflections of this sort, grounded in impatience as it is, looks for no more worthy solution of the difficulty than a sort of minimum language, a *lingua franca* of the modern world. Those who argue in this spirit invariably pride themselves on being 'practical,' and, like all 'practical' people, they are apt to argue without their host.

The opposed consideration is not as easy to state and can be so stated as to seem to be identical with the first. It should be put in something like the following form: An international auxiliary language should serve as a broad base for every type of international understanding, which means, of course, in the last analysis, for every type of expression of the human spirit which is of more than local interest, which in turn can be restated so as to include any and all human interests. The exigencies of trade or travel are from this point of view merely some of the more obvious symptoms of the internationalizing of the human mind, and it would be a mistake to expect too little of an organ of international expression. But this is not all. The modern mind tends to be more and more critical and analytical in spirit, hence it must devise for itself an engine of expression which is logically defensible at every point and which tends to correspond to the rigorous spirit of modern science. This does not mean that a constructed international language is expected to have the perfection of mathematical symbolism, but it must be progressively felt as moving in that direction. Perhaps the speakers of a national language are under profound illusions as to the logical character of its structure. Perhaps they confuse the comfort of habit with logical necessity. If this is so—and I do not see how it can be seriously doubted that it is—it must mean that in the long run the modern spirit will not rest satisfied with an international language that merely extends the imperfections and provincialisms of one language at the expense of all others.

These two opposing considerations seem to me to be the primary ones. They may be rephrased as "what can be done right now" and "what should be done in the long run." There are also other considerations that are of importance, and among them perhaps the most obvious is the attitude of people toward the spread or imposition of any national language which is not their own. The psychology of a language which, in one way or another, is imposed upon one because of factors beyond one's control, is very different from the psychology of a language that one accepts of one's free will. In a sense, every form of expression is imposed upon one by social factors, one's own language above all. But it is the thought or illusion of freedom that is the important thing, not the fact of it. The modern world is confronted by the difficulty of reconciling internationalism with its persistent and tightening nationalisms. More and more, unsolicited gifts from without are likely to be received with unconscious resentment. Only that can be freely accepted which is in some sense a creation of all. A common creation demands a common sacrifice, and perhaps not the least potent argument in favour of a constructed international language is the fact that it is equally foreign, or apparently so, to the traditions of all nationalities. The common difficulty gives it an impersonal character and silences the resentment that is born of rivalry. English, once accepted as an international language, is no more secure than French has proved to be as the one and only accepted language of diplomacy or as Latin has proved to be as the international language of science. Both French and Latin are involved with nationalistic and religious implications which could not be entirely shaken off, and so, while they seemed for a long time to have solved the international language problem up to a certain point, they did not really do so in spirit. English would probably fare no better, and it is even likely that the tradition of trade, finance, and superficial practicality in general that attaches to English may, in the long run, prove more of a hindrance than a help to the unreserved acceptance of English as an adequate means of international expression. One must beware of an over-emphasis on the word 'auxiliary.' It is perfectly true that for untold generations to come an international language must be auxiliary, must not attempt to set itself up against the many languages of the folk, but it must for all that be a free powerful expression of its own, capable of all work that may reasonably be expected of language and protected by the powerful negative fact that it cannot be interpreted as the symbol of any localism or nationality.

Whether or not some national language, say, English, or a constructed language, say Esperanto, is to win out in the immediate future, does not depend primarily on conscious forces that can be manipulated, but on many obscure and impersonal political, economic and social determinants. One can only hope that one senses the more significant of these determinants and helps along with such efforts as one can master. Even if it be assumed for the sake of argument that English is to spread as an auxiliary language over the whole world, it does not in the least follow that the international language problem is disposed of. English, or some simplified version of it, may spread for certain immediate and practical purposes, yet the deeper needs of the modern world may not be satisfied by it and we may still have to deal with a conflict between an English that has won a too easy triumph and a constructed language that has such obvious advantages of structure that it may gradually displace its national rival.

What is needed above all is a language that is as simple, as regular, as logical, as rich, and as creative as possible; a language which starts with a minimum of demands on the learning capacity of the normal individual and can do the maximum amount of work; which is to serve as a sort of logical touchstone to all national languages and as the standard medium of translation. It must, ideally, be as superior to any accepted language as the mathematical method of expressing quantities and relations between quantities is to the more lumbering methods of expressing these quantities and relations in verbal form. This is undoubtedly an ideal which can never be reached, but ideals are not meant to be reached: they merely indicate the direction of movement.

I spoke before about the illusions that the average man has about the nature of his own language. It will help to clarify matters if we take a look at English from the standpoint of simplicity, regularity, logic, richness, and creativeness. We may begin with simplicity. It is true that English is not as complex in its formal structure as is German or Latin, but this does not dispose of the matter. The fact that a beginner in English has not many paradigms to learn gives him a feeling of absence of difficulty, but he soon learns to his cost that this is only a feeling, that in sober fact the very absence of explicit guide-posts to structure leads him into all sorts of quandaries. A few examples will be useful. One of the glories of English simplicity is the possibility of using the same word as noun and verb. We speak, for instance, of "having cut the meat" and of "a cut of meat." We not only "kick a person," but "give him a kick." One may either "ride horseback" or "take a ride." At first blush this looks like a most engaging rule but a little examination convinces us that the supposed simplicity of word-building is a mirage. In the first place, in what sense may a verb be used as a noun? In the case of "taking a ride" or "giving a kick" the noun evidently indicates the act itself. In the case of "having a cut on the head" or "eating a cut of meat," it just as clearly does not indicate the act itself but the result of the act, and these two examples do not even illustrate the same kind of result, for in the former case the cut is conceived of as the wound that results from cutting, whereas in the latter case it refers to the portion of meat which is loosened by the act of cutting. Anyone who takes the trouble to examine these examples carefully will soon see that behind a superficial appearance of simplicity there is concealed a perfect hornet's nest of bizarre and arbitrary usages. To those of us who speak English from the earliest years of our childhood these difficulties do not readily appear. To one who comes to English from a language which possesses a totally different structure such facts as these are disconcerting. But there is a second difficulty with the rule, or tendency, which allows us to use the unmodified verb as a noun. Not only is the function of the noun obscure, but in a great many cases we cannot use it at all, or the usage is curiously restricted. We can "give a person a shove" or "a push," but we cannot "give him a move" nor "a drop" (in the sense of causing him to drop). We can "give one help," but we "give obedience," not "obey." A complete examination, in short, of all cases in which the verb functions as a noun would disclose two exceedingly cheerless facts: that there is a considerable number of distinct senses in which the verb may be so employed, though no rule can be given as to which of these possible senses is the proper one in any particular case or whether only one or more than one such meaning is possible; and that in many cases no such nouns may be formed at all, but that either nouns of an entirely different formation must be used or else that they are not possible at all. We thus have to set up such rather cranky-looking configurations as

$$\text{to help:help} = \text{to obey:obedience}$$
$$= \text{to grow:growth}$$
$$= \text{to drown:drowning,}$$

a set-up which is further complicated by the fact that such a word as 'drowning' not only corresponds to such words as 'help' and 'growth,' but also to such words as 'helping' and 'growing.' The precise disentanglement of all these relations and the obtaining of anything like assurance in the use of the words is a task of no small difficulty. Where, then, is the simplicity with which we started? It is obviously a phantom. The English-speaking person covers up the difficulty for himself by speaking vaguely of idioms. The real point is that behind the vagaries of idiomatic usage there are perfectly clear-cut logical relations which are only weakly brought out in the overt form of English. The simplicity of English in its formal aspect is, therefore, really a pseudo-simplicity or a masked complexity.

Another example of apparent, but only apparent, simplicity in English is the use of such vague verbs as 'to put' and 'to get.' To us the verb 'put' is a very simple matter, both in form and in use. Actually it is an amazingly difficult word to learn to use and no rules can be given either for its employment or for its avoidance. 'To put at rest' gives us an impression of simplicity because of the overt simplicity of the structure, but here again the simplicity is an illusion. 'To put at rest' really means 'to cause to rest,' and its apparent analogy to such constructions as 'to put it at a great distance,' so far from helping thought, really hinders it, for the formal analogy is not paralleled by a conceptual one. 'To put out of danger' is formally analogous to 'to put out of school,' but here too the analogy is utterly misleading, unless, indeed, one defines school as a form of danger. If we were to define 'put' as a kind of causative operator, we should get into trouble, for it cannot be safely used as such in all cases. In such a sentence as "The ship put to sea," for example, there is no implied causative relation. If English cannot give the foreigner clear rules for the employment of verbs as nouns or for such apparently simple verbs as 'put,' what advantage is derived by him from the merely negative fact that he has not much formal grammar to learn in these cases? He may well

feel that the apparent simplicity of English is purchased at the price
of a bewildering obscurity. He may even feel that the mastery of
English usage is, in the long run, much more difficult than the application of a fairly large number of rules for the formation of words, so
long as these rules are unambiguous.

English has no monopoly of pseudo-simplicity. French and German
illustrate the misleading character of apparent grammatical simplicity
just as well. One example from French will serve our purpose. There is
no doubt that the French speaker feels that he has in the reflexive verb
a perfectly simple and, on the whole, unambiguous form of expression.
A logical analysis of reflexive usages in French shows, however, that
this simplicity is an illusion and that, so far from helping the foreigner,
it is more calculated to bother him. In some cases the French reflexive
is a true reflexive; that is, it indicates that the subject of the sentence
is the same as the object. An example of a reflexive verb of this sort
would be *se tuer*, 'to kill oneself.' To French feeling this sort of verb is
doubtless identical with the type illustrated by *s'amuser*. Logically,
however, one does not 'amuse oneself' in the sense in which one 'kills
oneself.' The possibility of translating 'to amuse oneself' into 'to have
a good time' and the impossibility of translating 'to kill oneself' into
'to have a bad time killing,' or something of that sort, at once shows the
weakness of the analogy. Logically, of course, *s'amuser* is not a true
reflexive at all, but merely an intransitive verb of the same general
type as 'to rejoice' or 'to laugh' or 'to play.' Furthermore, the French
verb *se battre* gives the Frenchman precisely the same formal feeling as
se tuer and *s'amuser*. Actually it is a reciprocal verb which may be translated as 'to strike one another' and, therefore, 'to fight.' Finally, in such
a verb as *s'étendre*, 'to extend' or 'to stretch,' the Frenchman distinctly
feels the reflexive force, the stretching of the road, for instance, being
conceived of as a self-stretching of the road, as though the road took
itself and lengthened itself out. This type of verb may be called a
pseudo-reflexive, or a non-agentive active verb, the point being that
the action, while of a type that is generally brought about by an outside agency, is conceived of as taking place without definite agency. In
English, verbs of this kind are regularly used without the reflexive,
as in 'the road stretches,' 'the string breaks,' 'the rag tears,' 'the bag
bursts,' which are the non-agentive correspondents of such usages as
'he stretches the rubber band,' 'he breaks the string,' 'he tears the rag,'
'he bursts the balloon.' It should be clear that a linguistic usage, such as
the French reflexive, which throws together four such logically distinct
categories as the true reflexive, the simple intransitive, the reciprocal,

and the non-agentive active, purchases simplicity at a considerable price. For the Frenchman such usage is convenient enough and no ambiguity seems to result. But for the outsider, who comes to French with a different alignment of forms in his mind, the simplicity that is offered is puzzling and treacherous.

These examples of the lack of simplicity in English and French, all appearances to the contrary, could be multiplied almost without limit and apply to all national languages. In fact, one may go so far as to say that it is precisely the apparent simplicity of structure which is suggested by the formal simplicity of many languages which is responsible for much slovenliness in thought, and even for the creation of imaginary problems in philosophy. What has been said of simplicity applies equally to regularity and logic, as some of our examples have already indicated. No important national language, at least in the Occidental world, has complete regularity of grammatical structure, nor is there a single logical category which is adequately and consistently handled in terms of linguistic symbolism. It is well known that the tense systems of French, English and German teem with logical inconsistencies as they are actually used. Many categories which are of great logical and psychological importance are so haltingly expressed that it takes a good deal of effort to prove to the average man that they exist at all. A good example of such a category is that of 'aspect,' in the technical sense of the word. Few English-speaking people see such a locution as 'to burst into tears' or 'to burst out laughing' as much more than an idiomatic oddity. As a matter of fact, English is here trying to express, as best it can, an intuition of the 'momentaneous aspect'; in other words, of activity seen as a point in contrast to activity seen as a line. Logically and psychologically, nearly every activity can be thought of as either point-like or line-like in character, and there are, of course, many expressions in English which definitely point to the one or to the other, but the treatment of these intuitions is fragmentary and illogical throughout.

A standard international language should not only be simple, regular, and logical, but also rich and creative. Richness is a difficult and subjective concept. It would, of course, be hopeless to attempt to crowd into an international language all those local overtones of meaning which are so dear to the heart of the nationalist. There is a growing fund of common experience and sentiment which will have to be expressed in an international language, and it would be strange if the basic fund of meanings would not grow in richness with the interactions of human beings who make use of the international medium.

The supposed inferiority of a constructed language to a national one on the score of richness of connotation is, of course, no criticism of the idea of a constructed language. All that the criticism means is that the constructed language has not been in long-continued use. As a matter of of fact, a national language which spreads beyond its own confines very quickly loses much of its original richness of content and is in no better case than a constructed language.

More important is the question of creativeness. Here there are many illusions. All languages, even the most primitive, have very real powers of creating new words and combinations of words as they are needed, but the theoretical possibilities of creation are in most of these national languages which are of importance for the international language question thwarted by all sorts of irrelevant factors that would not apply to a constructed language. English, for instance, has a great many formal resources at its disposal which it seems unable to use adequately; for instance, there is no reason why the suffix -*ness* should not be used to make up an unlimited number of words indicating quality, such as 'smallness' and 'opaqueness,'' yet we know that only a limited number of such forms is possible. One says 'width,' not 'wideness'; 'beauty,' not 'beautifulness.' In the same way, such locutions as 'to give a kick' and 'to give a slap' might be supposed to serve as models for the creation of an unlimited number of momentaneous verbs, yet the possibilities of extending this form of usage are strictly limited. The truth is that sentiment and precedent prevent the national language, with its accepted tradition, from doing all it might do, and the logically possible formations of all kinds which would be felt as awkward or daring in English, or even in German, could be accepted as the merest matters of course in an international language that was not tied to the dictates of irrational usage.

We see, then, that no national language really corresponds in spirit to the analytic and creative spirit of modern times. National languages are all huge systems of vested interests which sullenly resist critical inquiry. It may shock the traditionalist to be told that we are rapidly getting to the point where our national languages are almost more of a hindrance than a help to clear thinking; yet how true this is is significantly illustrated by the necessity that mathematics and symbolic logic have been under of developing their own systems of symbolism. There is a perfectly obvious objection that is often raised at this point. We are told that normal human expression does not crave any such accuracy as is attained by these rigorous disciplines. True, but it is not a question of remodeling language in the spirit of mathematics and symbolic logic, but merely of giving it the structural means whereby it may refine itself in as economical and unambiguous a manner as possible.

It is likely that the foundations of a truly adequate form of international language have already been laid in Esperanto and other proposed international auxiliary languages, but it is doubtful if the exacting ideal that we have sketched is attained by any one of them, or is likely to be attained for some time to come. It is, therefore, highly desirable that along with the practical labour of getting wider recognition of the international language idea, there go hand in hand comparative researches which aim to lay bare the logical structures that are inadequately symbolized in our present-day languages, in order that we may see more clearly than we have yet been able to see just how much of psychological insight and logical rigour have been and can be expressed in linguistic form. One of the most ambitious and important tasks that can be undertaken is the attempt to work out the relation between logic and usage in a number of national and constructed languages, in order that the eventual problem of adequately symbolizing thought may be seen as the problem it still is. No doubt it will be impossible, for a long time to come, to give a definite answer to all of the questions that are raised, but it is something to raise and define the questions.

I have emphasized the logical advantages of a constructed international language, but it is important not to neglect the psychological ones. The attitude of independence toward a constructed language which all national speakers must adopt is really a great advantage, because it tends to make man see himself as the master of language instead of its obedient servant. A common allegiance to form of expression that is identified with no single national unit is likely to prove one of the most potent symbols of the freedom of the human spirit that the world has yet known. As the Oriental peoples become of more and more importance in the modern world, the air of sanctity that attaches to English or German or French is likely to seem less and less a thing to be taken for granted, and it is not at all unlikely that the eventual triumph of the international language movement will owe much to the Chinaman's and the Indian's indifference to the vested interests of Europe, though the actual stock of basic words in any practical international language is almost certain to be based on the common European fund. A further psychological advantage of a constructed language has been often referred to by those who have had experience with such languages as Esperanto. This is the removal of fear in the public use of a language other than one's native tongue.

The use of the wrong gender in French or any minor violence to English idiom is construed as a sin of etiquette, and everyone knows how paralyzing on freedom of expression is the fear of committing the slightest breach of etiquette. Who knows to what extent the discreet utterances of foreign visitors are really due to their wise unwillingness to take too many chances with the vagaries of a foreign language? It is, of course, not the language as such which is sinned against, but the conventions of fitness which are in the minds of the natives who act as custodians of the language. Expression in a constructed language has no such fears as these to reckon with. Errors in Esperanto speech are not sins or breaches of etiquette; they are merely trivialities to the extent that they do not actually misrepresent the meaning of the speaker, and as such they may be ignored.

In the educational world there is a great deal of discontent with the teaching of classical and modern languages. It is no secret that the fruits of language study are in no sort of relation to the labour spent on teaching and learning them. Who has not the uncomfortable feeling that there is something intellectually dishonest about a course of study that goes in for a half-hearted tinkering with, say, Latin and two modern languages, with a net result that is more or less microscopic in value? A feeling is growing that the study of foreign languages should be relegated to the class of technical specialties and that the efforts of educators should be directed rather toward deepening the conceptual language sense of students in order that, thus equipped, they may as occasion arises be in a better position to learn what national languages they may happen to need. A well-constructed international language is much more easily learned than a national language, sharpens one's insight into the logical structure of expression in a way that none of these does, and puts one in possession of a great deal of lexical material which can be turned to account in the analysis of both the speaker's language and of most others that he is likely to want to learn. Certain beginnings have already been made toward the adoption of international language study as a means toward general language work. Time alone can tell whether this movement is a fruitful one, but it is certainly an aspect of the international language question that is worth thinking about, particularly in America, with its growing impatience of the largely useless teaching of Latin, French, German, and Spanish in the high schools. The international language movement has had, up to the present time, a somewhat cliquish or esoteric air. It now looks as though it might take on the characteristics of an international Open Forum. The increasing degree to which linguists, mathematicians and scientists have been thinking about the problem is a sign that promises well for the future. It is a good thing that the idea of an international language is no longer presented in merely idealistic terms, but is more and more taking on the aspect of a practical or technological problem and of an exercise in the cleaning up of the thought process. Intelligent men should not allow themselves to become international language doctrinaires. They should do all they can to keep the problem experimental, welcoming criticism at every point and trusting to the gradual emergence of an international language that is a fit medium for the modern spirit.

The spirit of logical analysis should in practice blend with the practical pressure for the adoption of some form of international language, but it should not allow itself to be stampeded by it. It would be exceedingly unfortunate if an international language, whether Esperanto or English or some form of simplified English, were looked upon as thenceforth sacred and inviolate. No solution of the international language problem should be looked upon as more than a beginning toward the gradual evolution, in the light of experience and at the hand of all civilized humanity, of an international language which is as rich as any now known to us, is far more creative in its possibilities, and is infinitely simpler, more regular, and more logical than any one of them.

GRADING: A STUDY IN SEMANTICS*

The Psychology of Grading

The first thing to realize about grading as a psychological process is that it precedes measurement and counting. Judgments of the type "A is larger than B" or "This can contains less milk than that" are made long before it is possible to say, e.g., "A is twice as large as B" or "A has a volume of 25 cubic feet, B a volume of 20 cubic feet, therefore A is larger than B by 5 cubic feet," or "This can contains a quart of milk, that one 3 quarts of milk, therefore the former has less milk in it." In other words, judgments of quantity in terms of units of measure or in terms of number always presuppose, explicitly or implicitly, preliminary judgments of grading. The term *four* means something only when it is known to refer to a number which is "less than" certain others, say *five, six, seven*, arranged in an ordered series of relative *mores* and *lesses*, and "more than" certain others, say *one, two, three*, arranged in an ordered series of relative *mores* and *lesses*. Similarly, *a foot* as a unit of linear measure has no meaning whatever unless it is known to be more than some other stretch, say *an inch*, and less than a third stretch, say *a yard*.

Judgments of "more than" and "less than" may be said to be based on perceptions of "envelopment." If A can be "enveloped by" B, contained by it, so placed in contact with B, either actually or by the imagination, as to seem to be held within its compass instead of extending beyond it, it is judged to be "less than" B, while B is judged to be "more than" A. With only two existents of the same class, A and B, the judgments "A is *less than* B" and "B is *more than* A" can be translated into the form "A is *small*" and "B is *large*." In the case of the two cans of milk, we may say "There is *little* milk in this can" and "There is *much* milk in that can." Again, if there are three men in one room and seven in another, we may either say "The first room has *fewer* men in it *than* the second" and "The second room has *more* men in it *than* the first" or, if we prefer, "The first room has *few* men in it" and "The second room has *many* men in it."[1] Such contrasts as *small* and *large*, *little* and *much*, *few* and *many*, give us a deceptive feeling of absolute values within the field of quantity comparable to such qualitative differences as *red* and *green* within the field of color perception. This feeling is an illusion, however, which is largely due to the linguistic fact that the

* *Philosophy of Science*, 11 (1944): 93–116.
[1] "Few" and "many" in a relative sense, of course. More of this anon.

grading which is implicit in these terms is not formally indicated, whereas it is made explicit in such judgments as "There were *fewer* people there *than* here" or "He has *more* milk *than* I." In other words, *many*, to take but one example, embodies no class of judgments clustering about a given quantity norm which is applicable to every type of experience, in the sense in which *red* or *green* is applicable to every experience in which color can have a place, but is, properly speaking, a purely relative term which loses all significance when deprived of its connotation of "more than" and "less than." *Many* merely means any number, definite or indefinite, which is *more than* some other number taken as point of departure. This point of departure obviously varies enormously according to context. For one observing the stars on a clear night thirty may be but "few," for a proof-reader correcting mistakes on a page of galley the same number may be not only "many" but "very many." Five pounds of meat may be embarrassingly "much" for a family of two but less than "little" from the standpoint of one ordering provisions for a regiment.

Degrees of Explicitness in Grading

We may bring these remarks to a focus by saying that all quantifiables (terms that may be quantified) and all quantificates (terms to which notions of quantity have been applied) involve the concept of grading in four degrees of explicitness.

1. Every quantifiable, whether existent (say *house*) or occurrent (say *run*) or quality of existent (say *red*) or quality of occurrent (say *gracefully*), is intrinsically gradable. No two houses are exactly identical in size nor are they identical in any other feature that can be predicated of them. Any two houses selected at random offer the contrast of "more" and "less" on hundreds of features which are constitutive of the concept "house." Thus, house A is higher but house B is roomier, while existent C is so much smaller than either A or B that it is "less of a house" than they and may be put in the class "toy" or at best "shack." Similarly, the concept of "running," involving, as it does, experience of many distinct acts of running which differ on numerous points of "more" and "less," such as speed, excitement of runner, length of time, and degree of resemblance to walking, is as gradable as that of "house." Different examples of "red" similarly exhibit "mores" and "lesses" with respect to intensity, size of surface or volume characterized as red, and degree of conformity to some accepted standard of redness. And "gracefully" is quite unthinkable except as implying a whole gamut of activities which may be arranged in a graded series on the score of

gracefulness. Every quantifiable, then, not yet explicitly quantified, is gradable. Such terms may be called *implicitly gradable but ungraded.*

2. As soon as a quantifiable has been quantified, the resulting quantificate necessarily takes its place in an infinite set of graded quantificates. Thus, *three houses* and *the whole house* belong to infinite sets in which they are respectively "less than" *four houses, five houses, six houses, . . .,* and "more than" *half of the house, a third of the house, a fourth of the house, . . .* Such terms may be called *implicitly graded by quantification.* The process of grading is here of interest only insofar as quantification is impossible without it.

3. Instead of directly quantifying a quantifiable in terms of count or measure, e.g., *one hundred men* or *a gill of milk*, one may content oneself with an indirect quantification by means of quantifiers which are thought of as occupying positions in a sliding scale of values of "more" and "less," e.g. *many men* or *a little milk.* Such terms may be called *quantified by implicit grading.* Here the grading is of essential interest but is assumed as accomplished rather than stated as taking place. Such terms as *many* are psychologically midway between terms like *more than* and *hundred.* First, a set A is perceived as capable of envelopment by another set B, which latter is then declared to be "more than" A. Next, B is declared to be "many," the reference to sets of type $A_1, A_2, A_3, . . .$, all of which are "less than" B, being purely implicit. Finally, the "many" of B is discovered to consist of a definite number of terms, say "one hundred," at which point grading as such has ceased to be of interest. In the realm of quantity "one hundred" is a gradable but ungraded absolute in approximately the same sense in which in the realm of existents "house" is a gradable but ungraded absolute.

4. Instead, finally, of quantifying by means of terms which grade only by implication we may grade explicitly and say, e.g., "*More men* are in this room *than* in that." Such a statement emphasizes the fact of grading itself, the quantifying judgment (i.e. "*Many men* are in this room but *few* in that" or "*Few men* are in this room but *even fewer* in that") being left implicit. Such terms as "more men" may be called *explicitly graded and implicitly quantified.*

The following scheme conveniently summarizes the grading gamut:

1. Implicitly gradable but ungraded: *house; houses*

2. Implicitly graded by quantification: *half of the house; a house 20 ft. wide; ten houses*

3. Quantified by implicit grading: *much of the house; a large house; many houses*

4. Explicitly graded and implicitly quantified: *more of the house (than); a larger house; more houses (than)*

GRADING FROM DIFFERENT POINTS OF VIEW

Only the last two types of terms are of further interest to us here. We shall briefly refer to the quantifying elements of terms of class 3 as *implicitly graded quantifiers*, to explicitly grading terms as *graders* (*more* than, *less* than), and to the implicitly quantifying elements of terms of class 4 as *explicitly grading quantifiers*. It is very important to realize that psychologically all comparatives are primary in relation to their corresponding absolutes ("positives"). Just as *more men* precedes both *some men* and *many men*, so *better* precedes both *good* and *very good*, *nearer* (= *at a less distance from*) precedes both *at some distance from* and *near* (= *at a small distance from*). Linguistic usage tends to start from the graded concept, e.g. *good* (= *better than indifferent*), *bad* (= *worse than indifferent*), *large* (= *larger than of average size*), *small* (= *smaller than of average size*), *much* (= *more than a fair amount*), *few* (= *less than a fair number*), for the obvious reason that in experience it is the strikingly high-graded or low-graded concept that has significance, while the generalized concept which includes all the members of a graded series is arrived at by a gradual process of striking the balance between these graded terms. The purely logical, the psychological, and the linguistic orders of primacy, therefore, do not necessarily correspond. Thus, the set *near, nearer, far, farther,* and *at a normal distance from* and the set *good, better, bad, worse, of average quality*, show the following orders of complication from these three points of view:

A. LOGICAL GRADING

TYPE I. GRADED WITH REFERENCE TO NORM

1) Norm: *at a normal distance from; of average quality*
2) Lower-graded: *at a less than normal distance from* = *nearer* or *less far* (*from*) (explicitly graded), *near* or *not far* (*from*) (implicitly graded); *of less than average quality* = *worse* or *less good* (explicitly graded), *bad* or *not good* (implicitly graded)
3) Upper-graded: *at a more than normal distance from* = *farther* or *less near* (explicitly graded), *far* or *not near* (implicitly graded); *of more than average quality* = *better* or *less bad* (explicitly graded), *good* or *not bad* (implicitly graded)

TYPE II. GRADED WITH REFERENCE TO TERMS OF COMPARISON

1) Lower-graded: *at a less distance than* = *relatively nearer* or *relatively less far* (explicitly graded), *relatively near* or *relatively not far* (implicitly graded); *of less quality than* = *relatively worse* or *relatively less good* (explicitly graded), *relatively bad* or *relatively not good* (implicitly graded)
2) Upper-graded: *at a greater distance than* = *relatively farther* or *relatively less near* (explicitly graded), *relatively far* or *relatively not near* (implicitly

graded); *of greater quality than* = *relatively better* or *relatively less bad* (explicitly graded), *relatively good* or *relatively not bad* (implicitly graded)

Note on A (*Logical Grading*).—In type I, "graded with reference to norm," any "nearer" or "near" is nearer than any "farther" or "far," any "worse" or "bad" is worse than any "better" or "good;" correlatively, any "farther" or "far" is farther than any "nearer" or "near," any "better" or "good" is better than any "worse" or "bad." But in type II, "graded with reference to terms of comparison," "nearer" and "near" do not need to be near but may actually, i.e. according to some norm, be far, "worse" and "bad" do not need to be bad but may actually be good; correlatively, "farther" and "far" do not need to be far but may actually be near, "better" and "good" do not need to be good but may actually be bad. Hence specific "nears" and "bads" may factually be respectively farther and better than specific "fars" and "goods."

A warning: These are logical terms, not terms of actual usage, which exhibit great confusion. In certain cases usage preferentially follows type I, e.g. "more brilliant" and "brilliant" connote, as a rule, some degree of noteworthy ability, "more brilliant" being rarely equivalent merely to "not so stupid"; "good" follows type I, but "better" follows type II, being equivalent to "relatively better, not so bad," e.g. "My pen is *better than* yours, but I confess that both are bad" (on the other hand, "A is *more brilliant than* B, but both are stupid" is meaningless except as irony, which always implies a psychological transfer); "near" tends to follow type I, "nearer" follows type II, but "near" may frequently be used like a type II term, e.g. "From the point of view of America, France is on the *near* side of Europe," i.e. "*nearer than* most of Europe, though actually far." Interestingly enough, the correlatives of these terms do not exactly correspond. "Stupid" and "less stupid" follow type I, "less stupid" being never equivalent to "more brilliant" (except, again, ironically); "less brilliant" is still "brilliant" as a rule, just as "less stupid" is still "stupid." "Bad" and "less bad," differing in this respect from "good" and "better," both follow type I; "less bad" is still "bad" but "better" (with reference to another term) may be even worse. (The "more" of inverse terms, e.g. "more stupid" and "worse," has a negative direction, as we shall see later.) "Far" tends to follow type I, "farther" follows type II, but "far" may frequently be used like a type II term, e.g. "He is sitting at the *far* end of the table," i.e. "at the end that is *farther*, though actually near." Needless to say, a logical analysis must proceed regardless of linguistic usage. On the whole, usage tends to assign comparative terms to type II of grading, positive terms to type I of grading, though this tendency never hardens into a definite rule. The linguistic types will be tabulated under C below.

According to strict logic, we should start from, say, *good = of average quality* (type I) or *of a certain quality* (type II) and grade all other qualities as follows:

Type I: *better, less good* (explicit), corresponding to ordinary *better, worse; good indeed, indeed not good* (implicit), corresponding to ordinary *good, bad.*

Type II: *relatively better, relatively less good* (explicit); *relatively good indeed, relatively indeed not good* (implicit).

How embarrassing logically such linguistic couplets as *good:bad, far:near, much:little* really are comes out in asking a question. "How *good* is it?" "How *far* was he?" and "How *much* have you?" really mean "Of what *quality* is it?" "At what *distance* was he?" and "What *quantity* have you?" and may be answered, with a superficial character of paradox, by "Very bad," "Quite near," and "Almost nothing" respectively.

B. PSYCHOLOGICAL GRADING

(*a* is graded with reference to *b*, which is either some other term comparable to *a* or stands for some norm)

TYPE I. OPEN-GAMUT GRADING: a, b, c, . . ., n

1) Explicit: *a is less than b = b is more than a: a is nearer than b = b is farther than a, a is worse than b = b is better than a.* Similarly for a:c; . . .; a:n; b:c; . . .; b:n; . . .; c:n; . . .

2) Implicit: *a is little = b is much: a is near = b is far, a is bad = b is good.* Similarly for other cases.

TYPE II. CONJUNCT CLOSED-GAMUT GRADING: a, b, c, . . ., n [ ] o, p, q, . . ., t (e.g., series of colors graded from *a*, vivid green, to *t*, vivid yellow).

1) Explicit: *a is less green than b = b is greener than a; . . .* [judgments of more or less green or yellow] *o is less yellow than p = p is yellower than o; . . .* In the brackets [ ] we have indeterminate field of marginal greens and marginal yellows, in which $a_1:b_1$ is interpreted as b_1 *is less green than* $a_1 = a_1$ *is greener than* $b_1 = b_1$ *is yellower than* $a_1 = a_1$ *is less yellow than* b_1. In other words, at some point, *n*, crest of green is reached and *more green* as grader gives way to *more yellow*, with establishment in transition zone, [ ], of secondary *more green* always coming before *less green.*

2) Implicit: *a, b, c, . . ., n are shades of green;* [judgments of green or yellow]; *o, p, q, . . ., t are shades of yellow.* In the brackets [ ] we have *yellowish greens* and *greenish yellows.*

TYPE III. OPEN-GAMUT GRADING (I) INTERPRETED IN TERMS OF CONJUNCT CLOSED-GAMUT GRADING (II): "a, b, c, . . ., n" interpreted, by analogy of (II), as "a, b, c, . . ., g [ ] h, i, j, . . ., n [ ]."

1) Explicit: *a is less than b = b is more than a: a is less far than b = b is farther than a, a is less good than b = b is better than a; . . .* [　] *h is less near than i = i is nearer than h, h is less bad than i = i is worse than h; . . . .* In transition zone [　] we have psychologically indeterminate field of marginal fars (goods) and marginal nears (bads), in which $a_1:b_1$ is interpreted as *b_1 is less far (good) than a_1 = a_1 is farther (better) than b_1 = b_1 is nearer (worse) than a_1 = a_1 is less near (bad) than b_1.* In other words, at some point, g, crest of far (good) is reached and *farther (better)* as grader gives way to *nearer (worse)*, with establishment in transition zone, [　], of secondary *farther (better)* always coming before *less far (less good).* Type III, however, differs from type II in that it has a second psychologically indeterminate field of marginal nears (bads) and marginal gars (goods), in which $h_1:i_1$ is interpreted as *i_1 is less near (bad) than h_1 = h_1 is nearer (worse than i_1 = i_1 is farther (better) than h_1 = h_1 is less far (good) than i_1.* In other words, at some point, n, crest of near (bad) is reached and *nearer (worse)* as grader gives way to *farther (better)*, with establishment in second transition zone, [　], of secondary *nearer (worse)* always coming before *less near (less bad).* Obviously, our second [　] brings us back to a, b, c, . . ., g. Type III of psychological grading (*far-near, good-bad*) is circular in configuration, as we shall see more clearly later on, while type II (*violet-blue-green-yellow-orange-red*) is successively semicircular. Type II may be called *conjunct semicircular closed-gamut grading* or *conjunct closed-gamut grading with open ends;* type III, *conjunct circular closed-gamut grading* or *conjunct closed-gamut grading with meeting ends.*

2) Implicit: *a, b, c, . . ., g are far (good) in varying degree; h, i, j, . . ., n are near (bad) in varying degree.* In first transition zone [　] we have psychological blends of type *not near (bad), not really near (bad),* in second transition zone [　], psychological blends of type *not far (good), not really far (good).*

TYPE IV. DISJUNCT CLOSED-GAMUT GRADING: a, b, c, . . ., g [e.g. neither blue nor yellow] o, p, q, . . . t.

1) Explicit: *a is less blue than b = b is bluer than a; . . .* [zone of indifference in which neither *blue* nor *yellow* strictly applies] *o is less yellow than p = p is yellower than o; . . . .* There is no psychological interest in zone of indifference, [　], which is only gradually spanned with increasing experience and demand for continuity. When zone of indifference [　] is recognized as h, i, j, . . ., n, it may: (a), take on distinctive character, e.g. *green,* in which case type IV becomes identical with II, for with establishment of continuity certain blues now become *greenish blues, bluish greens* are created, and certain yellows now become *greenish yellows;* or (b), be characterized negatively, in which case we cannot do better than say *h is neither blue nor yellow, neither h nor i is blue or yellow, but h is more nearly blue than i and i is more nearly yellow than h, j is more nearly blue than yellow (is bluer than it is yellow), k is more nearly yellow than blue (is yellower than it is blue).* In other words, for grading are substituted other techniques, which have grading implications, e.g. intermediate placement (*between blue and yellow*), goal-gauging (*nearly blue*), graded goal-gauging (*more nearly blue, nearer yellow than*), negation of alternatives (*neither blue nor yellow*), compromise (*blue-yellow²*).

---

² To be understood as theoretical tag for *green.*

2) Implicit: *a, b, c, . . ., g are shades of blue; o, p, q, . . ., t are shades of yellow.* For zone of indifference [ ] see (1).

TYPE V. OPEN-GAMUT GRADING (I) INTERPRETED IN TERMS OF DISJUNCT CLOSED-GAMUT GRADING (IV): "a, b, c, . . ., n" interpreted, by analogy of (IV), as "a, b, c, . . ., e [ ] j, k, l, . . ., n."

1) Explicit; *a is less hot, old, brilliant, good than b = b is hotter, (even) older, more brilliant, (even) better than a; . . .* [zone of indifference in which neither *hot* nor *cold*, neither *old* nor *young*, neither *brilliant* nor *stupid*, neither *good* nor *bad* strictly applies] *j is less cold, young, stupid, bad than b = b is colder, younger, more stupid, worse than a; . . .* When zone of indifference [ ] is gradually recognized as f, g, . . ., i, it may: (a), take on distinctive character, e.g. *temperate, middle-aged, of normal intelligence, of average quality,* such terms establishing filling-in norms rather than mores and lesses of primary fields (e.g. *more than middle-aged* rather than *more middle-aged, of more than normal intelligence* rather than *more normal,* which would generally be understood as an ellipsis for *more nearly normal),* in which case type V becomes identical with type I, f, g, . . ., i being intercalated between j, k, l, . . ., n and reversed field e, d, c, . . ., a; or (b), be characterized negatively, e.g. *f is neither hot nor cold, neither f nor g is old or young but f is more nearly old than g, h is more nearly stupid than brilliant.* In other words, for grading are substituted other techniques, which have grading implication, e.g. intermediate placement (*betwixt old and young*), goal-gauging (*nearly good*), graded goal-gauging (*nearer cold than hot* = implicitly graded *cool*), negation of alternatives (*neither good nor bad*), compromise (*good or bad, depending on one's standard*).

2) Implicit: *a, b, c, . . ., e are hot, old, brilliant, good in varying degree; j, k, l, . . ., n are cold, young, stupid, bad in varying degree.* For zone indifference [ ] see (1).

Note on B (Psychological Grading).—It must be carefully borne in mind that these five psychological types of grading, which naturally do not preclude the possibility of still other, and more complex, grading configurations, are by no means mutually exclusive types. The same objective elements of experience, e.g. *good:bad,* may be graded according to more than one type. Thus, when we say "A is *better than* B," though A and B are both bad, we are obviously treating *better* as an incremental grader in an open series in which the movement is assumed to be toward the relatively good and away from the relatively bad. "A is *better than* B" therefore illustrates type I, open-gamut grading, which is the prototype of all logical grading. On the other hand, when we say "A is *worse than* B, which in turn is *fairly good,*" we do not mean to imply that A too is perhaps not too far from good, rather that A belongs distinctly to the lower end of the gamut, that *good* and *bad* are psychologically distinct qualities (not, like logically graded terms of type I, merely a more and a less of a single quality), but that these distinct qualities are psychologically contiguous and capable of being fitted into a single series with two crests or maxima. All of this means that in this case we are fitting the concepts of *good* and *bad* into a conjunct closed-gamut grading scheme, and since the natural, or rather logical, type to which *good:bad* belongs is type I, we speak of a transfer on the analogy of type II and create a blend type III. Finally, when we say "A is *better than* B but both are *good*, C is of quite a different order and is actually *bad*, while D, being *neither good nor bad*, is of no interest," we are thinking in terms of a type of grading in which psychologically distinct qualities are connected, by intercalation, into an open series of the disjunct closed-gamut grading type, namely type V.

Type I recognizes no crest, only a norm at best, which, in the logical form of the grading (A), sinks to an objective or statistical norm—in other words, an average. Type III recognizes two crests and two areas of blend, but no norm except at the points where psychology, via neutral judgments, fades away into logic. Type V recognizes two extreme and opposed crests and a trough of normality between them. Types I, II, and IV (*near:far, green:yellow, blue:yellow*) are given us directly through our sensations or perceptions. Type III is probably the most natural type for psychologically subjective, as contrasted with objective, judgments; even such simple contrasts as *near:far* and *good:bad* probably present themselves, first of all, as contiguous areas of contrasting quality, not as points above or below a norm with which they intergrade in an open series. After considerable experience with socially determined acceptances and rejections, familiarities and strangenesses, contrasting qualities are felt as of a relatively absolute nature, so to speak, and *good* and *bad*, for instance, even *far* and *near*, have as true a psychological specificity as *green* and *yellow*. Hence the logical norm between them is not felt as a true norm but rather as a blend area in which qualities grading in opposite directions meet. To the naive, every person is either good or bad; if he cannot be easily placed, he is rather part good and part bad than just humanly normal or neither good nor bad. Type V represents the most sophisticated type of judgment, for it combines psychological contrast with the objective continuum of more and less and recognizes the norm as a true area of primary grading, not as a secondary area produced by blending.

We can easily see now that the confused psychological state of our grading judgments and terminology, also the unsatisfactory nature of our logical grading terminology, is due to a number of factors, the chief of which are: 1, the tendency to conceive of certain points in an evenly graded series as primarily distinct and opposed to each other instead of directly capable of connection by grading in terms of more and less (this tendency is, of course, carried over even into the realm of abstract quantity, and even a mathematically trained person may find it some-what paradoxical to call 7 "many" and 100 "few," though the 7 belong to a context in which 9, say, is the maximum, and 100 to another context in which 500 is the norm); 2, the contrary direction of grading in two such contrasted qualities, the "more" of one being logically, but not quite psychologically, equivalent to the "less" of the other (e.g., logically *better = less bad, worse = less good*, but psychologically this is not quite true; contrast *nearer = less far, farther = less near*, where logic and psychology more nearly correspond); 3, a preference for the upper or favored quality, in its relative sense, as grader (e.g. *better* and *heavier* more easily serve as incremental upward graders, *of more quality* and *of more weight*, than do *worse* and *lighter* as incremental downward graders; this hangs together with 5); 4, the conflict with psychological grading brought in by a more sophisticated attempt to establish an absolute continuity of grading in a logical sense (problems of interpretation of how, of two contrasted terms, a and b, "more a" is related to "less b," and of whether the neutral area between a and b is to be understood as a "both and" area, a "neither nor" area, or logically as a tie between a and b, which thereupon lose their distinctiveness and one of which, in consequence, must change its direction of grading so that a complete open-gamut grading may be established); 5, the different psychological value of a given grade according to whether it is reached positively, e.g., *fairly good* from *poor*, or negatively, e.g., *fairly good* from *very good* (the latter "fairly good" is almost necessarily an "only fairly good," i.e. a "fairly good" with emotional coloring of "poor").

C. Linguistic Grading

(elaboration of terms)

TYPE I. EXPLICIT

1) Abstract: *more than, less than.* These terms are general upward and downward terms and carry no implication as to class of graded terms or as to presence or absence of norms or crests. Certain other terms, of originally specialized and normated application, such as *greater, larger,* and *smaller,* have taken on abstract significance (e.g. *a greater amount of = more . . . than, a larger number of = more . . . than, a smaller number of = less, fewer*). More and *less* apply to both count and measure. *Fewer,* as equivalent of *less,* applies to counted terms only, e.g. *fewer people = less people,* but is secondary as explicit grader, being based on *few,* which is implicitly graded. There is no special count term in English corresponding to *more. More* and *less* are old comparatives in form, but are not really referable to *much* and *little.*

2) Specialized. There are no explicit specialized graders in English which

are not based, generally by use of *more* and *less* or suffixing of comparative *-er*, on linguistically primary graded terms which imply above or below a logical norm. Thus, *heavier*, based on *heavy* (= *of more than average weight*), means *heavy to a greater extent* (*than another heavy object*) to begin with, and only secondarily takes on, in its specialized sphere of weight, the purely relative grading quality of *more*; similarly with *less heavy* as parallel to *less*. Such terms as *of more weight* or *more weighted, of less linear extent, of more temperature, less in volume* are not in ordinary use and have to be replaced by comparatives of such terms as *heavy, short, warm, small*, which are not neutral in reference as to graded area.

TYPE II. IMPLICIT

1) Abstract: *much* and *little* for measured terms; *many* and *few* for counted terms. Note that implicitly graded terms can themselves be taken as new points of departure for grading, e.g. *less than many, more than a few, many* and *a few* being respectively arrived at by grading upward and downward from a certain norm. "How *much?*" and "How *many?*" show how helpless language tends to be in devising neutral implicitly graded abstract terms; linguistically upper-graded terms for logically neutral ones are also used in such terms as *so and so many, as much as*.

2) Specialized. A great variety of terms, most of which appear as pairs of opposites. We may distinguish:

a) *One-term sets* (graded as *more* and *less*; there is no true contrary): *capacious, silvery, distant* (in its strictly scientific sense of *at such and such a distance, near* and *far* being "psychologized" forms of it). Such terms are either of notions of a relatively ungradable type or are of scientific rather than popular application. Such terms as "how *far?*," "how *long?*," "2 mm. *wide*," "how *warm?*," "*as heavy as* one tenth of a gram," "*old enough* to know better" again show how helpless language tends to be in devising specialized single terms which are logically neutral as to grading.

b) *Two-term sets*. Two types are both common: 1, *linguistically unrelated terms* indicating opposites, e.g. *good:bad, far:near, high:low, long:short, full: empty, heavy:light, friend:enemy, hard:soft, old:young*; 2, *linguistically related terms* which are implicitly affirmative and explicitly contrary (formally negative) terms, e.g. *friendly:unfriendly* (also type (b) 1, *friendly:hostile, inimical*), *usual:unusual, normal:abnormal, frequent:infrequent, discreet:indiscreet*. These formally negative terms frequently take on as distinctive a meaning as type (a) contraries and can be as freely graded, "upward" and "downward," e.g. *more* and *less infrequent* are as good usage as *rarer* and *less rare*.

Note on (*b*), *Two-term sets*. As regards grading relations, two-term sets (contrary terms) tend to fall into three types:

I. SYMMETRICALLY REVERSIBLE, e.g.

far, farther	*near, nearer*
not near, less near	*not far, less far*

II. PARTLY REVERSIBLE, e.g.

good, better	*bad, worse*
not bad, less bad	*not good, less good*

III. Irreversible, e.g.

brilliant, more brilliant	*stupid, more stupid*
not stupid, less stupid	*not brilliant, less brilliant*

Note that implicitly graded specialized terms can themselves be taken as new points of departure for grading, e.g., *more than good, less than bad = better than bad.*

c) *Three-term sets.* These are not as common as type (b) (two-term sets) in ordinary usage but are constantly required for accurate grading. Generally one takes opposite terms of type (b) and constructs a middle term by qualifying the upper-graded one, e.g. *bad, averagely* (or *moderately* or *normally*) *good, good.* Sometimes a middle term comes in by way of transfer from another field, e.g. *bad, fair, good.* Specific middle terms, however, tend to gravitate toward one or the other of the two opposites, e.g. *fair,* on the whole, leans more to good than bad. If we further insert *poor,* again transferred from another field, we get type (d), four-term sets: *bad, poor, fair, good.* (The reason why *poor,* when transferred to the *bad:good* scale, does not quite fall in with *bad* is that *poor:rich* has not quite as great a scale amplitude as *bad:good* (zero to maximum) but is felt as corresponding rather to a scale of little to maximum. *Zero, lower average, higher average, much* is the implicit measure of *having nothing* (= *destitute, penniless*), *having little* (= *poor*), *having a moderate amount* (= *fairly well off*), *having much* (= *rich*). Hence *poor* stresses *something, though little* and cannot entirely parallel *bad,* which includes its logical extreme. On the whole, three-term sets do not easily maintain themselves because psychology, with its tendency to simple contrast, contradicts exact knowledge, with its insistence on the norm, the "neither nor." True three-term sets are probably confined to such colorless concepts as: *inferior, average, superior,* in which the middle term cannot well be graded.

d) *Four-term sets: cold, cool, warm, hot.* These are formed from type (b) by grading each of the opposites into a psychologically lower and higher. The new terms become psychological opposites (or sub-opposites) of a smaller scale. It is important to note that the two middle terms do not correspond to the middle term of type (c) (three-term sets), i.e. *warm* is psychologically no nearer to *cool* than *superior* is to *inferior.* In other words, *cold-cool* contrasts with *warm-hot* precisely as does *very bad-bad* with *good-very good.* The problem of connecting *cool* and *warm* has to be solved, psychologically, by blend-grading (*coolish; warmish, lukewarm*) or, more objectively, by norming (*of ordinary, normal, temperature*). As usual, the normed term is quasi-scientific rather than popular in character.

More complex linguistic sets are of course possible. We may summarize these analyses of the grading process by saying that logical grading is of the open-gamut type and may be with or without reference to an objective norm or statistical average, while psychological grading and linguistic grading tend strongly to emphasize closed-gamut grading, whether of the conjunct or disjunct type, and have difficulty in combining the notions of grading and norming into that of a normed field within which grading applies. Furthermore, it is worth noting that the difference between explicit and implicit grading is of little importance logically, of considerable importance psychologically (with constant conflict of the relative and fixed points of view), and of paramount importance linguistically.

IMPLICATIONS OF MOVEMENT IN GRADING

The main operational concepts that we have used in developing our notions of grading up to this point have been: the successive envelopment of values by later ones (giving us a set of "lesses" in an open series); the establishment of a norm somewhere in such an open series; the placement of values "above" and "below" this norm; the contrasting of specific gradable values which belong to the same class; the establishment of continuity between such contrasting values by means of intercalation; and certain implicit directional notions (upward,[3] e.g. *good:better, bad:less bad;* downward,[3] e.g. *good:less good, bad:worse;* contrary, e.g. *good-better:bad-worse*).

The directional ideas so far employed have merely implied a consistent increase or decrease in value of the terms which are seriated and graded. Thus, of a set of terms "a, b, c, . . ., n," in which a is less than any of the terms "b, c, . . ., n," and b is less than any of the terms "c, . . ., n," and c is less than any of the terms ". . . n," and no term is more than n, we have established an upward grading direction, consistently from less to more, but the terms themselves are not necessarily thought of as having been arrived at either by moving up from a or down from, say, c. Logically, as mathematically, *b increased from a = b decreased from c.* Psychologically, however, and therefore also linguistically, the explicit or implicit trend is frequently in a specific direction. It is this tendency to slip kinaesthetic implications into speech, with the complicating effects of favorable affect linked with an upward trend and of unfavorable affect linked with a downward trend, that so often renders a purely logical analysis of speech insufficient or even misleading.

We can easily test the kinaesthetic aspect of grading by observing the latent direction and associated feeling tone of an implicitly graded term like "few." If some one asks me "How many books have you?" I may answer "A few," which is, on the whole, a static term which, though indefinite, takes the place of any fixed quantity, say 25, deemed small in this particular context. But if I answer "I have few books," the questioner is likely to feel that I have said more than is necessary,

---

[3] "Upward" and "downward" are used in the sense of "in the direction of increase" and "in the direction of decrease" respectively. This purely notional kinaesthesis may be, and probably generally is, strengthened by a concomitant spatial kinaesthesis.

for I have not only fixed the quantity, namely "a few," but implicitly added the comment that I might be expected to have a larger number. In other words, "few" suggests grading downward from something more, while "a few" is essentially noncommittal on the score of direction of grading. The difference here in implicit grading is not one of magnitude, but of direction only. The psychological relation between "a few" and "few" is very similar to the psychological relation between "nearly" and "hardly," which belong to the conceptual sphere of gauging.

Can "a few" be given an upward trend? Not as simply and directly as the change to "few" gives a downward trend, but there are many contexts in which the upward trend is unmistakable. If I am told "You haven't any books, have you?" and answer "Oh yes, I have a few," there is likely to be a tonal peculiarity in the reply (upward melody of end of "few") which suggests upward grading from zero. Language, in other words, here ekes out the notional and psychological need for an upward-tending quantitative term as best it can. If I use "quite," which has normally an upward-tending feeling tone, and say "Quite a few," the kinaesthetic momentum carries me beyond the static "a few," so that "quite a few" is well on toward "a considerable number."

The kinaesthetic feeling of certain graded terms can easily be tested by trying to use them with terms whose kinaesthetic latency is of a different nature and noting the baffled effect they produce due to implied contradictions of movement. Thus, we can say "barely a few" or "hardly a few" because "a few" is conceived of as a fixed point in the neighborhood of which one can take up a position or toward which one can move, positively or negatively. But "nearly few" is baffling, and even amusing, for there is no fixed "few" to be near to. "Hardly few" is psychologically improper too, for "hardly" suggests a falling short, and inasmuch as "few" is downwardly oriented, it is hard to see how one can fall short of it. "Hardly few" has the same fantastic improbability as the concept of A moving on to a supposedly fixed point B, which it "hardly" expected to reach, and finding that B was actually moving toward A's starting point, and eventually reaching it, without ever passing A. Again, "all but" requires a psychologically fixed term to complete it, e.g. "all but half," "all but a few." "All but few" suggests a remainder which is not even a remainder. Again, "all but quite a few," even if "quite a few" is no more factually than a small proportion of the whole, is psychologically difficult because "quite a few" is no more static than "few." The "all but" form is implicitly static, hence "all but few" and "all but quite a few" ring false, involving, as they do, down-tending and up-tending elements respectively.

THE CONCEPT OF EQUALITY

We are now in a position to arrive at a simple psychological conception of "equal to." "Equal to" may be defined as the quantitative application of the qualitative "same as," ' more than" and "less than" being the two possible kinds of quantitative "different from." But it seems more satisfactory, on the whole, to define "equal to" in a more negative spirit, as a more or less temporary point of passage or equilibrium between "more than" and "less than" or as a point of arrival in a scale in which the term which is to be graded is constantly increasing or diminishing. In other words, if we take q as defined to begin with, we can give meaning to $a = q$ by saying that: (1) a is less than q to begin with, gradually increases while still less than q, and is later found to be more than q, having passed through some point at which it was neither less than nor more than q; or (2) a is more than q to begin with, gradually decreases while still more than q, and is later found to be less than q, having passed through some point at which it was neither more than nor less than q: or (3) a is less than q to begin with, gradually increases while still less than q, and finally rests at some point at which it is neither less than nor more than q; or (4) a is more than q to begin with, gradually decreases while still more than q, and finally rests at some point at which it is neither more than nor less than q. These four types of equality may be classified as:

I. Explicitly dynamic $\begin{cases} \text{(1) While increasing toward and away from} \\ \text{(2) While decreasing toward and away from} \end{cases}$

II. Implicitly dynamic $\begin{cases} \text{(1) Having increased toward} \\ \text{(2) Having decreased toward} \end{cases}$

A fifth type of equality, that of kinaesthetic indifference, is the limiting or neutral type which alone is recognized in logic:

III. Non-dynamic: Statically "equal to."

So far are these psychological distinctions from being useless that, as a matter of fact, a little self-observation will soon convince one that it is hardly possible to conceive of equality except as a medium state or equilibrated state in an imagined back and forth of "more than" and "less than." It is safe to say that if we had no experience of lesses increasing and of mores decreasing, one could have no tangible conception of how obviously distinct existents, occurrents, and modes could be said to be "equal to each other" in a given respect.

The Classification of Types of Grading Judgment

The classification of "equals" applies, of course, equally well to "mores" and "lesses," so that we have, psychologically speaking, 15 fundamental judgments of grading to deal with, of which the 3 logical ones ("more than," "equal to," and "less than") are the kinaesthetically neutral judgments. The best way to understand this enlarged grading scheme is to express it symbolically. Let $a \rightarrow q$ be understood to mean "a is less than q and is increasing toward it," $a \leftarrow q$ to mean "a is less than q and is decreasing away from it," $q \rightarrow a$ to mean "a is more than q and is increasing away from it," $q \leftarrow a$ to mean "a is more than q and is decreasing toward it." In other words, "to the left of" means "less than," "to the right of" means "more than," while an arrow pointing to the right means "increasing," an arrow pointing to the left means "decreasing." An arrow pointing downward will mean "having increased," an arrow pointing upward will mean "having decreased," and an arrow superimposed will mean "equal to, with implication of actual or prior movement." We then have the following symbolically expressed notional scheme of grading judgments which can be made of two entities of the same class, a and q, of which q is supposed to be known and fixed. In the symbolism a will be understood as the subject of the implied proposition.

Types of Grading Judgment

I. Explicit dynamic	*Increasing* 1. $\rightarrow$ q *Decreasing* 2. $\leftarrow$ q	6. $\vec{q}$ 7. $\overleftarrow{q}$	11. q $\rightarrow$ 12. q $\leftarrow$
II. Implicit dynamic	*Increased* 3. $\downarrow$ q *Decreased* 4. $\uparrow$ q	8. $\overset{\downarrow}{q}$ 9. $\overset{\uparrow}{q}$	13. q $\downarrow$ 14. q $\uparrow$
III. Nondynamic	5. $\begin{cases} a<q \\ q>a \end{cases}$	10. $\begin{cases} a = q \\ q = a \end{cases}$	15. $\begin{cases} a>q \\ q<a \end{cases}$

These symbols may be read as follows:

1. "is being less than q, though increasing" (= "still falls short of")

2. "is being less than q, and decreasing" (= "falls shorter and shorter of")

3. "is less than q, though increased from still less" (= "is still short of")

4. "is less than q, and decreased from more" (= "is even short of")

5. "a is less than q" (= "is short of") = "q is more than a"

6. "is equalling q, on its way from less to more"

7. "is equalling q, on its way from more to less"

8. "is equal to q, having increased to it"

9. "is equal to q, having decreased to it"

10. "is equal to q"

11. "is being more than q, and increasing" (= "exceeds more and more")

12. "is being more than q, though decreasing" (= "still exceeds")

13. "is more than q, and increased from less" (= "is even in excess of")

14. "is more than q, though decreased from more" (= "is still in excess of")

15. "a is more than q" (= "is in excess of") = "q is less than a."

The symbols for nos. 5, 10, and 15 are of course the ordinary mathematical ones, $a < q$ and $q > a$ being considered equivalent notations. The sign of equality, $=$, may, if one likes, be looked upon as the neutralized forms of nos. 6 and 7: $\leftrightarrows$.

In order to give more reality to these theoretically distinct types of grading, it may be of some service to give simple examples of them. For this purpose we shall take *5 (miles, pounds, hours)* as illustrative of q, thus applying our notions of grading to the sphere of quantity,

1. "He has run *less than five miles*" : $\rightarrow 5$ (answer to question: "How far has he run by now?")

2. "He has *less than five hours* to finish his job" : $\leftarrow 5$ (answer to question: "How much time can he count on to finish his job?")

3. "He ran until he came to a point that was *less than five miles* from his starting point": $\downarrow 5$ (answer to question: "How far had he got when he stopped running?")

4. "He got weaker and weaker until he could lift *less than five pounds*" : $\uparrow 5$ (answer to question: "How much could he still lift when he had to give up?")

5. "Jersey City is *less than five miles* from New York": $a < 5$ (answer to question: "How far [a, i.e., required distance] is Jersey City from New York?")

6. "He has run *(as much as) five miles*": $\overrightarrow{5}$ (answer to question: "How far has he run by now?")

7. "He has *(just, still) five hours* to finish his job: $\overleftarrow{5}$ (answer to question: "How much time can he count on to finish his job?")

8. "He ran until he came to a point that was *(just, as much as, al-*

ready)[4] *five miles* from his starting point": 5 ↓ (answer to question "How far had he got when he stopped running?")

9. "He got weaker and weaker until he could lift (*just, only, no more than*) *five pounds*": 5 ↑ (answer to question: "How much could he still lift when he had to give up?")

10. "A is (*just*) *five miles* from B": a = 5 (answer to question: "How far [a] is A from B?")

11. "He has run *more than five miles*": 5 → (answer to question: "How far has he run by now?")

12. "He (*still*) has *more than five hours* to finish his job": 5 ← (answer to question: "How much time can he count on to finish his job?")

13. "He ran until he came to a point that was (*even*) *more than five miles* from his starting point": 5 ↓ (answer to question: "How far had he got when he stopped running?")

14. "He got weaker and weaker until he could lift *hardly more than five pounds*": 5 ↑ (answer to question: "How much could he still lift when he had to give up?")

15. "Philadelphia is *more than five miles* from New York": 5 < a (answer to question: "How far [a] is Philadelphia from New York?")

AFFECT IN GRADING

It will be observed that such terms as *as much as, just, still, already, only, no more than, even, hardly,* and others not illustrated in our examples help along, as best they can, to bring out the latest kinaesthetic element in the logical concepts "less than," "equal to," and "more than" when these are applied to experience, but at best they are only a weak prop. Most languages suffer from the inability to express the explicitly dynamic, implicitly dynamic, and non-dynamic aspects of grading in an unambiguous manner, though the notional framework of fifteen grading judgments that we have developed is intuited by all normal individuals. Such English terms as we have suggested are really unacceptable for two reasons: 1, they are transfers from other types of judgment than dynamic and non-dynamic grading (e.g., "only" is properly an exclusive limiter; "hardly" and "just" are goal-gauging limiters; "still" has time implication, at least in origin); and 2, they unavoidably color the judgment with their latent affect of approval or disapproval (e.g., "as much as" smuggles in a note of satisfaction; "only" and "hardly" tend to voice disappointment).

[4] More idiomatic in German: *schon.*

Even the simple graders "more than" and "less than" tend to have a definite affective quality in given contexts. Thus, if a quantitative goal is to be reached by increase, say "ten pages of reading," *more than* necessarily has an approving ring (e.g., "I have *already* read *more than three pages*," though it may actually be less than four), *less than* a disapproving ring (e.g., "I have *only* read *less than eight pages*," though it may actually be more than seven). On the other hand, if the quantitative goal is to be reached by decrease, say "no more reading to do," *more than* has a disapproving ring (e.g., "I have *still more than three pages* to do," though actually less than four remain to be done), *less than* an approving ring (e.g., "I have *less than eight pages* to do," though more than seven pages remain to be done out of a total of ten). In other words, grading and affect are intertwined, or, to put it differently, *more than* and *less than* tend to have both an objective grading value and a subjective grading value dependent on a desired or undesired increase or decrease. This means that linguistic awkwardnesses arise when it is desired to combine an objective *more than* with a subjectively desired decrease or an objective *less than* with a subjectively desired increase. Thus, if the *more than three days* in "I have *more than three days* to wait" is to convey the approving connotation of "only four or five days," we cannot say "I have *only more than three days* to wait" (as contrasted with a possible *more than ten days*) but must recapture the note of approval by minimizing the implied excess, hence "I have *only a little more than three days* to wait." An approved *more than* (slight quantity) in a desiredly decreasing scale, though logically defensible, goes against the psychological grain of language. Again, it is hard to say "I have *only more than fifty dollars* in the bank," for *fifty dollars* plus *a slight amount* (by implication) is on an upgoing trend, as it were. We have to grade down from *fifty-one dollars*, say, and say "I have *less than fifty-one dollars* in the bank." To put it differently, if $50.99 is disapproved of, it must be graded downward as *less than fifty-one dollars;* if $50.01 is approved of, it can be graded upward as *more than fifty dollars*. The difficult word *hardly* frequently reorients the normally implied affect, hence "I have *hardly more than three days* to wait" (approval), "I have *hardly more than fifty dollars* in the bank" (disapproval).

If we had a subjective grading symbolism that was independent of objective grading, it would be possible to convey very compactly every possible type of grading judgment—static, implicitly dynamic, and explicitly dynamic grades independently combined with neutral, approving, not disapproving, disapproving, and not approving affect.

How complex, in actual speech, our grading judgments, or rather intuitions, really are from a psychological standpoint, however simple they may seem to be from a purely logical or merely linguistic standpoint, may be exemplified by considering the meanings of such apparently simple statements as "I have *three pages* to read," "I have *more than three pages* to read" and "I have *less than three pages* to read." In the first place, it makes a difference if "three pages" (or "reading matter equal to three pages") is conceived non-dynamically or dynamically, e.g. "three pages as an assigned task" (grade 10: non-dynamic "equal to") or "more than three pages in a rapidly accumulating series of MS pages submitted for approval" (grade 11: explicit dynamic increasing "more than") or "more than three pages still to do in the passage from a total of ten pages to do to the goal of no pages left to do" (grade 12: explicit dynamic decreasing "more than") or "less than three pages yet accumulated in a long MS report which one desires to read" (grade 3: implicit dynamic increased "less than"). Ordinarily the affective valuation involved in such statements does not clearly rise in consciousness because "more than" and "less than" pool the energies, as it were, of the grading process itself and the approval or disapproval of increase (growing exhilaration, growing fatigue) or decrease (growing relief, growing disappointment). We cannot possibly go into all the involvements of this very difficult field of inquiry, but a general idea of its nature may be had by considering one case, say the explicit dynamic decreasing forms of "less than" (grade 2), "equal to" (grade 7) and "more than" (grade 12).

Our type statements will be "less than three pages [to read]," "[still as much as] three pages (to read)," and "more than three pages [to read]." These will be symbolized, in the first instance, by ← 3, $\overleftarrow{3}$, and 3 ← respectively. If, in the statement "I have less than three pages to read," the reading is conceived of as a task which is to be accomplished, say a certain amount of Latin to be prepared for translation, the statement will be normally interpreted as implying approval of decrease (growing relief), the implication being that of "only." Had we wished to imply disapproval of increase (growing fatigue), we should normally have put it not at "less than three pages" but at "more than two pages," with an implication of "still." We could combine the form of approving "less than" statement with that of disapproving "still" and say "I have less than three pages to read, *to be sure, but* there is *still* some of my assignment to read." In other words, when the goal, zero, is approved, any form of statement implying decrease toward that goal involves approval, and the factual disapproval of having still so much left to do has normally to be rendered by terms implying reversal of judgment, such as *to be sure, but, still*. Our linguistic awkwardness in expressing disapproval of a state which is kinaesthetically committed, as it were, to approval, is on a par with, though less obviously helpless than, such periphrases for the potential mode as "He will come, he will not come," a naive substitute for "Perhaps he will come" or "He may come." Let us, for the sake of brevity, reduce the complete circle of valuation in judgment to the two simple forms of approval and disapproval, symbolized respectively by $'$ and $\grave{}$. Then $\underleftarrow{'}3$ symbolizes an explicit dynamic decreasing "less than 3" which is approved of, the "less than 3" of growing relief inadequately rendered in English by "less than 3" or the rather unidiomatic "already less than 3" or the round-about "only 3, in fact less." And

$$\underleftarrow{'}3$$

symbolizes an explicit dynamic decreasing "less than 3" which is dis⁻ approved of, the "less than 3" of growing fatigue, which cannot easily be rendered in English except by such periphrases as "still some, though less than 3."

Further consideration of the implied "only" and "still" of these statements shows that they may indicate exactly the opposite affects if we assume that the goal of decrease is not desired but resisted. Thus, if my desire is to read all I can get, an approving $\underleftarrow{'}3$ cannot imply that I am relieved to find that what I still have left to read is even less than three pages, but that I am glad to know that while there are less than three pages left, at least there is *still* left more than nothing. This, then, is an approving "still." Correlatively, the disapproving "only" of $\underleftarrow{'}3$ implies that neither the quantity on hand nor its proximate extinguishment is approved of. In other words, two distinct affective judgments are involved, that of the grade itself and that of the goal of its implied tendency. How can we distinguish the $\underleftarrow{'}3$ of growing fatigue from the $\underleftarrow{'}3$ of growing disappointment? Obviously we must have some way of indicating the affect attaching to the factual goal, which gives the whole grading process its significance. We shall therefore use a symbol for limit of tendency, $\overset{|}{q}$, in which q stands for any quantity, and express the four affective types of explicit dynamic decreasing "less than" as follows:

1. $\overset{'}{\underset{|}{\textposition}}\;\underleftarrow{'}3$ (both decreasing quantity and zero-limit are approved: "I have *only* [a little] less than 3 pages [still] to read"

2. $\overset{'}{\underset{|}{\textposition}}\;\underleftarrow{'}3$ (quantity disapproved, zero-limit approved: "I have *still* to read [only a little] less than 3 pages," "I have *hardly* less than 3 pages [still] to read"

3. $\overset{\prime}{\underset{|}{|}}$ $\underset{\leftarrow}{\prime}3$ (quantity approved, zero-limit disapproved: "I *still* have for reading [but a little] less than 3 pages")

4. $\overset{\prime}{\underset{|}{|}}$ $\underset{\leftarrow}{\prime}3$ (both decreasing quantity and zero-limit are disapproved: "I have *merely* less than 3 pages left for reading")

The four affective types of explicit dynamic decreasing "more than" are as follows:

1. $\overset{\prime}{\underset{|}{|}}$ $3\overset{\prime}{\underset{\leftarrow}{\smile}}$ ("I have *only* [a little] more than 3 pages [still] to read," "I have *hardly* more than 3 pages [still] to read"

2. $\overset{\prime}{\underset{|}{|}}$ $3\overset{\prime}{\underset{\leftarrow}{}}$ ("I have *still* to read more than 3 pages")

3. $\overset{\prime}{\underset{|}{|}}$ $3\overset{\prime}{\underset{\leftarrow}{\smile}}$ ("I *still* have for reading more than 3 pages")

4. $\overset{\prime}{\underset{|}{|}}$ $3\overset{}{\underset{\leftarrow}{\smile}}$ ("I have *merely* [a little] more than 3 pages left for reading," "I have *hardly* more than 3 pages left for reading")

And the four affective types of explicit dynamic decreasing "equal to" or "as much as" are as follows:

1. $\overset{\prime}{\underset{\circ}{|}}$ $\underset{3}{\overset{\prime}{\leftarrow}}$ ("I have *only* [no more than] 3 pages [still] to read")

2. $\overset{\prime}{\underset{\circ}{|}}$ $\underset{3}{\overset{\prime}{\leftarrow}}$ ("I have *still* to read [no less than, as much as] 3 pages")

3. $\overset{\prime}{\underset{\circ}{|}}$ $\underset{3}{\overset{\prime}{\leftarrow}}$ ("I *still* have [no less than, as much as] 3 pages for reading")

4. $\overset{\prime}{\underset{|}{|}}$ $\underset{3}{\overset{\prime}{\leftarrow}}$ ("I have *merely* [as much as] 3 pages left for reading")

Needless to say, analogous distinctions are to be made for the other grading cases. Here, as in every other phase of linguistic inquiry, we find that the more closely we study actual linguistic forms, the more we are driven to realize that they never express merely static, affectively neutral, concepts and judgments, but classes of concepts and judgments in which nuclear notions, capable of logical definition, are colored by unavowed dynamic and affective determinants. These determinants must be laboriously ferreted out and set in their own configuration of possible scale or types, so that the nuclear notions themselves may stand out with logical rigor. Certain of these dynamic and affective determinants are primary or typical, because arising naturally in experience; others are complex, involving a blending of features in logically permissible but psychologically atypical form, as when a logically static concept is blended with a dynamic implication and two opposed affects. So far as the primary, maximally natural, blends of dynamic tendency and affect with logically static grading concepts are concerned, we have probably to reckon with the following five types:

1. "More than" of growing exhilaration: $q \overset{\prime}{\rightarrow} \underset{a}{|}$

2. "More than" of growing fatigue: $q \xrightarrow{\quad}_{a}$

3. "Less than" of growing relief: $\lceil\; \underset{a}{\angle}\; q$

4. "Less than" of growing disappointment: $\lceil\; \underset{a}{\angle}\; q$

5. "Equal to" of balanced satisfaction: $\begin{cases} a \xrightarrow{\;} q \\ q \leftarrow a \end{cases}$

The neutral, logical, "more than" is probably derived from nos. 1 and 2 by progressive elimination of upward tendency (stage 1: q → ; stage 2: q ↓ ; stage 3: q <) and affect; the neutral, logical, "less than" is probably derived from nos. 3 and 4 by progressive elimination of downward tendency (stage 1: ← q; stage 2: ↑ q; stage 3: < q) and affect; the neutral, logical, "equal to" is probably derived from no. 5 by elimination of balancing (stage 1: $\begin{cases} a \xrightarrow{\;} q \\ q \xleftarrow{\;} a \end{cases}$; stage 2: a $\overset{\frown}{=}$ q) and affect (stage 3: a = q). Once the kinaesthesis and affect are rooted out of the psychology of grading, the human spirit is free to create richer and more complex meanings by recombining the elements of grading, of direction, of movement, halt, and status, and of immediate and prospective affect, into novel configurations in which inhere conflicts that have been reconciled.

THE SUPERLATIVE

"More than," "less than," and "equal to" are the most general grading terms and concepts we have. Owing to our habit of thinking of such triplets as *good—better—best, bad—worse—worst, famous—more famous—most famous*, and *famous—less famous—least famous* as possessing a logical structure which is analogous to their linguistic form, we tend to consider the concepts expressed by *most* and *least* as of the same nature as *more than* and *less than*. A little reflection shows that this feeling is an illusion and that the linguistically suggested proportion *good:better = better:best* is logically incorrect. If a, b, and c are arranged in a series of relative qualities, a may be said to be "good," b "better than" a, and c "better than" b. But c is just as truly "better than" a as it is "better than" b, in fact more unreservedly or *a fortiori* so. We cannot say that c is "best" unless we know either (a), that a, b, and c are the only members of the series that are to be graded, in which case c is "best," not because it is better than b as well as better than a, but because there is no other member of the series which is better than it;

or (b), that the quality possessed by c is equal to that grade which is known not to be exceeded by any other possible member of the whole class of gradable members. In the former case c may soon cease to be "best" as other members (d, e, f, . . ., n) are added to the series, though it always remains "better than" certain other fixed members of it. In the latter case c remains "best" throughout. These two meanings of the superlative form are really quite distinct, though they are often confused linguistically. Type (a), e.g. *the most . . . of them, the least . . . of them, the farthest of them, the best of them, the nearest of them, the worst of them,* may be called the "conditioned superlative" or "relative superlative." The other type, (b), e.g. *the most . . . possible* (= *as . . . as possible*), *the least . . . possible, the farthest (possible), the best (possible), the nearest (possible), the worst (possible),* may be called the "unconditioned superlative" or "absolute superlative." Both represent unique grades, though in differently ordered contexts, at the upper or lower end of a series. If we characterize a class of individuals, say as "good," the criterion of membership, *good,* applies to all; *better* (or *less bad*) applies to all but one of the class, which is thought of as *least good* (or *worst*); *less good* (or *worse*) applies to all but one of the class, polar to the member excluded from the sub-class "better," which is thought of as *best* (or *least bad*); *best* (or *least bad*) applies to only one member, the extreme of the sub-class "better"; and *least good* (or *worst*) applies to only one member, the extreme of the sub-class "less good."

Whether the terms *worst* and *least bad* properly apply to any of the members of the class depends, of course, on whether *good* and *bad* are thought of as mutually exclusive classes separated by a normative line of division (logical grading: A, I, with reference to norm) or as relative terms applying to the "more" and "less" of a single class (logical grading: A, II, with reference to terms of comparison). Hence arise certain ambiguities in the use of *least*. *Least good* may either mean *the least good of good individuals,* i.e. the first grade toward "best" beyond the dividing line of neutrality, as when we say *"The least good,* if good at all, will do"; or, more naturally, *the least good of good and bad individuals,* i.e. *the worst,* as when we say *"The least good* is indistinguishable from the worst." Similarly with *least bad,* except that here it is the normative usage that seems the more natural. Correlative ambiguities, though less easily, may arise for *most.* Paradoxically enough, language so handles *least* and *most* that *least good* (*of good ones*) and *least bad* (*of bad ones*) are often next door to each other, though *least good* and *least bad* may in other contexts be polar extremes, while *best* and *worst* are typically polar extremes. The set *best* (*of bad ones*) and *worst* (*of good ones*) is not generally thought of as a natural neighborhood. It is only in "open-gamut grading" (psychological grading: B, 1) that *least* and *most* can be defined as identical concepts arrived at by opposite movement of grading (*farthest* = *least near, nearest* = *least far*). We may conveniently speak of "open-gamut superlatives" (of which there are only two possible in the unconditioned type, namely *most* and *least*, e.g. *best* and *worst*) and of "closed-gamut superlatives" (of which there are typically four in the unconditioned type, e.g. *best, least good, least bad, worst;* or any higher even number, depending on the nature of the grading).

It is interesting to note that the superlative form is often used to denote a high grade, but not necessarily an apical grade, of the graded quality. Thus, Latin *amatissimus* means not only "most beloved, the most beloved" but also "greatly beloved." Similarly, we say in English, "He had a *most pleasing* personality," i.e., not *"the most pleasing* personality" among some implied number of individuals but simply "a *very pleasing* personality." It is probable that this logically unreasonable, but psychologically somehow inevitable, usage is due to a transfer of conditioned superlatives (type a) to the grading gamut in which unconditioned superlatives (type b) occur as polar points. The following diagram illustrates the process for unnormed grading:

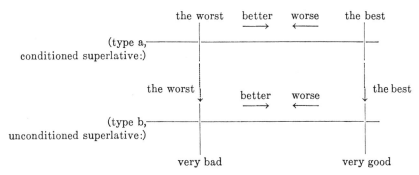

In other words, a conditioned superlative, true of some limited range of instances, becomes, when seen in the wider perspective of all possible instances, not a true superlative at all but an up-graded or down-graded comparative fixed at some point psychologically near the unconditioned extremes. This process at the same time involves a translation of explicit superlative grading into implicitly quantified grading, a more sophisticated type of grading judgment. Hence, to reverse the direction of transfer, it seems natural, because psychologically archaic, to see such judgments as "very bad" or "very good" as conditioned superlatives in an imaginary series in which all other graded terms fall below. It is as though one felt that what is merely "very good" in this context or the context of all values is actually "the best" in some other imagined context.

POLAR GRADING

At first sight it seems that the differences between explicit and implicit grading cannot be carried out for the superlative. But there are, as a matter of fact, quite a number of implicitly superlative terms which have, however, this linguistic and psychological peculiarity, that they are not felt as end points of a graded series but as points of polar normality. These outer points, though logically arrived at by the cumulative grading process that gives us "most" and "least," are not, psychologically speaking, worked up to *via* "more than" but can only be fallen short of *via* "less than." If, for instance, a series

a, b, c, . . ., k, l, m, n

is graded via increments of "more than" up to n, "the most," and we then accept this n as a new norm, we note: 1, that there can be no upgraded terms which are "more than" n; 2, that such terms as c, . . ., l, m, which could in the first instance be defined as progressively "more than" such lower terms as b, . . ., k, l, respectively, can now only be defined in an opposite sense as progressively "less than" the unique term n. We thus arrive at what amounts to a new type of grading, which we may term "polar grading."

A good example of a transfer from ordinary grading to polar grading is shown in the following normed scheme:

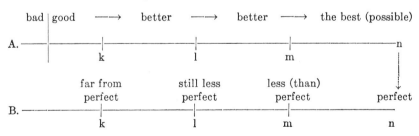

Observe that the "less perfect" of B is really as illogical as "more perfect" would be. It may be considered an ellipsis for the logical "less than perfect" or "less nearly perfect" based on a secondary extension of the range of meaning of the term "perfect." The superlative implication of "perfect," which should make of it a unique and ungradable term, tends to be lost sight of for the simple reason that it belongs to the class of essentially gradable terms (e.g. "good"). Such terms as "less perfect" are psychologically blends of unique terms of the type "perfect" and graded terms of the type "less good." The polar term is stretched a little, as it were, so as to take in at least the uppermost (or nethermost) segment of the gradable gamut of reality. Observe that at the worst the term which is farthest in significance from the unique value of the polar term under which it comes does not ordinarily relapse into the normal area of the term which implicitly underlies this polar term. Thus, "least perfect" is generally better than the merely normal "good," e.g. "the least perfect of these poems," which could hardly be said of a poem that did not belong to a set of poems which could be described, most of them, as "perfect." On the other hand, a complication arises when we fix the polar point not so much objectively as on the basis of a desired upper norm, as when we say "even the least perfect of God's creatures," which is a way of saying "even the worst of God's creatures, of whom we would all were perfect." As a result of such affective interferences, polar terms may be secondarily graded down (or up) to their polar contraries.

"Perfect" is perhaps the best example of a polar term. "Complete" and "full" are others of the implicitly up-graded type; "empty" and "barren," of the implicitly down-graded type. Implicit superlatives and polar grading offer many psychological subtleties, of which we have only touched the more obvious. Through the habit of using polar terms only to indicate some measure of falling short of their proper significance they may finally take on a less than polar function. Thus, "perfect" comes to mean to some people, and to all people in certain contexts, merely "very good." This paves the way for the secondary grading of polar terms in a positive direction, e.g. "more perfect" and "most perfect." Logically such terms might be interpreted to mean "more nearly perfect" and "most nearly perfect" (conditioned superlative with polar goal); actually, that is psychologically, they denote rather "better" and "best" in an upper tract of "good."

This paper was finished, in essentially its present form, many years ago as part of a larger study carried on, in collaboration with Professor W. Collinson, for the International Auxilary Language Association (IALA). My original purpose was to carry the analysis of grading considerably further but it seems best to offer this fragmentary contribution to semantics in the hope that others may be induced to explore the sadly neglected field of the congruities and non-congruities of logical and psychological meaning with linguistic form.

My thanks are due the IALA and Mrs. Alice V. Morris for permission to publish this paper here. I am also indebted to Mrs. Morris for her careful reading of the manuscript and for a number of critical observations from which I have profited greatly.

THE GRAMMARIAN AND HIS LANGUAGE*

THE NORMAL MAN of intelligence has something of a contempt for linguistic studies, convinced as he is that nothing can well be more useless. Such minor usefulness as he concedes to them is of a purely instrumental nature. French is worth studying because there are French books which are worth reading. Greek is worth studying—if it is— because a few plays and a few passages of verse, written in that curious and extinct vernacular, have still the power to disturb our hearts—if indeed they have. For the rest, there are excellent translations.

Now it is a notorious fact that the linguist is not necessarily deeply interested in the abiding things that language has done for us. He handles languages very much as the zoölogist handles dogs. The zoölogist examines the dog carefully, then he dissects him in order to examine him still more carefully, and finally, noting resemblances between him and his cousins, the wolf and the fox, and differences between him and his more distant relations like the cat and the bear, he assigns him his place in the evolutionary scheme of animated nature, and has done. Only as a polite visitor, not as a zoölogist, is he even mildly interested in Towzer's sweet parlor tricks, however fully he may recognize the fact that these tricks could never have evolved unless the dog had evolved first. To return to the philologist and the layman by whom he is judged, it is a precisely parallel indifference to the beauty wrought by the instrument which nettles the judge. And yet the cases are not altogether parallel. When Towzer has performed his tricks and when Porto has saved the drowning man's life, they relapse, it is true, into the status of mere dog—but even the zoölogist's dog is of interest to all of us. But when Achilles has bewailed the death of his beloved Patroclus and Clytaemnestra has done her worst, what are we to do with the Greek aorists that are left on our hands? There is a traditional mode of procedure which arranges them into patterns. It is called grammar. The man who is in charge of grammar and is called a grammarian is regarded by all plain men as a frigid and dehumanized pedant.

It is not difficult to understand the very pallid status of linguistics in America. The purely instrumental usefulness of language study is recognized, of course, but there is not and cannot be in this country that daily concern with foreign modes of expression so natural on the continent of Europe, where a number of languages jostle each other in

* American Mercury, 1 (1924): 149–155.

everyday life. In the absence of a strong practical motive for linguistic pursuits the remoter, more theoretical, motives are hardly given the opportunity to flower. But it would be a profound mistake to ascribe our current indifference to philological matters entirely to the fact that English alone does well enough for all practical purposes. There is something about language itself, or rather about linguistic differences, that offends the American spirit. That spirit is rationalistic to the very marrow of its bone. Consciously, if not unconsciously, we are inclined to impatience with any object or idea or system of things which cannot give a four-square reckoning of itself in terms of reason and purpose. We can see this spirit pervading our whole scientific outlook. If psychology and sociology are popular sciences in America today, that is mainly due to the prevailing feeling that they are convertible into the cash value of effective education, effective advertising, and social betterment. Even here, there is, to an American, something immoral about a psychological truth which will not do pedagogical duty, something wasteful about a sociological item which can be neither applied nor condemned. If we apply the rationalistic test to language, it is found singularly wanting. After all, language is merely a level to get thoughts "across." Our business instinct tells us that the multiplication of levers, all busy on the same job, is poor economy. Thus one way of "spitting it out" is as good as another. If other nationalities find themselves using other levers, that is their affair. The fact of language, in other words, is an unavoidable irrelevance, not a problem to intrigue the inquiring mind.

There are two ways, it seems, to give linguistics its requisite dignity as a science. It may be treated as history or it may be studied descriptively and comparatively as form. Neither point of view augurs well for the arousing of American interest. History has always to be something else before it is taken seriously. Otherwise it is "mere" history. If we could show that certain general linguistic changes are correlated with stages of cultural evolution, we would come appreciably nearer securing linguistics a hearing, but the slow modifications that eat into the substance and the form of speech and that gradually remold it entirely do not seem to run parallel to any scheme of cultural evolution yet proposed. Since "biological" or evolutionary history is the only kind of history for which we have a genuine respect, the history of language is left out in the cold as another one of those unnecessary sequences of events which German erudition is in the habit of worrying about.

But before pinning our faith to linguistics as an exploration into form, we might cast an appealing glance at the psychologist, for he is likely to prove a useful ally. He has himself looked into the subject of language, which he finds to be a kind of "behavior," a rather specialized type of functional adaptation, yet not so specialized but that it may be declared to be a series of laryngeal habits. We may go even further, if we select the right kind of psychologist to help us, and have thought put in its place as a merely "subvocal laryngeating." If these psychological contributions to the nature of speech do not altogether explain the Greek aorists bequeathed to us by classical poets, they are at any rate very flattering to philology. Unfortunately the philologist cannot linger long with the psychologist's rough and ready mechanisms. These may make shift for an introduction to his science, but his real problems are such as few psychologists have clearly envisaged, though it is not unlikely that psychology may have much to say about them when it has gained strength and delicacy. The psychological problem which most interests the linguist is the inner structure of language, in terms of unconscious psychic processes, not that of the individual's adaptation to this traditionally conserved structure. It goes without saying, however, that the two problems are not independent of each other.

To say in so many words that the noblest task of linguistics is to understand languages as form rather than as function or as historical process is not to say that it can be understood as form alone. The formal configuration of speech at any particular time and place is the result of a long and complex historical development, which, in turn, is unintelligible without constant reference to functional factors. Form is even more liable to be stigmatized as "mere" than the historical process which shapes it. For our characteristically pragmatic American attitude forms in themselves seem to have little or no reality, and it is for this reason that we so often fail to divine them or to realize into what new patterns ideas and institutions are balancing themselves or tending to do so. Now it is very probable that the poise which goes with culture is largely due to the habitual appreciation of the formal outlines and the formal intricacies of experience. Where life is tentative and experimental, where ideas and sentiments are constantly protruding gaunt elbows out of an inherited stock of meagre, inflexible patterns instead of graciously bending them to their own uses, form is necessarily felt as a burden and a tyranny instead of the gentle embrace it should be. Perhaps it is not too much to say that the lack of culture in America is in some way responsible for the unpopularity of linguistic studies, for these demand at one and the same time an intense appreciation of a given form of expression and a readiness to accept a great variety of possible forms.

The outstanding fact about any language is its formal completeness. This is as true of a primitive language, like Eskimo or Hottentot, as of the carefully recorded and standardized languages of our great cultures. By "formal completeness" I mean a profoundly significant peculiarity which is easily overlooked. Each language has a well defined and exclusive phonetic system with which it carries on its work and, more than that, all of its expressions, from the most habitual to the merely potential, are fitted into a deft tracery of prepared forms from which there is no escape. These forms establish a definite relational feeling or attitude towards all possible contents of expression and, through them, towards all possible contents of experience, in so far, of course, as experience is capable of expression in linguistic terms. To put this matter of the formal completeness of speech in somewhat different words, we may say that a language is so constructed that no matter what any speaker of it may desire to communicate, no matter how original or bizarre his idea or his fancy, the language is prepared to do his work. He will never need to create new forms or to force upon his language a new formal orientation—unless, poor man, he is haunted by the form-feeling of another language and is subtly driven to the unconscious distortion of the one speech-system on the analogy of the other. The world of linguistic forms, held within the framework of a given language, is a complete system of reference, very much as a number system is a complete system of quantitative reference or as a set of geometrical axes of coördinates is a complete system of reference to all points of a given space. The mathematical analogy is by no means as fanciful as it appears to be. To pass from one language to another is psychologically parallel to passing from one geometrical system of reference to another. The environing world which is referred to is the same for either language; the world of points is the same in either frame of reference. But the formal method of approach to the expressed item of experience, as to the given point of space, is so different that the resulting feeling of orientation can be the same neither in the two languages nor in the two frames of reference. Entirely distinct, or at least measurably distinct, formal adjustments have to be made and these differences have their psychological correlates.

Formal completeness has nothing to do with the richness or the poverty of the vocabulary. It is sometimes convenient or, for practical reasons, necessary for the speakers of a language to borrow words from foreign sources as the range of their experience widens. They may extend the meanings of words which they already possess, create new words out of native resources on the analogy of existing terms, or take over from another people terms to apply to the new conceptions which they are introducing. None of these processes affects the form of the language, any more than the enriching of a certain portion of space by the introduction of new objects affects the geometrical form of that region as defined by an accepted mode of reference. It would be absurd to say that Kant's "Critique of Pure Reason" could be rendered forthwith into the unfamiliar accents of Eskimo or Hottentot, and yet it would be absurd in but a secondary degree. What is really meant is that the culture of these primitive folk has not advanced to the point where it is of interest to them to form abstract conceptions of a philosophical order. But it is not absurd to say that there is nothing in the formal peculiarities of Hottentot or of Eskimo which would obscure the clarity or hide the depth of Kant's thought—indeed, it may be suspected that the highly synthetic and periodic structure of Eskimo would more easily bear the weight of Kant's terminology than his native German. Further, to move to a more positive vantage point, it is not absurd to say that both Hottentot and Eskimo possess all the formal apparatus that is required to serve as matrix for the expression of Kant's thought. If these languages have not the requisite Kantian vocabulary, it is not the languages that are to be blamed but the Eskimo and the Hottentots themselves. The languages as such are quite hospitable to the addition of a philosophic load to their lexical stock-in-trade.

The unsophisticated natives, having no occasion to speculate on the nature of causation, have probably no word that adequately translates our philosophic term "causation," but this shortcoming is purely and simply a matter of vocabulary and of no interest whatever from the standpoint of linguistic form. From this standpoint the term "causation" is merely one out of an indefinite number of examples illustrating a certain pattern of expression. Linguistically—in other words, as regards form-feeling—"causation" is merely a particular way of expressing the notion of "act of causing," the idea of a certain type of action conceived of as a thing, an entity. Now the form-feeling of such a word as "causation" is perfectly familiar to Eskimo and to hundreds of other primitive languages. They have no difficulty in expressing the idea of a certain activity, say "laugh" or "speak" or "run," in terms of an entity, say "laughter" or "speech" or "running." If the particular language under consideration cannot readily adapt itself to this type of expression, what it can do is to resolve all contexts in which such forms are used in other languages into other formal patterns that eventually do the same work. Hence, "laughter is pleasurable," "it is pleasant to laugh," "one laughs with pleasure," and so on *ad infinitum*, are functionally equivalent expressions, but they canalize into entirely distinct form-feelings. All languages are set to do all the symbolic and expressive work that language is good for, either actually or potentially. The formal technique of this work is the secret of each language.

It is very important to get some notion of the nature of this form-feeling, which is implicit in all language, however bewilderingly at variance its actual manifestations may be in different types of speech. There are many knotty problems here—and curiously elusive ones— that it will require the combined resources of the linguist, the logician, the psychologist, and the critical philosopher to clear up for us. There is one important matter that we must now dispose of. If the Eskimo and the Hottentot have no adequate notion of what we mean by causation, does it follow that their languages are incapable of expressing the causative relation? Certainly not. In English, in German, and in Greek we have certain formal linguistic devices for passing from the primary act or state to its causative correspondent, e.g., English *to fall, to fell,* "to cause to fall"; *wide, to widen;* German *hangen,* "to hang, be suspended"; *hängen,* "to hang, cause to be suspended"; Greek *pherō,* "to carry"; *phoreō,* "to cause to carry." Now this ability to feel and express the causative relation is by no manner of means dependent on an ability to conceive of causality as such. The latter ability is conscious and intellectual in character; it is laborious, like most conscious processes, and it is late in developing. The former ability is unconscious and nonintellectual in character, exercises itself with great rapidity and with the utmost ease, and develops early in the life of the race and of the individual. We have therefore no theoretical difficulty in finding that conceptions and relations which primitive folk are quite unable to master on the conscious plane are being unconsciously expressed in their languages—and, frequently, with the utmost nicety. As a matter of fact, the causative relation, which is expressed only fragmentarily in our modern European languages, is in many primitive languages rendered with an absolutely philosophic relentlessness. In Nootka, an Indian language of Vancouver Island, there is no verb or verb form which has not its precise causative counterpart.

Needless to say, I have chosen the concept of causality solely for the sake of illustration, not because I attach an especial linguistic importance to it. Every language, we may conclude, possesses a complete and psychologically satisfying formal orientation, but this orientation is only felt in the unconscious of its speakers—is not actually, that is, consciously, known by them.

Our current psychology does not seem altogether adequate to explain the formation and transmission of such submerged formal systems as are disclosed to us in the languages of the world. It is usual to say that isolated linguistic responses are learned early in life and that, as these harden into fixed habits, formally analogous responses are made, when the need arises, in a purely mechanical manner, specific precedents pointing the way to new responses. We are sometimes told that these analogous responses are largely the result of reflection on the utility of the earlier ones, directly learned from the social environment. Such methods of approach see nothing in the problem of linguistic form beyond what is involved in the more and more accurate control of a certain set of muscles towards a desired end, say the hammering of a nail. I can only believe that explanations of this type are seriously incomplete and that they fail to do justice to a certain innate striving for formal elaboration and expression and to an unconscious patterning of sets of related elements of experience.

The kind of mental processes that I am now referring to are, of course, of that compelling and little understood sort for which the name "intuition" has been suggested. Here is a field which psychology has barely touched but which it cannot ignore indefinitely. It is precisely because psychologists have not greatly ventured into these difficult reaches that they have so little of interest to offer in explanation of all those types of mental activity which lead to the problem of form, such as language, music, and mathematics. We have every reason to surmise that languages are the cultural deposits, as it were, of a vast and self-completing network of psychic processes which still remain to be clearly defined for us. Probably most linguists are convinced that the language-learning process, particularly the acquisition of a feeling for the formal set of the language, is very largely unconscious and involves mechanisms that are quite distinct in character from either sensation or reflection. There is doubtless something deeper about our feeling for form than even the majority of art theorists have divined, and it is not unreasonable to suppose that, as psychological analysis becomes more refined, one of the greatest values of linguistic study will be in the unexpected light it may throw on the psychology of intuition, this "intuition" being perhaps nothing more nor less than the "feeling" for relations.

There is no doubt that the critical study of language may also be of the most curious and unexpected helpfulness to philosophy. Few philosophers have deigned to look into the morphologies of primitive languages nor have they given the structural peculiarities of their own speech more than a passing and perfunctory attention. When one has the riddle of the universe on his hands, such pursuits seem trivial enough, yet when it begins to be suspected that at least some solutions of the great riddle are elaborately roundabout applications of the rules of Latin or German or English grammar, the triviality of linguistic analysis becomes less certain. To a far greater extent than the philosopher has realized, he is likely to become the dupe of his speech-forms, which is equivalent to saying that the mould of his thought, which is typically a linguistic mould, is apt to be projected into his conception of the world. Thus innocent linguistic categories may take on the formidable appearance of cosmic absolutes. If only, therefore, to save himself from philosophic verbalism, it would be well for the philosopher to look critically to the linguistic foundations and limitations of his thought. He would then be spared the humiliating discovery that many new ideas, many apparently brilliant philosophic conceptions, are little more than rearrangements of familiar words in formally satisfying patterns. In their recently published work on "The Meaning of Meaning" Messrs. Ogden and Richards have done philosophy a signal service in indicating how readily the most hardheaded thinkers have allowed themselves to be cajoled by the formal slant of their habitual mode of expression. Perhaps the best way to get behind our thought processes and to eliminate from them all the accidents or irrelevances due to their linguistic garb is to plunge into the study of exotic modes of expression. At any rate, I know of no better way to kill spurious "entities."

This brings us to the nature of language as a symbolic system, a method of referring to all possible types of experience. The natural or, at any rate, the naïve thing is to assume that when we wish to communicate a certain idea or impression, we make something like a rough and rapid inventory of the objective elements and relations involved in it, that such an inventory or analysis is quite inevitable, and that our linguistic task consists merely of the finding of the particular words and groupings of words that correspond to the terms of the objective analysis. Thus, when we observe an object of the type that we call a "stone" moving through space towards the earth, we involuntarily analyze the phenomenon into two concrete notions, that of a stone and that of an act of falling, and, relating these two notions to each other by certain formal methods proper to English, we declare that "the stone falls." We assume, naïvely enough, that this is about the only analysis that can properly be made. And yet, if we look into the way that other languages take to express this very simple kind of impression, we soon realize how much may be added to, subtracted from, or rearranged in our own form of expression without materially altering our report of the physical fact.

In German and in French we are compelled to assign "stone" to a gender category—perhaps the Freudians can tell us why this object is masculine in the one language, feminine in the other; in Chippewa we cannot express ourselves without bringing in the apparently irrelevant fact that a stone is an inanimate object. If we find gender beside the point, the Russians may wonder why we consider it necessary to specify in every case whether a stone, or any other object for that matter, is conceived in a definite or an indefinite manner, why the difference between "the stone" and "a stone" matters. "Stone falls" is good enough for Lenin, as it was good enough for Cicero. And if we find barbarous the neglect of the distinction as to definiteness, the Kwakiutl Indian of British Columbia may sympathize with us but wonder why we do not go a step further and indicate in some way whether the stone is visible or invisible to the speaker at the moment of speaking and whether it is nearest to the speaker, the person addressed, or some third party. "That would no doubt sound fine in Kwakiutl, but we are too busy!" And yet we insist on expressing the singularity of the falling object, where the Kwakiutl Indian, differing from the Chippewa, can generalize and make a statement which would apply equally well to one or several stones. Moreover, he need not specify the time of the fall. The Chinese get on with a minimum of explicit formal statement and content themselves with a frugal "stone fall."

These differences of analysis, one may object, are merely formal; they do not invalidate the necessity of the fundamental concrete analysis of the situation into "stone" and what the stone does, which in this case is "fall." But this necessity, which we feel so strongly, is an illusion. In the Nootka language the combined impression of a stone falling is quite differently analyzed. The stone need not be specifically referred to, but a single word, a verb form, may be used which is in practice not essentially more ambiguous than our English sentence. This verb form consists of two main elements, the first indicating general movement or position of a stone or stonelike object, while the second refers to downward direction. We can get some hint of the feeling of the Nootka word if we assume the existence of an intransitive verb "to stone," referring to the position or movement of a stonelike object.

Then our sentence, "The stone falls," may be reassembled into something like "It stones down." In this type of expression the thing-quality of the stone is implied in the generalized verbal element "to stone," while the specific kind of motion which is given us in experience when a stone falls is conceived as separable into a generalized notion of the movement of a class of objects and a more specific one of direction. In other words, while Nootka has no difficulty whatever in describing the fall of a stone, it has no verb that truly corresponds to our "fall."

It would be possible to go on indefinitely with such examples of incommensurable analyses of experience in different languages. The upshot of it all would be to make very real to us a kind of relativity that is generally hidden from us by our naïve acceptance of fixed habits of speech as guides to an objective understanding of the nature of experience. This is the relativity of concepts or, as it might be called, the relativity of the form of thought. It is not so difficult to grasp as the physical relativity of Einstein nor is it as disturbing to our sense of security as the psychological relativity of Jung, which is barely beginning to be understood, but it is perhaps more readily evaded than these. For its understanding the comparative data of linguistics are a *sine qua non*. It is the appreciation of the relativity of the form of thought which results from linguistic study that is perhaps the most liberalizing thing about it. What fetters the mind and benumbs the spirit is ever the dogged acceptance of absolutes.

To a certain type of mind linguistics has also that profoundly serene and satisfying quality which inheres in mathematics and in music and which may be described as the creation out of simple elements of a self-contained universe of forms. Linguistics has neither the sweep nor the instrumental power of mathematics, nor has it the universal aesthetic appeal of music. But under its crabbed, technical, appearance there lies hidden the same classical spirit, the same freedom in restraint, which animates mathematics and music at their purest. This spirit is antagonistic to the romanticism which is rampant in America today and which debauches so much of our science with its frenetic desire.

THE STATUS OF LINGUISTICS AS A SCIENCE*

Linguistics may be said to have begun its scientific career with the comparative study and reconstruction of the Indo-European languages. In the course of their detailed researches Indo-European linguists have gradually developed a technique which is probably more nearly perfect than that of any other science dealing with man's institutions. Many of the formulations of comparative Indo-European linguistics have a neatness and a regularity which recall the formulae, or the so-called laws, of natural science. Historical and comparative linguistics has been built up chiefly on the basis of the hypothesis that sound changes are regular and that most morphological readjustments in language follow as by-products in the wake of these regular phonetic developments. There are many who would be disposed to deny the psychological necessity of the regularity of sound change, but it remains true, as a matter of actual linguistic experience, that faith in such regularity has been the most successful approach to the historic problems of language. Why such regularities should be found and why it is necessary to assume regularity of sound change are questions that the average linguist is perhaps unable to answer satisfactorily. But it does not follow that he can expect to improve his methods by discarding well tested hypotheses and throwing the field open to all manner of psychological and sociological explanations that do not immediately tie up with what we actually know about the historical behavior of language. A psychological and a sociological interpretation of the kind of regularity in linguistic change with which students of language have long been familiar are indeed desirable and even necessary. But neither psychology nor sociology is in a position to tell linguistics what kinds of historical formulations the linguist is to make. At best these disciplines can but urge the linguist to concern himself in a more vital manner than heretofore with the problem of seeing linguistic history in the larger framework of human behavior in the individual and in society.

The methods developed by the Indo-Europeanists have been applied with marked success to other groups of languages. It is abundantly clear that they apply just as rigorously to the unwritten primitive languages of Africa and America as to the better known forms of speech of the more sophisticated peoples. It is probably in the languages of

* *Language*, 5 (1929): 207–214. Read at a joint meeting of the Linguistic Society of America, the American Anthropological Association, and Sections H and L of the American Association for the Advancement of Science, New York City, December 28, 1928.

these more cultured peoples that the fundamental regularity of linguistic processes has been most often crossed by the operation of such conflicting tendencies as borrowing from other languages, dialectic blending, and social differentiations of speech. The more we devote ourselves to the comparative study of the languages of a primitive linguistic stock, the more clearly we realize that phonetic law and analogical leveling are the only satisfactory key to the unravelling of the development of dialects and languages from a common base. Professor Leonard Bloomfield's experiences with Central Algonkian and my own with Athabaskan leave nothing to be desired in this respect and are a complete answer to those who find it difficult to accept the large-scale regularity of the operation of all those unconscious linguistic forces which in their totality give us regular phonetic change and morphological readjustment on the basis of such change. It is not merely theoretically possible to predict the correctness of specific forms among unlettered peoples on the basis of such phonetic laws as have been worked out for them—such predictions are already on record in considerable number. There can be no doubt that the methods first developed in the field of Indo-European linguistics are destined to play a consistently important rôle in the study of all other groups of languages, and that it is through them and through their gradual extension that we can hope to arrive at significant historical inferences as to the remoter relations between groups of languages that show few superficial signs of a common origin.

It is the main purpose of this paper, however, not to insist on what linguistics has already accomplished, but rather to point out some of the connections between linguistics and other scientific disciplines, and above all to raise the question in what sense linguistics can be called a 'science.'

The value of linguistics for anthropology and culture history has long been recognized. As linguistic research has proceeded, language has proved useful as a tool in the sciences of man and has itself required and obtained a great deal of light from the rest of these sciences. It is difficult for a modern linguist to confine himself to his traditional subject matter. Unless he is somewhat unimaginative, he cannot but share in some or all of the mutual interests which tie up linguistics with anthropology and culture history, with sociology, with psychology, with philosophy, and, more remotely, with physics and physiology.

Language is becoming increasingly valuable as a guide to the scientific study of a given culture. In a sense, the network of cultural patterns of a civilization is indexed in the language which expresses that civilization. It is an illusion to think that we can understand the significant outlines of a culture through sheer observation and without the guide of the linguistic symbolism which makes these outlines significant and intelligible to society. Some day the attempt to master a primitive culture without the help of the language of its society will seem as amateurish as the labors of a historian who cannot handle the original documents of the civilization which he is describing.

Language is a guide to 'social reality.' Though language is not ordinarily thought of as of essential interest to the students of social science, it powerfully conditions all our thinking about social problems and processes. Human beings do not live in the objective world alone, nor alone in the world of social activity as ordinarily understood, but are very much at the mercy of the particular language which has become the medium of expression for their society. It is quite an illusion to imagine that one adjusts to reality essentially without the use of language and that language is merely an incidental means of solving specific problems of communication or reflection. The fact of the matter is that the 'real world' is to a large extent unconsciously built up on the language habits of the group. No two languages are ever sufficiently similar to be considered as representing the same social reality. The worlds in which different societies live are distinct worlds, not merely the same world with different labels attached.

The understanding of a simple poem, for instance, involves not merely an understanding of the single words in their average significance, but a full comprehension of the whole life of the community as it is mirrored in the words, or as it is suggested by their overtones. Even comparatively simple acts of perception are very much more at the mercy of the social patterns called words than we might suppose. If one draws some dozen lines, for instance, of different shapes, one perceives them as divisible into such categories as 'straight,' 'crooked,' 'curved,' 'zigzag' because of the classificatory suggestiveness of the linguistic terms themselves. We see and hear and otherwise experience very largely as we do because the language habits of our community predispose certain choices of interpretation.

For the more fundamental problems of the student of human culture, therefore, a knowledge of linguistic mechanisms and historical developments is certain to become more and more important as our analysis of social behavior becomes more refined. From this standpoint we may think of language as the *symbolic guide to culture*. In another sense too linguistics is of great assistance in the study of cultural phenomena. Many cultural objects and ideas have been diffused in connection with their terminology, so that a study of the distribution of culturally significant terms often throws unexpected light on the history of inventions and ideas. This type of research, already fruitful in European and Asiatic culture history, is destined to be of great assistance in the reconstruction of primitive cultures.

The values of linguistics for sociology in the narrower sense of the word is just as real as for the anthropological theorist. Sociologists are necessarily interested in the technique of communication between human beings. From this standpoint language facilitation and language barriers are of the utmost importance and must be studied in their interplay with a host of other factors that make for ease or difficulty of transmission of ideas and patterns of behavior. Furthermore, the sociologist is necessarily interested in the symbolic significance, in a social sense, of the linguistic differences which appear in any large community. Correctness of speech or what might be called 'social style' in speech is of far more than aesthetic or grammatical interest. Peculiar modes of pronunciation, characteristic turns of phrase, slangy forms of speech, occupational terminologies of all sorts—these are so many symbols of the manifold ways in which society arranges itself and are of crucial importance for the understanding of the development of individual and social attitudes. Yet it will not be possible for a social student to evaluate such phenomena unless he has very clear notions of the linguistic background against which social symbolisms of a linguistic sort are to be estimated.

It is very encouraging that the psychologist has been concerning himself more and more with linguistic data. So far it is doubtful if he has been able to contribute very much to the understanding of language behavior beyond what the linguist has himself been able to formulate on the basis of his data. But the feeling is growing rapidly, and justly, that the psychological explanations of the linguists themselves need to be restated in more general terms, so that purely linguistic facts may be seen as specialized forms of symbolic behavior. The psychologists have perhaps too narrowly concerned themselves with the simple psycho-physical bases of speech and have not penetrated very deeply into the study of its symbolic nature. This is probably due to the fact that psychologists in general are as yet too little aware of the fundamental importance of symbolism in behavior. It is not unlikely that it is precisely in the field of symbolism that linguistic forms and processes will contribute most to the enrichment of psychology.

All activities may be thought of as either definitely functional in the immediate sense, or as symbolic, or as a blend of the two. Thus, if I shove open a door in order to enter a house, the significance of the act lies precisely in its allowing me to make an easy entry. But if I 'knock at the door,' a little reflection shows that the knock in itself does not open the door for me. It serves merely as a sign that somebody is to come to open it for me. To knock on the door is a substitute for the more primitive act of shoving it open of one's own accord. We have here the rudiments of what might be called language. A vast number of acts are language acts in this crude sense. That is, they are not of importance to us because of the work they immediately do, but because they serve as mediating signs of other more important acts. A primitive sign has some objective resemblance to what it takes the place of or points to. Thus, knocking at the door has a definite relation to intended activity upon the door itself. Some signs become abbreviated forms of functional activities which can be used for reference. Thus, shaking one's fist at a person is an abbreviated and relatively harmless way of actually punching him. If such a gesture becomes sufficiently expressive to society to constitute in some sort the equivalent of an abuse or a threat, it may be looked on as a symbol in the proper sense of the word.

Symbols of this sort are primary in that the resemblance of the symbol to what it stands for is still fairly evident. As time goes on, symbols become so completely changed in form as to lose all outward connection with what they stand for. Thus, there is no resemblance between a piece of bunting colored red, white, and blue, and the United States of America—itself a complex and not easily definable notion. The flag may therefore be looked upon as a secondary or referential symbol. The way to understand language psychologically, it seems, is to see it as the most complicated example of such a secondary or referential set of symbols that society has evolved. It may be that originally the primal cries or other types of symbols developed by man had some connection with certain emotions or attitudes or notions. But a connection is no longer directly traceable between words, or combinations of words, and what they refer to.

Linguistics is at once one of the most difficult and one of the most fundamental fields of inquiry. It is probable that a really fruitful integration of linguistic and psychological studies lies still in the future. We may suspect that linguistics is destined to have a very special value for configurative psychology ('Gestalt psychology'), for, of all forms of culture, it seems that language is that one which develops its fundamental patterns with relatively the most complete detachment from other types of cultural patterning. Linguistics may thus hope to become something of a guide to the understanding of the 'psychological geography' of culture in the large. In ordinary life the basic symbolisms of behavior are densely overlaid by cross-functional patterns of a bewildering variety. It is because every isolated act in human behavior is the meeting point of many distinct configurations that it is so difficult for most of us to arrive at the notion of contextual and non-contextual form in behavior. Linguistics would seem to have a very peculiar value for configurative studies because the patterning of language is to a very appreciable extent self-contained and not significantly at the mercy of intercrossing patterns of a non-linguistic type.

It is very notable that philosophy in recent years has concerned itself with problems of language as never before. The time is long past when grammatical forms and processes can be naïvely translated by philosophers into metaphysical entities. The philosopher needs to understand language if only to protect himself against his own language habits, and so it is not surprising that philosophy, in attempting to free logic from the trammels of grammar and to understand knowledge and the meaning of symbolism, is compelled to make a preliminary critique of the linguistic process itself. Linguists should be in an excellent position to assist in the process of making clear to ourselves the implications of our terms and linguistic procedures. Of all students of human behavior, the linguist should by the very nature of his subject matter be the most relativist in feeling, the least taken in by the forms of his own speech.

A word as to the relation between linguistics and the natural sciences. Students of linguistics have been greatly indebted for their technical equipment to the natural sciences, particularly physics and physiology. Phonetics, a necessary prerequisite for all exact work in linguistics, is impossible without some grounding in acoustics and the physiology of the speech organs. It is particularly those students of language who are more interested in the realistic details of actual speech behavior in the individual than in the socialized patterns of language who must have constant recourse to the natural sciences. But it is far from unlikely that the accumulated experience of linguistic research may provide more than one valuable hint for the setting up of problems of research to acoustics and physiology themselves.

All in all, it is clear that the interest in language has in recent years been transcending the strictly linguistic circles. This is inevitable, for an understanding of language mechanisms is necessary for the study of both historical problems and problems of human behavior. One can only hope that linguists will become increasingly aware of the significance of their subject in the general field of science and will not stand aloof behind a tradition that threatens to become scholastic when not vitalized by interests which lie beyond the formal interest in language itself.

Where, finally, does linguistics stand as a science? Does it belong to the natural sciences, with biology, or to the social sciences? There seem to be two facts which are responsible for the persistent tendency to view linguistic data from a biological point of view. In the first place, there is the obvious fact that the actual technique of language behavior involves very specific adjustments of a physiological sort. In the second place, the regularity and typicality of linguistic processes leads to a quasi-romantic feeling of contrast with the apparently free and undetermined behavior of human beings studied from the standpoint of culture. But the regularity of sound change is only superficially analogous to a biological automatism. It is precisely because language is as strictly socialized a type of human behavior as anything else in culture and yet betrays in its outlines and tendencies such regularities as only the natural scientist is in the habit of formulating, that linguistics is of strategic importance for the methodology of social science. Behind the apparent lawlessness of social phenomena there is a regularity of configuration and tendency which is just as real as the regularity of physical processes in a mechanical world, though it is a regularity of infinitely less apparent rigidity and of another mode of apprehension on our part. Language is primarily a cultural or social product and must be understood as such. Its regularity and formal development rest on considerations of a biological and psychological nature, to be sure. But this regularity and our underlying unconsciousness of its typical forms do not make of linguistics a mere adjunct to either biology or psychology. Better than any other social science, linguistics shows by its data and methods, necessarily more easily defined than the data and methods of any other type of discipline dealing with socialized behavior, the possibility of a truly scientific study of society which does not ape the methods nor attempt to adopt unrevised the concepts of the natural sciences. It is peculiarly important that linguists, who are often accused, and accused justly, of failure to look beyond the pretty patterns of their subject matter, should become aware of what their science may mean for the interpretation of human conduct in general. Whether they like it or not, they must become increasingly concerned with the many anthropological, sociological, and psychological problems which invade the field of language.

STUDIES OF AMERICAN INDIAN LANGUAGES

EDITOR'S PREFACE

T HE PAPERS *of this section are representative of Sapir's chief field of specialization. The major part of his research was concerned with American Indian languages; only a few facets of this work of more than thirty years can be shown here.*

The lead article is more than an encyclopedia piece giving a brief résumé of the subject, for it presents a reduction of the linguistic families of North America which goes far beyond those which had previously been suggested. Sapir's intention was to provide a working hypothesis, to place on record his best estimates of the genetic relationships which might be proved as a result of future work. His warning that the scheme is "suggestive but far from demonstrable in all its features at the present time" has occasionally gone unheeded and the six "superstocks" are sometimes referred to as though fully established.

By no means all of the scheme is simply a matter of hunch. Sapir himself provided confirmatory data for several divisions of it. Thus a good part of the rationale for the establishment of Uto-Aztecan is given in Sapir's important "Southern Paiute and Nahuatl, a Study in Uto-Aztekan" (1913, 1914, 1915). Considerable evidence for Na-dene is given in "The Na-dene Languages, a Preliminary Report" (1915). The Algonkin-Ritwan category was discussed in "Wiyot and Yurok, Algonkin Languages of California" (1913); and further evidence was presented in papers of 1915 and 1923. The Hokan-Coahuiltecan grouping was justified in two papers of 1917 and especially in a study which American Indian linguists consider to be one of the very best of Sapir's technical analyses, "The Hokan Affinity of Subtiaba in Nicaragua" (1925).

Sapir also contributed an important share of the descriptive studies which provide the basic data for the historical formulations. Among the more extensive of his descriptive works are "The Takelma Languages of Southwestern Oregon" (1922) and "Southern Paiute, a Shoshonean Language" (1930–1931). Penetrating observations concerning general processes in American Indian languages are to be found scattered through these papers: the titles sometimes give little hint of the scope of the observations, for once Sapir worked into a problem he was apt to follow it through to distant ramifications. Even such writings as his two reviews, published in 1917, of some of Uhlenbeck's work, include novel and significant statements about North American languages.

Save for the first, the papers in this section are arranged in chronological order and illustrate various kinds of linguistic analyses. The Nootka article deals with "the historical connexion between various linguistic and stylistic processes involving the symbolic use of sounds." The treatment of a Chinookan phonetic law not only ascertains the specific pattern involved, but discusses briefly the possibility of the diffusion of phonetic patterns. The article on the variant forms of speech used by males and females among the Yana describes a phenomenon which has wide interest. What Sapir called "linguistic archeology" is exemplified in the paper concerning the linguistic evidence suggestive of the northern origin of the Navaho.

The manner in which Sapir could marshal a vast array of evidence to demonstrate a linguistic process is illustrated in the study of glottalized continuants in three American Indian languages. The insight so derived is then applied to illuminate phonological developments in Indo-European. This paper has special importance for the Indo-European field, since it contains a brief but trenchant exposition of Sapir's ideas on the Indo-European laryngeal hypothesis.

CENTRAL AND NORTH AMERICAN LANGUAGES*

THE POPULATION of aboriginal America north of Mexico (about 1,150,000) at the time of the discovery of America by Columbus spoke an astonishing number of languages, most of which are still spoken, though in many cases by only a bare handful of individuals. Certain of them, like Sioux and Navaho, are still flourishing languages.

They consist of a number of distinct stocks, which differ fundamentally from each other in vocabulary, phonetics, and grammatical form. Some of these stocks, such as Algonkin, Siouan, and Athabaskan, consist of a large number of distinct languages; others seem to be limited to a small number of languages or dialects or even to a single language. The so-called "Powell classification" of languages north of Mexico recognizes no less than 55 of these "stocks" (see the revised map of 1915 issued by the Bureau of American Ethnology), excluding Arawak, a South American stock originally represented in the West Indies and perhaps also on the southwestern coast of Florida.

The distribution of these 55 stocks is uneven: 37 of them are either entirely or largely in territory draining into the Pacific, and 22 of these have a coast line on the Pacific. Only 7 linguistic stocks had an Atlantic coast line. Besides the Pacific coast, in the lower Mississippi and Gulf coast languages of 10 stocks were spoken (apart from Arawak). The most widely distributed stocks are: *Eskimoan*, which includes Eskimo dialects ranging from east Greenland west to southern Alaska and East Cape, Siberia, as well as the Aleut of Alaska Peninsula and the Aleutian Islands; *Algonkian*, which embraces a large number of languages spoken along the Atlantic coast from eastern Quebec and Cape Breton Island south to the coast of North Carolina, in the interior of Labrador, in the northern part of the drainage of the St. Lawrence, in the country of the three upper Great Lakes and the upper Mississippi, and west into the plains of the Saskatchewan and the upper Missouri; *Iroquoian*, which consists of languages originally spoken in three disconnected areas—the region of Lakes Erie and Ontario and the St. Lawrence, eastern Virginia and North Carolina, and the southern Alleghany country (Cherokee); *Muskogian* (including Natchez), which occupies the Gulf region from the mouth of the Mississippi east into

* *Encyclopaedia Britannica* (14th ed.; London and New York, Encyclopaedia Britannica Co., 1929), 5: 138–141.

Florida and Georgia and north into Tennessee and Kentucky; *Siouan*, divided into four geographically distinct groups—an eastern group in Virginia and North and South Carolina, a small southern contingent (Biloxi) in southern Mississippi, the main group in the valley of the Missouri (eastern Montana and Saskatchewan southeast through Arkansas), and a colony of the main group (Winnebago) in the region of Green Bay, Wisconsin; *Caddoan*, spoken in the southern Plains (from Nebraska south into Texas and Louisiana) and in an isolated enclave (Arikara) along the Missouri in North and South Dakota; *Shoshonean*, which occupies the greater part of the Great Basin area and contiguous territory in southern California and the southwestern Plains (Texas), also, disconnected from this vast stretch, three mesas in the Pueblo region of northern Arizona (Hopi); *Athabaskan*, divided into three geographically distinct groups of languages—Northern (the valleys of the Mackenzie and Yukon, from just short of Hudson's Bay west to Cook Inlet, Alaska, and from Great Bear Lake and the Mackenzie delta south to the headwaters of the Saskatchewan), Pacific (two disconnected areas, one in southwestern Oregon and northwestern California, the other a little south of this in California), and Southern (large parts of Arizona and New Mexico, with adjoining regions of Utah, Texas, and Mexico)—besides isolated enclaves in southern British Columbia, Washington, and northern Oregon; and *Salishan*, in southern British Columbia, most of Washington, and northern Iadho and Montana, with two isolated offshoots, one (Bella Coola) to the north on the British Columbia coast, the other (Tillamook) to the south in northwestern Oregon.

The remaining 46 stocks, according to Powell's classification, in alphabetical order, are: *Atakapa* (Gulf coast of Louisiana and Texas); *Beothuk* (Newfoundland; extinct); *Chimakuan* (northwestern Washington); *Chimariko* (northwestern California); *Chinook* (lower Columbia River, in Washington and Oregon); *Chitimacha* (southern Louisiana); *Chumash* (southwestern California); *Coahuiltecan* (lower Rio Grande, in Texas and Mexico); *Coos* (Oregon coast); *Costanoan* (western California south of San Francisco Bay); *Esselen* (southwestern California; extinct); *Haida* (Queen Charlotte Islands and part of southern Alaska); *Kalapuya* (northwestern Oregon); *Karankawa* (Texas coast); *Karok* (northwestern California); *Keres* (certain Rio Grande pueblos, New Mexico); *Kiowa* (southern Plains, in Kansas, Colorado, Oklahoma, and Texas); *Kootenay* (upper Columbia River, in British Columbia and adjoining parts of Idaho and Montana); *Lutuami*, consisting of Klamath and Modoc (southern Oregon and northeastern California); *Maidu* (eastern part of Sacramento Valley, California); *Miwok* (central California); *Piman* or Sonoran (southern Arizona and south into Mexico as far as the state of Jalisco); *Pomo* (western California north of San Francisco Bay); *Sahaptin* (middle Columbia River valley, in Washington, Oregon, and Idaho); *Salinan* (southwestern California); *Shastan* or Shasta-Achomawi (northern California and southern Oregon); *Takelma* (southwestern Oregon); *Tanoan* (certain pueblos in New Mexico, Arizona, and originally also in Chihuahua, Mexico); *Timuqua* (Florida; extinct); *Tlingit* (southern Alaska); *Tonkawa* (Texas); *Tsimshian* (western British Columbia); *Tunica* (Mississippi River, in Louisiana and Mississippi); *Waiilatpuan*, consisting of Molala and Cayuse (northern Oregon); *Wakashan*, consisting of Kwakiutl and Nootka (coast of British Columbia); *Washo* (western Nevada and eastern California); *Wintun* (north-central California); *Wiyot* (northwestern California); *Yakonan* (Oregon coast); *Yana* (northern California); *Yokuts* (south-central California); *Yuchi* (Savannah River, in Georgia and South Carolina); *Yuki* (western California); *Yuman* (lower Colorado River valley, in Arizona, southern California and south into all or most of lower California); *Yurok* (northwestern California); *Zuñi* (pueblo of New Mexico). To these was later added, as distinct from Yakonan, *Siuslaw* (Oregon Coast).

This complex classification of native languages in North America is very probably only a first approximation to the historic truth. There are clearly far-reaching resemblances in both structure and vocabulary among linguistic stocks classified by Powell as genetically distinct. Certain resemblances in vocabulary and phonetics are undoubtedly due to borrowing of one language from another, but the more deeplying resemblances, such as can be demonstrated, for instance, for Shoshonean, Piman, and Nahuatl (Mexico) or for Athabaskan and Tlingit, must be due to a common origin now greatly obscured by the operation of phonetic laws, grammatical developments and losses, analogical disturbances, and borrowing of elements from alien sources.

It is impossible to say at present what is the irreducible number of linguistic stocks that should be recognized for America north of Mexico, as scientific comparative work on these difficult languages is still in its infancy. The following reductions of linguistic stocks which have been proposed may be looked upon as either probable or very possible: (1) *Wiyot* and *Yurok*, to which may have to be added Algonkian (of which Beothuk may be a very divergent member); (2) *Iroquoian* and *Caddoan*; (3) *Uto-Aztekan*, consisting of Shoshonean, Piman, and Nahuatl; (4) *Athabaskan* and *Tlingit*, with *Haida* as a more distant relative; (5)

Mosan, consisting of Salish, Chimakuan, and Wakashan; (6) *Atakapa, Tunica*, and *Chitimacha*; (7) *Coahuiltecan, Tonkawa*, and *Karankawa*; (8) *Kiowa* and *Tanoan*; (9) *Takelma, Kalapuya*, and *Coos-Siuslaw-Yakonan*; (10) *Sahaptin, Waiilatpuan*, and *Lutuami*; (11) a large group known as *Hokan*, consisting of Karok, Chimariko, Shastan, Yana, Pomo, Washo, Esselen, Yuman, Salinan, Chumash, and, in Mexico, Seri and Chontal; (12) *Penutian*, consisting of Miwok-Costanoan, Yokuts, Maidu, and Wintun.

A more far-reaching scheme than Powell's, suggestive but far from demonstrable in all its features at the present time, is Sapir's.

These linguistic classifications (shown below) do not correspond at all closely to the racial or subracial lines that have been drawn for North America, nor to the culture areas into which the tribes have been grouped by ethnographers. Thus, the Athabaskan stock counts among its tribes representatives of four of the major culture areas of the continent: Plateau-Mackenzie area, southern outlier of West Coast area, Plains area, and Southwestern area.

PROPOSED CLASSIFICATION OF AMERICAN INDIAN LANGUAGES
NORTH OF MEXICO (AND CERTAIN LANGUAGES OF
MEXICO AND CENTRAL AMERICA)

I. *Eskimo-Aleut*

II. *Algonkin-Wakashan*

1. Algonkin-Ritwan
    (1) Algonkin
    (2) Beothuk (?)
    (3) Ritwan
       (a) Wiyot
       (b) Yurok

2. Kootenay
3. Mosan (Wakashan-Salish)
    (1) Wakashan (Kwakiutl-Nootka)
    (2) Chimakuan
    (3) Salish

III. *Nadene*

1. Haida
2. Continental Nadene
   (*see opposite*)

Continental Nadene
    (1) Tlingit
    (2) Athabaskan

IV. *Penutian*

1. Californian Penutian
    (1) Miwok-Costanoan
    (2) Yokuts
    (3) Maidu
    (4) Wintun
2. Oregon Penutian
    (1) Takelma
    (2) Coast Oregon Penutian
       (a) Coos
       (b) Siuslaw
       (c) Yakonan

    (3) Kalapuya
3. Chinook
4. Tsimshian
5. Plateau Penutian
    (1) Sahaptin
    (2) Waiilatpuan (Molala-Cayuse)
    (3) Lutuami (Klamath-Modoc)
6. Mexican Penutian
    (1) Mixe-Zoque
    (2) Huave

V. *Hokan-Siouan*

1. Hokan-Coahuiltecan
   A. Hokan
     (1) Northern Hokan
       (a) = $\begin{cases} \text{Karok} \\ \text{Chimariko} \\ \text{Shasta-Achomawi} \end{cases}$
       (b) Yana
       (c) Pomo
     (2) Washo
     (3) Esselen-Yuman
       (a) Esselen
       (b) Yuman
     (4) Salinan-Seri
       (a) Salinan
       (b) Chumash
       (c) Seri
     (5) Tequistlatecan (Chontal)
   B. Subtiaba-Tlappanec
   C. Coahuiltecan
     (1) Tonkawa

    (2) Coahuilteco
      (a) Coahuilteco proper
      (b) Cotoname
      (c) Comecrudo
    (3) Karankawa
2. Yuki
3. Keres
4. Tunican
  (1) Tunica-Atakapa
  (2) Chitimacha
5. Iroquois-Caddoan
  (1) Iroquoian
  (2) Caddoan
6. Eastern group
  (1) Siouan-Yuchi
    (a) Siouan
    (b) Yuchi
  (2) Natchez-Muskogian
    (a) Natchez
    (b) Muskogian
    (c) Timucua (?)

VI. *Aztec-Tanoan*

1. Uto-Aztekan
     (1) Nahuatl
     (2) Pima
     (3) Shoshonean

2. Tanoan-Kiowa
     (1) Tanoan
     (2) Kiowa
3. Zuñi (?)

The aboriginal languages of North America differ from each other in both phonetic and morphological respects. Some are polysynthetic (or "holophrastic") in structure, such as Algonkian, Yana, Kwakiutl-Nootka, or Eskimo. Others, like Takelma and Yokuts, are of an inflective cast and may be compared, for structural outlines, to Latin or Greek; still others, like Coos, while inflective, have been reduced to the relatively analytic status of such a language as English; agglutinative languages of modern complexity, comparable to Turkish, are common, say Shoshonean or Sahaptin.

The term "polysynthetic" indicates that the language is far more than ordinarily synthetic in form, that the word embodies many more or less concrete notions that would in most languages be indicated by the grouping of independent words in the sentence. The Yana word *yābanaumawildjigummaha'nigi* "let us, each one [of us], move indeed to the west across [the creek]!" is "polysynthetic" in structure. It consists of elements of three types—a nuclear element or "stem" (*yā-* "several people move"); formal elements of mode (*-ha-*, hortatory) and person (*-nigi* "we"); and elements of a modifying sort which cannot occur independently but which nevertheless express ideas that would ordinarily be rendered by independent words (-*banauma*- "everybody," -*wil*- "across," -*dji*- "to the west," -*gumma*- "indeed"). Such constructions are not uncommon in native America but are by no means universal.

Phonetically these languages differ enormously. Some, like Pawnee (Caddoan stock), have a simple consonantal structure; others make all manner of fine consonantal discriminations and possess many strange types of consonants, such as voiceless *l*-sounds, "glottalized" consonants, and velar *k*-sounds, that are infrequent elsewhere. Kutchin, an Athabaskan language of Alaska, possesses no less than 55 consonantal "phonemes," distinct consonantal elements of the total phonetic pattern. A considerable number of the native languages of North America are pitch languages, *i.e.*, they use pitch differences in otherwise similar syllables to make lexical or grammatical distinctions. Such languages are Tlingit, Athabaskan (certain dialects of this group have lost pitch as an inherently necessary element of language), Takelma, Shasta-Achomawi, Yuman, Tanoan. Navaho may serve as an example of such a pitch language. Every syllable in its words is definitely high or low in pitch, or, less frequently, has a falling or rising tone. Thus, *binī'* means "his nostril" if the two syllables have a high tone, "his face" if they have a low tone, and "at his waist, center" if the first syllable is low and the second high; *yāzīd* means "you pour it [sandy mass] down" if the first syllable is low and the second high, but "I have poured it down" if both are low.

The six major linguistic groups of Sapir's scheme may be characterized as follows:

I. The *Eskimo-Aleut* languages are "polysynthetic" and inflective; use suffixes only, never prefixes, reduplication, inner stem modification, or compounding of independent stems; have a great elaboration of the formal aspect of verb structure, particularly as regards mode and person; and make a fundamental distinction between the transitive and intransitive verb, to which corresponds the nominal case distinction of agentive-genitive and absolutive (or objective).

II. The *Algonkin-Wakashan* languages, too, are "polysynthetic" and, especially as regards Algonkian, inflective; make use of suffixes; to a much less extent, particularly in Algonkian and Ritwan, of prefixes; have important inner stem modifications, including reduplication; have a weak development of case; and illustrate to a marked degree the process of building up noun and verb themes by suffixing to stems local, instrumental, adverbial, and concretely verbalizing elements.

III. The *Nadene* languages, probably the most specialized of all, are tone languages and, while presenting a superficially "polysynthetic" aspect, are built up, fundamentally, of monosyllabic elements of prevailingly nominal significance which have fixed order with reference to each other and combine into morphologically loose "words"; emphasize voice and "aspect" rather than tense; make a fundamental distinction between active and static verb forms; make abundant use of postpositions after both nouns and verb forms; and compound nominal stems freely. The radical element of these languages is probably always nominal in force and the verb is typically a derivative of a nominal base, which need not be found as such.

IV. The *Penutian* languages are far less cumbersome in structure than the preceding three but are more tightly knit, presenting many analogies to the Indo-European languages; make use of suffixes of formal, rather than concrete, significance; show many types of inner stem change; and possess true nominal cases, for the most part. Chinook seems to have developed a secondary "polysynthetic" form on the basis of a broken down form of Penutian; while Tsimshian and Maidu have probably been considerably influenced by contact with Mosan and with Shoshonean and Hokan respectively.

V. The *Hokan-Siouan* languages are prevailingly agglutinative; tend to use prefixes rather than suffixes for the more formal elements, particularly the pronominal elements of the verb; distinguish active and static verbs; and make free use of compounding of stems and of nominal incorporation.

VI. The *Aztec-Tanoan* languages are moderately "polysynthetic"; suffix many elements of formal significance; make a sharp formal distinction between noun and verb; make free use of reduplication, compounding of stems, and nominal incorporation; and possess many postpositions. Pronominal elements, in some cases nouns, have different forms for subject and object but the subject is not differentiated, as in types I and IV, for intransitive and transitive constructions.

Mexican and Central American Languages

The classification of the native languages of Middle America is not in quite so advanced a stage as that of the many languages spoken north of Mexico. The languages are, some of them, spoken by large populations, numbering millions, as in Nahuatl (or Mexican) and the Maya of Yucatan; others are confined to very small groups, like the Subtiaba-Tlappanec of Nicaragua and Guerrero, or are extinct, as is Waïcuri in Lower California. Nahuatl, Maya (with Quiche, Kekchi, and Cakchiquel, which belong to the Mayan stock), and Zapotec were great culture languages which had developed ideographic methods of writing.

The languages of Middle America may be conveniently grouped into three main sets: A, southern outliers of stocks located chiefly north of Mexico; B, stocks spoken only in Mexico and Central America, so far as is known at present; C, northern outliers of South American stocks. It is quite probable that relationships will eventually be discovered between some of the languages of group B and languages lying farther north.

To group A belong three distinct stocks: *Uto-Aztekan*, with two subdivisions, *Sonoran* (or *Piman*), spoken in a large number of dialects in northern Mexico, and *Nahuatl* (or *Aztek*), spoken in central Mexico and in a number of isolated southern enclaves—the Pacific coast of Oaxaca (Pochutla), three disconnected areas in Salvador and Guatemala (Pipil), two areas in Nicaragua and one in Costa Rica (Nicarao), and the Chiriqui region of Costa Rica (Sigua), of which dialects Nicarao and Sigua are now extinct—with *Cuitlateco* of Michoacan as a doubtful member of the stock; *Hokan-Coahuiltecan*, represented by *Hokan* proper, which includes Seri (coast of Sonora), Yuman (in Lower California), and Tequistlateco or Chontal (coast of Oaxaca), by *Coahuiltecan* (Pakawan), of the lower Rio Grande, and by *Subtiaba-Tlappanec*, which is spoken in two small areas in Guerrero, one in Salvador, and one in Nicaragua; and *Athabaskan* (Apache tribes of Chihuahua and Coahuila).

The Middle American languages proper (group B) may, with reservations, be classified into 15 linguistic stocks, which, in alphabetic order, are: *Chinantec* (Oaxaca and western Vera Cruz); *Janambre* (Tamaulipas: extinct); *Jicaque* (northern Honduras); *Lenca* (Honduras and Salvador); *Mayan* (Yucatan and neighboring states of southern Mexico, British Honduras, western Honduras, and Guatemala), with an aberrant dialect group, *Huastec*, in the northeastern coast region of Mexico (Vera Cruz, San Luis Potosi, Tamaulipas); *Miskito-Sumo-Matagalpa*, consisting of three quite distinct language groups: *Miskito* (coast of Nicaragua and Honduras), Sumo-Ulua (eastern Nicaragua and southern Honduras), and *Matagalpa* (Nicaragua; a small enclave, Cacaopera, in Salvador); *Mixe-Zoque-Huave*, spoken in four disconnected groups, *Mixe-Zoque* (Oaxaca, Vera Cruz, Chiapas, and Tabasco), *Tapachultec* (southeastern Chiapas; extinct), *Aguacatec* (Guatemala; extinct), and *Huave* (coast of Oaxaca); *Mixtec-Zapotec*, a group of languages that some students still prefer to consider as composed of four independent stocks: *Mixtec* (Guerrero, Puebla, and western Oaxaca), *Amusgo* (Guerrero and Oaxaca), *Zapotec* (Oaxaca), and *Cuicatec* (northern Oaxaca); *Olive* (Tamaulipas; extinct); *Otomian*, consisting of three distinct groups: *Otomi* (large part of central Mexico),

Mazatec (Guerrero, Puebla, Oaxaca; includes *Trique* and *Chocho*), and the geographically distant *Chiapanec-Mangue* (*Chiapanec* in Chiapas; *Mangue* and related languages in three disconnected areas in Nicaragua and Costa Rica); *Paya* (Honduras); *Tarascan* (Michoacan); *Totonac* (Hidalgo, Puebla, and coast of Vera Cruz); *Waïcuri* (southern part of Lower California; extinct); *Xinca* (southeastern Guatemala).

The outliers from South America are two: *Carib* (coast of Honduras and British Honduras; transferred in post-Columbian times from the Antilles); *Chibchan* (Costa Rica and Panama). In the West Indies two South American stocks were represented, *Carib* and *Arawak*, the latter constituting an older stream which had overrun the Greater Antilles and perhaps penetrated into Florida.

As to languages of group B, some connect Chinantec, Mixtec-Zapotec, and Otomian in one great linguistic stock, *Mixtec-Zapotec-Otomi*. Both Xinca and Lenca (also Paya and Jicaque?) may be remote southern outliers of the Penutian languages of North America. Waïcuri may have been related to Yuman. It is by no means unlikely that such important Middle American stocks as Mayan, Totonac, and Tarascan may also belong to certain of the larger stock groupings that have been suggested for North America; *e.g.*, Maya may fit into the Hokan-Siouan framework, Tarascan into Aztek-Tanoan.

Middle America, in spite of its special cultural position, is distinctly a part of the whole North American linguistic complex and is connected with North America by innumerable threads. On the other hand, there seems to be a much sharper line of linguistic division, distributionally speaking, between Middle America and South America. This line is approximately at the boundary between Nicaragua and Costa Rica; allowances being made for Nahuatl and Otomian enclaves in Costa Rica and for an Arawak colony in Florida, we may say that Costa Rica, Panama, and the West Indies belong linguistically to South America. The Chibchan, Arawak, and Carib stocks of the southern continent were obviously diffusing northward at the time of the Conquest, but evidence seems to indicate that for Mexico and Central America as a whole the ethnic and linguistic movement was from north to south. Middle America may be looked upon as a great pocket for the reception of a number of distinct southward-moving peoples and the linguistic evidence is sure to throw much light in the future on the tangled problem of unraveling the ethnic and culture streams which traversed these regions.

Two linguistic groups seem to stand out as archaically Middle American: Miskito-Sumo-Matagalpa, in Central America, and Mixtec-Zapotec-Otomi, with its center of gravity in southern Mexico. The latter of these sent offshoots that reached as far south as Costa Rica. The Penutian languages, centered in Oregon and California, must early have extended far to the south, as they seem to be represented in Mexico and Central America by Mixe-Zoque, Huave, Xinca, and Lenca. These southern offshoots are now cut off from their northern cognate languages by a vast number of intrusive languages, *e.g.*, Hokan and Aztek-Tanoan. The Mayan languages, apparently of Hokan-Siouan type, may have drifted south at about an equally early date. Presumably later than the Penutian and Mayan movements into Middle America is the Hokan-Coahuiltecan stream, represented by at least three distinct groups—Coahuiltecan (N. E. Mexico), Subtiaba-Tlappanec (Guerrero, Nicaragua), and a relatively late stream of Hokan languages proper (Yuman; Seri; and Chontal in Oaxaca). Not too early must have been the Uto-Aztekan movement to the south, consisting of an advance guard of Nahuatl-speaking tribes, a rear guard of Sonoran-speaking tribes (Cora, Huichol, Tarahumare, Tepehuane). The Nahuatl language eventually pushed south as far as Costa Rica. Last of all, the Apache dialects of Chihuahua brought into Mexico the southernmost outpost of the Nadene group of languages, which extend north nearly to the Arctic.

ABNORMAL TYPES OF SPEECH IN NOOTKA*

AN INTERESTING linguistic and cultural problem is the use in speech of various devices implying something in regard to the status, sex, age, or other characteristics of the speaker, person addressed, or person spoken of, without any direct statement as to such characteristics. When we say "big dog make bow-wow" instead of "the dog barks," it is a fair inference that we are talking to a baby, not to a serious-minded man of experience. Further, when we hear one use "thee" where most would say "you," we suspect that we are listening to an orthodox Quaker. In neither of these cases is there an explicit reference to a baby as person addressed or to a Quaker as person speaking. Such implications are common in all languages and are most often effected by means of the use of special words or specific locutions. Thus, in Nootka there are special words used in speaking of obscene matters to or in the presence of women; a number of "baby-words" also exist. Generally it is the speaker or person addressed that is thus signalized, but it is quite possible, though less frequent, to thus imply something also in regard to the third person. A more specialized type of these person-implications is comprised by all cases in which the reference is brought about not by the use of special words or locutions, that is, by lexical, stylistic, or syntactic means, but by the employment of special grammatical elements, consonant or vocalic changes, or addition of meaningless sounds, that is, by morphologic or phonetic means.

To enumerate all the possible types of person-implication expressed in language, from the point of view of resulting classifications of human beings, would lead one far afield. Two types, however, seem to stand out most prominently—those referring to sex-discrimination and to rank-discrimination. Several languages make a distinction between words or forms used by males and such as are restricted to females. Such a distinction, for instance, is made by certain Eskimo dialects, in which, at least in earlier times, according to Boas,[1] final p, t, k, and q[2] were pronounced by the women as the corresponding nasals m, n, η, and η. In Yana, an isolated linguistic stock of northern California, the forms used by the women, whether in speaking to one another or to males, differ from the fuller forms used by the latter in the unvoicing

---

* Canada, Geological Survey, Memoir 62, Anthropological Series No. 5 (Ottawa, Government Printing Bureau, 1915).

[1] Franz Boas, *Handbook of American Indian Languages*, Bureau of American Ethnology, Bulletin 40, pt. 1 (Washington, G. P. O., 1911), p. 79.

[2] See Phonetic Key at end of this paper.

of final vowels; final -*na* (-*hi* in Southern Yana), a common noun ending, is replaced by aspiration in the speech of the women, who further lengthen final vowels to express the interrogative, while the males suffix an element -*n*. Most languages that make such sex distinctions differentiate the sexes as speakers. In Yana, however, a further discriminating factor is the sex of the person spoken to, in so far as the men in speaking to the women use the forms characteristic of the latter.

More widespread in language seems to be a discrimination of forms according to the rank or social status of the person speaking, addressed, or spoken of. Here belong the etiquette forms characteristic of several East Asiatic and Indonesian languages, by which the social grading of the speakers as inferiors or superiors in reference to one another is clearly reflected in their speech. An analogous American instance is the use in Nahuatl of reverential forms to imply respect to the person addressed or spoken of. These are morphologically nothing but indirectives or causatives in -*lia*, -*tia*, or -*ltia* with reflexive pronominal prefixes; "he sleeps" is thus more politely expressed as "he causes himself to sleep." Here belongs also the use in so many European languages (French, German, Russian, and others) of second or third person plurals, instead of the more logical second person singulars, in speaking to people with whom one is not on the most intimate terms. This usage has its parallel in Yana, where brothers and sisters address each other in the plural[3]; other Californian examples of a similar nature have been given by Goddard[4] and Kroeber.[5]

These preliminary remarks are intended merely to indicate the general class of linguistic phenomena to which belong the more specialized Nootka examples to be given presently. At the same time they will serve to render these latter less glaringly bizarre by providing them with parallels of a more general character. The data here presented were chiefly obtained in November, 1910, in the course of ethnologic and linguistic research for the Geological Survey of Canada among the Nootka Indians of Alberni canal, Vancouver island; the informant was Dan Watts, the young chief of the *Hōpátcĺas'atʜ*ᵃ tribe. Further data on this subject were obtained in the winter of 1913–14 from Alex Thomas, a young Indian of the *Tsĺicá'atʜ*ᵃ tribe of the same region.

It is possible and often customary in Nootka to imply in speech some physical characteristic of the person addressed or spoken of, partly by

---

[3] Sapir, *Yana Texts*, Univ. Calif. Publ. Am. Arch. and Ethn., 9 (1910): 95, n. 139: 101, n. 150.
[4] Goddard, *Kato Texts*, ibid., 5 (1909): 142, fn. 185.
[5] Kroeber, *The Languages of the Coast of California North of San Francisco*, ibid., 9 (1911): 321 (Pomo).

means of suffixed elements, partly by means of "consonantal play." Consonantal play consists either in altering certain consonants of a word, in this case sibilants, to other consonants that are phonetically related to them, or in inserting meaningless consonants or consonant clusters in the body of the word. The physical classes indicated by these methods are children, unusually fat or heavy people, unusually short adults, those suffering from some defect of the eye, hunchbacks, those that are lame, left-handed persons, and circumcised males.

In speaking to or about a child it is customary to add the regular diminutive suffix -*'is* to verb or other forms, even though the word so affected connotes nothing intrinsically diminutive; affection may also be denoted by it. The -*'is* comes before temporal, modal, and pronominal suffixes. Thus, the normal *qwístci'* "do so!" (*qwís-* "to do thus;" -*tci'* second person singular imperative, "go and . !") is changed to *qwís'ístci'* "do so, little one!" when speaking to a child. Similarly, *qwísma'* "he does so" (-*ma'* third person present indicative) is changed to *qwís'isma'* when one is speaking about a child. In speaking about oneself or others when addressing a child, it does not seem to be customary to use the diminutive suffix except to show affection at the same time. Thus, the word *walcíLaH* "I am going home" (*wal-* "to return home"; -*ciL-* inceptive; -*aH* "I") may be changed to *walcíL'isaH* "I am going home, little one" when addressed to a child for whom one wants to show love, but this form would not be used in speaking to a child that is a stranger. As might be expected, diminutive verbal and other forms occur in lullabies, in some of which the child is represented as speaking about itself. Thus, in a lullaby supposed to be sung by a whale mother to its child, occur the words *'oH^a'ésǫk^c 'émiti'* ("my) little name is" (*'oH^a-* "to be"; -*'is-* diminutive; -*ǫk^e* "of, belonging to"; *'émiti'* "name"). Some people were said by Dan to have the habit of using the diminutive suffix in order to belittle others, as though the persons addressed or referred to were of no more importance than children as compared to themselves. If a chief does this to too great an extent, he is set down as haughty.

In talking to or about fat people or people of unusual size, the suffixed element -*aq'* is used in a manner analogous to the diminutive -*'is*. Thus, the normal *hint'ciLwe'in^i* "he comes, it is said" (*hin-* "empty" verb stem "to be, do"; -*t'-*, shortened form of -*in^i* "to come"; -*ciL-* inceptive; -*we'in^i* quotative) becomes *hint'ciLaq'we'in^i*; *'ǫtsátciLma'* "he goes to it" (*'ǫ-* "empty" noun stem meaning "something"; -*tsa-* "to start for, go to"; -*tciL-* inceptive, used after vowels; -*ma'* third person present indicative) becomes *'ǫtsatciLáq'ma'*. Other examples are: *ha'ókwaq'ma'* "he, clumsy one, eats"; (*ha'w-* "to eat"; *-okw-* intransitive verbal suffix); and *ha'okwáqit'ᴴak'* "did you eat, fatty?" (*-it'* tense suffix denoting past time; *-ᴴa-* interrogative; *-k'* second person singular).

People who are abnormally small are spoken of in forms with the diminutive suffix; moreover, in such cases, all sibilant consonants (*s, ts, ts!; c, tc, tc!*) become palatalized *c-* sounds (*š, tš, tš!* compare, for *š*, Polish *ś* and Sanskrit *ç*; for *tš*, compare Polish *ć*), which sound acoustically midway between *s-* and *c-* sounds; the diminutive *-'is* itself becomes *-'iš*. Thus, *hínt'ciᴸwe'inⁱ* "he comes, they say" is changed to *hínt'šiᴸ-'išwe'inⁱ* "he, little man, comes, they say." These *š-* forms are also used to refer to small birds, such as sparrows and wrens. Sometimes a meaningless *š* is added to the word, as in *wikấᴴᵃš tóᴴauk'* from *wikấᴴᵃ tóᴴauk'* "I am not afraid" (*wik-* verb stem "to be not"; *-āᴴᵃ* first person singular present indicative; *tōᴴ-* verb stem "to be afraid"; *-uk'*, diphthongized to *-auk'* because of preceding *a-* timbred *ᴴ*, intransitive suffix). We shall meet this consonantal change again further on in another connexion.

Quite analogously to dwarfs, are addressed or spoken of those suffering from some defect of the eye. Under this category are included cross-eyed people, those who squint, and such as have one eye run out, but not the blind. Here again the diminutive suffix is used, with the added feature that all *s-* sounds and *c-* sounds are converted into the corresponding voiceless lateral stops or spirants (*s* and *c* become *ł*; *ts* and *tc* become *ᴸ*; *ts!* and *tc!* become *ᴸ!*); the diminutive *-'is* itself becomes *-'ił*. This style of speech is termed *ᴸ!aᴸ!átck!inⁱ* "to talk in sore-eyed fashion" (cf. *ᴸ!aᴸ!átck'sul* "one-eyed person"). Thus, *qwísma'* "he does so" is changed to *qwíł'ilma'*. Similarly, *tc!ítciᴸma'* "he cuts" (*tc!i-* "to cut"; *-tciᴸ-* inceptive; *-ma'* third person present indicative) becomes *ᴸ!íᴸiᴸ'iłma'*. A full-grown Indian named Sammy (or *Sê'mi* as pronounced in Nootka), who is cross-eyed, is referred to as *łê'mi'ił* "little cross-eyed Sammy." Another Indian of the same tribe, *Tô'mic*, who has only one good eye, is, in parallel fashion, referred to as *Tô'mil'ił* "little one-eyed Tô'mic." It should be remarked that such people, particularly when adult, are apt to become offended if addressed in this fashion, and that one would not use such forms in their presence unless with the express purpose of showing contempt or of teasing. As will be seen again later on, *ᴸ!aᴸ!átck!inⁱ* forms are used also in referring to the deer[6] and mink. Thus, the mythological Mink, *tc!ástimits'mit'* "Mink-son," is generally referred to as *ᴸ!áłtimiᴸ'mit'*.

[6] Deer is associated with sore eyes also in other Indian mythologies. An Ojibwa example may be found in P. Radin, *Some Myths and Tales of the Ojibwa of Southeastern Ontario*, Geological Survey of Canada, Memoir 48 (No. 2, Anthropological Series), p. 3 (episode *d*).

Hunchbacks (*k!wápi̧*) are also addressed or spoken of in forms provided with the diminutive suffix, a further peculiarity in these being the change of ordinary *s*- sounds and *c*- sounds to peculiar thickish *c*-sounds, pronounced with the lower jaw held in front of the upper; the diminutive *-'is* appears as *-'i̧ç*. We may represent these *c*- sounds by *ç*. In this hunchback talk *qwísma'* becomes *qwí̧ç'i̧çma'*. Other examples are: *yátçuk"'i̧çma'* "he is walking" (*yāts,-* "to walk"; *-uk'-* intransitive verb suffix); *tçlótçk"'miniɪ̯ᴴᵃ'i̧çma'* "all of them are" (*tclótck'-* "to be all"; *'miniɪ̯ᴴᵃ-* plural); and *tçláx̧çi̧ʟ'i̧çma'* "he spears" (*tsla̧x-* "to spear"; *-çi̧ʟ-* inceptive). Here again these distinctive forms are generally avoided when in the presence of humpbacked people, for fear of giving offence. However, a humpbacked child who is well known to the speaker would hardly take offence and would be addressed as described. Or, if an old humpbacked woman is good-natured, *ç*- forms may well be used when she is about, as though to show that she is happy and not easily ruffled. Here the notions of contempt and affection commingle.

In speaking of lame people the diminutive suffix is again used, this time in its normal form. Besides this, the meaningless element *ʟc or ʟci* is inserted in the body of the word somewhere before the diminutive suffix, its exact position apparently depending on the whim of the speaker. Thus, *hiníni'aʟma'* "he comes now" (*hin-* "empty" verb stem; *-ini-* "to come"; *-'aʟ-* determinative suffix marking point of time, "now"; *-ma'* third person present indicative) becomes *hiníniʟci̧'-its!aʟma'* (diminutive *-'is* and *-'aʟ* regularly combine to form *-'its!aʟ*) or *hiʟcníni'its!aʟma'* "the lame chap is coming." Similarly, the verb *tclíitci'aʟma'* "he cuts now" (inceptive *-tci̧ʟ* and *-'aʟ* combine into *-tci'aʟ*) is changed to *tclíitci̧ʟc'i̧ts!aʟma'* when a lame person is spoken of. The word *t!a'nȩ'is'i̧'* "the child" (*t!a'na-* "child, son, daughter"; *-'is* diminutive suffix, *i* causing preceding *a* to become umlauted to *ȩ*; *-'i̧'* nominalizing element, about equivalent to our definite article) becomes *t!aʟcnȩ'is'i̧'* "the young lame fellow," which may be used in speaking to children.

In speaking of or to left-handed people the diminutive suffix is used in its normal form, besides which the meaningless element *tcᴴᵃ* is inserted after the first syllable of the word. Thus, *yā̧l'aʟma'* "there now he is" (*yāl-* "to be there"; *-'aʟ* and *-ma'* as above) becomes *yā̧ltcᴴᵃ'its!aʟma'* (*-'is* and *-'aʟ* combine to form *-'its!aʟ*) "there now he is, poor little left-handed chap!" Similarly, from *sukwí'aʟma'* "now he takes it" (*su-* verb stem "to take"; *-kwiʟ* inceptive suffix, changed to *-kwi-* before *-'aʟ*) is formed *sútcᴴᵃkwiʟ'its!aʟma'*. The diminutive suffix may also be omitted. Examples are: *hitcᴴᵃníni̧* from *hiníni̧* "to come"; and *t!itcн^ₐtciʟaн* from *t!itciʟaн* "I throw it down" (*t!i-* "to throw"; *-tciʟ* inceptive suffix; *-aн* first person singular indicative). Such a form as the last might be appropriately used in speaking to a left-handed person that one is well acquainted with and who will not take offence at being thus twitted. It is customary, particularly for jokers, to use these left-hand forms also in talking about bears, who are supposed to be left-handed.[7]

In speaking of or to circumcised males, forms known as *'i'ict'k!in^i* "to make *ct'*- sounds" are used. In these the meaningless element *ct'* is inserted after the first syllable of the word. One of the *Ts!icá'atн^ₐ* Indians, named *T!óx̣mis* "Slaying-while-moving-from-beach-to-beach," is often humorously referred to as *T!óctx̣mis* because of his having been born circumcised. Other examples of this class of forms are: *hict'ninıma'* from *hininıma'* "he comes"; and *háct''ǫk'^ᵘ* from *há'ǫk'^ᵘ* "to eat."

Similar phonetic changes are made in forms used to refer to one or two classes of individuals characterized by some mental quality. Thus, greedy people are addressed or referred to in forms having a meaningless *tcx* inserted after the first syllable of the word. Thus, from *'oн^ₐsámaн* "I hunger for it" (*'o-* "empty" stem which may be rendered by "something" or "so and so"; *-н^ₐsā-* verbifying suffix "to desire to eat"; *-maн* first person singular present indicative, used after vowels) is formed *'utcxнsámaн*. Similarly, *hinínı'aʟma'* "now he comes" becomes *hitcxnínı'aʟma'* "now he comes, greedy fellow that he is." These *tcx*-forms are also used to refer to ravens, regularly to the mythological Raven, a character noted for his gluttony.

Cowards may be satirized by "making one's voice small" in referring to or addressing them, in other words by speaking in a thin piping voice that suggests timidity.

It is interesting to notice that in several of the above usages, the notions of mere smallness, of contempt, and of affection are found side by side, and doubtless the precise nuance of feeling expressed depends much on the relations subsisting between the speaker and the person addressed or spoken of. What is meant in the spirit of pitying affection for a poor lame or humpbacked child or for a good-natured squinting old grandpa, might be intended to convey contempt when addressed to a young man and would be promptly resented as an insult. It is significant that the various types of abnormal forms of speech that we have reviewed are used with little or no reserve when speaking

---

[7] According to Dr. Paul Radin, the Winnebago also consider the bear to be left-handed. In the bear clan feast of these Indians the guests eat with a spoon in their left hand.

of the persons referred to or when addressing children, but are, on the whole, avoided when within ear-shot of adults so referred to. It seems further significant that the traits satirized are chiefly such as are inherent in a person, not merely acquired in the accidental course of events, whereby he is set apart by nature as falling short in some respect of the normal type of individual and is to that extent stamped as inferior. This may explain why blindness, which is more often acquired rather late in life than congenital, is not made the subject of speech-mockery. Added to this may be the feeling that blindness is too grave an affliction to be treated light-heartedly, an explanation which gains weight when the well-known sensitiveness of the Indian is considered.

Outside of the normal use of the diminutive in addressing or referring to children, the peculiar forms of speech that we have seen to obtain in Nootka are not easily paralleled in America. For diminutive verbal forms of the Nootka type Uto-Aztekan affords a close parallel. In Southern Paiute the regular diminutive suffix -*tsi*-, which is employed to form diminutive nouns and adverbs of all sorts, is also used as a verb suffix when speaking to or of a child. Cognate with this element is the diminutive suffix -*tzin*(*tli*) of Nahuatl. Derived from this is the verb suffix -*tzinoa*, "which," according to Rémi Siméon,[8] "serves to denote respect or love"; it is generally, like reverentials of the type already referred to, employed with reflexive prefixes. Examples given by Rémi Siméon are: *otechmo-chiuilitzino in Totecuyo* "our Lord created us" (*o* preterit prefix; *tech-* first person plural objective prefix; *mo-* third person reflexive prefix; *chiui-*, from *chiua*, because of following -*li*-, verb stem "to make"; -*li* dative suffix, *mo-* . . . -*li* "for himself"; -*tzino* reverential, final -*a* being dropped because of preterit tense; *in* definite article, "the"; *to-* first person plural possessive prefix; *tecuyo* noun stem "lord"); and *timo-çauhtzinoa* (quoted from Olmos) "you fast" (*ti-* second person singular subject; *mo-* reflexive;[9] *çauh-*, from *çaua* verb stem "to fast"; -*tzinoa* reverential). These forms may be rendered in some such fashion as: "our Lord has created us for himself, revered one," and "you fast, honoured sir."

Strikingly similar psychologically to the cases of consonantal play in Nootka just considered are the peculiar consonant changes characteristic of Chinookan, employed to convey diminutive and augmentative notions respectively in all parts of speech.[10] The change here of *c-*

---

[8] *Dictionnaire de la Langue Nahuatl ou Mexicaine* (Paris, 1885), s.v. *tzinoa*.
[9] This verb is intrinsically reflexive.
[10] See Sapir, "Preliminary Report on the Language and Mythology of the Upper Chinook," *American Anthropologist*, n.s., 9 (1907): 537, 538; and, in greater detail, *idem*, section on "Diminutive and Augmentative Consonantism in Wishram," in Boas, *Handbook of American Indian Languages*, pp. 638–645.

consonants to *s*- consonants to express the idea of diminution further illustrates the tendency of sibilants in America to be subject to consonantal play. In Yana the phenomenon of diminutive consonantism is illustrated in the change of *l* to *n*. This process takes place regularly in forming diminutive nouns in -*p!a*; thus, *nínimaup!a* "little nose," from *lílimau(na)* "nose." The *l-n* type of consonantal play is another one of some currency in America, and seems to obtain also in Sahaptin. This matter of consonantal play to express modalities of attitude is doubtless a fruitful field for investigation in American linguistics and should receive more attention than has hitherto been accorded it. It may be expected to turn up particularly in connexion with notions of smallness, largeness, contempt, affection, respect, and sex-differences.

Such consonant changes and increments as have been considered are evidently of a rhetorical or stylistic as much as of a purely grammatical sort. This is borne out by the fact that quite analogous processes are found employed as literary devices in American myths and songs. I have already drawn attention to the fact,[11] that in American mythology certain beings are apt to be definitely characterized by speech peculiarities. The employment of consonantal play or of similar devices in such cases seems always to have a decidedly humorous effect. The culture-hero *Kwátiyāt* of Nootka mythology is in the habit of inserting a meaningless *x* after the first vowel of a word; thus, the normal form *hínuse'i* "come up out of the water!" (*hīn-* empty stem "to do, be"; -*use*-, umlauted from -*usa*- because of following *i*, "to move up out of the water"; -'*i* imperative singular) becomes, at the same time, inasmuch as it occurs in a song, with song-vocalism, *hīxnusa'ê*. In the speech of the Deer and Mink all sibilants, whether of the *s* or *c* series, are transformed into the corresponding laterals (*s* and *c* to *ɫ*, *ts* and *tc* to *L*, *ts!* and *tc!* to *L!*). Thus, the Deer says *ɫɪmɪɫ* for *tcɪmis* "black bear"; *L!ápaL* for *tc!ápats* "canoe." The Nootka Deer and Mink style of talking is of particular interest for two reasons. In the first place, it will have been noticed that the consonantal changes are identical with those employed in speech about or addressed to those that have some defect of the eye, the latter type of forms, of course, be'ng further characterized by the use of the diminutive suffix -'*iɫ* (from -'*is*). Here we see at once the intimate connexion between the two types of consonant play. In the second place, the speech of the Nootka Deer and Mink offers an interesting parallel, or rather contrast, to that of the

[11] Sapir, "Song Recitative in Paiute Mythology," *Journal of American Folk-Lore*, 23 (1910): 445–472. Takelma, Ute, Chinookan, and Nootka examples are there given, p. 471.

Kwakiutl Mink. This latter character regularly transforms all laterals to corresponding *s*- sounds (*ł*, *L*, *ʟ̣*, and *L!* become respectively *s*, *ts*, *dz*, and *ts!*), the exact reverse of the Nootka process. From the point of view of the psychology of phonetics, it is significant to observe that both Nootka and Kwakiutl have a feeling for the interchangeability of the sibilant and lateral series of consonants. But the Mink of the Kwakiutl is not content with this. He also regularly transforms all anterior palatals to corresponding sibilants (*x·*, *k·*, *g·*, and *k·!* become respectively *s*, *ts*, *dz*, and *ts!*). There are still other phonetic changes to be found in Boas' Mink texts, but they seem less regular in character than these two; the changes at times of *l* and *'l* to *y* and *'y* may be instanced as one of these (thus *sᴇ'yḗ* for *lᴇ'lḗ* "dead").[12] Now it is perhaps significant that the change in Kwakiutl of anterior palatals to sibilants is curiously like the change of original Wakashan (Kwakiutl-Nootka) anterior palatals, as preserved in Kwakiutl, to *c*- consonants in Nootka.[13] Thus, a Mink form *nᴇdzḗ* in Kwakiutl for normal *nᴇg·ḗ* "mountain" is strikingly similar to the regular Nootka cognate *nutcî'*. Suggestive also, à propos of the use by Mink of sonant palatal spirants (*y* and *'y*) for normal sonant laterals (*l* and *'l*), is the fact that in Nootka so-called "hardening" suffixes change immediately preceding *l* to *'y*, corresponding in such cases to Kwakiutl *'l*.[14] The bearing of these facts on mythological consonant play in Kwakiutl is not easy to determine; a possibility will be suggested farther on.

Consonant play as a device in mythology is not confined to America. In reading some recently published Bushman literature the writer came across striking parallels. The Bushman Mantis, who, like the Kwakiutl Mink, is a trickster, consistently changes all the cerebral clicks of normal speech into lateral clicks.[15] Similarly, the Baboon transforms all the clicks of ordinary speech into a compound click, consisting of cerebral followed by dental click.[16] Evidently a comic effect is aimed at in both these cases.

[12] For data on Mink's peculiarities of speech, see F. Boas and G. Hunt, *Kwakiutl Texts, Second Series*, Publ. Jesup North Pacific Expedition, 10 (1906): 82–154, notes; and Boas, *Kwakiutl Tales*, Columbia University Contributions to Anthropology, 2 (1910): 126–154.

[13] See Sapir, "Some Aspects of Nootka Language and Culture," *American Anthropologist*, n.s., 13 (1911): 16.

[14] See Boas, *Handbook of American Indian Languages*, pp. 430, 435; Sapir, "Some Aspects of Nootka Language and Culture," p. 16.

[15] W. H. Bleek and L. C. Lloyd, *Specimens of Bushman Folklore* (London, Allen, 1911), notes, pp. 6, 8.

[16] *Ibid.*, notes, pp. 18, 22. At least this is indicated by Bleek's orthography, though possibly the compound sign is meant to indicate a special click not otherwise found.

The phenomenon of consonant and vocalic play is also well illustrated in Indian songs. Song diction is an extremely important, though rather neglected, field of primitive lore, and only one phase of it can be touched on here. Song texts often represent a "mutilated" form of the language, but study of the peculiarities of song forms generally shows that the normal forms of speech are modified according to definite stylistic conventions, which may vary for different types of songs. Sometimes sounds are found in songs which do not otherwise occur in the language. Where the texts of a type of songs are in the language of another tribe, as happens so often in America, such an abnormal sound may be simply borrowed from the foreign language, as is the case with the mourning songs of the Southern Paiute, which, sung to supposedly Mohave texts, contain many examples of *l*, a sound otherwise unknown in Paiute. On the other hand, new sounds may be developed spontaneously or in imitation of foreign sounds. The former is probably the case in the frequent Nootka use of *η*, a sound quite foreign to normal Nootka speech, in certain classes of songs; the latter explanation is more plausible in the case of the regular Nootka change of *n* to *l* in many songs. This *n-l* interchange, again, is significant in so far as Kwakiutl, doubtless agreeing in this respect with primitive Wakashan, has both *n* and *l*, while Nootka, when cognate words are compared, is seen to have only *n* to correspond to both. Of particular interest in this connexion is the fact that such special song-sounds (Paiute *l*; Nootka *l* and *η*) are, at least so it would seem, pronounced with difficulty by Indians under ordinary circumstances, as in the handling of English words that contain them. The obvious inference is that one may react quite differently to the same speech-sound entering into dissimilar associations. This fact, has, of course, a much wider psychological significance.[17] Conventional consonant changes in songs are no more restricted to America than, as we have seen, are parallel changes in mythology. An example that happens to have come to the writer's attention lately is the change of voiceless stops to corresponding nasals plus voiced stops in the songs of the Karesau-Papua of German New Guinea. Thus, the normal *apil* becomes *ambil* in songs.[18]

[17] Sounds falling outside the regular phonetic system of the language may be spontaneously developed also by the operation of other systems of consonantal (or vocalic) play than are found in song diction. Thus, in Wishram (Upper Chinookan), the analogy of certain consonant changes of augmentative value (as of *p* to *b*, *t* to *d*, *k* to *g*) brought about the creation of *dj*, a sound otherwise unknown in Chinookan, as the augmentative correlate of *tc* or *ts* sounds. See Boas, *Handbook of American Indian Languages*, pp. 638, 639, 640.

[18] See Father W. Schmidt, abstract of *Über Musik und Gesänge der Karesau-Papuas, Deutsch Neu-Guinea*, Bericht über den III. Kongress der Internationalen Musikgesellschaft (1909), p. 297.

In seeking some comparatively simple basic phenomenon, from which, as a starting point, the various types of consonant play we have illustrated from Nootka could have originated, one easily thinks of the vocalic changes or consonant substitutions that take place in the speech of those who have some specific speech defect. The most familiar case of this sort in English is lisping, which simply means that the ordinary alveolar sibilants (sometimes also stops) are changed to the corresponding dental sibilants or even interdental fricatives (and sometimes correspondingly for stops). Information was obtained of five types of speech defects found among the Nootka. The first of these is called *níniklini* (*nini*- reduplicated stem; *-klini* "to make a sound of") and consists of the involuntary nasalizing of all vowels and continuants. Thus, the normal *hayā́'akaн* "I do not know" (*-aн* first person singular present indicative) is pronounced by people who have this defect *hạyā̧''ạkạн*. The father-in law of Dan Watts, who is a Ucluelet Indian that came to visit his son-in-law, was observed by the writer and definitely stated by Dan to have this "nasal twang," which is due to an inability, muscular or nervous, to raise the velum so as to shut off the passage of the outgoing breath through the nose. In speaking of the elk, *nínıklini* forms are used.

A second type of defective articulation is termed *hahát'klini* or *hahátlini* (*hahat'*- reduplicated stem; *-klini* "to make a sound of"), and is supposed to be due to a hole in the palate. I have no clear idea as to just what the organic basis of the faulty articulation is, but, judging from the examples given of it, it seems evident that those subject to it have difficulty in articulating against the hard palate. Perhaps the speech defect is due to cleft palate. All *ts* and *tc* affricatives (presumably also lateral affricatives) become simple *t*- sounds (dental), while *s*, *c*, and *l* become interdental fricatives (θ). The acoustic effect is that of an exaggerated lisp. Thus, *tclótck'* "all" becomes *tlót'k'*; *'ọtsị'-yukwaн* "I go to it" (*'ọ*- empty noun stem "something"; *-tsị'yukw-* "to go to"; *-aн* "I") becomes *'ọtï'yukwaн*; and *tclọp'tclọ́p'cinıl* "stretch around the neck; sweater" (*tclọp'tclọp'c*- reduplicated stem; *-inıl* "at the neck") becomes *tlọp'tlọ́p'θinıθ*. This latter rests on the authority of Dan Watts; Alex Thomas, starting from a form *tclọp'tclọ́p'cimıl* for "sweater," gave *tlọp'tlọ́p'timıl* as its *hahátlini* correspondent. Those who are *hahát'klini* thus confound three distinct series of consonants in a single dental or interdental series. Such persons are imitated when addressed. The outward resemblance with the phenomena of consonant play is quite striking here.

This resemblance becomes even stronger in the case of the third

Nootka speech defect of which information was obtained, that known as *tsȋska'* (*tsȋsk-* verb stem; *-a'* verb suffix of continuative significance) or *tsȋskaq'sul* (*tsȋsk-* verb stem; *-aq'sul*, perhaps misheard for *-ak'sul* "at the lips"). Such as are subject to it are supposed always to keep their teeth open and to be saying *ts* +. As a matter of fact, those who are *tsȋska'* change all *s* and *c-* sounds to palatalized sibilants (*ś*). Thus, *'otsȋ'yukwaн* "I go to it" becomes *'otśȋ'yukwaн*; *sȋ'yāsaн* "it is mine" (*sȋ'yās-* "to be mine," from independent pronoun *sȋ'ya'* "I"; *-aн* first person singular present indicative) becomes *śȋ'yāśaн*. It will be remembered that these consonant changes are characteristic of the forms used in addressing or speaking about abnormally small adults, except that such discourse is further characterized by the use of the diminutive suffix *-'iś* (from *-'is*). Here there is a tangible connexion between the involuntary consonant changes brought about by a speech defect and the consonant play used to symbolize a body defect, though it is far from obvious in this particular case what association there can be between a kind of lisp and a dwarfed condition of the body. A further point of interest is that those who are *tsȋska'* are generally imitated when spoken of. The significance of this in the argument is obvious.

Somewhat similar to the *hahátlin^i* speech defect, yet not to be confused with it, is that known as *kakát' 'win^i* "to talk as one with missing teeth" (cf. *kátxwak'sul* "to have teeth missing in one's mouth"). Such persons speak with a decided lisp, substituting *θ* for *s* and *c*, *tθ* for *ts*, *tθ!* for *ts!* and *tc!*, but, it would seem, *t* for *tc*. Examples are: *'ê'pınıθ* from *'ê'pınıs* "apples"; *'ô'yıntaθ* from *'ô'yıntcas* "oranges"; *tímıθ* from *tcímıs* "bear"; *tθ!ōtk'* from *tc!ōtck'* "all"; *tθ!ápatθ* for *tc!ápats* "canoe" (contrast the corresponding *hahátlin^i* form: *t!ápat'*). Here again, one who is afflicted with this speech defect is imitated when addressed; thus, Alex Thomas, before he had caps put on his vestiges of teeth, used to be mocked *kakát' 'win^i*—fashion.

A fifth, not uncommon, speech defect among the Nootka is stuttering. Stutterers, like all other persons who have something abnormal about their speech, are derided by being imitated.

The West Greenland speech defect known as *kutät·oq*[19] is particularly instructive in that an individual speech-peculiarity, which, however, seems to be a common one in the Eskimo settlements along the coast, has become one of the dialectic peculiarities of the northern settlements of the Upernavik district. The *kutät·oq* habit consists in substituting ordinary gutturals (*k-* sounds) for velars (*q-* sounds),

[19] See W. Thalbitzer, "A Phonetical Study of the Eskimo Language," *Meddelelser om Grönland*, 31 (1904): 178–180.

and is evidently due to the greater difficulty of bringing about a contact between the root of the tongue and the velum than farther front in the mouth. This defect, it should be noted, brings with it the confusion of two etymologically distinct series of consonants with resulting grammatical or lexical ambiguities, at least theoretically. In this respect *kutät·oq* forms are parallel to the forms resulting in Nootka from speech defects or the use of consonantal play. Children are particularly apt to be *kutät·oq*, but generally lose the habit as they grow older. However, certain adults, particularly women, always remain *kutät·oq*, whether because of the mere force of habit or because of a physiological or anatomical impediment. As for the Upernavik peculiarity, it seems clear that the *kutät·oq* habit can hardly be due to the individual disability or carelessness of all the members of the district, but that what was originally a speech defect has become socialized into a dialectic peculiarity. The analogy with the forms employed in Nootka in speaking of or addressing certain classes of people that are ill-favoured by nature is striking.

The explanation and genesis of the various types of speech mutilation in Nootka can hardly be more than guessed at, yet certain probabilities, in part already suggested, seem to stand out. In the first place, the use of definite morphological elements to indicate some characteristic of the person spoken to or of (Nootka *-'is* and *-aq'*; Paiute *-tsi-*; Nahuatl *-tzinoa*) needs no particular comment, at least from the purely linguistic point of view. Further, definite points of contact have been established between speech defects and "mocking-forms," with consonantal play, on the one hand, and between the latter and myth-character forms with consonantal play, on the other. I am inclined to believe that the observation of consonant substitutions such as take place, with involuntarily humorous effect, in the speech of those that articulate incorrectly, has set the pace for the consciously humorous use of the same or similar substitutions in both mocking and, directly or indirectly, myth-character forms. The Nootka mocking-forms, with their use of the diminutive affix and of consonant play, represent a combination, both linguistically and psychologically, of the pity and affection symbolized by the use of the diminutive element and of the contempt or jesting attitude implied by the imitation of a speech defect. A myth character whom it is desired to treat humorously may, among other possibilities, be relegated either to the class of poor talkers or to that of nature's step-children. Hence the consonant play of such characters is in part traceable either to speech defects or to mocking-forms. In passing it may be observed that the "enfant terrible" motive is fairly clear in the treatment of many humorous characters of American mythology, and that consonant play may in some cases be taken to symbolize this attitude. The socializing of the *kutät·oq* habit among certain of the Eskimo forcibly suggests the influence of the speech of children as a contributing factor in the creation of myth-character forms. The Kwakiutl Mink is a very likely example of the "enfant terrible," both in action and speech. The possibility should not be lost sight of, of the use of myth-character forms to apply to a class of people or to an individual in ordinary life. This would be an extension of the well-known American Indian habit of comparing one that is marked by some peculiarity of temper or habit with a favourite mythological character.[20]

There is, however, another factor which has undoubtedly exercised a great influence both on the forms of speech used by myth-characters and on the forms peculiar to songs. This is the comic or novel effect produced by the imitation of the speech of foreigners, particularly of such as speak a dialect divergent enough from the home-dialect to be funny or impressive, yet not so different as to be unintelligible and, therefore, lacking in interest. Hence we often find mythological characters in America making use of a neighbouring dialect of the language, as in the case of the Nass River *TxämsEm* and other characters, who talk in the dialect of the Tsimshian proper of Skeena river.[21] Examples of songs whose texts are in a divergent dialect, not to speak of the common use of a totally distinct language, are frequently met with in and out of America. A well-known instance is the use by Melanesian tribes, according to Codrington, of the dialect of some neighbouring tribe for their own song diction; thus, the Melanesians of Mota (Norfolk island of Banks islands) use for their songs the dialect of Saddle island. Also in the clownish episodes of rituals, which are so characteristic of America, the impersonation and imitation of the speech peculiarities of foreigners are often resorted to and never fail to arouse a hearty laugh. In all these cases, it is rather important to observe, real accuracy of imitation is not generally attained or even aimed at, so that the foreign style often tends to reduce itself to a number of conventional vocalic and consonantal displacements. In dealing above with the change of anterior palatal *k-* sounds to *ts-* sounds in the language of the Kwakiutl Mink, I pointed out that a similar change was involved in the passage

[20] A few interesting examples are given by A. Skinner, *Notes on the Eastern Cree and Northern Salteaux*, American Museum of Natural History, Anthropological Papers, 9 (1912): 82.
[21] See Boas, *Tsimshian Texts*, Bureau of American Ethnology, Bulletin 27 (Washington, G. P. O., 1902), pp. 8, 18, 20, 30, 35, 46, 61–64, 78, 171.

of original Wakashan anterior palatal *k*- sounds to Nootka *tc*- sounds. It is just possible that the Mink *ts*- sounds are in such cases due to an imitation of the speech of the northern Nootka tribes. The difficulty with this interpretation is that Nootka and Kwakiutl are altogether too divergent to afford more than a quite inconsiderable number of illustrative cases of the *k*- *tc* change, and of these but few would strike the naïve mind. It seems more plausible, on the whole, to assume that both the Mink and Nootka consonant changes rest on a common Kwakiutl-Nootka tendency, perhaps a tendency on the part of children to pronounce anterior palatals as sibilants. Data on the speech peculiarities of Kwakiutl children would be valuable here.

The Nootka Indians of one tribe frequently imitate the real or supposed speech peculiarities of those belonging to other Nootka tribes, the stress being primarily laid not so much on peculiarities of vocabulary and grammatical form as on general traits of intonation or sound articulation (cf. our New England "nasal twang" and Southern "drawl"). For the purposes of this paper the Nootka now spoken by the *Ts!icá'atн* and *Hōpátc!as'atн* of Barkley sound and the head of Alberni canal may be taken as the normal form of Nootka speech; this is, of course, purely arbitrary, but so would any other point of departure be. It is instructive to note that one or two of these tribal speech peculiarities coincide with individual speech defects.

According to the *Ts!icá'atн* Indians, the нoutcúq'ʟis'atн* tribe of Uchucklesit harbour, a western inlet of Alberni canal, speak or spoke (for there are few of them left now) in a rumbling fashion (ʟ!oʟ!o̜'én*); they are said to use their throat more than the other tribes. The peculiarity referred to seems to be a more than ordinary use of velar resonance, due to a tightening of the passage between the root of the tongue and the velum or perhaps the throat.

The *Hō'ái'atн* Indians of Sarita river and the southern shore of Barkley sound are said to speak ʟ!áʟ!atc!in*, a spluttering effect being apparently referred to. As far as can be made out, their speech peculiarity consists in a more liberal use of *tc* sounds than ordinarily. Thus, according to Alex Thomas, the *Hō'ái'atн* say 'nátcciʟ instead of 'nácciʟ "to look at" (as a matter of fact,this usage is probably etymologically justified, as 'nac- and, in other forms, 'natc- are both used as verb stems in *Ts!icá'atн* itself); instead of pronouncing *tc!ayí'is* "give me water" (*tc!a*- noun stem "water"; -*yī*- verbifying suffix "to give"; -'*is* second person singular imperative with first person singular object) they say something like *tc!atyí'is*, though Alex maintained that it was not a full clear-cut *tc* that was inserted. At any rate, the *Ts!icá'atн* have seized upon the *tc-* insert as a convenient means of poking fun at their *Hōˈái'atн^a* kinsmen, using it in ways that are certainly not, nor meant to be, accurate renderings of the tribal peculiarity. Thus, the tribe itself is humorously referred to as *Hōtcˈái'atн^a*; *Numáqemiyis*, the main inlet of their country, is similarly termed *Nutcmáqemiyis*. Evidently, we have here an example of a mocking usage, based on a tribal peculiarity, that is in form perfectly analogous to certain myth-character and cripple-mocking usages (cf. inserted *x* for Kwatiyāt and inserted *tcн^a* for left-handed people.)

The northern Nootka tribes, beginning with the *La'ókwi'atн^a* of Clayoquot sound and proceeding north, are said to speak *tāнtáнa'*, which refers to a drawling or long drawn out manner of talking. Apparently the peculiarity, which is often imitated in jest, consists not so much in lengthening out vowels as in a somewhat exaggerated rise in pitch towards the end of a sentence, which gives the flow of speech a sliding cadence. The most northern Nootka tribe, the *Tclī'q'Lis'atн^a*, are said to be all stutterers and are accordingly imitated in jest.

In imitating the Nitinats (*Nĭtĭna'atн^a*), a group of Nootka tribes to the south of Barkley sound that speak a very divergent dialect, the meaningless syllable -'*aq'* is always added to the word, as this syllable is supposed to be a very common one in Nitinat. This device is strikingly similar to the use of suffixed -*aq'* for large persons.

The real old *Hōpátclas'atн^a* Indians, whose earliest homes were in the interior of the island along Somass river and about Sproat and Great Central lakes, were said to talk *tsíska'*, that is, to confound *s* and *c* sounds. As we have seen, this is also a well-recognized individual speech defect among the Nootka. In the case of the *Hōpátclas'atн^a*, the *tsíska'* habit was simply due to the fact that they carried over into Nootka speech a linguistic peculiarity found in the Salish dialect which they originally spoke (a dialect apparently identical with or closely related to Boas' Pénlatc; recognized as *PinLlá'atc* by Tyee Bob, the leading man among the *Hōpátclas'atн^a* to-day and whose father is still remembered to have spoken *tsíska'*).

As for the *Tslicá'atн^a* themselves, they are said by the other tribes to talk very fast. If one anywhere among the Nootka Indians talks too fast, the proverbial saying is that he is a *Tslicá'atн^a*.

It will, as we have seen, have to be admitted, that mocking forms for various classes of people are connected not only with speech defects and mythological devices, but, to a large extent, also with tribal speech peculiarities.

Finally, the possibility of a direct psychological relation between the consonant change and the type of individual or attitude it symbolizes should not be summarily ruled out of court. That such an association once established by historical causes will be felt as a direct and simple psychological association is quite obvious, also that it may become productive, by analogy, of further associations of a related sort. I would, however, even be inclined to suppose, though proof may be difficult or impossible, that certain associations of sound and character or form arose more or less spontaneously, or, to put it more correctly, by virtue of the inherent associative value of the otherwise unconnected phenomena in the mind of a particular individual or group of individuals. Such an individual association, if given outward expression, can become socialized in the same way in which any individual idea becomes socialized. The type of association here thought of is quite parallel to the sound-colour associations familiar enough in psychology. It may be not uninteresting as a psychological datum to note that the writer himself feels, or thinks he feels, the intrinsically diminutive or augmentative value of certain consonant changes in Wishram. Moreover, the association of c- consonants with humpbackedness in Nootka seems not so far-fetched after all. The thickish quality of these consonants, together with the protrusion of the lower jaw in pronouncing them, suggests to me the same squat clumsiness as the image of a hunchback. All this may, of course, be merely auto-suggestion *ad hoc.*

To summarize, evidence has been presented of the historical connexion between various linguistic and stylistic processes involving the symbolic use of sounds. These are diminutive and augmentative forms of speech, mocking-forms, myth-character and animal forms, and song forms. Moreover, further evidence has been presented to show the historical connexion of these quite specialized tricks of language with the far simpler phenomena of speech defects, children's language, and imitation of the phonetic peculiarities of foreigners. The direct association of some of the former with the types they symbolize, after the manner of primary association betwen data of distinct sense, has also been suggested as a possibility.[22]

PHONETIC KEY

a, short as in German *Mann; e*, short and open as in English *met; i*, short and open as in English *it; o* short and open as in German *voll; u*, short and open as in English *put; ę*, short and close as in French *été; i*, short and close as in French *fini; ǫ*, short and close as in French *chaud.*

ā, long as in German *Bahn; ē*, long and close as in German *See; ī*, long and

---

[22] A table published in the original version, listing the linguistic classes described in the paper, is not reproduced here.—ED.

close as in German *Sie; ō,* long and close as in German *roh; ê,* long and open as in French *fête; ŏ,* long and open as in English *saw,* yet with back of tongue not so low.

E (Kwakiutl), short obscure vowel like *e* of German *Rose; I* (Nootka), short open *i*-vowel of rather unclear quality; *ⁱ* (Nootka), occurring as syllabic final after *n* and *m,* barely articulated or murmured (yet not voiceless or whispered) *I; ᵃ* (Nootka), denotes *a*-timbre of preceding *H* (see below).

c, like *sh* in English *ship: tc,* corresponding voiceless affricative, *ch* of English *church* (in Nahuatl *ch* is used for *tc*); *dj,* corresponding voiced affricative, *j* of English *joy; s* and *ts,* as in English *sit* and *hats* (in Nahuatl *z* and *tz* are respectively used instead); *š* and *tš,* palatal voiceless sibilant and affricative, acoustically midway between *s-c* and *ts-tc* respectively; *ç* and *tç, c* and *tc* pronounced with lower teeth in front of upper; *θ,* interdental voiceless spirant, like *th* in English *thin.*

q, voiceless velar stop like Semitic *qōf; qw,* labialized form of same; *x,* voiceless spirant of *q*-position; *x̣,* voiceless spirant of *k*-position, not pronounced as far back as German *ch* of *Bach; k·* and *g·* (Kwakiutl), anterior palatal stops (pala· talized k-stops), approximately *ky* and *gy; x·* (Kwakiutl), voiceless spirant of *k·*-position, *ch* of German *ich; η,* voiced nasal of *k*- position, *ng* of English *sing; ɲ* (Eskimo), voiced nasal of *q*- position.

ł, voiceless lateral spirant; *L,* corresponding voiceless lateral affricative (written *tl* in Nahuatl); *Ł* (Kwakiutl), corresponding voiced affricative.

', glottal stop; *!*(Nootka), strangulated-sounding laryngeal stop, similar in resonance to Arabic *'ain; H* (Nootka), strangulated-sounding laryngeal spirant, Arabic *ḥa; ',* aspiration or breath-release of preceding vowel or consonant (*p',* *t', k',* and *q'* are aspirated voiceless stops); *!* denotes glottalized stops and affricatives (*p!, t!, k!, q!, L!, ts!, tc!, tš!, tç!, k·!*), that is, such as are pronounced with simultaneous closure of glottis, but with oral release prior to that of glottal release. All other consonants as in English.

', stress accent; *˙,* denotes preceding long consonant (except in Kwakiutl *k·*-sounds); *ˌ,* denotes nasalization of vowel under which it is placed; *+,* denotes excessive length of preceding vowel or consonant.

A CHINOOKAN PHONETIC LAW*

It is the purpose of this paper to show how the operation of a phonetic law, hitherto unnoticed, brought about a number of irregularities in the use of pronominal elements in Chinookan. Certain incidental inferences on more fundamental points of Chinookan linguistic history also suggest themselves. These will be briefly referred to at the end of the paper.

If we examine the Chinookan system of transitive and intransitive pronominal prefixes of the verb and corresponding possessive prefixes of the noun[1], we shall note three apparently unrelated irregular features which involve an alternation of g (which may be modified to k or $k\chi$[2]) and the palatal sibilant affricate tc. These are as follows:

1. The possessive prefix for the third person singular feminine ("her") is -ga- when the noun itself is feminine, neuter, dual, or plural, i.e. is preceded by the gender-number prefixes:

	Lower Chinook	Wishram[3]
sing. fem.	$\bar{o}$-	(w) a-
neut.	L-	$i\dot{t}$-
du.	c-, s-	ic-, is-
plur.	t-	id- (it-)

but is -tca- when the noun itself is masculine, i.e. is preceded by the gender-number prefix:

masc. sing.	$\bar{e}$-, i-	$(w)i$-

Examples (Wishram dialect) are:

Absolute		Possessive: "Her"
wa-$ska'n$	cup	a-ga'-$skan$
$i\dot{t}$-$tcqwa'$	water	$i\dot{t}$-ga'-cq
is-$qxu's$	eyes	is-ga'-xus
$i't$-q^uli	house	it-ga'-q^ul
		($-k\delta'$-q^ul)

but:

wi'-$lxam$	village	i-tca'-$lxam$

---

* *International Journal of American Linguistics*, 4 (1926): 105–110.
[1] See F. Boas, "Chinook" in his *Handbook of American Indian Languages*, Bureau of American Ethnology, Bulletin 40, pt. I (Washington, G. P. O., 1911), pp. 559–677, particularly pages 580, 581, and 585.
[2] For consistency's sake I am preserving Boas' Chinook and my own Wishram orthography without modification.
[3] An Upper Chinookan dialect. I quote from my MS data

2. The possessive prefix for the first person singular ("my") is -gE- (Wishram -g-, -k-; -x̱- before k-stops) when the noun is feminine, neuter, dual, or plural, but -tcE-, -tcî- (Wishram -tc-) when the noun is masculine. Lower Chinook (C.) and Wishram (W.) examples are:

ABSOLUTE		POSSESSIVE: "MY"
C. ō'-ᴘʟ!îke	bow	ō-gu'-ᴘʟ!îkē (-gu- labialized from -gE- because of preceding ō-)
W. a-knî'm	canoes	a-x̱-knî'm
C.		ʟ-gE'-qacqac my grandfather
W. is-qxu's	eyes	is-k-xu's
W. i't-pc	feet	i't-k-pc

but:

C. i-ts!E'mEnō	wooden spoon	i-tcE'-ts!EmEnō
W. wi'-łq	body	i'-tc-łq

3. Aside from certain secondary irregularities in the third person dual and third person plural which do not concern us here, the pronominal subject of the transitive verb differs from the pronominal subject of the intransitive verb (and pronominal object of the transitive verb) only in the case of the third person singular masculine and third person singular feminine, the difference between the two sets of forms being for the most part indicated by position (the subjective pronominal prefix preceding the objective pronominal prefix) and, in part, by the use of a "postpronominal" particle -g- which indicates that the preceding pronominal element is used as the subject of a transitive verb. For "he" (and "him") and "she" (and "her"), however, the following distinctive forms are used:

TRANSITIVE		INTRANSITIVE	
3d person singular, masc.		tc- he	i-he, him
fem.		g- she	a-she, her

The forms will be better understood from the following Wishram examples:

i-tc-i'-uwaq   he killed him (i- is temporal; tc- "he"; -i- "him")
i'-ipx̱   he comes out of the house (i- "he")
i-g-i'-uwaq   she killed him (-g- "she")
a'-tpx̱   she comes out of the house (a- "she")
    Contrast:
i-m-i'-uwaq   you (sing.) killed him (-m- "thou")
a-m-tha'y-a   you will come out of the house (a- is temporal)

i-tc-m-u'woq he killed you,
in which *-m-* "thou, thee" is used both as transitive subject and as intransitive subject and transitive object.

How are we to explain these irregularities? The distribution of the forms in question is such as to make it probable that we are dealing with a phonetic factor rather than a morphological one in the first instance. Cases 1 and 2 are parallel phonetically:

1. *a-ga-* "her" (fem. noun): *i-tca-* "her" (masc. noun)
2. *a-g-* "my" (fem. noun): *i-tc-* "my" (masc. noun)

and suggest at once that the masculine prefix *i-* palatalized the older *-ga-* "her", *-g*(ᴇ)· "my", to *-tca-*, *-tc*(ᴇ)-, perhaps via palatalized *k*-sounds (*-*ga̯-*, *-*gɔ̯-*). But how account for the forms in case 3 (fem. *g-*: masc. *tc-*), and why should only these forms be exclusively characteristic of the subjective transitive verbal paradigm? If we venture to reconstruct them in accordance with cases 1 and 2, we get:

ag- "she" (transitive subject)
itc- "he" (transitive subject)

$$< \text{*}ig\text{-}$$

The phonetic parallelism would then be perfect in the three cases. If we compare the theoretical forms *ag-* "she" and *itc-* "he" with the remaining subjective forms of the transitive verb, we obtain at once a perfectly regular and intelligible set of forms. Including the "post-pronominal" *-g-*, the system is as follows:

1st pers. sing.	*n-*
exclusive dual	*nt-g-*
exclusive plural	*nc-g-* (also heard as *ntc-g-*, with *t*-glide)
inclusive dual	*tx-g-* (simplified in Wishram to *t-g-*)
inclusive plural	*lx-g* (simplified in Wishram to *l-g-*)
2nd pers. sing.	*m-*
dual	*mt-g-*
plural	*mc-g-*
3d pers. sing. masc.	* *i-tc-* < * *i-g-*
sing. fem.	* *a-g-*
sing. neut.	*l-g-*
dual.	*c-g-*
plural	*t-g-*

Compare these pronominal prefixes with the corresponding intransitive subjects (and transitive objects):

1st pers. sing.	*n-*
exclusive dual	*nt-* (*nd-*)
exclusive plural	*nc-* (*ntc-*)
inclusive dual	*tx-*
inclusive plural	*lx-*
2nd pers. sing.	*m-*
dual	*mt-* (*md-*)
plural	*mc-*
3d pers. sing. masc.	*i-* (*y-* before vowels)
sing. fem.	*a-*
sing. neuter	*ł-*
dual	*c-* (in certain cases *ct-*, *cd-*)
plural	*t-* (in certain cases *u-gwa-*, Lower C. *o-gō-*)

Aside from the irregular intransitive subjective (not objective) forms in the third person dual and plural (*ct-*; *u-gwa-*), whose use is limited to certain cases, the transitive paradigm obviously derives from the intransitive by the addition of a transitivizing particle -*g-* to the pronominal element, except in the first person singular (*n-*) and second person singular (*m-*), in which cases position alone differentiates the transitive and intransitive subjective uses. If our analysis is correct, the actual transitive subjects for the third person singular, masc. *tc-* and fem. *g-*, are not true pronominal forms in origin; the older pronominal elements, *i-* and *a-* respectively, still in evidence in the intransitive paradigm, have disappeared as such but have left their trace in the different treatment of the old transitivizing -*g-*, which now appears in twofold form and with transferred function as *tc-* "he" and *g-* "she."

We may therefore reasonably infer that in all three cases what now appears as a peculiar morphological alternation of *g* : *tc* is really a survival of an old phonetic law, according to which *g* (*k*) was palatalized by immediately preceding *i* to anterior palatal *g̒* (*k̒*), which in turn shifted at an early period of Chinook history to *tc*. Presumably an old *ik̒! shifted to *itc!*, but I have no evidence of this. The law is no longer operative as such. It had run its course long before Chinookan split up into its present dialects, its consequences are now of a strictly functional character, and its operation was probably checked at an early period by analogical leveling. There may at one time have been such alternations as *i-tca'la* "man" : *it-ka'lukc* "men" or *n-i'-tcim* "he said" : *n-a'-kim* "she said", which were then leveled out to the forms

i-ka'la: *it-ka'lukc*, *n-i'-kim*: *n-a'-kim* that we now possess. But there is
nothing to prove this and it is more probable that the phonetic law had
ceased to operate before the welding of noun and verb stems with
pronominal and with gender-number class prefixes. It is not at all
unlikely that such elements as *i-*, *wi-* of masculine nouns and *n-i-*, *n-a-*
of verb forms were independent elements or assemblages of elements
(e.g. **w-i* "he"; **n-i* "then-he", **n-a* "then-she"), which became attached to noun and verb stems at a comparatively recent date. On the
other hand, we must assume that such assemblages as **i-tca* < **i-ga*
"hers" (masc.), **i-tcə* < **i-gə* "mine" (masc.), and **i-tcə* < **i-gə* "he"
(transitive subject), **a-gə* "she" (transitive subject) and **c-gə* "they
two" (transitive subject) formed firm units at a much earlier date.
Within such units the phonetic law could operate but not outside of
them.

Comparative evidence, making use of data outside of Chinookan,
may some day succeed in confirming our phonetic law by showing that
certain cases of *tc* in stems go back to *g* (*k*) after *i* (say *-itc*, fem., "tail
of quadruped"), but at present we cannot do this. So far I know of
only one other case of *tc* which may be presumed, with some plausibility,
to derive from palatalized *k*. This is Upper Chinook *-i-tc(i)*, which
forms personal plurals of demonstrative and personal pronouns, e.g.
Kathlamet Lа-*i-tci* "those" (indef.), *ta-i-tci* "those" (def.), based on
pronominal stems Lа- "it", *ta-* "they"; Wishram *da'-i-tc*, *la'-i-tc*, *a'i-tc*
"they", based on pronominal stems *da-* "they", *la-* "it", *a-* "she";
Wishram *da'uda-i-tc* "these people", *la'xia-i-tc* "yon (indef.) people",
based on demonstrative *da'uda*, *la'xia*[4]. This suffix corresponds morphologically to *-kc*, *-di-kc*, *-i-kc* of other forms (e.g. nominal plural
-kc in cases like W. *it-ka'-lu-kc* "men"; W. *la'it!i-kc* "they too", cf.
la'it!a "it too"; *da'-ima-di-kc* "they alone", cf. *da'ima*; Kathlamet
tatā-i-kc "these people", cf. *talā'-x* "these"). Presumably Upper Chinook
-i-kc is umlauted from older **-a-kc* < **-a-ki-c* (cf. *la'it!a*: *la'it!i-kc*;
-di-kc < **da-ki-c*, personal plural in **-ki-c* of *da-* "they"). In Lower
Chinook plural forms in *-kc*, *-ikc*, and *-tikc* occur plentifully with nouns,
both animate and inanimate (e.g. L-*q!ēLxā'pu-kc* "coats", *t-iā'-gala-i-kc*
"his fins", *iā'wux-ti-kc* "his younger brothers"), but not with demonstrative or personal pronouns. The Lower Chinook suffix for personal
plurals in the demonstrative is *-c* (e.g. *x·īta-c* "those people", visible,
qōta-c "yon people", invis.), probably the same element as the *-c-* of
prefixed *nc-* "we" (excl.) and *mc-* "ye" (cf. *n-* "I", *m-* "thou"). The best

---

[4] Boas, *op. cit.*, pp. 623, 625, 627.

way to explain the various plural suffixes in Chinookan seems to be to
assume an old element *ki, preserved in palatalized form in Upper
Chinook -i-tc(i); a plural element -c; and a double plural -kc < *-ki-c.

Another survival of the old *-ki plural may be Lower C. ʟ-a-tct
"mothers" < *l-a-ki-t: ʟ-aa "mother".

The data presented in this paper suggest a number of further problems, which we can hardly do more than touch upon.

1. The disappearance of *i- and *a- in the old forms *itc(ə)- "he"
and *agə- "she" is merely an early phase of a phenomenon that seems
to have been characteristic of Chinookan at all times, the loss of short
unaccented vowels. The accent of Chinook is a strongly expiratory one,
seems to have been regulated by morphological considerations (contrast W. galu'pa "she went out of the house" with aluba'ya "she will
go out of the house"; future -a, as shown also by Lower Chinook evidence, shifts the accent forward), and has left in its train a number of
phonetic consequences, both early and dialectic, the chief of which are
the disappearance of short vowels (cf. vowelless stems like -lq "body",
-tcktc "to wash"; alternations like n- "I", as verb prefix, with independent na'-, W. -g- "my" with Lower C. -gᴇ'-; loss of final vowels
which reappear in protected forms, e.g. Lower C. i-sā'mᴇl' "lid" <
*-sa'məlga: ʟ-iā'-sᴇmᴇlqa-ks "their lids" < *-saməʾlqa-), the shortening
of unaccented and the lengthening of accented vowels (e.g. Lower C.
*i-cā'yim "grizzly bear": plur. ʟ-cayā'm-u-kc < early Chinook *ca'yam:
*caya'm-), and the weakening of consonants after unaccented vowels
(cf. above examples of W. 'p: b'; Lower C. 'q:'g').

2. As regards the old unaccented *i- and *a- which we must suppose
to have disappeared before transitivizing *-gə-, we may note that it is
characteristic of all transitive forms that the pronominal subject is
unaccented, while in many instances the intransitive subject receives
the accent. Lower Chinook seems to preserve the old accentual conditions better than the upper dialects, which have undergone further
shifts of accent with resulting loss of reduced vowels (e.g. Lower C.
atcᴇ'tax "he made them": W. gatctúx). A good example of such accentual
alternation is Lower C. ʟᴇ'- "it" (intr. subj.): ʟ- "it" (tr. subj.) in
aʟᴇ'nkatka "it comes flying above me": aʟgigᴇ'ltcxᴇm "it sings for
him[5]". This is not the place to pursue the matter further, but we may
at least point out that the transitivizing *-gə- is in all probability identical with the -gᴇ- of the "adverbial prefixes" -gᴇ-l- "for, on account of"
and -gᴇ-m- "with, near". It is remarkable that the pronominal element (indirect object) to which -gᴇl- and -gᴇ̇m- are suffixed never receives the accent,

---

[5] Boas, *op. cit.*, p. 588.

which either strikes the -ɢᴇ- or some syllable following it. In other words, the treatment of pronominal element + transitivizing *-gə- and that of pronominal element + indirective -ɢᴇl-, -ɢᴇm- are parallel. But note that the pronominal element (indirect object) is frequently, even typically, accented before the "adverbial prefix" (really postposition) -l- "to, for", with which -ɢᴇl- is compounded; e.g. W. *inia'lut* "I gave it (masc.) to her," Lower C. ʟā'lōc "it was to her". If -l- and -ɢᴇl- were strictly parallel elements, it should be possible to have such parallel forms as *a'-l-* "to her" and *a'-ɢᴇl-* "for her", whereas we consistently have *a'-l-* "to her" but *a-ɢᴇ'l-* or *a-ɢᴇl-'* "for her." This can only mean that -l- and -ɢᴇl- are not morphologically parallel, but that -ɢᴇ- is an element which somehow displaces the pronoun and draws the accent to itself. Its power to take the accent away from preceding elements is further indicated by the fact that it regularly occurs with voiced g, not with voiceless k or affricative kx (cf. remarks in 1.).

What is this old element *-gə'-, which now appears as transitivizing -g(ᴇ)-, as third person singular masculine and feminine transitive subject (*tc*[ᴇ]- "he", *g*(ᴇ)- "she"), and as first component of the verb prefixes -ɢᴇl- "for" and -ɢᴇm "with"? It seems likely that it is an old demonstrative or deictic stem which is either predicatively related to the preceding pronominal element or which serves to emphasize or displace the pronominal element and to which the postposition (-l-, *-m-) is attached as an enclitic. A cluster of elements like *i-ɢᴇl-* "for him" originally meant *i-ɢᴇ'-l-* "him *-that one*-to, for *him*". Similarly, at a far earlier stage, a transitive cluster like *t-ɢᴇ'-n-* (W. *t-g-n-'*) "they (subj.) -me (obj.) " or **i-ɢᴇ'-m-* > **i-tcᴇ'-m-* > *tcᴇ'-m-* (W. tc-m-') "he (subj.) -thee (obj.)" really indicated "they-*that* (it is) -me", "he -*that* (it is) -thee." If this is correct, the original difference between the intransitive and transitive phrase must have been one of sentence idiom. "He goes" was expressed as "*he* goes," but "he kills her" as "he *that* (*is*) (who) kills her."

This deictic or demonstrative *gə'- can only be a reduced form of post-accentual -ka, which occurs freely in Chinookan numerals, pronouns, and adverbs as deictic element ("only, just"). Examples are W. *i'xt-ka* "just one," *na'i-ka* "I," *a'x-ka* "she," Lower C. *nā'm-ka* "I alone," *ē'-ka* "thus," *kawa't-ka* "soon," *nau'it-ka* "indeed," W. *iwa't-ka* "to yon (place)." This deictic *'-ka*, in turn, is obviously merely an enclitic use of an old demonstrative stem *ka* "that" which is no longer in free Chinookan use but which survives in Lower C. *ka*, *c-ka* "and" and as petrified temporal *ka-* "that (time)" in Lower C. *ka-wa't-ka* "soon" (< "to just that [time]", parallel in form to W. *i-wa't-*

ka "to just yon [place]") and *ka-wī'x·* "early" (cf. *wux'ī'* "tomorrow," W. *wax* "dawning"); cf. also W. tense prefix *ga-*, *ga-l-* of remote past time. All these Chinookan elements (*ka*, *ka-*, *-ka*; *ga-*; *-g*ᴇ-), finally, are reflexes of a wide-spread demonstrative stem **ka* "that," often used as a general term of reference, found in other Penutian languages (e.g. Coos *-kä* in *xä-kä* "he"; Takelma *ga* "that"; Yokuts *ka* "that" [viz.]; Miwok *i-ka* "that"; Tsimshian *-g*ᴇ absent connective, *-ga'* absent demonstrative added to final noun in sentence).

3. It is fairly clear that the two fundamental factors in the development of the somewhat irregular morphology of Chinookan were a strong and movable stress accent and, as a result of this, the tendency for vowels to drop out and for originally independent elements to melt together into complex assemblages. Thus the old sentence, which seems to have been constructed on rather simple, analytical, lines, tended more and more to petrify into a highly synthetic sentence-word. We have already hinted at the probability that the phonetic change of *g* to *tc* antedated the inclusion of certain elements in the verb. Internal evidence makes it practically certain that at least the tense prefixes were late in coming into the verb complex. In the first place, the tense prefixes of Lower Chinook differ considerably from those of the upper dialects,[6] so that it looks as though an old set of temporal particles or adverbs (Lower C. *a*; *n-*; W. *a*, *a-l*; *i*, *i-g*; *na*, *na-l*; *ni*, *ni-g*; *ga*, *ga-l*; *n-*) had coalesced with the following pronominal prefixes of the verb in the independent life of the various dialects. Moreover, these elements do not behave as though they had ever coalesced into a phonetic group with the early Chinookan forms of the transitive forms for "he" (**itcə-*) and "she" (**agə-*). Thus, in Wishram we have forms like *i-g-i'-ux* "she made him," in which the tense prefix *i-* does not palatalize the following *-g-* to *-tc-*, no doubt because it did not enter into the verb complex until long after the palatalizing effect of an *i-* had spent its force. If the *i-* had been prefixed at the time that the pronominal element *g-* "she" still existed in the fuller form **agə-*, it would have required an intervocalic *-g-* and the form **ig-agə'-* would have arisen (cf. modern forms like *ig-a'- -tpa* "she came out of the house"). Similarly, a form like Lower Chinook *atc*ᴇ*'tax* "he made them" evidently arose before the tense prefix *a-* was part of the verb complex, for *a-* could not have palatalized an original **-gə-* to **tcə-*, while the older pronominal form **itcə-* would have required as tense prefix the prevocalic *n-*, hence **n-itcə'-*.

4. It is a well known linguistic phenomenon that similar or identical

[6] Boas, *op. cit.*, pp. 577–579.

sounds, groupings of sounds into phonetic patterns, or phonetic processes may characterize a number of independent languages or even linguistic stocks within a continuous area. Such examples are suggestive of phonetic interinfluences between distinct languages presumably through the medium of bilinguals. The change of *g* or *k* to *dj* or *tc* because of the palatalizing influence of a preceding or following front vowel (*i* or *e*) is perhaps too general a process to warrant our attaching much importance to its occurrence in a number of contiguous languages. Nevertheless it is of some interest, and, it may be, of historical significance, to point out that the change of *k*- sounds or of palatalized *k*-sounds to *tc*- sounds is found in a continuous or nearly continuous area from a northern point on the west coast of Vancouver Island south to the mouth of the Columbia. All the Nootka dialects, both Nootka proper and Nitinat-Makah, have altered the original Wakashan anterior palatal *k*- sounds, preserved in Kwakiutl, to corresponding palatal sibilant affricatives; Kwakiutl *g·* (*g̣*) and *k·* (*ḳ*) appear as Nootka *tc*; *k·!* (*ḳ'*) as *tc'*; and *x* (*x̣*) as *c*. A large number of Salish dialects, furthermore, have altered the original unlabialized *k*-sounds to *tc*-sounds. I am quoting Dr. Boas' personal statement on this point and am unable to give the geographical distribution of the Salish *tc*-dialects. I should perhaps add that the Lower Chinook *k·*- (*ḳ*-) sounds, which correspond to ordinary *k*- sounds in Wishram, are a comparatively recent dialectic development before *i*-vowels and that they have nothing whatever to do with the old, general Chinookan, change of *g* to *tc* after *i*-vowels which is the subject of this paper.

MALE AND FEMALE FORMS OF SPEECH
IN YANA*

IT IS A well known peculiarity of some languages that they distinguish forms used by males from those that are used by females. This peculiarity has, of course, nothing to do with gender. In this paper I propose to call attention to the sex forms of Yana, a language of northern California which is (or was) spoken in four distinct dialects—Northern, Central, Southern, and Yahi. It is the first two dialects which will be utilized here, though the main facts apply to all four of them.[1] There are probably few languages which carry the distinction between male and female forms so far as Yana. The facts presented in this paper will therefore, I hope, prove of general interest to students of language and of linguistic psychology.

In order to clear the ground, it may be pointed out that there is no gender in Yana. On the other hand, there is a small number of verb stems which apply exclusively to activity carried on by a male or by a female; e.g., *ni-*, *nī-* "a male goes" but *'a-* "a female goes," *bu-ri-*, *bu-rī-* "a man dances" but *dja-ri*, *dja-rī-* "a woman dances." In the latter case the difference of verb probably reflects an actual difference in the style of dancing. Furthermore, a number of verbs implying a more or less abnormal kind of appearance add a suffixed *-yai-* when the reference is to a female, e.g. *lulmai-'a-* "to be blind" (of a male), but *lulmai-yai-'a-* "to be blind" (of a female). This *-yai-* is the incorporated form of the suffixed element *-ya* "female," which is common in nouns, e.g. *k!ūwi* "medicine-man" but *k!uwi-ya* "medicine-woman," *bai-djū-si* "male hunter" but *bai-djū-ya* "female hunter."

The great majority of Yana words have two forms, the full or male form and the reduced or female form. The terms "male" and "female" are not entirely adequate, for the male forms are used only by males in speaking to males, while the female forms are used by females in speaking to males or females and by males in speaking to females. In other words, the female forms are used about three times as frequently as the male forms. There is apparently no question of the male forms being

* St. W. J. Teeuwen, ed., *Donum Natalicium Schrijnen* (Nijmegen-Utrecht, 1929) pp. 79–85.
[1] For data on Yana, see E. Sapir, *Yana Texts*, Univ. Calif. Publ. Am. Arch. and Ethn., 9 (1910): 1–235; *The Position of Yana in the Hokan Stock*, ibid., 13 (1917): 1–34; *Yana Terms of Relationship*, ibid., 13 (1918): 153–173; *The Fundamental Elements of Northern Yana*, ibid., 13 (1922): 215–234; *Text Analyses of Three Yana Dialects*, ibid., 20 (1923): 263–294. The Yana orthography here used is explained in these papers.

tabooed to the females, for a female uses the male forms without hesitation when she quotes the words of a male speaking to a male, as in relating a myth in which one male character speaks to another.

There seem to be two distinct methods of distinguishing male and female forms, depending on specific phonetic and grammatical factors. The male form may be identical with the absolute, or theoretically fundamental, form of the word, in which case the female form is derived from it by phonetic reduction of the final syllable; or the female form may be identical with the theoretically fundamental form of the word, in which case the male form is derived from it by the addition of a syllable which varies from one formal category to another. In either case the male form is longer than the female form. The interrogative shows rather peculiar sex contrasts, as we shall see later. It should be carefully observed that the formal sex differences apply to complete words only, not to stems or suffixed elements as such. Thus, the male *'au-na* "fire," *'au-'nidja* "my fire," corresponds to the female *'au'* "fire," *'au-'nitc'* "my fire"; the contrast between *'au-na* and *'au'* ceases to operate as soon as a suffixed element (e.g. "my") is added to the absolute or thematic form *'au-*. Similarly, the male *k/ūwi* "medicine-man," *k/ūwi-ya* "medicine-woman," corresponds to the female *k/ūwⁱ* (*-wi* has here become voiceless *w* followed by voiceless *i*, or voiceless *w* with *i-* timbre), *k/ūwi-yᵃ* (*-ya* has become voiceless *y* with *a-* timbre); the contrast between *k/ūwi* and *k/uwⁱ* is of no interest in the form "medicine-woman" because the suffixed *-ya* protects the element *k/ūwi-* from reduction.

It will naturally be impossible to give a complete account in this paper of all the rules of formation of sex forms, as this would involve too much grammatical detail. All we can do is to illustrate the main lines of phonetic and morphological contrast.

One great class consists of all non-monosyllabic nominal and many verbal forms in which the absolute form, which is also the male form, ends in a short vowel (*a, i, u*; but not *e, o*). The corresponding female form unvoices the final vowel and also the preceding consonant, if it is not already voiceless. The "intermediate" or "voiceless lenis" stops (*b, d, g, dj*) become aspirated tenues (*p', t', k', tc'*). Hence a female form of type *-t'ⁱ* may be reduced from either *-t'i* or *-di*; e.g. male *ni-sā-t'i*, female *ni-sā-t'ⁱ*, "it is said he goes away," male *p'adi*, female *p'at'ⁱ*, "place."

The following table of male and female finals covers the actual cases, *-a* standing for *-a, -i,* or *-u*:

	MALE	FEMALE
Glottal stop	-'a	-'ᵃ
Intermediate stops	-ba -da -ga -dja	-p'ᵃ -t'ᵃ -k'ᵃ -tc'ᵃ
Aspirated tenues	-p'a -t'a -k'a -tc'a	-p'ᵃ -t'ᵃ -k'ᵃ -tc'ᵃ
Glottalized stops	-p!a -t!a -k!a ts!a	-p!ᵃ -t!ᵃ -k!ᵃ -ts!ᵃ
Spirants	-ha, -xa -sa, -ca	-xᵃ -sᵃ, -cᵃ
Semivowels	-wa -ya	-wᵃ -yᵃ
Liquids and nasals	-la -ra -ma -na	-lᵃ, -l'ᵃ -rᵃ -mᵃ, -m'ᵃ -nᵃ, -n'ᵃ
Liquids and nasals preced. by glottal stop	-'la -'ma -'na	-'lᵃ, -l'ᵃ -'mᵃ, -m'ᵃ -'nᵃ, -n'ᵃ

Examples are:

MALE	FEMALE
mô'i "to eat"	mô'ⁱ
imamba "deer liver"	imamp'ᵃ
wawip!a "little house"	wawip!ᵃ
sigāga "quail"	sigāk'ᵃ
gāgi "crow"	gāk'ⁱ
mal'gu "ear"	mal'k'ᵘ
p'adja "snow"	p'atc'ᵃ
mits!li "coyote"	mits!ˡⁱ
dāha "river"	dāxᵃ
'īsi "man"	'īsⁱ
cūcu "dog, horse"	cūcᵘ
ts!orêwa "elk"	ts!orêwᵃ
'iya "trail"	'īyᵃ
wêyu "horn"	wêyᵘ
'ī'lala "star"	'ī'lalᵃ
īwūlu "inside"	īwūlᵘ
wak!āra "moon"	wak!ārᵃ
p'att!ama "bird sp."	p'att!am'ᵃ
ba'nīnu "dentalia"	ba'nīn'ᵘ
'ak!āli'li "lake"	'ak!ālil'ⁱ
mari'mi "woman"	mari'mⁱ

Very few types have a final glottal stop preceded by vowel in the absolute and male form. The best example is the ending of the mild imperative, -*magara'*, which forms -*magar'ᵃ* in the female form, e.g., *t'immagarᵃ'* "pray tell him!" female *t'immagar'ᵃ*.

A peculiar sub-type of the first main class of forms is the second person singular in -*numa* (male), e.g. *t'īsi'numa* "you say," *t'imsiwa'-numa* "you are said to, he says to you," *'au'numa* "your fire." The parallel female form is not *-*num'ᵃ*, as might be expected, but simply -*nu*. But the male form is not to be analyzed as absolute -*nu* plus male element -*ma*, in accordance with the second class of forms, but as identical with an absolute -*numa*. This is clear from the fact that -*numa* must be presupposed for both male and female forms in the interrogative, e.g. male *t'īsi'numán* "do you say?" female *t'īsi'numā̃*. The final -*ma*, moreover, occurs without preceding -*nu*- in such forms as male *t'imsiwā'ma* "I say to you," female *t'imsiwā'mᵃ*.

The second class of forms includes all noun forms which do not end in a short vowel in the theme, all monosyllabic noun themes, demonstratives, and a large number of verb forms. All these forms are characterized by an added male syllable. All nouns whose themes end in a long vowel (*ā, ī, ū, ê, ô*), a diphthong (*ai, au, ui*), or a consonant, and all monosyllabic noun themes, suffix -*na* in the male form, but are unchanged in the female form except for a breath release (-'). Examples are:

MALE	FEMALE
'i-na "tree, stick"	'i'
yu-na "shelled acorn"	yu'
ba-na "deer'	ba'
yā-na "person"	yā'
yūtc'ai-na "acorn mush"	yūtc'ai'
'ik!īwau-na "moccasin"	'ik!īwau'
'itc!in-na "wildcat"	{ 'itc!in' (Central) { 'itc!it' (Northern)
t'en'-na "grizzly bear"	t'et'

The rule is slightly obscured in certain cases by the operation of phonetic laws: e.g. syllabically final *n* and *m*, unless protected by immediately following nasal, become *t* and *p* in the Northern dialect; further, *t'* and *p'* become voiceless nasals plus glottal stop before nasal consonants. If the theme ends in *l* or voiceless *l'*, the suffix -*na* becomes assimilated to -*la*; e.g. male *dal-la* "hand," female *dal'*. In the Yahi dialect *-na* (*-la*) is used in certain cases (e.g. male, *'au-na* "fire"), *-hi* in others (e.g. male *yā-hi* "person").

The demonstratives, which end in *-e*, add *-'e* to form the male forms. Thus, male *aidje'e* "that one," female *aidje*; male *aiye'e* "that one yonder," female *aiye*; male *aige'e* "(to) that one yonder," female *aige*.

A considerable number of forms, chiefly verbal, add *-'a* or *-'i* to the absolute form, which is used by females. Among these are:

1. Third person future *-si-'i*, e.g. male *t'ūsi'i* "he will do," female *t'ūsi*. Contrast male *t'ūsi* "he does," female *t'ūsⁱ*.

2. First person future *-sik!ô-'a*, e.g. male *t'ūsik!ô'a* "I shall do," female *t'ūsik!ô*.

3. Third person usitative *-ma-'a*, e.g. male *t'ūma'a* "he is accustomed to do," female *t'ūma*.

4. Third person dubitative *-k!u-'i*, e.g. male *nisāk!u'i* "he might go away," female *nisāk!u*.

5. Third person passives in *-wa-'a*, e.g. male *ap'djīsiwa'a* "he is killed," female *ap'djīsiwa*.

6. Certain third person contracted causative forms, e.g.:

	PRIMARY		CAUSATIVE
Future............................	Male	-si'i	-sê'a
	Female	-si	-sê
Usitative........................	Male	-ma'a	-mā'a
	Female	-ma	-mā
Dubitative......................	Male	-k!u'i	-k!ô'a
	Female	-k!u	-k!ô
Quotative........................	Male	-t'i	-t'e'a
	Female	-t'ⁱ	-t'ê

Thus, from *mô-* "to eat" are formed: male *môt'i* "it is said he eats," female *môt'ⁱ*, male *môt'ê'a* "it is said he gives to eat," female *môt'ê*.

7. Possessive verbal and nominal forms, also adverbial constructions, in *-k'i-'a*, e.g. male *laut'k'i'a* "his is said to be strong" (contracted from quotative *-t'i* and possessive *-k'i'a*), female *laut'k'i*, male *mômauk'i'a* "[he eats] his (i.e. another's) food," female *mômauk'i*, male *bāwisak'i'a* "in the evening," female *bāwisak'i*.

A peculiar set of verb forms is constituted by the imperatives. The male *-'i'* and *-'a'* correspond to the female *-'ⁱ* and *-'ᵃ*. i.e. the final glottal stop does not appear in the female forms, e.g. male *nisā'i'* "go away!" female *nisā'ⁱ*. This absence of the final glottal stop is peculiar also to the female imperatives with first person object, e.g. male *diwai-dja'* "see me!" female *diwai-tc'ᵃ*, male *diwai-k'ĩgi*, "see us!" female *diwaik'ĩk'ⁱ*.

Interrogative forms differ from the two classes of forms that we have discussed in that the males and females each use distinctive suffixes or enclitics. The ordinary interrogative has an added -*n* for the male forms, with stress accent and falling (not rising) tone on the preceding vowel, e.g. *'au'asĩn* "is there fire?" The corresponding female form has a final lengthened vowel, generally of the same quality as the original vowel, with stress accent and falling tone, e.g. *'au'asĩ* "is there fire?" But certain forms in -*a* have the female interrogative in -*i*, e.g. male *ts!êwal'awa-randján* "did I make a noise?" female *ts!êwal'awarandjĩ*; further, forms ending in a diphthong or consonant take -*yĩ* in the female form, e.g. male *ga'lāyau-nán* "crying," female *ga'lāyau-yĩ*. The female interrogative of the demonstrative lengthens the male -*'e*, e.g. male *aidje'én* "that one?" female *aidje'ê*.

Another interrogative, more emphatic than the preceding, is really an enclitic, male *nắ* and female *gắ*, appended to the appropriate sex form, e.g. male *ts!êwal'asi'nuga nắ* "are you (pl.) making a noise?" female *ts!êwal'asi'nuk'gắ*.

As we have seen, most Yana words have distinct male and female forms. There are certain words, however, which are alike in the speech of both sexes. These are: 1. the syntactic particles (*ai*, third person subjective; *aitc'*, article; *dji*, article with first person possessive; *dju*, article with second person possessive; *k'*, possessive of third person; *gi*, objective particle); 2. the substantive verbs *u* "it is" and *bê* "it is . . . who . . ."; 3. certain passive forms which end in a long vowel (e.g. *ap'djīwarā* "he was killed", *t'im'ĩ* "to be told").

Furthermore, final short vowels are elided before words beginning with a smooth vowel, so that within the sentence or phrase the distinction between the sex forms sometimes disappears. In such cases the original form of the consonant appears, e.g. male *p'adi* "place" and female *p'at'ⁱ* appear as male *aitc' p'ad aidja* "the place there" and *aitc' p'ad aitc'ᵃ* respectively. There are also morphological processes that demand a reduction of absolute forms within the word to a form that corresponds to the female form, e.g. male *dalūwi* "both hands," female *dalūwⁱ*, takes the form *dalūwⁱ-* in certain cases, e.g. male *dalūwⁱk'i'a* "his hands", female *dalūwⁱk'i*.

The sex forms of Yana, to summarize our data, seem to be derived from two psychologically distinct sources. In the minority of cases we are dealing with distinctive sex particles. In the great majority of cases the female forms can be best explained as abbreviated forms which in origin had nothing to do with sex but which are specialized female applications or reduced forms suggested by the phonetic and morphologic economy of the language. Possibly the reduced female forms constitute a conventionalized symbolism of the less considered or ceremonious status of women in the community. Men, in dealing with men, speak fully and deliberately; where women are concerned, one prefers a clipped style of utterance! However this may be, the female forms of Yana are now a complex and completely formalized system which contrasts in many ways with the parallel system of forms used by males in addressing males.

INTERNAL LINGUISTIC EVIDENCE SUGGESTIVE
OF THE NORTHERN ORIGIN OF THE NAVAHO*

INTERNAL linguistic evidence for inferences as to cultural antecedents is not in much favor among cultural anthropologists at the present time, and this for two reasons. Such linguistic evidence is often, if not generally, tricky as to what of a factual nature can be gathered from it, for words may change their meanings radically and, furthermore, it is often difficult to tell whether community of nomenclature rests on early linguistic relationship or on linguistic borrowing attending cultural diffusion. In the second place linguistic evidence is difficult to handle, full of phonologic pitfalls, requiring a closeness of knowledge that is often out of proportion to what little can be obtained from it for tangible cultural inference. Nevertheless at its best linguistic evidence, properly controlled, may throw an unexpected light on remote cultural perspectives. There is reason to think that as our descriptive and comparative knowledge of unwritten languages increases, their value for cultural reconstructions and other kinds of inference—not least among which is elimination of theoretically conceivable possibilities—will grow in importance. It is natural that in the Americanistic field linguistic evidence has yet yielded but a scanty return to the historian of culture, but this need not continue to be the case indefinitely.

I shall try to show that there is tangible evidence in Navaho itself for the secondary origin of apparently fundamental elements of Navaho culture, such as agriculture, and that such evidence seems to point to an early association of the culture of these people with a more northern environment than their present one. It may be said—and with justice— that the distribution of the Athapaskan languages is such as to make this historical theory as good as certain, but dialectic distribution is external, rather than internal, linguistic evidence. It is conceivable, if not plausible, that the Athapaskan-speaking tribes were originally massed in the South-west and gradually rayed out to the north in successive waves of migration. One might argue that the Navaho and, to a greater degree, the various Apache tribes present the non-Pueblo aspect they do, not because of their relative recency in the area of Pueblo cultural development but because, like the Walapai and other Yuman tribes of Arizona, they represent a simpler and more archaic Southwestern culture, which proved impervious, aside from a late Pueblo veneer, to the influence of the more elaborate cultures in their neighborhood. It is true that the

* *American Anthropologist*, n. s., 38 (1936): 224–235.

linguistic homogeneity of the Southern Athapaskan dialects is such and
the dialectic cleavages in the Northern Athapaskan area are so profound
that the suggested theory fails to carry conviction either to the linguist
or to the ethnologist, but here again we are dealing with external linguistic evidence. This external evidence is far more compelling than can
be any evidence derived from details of dialectic structure or vocabulary,
for it is more direct and sweeping. None the less, the more elusive internal
linguistic evidence has its place in giving confirmation to a hypothesis
based on linguistic distributions.

There is undoubtedly a large amount of relevant cultural evidence
packed away in the vocabularies of Navaho and Apache. For the present
I must content myself with considerations based on the study of four
words or groups of words.

1. The Navaho word for "gourd" is 'àdè·'.[1] The word is used both for
the plant and for the "gourd dipper, ladle."[2] The "gourd rattle," on the
other hand, is otherwise named ('àɣá·l).[3] But 'àdè·' means not only
"gourd ladle" but "dipper, ladle, spoon" in general, the gourd ladle being
the ladel or spoon *par excellence*. Hence we find the earthen spoon called
"mud 'àdè·' " or "earth 'àdè·'," while the modern tablespoon is called
"metal (<flint) 'àdè·'."[4] Now the term 'àdè·' (in form a possessed
noun -dè·' with indefinite possessive prefix 'à- "somebody's" or "something's") means not only "gourd," "gourd ladle," and "ladle, spoon" in
general, a natural family of words, but also "horn" or rather "somebody's, some animal's horn" (dé "horn" as absolute; 'à-dè·' "an animal's
horn," parallel to bì-dè·' "his [animal's] horn"). In no other Athapaskan
dialect does 'àdè·' or its dialectic equivalent mean "gourd" or "gourd
ladle," while, so far as I can discover, it is only in Apache that it means
not only "horn" but also "ladle" in general. In Chiricahua Apache[5] we
have possessed -dè·' "horn (of animal)" and 'ìdè·' "cup, dish, dipper";
in Mescalero Apache -dè· "horn (of animal)" and 'ìdè· "cup, dish,
dipper." In both Navaho and Apache 'àdè·', 'ìdè·', 'ìdè·, in its meaning
of "gourd ladle" or "dipper," keeps its indefinite possessive prefix
'à-, 'ì-, when itself possessed, e.g., Nav. bè-'èdè·' (assimilated from
*bì-àdè·') "his gourd ladle," Chiricahua Apache bì-'ìdè·' "his dipper,"
Mescalero Apache bì-'ìdè·. This does not in the least prove that Navaho

---

[1] See, e.g., Franciscans, *A Vocabulary of the Navaho Language*, 2 vols. (St.
Michaels, Arizona, 1912), 1: 99, *sub* "gourd"; 2: 13, *sub* ădē', where it is defined as
Cucurbita.

[2] See Franciscans, *An Ethnologic Dictionary of the Navaho Language* (St Michaels, Arizona, 1910).

[3] *Ibid.*, p. 401.

[4] *Vocabulary*, 1: 186, *sub* "spoon."

[5] My Chiricahua and Mescalero Apache forms are quoted from manuscript
material kindly put at my disposal by Dr Harry Hoijer.

'à-dè·' "one's horn" and 'àdè·' "gourd ladle" are unrelated words; for we have other examples in Southern Athapaskan of double possessives of type "his-one's . . ."; e.g., Navaho bì-t'à' "his (i.e., bird's) feather," 'à-t'à' "a (bird's) feather," but bè-'èt'à' "his-one's-feather," i.e., "his (secondarily owned) feather, his plume (used in hair decoration)." All this suggests that Navaho 'àdè·' "gourd ladle" originally meant "ladle" in general and that this word in turn originally meant "an animal's horn," reinterpreted as "horn spoon," very much as our musical instrument, the "horn," originally a "ram's horn" used for blowing, is now a brass instrument with no obvious relation to an animal's horn. The semantic history of 'àdè·' would, then, be: (1) an animal's horn; (2) ladle made of horn; (3) any ladle; (4) gourd ladle; (5) the gourd, *Cucurbita*, of which ladles are made. Stage 1 would be proto-Athapaskan; 2, a dialectic Northern and Pacific, and presumably early Southern, development based on the wide-spread use of horn for spoons; 3, a Southern Athapaskan transfer of meaning due to the fact that spoons were no longer made of horn; and 4 and 5, a specific Navaho (in part perhaps also Apache) development. Inasmuch as stage 2 no longer has validity in Navaho, the meanings of the word group into two disconnected sets (1; 3–5), so that 'àdè·' is now felt to be two distinct and unrelated words, the more so as it is tabooed among the Navaho to use the horn of the deer for the making of spoons. My interpreter Albert Sandoval once volunteered surprise that identically the same Navaho word meant both "a horn" and "gourd, gourd ladle."

If we turn to other than Southern Athapaskan dialects, we find that the absolute *dé "horn," the possessed *-dè·' "horn of . . . ," and the form with indefinite possessive prefix *k̆ĕ-dè·' "an animal's horn" are found in both of the two other Athapaskan areas. Corresponding to Navaho dé we have, e.g., Kutchin ʐ̌í "horn" and Hupa -de·- (in compounds); corresponding to Navaho -dè·' we have Carrier -de, Chipewyan -dé (Li) (Chipewyan high tone = Athapaskan [Navaho, Apache, Sarsi, Kutchin] low tone), Hare -de, Loucheux -ʐi, Kutchin ʐ̌ì', Beaver -de', Sarsi -dà', Hupa -de', Kato -de', and Mattole -de'; while Navaho 'à-dè·' has an exact correspondent in Chipewyan 'ɛ-dɛ, Hare e-de, Loucheux e-ʐi, Kutchin č'í-ʐ̆ì', Bâtard Loucheux e-dʸe, and Hupa k̂i-de', all meaning "an animal's horn." The early use of horn for spoons, which can only be inferred for Southern Athapaskan, is linguistically reflected in Hupa k̂ide·-k̟in', literally "a horn's handle," whence "spoon," and in Hare ede-k̄ʷa "cuiller en corne" (Petitot: k̄ʷa "plate, bowl") and Sheep Indian (ɛsbatahot'ine) ede-k̄a "corne aplatie" (Petitot), whence "spoon." Obviously, to the Navaho mind 'àdè·' in its meaning of "gourd" must be referred to the beginning of things, for the term is used in ritual and mythology, for example in the compound term Gourd Children,[6] but the feeling of the Navaho is of no more importance in the historic problem than their conviction that ł{' always meant "horse" (though we can easily prove from comparative evidence that its original meaning was "dog") and that their ancestors became acquainted with the horse not too long after the Emergence, as indicated by the origin legend for the creation of the horse in the four cardinal points out of the four ritual-istically proper materials.

Our linguistic analysis, in short, points unmistakably to two things of historical interest: that the gourd is not an original element of Southern Athapaskan culture; and that horn spoons, not directly given by present-day Navaho culture, must be assumed to have been known to the remoter Athapaskan-speaking ancestors of the Navaho or, at the least, to early Southern Athapaskan culture. These inferences go well with a theory of immigration of the Navaho and Apache from the north (or east) into the Southwest. Even if one goes no further than to infer the absence of the gourd and the presence of horn spoons in an early phase of the culture of the Navaho-Apache tribes, the illumination brought by a close analysis of Navaho 'àdè·' and its Apache cognates is useful for the reconstruction of the period antedating the massive influence of the Pueblos on the Navaho and the Apache tribes.

2. The Navaho verb for "seed lies" is -sàs, a perfective neuter, e.g., sìsàs "the seed lies," ńsàs "the seed lies in a row." The original meaning of these forms is obviously not specifically "the seed lies" but, more gen-erally, "the mass of finely divided particles (e.g., grain, sand) lies." A cor-responding active verb, nà·sàs, means, for instance, not merely, "I scatter the seed,"[7] but also "I let the mass (of grain, sand) spill (e.g., out of a bag); I sprinkle it (e.g., sand, water)." I can find no cognate for these verbs in the material available to me from other Athapaskan dialects, and the inference—as so often in analogous Athapaskan cases of apparently isolated verbs—is that we probably have here a dialectic denominative formation, i.e., a secondary set of verbs based on a noun.

Now it is perfectly clear from Navaho phonology that all verb stems beginning in s (after vowels) are contracted products of a "classifier" -ł- and either z or y; in other words, -sàs must go back to either -ł-zàs or -ł-yàs. The perfective neuter *sì-ł-zàs or *sì-ł-yàs is analogous in form to such a perfective neuter verb as sìłcò·z[8] "the fabric lies." But what is the underlying zàs or yàs? Quite obviously, "snow," Navaho zàs, yàs (these two forms, of which the latter is the more archaic, constitute one of the few cases of dialectic difference within Navaho). Hence the verb sìsàs

[6] *Ethnologic Dictionary*, pp. 351, 353.
[7] See, e.g., *Vocabulary*, *sub* "broadcast (in sowing)."
[8] c = ts.

must have meant, originally, "it lies like (flakes of) snow," whence "the seed lies"; the derived active verb nà·sàs originally meant "I scatter it about (so that it lies) like snow," whence "I sow the seed broadcast."

As in the preceding case, while the present cultural term is not widespread in Athapaskan but is confined to Navaho (or Southern Athapaskan), it is not difficult to establish a close connection with a universal Athapaskan term of differing cultural connotation. Athapaskan *yáxs[9] "snow" is found in the majority of Athapaskan dialects: Ingalik yiθ, Babine yìs (Jenness), Carrier yəs̲, Chipewyan yàθ (Li), Slave žah, Hare, Dogrib ž▸ah, Loucheux z̲iow, Kutchin z̲áh, Kaska zȧs (Jenness), Beaver yas, Sarsi zạs, Kwalhioqua yaxs, Hupa yahs,[10] Kato yas, Mattole yas, Jicarilla Apache zas, Mescalero, Chiricahua zàs. The original meaning of the Athapaskan word is not "snow" in general but specifically "snow lying on the ground;"[11] another common Athapaskan term, represented by Navaho čí·l, means "snowdrift" or "falling snow." This restricted meaning, "snow lying on the ground," is clearly the prototype of the present Navaho term for "the seed lies." To summarize, a non-agricultural term ("snow lying on the ground") takes on a transferred and more general meaning in a classificatory verb "the finely divided particles lie [snow-like] on the ground") and, in a secondary, agricultural environment, advances to the technical meaning of "the seed lies." No other sequence of meanings fits the linguistic facts.

3. The Navaho word for "corn" is nà·dą́·'. The second element, -dą́·', occurs in a number of compound nouns referring to plants in which it tends to be translated "corn" by Navaho interpreters, e.g., hà·ščé·'dą́·' "box-thorn," approximately "god-corn" (hà·ščé·' is a familiar Navaho god name and, in slightly abbreviated form, is the first element in the native term for the Talking God); čí'·dą́ "buckthorn," perhaps "bitter corn" (cf. díčí·' "it is bitter"); mà·'ì·dą́·' "cedar-berries," literally "coyote-corn;" gàhcòhdą́·' "winterfat," literally "jackrabbit-corn." The reason why, in compounds such as these, -dą́·' is translated "corn" rather than "food," which is obviously more logical in such terms as "coyote-food" and "jackrabbit-food," is probably the use of the abbreviated -dą́·' for "corn" in possessed forms (e.g., šìdą́·' "my corn") instead of the fuller nà·dą́·' of the absolutive. But it is quite easy to prove that -dą́·' is not, in any true sense, abbreviated from nà·dą́·' "corn" but,

---

[9] My reason for reconstructing to high-toned *yáxs rather than low-toned *yàxs is too technical to give here.

[10] The Hupa word means not "snow" but "white frost (on trees)."

[11] See, e.g., Fang-Kuei Li, "A List of Chipewyan Stems," *International Journal of American Linguistics,* 7 (1933): 146: "yàθ snow on the ground," similarly, for Chipewyan, L. Le Goff, *Dictionnaire Français-Montagnais* (Lyons, Marseilles, and Rome, 1916), *sub* "neige tombée"; for Carrier see A. G. Morice, *The Carrier Language,* 2 vols. (Mödling bei Wien, 1932), 1:25, where yeš (our yəs̲) "snow" contrasts with cel (our šəł) "snow (heavy and not yet settled)."

on the contrary, is an old term for "food" which lingers, somewhat disguised, in such compounds as have been quoted and in possessed forms for "corn" (šìdą́·' "my food" *par excellence*, whence "my corn"). This interpretation, not clear to the Navaho himself because the word in actual use for "food" is čì·yá·n and he therefore feels that the primary meaning of -dą́·' is, or should be, "corn," is at once made plausible from within Navaho when we compare -dą́·' with the mediopassive imperfective neuter verb -dą́ "to be eatable" (e.g., yìdą́ "it is eatable"), itself closely related to the durative transitive verb -yą́ "to eat it" (from which čì·yá·n above is independently derived). It looks, therefore, as if -dą́·' originally meant "what is eatable," i.e., "food," secondarily "corn" in possessed forms.

The nà·- or nà·dą́·' is quite obscure to the Navaho. It seems to follow no obvious analogy and cannot be equated with the common nà·- "about, here and there" of continuative verbs. One might venture nà·dą́·', originally "corn is here and there," whence "planted corn, standing corn," finally generalized to "corn." This is to be taken no more seriously, however, than an attempt to see our common word tide in the -tide of eventide, whereas every historical student of English knows that this compounded -tide is a survival of an old word tide synonymous with time and cognate with Danish tid and German Zeit. Our problem cannot be considered completely solved until we have done more than plausibly surmise that -dą́·' originally meant "food" and have found a linguistically unforced explanation of nà·-. The former requirement is met by a consideration of Athapaskan cognates, which reconstruct to *dán-ĕ́ (itself reduced from *dĕ-hán-ĕ́ "that which is eaten, food," relative form in *-ĕ́ of *dĕ-hán, whence *-dán, "to be eaten, to be eatable"), possessed form *-dán-è', *-dán-ĕ̀' "food of ...." Chipewyan dàṇè (Li), possessed -dàṇè, Sarsi dą́ní, Mescalero Apache dán, possessed -dán and -dą́·', Chiricahua Apache dán, possessed -dán (also -dą́·' in nà·dą́·' "corn," perhaps borrowed from Navaho), Hupa possessed -da·n' in -da·n' sa'a·n "food of ... is lying" = "... is saving with food," Mattole possessed -da·ne' "possession, property" (presumably a meaning enlarged from "food"). These forms enable us to understand the exact status of Navaho -dą́·'. It is not the reflex of the primary *dánĕ́ "food" but of its possessed form *-dánĕ̀' "food of ..."; the former (exemplified by Chipewyan dàṇè, Sarsi dą́ní, and Apache dán [read dáń, for an old Southern Athapaskan *dàn, monosyllabic, would have yielded Navaho, Apache *dàn, while an old Athapaskan *dán would have given Navaho, Apache *dą́]) would have resulted in Navaho *dání, *dáń. The Apache possessed forms in -dáń are merely generalized from the absolutive dáń, the variant Mescalero -dą́·' "food of ... " being the true reflex of Athapaskan -*dán-ĕ̀' and an exact cognate of Navaho -dą́·' "corn." We see, therefore, that on strictly linguistic grounds such Navaho forms as mà·ì·dą́·' mean, not "coyote-food," but "coyote's food." This makes it doubly impossible to interpret nà·dą́·' as "corn here and there," which form, if it ever existed, would have to yield *nà·dą́ń in Navaho. We are driven to infer that nà·dą́·' originally meant "food of nà·-," whatever nà·- may be.

Once we see that nà·- must have referred to certain beings, human or animal, whose food was corn, we advance rapidly to a satisfactory linguistic solution. Many Athapaskan dialects have reflexes of an old word for "enemy, aliens," occurring in two forms (*nà·', nà·- in compounds, and, with indefinite possessive prefix, *ḳĕ-(dĕ-)nà·', *ḳĕ-na·- in compounds). These words are frequently used to refer to specific neighboring tribes. Examples of *ḳĕ-nà·', *ḳĕ-dĕ-nà·' (*dĕ- is collective) and compounded *ḳĕ-nà·- are: Carrier ə-d-na, Chipewyan 'ɛ́-ná (Li) "enemy, Cree Indian," Slave e-na-kie "Eskimo," Hare e-h-da "enemy," e-na-ke "Eskimo," Dogrib e-h-da, Loucheux ə-ne "enemy, Eskimo," Bâtard Loucheux a-ra-ke "Eskimo," Kutchin čè·kʷói (contracted from *ča-nè·-) "Eskimo," Hupa ḳi-na' "Yurok Indian," Navaho 'à-nà·', Mescalero, Chiricahua Apache 'ì-ndà·. (The -kie, -ke, -kʷói of some of these forms, analogous to Navaho -ké, is a plural animate suffix.) The old compounded form without indefinite prefix, *nà·-, is illustrated in Chipewyan na-tʼį-i "enemy" (Petitot) (literally, "the one who acts as an enemy") and, presumably, in Kato na-čəl "orphan" (from "alien" + "child, little"). In Navaho this nà·- is found in compound nouns, particularly such as refer to foreign peoples, e.g., nà·łáń "Comanche Indians" (from "enemy-many-the"), nà·-štʼéží "Zuñi Indians" (contracted from nà·yìštʼéží "enemy" + "the ones who are blackened"), nà·sgálí (apparently made over, in accordance with the Navaho tribal name pattern, from mà·sgálí "Mescalero"),[12] nà·tò·hó "Laguna Indians" (apparently also "Isleta Indians"?). The last of these tribal names is interpreted as "enemies at the water" by the Franciscan Fathers[13] but a more natural interpretation is to take the name as a relative in -í (assimilated to -ó) from nà·tò·h "enemy-river," presumably an old name for the San Jose (and Rio Grande?), in contrast to the two normal interpretations of tò·h, namely San Juan River and Little Colorado River, the two rivers in or near the old Navaho habitat which never completely dry up. This is confirmed by the place name nà·tò·(h) sìḳà̀i' given by the Franciscan Fathers for Grant, New Mexico (nātqo săḳai'),[14] literally "the enemy river has its legs distended," "(where) the San Jose turns crotch-wise." The point is

---

[12] See *Vocabulary*, 1:127, *sub* "Mescalero Apache."

[13] *Ibid.*, 2:135, *sub* nátqoho; better "at the river," for this name is based on tò·h, possessed -tò·h, "river which does not dry up," rather than on tó "water."

[14] *Ibid.*, 1:226.

of some importance linguistically as indicating that Navaho compounds in nà·- "enemy" not only mean ". . . enemies" but also "enemy . . ." In other words, both nà·tò·h and nà·dá̜' are archaic Navaho words which qualify basic nouns ("river" and "food") by referring them to the enemy, in this case the Pueblo Indians.

The Navaho word for "corn," nà·dá̜·', in summary, which can be analyzed with great probability into an older "food of the enemy," "Pueblo food," implies that there was a time when the Navaho, an agricultural people in historic times, were still thinking of corn as an alien food. Later on, when they had adopted corn as a staple and had built so much of their myth and ritual around it that it was inconceivable to them that there could be anything alien about it, they could not possibly feel the nà·- of their word for "corn" as akin to the -nà·' of 'ànà·' "enemy" and the nà·- of tribal names. The sentiments clustering about the two terms had become irreconcilable.

4. There is a curious verb stem in Navaho which seems to be used only in certain quite specialized verbs; this stem has the forms: imperfective -ké·h (probably error for -kè·h), perfective -kí, progressive and future -ké·ł, usitative and iterative -ké·h, optative -ké·ł. It is used in an idiomatic verb referring to sleeplessness, e.g., iterative bìł sìɔ́ánáké·h "sleeplessness always bothers me," perfective bìł sìɔ́áṅkí "I have been sleepless." The form of the verb is such (bìł "sleep" is subject; -ɔ́á- "away from" is preceded by the indirect pronominal object) as to suggest that the verb stem refers to a specific type of movement. My interpreter, Albert Sandoval, had no notion what the underlying metaphor was but said he felt, somehow, that there was a reference to gliding movement in it: "sleep glides (slips) away from me." There is no linguistic support for this feeling, which is hardly more than an *ad hoc* interpretation to fit the linguistic form. This obscure verb, as Sandoval pointed out, must have the same stem, in its progressive form (-ké·ł), as the sacred name of the owl, ɔ̌àhàłxè·ł yìł ná·kéłí "darkness with-it the-one-who-comes-gliding(?)-back, the one who comes gliding (?) back with darkness." The image of gliding is not so apposite here. The simple progressive form, which would be *yìké·ł "it glides (?) along," is not in use in Navaho. There is nothing to be done with these isolated forms except to see in them survivals of an old set of verbs of movement which perhaps still occur in other Athapaskan dialects.

Turning to Chiricahua Apache, we find the verb stem: imperfective momentaneous -kè· (continuative -ké), perfective -kí, progressive and future -ké·ł, usitative and iterative -ké, optative (evidently transferred from imperfective) momentaneous -kè· (continuative -ké). Its meaning is given as "several run, trot," which is by no means easy to reconcile with the hypothetical "glide" of the Navaho words. If the Navaho and Chiricahua Apache words are historically related, as is indicated by their strict formal parallelism, it must be because each dialect has developed specialized meanings that diverge from a third term. Now the distribution of the meanings of the Northern and Pacific Athapaskan verb stems which are demonstrably cognate to the Southern Athapaskan stems is such as to leave little doubt of what this third term must have been. The following table of stem forms gives a summary of dialectic meanings and of phonetic equivalents for four selected stems of the set:

	MOMENTANEOUS IMPERFECTIVE	PERFECTIVE	PROGRESSIVE	CONTINUATIVE IMPERFECTIVE
Athapaskan	*-kè·ⁿx̣	*-kén	*-ké·ⁿł	*-ké
1. Ingalik "to travel by canoe"	-kaix̂	-kan	-kał	
2. Loucheux (ditto)	-kəi	-kę	-ka	
3. Kutchin (ditto)	-kʷòi	-kʷǫ́i	-kʷá·	
4. Carrier (ditto)	-keh	-kei	-kəł	
5. Beaver (ditto)	-kɛ (read -kɛh?)	-ki̧	-kɛł	-kɛ
6. Hare (ditto)	-kɛ		-kɛ	
7. Chipewyan (ditto)	-kə́ih	-ki̧	-kəł	
8. Sarsi "to travel by canoe; to go for trade"	-kàh	-kí (-kín- before vocalic suffix)	-káł	
9. Ts'ets'aut "to travel by canoe"	-ki·			-kɛ·
10. Chasta Costa (ditto)				-xɛ
11. Hupa "to travel by canoe; several objects float"	-xiw	-xiŋ	-xił	-xɛ·
12. Mattole "to travel by canoe"	-kx̣i·x	-kx̣iŋ	-kx̣i·l (relative form)	
13. Kato "several bathe"				-kɛ· (transferred from cont. pf., it., and opt.?)
14. Chiricahua Apache "several run, trot"	-kè·	-kí	-kè·ł	-kɛ
15. Navaho (only as survival in obscure forms)	-kɛ́·h (read -kè·h?)	-kí	-kɛ́·ł	

The history of the meaning of these verb stems is now reasonably clear. The primary meaning of the Athapaskan verb stems may have been "several objects (*or* persons) move in the water, float" (see Hupa and Kato above), whence "the group travels on the water, to travel by canoe (as one of a canoe-party)." Both meanings are preserved in Hupa. The latter meaning, however, may well have been the primary one. The specific meaning of a group traveling by water seems, under changed environmental conditions, to have taken on a new meaning in Chiricahua Apache ("several run, trot"), though the old plural or collective implication is still preserved. In Sarsi the meaning of "to travel by canoe" is now felt to be rather archaic and to belong to myth and story. The natural meaning today is "to go to trade, to go (by foot or horse-back) in order to shop;" this is developed from "to go by boat (*or* canoe) in order to trade at a Hudson's Bay Co. trading post," itself specialized from the common Athapaskan meaning "to travel by canoe." Here too the gradual passage to a typical Plains life, with little or no use of water craft, has brought about a redefinition of a familiar set of words. The Navaho words seem to stem from an old meaning "to travel by canoe," naturally entirely effaced from tribal memory. A generalized meaning "to float," applying to singular as well as plural subject, cannot be assumed for early Navaho because there is no evidence anywhere in Athapaskan for a reflex of *-kè·ⁿx̣ in the sense of "one person floats" and because all Athapaskan dialects are peculiarly sensitive to the difference between singular and plural forms of verb stems referring to characteristic types of movement. "I become sleepy," in other words, seems originally to have meant "Sleep paddles away from me;" the Owl was ritualistically described as "he who brings Darkness back in his canoe." Such locutions seem to stem from a cultural setting in which travel by canoe was so much a matter of course that it could be transferred to the supernatural world.

The Navaho ná·ké·ł "he comes 'gliding' home" (of which ná·kełí in the sacred name of the owl is the relative form) is contracted from an old Athapaskan progressive *ná-γě-(dě-)ké·ⁿł, of which there are exact reflexes in many of the other dialects, e.g., Sarsi ná-γì-kál "he's coming back on a boat, he's returning from shopping;" Beaver na-γa-kił (read -keł?) "he is paddling back;"[15] Carrier na-s-keł (contracted from *ná-γě-š-ké·ⁿł) "I am again navigating, I am returning by boat;"[16] Ingalik nə-γə-də-kał "he paddles again."[17]

[15] Pliny Earle Goddard, *Beaver Dialect*, American Museum of Natural History, Anthropological Papers, 10 (1917): 506.

[16] Morice, *The Carrier Language*, 1: 279.

[17] John W. Chapman, *Ten'a Texts and Tales from Anvik, Alaska*, American Ethnological Society, Publications, 6 (1914): 158, 1.1.

The evidence collected in this paper may now be summarized. (1) It is assumed that there is important external linguistic evidence, distributional in character, to provide a *prima facie* probability of the northern origin of the Navaho and Apache. All the Southern Athapaskan dialects (Navaho, Western Apache, Mescalero and Chiricahua Apache, Jicarilla Apache, Lipan, and Kiowa Apache) obviously form a close-knit dialectic unity which contrasts with the more complex dialectic ramifications of Pacific and Northern Athapaskan. The geographical center of gravity of these languages, in short, lies in the north. (2) If we could find internal linguistic evidence in Navaho, of cultural implications, tending, as it were, to free Navaho and Navaho culture from their present Southwestern environment, the initial probability of a northern provenience would be strengthened. Such supplementary strengthening of an inherently probable hypothesis is suggested by the linguistic analysis of four Navaho words having cultural connotations. The cultural inferences that may be derived from this analysis are: that the gourd was not originally an element of Southern Athapaskan culture; that spoons in this culture were originally made of horn; that broadcast sowing of seed was foreign to the culture; that maize, a staple in historic times, was at one time felt to be an alien food—in other words, that the Southwestern agricultural complex was originally lacking; and that a glimpse, faint but not to be lightly argued away, may be had of a time when the Navaho, or Southern Athapaskans collectively, made use of canoes. (3) All of these inferences deepen, in a historical sense, the cultural gap between the Navaho and the Pueblos. This gap is already given, in a descriptive sense, though in lesser degree, by the modern ethnologic evidence. The first four of the cultural inferences we have listed are theoretically compatible with a non-Pueblo Southwestern cultural setting and, equally, with a more northern setting. The last of these inferences, if valid, points more positively to a northern setting.

"Northern origin" does not in the least imply a direct line of movement from north to south across the Great Basin. Such a line of migration is most improbable. It is far more likely that the movement of these peoples proceeded *via* the western plains. If this is correct, an analysis of Southern Athapaskan culture would aim to reveal four strata: a fundamental northern layer, comparable to the culture of the tribes of the Mackenzie basin; an early western Plains adaptation, more archaic in its outlines than the specialized culture of the Plains as now defined by ethnologists; a first Southwestern influence, tending to assimilate these tribes to the relatively simple non-Pueblo culture of the Southwest; and a second, distinctively Pueblo, Southwestern influence. To these must, naturally, be added a good deal of Navaho specialization on the basis of the Pueblo influence. The disentangling of these various layers is work for the future and, in any event, is hardly likely to be ever more than fragmentary. Meanwhile, the geographical sequence: Chipewyan, Sarsi, Kiowa Apache, Jicarilla Apache, Navaho, may stand as a suggestion of the reality of the historical problem, though, no doubt, the Plains character of Sarsi and Kiowa Apache culture is in each instance of a much later type than the hypothetical Plains influence to be worked out for Navaho cultural antecedents.

GLOTTALIZED CONTINUANTS IN NAVAHO, NOOTKA, AND KWAKIUTL

(WITH A NOTE ON INDO-EUROPEAN)*

1. IT IS WELL KNOWN that a very large number of American Indian languages number among their phonemes glottalized stops and affricates (e.g. $\acute{p}$, $\acute{t}$, $\acute{k}$, $\acute{q}$, $\acute{k}^w$, $\acute{q}^w$, $\acute{c}$, $\acute{\check{c}}$). Examples of such languages or groups of languages are Dakota, Winnebago, Ponca and other Siouan languages; Tonkawa; Chitimacha; Kootenay; Salish languages; Sahaptin languages; Chinookan; Tlingit; Haida; Tsimshian; Kwakiutl and Nootka[1]; Chimakuan; Athapaskan languages (e.g. Navaho)[1] Alsea; Siuslaw; Coos; Takelma; Karok; Shasta; Achumawi and Atsugewi; Pomo; Chimariko; Yana; Klamath and Modoc; Kalapuya; Yana; Yurok; Yuki; Wintun; Yokuts; Washo; Keres; Tanoan languages; Kiowa; Mayan languages; Quechua. In most of these languages the glottalized consonants are fortes, as in Chinookan and Athapaskan; in others, as in Chitimacha and Taos (Tanoan),[2] they are lenes. In the overwhelming majority of cases the glottal release is posterior to the oral release, precisely as in Georgian and other Caucasic languages. These glottalized consonants are sometimes known as 'ejectives'. In some languages, however, the oral and glottal releases are synchronous. An example of a language having glottalized consonants of this type is Southern Paiute (Shoshonean), where they are not true phonemes, however, as they may always be analyzed into stop (or affricate) + ?.

2. Less common than glottalized stops and affricates are glottalized continuants. Voiceless spirants with glottal affection are well attested in Tlingit, where we have the series: $\acute{s}$, $\acute{x}$, $\acute{x}^w$, $\acute{\dot{x}}$, $\acute{\dot{x}}^w$, which must be carefully distinguished from the parallel series of glottalized stops and affricates: $\acute{c}$, $\acute{k}$, $\acute{k}^w$, $\acute{q}$, $\acute{q}^w$. In Chasta Costa (Athapaskan) $\acute{\dot{x}}$ is the regular reflex of Athapaskan $\acute{k}$, whose more common dialectic reflexes are $\acute{k}$ (e.g. Navaho), or $\acute{q}$ (e.g. Hupa).

* *Language*, 14 (1938): 248–274.
[1] The Navaho forms cited in this paper are from the author's field notes. The Nootka forms are quoted from E. Sapir and M. Swadesh, *Nootka Texts*, William Dwight Whitney Linguistic Series (Philadelphia, Linguistic Society of America, 1939). The Kwakiutl forms are quoted from F. Boas' writings on Kwakiutl, particularly: "Kwakiutl," in his *Handbook of American Indian Languages*, Bureau of American Ethnology, Bulletin 40, pt. 1 (Washington, G.P.O., 1911), pp. 423–557; *Ethnology of the Kwakiutl, pt. 2*, Bureau of American Ethnology, 35th Annual Report (Washington, G.P.O., 1921), Vocabulary, pp. 1389–1466; "A Revised List of Kwakiutl Suffixes," *International Journal of American Linguistics*, 3(1924): 117–131; "Notes on the Kwakiutl Vocabulary," *ibid.*, 6(1931):163–178.
[2] *Fide* Morris Swadesh and George L. Trager respectively.

Of greater frequency, it would seem, than glottalized voiceless spirants are glottalized sonorant consonants (*y, w, m, n, ɴ, l*): *ẏ, ẇ, ṁ, ṅ, ̇ɴ, ̇l.* In these consonants the glottal closure is synchronous with the momentarily voiceless initial phase of the continuants, its release being immediately followed by the voiced phase of the continuant. A pronunciation *ʔ + y*, for instance, is always resisted by the native's ear as incorrect, particularly as such clusters may occur as well. In Nootka, for instance, *taṅa* 'child' cannot be syllabified *taʔ-na*, as there are no syllables ending in *ʔ*. The *ṅ* is a true phoneme, beginning its syllable, and a syllable can only begin with a single consonant. In Navaho the same phoneme, *ṅ*, must be carefully distinguished from the cluster *ʔn*; the former occurs, e.g., in *xàná·ṅàʔ*[3] 'he has crawled out back again', the latter in *xàʔnà·* 'across'. A few indications of the occurrence of these sounds may be welcome. Haida possesses *ẏ, ẇ, ṁ, ṅ, ̇ŋ*, and *̇l*; *ẏ* and *ẇ* are actually more common phonemes than *y* and *w*, though these are not absent. Yokuts, Tsimshian, and Kwakiutl have *ẏ, ẇ, ṁ, ṅ*, and *̇l*. Nootka has *ẏ, ẇ, ṁ*, and *ṅ*. Navaho possesses *ṅ* and *ṁ* and, very rarely, *ẏ*; these can only occur as stem initials, never as word initials.

3. Examples of these phonemes as initials in Nootka are: *ẏaṁa* 'salal-berries'; *ẏa·q* 'long' (contrast *yaq-ʔi·tq* 'he who is'); *ẏowa·-ƛ* 'filled with surprise, grateful' (contrast *yoxʷa·* 'heating up, giving off hot air'); *ẇa·-* 'ashamed, bashful' (contrast *wa·* 'to say'); *ẇaẇal* 'the temples' (contrast *wal-šiƛ* 'to go home'); *ẇi·-ya* 'to split into thin slabs' (contrast *wi·-ẏa* 'never'); *ẇic-a·* 'to nod one's head' (contrast *wica-* 'well to do'); *ṁa-* 'holding in the mouth' (contrast *ma-* 'to dwell'); *ṁa·t-il* 'captive' (contrast *mat-* 'to fly'); *ṁo·q* 'throwing off sparks from fire-drill twirler' (contrast *moq-* 'having liquid in the mouth'); *ṅa·pi* 'there is moonlight' (contrast *na·p-a·* 'to get coiled up'); *ṅaš-* 'to look' (contrast *naš-ok* 'strong, firm'); *ṅixʷ-* 'salmon roe, kidneys' (contrast *nixʷ-ak* 'cheap'); *ṅoč-šiƛ* 'to cook food by steaming' (contrast *noč-i·* 'mountain'). Non-initial examples are: *ƛol-i·ẏol* 'well-throated, having a good voice' (contrast *ʔo·-yoqʷa* 'doing to him'); *-ẇi, -ẇi·* 'mark of . . . ' (contrast *-wi, -wi·* 'first'); *-ṁa, -ṁa·* 'as far as . . . ' (contrast *-ma·ʔaƛ* 'intending to . . . '); *ʔo·ṅaqi·l* 'to find it' (contrast *ʔo·-naqa* 'using it as bait').

4. It is obvious, from the behavior of *ẏ, ẇ, ṁ*, and *ṅ* in Nootka, that these are true phonemes, sharply distinguishable from the non-glottalized *y, w, m*, and *n* and etymologically irreducible, at least in the first instance, to *ʔ +* sonorant consonant (or sonorant consonant *+ ʔ*). So singular are these consonants, however, that it is tempting to seek evi-

---

[3] ́, high tone; ̀, low tone.

dence accounting for their origin, though in a purely descriptive treatment of the phonemes of a language no such evidence need be considered.
We may turn for a moment to Navaho, for neither *ṅ*, *ṁ*, nor *ẏ* is an original Athapaskan phoneme and a comparative study of Athapaskan sounds
must account for their appearance in Navaho. Fortunately this is an
easy task. It is true that there are, or seem to be, a few stems in which an
initial *ṅ* must be accepted as an unanalyzable phoneme, e.g. *-ṅé·h* (ipf.),
-ṅà? (pf.) 'to crawl'. But in other cases an apparently irresolvable *ṅ* can
be plausibly shown to result from a contraction of *d + n*. Thus, the stem
-ṅì? of *?ì·ṅì?* 'thunder' and the stem *-ṅí* of *dìṅí* 'he moans' are best
explained as resulting from an earlier **-d-nì?* and **-d-ní* respectively.
The *-d-* of **-d-nì?* is reduced from the *di-* of the verb *di-...-ní* 'to say',
whose stem (*-ní* 'to make a sound') is identical with the *-ní* which
underlies the *-ṅí* of 'to moan' and closely related to the *-nì?* underlying
the *-ṅì?* of 'thunder'. That this is the case can be shown by the testimony
of related languages, in which we either have actual combinations of
d + n or the proper reflexes of *-dn-* in the words for 'thunder'. In Navaho
dìṅí 'he moans' the prefix *di-* is the same sound-referring element which
we have in *di-...-ní* 'to say' and in countless other verbs having to do
with sound, word, or speech, while the *-d-* of earlier **-d-ní* is a self-
referring element; *dìṅí* is, therefore, etymologically something like 'he
says, makes a sound, with reference to himself', i.e. 'he makes a sound
without purpose of communication'. It will be seen that the glottal
element of *ṅ* in *-ṅì?* and *-ṅí*, while going back to the same stopped
consonant, is not derivable from the same morphological element. In
other words, we are dealing here with a purely mechanical morphophonemic emergent, *ṅ*, due to the coalescence of two originally distinct
phonemes, *d* and *n*, of whatever etymological value. Owing to the great
semantic distinctiveness of 'thunder' and 'to moan' as compared with
'to say' and the lack of obvious paradigmatic relationship of *?ì·ṅì?* and
dìṅí to *di-...-ní*, it is safe to assume that the analyses that we have given,
however clear to the dissecting linguist, have not the 'configurative
pressure' that would justify our considering the phoneme *ṅ* as merely a
resultant of *d + n*. If such an interpretation was at one time possible, it
is probably no longer the case from a purely descriptive point of view.
-ṅé·h (*-ṅà?*), *-ṅì?*, *-ṅí*, and other stems of this sort are best listed, for
descriptive purposes, as possessing a distinct phoneme, *ṅ*, whose remoter
history has no compelling relevance for its placement in the scheme of
Navaho phonemes.

There are, however, two important considerations which weaken the
force of the negative argument. All other consonantal phonemes (aside

from the rare *m̊* and *ẙ*, of which a word later on), 32 in number, not only occur as stem initials but as word initials, while *n̊*, *m̊*, and *ẙ* can only occur as non-initial stem initials. This at once suggests, and quite aside from historical or morphological considerations, that *n̊*, *m̊*, and *ẙ* have a secondary, derivative, phonemic status. This surmise is borne out by the second and more important consideration, that all cases of *m̊* and *ẙ* (there are only a few) and the great majority of cases of *n̊*, a common phoneme, are not as isolable or as relatively isolable as those we have just spoken of but occur in a clear-cut morphophonemic relation to *m*, *y*, and *n* respectively. To make this clear, we shall have to go into certain details of Navaho morphology. An important feature of the structure of Navaho verb-paradigms is the appearance of what may be called a *d*-effect at certain points in the total configuration. There are chiefly two such points: the first person dual-plural subjective pronoun prefix (-*ì*- < *-*ì·d*-) and the mediopassive forms (characterized by an old element *-*d*-). For these two groups of forms it is necessary to modify either the stem initial or the form of a consonantal prefix immediately preceding the stem or, very frequently, both. Thus, a *d*-modified stem initial, even when such modification is only implicit (in cases where the earlier *-*d*- disappeared without leaving an overt trace, e.g. before stops and affricates), requires that the perfective prefix -*z*- in the third person of a very large 'class' of verbs (the most numerous of the four 'classes') take the form characteristic of the other three classes, namely -*s*-; thus, *yì-dè·z-ʔą́* (pf. stem -*ʔą́* of ipf. -*ʔà·h* 'to handle the round object') 'he has gone off with it (an object of a certain semantic classification)', but passive *dè·-s-ìą́* 'it has been gone off with' < **dè·-z-d-ʔą́*. Similarly, *yì-dè·-z-ką́* (pf. stem -*ką́* of ipf. -*kà·h* 'to handle the container with its contents') 'he has gone off with it (an object of another semantic classification)', but *dè·-s-ką́* 'it has been gone off with' < **dè·-z-d-ką́*. Again, *dì·ìà·h* 'we 2 go off with the round object' < **d-ì·d-ʔà·h* : *dìš̥ʔà·h* 'I go off with it'; while in *dì·kà·h* 'we 2 go off with the container with its contents': *dìškà·h* 'I go off with it' there is no overt difference between *d*-effect and its absence. It may be remarked that in certain Athapaskan dialects, e.g. Hupa, the theoretical *-*d*- of Navaho actually appears as a syllable of type -*di*-. The table of *d*-modified stem initials, aside from irregularities which do not interest us, is as follows:

PRIMARY CONSONANT	D-MODIFIED
ʔ	*ì*
s, z	*ʒ*
š, ž	*ǯ*
γ	*g*; sometimes *ʒ*

PRIMARY CONSONANT *(cont.)*	D-MODIFIED *(cont.)*
y	*ẓ*; rarely *ẏ*
m	*m̓*
n	*n̓*
ł, l	*λ*

In the forms analogous to those which require a change of *ʾ* to *i̓*, *n* becomes *n̓*. Hence, analogously to *yìde·z̓ʾą́*, *dè·si̓ą́*, *dìš̓ʾà·h* and *dì·tà·h*, we have *yìdè·zn̓ìl* (pf. stem *-nìl* of ipf. *-ni̓·l* 'to handle the group of objects') 'he has gone off with them', *dè·sn̓ìl* 'they have been gone off with', *dìšn̓ì·l* 'I go off with them', *dì·n̓ì·l* 'we 2 go off with them'. Again, within the paradigm of the verb *dì-...-ni̓* 'to say', the stem *-ni̓*, pf. *-ni̓·d*, must be modified to *-n̓í*, *-n̓ì·d*, e.g. *dì·n̓í* 'we 2 say' (homonymous with *dì·n̓í* 'we 2 moan' but referable to *dìšní* 'I say', not to *dìšn̓í* 'I moan'), *hòdò·n̓ì·d* 'it has been said' (contrast *dì·nì·d* 'I have said').

5. In Navaho *ẏ* only occurs in morphophonemic alternation with *y* in the stem *-yói*, e.g. *hòn̓šyói* 'I have bravery, am able to endure', *hònì·ẏói* 'we 2 have bravery'; *i̓ó· ʾòhàyói* 'they are in great number', *i̓ó· ʾòhònì·ẏói* 'we are in great number'. We should have expected *-ẓói* in the *d*-modified forms of *-yói* but, for reasons which seem totally obscure at present, *-yói* here follows the analogy of stems with initial *n* and *m*. *m̓* is the regular *d*-modified form of *m*, not a common phoneme, and occurs almost exclusively as its morphophonemic pendant. Examples are *nànì·m̓à?ì·* 'we 2 are vagabonds': *nànšm̓à?ì·* 'I am a vagabond, roam about like a coyote', a denominative verb based on *mà?ì·* 'coyote'; *nè·m̓às* 'we 2 have got round': *ném̓às* 'I have got round', *nè·zmàs* 'he has got round'.[4]

It would seem, therefore, that the class of glottalized voiced continuants in Navaho, consisting of *n̓*, *m̓*, and *ẏ*, of which the two latter are but sparsely represented, arose in the first place as secondary phonemes, owing to the coalescence of an old *d* with an immediately following *n* or *m*, irregularly also with an immediately following *y*. The processes *-dn-*, *-dm-* > *-n̓-*, *-m̓-* may be considered true phonetic laws but *-dy-* > *-ẏ-* contravenes all known analogies, which suggest *-ẓ-* as the regular phonetic development. We shall therefore infer that *ẏ* arose, not by the operation of a normal phonetic law, but by a peculiar type of morphophonemic analogy. Perhaps analogies of this sort have played a greater part in linguistic history than is generally suspected. In Navaho we have the interesting spectacle of a peculiar class of phonemes 'on the make', as it were. Their functional dependence on the more common, non-

[4] I owe these forms of the verb 'to get round' to Father Berard Haile, O.F.M.

glottalized, forms of the voiced continuants (*n*, *m*, *y*) is still entirely clear, yet cases like -*n̓é·h* 'to crawl', which cannot easily be traced to an earlier *-*d-né·h*, though that is almost certainly what it does go back to, already show that there is a tendency for the glottalized voiced continuants to establish for themselves a more independent position in the configuration of Navaho phonemes.

6. We must now return to Nootka. This language is at the opposite extreme from Navaho, for its glottalized voiced continuants show little sign of a relationship to the corresponding non-glottalized voiced continuants. The glottalized varieties have obviously been completely independent phonemes for a very long time and comparison with Kwakiutl, a remotely related language,[5] confirms this, for in both languages these consonants occupy the same position. Among the cognates are examples illustrating them, e.g. Nootka *n̓op-* 'one' : Kwakiutl *n̓əm-* 'one' (syllabically final *m* becoming *p* in Nootka; before this *p* original *ə* labialized to *o*, phonetically open *u*). As no obvious biconsonantal prototype can be suggested for either Nootka or Kwakiutl *n̓-* in this word and in similar words, we must ascribe the phoneme *n̓*, and with it also *y̓*, *w̓*, *m̓*, and *l̓*, to the early Wakashan[6] period.

There are, however, certain processes which strongly suggest that Nootka *y̓*, *w̓*, *m̓* , and *n̓* are of secondary origin, at least in part. These processes are shared by Nootka and Kwakiutl, so that the emergence of the glottalized voiced continuants is at least as old as the Wakashan period. One of the most important of these processes is the 'hardening' of consonants when they are immediately followed by suffixes with inherently 'hardening' power. In the main the 'hardening' process consists of glottalization. Thus, in Kwakiutl *p*, *t*, *kʷ*, *c*, *q*, *l*, *xʷ*, to single out a number of consonants, are 'hardened' to *p̓*, *t̓*, *k̓ʷ*, *c̓*, *q̓*, *l̓*, *w̓* respectively; *q̓*, undoubtedly a Wakashan phoneme, develops to Nootka *ʔ*, a laryngeated ('strangulated') glottal stop, phonemically distinct from *ʔ*, while -*l̓*- develops to Nootka -*y̓*-. The other of these 'hardened' consonants remain in Nootka. Thus, to give only a few Nootka examples, *hap-* 'hair' + '-*itol* [R] 'dreaming of . . .'[7] yields *hahap̓itol* 'dreaming of hair'; *hopt-* 'in hiding' + '-*a·ʔa* 'on the rocks' yields *hopt̓a·ʔa* 'in hiding on the rocky (shore)'; *ʔi·kʷ-* 'pair of brothers' + '-*akλi* 'at the rear, last'

[5] The degree of genetic relationship of Nootka and Kwakiutl is hardly greater than that of, say, Russian and German.

[6] Wakashan is the term employed by Americanists for a linguistic group which includes two main branches: Kwakiutl, consisting of Kwakiutl proper, Bella Bella, and Kitamat; and Nootka, consisting of Nootka proper (also known as Aht), Nitinat, and Makah. This synthesis was first established by Boas.

[7] '- is a symbol to indicate the 'hardening' effect of a suffix. R indicates that the suffix causes reduplication of stem; L, that the suffix causes lengthening of stem vowel.

yields *ɬiˑƙʷak̓ƛi* 'the two brothers (are) at the rear, come last'; *ɬoc* 'large
sea-egg' + absolutive suffix '-*op* yields *ɬoċop*; *čikit-q-* stem abstracted
(because of current relation of Nootka -*t-q-:-n-*) from *čikinis*, borrowed
from English 'chickens', + '-*is* 'eating . . .' yields *čikitːis* 'eating chicken';
hoɬ- 'dancing' + '-*as* 'outdoors, in the village' yields *hoẏas* 'dancing in
the village'; *ʔoxʷ-* 'paddle' (absolutive *ʔoxʷaˑp*) + '-*ahs* 'in a vessel'
yields *ʔoẇahs* 'a paddle (is) in the canoe'. In part, therefore, non-initial
ẏ, *ẇ*, *ṁ*, and *ṅ*, like other non-initial glottalized consonants, can be
shown to go back to the 'hardening' of glottalized continuants, such as
-*ɬ-* and -*xʷ-*. The chief types of Nootka 'hardening' to these consonants
are:

-*n*-	'hardened' to -*ṅ*-	
-*m*-	"	" -*ṁ*-
-*ɬ*-	"	" -*ẏ*-, sometimes -*ẇ*-
-*s*-	"	" -*ẏ*-
-*š*-	"	" -*ẏ*-
-*xʷ*-	"	" -*ẇ*-
-*ḥ*- (rarely)	"	" -*ẇ*-

Nootka *š* goes back, in the main, to Wakashan *x* (voiceless prepalatal
spirant); -*ḥ*- (laryngeated *h*, similar to Arabic *ḥ*) is developed from -*x*-
(voiceless velar spirant) or its labialized form, -*xʷ*-, 'hardening' of *ḥ*
to -*ẇ*- always implying an underlying Wakashan -*xʷ*-. Of the four
glottalized voiced continuants, therefore, two (*ṅ* and *ṁ*) may be direct
resultants of a glottalizing process dependent on an initial peculiarity of a
suffixed element, and two (*ẏ* and *ẇ*) may result, more indirectly, from
glottalization, voicing and loss of spirantal friction or shift in articulatory
position, of voiceless spirants or their prototypes (*ɬ*, *s*, **x*, *xʷ*, **xʷ*),
dependent on the same initial peculiarity of a suffixed element. No
doubt the three etymological sources for *ẏ* and the two (or three)
etymological sources for *ẇ* were originally reflected in five distinct
glottalized phonemes (perhaps -*ɬ̓*-, -*ƚ̓*-, -*γ̓*-, -*γ̓ʷ*-, -*γ̓ʷ*-). This is confirmed
by the fact that in Kwakiutl the 'hardened' forms of -*ɬ*-, -*s*-, and *x* are
respectively -*ɬ̓*-, -*ċ*-, and -*ṅ*-, the last of which suggests that 'hardened'
Wakashan -*γ̓*- was a different phoneme from the primary *ẏ* shared by
Kwakiutl and Nootka.

What this 'initial peculiarity of a suffixed element' was we cannot be
sure of at present. That it was not the simple presence of a glottal stop is
likely, for there are several suffixes which begin with *ʔ* that remains
unabsorbed by the preceding consonant, such as -*ʔato* 'to fall off, come
off', -*ʔokt* 'obtained by . . .', -*ʔaɬ* 'aware of . . .'; thus *his-* 'to hit' + -*ʔokt*

yields *his-ʔokt* 'obtained by violence', not *hiẏokt (contrast *hiẏo·ƛ* 'to hit
on the rocks' < *his-* + *'-o·ƛ* 'on the rocks', momentaneous aspect).
There may have been a weak consonant, say *-h-*, following the ʔ in the
case of 'hardening' suffixes, which had the effect of throwing the ʔ back
on the preceding syllable, with resultant glottal absorption or 'hardening', while the *h* was left to begin the following syllable. Later, when
nearly all but analogical *h*'s (chiefly in reduplication, e.g. *hihis-*, distributive form of *his-*) disappeared in non-initial position, the syllabic
division was shifted and the appearance created of simple glottal absorption. If this view is correct, *hisʔokt* derives from an early *his-ʔokt*, but
ƛoƛoẏi·h 'fishing for herrings' < *ƛos-* 'herring' (absolutive *ƛos-mit*)
+ *'-i·h* [ʀ] 'hunting, collecting . . .' derives from **ƛoƛos-ʔhi·x̣⁽ʷ⁾* >
**-ƛoṡhi·x̣⁽ʷ⁾* > **-ƛoźi·x̣⁽ʷ⁾* > Nootka *-ƛoẏi·h*; the *-ʔ-* of the suffix would
be responsible for the glottalization of the emergent *-ẏ-*, the former *-h-*
for the 'softening' (see below) of the glottalized spirant (*-ṡ-* ?) lying back
of the present *-ẏ-*. Be this as it may, it can be shown from a comparison
of Kwakiutl and Nootka elements that consonant + ʔ does not yield a
'hardened' consonant; in other words, that the difference between retained ʔ and 'hardening' of preceding consonant is not simply a matter of
difference of chronology, the 'hardening' process being due to an early,
Wakashan, glottalizing, but the mechanical preservation of ʔ to a later
Nootka process. An example of preserved consonant + ʔ that must go
back to the Wakashan period is Kwakiutl *-x̣ʔənx̣* '. . . year', Nootka
-qʔič̣, Wakashan **-qʔəḳx̣* (voiceless stopped consonants are spirantized
before certain consonants in Kwakiutl; for earlier Kwakiutl **-x̣ʔəx̣x̣*
> *-x̣ʔənx̣*, cf. 'hardening' of *-x̣-* to *-ṅ-* above).

7. The theory that Nootka and Kwakiutl 'hardening' are due to the
pooling of two historically distinct processes, glottalization and 'softening', receives some weight from the fact that there is an independent
but related 'softening' effect exerted by several suffixes on the immediately preceding consonant. The 'softening' effect is very clear in
Kwakiutl, which possesses three distinct series of stops and affricates
('intermediate' or voiceless lenis, aspirated voiceless fortis, and glottalized: e.g. *b*, *p*, *ṗ*). The 'softening' suffixes change aspirated voiceless
stops and affricates to their corresponding intermediates (e.g. *t* to *d*,
c to *ʒ*). As Nootka has pooled the old intermediates and aspirates in a
single voiceless fortis series (unaspirated before vowels, aspirated as
syllabic finals), the old 'softening' process is visible only with spirants
and here only in considerably diminished range. Those suffixes (like
'*-iƚ*[8] 'in the house' and '*-is* 'on the beach') which have the 'softening'

[8] '- indicates 'softening'.

effect change *l* to *y* (or *w*), *s* and *š* to *y*, and *xʷ* and *ḥ* (if < *xʷ*) to *w*; e.g. *-ol* 'place of . . .' + '-*is* yields *-owis* '. . . place on the beach', *ʔi·ḥ-* 'big' + '*-a-čiλ* (inceptive) yields *ʔi·wačiλ* 'to get big', *-mal* 'moving about' + '*-il* 'in the house' yields *-mayil* > *-mail* > *-mi·l* 'moving about in the house' (older *ai* and *au* become monophthongized to Nootka *i·* and *o·* respectively). It cannot be argued that 'softening' is simply due to the mechanical lenition of an immediately following smooth vowel, for in both Kwakiutl and Nootka a very large number of suffixes which begin with a vowel leave the preceding consonant unaffected. Both 'softening' and 'hardening', therefore, with their parallel effects, must have a phonological feature in common which goes back to the Wakashan period and this feature is most likely to have been a weak consonant that has now disappeared. Now *h* is a very common initial consonant in both Kwakiutl and Nootka but is rare in other positions. As we have seen, it occurs postvocalically in reduplicated forms, where its presence is readily explained as due to analogy (an irregular *hi·s-* 'several hit' < *hihis-*, distributive of *his-*, could hardly have withstood analogical restoration under the pressure of thousands of regular forms like *mimis-* 'several smell', distributive of *mis-*). Significantly enough, present intervocalic *h* shows a tendency itself to 'soften' and palatalize to *-y-* after *i* in certain very common stems, e.g. *hiyil* < *hihil*, distributive of *hil* 'at that place, there'; *hiyiq-* and *hihiq-* 'various things', distributive of *hiq-* 'all'. 'Hardening' is not a process opposed to 'softening', as originally conceived by Boas for Kwakiutl, but a 'glottalized softening'. 'Lenition' (due to former *-h-* ?) and 'glottalized lenition' (due to former *-ʔh-* ?) would seem to be the linguistically preferable terms.

It may be pointed out that it is at least conceivable that the '*-i-* of '*-il* and '*-is*, the two most common 'softening' suffixes of Nootka (and Kwakiutl: '*-i·l*, '*-i·s*) is an old demonstrative stem *hi*, which obviously occurs in an important series of local and referential stems: *hita-*, *hin-*, *hina-* empty stem or peg for attachment of semantically significant suffixes; *his-*, *hist-*, *hisa-*, *hista-*, *hil* 'at that place, there' (referential). The last series of stems is formally parallel to *ya·s-*, *ya·st-*, *ya·l*, *ya·* 'there, that' and to *yi·s-*, *yi·st-*, *yi·l*, *yi·* 'yonder', enabling us to isolate *hi* without difficulty. The meanings 'in the house' (often also 'inside' without reference to human abode) and 'on the beach' (originally, as can be shown, 'on a level stretch') are clumsy renderings of a more generalized type of orientation.

8. 'Hardening' is a process that had worked itself out long before the dialectic Nootka period. We cannot directly prove the presence of an old *-ʔ-* to account for it, because the *-ʔ-* which appears before a 'harden-

ing' suffix when the monosyllabic stem ends in a vowel (e.g. λa- 'stick-like object standing up' + '-a·ʔa 'on the rocks' yields λaʔa·ʔa '[tree, stick] standing up on the rocky place') is found also with 'softening' suffixes under the same conditions (e.g. λa- + '-is 'on the beach' yields λeʔis standing up on the beach', umlauted < *λaʔis); this glottal stop, while it may be a survival of the phoneme that actually caused the 'hardening', can also be a mere hiatus-filler, for a syllable must begin with a consonant and vocalic contraction cannot take place between an initial mono-syllabic stem ending in a vowel and an initial vowel of a suffix that 'hardens', 'softens' or begins with inherent -ʔ-, though such contraction does take place in subsequent syllables or when the suffix begins with a smooth vowel that has no disturbing effect on a preceding consonant (e.g. not only λa- + '-a·ʔa = λaʔa·ʔa, λa- + '-is = *λaʔis, but also λa- + -ʔi·-ʔa 'to get to be on the rocks' = *λaʔi·ʔa 'stick gets to be standing on the rocks' > λeʔi·ʔa; contrast λa- + -a·s 'on a surface' = λa·s '[stick] standing on [it]' and distributive λaλa·ʔa 'several trees standing on the rocks'). What probably happened is that original forms of type *λa-ʔi·- remained, that forms of type *λa-a·s contracted early, and that original forms of type *λa-ʔha·ʔa ('hardening') lost their -h- and thus leveled with the first type in this particular category of cases. The fourth original type, e.g. *λa-his ('softening') also lost its -h- and yielded at first dissyllabic *λais, analogically remodeled to *λaʔis, instead of eventually monophthongizing to *λi·s. Hence resulted a leveling, in forms involving retained -ʔ-, between 'hardening' and 'softening'.[9]

9. We have a few interesting cases in Nootka of forms in -ʔ- + vowel + voiced continuant which alternate with glottalized voiced continuant, suggesting that this class of consonants could also arise from an absorption of a ʔ by a following consonant when the intervening vowel had dropped out. Such cases are mere survivals of what was probably at one time an active process. Thus, the stem koʔoq- 'to berate, vituperate', probably monophthongized from earlier *koʔauq-, alternates with

---

[9] That -ʔ- of λeʔ *is* is merely analogical seems also to be indicated by the fact that a number of smooth-vowel suffixes, which neither 'harden' nor 'soften' pre-ceding consonants, also insert -ʔ- after a final vowel of the syllable. Thus, ča- 'island', ċa- 'stream', and ča- 'water' form absolutive (or durative) čaʔak, ċaʔak, čaʔak (cf. indifferent effect of -ak in such words as kimt-ak 'long pole extending from end to end', k̫as-ak 'dead limb, twig') distributive čača·k, ċaċa·k, čača·k. On the other hand, the 'softening', as well as 'hardening', in Kwakiutl of original -y-, -w-, -n-, -m-, -l- to -ẏ-, -ẇ-, -ṅ-, -ṁ-, -l̇- (e.g., han- 'hollow vessel is somewhere' + '-iˑl yields haṅiˑl 'kettle on floor'; see Boas, "Kwakiutl", in his *Handbook* of *American Indian Languages*, pp. 430, 473) might be interpreted to mean that 'softening' too is the result of an old absorption of a glottal stop, though it seems much simpler to assume that in Kwakiutl types -nʔh- and -nh- leveled to -ṅ-. Possible confirmation of this will be pointed out below, when Kwakiutl initial glottalized voiced continuants are discussed.

koẃaq-; in other words, an underlying **koʔawaq-* either reduces to **koʔawq-* (with loss of second *-a-*) > *koʔoq-* or to **koʔwaq-* (with loss of first *-a-*) > *koẃaq-*, syllabically final *ʔ* being impossible in Nootka, though very frequent in Kwakiutl. Much clearer than this example is the obviously archaic alternation of *ʔeʔim* 'at first, immediately', umlauted from **ʔaʔim*, with *ʔaṁa-* 'at a proximate time (immediately before or immediately after), immediately, at first, for the first time'. In order to understand these forms, it is necessary to know that syllabically final *m* and *n* have a light *i*-murmur release, that they go back to original *m, n* + vowel (*a, i,* or *o*; original syllabically final *m* and *n* become *p* and *t*), and that original *a* preceding such elements (*mⁱ, nⁱ*) regularly thins to *i*. After a non-initial consonant *-ama* (*-ami, -amo*) and *-ana* (*-ani, -ano*), except under conditions which we need not attempt to define here, develop to *-in* (i.e. *inⁱ*) and *-im* (i.e. *-imⁱ*) respectively, whether in final or non-final position (e.g. *-ła·, -ła* 'having ... as name', durative, forms momentaneous *-ła·noχ*, alternating with **-łanoχ* > *-łinχ*, i.e. *-łinⁱχ*; similarly, *-ma* 'thing', when combined with *-ẃana-, -ẃinⁱ* 'in the middle', forms *-ẃanimⁱ* 'thing in the middle'). This means that *ʔeʔim* is not only closely related in meaning to *ʔaṁa-* but, in all likelihood, goes back to a form, **ʔaʔama*, that is originally nothing but a phonetic variant of *ʔaṁa-*. It is quite possible that **ʔaʔama* was originally the independent form, as which (*ʔeʔim*) it is still used, while *ʔaṁa-* was always used as the base for derivations, as which alone it is found today. Present cases of *ʔeʔim-* with derivational suffixes (which, if 'hardening' or 'softening', require an inserted *-ʔ-* after *m*, in other words *ʔeʔimⁱ-ʔ-*) are perhaps merely analogical, as derivations are often secondarily based on abso-lutive or durative forms rather than on the proper 'combining forms'. This interpretation of the relation between *ʔeʔim* and *ʔaṁa-* seems simpler than to consider the former a reduplicated form of *ʔaṁa-*, for *ʔeʔim* is not, as a matter of fact, the distributive of *ʔaṁa-*. Both of these stems are, then, divergent forms of an inherently reduplicated **ʔaʔama-*, which we cannot analyze further at present. Presumably, when the final *a* of this stem was non-final, the second *a* was elided (original stress patterns: **ʔaʔáma* but **ʔàʔamá-* ? but stress is not functional in Nootka today), the resulting **ʔaʔma-* yielding *ʔaṁa-*.

10. Far more numerous than such isolated cases are those in which *-ẏ-, -ẃ-, -ṁ-, -ṅ-* alternate with *-y-, -w-, -m-, -n-* without a trace of preceding *-ʔ-*. Cases in point are: *-ṅok*, momentaneous *-ṅokʷiχ : -nkʷ-*[R] 'at, on, of the hand' (e.g. *λiλis-ṅok* 'white-handed', *ya·ya·k-ṅok* 'sore-handed': *sosi-nkoχ* 'to get hold of by the hand' < **soso-nokʷi-λ, titinkom* 'hand-wiper' < **titi-nokʷi-ma* 'thing for wiping the hands', *kʷikʷi-nk-so*

'hand' with obscure stem k^wi- and suffix -*so*, possibly also in *holi-nk* 'benumbed of hand')[10]; -*ńi*, -*ńi·* : -*n* 'to come' (e.g. *ʔo-ńi·* 'that one comes' : *hini-n* 'to come' < empty stem *hina-* + *-ni*); -*ńiq-*, -*ńi·q-* 'down a slope' : -*nq-* (e.g. *po-ńi·q-saχ* 'several run down a slope to the beach' : *hiti-nq-is* 'down a slope on the beach' > 'the beach' < empty stem *hita-* + *-niq-* + '-*is*); -*cowat*[L] 'on . . . side, on the . . . side' : -*co·t* 'on . . . side' (= theoretical *-cowt* ?); -*wilta* 'out of a canoe' : -*olta* (= theoretical *-wlta*; e.g. *taq-wilta* 'to get directly out of the canoe' : *hinolta* 'to come out of the canoe' < empty stem *hina-* + *-wlta*); *nayaq-* 'baby', absolutive *nayaq-ak* : *na·ni·q-a* 'lulling to sleep' < reduplicated **na·naiq- = *na·nayq-*, probably a denominative verb based on an older form of stem underlying *nayaq-*.

It is fairly obvious that in cases of this sort we are dealing with divergent developments of a single element under differing phonetic conditions. To understand these developments we must take account of the fact that the sequence vowel + ? + vowel, when the first vowel is in the second or a following syllable of the word, contracts to a long vowel, which may then be secondarily shortened. The rules of contraction are quite complex as to detail and a few examples must suffice: *ma-* 'to dwell' + '-*as* 'on the ground' yields *maʔas* 'tribe', but its plural, with reduplication and lengthening *t*-infix, is *ma·tma·s* 'tribes'; *χa-* + '-*akχi* 'at the rear' yields *χaʔakχi* 'the (stick) is standing at the rear', but *hayo* 'ten' + '-*akχi* yields *haya·kχi* 'having ten at the rear', distributive *hahayakχi*; *ti-* 'boulder' + '-*akχi* = *tiʔakχi* 'boulder at the rear', but -'*akχi* + inherently possessive '-*at* = '-*akχat*, e.g. *ya·k̓ʷakχat* 'having one's buttocks sore'. If, now, we examine cases like postconsonantal -*ńok^w-* : postvocalic -*nk^w-*, we shall be led to surmise that these divergent forms are independent reflexes of a basic -ʔ v*nok^w-* (in which v means *a*, *i*, or *o*); that -ʔv- contracted with preceding *a*, *i*, or *o* to -v·-, whence frequently shortened -v-, which united with following -*no*- to -*in*-, i.e. -*in^i*-; and that, on the other hand, when v was itself elided, the ?, inasmuch as it could not be absorbed by the preceding syllable-ending consonant, coalesced with the following *n* to *ń*. Thus, **χiχisʔanok^w* (assuming that v = *a*) > **χiχisʔnok^w* > *χiχisńok*, but **titiʔanok^wima* > **tita·nok^wima*, shortened (because of reduplicated form of word?) to **titanok^wima* > *titin^ikom^i*. Similarly, an old **naʔayaq-* > **naʔyaq-* > *nayaq-*, but *na·naʔayaq-* > **na·na·yaq-* > **na·nayq-* > *na·ni·q-*. In other words, the alternations *n* : *ń*, *m* : *m̓*, *y* : *y̓*, *w* : *w̓*, in non-initial position, are correlates of such

---

[10] There is a survival of -*nk^w-* 'at the hand' [R] in Kwakiutl *cancank^w-a* 'to wash the hands', with secondary stem *cank^w-*; cf. Kw. *co·x^w-* 'to wash', N. *co-*. This seems to imply that the Nootka alternation of glottalized and non-glottalized *n* is of Wakashan age.

syllabic alternations as *maʔas* : *-ma·s*. If we may generalize from these cases and from those due to 'hardening', it would appear that many, eventually perhaps all, examples of glottalized voiced continuants in Nootka in medial position are due to glottal absorption, the ʔ responsible for this process either preceding or following the continuant (e.g. *-ʔn-* > *-ṅ-*; *-nʔh-* > *-ṅ-*).

11. A careful scrutiny of the Kwakiutl and Nootka lexical materials would undoubtedly yield confirmatory comparative evidence. One striking instance is Kwakiutl '*-aʔano·*[11] 'rope, line' (e.g. *səg-aʔano·* 'harpoon line') : Nootka *-aṅo-ł*, *-a·ṅo-ł* [L] 'all along, on a long thing' (durative), *-aṅo·-ƛ*, *-a·ṅo·-ƛ* (momentaneous), often *-aṅo·-*, *-a·ṅo·-* in combinations (e.g. *hi·n-a·ṅo-ḥsim* 'whaling spear' < *hin-* empty stem + *-a·ṅo·-* [L] + '*-aḥs* 'in the canoe' + *-im* 'thing'). Here the **-aʔano·-*, **-a·ʔano·-* required by theory to explain Nootka *-aṅo·-*, *-a·ṅo·-* is directly given by its Kwakiutl cognate, *-aʔano·*. We do not know enough about Wakashan phonology as yet to explain why absorption took place in Nootka but not in Kwakiutl. Apparently contraction processes of various sorts were more far-reaching in Nootka than in Kwakiutl.

Nevertheless, there seem to be a few examples in Kwakiutl too of glottalized voiced continuants in medial position resulting from a coalescence of ʔ with following *y*, *w*, *m*, *n*, *l*. Thus *ʔaʔams* 'bad luck, defiled' : *ʔaṁe·la* 'to spoil, to make a mistake' < **ʔaʔams-* + '*-la* (*-y-*, 'softened' from *-s-*, vocalized to *-e·-* before consonant); *ʔaẏo·s-əla* (durative) 'to understand' < **ʔaʔayo·s-* with primary reduplication : regularly reduplicated *ʔaʔayo·ċ-a* 'to try to understand' < unreduplicated base *ʔayo·s-* + '*-a* [R] 'to endeavor to . . .'; *ʔaẏaso·* 'hand' with primary reduplication[12] < **ʔaʔayaso·* (cf. Nootka *kʷikʷinkso* above); *ʔawał-iłɛ·la* 'to walk about searching for something' < **ʔaʔawał-* (reduplicated from **ʔawał-* ?; cf. reduced form of stem in *ʔo·ł-əla* 'to turn a corner' < **ʔauł-*) + *-iłɛ·la* 'about' (this suffix, though not regularly reduplicating, seems to favor reduplicated forms, e.g. *do·dəqʷiłɛ·la* 'to look about' : *do·qʷ-* 'to see'; note weakening of *do·qʷ-* to *-dəqʷ-* as of **ʔawał-* to **-ʔwał-*); *ʔaṅa·k̲* 'enough', reduplicated from **ʔaʔana·-k̲* ? (cf. Nootka *ʔana* 'only' ?).

In view of the possibilities of dialectic development of glottalized voiced continuants, it is not surprising that it sometimes happens that Nootka has what seems to be a permanent glottalization where Kwakiutl shows the more archaic alternation. A case in point is Nootak

---

[11] Boas writes *-aanō* (*op. cit.* 511) but all cases of Kwakiutl v- and -vv₁- are to be interpreted as ʔv- and -vʔv₁-. Smooth vowel initials and combinations of vowel and smooth vowel are impossible in Kwakiutl and Nootka.

[12] Such primary reduplications occur with other Kwakiutl nouns for paired body-parts, e.g. eye, ear, foot, kidney.

ḥanaḥ 'naked', corresponding to Kwakiutl *x̣aṅa·-la* 'naked', which point to a Wakashan **x̣aṅax̣*, **x̣aṅa·-*. So far as Nootka is concerned, the *ṅ* is a primary phoneme, but Kwakiutl *x̣ən-x̣ʔi·d* (momentaneous) 'to undress' suggests that here too *ṅ* is secondary.

In Kwakiutl an enormous number of secondary cases of *ẏ* and *ẇ* arise when the vowels *e·* (*ε·* < *aya*) and *o·* (*ɔ·* < *awa*) are resolved into *ay* and *aw* respectively and these heterosyllabic groups are then 'hardened' to *aẏ* and *aẇ*. Thus, *ʔa·ẇage·ʔ* 'the place between, inside' < *ʔo·-* stem of location + *'-ag-* 'among' + noun-forming *-e·ʔ*; *na·naqaẇa* 'to try to meet' < *na·qo·* 'to meet' + *'-a* [R] 'to endeavor to . . .'; *ca·caẏa* 'to try to draw water' < *cε·*(< **cay-a*) 'to draw water' + *'-a* [R]. Of greater interest to us is a group of cases, equally numerous, in which *e·ʔ* and *o·ʔ* are resolved before vowels into *aẏ* and *aẇ*. Thus, *nɔ·qaẏas* 'his mind' < *nɔ·qe·ʔ* 'mind' + *-as* 'his'; *λəẇe·s* 'and his' < *λo·ʔ* 'and' + *-e·s* 'his'; *ʔaẏəlkʷ* 'attendants' < **ʔe·ʔəlkʷ*, reduplicated plural of *ʔəlkʷ* 'attendant'. And, further, secondarily labialized gutteral and velar spirants (*xʷ*, *x̣ʷ*) develop *ẇ* because of immediately following *ʔ*, e.g. *bo·x̣uẇi·d* 'to leave' < *bo·-* + momentaneous *-x̣ʔi·d*.

12. It is hardly to be expected that we should have reflexes initially of an old alternation in Wakashan between glottalized voiced continuant and *ʔ* + vowel + voiced continuant, for both Nootka and Kwakiutl are non-prefixing languages and, as these alternations, if present, could not easily develop systematic morphophonemic significance (except perhaps in connection with reduplication), they would inevitably tend to be ironed out by analogy. Nevertheless there are a few cases which are suggestive, though obscure. Nootka *ẏaq-* 'long' may be interpreted as reduced from an old *ʔaya-* 'much' + **-q-* 'in length (?)' (this hypothetical *-q-* is perhaps preserved in Nootka *-q-ʔič̣ḥ* '. . . year, for . . . many years' : *-ʔič̣ḥ*, *'-ič̣ḥ*, *'-i·č̣ḥ* 'season of . . .'). Much clearer is dialectic (Ucluelet and N. Nootka) *ṅi·c*, *ṅi·c- ʔis* 'short', which is synonymous with Tsishaath[13] *ʔa·ne-ʔis*. *-ʔis* is diminutive; *ʔa·ne-* is umlauted from *ʔa·na-*, based on *ʔana* 'only that; thus much, thus many', 'short' in effect meaning 'diminutively thus much (in length)'. Now the older form of *-ʔis* is **-ʔic*, as is shown by the compounded *-ʔic-aλ* (diminutive + *'-aλ* 'now, then') and this older form is preserved in *ṅi·c* < **ṅaic* < **ʔana-ʔic*, a parallel form to early **ʔa·na-ʔic*; *ṅi·c-ʔis* is probably a later pleonastic form, with double diminutive. A further example is *ṅama-* 'only', probably related to *ʔana-* (see above). The element *-ma-* is probably a variant of *-ṁa*, *-ṁa·* '. . . far off, as far as . . .; . . . in quantity, degree', an original **ʔana-ʔama-* 'only to that degree', after contracting to **ʔanama-*

---

[13] Which we take as our basic Nootka dialect.

(see above), still further reducing to *ṅama-*. The verb *ẇaqʔoˑ* (durative and momentaneous) 'to go to a feast in response to an invitation', combining form *ẇaqʔo-q-*, is probably reduced from an irregularly reduplicated *ʔawa-q-ʔauq-*, *ʔawaqʔaw-a*. If this analysis is allowed, an etymology is suggested which may or may not be true. With reduplicated *ẇa-...-ʔoˑ* compare *ẇa-čk-* (*ẇa-šk-*, *ẇi-ṅčk-*) 'living beings bunched together' and with reduplicating *-q-* (*..-q-*) compare *-q*[ʀ] 'traveling in ... vehicle, canoe'; in other words, *ẇaqʔoˑ* would properly mean 'to come (as invited guest) in a canoe, crowded with one's people', which fits the cultural requirements.

Turning to Kwakiutl, we have two striking examples of *ẇ-* alternating with *ʔ-* + vowel + *-w-*. These are *ẇaˑ-la-s* 'large' (sg.) : *ʔawoˑ* 'great' (pl.) (also with suffixes, e.g. *ẇaˑla-ʔas* 'distance' but *ʔawoˑ-ẓəm* 'great tribes'); and *ẇa-* 'size, measure' (sg.) : *ʔawa-*, *ʔawɔˑ-* (pl.) (only with suffixes, e.g. *ẇaˑ-xa-ċoˑ* 'measure inside' : *awɔˑ-xa-ċoˑ* 'measures inside'). These common and important words seem to point to original *ʔawáˑ-la-* : *ʔáwaw* and *ʔawáˑ*:*ʔáwa-*, *ʔáwawa-* respectively. A probable example of *ṁ-* : *ʔam-* in Kwakiutl is *ʔama-* 'small' (pl.), also an extended form, apparently, *ʔamay-* (*ʔameˑẋʔid* 'to become small' < *ʔamai-*; *ʔamaʔinx-e·ʔ* 'youngest child' = *amaẏ-ənx-e·ʔ* 'the youngest in season, time'?; *ʔamaˑẏace·* 'fifth child'):Koskimo (Kw. dialect) *-ṁən* 'young of an animal' (= N. *-ṁit, -ṁiˑt* 'son of ...'), Kw. *-ṁane·xʷ* 'small' (pl.) (= N. *ṁiniⁱḥ* plural suffix; *-ḥ, -iˑḥ* is a common plural suffix in Nootka, Kw. *-e·xʷ* probably a survival of this element, hence N. *-ṁiniⁱḥ* probably extended in meaning from 'small ones').

13. Still further examples of the probable emergence of initial glottalized voiced continuants appear when we compare Kwakiutl and Nootka. There are enough examples of the correspondence in the two languages of these phonemes in initial position to make it reasonably certain that the glottalized voiced continuants had become phonemic in character in the Wakashan period or, at the least, that *ʔ* + *y, w, m, n, l* were allowable initial consonant clusters at that time; e.g., besides Nootka *ṅop-* 'one': Kwakiutl *ṅəm-*, already quoted, may be noted:N. *ẏak-* 'in view, peering out; having one's neck stretched' < *ẏaxʷ-* (perhaps related to suffixed *-ẏoˑč* [ʟ] 'extending out, in view' < *-ẏaxʷ-ḳ*): Kw. *ẏəxʷ-a* 'land looms up'; N. *ẏas-*, *ẏas-x-*, *ẏas-xʷ-* 'opened out, having the legs spread out':Kw. *ẏɨl-* 'to spread the legs' (perhaps < *ẏəy-l-*, 'softened' from *ẏəs-*); N. *ṁinaˑl-i* 'fishing bank' : Kw. *ṁənaˑla* 'fish gather at mouth of river'; N. *ṁokʷ-* 'stone':Kw. *ṁəkʷ-* 'a round thing is somewhere' (e.g. *ṁəkʷ-ayind* 'to put [a stone] on top'); N. *ṁačk-* 'having the jaws closed' < *ṁaḳxʷ-* : Kw. *ṁəkʷ-*, *ṁəḳ-əxɔ* 'to choke'; N. *ṁoš-*

'closed', *m̓oš* 'fish weir' < **m̓əxʷ-x̣* : Kw. *m̓əu̓-a* 'salmon weir' < **m̓əxʷ-* + *'-a* 'on the rocks'; N. *m̓au̓-a·* 'delivering, taking a thing to its destination' : Kw. *m̓axʷ-* 'to carry property'; N. *m̓ay-ink-šiχ̣* (momentaneous) 'dancers join in completing a circle' (*-ink* 'together') < **m̓al-*[14] : Kw. *m̓əl-* 'to plait a rope, to take a turn on a trail'; N. *m̓oqʷ-* 'phosphorescent, glowing' < **m̓əl-qʷ-* : Kw. *m̓əl-* 'white'; N. *n̓a·-s* 'daylight' : Kw. *n̓a·-la* 'day, light'; N. *n̓o꞉aq-* < **n̓əq̓ʷ-aq-* (for *'-aq-* cf. *'-aqχ* 'in, into') 'to swallow' : Kw. *n̓aqʷ-* 'to swallow'.

But by no means all cases of *y̓-, u̓-, m̓-, n̓-, l̓-* which appear in these can be as archaic as the examples that we have just given presumably are. Some of them are secondary or point to an old Wakashan alternation of type *y̓-* : *ʔay-*. Such are: N. *m̓isk-* 'dull, without power' < **m̓əsxʷ-* < **ʔm̓əsxʷ-* : Kw. *ʔaʔo·ms* 'man of ordinary power' < reduplicated **ʔaʔaums* (< **ʔaʔaməsxʷ* ?); N. *m̓a-* 'holding in the teeth, in the mouth', *m̓ač-* 'to close the teeth', *m̓ačk-* 'having the jaws closed', Kw. *m̓ək̓ʷ-* 'to choke' (see above) : Kw. *ʔam-* 'closed up, tight'; N. *n̓oš-* 'to distribute property in a potlatch (after the more important gifts have been made to chiefs)' < **ʔn̓axʷ-* *x̣-* : Kw. *ʔane·xʷ-s꞊ʔɔ·-ʔe·* 'what is left over' (cf. *-s꞊ʔɔ·-la* 'deserted'); N. *n̓eʔiχ̣-* 'lit up, light' < **ʔn̓aʔ-* : Kw. *ʔan̓ʔq-a* 'to light fire, charcoal' (this alternation is likely to be old, cf. Kw. *n̓aq̆u-la* 'light' and N. *n̓a·-s* above); perhaps also N. *ʔana, n̓a-ma-* 'only' (see above) : Kw. *n̓a·xŭ-la* 'alone' (related to Kw. *n̓a·xʷ-* 'all'?).

14. There are a number of Kwakiutl words in *ha-* which look as if they were irregularly reduplicated forms. As this *ha-* occurs rather more frequently before *y̓, u̓, m̓, n̓, l̓* than pure chance would render likely, in view of the relative infrequency of these phonemes, we are confronted by the possibility that another source of the glottalized voiced continuants in Kwakiutl is *h* + voiced continuant. Early **hya-* would yield *y̓a-*, according to this theory, and early reduplicated **hahya-* would yield *haya-*; later on *y̓a-* would of course reduplicate to *y̓ay̓a-*. Examples in point may be: *hay̓əxʷ-ano·ma* 'to come to dance' < **hahyəxʷ-* (see below for Nootka confirmation): *y̓əxʷ-* 'to dance'; *hayano·* 'round-headed club' < **hahyano·* ?; *hayamo·t* 'mark, sign' < **hahya-mo·t* (*-mo·t, -mu·t, -mut* 'remains of. . .' reduplicates, e.g. *xʷa·x̣ul-mu·t* 'what is left over from cutting salmon': *xʷa·χ-a* 'to cut salmon', hence *haya-mo·t* is self-defined as reduplicated); *hau̓i·nal-əla* 'to frighten away' (plur.) < **hahwi·nal-əla* : *u̓i·nal-əla* (sing.) [read *u̓i·natəla* ?]; *ham̓o·* 'pigeon' < **hahmo·* (for similar reduplicated animal name cf. *ho·mho·m*

---

[14] There is no properly phonemic *l̓* in Nootka. Wakashan *l̓* almost certainly developed to Nootka *y̓*; cf. 'hardening' of Nootka *l* to *y̓* (*u̓*), 'softening' to *y* (*w*), as against Kwakiutl *l̓* and *l* respectively.

'blue grouse'); *haməlq̇ŭ-la* 'to remind' < **hahməlq̇ʷ-* [read *haməlq̇ŭ-* ?] : *m̓əlq̇ŭ-la* 'to remember'; *hańakʷ-e·la* 'to do quickly' < **hahnakʷ-* = **hah-nakʷ-* ? (cf. *ha-* 'quickly'); *hańas-x̣aw-e·ʔ* 'collar-bone of porpoise' < **hahnas-x̣aw-* (*-x̣aw-* = *-x̣o·* 'neck' ? cf. *ʔo·-x̣a·w-e·ʔ* 'neck'); *hala̓-ba-la* 'quickly' < **hahla-* (*hala,-* *hala·-* of many derivatives, e.g. *hala·-ga* 'go away!', *hala-k̓a·la* 'to tell to hurry', *hala·x̣ʷa* 'to eat quickly', probably represents the unreduplicated form); *hala̓·-la* 'to hesitate' < **hahla·-* (probably based on an old **hala·-, *hala-* > N. *haya·-ʔak, hayi-m̓h̓* 'to be ignorant'). An example of *hay-* : *y̓-* (<*hy-*) is *hayo·t* 'rival' (<*haya-* 'to go along' [?] in *haya·qa* 'to pass', *haye·gi* 'to imitate', *hayo·l̓a·la* 'to bring out of woods' + *-o·t* 'fellow') : *y̓a-gas* 'woman friend' < **hya-* (reduced from *haya-*) + *-gas* 'woman'. Not all of these examples are certain but several are highly suggestive. The cluster **-hm̓-* would naturally become *-m̓-*; an example is *he·m̓a-ʔ o·mas* 'kinds of food' < plural-reduplicated **he·hm̓a-* : *ham̓(a)-* 'to eat'.

There are also cases in Kwakiutl in which *ha-* is a formative element (reduplicating syllable?) before non-glottalized voiced continuant (e.g. *hamanxŭ-lal* 'smiling dance' : *manx̣ʷ-* 'to smile'; *hawa·x̣ʔ-əla* 'to beg, to pray' : *wa·x̣ʔ-* 'to have mercy'; perhaps also *hawa·k̓as* 'great, dreadful', *hamane·kʷ-a* 'to be dazed', *hamase·lalis* 'grebe', *hane·naxʷ* 'to desire to go in company'). Some of these may be cases of early (aspirate) or late (glottal) dissimilation, e.g. *wa·x̣ʔ* < **u̓ba·x̣ʔ-* < **hwa·x̣ʔ-?*; *hane·naxʷ* < **hahnaihnaxʷ*? Cases of *hay-* (e.g. *hayatilagas* 'invisible spirit', *hayal̓cama* 'to keep secret', *haya·x̓o·-la* 'to warn' : *ya·x̓o·* 'take care') are likely to be dissimilated from **hah-* (cf. Nootka *hiyil̓* for **hihil̓*, distributive of *hil̓* 'there').

15. In Nootka **hy-, *hw-, *hm-, *hn-* did not become glottalized voiced continuants but simply dropped the *h-*. This is not only suggested by the absence of forms of type *hay-* which could be explained as developed from type *hahy-* but is directly indicated by the verbs *weʔič* 'sleeping' (sg.), momentaneous *weʔičo-ƛ* : *ho·ʔič* 'sleeping' (pl.) < **waʔiḳo* : **hawʔiḳo* < **hwaʔiḳo* : reduplicated **hahw(a)ʔiḳo*. This interpretation, curiously enough, is confirmed by the baby word for 'sleep', *ho·š*, which reconstructs to a **haux̣* that must have been the old simplification, in baby talk, of **hawaʔiko*, the prototype of reduced **hwaʔiḳo*. There are also cases of Kwakiutl glottalized voiced continuant which seem to be in relation to Nootka forms with *h-*, e.g. Kw. *y̓əxʷ-* 'to dance', *hay̓əxʷ-ano·ma* 'to come to dance' (see above) : N. *ho·ya·l̓* 'dancing', an irregular reduplicated durative, < **hohyaxl̓* < **həx⁽ʷ⁾hyax⁽ʷ⁾-la* (there are several such cases of N. durative *-l̓* < voiceless spirant + Wakashan durative *-la*, preserved in Kwakiutl

but lost as such in Nootka), from which was then abstracted the stem form *ħəx*^{w}*l-* > *hol-* (e.g. *hol-ma·s* 'going from house to house dancing'); Kw. *ýa 'oh!'*, *ýo·* (call from a distance), *ýɛ·* (exclamation of disgust) < *ħya*, *ħyawa*, *ħyaya*, reduced from exclamations of type *ħaya*, which represents a well-nigh universal pattern : N. *hay* (shout used in various rituals; interjection to attract attention), *ha·yi* 'I told you so!' (if this is correct, N. *ýo·ýo·-wa*ʔ*a·l* 'welcoming one heartily', which looks like an iterative of *-wa* 'to say...', hence < 'to keep saying *ýo·*', is based on a ceremonial *ýo·* borrowed from Kwakiutl *ýɔ·*); Kw. *ẃŭn-* 'to hide' < *ħwun-* < *ħwəmn-* : N. *hopt-* 'in hiding' < *ħomn-* < *ħwəmn-*; Kw. *ẃat-* 'kelp' < *ħwat-* : N. *hos-min*, *hoc-smin* 'kelp' < *ħot-smin* < *ħwət-sma-*; Kw. *ẃa·l-* 'to stop' < *ħwa·l-* : N. *hawi-ł-*, *hawi·-*, momentaneous *hawi-ƛ* 'to stop' < *ħawa·y-* < *ħawa·l-*.

Aside from cases such as these, in which *h* was preserved before a vowel or before an *o* which resulted from *w* + reduced vowel, *h* was bound to disappear, as in *we*ʔ*ič* above. Thus, we may deduce from correspondences of type Kw. *ý* : N. *y* an older (possibly Wakashan) *hy*. Examples are: Kw. *ẃe·-* 'how, where' < *ẃay-* < *ħway-* ('softened' from *ħwas-* ?) : N. *wa·s-*, *wa·s-t-*, *wa·s-a-*, *wa·s-i* 'where?', *wa·y-aq-* 'which?' < *ħwa·s-* ('softened' to *ħwa·y-*); Kw. *ẃe·ḵ-* 'to carry long, stiff thing (firewood, pole) on shoulder' < *ħwaiḵ-* : N. *wača-* 'piled up firewood' < *ħwaḵa-*; Kw. *ẃas-* 'dog' < *ħwas-* : N. *wa·win* 'hunting deer in the manner of wolves, employing wolf howls to scare out the deer', contracted < *ħwa-hwa-*ʔ*in* (*ħwahwáy-in* ?) (originally 'making the sound of dogs') < *ħwa(s)-* + *'-in* [ʀ] 'making the sound of ..'; Kw. *ṁa*ʔ*o·s-* 'to work' < *ħma*ʔ*au-s-* : N. *mamo-* 'working' < *ħmahmaw-*. This type of correspondence applies also in medial position, e.g. Kw. *hańak*^{w}*-e·la* 'to do quickly' < *ħahnak*^{w}*-* (see above) : N. *nawit* 'to do, finish, quickly' < *ħnax*^{w}*-* (*hnak*^{w}*-* ?) + *'-it*; Kw. *x̣aẃe·* 'loon' : N. *ħa·wi* 'small variety of loon' < *x̣aħwi*. An original *hn-* can also be inferred for Nootka when it has *n-* corresponding to Kwakiutl *han-*, e.g. N. *na*ʔ*o·-*, *na*ʔ*-o* 'accompanying, following' < *ħna*ʔ*aw-* ('softened' from *ħna*ʔ*ax*^{w}*-* ?) : Kw. *hane·nax*^{w} 'to desire to go in company' (see above); N. *ni-* 'hollow object, container', *ni-čiƛ* 'to carry in packbasket' < *hni-* : Kw. *han-* 'an open vessel is somewhere' (sg.), *han-x̣ƛa·-la* 'kettle'.

As syllabically final ʔ or glottalized consonant is not possible in Nootka, certain cases of initial glottalized voiced continuant in Nootka are likely to be due to absorption of such a glottal element. A clear case is N. *ṁo-* 'burning; setting on fire' < *ṁəl-* < *mə*ʔ*l-* or *məl*ʔ*-* : Kw. *məl-* 'to light a fire', *mal-e·*ʔ 'torch'. There are, however, also a number of cases of glottalized voiced continuant in Nootka which correspond to an unglottalized consonant in Kwakiutl, e.g. N. *ṅoẇi-*, *ṅoẇi-c-*, *ṅoẇi·-qso* 'father' (*ṅoẇi·-* 'softened' from **ṅoẇas-* ?) : Kw. *no·mas* 'old man' (for N. *-ẇ-* : Kw. *-m-* cf. perhaps also N. *haẇa-* 'to eat' : Kw. *ham̓(a)-* 'to eat' alternating with *ham-* in certain derivatives); N. *ṅiX̣-* 'supine', momentaneous *ṅiX̣-šiX̣* 'to lean, fall, back' : Kw. *nǝX̣-a* 'to lie on back'; N. *ẏo·-qʷa·* 'likewise' (probably compounded of a demonstrative *ẏo·-* and *qʷa·* 'thus, such, so') : Kw. *yu·* 'that near thee'. The reason for this divergence is far from clear. In at least one case Nootka *ṅ-* may go back to *ʔn-* (*ʔ* is a laryngeated glottal stop, regularly equivalent to Kwakiutl *q̓*) : *ṅi-* (durative *ṅi-ya·*), *ṅiq-* (durative *ṅiq-a·*) 'to sew' < **ʔni-*, **ʔniq-* < **q̓ni-*, **q̓niq-* : Kw. *q̓ǝn-*, *q̓an-* 'to sew' (this relation would seem to be parallel to that of N. *ni-* : Kw. *han-*, see above). Other, Kwakiutl, examples of alternation between glottalized and unglottalized consonants, in initial position, are: *mo·-* 'to pile up', *ma·w-a* 'to move', *mǝ·-x̣s* 'to load canoe' (cf. N. *maw-iqs* 'covered box' < 'box for storage of goods') : *m̓ǝw-e·s* 'heap on beach' (but plur. *mǝx̣mǝw-e·s*), *m̓ǝmw-a·la* 'cargo of canoe' (cf. probably also Kw. *m̓axw-* 'to carry property' : N. *maẇa·-* above); *ẏo·-ẏa* 'cold wind' : *yo·x̣ʷ-* 'wind', absolute *yo·la* < **yaw-ala*, *ya·w-ap-a* 'to set sail' (cf. N. *yo-*, durative *yo·ʔi*, 'wind blowing', *yox̣-ɬ-* 'to get blown by the wind'); *wǔl-* 'to stop, to arrest' : *ẇa·l-* 'to stop' (see above); *m̓ǝns-* 'to measure' : *mǝny-ayo* 'measure' < *mǝns-* + *'-ayo* 'instrument of. . .'.

16. The last example takes us back to our hypothesis (see 7 and note 8) that 'softening' in Kwakiutl and Nootka is due to the effect left behind by a former *-h-*. In that case an older **hmǝns-hayo* could have dissimilated to **mǝnshayo* > **mǝnzayo* > *mǝnyayo*. Again, there are many cases of instrumental and passive *-ẏo·*, *-ẏo* in Kwakiutl instead of normal *'-ayo*, *'-a·yo*, e.g. Koskimo *nǝl-ẏo·* 'song' < 'singing instrument'[15] (instead of expected **nǝla·yo* < *nǝl-* 'to sing' + *'-a·yo*), *cɛ·la-ẏo* 'dipper', *tǝḳo-ẏo* 'blown off by steam', Koskimo *lǝm-ẏo* 'rope', *no·ẏo* 'medicine put near back of pregnant woman' (: *nǝx̣ʷ-* 'near'); but also *q̓ǝn-yo* 'thread' < 'instrument of sewing' (**q̓ǝn-ẏo* dissimilated to *q̓ǝnyo* ?), *degǝm-yo* 'towel for face'. To Kw. *'-a·yo*, *'-ayo*, *-ẏo·*, *-ẏo* probably corresponds N. *-yo*, *-yo·* (after consonants), *-čo*, *-čo·* (after vowels) 'having been . . -ed'. These various forms are best reconciled on the basis of a Wakashan **-hayo*, **-ha·yo*, alternating, with loss of *-a-*, with **-hyo·*, **-hyo* > Kw. *-ẏo·*, *-ẏo*, N. *-yo·*, *-yo*; N. *-čo·*, *-čo* < **-g̣o·*, **-g̣o* < **-g̣-hyo·*, **-g̣-hyo* with intercalated *-g̣-*, frequent in both Kwakiutl and Nootka

[15] In Nootka too various types of songs are named with *-ẏak*, *-čak* 'instrument of . . .'.

(as -*č*-). But the Nootka instrumental, corresponding to Kwakiutl normal '-*ayo*, '-*a·yo*, is -*y̓ak* (after consonants), -*čak* (after vowels) < *-*y̓o-ʔak*, *-*čo-ʔak* (< *-*ḳo-* < *-*g̓-y̓o-*). It looks, therefore, as though Wakashan, like Nootka, distinguished an instrumental *-*ʔayo*, *-*ʔyo* (*-*ʔhayo*, *-*ʔhyo* ?) from a passive *-*hayo*, *-*hyo* and that the two formations merged in Kwakiutl because of the leveling of *-*ʔyo* and *-*hyo* to *y̓o* and because of the leveling of *-*ʔhayo* and *-*hayo* in certain cases (e.g. *-*n-ʔhayo* and *-*n-hayo* > -*n̓-ayo*). In this way would also be explained why a few important instrumental nouns, likely to be archaic formations, having 'hardening' '-*ayo* instead of the regular and far more common '-*ayo*, e.g. *təmy̓-ayo* 'baton' (*təms-* 'to beat time'), *se·w̓-ayo* 'paddle' (*se·x^w-* 'to paddle').

17. We see, then, that these rather curious phonemes can be shown to go back to coalescences of *ʔ* or *h* with following or preceding *y, w, m, n, l*, also to coalescences of other consonants, such as *d*, with following voiced continuants. The details naturally differ for the different languages but all the cases here considered have this in common, that a relatively weak consonantal phoneme, instead of disappearing entirely when in a cluster with a sonorant consonant, is absorbed by the latter, so that new consonantal phonemes emerge. These new phonemes, characterized by glottal affection, tend at first to be in a morphophonemic relation with the simple sonorant consonants. In time, however, they tend to take on the status of isolated phonemes. It would be interesting to analyze the status of these consonants in Haida, Tsimshian, Yokuts, and other American Indian languages in which they occur to see if there too there is reason to think that they are phonemic emergents due to absorption. Essentially, consonants of this sort are on a par with the nasalized vowels of so many languages, the *n* or *m* originally following a vowel becoming absorbed in the vowel, whence a new set of phonemes results. The French nasalized vowels are, of course, the most familiar example. The methodologically interesting point is suggested by cases of this sort that if a language has two sets of phonemes, one of which, B, can be reasonably defined as identical with the other, A, except for a definite qualitative plus which linguistic experience shows to be relatively infrequent, then the set B may be *suspected*, certainly not *assumed*, to have emerged from some type of absorption in the set A of, or from modification of the set A by, a phoneme (or group of phonemes) having something of the character of this qualitative plus. Entirely new phonemic categories, such as nasalization, glottalization, aspiration, rounding, palatalization, laryngealizing, emphasis, tonal distinctions, may thus arise as absorption products.

For the rest of this paper we should like to show how the phenomena we have considered for Navaho and, more particularly, for Nootka and Kwakiutl, may help us to understand certain Indo-European phonological developments, specifically in the prehistory of Greek. Assuming that Indo-European possessed four 'laryngeal' consonants, namely ' (a glottal stop followed by *e*-timbre of full grade vowel in its primary form), ? (another glottal phoneme followed by *a*-timbre of full grade vowel in its primary form), *x* (presumably a voiceless velar spirant = *ḫ*-, -*ḫḫ*- of Hittite), and γ (presumably a voiced velar spirant, Arabic 'ghain', = *ḫ*-, -*ḫ*- of Hittite), we have not the right to take it for granted that when a vowel dropped out between such a preceding 'laryngeal' and a following consonant, the laryngeal necessarily disappeared without a trace. To do this is to project back into the earliest period the feeling for vocalic syncope that developed in the later stages of many Indo-European dialects. If, for instance, Greek ἀμέλγω, ἀμολγή, with its 'prothetic' ἀ-, leads us, in accordance with the laryngeal hypothesis, to posit a base *xamelĝ- (or rather *xamelAĝ-[16]) or *?amelĝ- (or rather *?amelAĝ-), we must not implicitly abandon this same hypothesis when we deal with reduction products and allow the *x*- or ?- to disappear with the -*a*-. The fact that we have forms in *m*- (e.g. OIr. *bligim* < *mligim*, Goth. *miluks*, Toch. A *malke*) in the later dialects is far from justifying our dealing with an ablaut *xamel- : *mel- for the earliest period. We must either believe in our 'laryngeals' and speak of an ablaut *xamel- : *xmel- or discard them and deal only with the conventional *amel- : *mel-. It may well be that in the vast majority of cases such Indo-European sequences as *xm-, *'w-, *?y-, and *γl- simply became *m*-, *w*-, *y*-, and *l*-, or their appropriate reflexes, but we have no more right to assume this than to assume that, at a later period, the treatment of pre-Greek *sm*- was identical with that of *m*-. 'Losses' of elements are frequently fallacious because of our tendency not to look closely enough into the possibilities of absorption phenomena.

If, now, we posit an IE series 'y-, 'w-, 'm-, 'n-, 'l-, 'r-, a series ?y-, ?w-, ?m-, ?n-, ?l-, ?r-, and a series *xy*-, *xw*-, *xm*-, *xn*-, *xl*-, *xr*-, we have to inquire what happened to these clusters (initially and in other positions) in each of the main branches of IE. In the end it will undoubtedly prove far more economical of effort to assume little or nothing in the way of

---

[16] We use '*A*' to indicate any one of the four laryngeal consonants when it is desired to speak in general terms or when we have reason to suspect a laryngeal consonant (in this case chiefly because of the 'Stosston' of Lithuanian *mélžu*) but have not enough evidence to determine which one is involved. Similarly, it is convenient often to use '*A*' for a laryngeal which must have been either ? or *x*, say because of the *a*-timbre of the following vowel, but between which we cannot decide. This is, as a matter of fact, a frequent contingency.

sweeping reductions of these, to us, uncomfortable clusters and to keep our eyes open for distinctive reflexes of them in the IE dialects than to oversimplify our task by assuming radical reductions in the IE period. Hittite *xwantes* 'winds' (*ḫu-u-wa-an-te-eš*) should warn us. Applying this principle to the Greek reflexes of this very base (IE **xawe'-*, conventionally **wē-*, 'to blow'), we are helped forward at once to a valuable hypothesis with regard to early Greek phonology. An old **xawe'-* : **xwe'-*, we may surmise, need not have developed an early Greek **awē-* : **wē-*, for there is no reason for certainty that a prevocalic *x-* would behave the same way as a *x-* caught in a consonantal cluster *xw-*. The actual course of the development may very well have been something like this:

1. **xawe'-* or **xəwe'-*[17] (tautosyllabic) : **xwe'-*
2. **hawe'-* (or **həwe'-*) : **hwe'-*
3. **hawe'-* (or **həwe'-*) : **ẘe'-*
4. **hawē-* (or **həwē-*) : **ẘē-*
5. **awē-* (or **əwe-*) : **ẘē-*
6. **awē-* : **hē-*

By *ẘ* is meant a *w* which had absorbed the preceding aspiration, therefore probably a voiceless *w*, but we do not claim to be able to say whether such a *ẘ* (stages 3–5) was a true phoneme or merely a consonant cluster. When it was in regular morphophonemic relation to *h* it may have been felt as a cluster, like *sk-* or *tl-*, but when many such irregular relations as *aw-* : *ẘ-* had developed, it is more likely to have constituted a true phoneme. The Greek forms which actualize this construction are, needless to say, ἄη-σι 'it blows' : αἴ-ν-ω 'I winnow' < **ẘə-n-yó* < IE **xwə(')-n-yó-A*.

Similarly, while it is easy to dispose of Greek ἕλκω, ὁλκός, ὁλκή, ὁλκάς by assuming an IE **selk-* and comparing with Latin *sulcus*, AS *sulh* 'plow', sound method requires that we refuse to disconnect ἕλκω from its uncomfortable Greek relatives. Just as we insisted on keeping ἄησι and αἴνω together, thereby arriving at a valuable hypothesis in regard to the treatment of IE *xw-* in early Greek, so here we may not disconnect ἕλκω from ἄλοξ, αὖλαξ, ὦαξῶ, Hom. ὦλξ, 'furrow', Laconian εὐλάκᾱ 'plow'. When we deal with this series, we are driven to posit **Aawelk-* as our base and the difficulty of equating ἕλκω with the obvious Lithuanian parallel *velkù* (OCS *vlěką*) disappears. Greek *he-* : Lithuanian

---

[17] '*ə*' should be used by those who hold to the laryngeal hypothesis only for a real schwa, a simple murmur vowel reduced from a full grade short vowel. The so-called 'schwa indogermanicum', for which '*ə*' is in general use, will have to yield to the series *ə'*, *ə!*, *əx*, *əγ*.

ve-, in other words, means IE **xwe-* or **ꭵwe-* or **'we-* and the Greek words
for 'plow' narrow the choice down, in spite of difficulties of detail, to
an *a*-timbred laryngeal, hence base **Ḁawelk-* = **xawelk-* or **ꭵawelk-*.
Again, ἕ-τερος, which may be etymologically distinct from its dialectic
variant ἄ-τερος, is a difficult word and no satisfactory etymology has
been given. If we define it as '(one or) the other' and connect with
ἠέ 'or', Latin *aut-*, *ve-*, Skr. *vā*, we arrive at a base **Ḁawe-*; *Ḁwé-teros
(**xwe-* or **ꭵwe-*) yields *hwé-teros or *ꭵwe-teros, either of which, via
voiceless *w*, results in *hé-teros*. The Latin ablaut *au-* : -*ve* is then seen
to be in significant relation to the Greek *h-*. In this way, too, we are
now free to hold to Gk. ἕσπερος, ἑσπέρᾱ : Latin *vesper* and Gk. ἑστίᾱ :
Latin *Vesta* without difficulty. We cannot at present decide if IE *xw-*,
ꭵw- and *'w-* fell together in the pre-Greek period into, say, *hw-* or *'w-*
or voiceless *w*, or simplified to *xw-* and *'w-* whence later *hw-*, or kept
apart for a very long time. All we can say now is that the reflexes of
IE *xw-*, *ꭵw-* and *'w-* seem to be different from that of *w-* in Greek as we
know it.

The same result is reached when we investigate the Greek reflexes
of so-called IE *y-* (*i̯-*). Current theory states that this phoneme regularly yields Greek *h-* (e.g. ὅς : Skr. *yás* < IE *yó-s) but that there are
a number of strays (e.g. ζυγόν : Skr. *yugám*; ζέω : Skr. *yásāmi*; ζωστός :
Lith. *jústas*) in which we have an 'irregular' ζ- instead of the 'regular'
h-. Why should a voiced continuant (*y*) branch into a voiceless continuant
(*h*) and a voiced affricate (*dz*) when nearly all the relevant analogies in
Greek indicate that Greek *h* is of voiceless origin (e.g. < *s*) and that
voiced consonants before vowels keep their voice unless unvoiced by
voiceless consonants that precede them (e.g. *dy-* > *dz-*; but *sw-* >
hw- > *h-*)? It is only statistical evidence that leads to the assumption
that *y-* > *h-* is the type development and *y-* > *dz-* the aberrant one.
It would seem far more natural to suppose that *y-* regularly yielded
dz- (cf. Lat. *mājor* > Italian *maggiore*, *jocus* > *giuoco*) but that a
reflex *h-* is due to an unvoicing of the old *y-* by some voiceless consonant
that has disappeared as such. The laryngeal hypothesis implies the
possibility that, as with IE *w-*, we have here two distinct prototypes: IE *y-*
and IE *'y-*, *ꭵy-*, *xy-*, *y'-*, *yꭵ-*, *yx-*, the former of which led to ζ-, while clusters
of the latter type eventually led to *h-*, perhaps via two distinct phonemes,
ẏ- and *ẏ-*. In examples like ζυγόν and ζέω all the available evidence
points to simple IE *y-*; in other words, there is nothing to show that IE
yewg-* and **yes-* are reduced from bases of type **'eyewg-* (ꭵayewg-*,
xayewg-*) and **'eyes-* (ꭵayes-*, **xayes-*). In Gk. ὅς : Skr. *yás*, however,
we are not dealing with a primary *yó-s but with a reduced form of the

base *'eye/o- (cf. Skr. ayá-m, Lat. ea < *'eya-Ḁ), hence properly *'yó-s. Again, in Gk. ἅγιος: Skr. yaj-, it cannot be an original *yaĝ- that we have to posit, for a full-grade a is itself defined by the laryngeal hypothesis as colored from e by a preceding ꞏ or x, hence we must posit *yḀaĝ-, i.e. *yꞏaĝ- or *yxaĝ-. At what time the y- of this base was glottally affected or unvoiced to ẏ- we do not know. Possibly there were IE forms of type *ẏaĝ- < *yꞏaĝ- long before later Greek ones of type *ẏo- developed from *'yo- (incidentally, now note an easy explanation of why Vedic Skr. yaj- reduces, not to ij-, but to īj- < *iꞏĝ- or *ixĝ- = theoretical *yꞏĝ- or *yxĝ-). Significantly enough, there seem to be no primary examples of Gk. ζα- < IE *ya-. There was no IE *ya- (there might, of course, be a *yaꞏ- or *yax- > later *yā-) but only *ye-, *yo-, *yə-.

With r-, too, we can now see why our Greek reflexes are partly er- (e.g. ἐρυθρός : Skr. rudhiráḥ), partly hr- (ῥ-). A smooth r- developed a true prothetic vowel e- (not to be confused with the large class of pseudo-prothetic vowels which are the remnants of laryngeal + vowel, generally reduced, which originally began the base, e.g. Gk. ὄνομα : Lat. nōmen < *ĝənəγ-mən : *ĝneγ-mən, hence palatalized ñ- in Toch. A ñom), while the series 'r-, ꞏr-, xr- eventuated in ῥ-, possibly via two distinct phonemes ŕ- and ȓ-. In this way it easy to understand why preserved initial r always takes the rough breathing in Greek. This characteristic can hardly have been a spontaneous development of early Greek r- but may be due to the fact that the vast majority of cases of initial r- in Greek as we have it are reduced from initials of type 'er-, ꞏar-, xar-, plus a later group of cases of type sr-. A case in point is ῥύζειν 'to growl, snarl' : Hom. ἐρυγόντα 'bellowing' < *'ruĝ- : *'eruĝ-.

Thus, the Greek history of IE w-, y-, r-, which, as generally presented, is full of unsolved problems, becomes a symmetrical and phonetically intelligible series of events from the standpoint of the laryngeal hypothesis:

IE	PRE-GREEK	GREEK
⎰ we-	we-	we- > e- (secondarily ewe- > ee-)
⎱ 'we-, ꞏwe-, xwe-	u̇e-, u̇e-	he-
⎰ ye-	ye-	dze- (perhaps via dye-)
⎱ 'ye-, ꞏye-, xye-	ẏe-, ẏe-	he-
⎰ re-	re-	ere-
⎱ 're-, ꞏre-, xre-	ŕe-, ȓe-	hre-

It would be difficult to present the known facts in a simpler light. There will still be numerous refractory problems of detail, but it is not a bad test of the validity of a theory (the laryngeal hypothesis) which uses entirely different evidence for its establishment that it incidentally seems to set the house in order for the difficult phonology of IE 'w-', 'y-', and 'r-' in Greek.

Undoubtedly there are still other types of absorption of the laryngeals in Greek, and elsewhere. It is very likely, for example, that Greek at one time had a true phoneme η (not merely the assimilated η of -ηg-, -ηk-, -ηkh-, written -γγ-, -γκ-, -γχ-), for otherwise it would be hard to understand why γ was chosen to represent this sound instead of ν. If Greek γ were always of conditional origin, as in ἔγγαιος 'in the earth' < *én-gaios*, it would have been almost unavoidably written n, e.g. *ἔνγαιος. That the η was regularly indicated by -γ-, an intrinsically poor symbol for the purpose, indicates that it may, like the parallel ν and μ, also have been a free phoneme. It is therefore possible that quite a number of words that are now considered as having a stopped g were in the earlier period pronounced with η. If, further, we ask how such a phoneme could arise in Greek, we have not far to seek for an answer. Either IE x or IE γ might be expected to be absorbed in a preceding or following m or n, yielding η. Just which, if any, of the clusters xm, xn, γm, γn, mx, nx, $m\gamma$, $n\gamma$ actually yielded η, and under what conditions, is a matter for detailed research. Two cases may be given for illustrative purposes.

The IE words for 'naked' are known to be difficult. Starting with Lith. *nůgas*, we know at once, if we apply the principles of the laryngeal hypothesis, that there must have been a laryngeal consonant before the -g-, IE -g^w-. This can only have been -γ-, the laryngeal which united with a preceding e to form a secondary $ō$ in many (but not all) IE dialects, an altogether different entity from the lengthened grade of o. We have, then, *néγg^wos* as the primary form. Other dialects used various suffixes, with shift of stress and zero grade in the first syllable. One of these derivatives was *nγəg^wnós* > pre-Gk. *ŋəg^wnós* > *ŋug^wnós* > *ŋubnós* > *ŋumnós*, probably the early pronunciation of γυμνός. Another form of the -nó- derivative was, apparently, *nγeg^wnós* > *nog^wnós* in those dialects (by no means all) in which IE γe- fell together with o-, hence Skr. *nagnáḥ*, Avestan *maγna*- (perhaps the curious divergence between Indic n- and Iranian m- is due to the fact that each represents an independent development of a η- which either developed independently in Indo-Iranian or goes back, with Greek γ-, to an IE η- < $n\gamma$-). The persistent o-timbre of the IE word for 'night' (Lat.

noct-), undoubtedly, as Sturtevant has pointed out, related to 'naked', and the υ of Gk. νμκτ- are both of them characteristic traces of the γ-laryngeal (cf., e.g., Gk. ἀν-ώνυμος). We now understand why Hittite has *e* (not *a* < IE *o*) in the related words: *neku-mant-s* 'naked', *nekut-s* 'bed-time' (read *nekᵘ-mant-s, nekᵘt-s* ?), for IE γe did not yield Hittite *a* < *o*. Hit. *nekut-* : Lat. *noct-* is therefore not an example of *e* : *o* ablaut, something otherwise unknown for this group of words, but represents independent reflexes of IE *nγegʷ-t-* 'bed-time' > 'night'. Here, then, the assumption of an IE *nγ-* cluster (or, perhaps less likely, its early reflex, *ŋ-*, in which case Hit. *neku-* is < IE *ŋegʷ-* < *nγegʷ-*), so far from merely explaining Greek γυμνός, throws all the related IE forms into a more intelligible focus.

We may return to *xamelAĝ-* (or *ɪamelAĝ-*) 'to milk'. In most IE dialects its reduced parallels, *xmelAĝ-* (or *ɪmelAĝ-*) lost the initial laryngeal. But the form *xm(ə)ləAĝ-t* (or -*d*) 'milk' seems to have yielded *ŋ(ə)ləAk-t* in that dialect or dialect group which, for Greek, yielded *ŋalakt* > γάλα, γάλακτ-, and, for Latin, *ŋlakt* > lac, *lact-*. It is not necessary to suppose, should it later appear that IE *xm-* regularly yielded Latin *m-*, as is probable, that *lact-* is a proper Italic form. It may be a cultural loan-word from an IE dialect in which the indicated course of development was regular, as indeed may the Greek word. All we need to note is that, granted a base *xamelAĝ-* (rather than *ɪamelAĝ-* ?) on the basis of Gk. ἀμέλγω, ἀμολγή, we have a right to expect forms in *xmeleAĝ-* > *ŋeleAĝ-*.

STUDIES OF INDO-EUROPEAN AND SEMITIC LANGUAGES
EDITOR'S PREFACE

THE LANGUAGES *dealt with in the papers of this section were the subjects of Sapir's earliest linguistic interest. Hebrew he had known from boyhood. His first academic concentration was in Germanics. And in the last few years of his life, he turned again to an intensive study of problems in Semitic and Indo-European. Thus the subject of one of his last articles, an unfinished piece published posthumously in 1939, was the same as that of his very first etymological analysis to be printed, on some Indo-European words for "tear." The later papers contain several references to further studies of these language families, studies for which Sapir had collected materials, but which were not to achieve completion.*

Of the articles here selected, first in chronological order is "Notes on Judeo-German Phonology" (1915). Although Sapir refers to these notes as "sketchy phonological observations," students of Germanic dialects still find his comments illuminating, especially his discussion of the archaic features retained by Yiddish.

The influence of a Sinitic language on an Indo-European tongue is treated in "Tibetan Influences on Tocharian" (1936). This paper is one of the very few in Sapir's bibliography which utilizes Sinitic materials, though for many years Sapir worked intermittently with Sinitic data, keeping record of forms which might possibly be related to certain American Indian forms. He sometimes spoke of intriguing research leads he had turned up in this project, but apparently never satisfied himself that he had yet collected evidence firm enough for publication.

In the 1937 analysis of the Hebrew word for helmet, there is again an example of wide historical implications being drawn from the analysis of a single word. The 1937 review of the work by Montgomery and Harris provides new lights for scholars in the Semitic field on the classification of the Semitic languages. The two brief studies published under the title "From Sapir's Desk" (1939) similarly contain insights which extend beyond the immediate subject of the analysis.

NOTES ON JUDEO-GERMAN PHONOLOGY*

A GRATIFYING phase of Germanic study in recent years is the constantly increased attention paid to the modern spoken dialects. That the dialects still spoken by the rural population of Germany, for instance, have often preserved archaic features in vocabulary, phonology, morphology, and syntax, where the literary 'Gemeinsprache' is less conservative, is well known. Thus, attention may be called in passing to the fact that many of the dialects in Middle and Upper Germany still observe the distinction in pronunciation between short open e (<O.H.G. and M.H.G. ĕ, as in gĕban, gĕben) and short close ẹ due to i-umlaut of a (as in O.H.G. bĕẓẓiro, cf. Gothic batiza), while, as is well known, the 'Gemeinsprache' has levelled the distinction completely. By such archaic features the modern dialects are often able to throw a great deal of light on the history of the language; moreover, they are generally more easily handled, from the purely linguistic standpoint, than the literary monuments of Old and Middle High German, in that they are immediately accessible to study and are not distorted, particularly in regard to phonetics, by orthographic imperfections.

While the German dialects now spoken within the confines of Germany, Austria, and Switzerland are being diligently and profitably studied, little has as yet been done in the way of scientifically examining the various dialects spoken by the Jews of Lithuania, Russian Poland, Galicia, southern Russia, and Roumania.[1] When one recollects that these Judeo-German or 'Yiddish' dialects have, since the beginning of

* The Jewish Quarterly Review, n.s., 6 (1915): 231–266.

[1] Besides Leo Wiener's two articles on Judeo-German in The American Journal of Philology, 14: 41–67, 456–482 (phonologically unreliable because modern literary German, instead of Middle High German, is taken as the point of departure), and L. Sainéan's study "Essai sur le Judéo-Allemand et spécialement sur le dialecte parlé en Valachie" in Mémoires de la Société de Linguistique de Paris, 12: 90–138, 176–196 (treats of Roumanian Judeo-German), we have Jacob Gerzon's Die jüdisch-deutsche Sprache, eine grammatisch-lexikalische Untersuchung ihres deutschen Grundbestandes (Frankfurt am Main, 1902), treating mainly of the Lithuanian Judeo-German of Homel (Government of Mohilev). Valuable as Gerzon's work is, it is much less satisfactory in its treatment of the phonology (pp. 20–35) than of the morphology and syntax; in particular Gerzon has failed to point out the absence of quantitative differences in the vowels of stressed syllables and the development of voiced stops in final position, both of which are characteristic features of Judeo-German when contrasted with other High German dialects. The present study, though late to appear, was completed before access was had to Gerzon's work, so that the material here presented is the result of independent investigation. The dialect here treated is the form of Lithuanian Judeo-German spoken in the Government of Kovno. Further references to works on special points in Judeo-German may be found in L. Wiener's History of Yiddish Literature in the Nineteenth Century (New York, 1899), pp. 12–24 (chapter on "The Judeo-German Language").

the modern period (in the early part of the sixteenth century), developed in comparative isolation from the main body of German dialects and that they have been subjected to the influence, chiefly lexical, of the Slavic vernaculars (Polish, Russian, and Little Russian) on the one hand, and of the sacred Hebrew tongue on the other, it becomes clear that we are here dealing with a complex of linguistic conditions that must prove highly instructive to the student of language.[2] The conditions are, in fact, not dissimilar to those that obtained in the development of the English language—isolation from the main body of the vernacular and considerable foreign influence. On the whole, the student of Judeo-German will be inclined to see a less extensive foreign influence in the case of Judeo-German than in that of English; the basis has remained thoroughly German, the foreign accretions and influences are, at best, of only secondary importance.

Before proceeding to the sketchy phonological observations I have to offer, it may not be inappropriate to call attention, by way of illustration, to some of the more interesting archaic features that Judeo-German presents. In vocabulary many Middle High German words now obsolete or, at any rate, not in common use in literary German, have been preserved in full vigour by Judeo-German. Such are $\acute{e}dm$ 'son-in-law' (<M.H.G. *eidem*); *šver* 'father-in-law' (<M.H.G. *swëher*); *šnur* 'daughter-in-law' (<M.H.G. *snur*); *tor* 'dare' (<M.H.G. *tar, gitar*); *zégr* 'clock' (<M.H.G. *seiger*); *haint* 'to-day' (<M.H.G. *hînt* 'this night'); and many others. In phonetics, Judeo-German has, for instance, not levelled M.H.G. *î* and *ei* into *ai*, but has kept them apart as *ai* and *ẹ* respectively; e.g. *vais* 'white' and *ix vẹs* 'I know' (<M.H.G. *wîẓ* and *ich weiẓ* respectively; contrast modern literary German *weiss* for both). In the case of *zamd* 'sand' an Indo-Germanic *m* has been preserved that has in practically all other Germanic dialects been assimilated to *n*—cf.

[2] The following taken from Grätz's *Geschichte der Juden* (9:64) will serve as historical basis of the above remarks. Grätz's statements apply to the period 1496–1525. "Aber nicht bloss deutsche Talmudkunde haben die jüdisch-deutschen Flüchtlinge nach Polen verpflanzt, sondern auch die deutsche Sprache—in ihrer damaligen Beschaffenheit; sie impften sie den eingeborenen Juden ein und verdrängten nach und nach aus deren Munde die polnische oder ruthenische Sprache. Wie spanischen Juden einen Teil der europäischen oder asiatischen Türkei in ein neues Spanien verwandelt haben, so machten die deutschen Juden Polen, Littauen und die dazu gehörigen Landesteile gewissermassen zu einem neuen Deutschland. ... Mehrere Jahrhunderte hindurch zerfielen daher die Juden in *spanisch Redende* und *deutsch Sprechende*, gegen welche die Italiens als eine wenig zählende Klasse verschwand, da auch hier die Juden Spanisch oder Deutsch verstehen mussten. ... [Die polnischen Juden] verehrten [die deutsche Sprache] wie ein Palladium, wie eine heilige Erinnerung, und wenn sie sich auch im Verkehr mit Polen der Landessprache bedienten, im trauten Familienkreise, im Lehrhause und im Gebete behielten sie das Deutsche bei. Sie galt ihnen nächst dem Hebräischen als eine heilige Sprache."

Greek ἄμαθος 'sand' <*samadhos*. A large number of archaic features are found also in the morphology. The old dative singular in -*en* of weak feminines (M.H.G. *der zungen, der mitten,* but modern German *der Zunge, der Mitte*) is preserved in stereotyped phrases like *in dr̩ mit̩n drı̄n* 'right in the midst of it'. The M.H.G. feminine noun *heit* 'manner' preserved in modern German only as derivative suffix in abstract nouns (e.g. *Kühnheit, Menschheit*) survives in Judeo-German in adverbial genitives in -*r̩(h)ét* (e.g. *blindr̩ ét* 'blindly' <*blinder heit*). The preterito-present verb M.H.G. *touc* has in modern German been levelled to the great class of other verbs, while Judeo-German still has *er tég* 'he is of account' (contrast modern German *er taugt*). The old imperative *lâ* 'let' survives in phrases like *ló mir* (or *ló mix*) 'let me' (contrast modern German *lass mich*). In syntax, the double negative may be mentioned as an archaic feature, though something should here be perhaps ascribed to Slavic influence.

It would, however, be erroneous to suppose that the Judeo-German dialects are on the whole more archaic than modern literary German. They are not. In morphology particularly great simplification has taken place. The preterite has disappeared in favour of the periphrastic perfect (e.g. *er hot gı̆zén = er sah*). The dative and accusative (at least in Lithuanian Judeo-German, which dialect alone is here considered) have disappeared as such and have been merged into an objective case, partly dative and partly accusative in form (e.g. *er gı̆t mir = er gibt mir; er zét mir = er sieht mich*). The ending -*er* preceded by umlaut and umlaut alone have greatly spread as plural signs (e.g. *plétsr̩* 'places'; *teg* 'days' <*tège* for *tage*). The umlaut of the second and third persons singular of strong verbs has in most cases been levelled out (*er zét = er sieht; er fâlt = er fällt; er léft = er läuft,* cf. *ix léf = ich laufe*). A number of weak verbs have followed the analogy of strong verbs in their participle (e.g. *gı̆króg̩n* 'obtained' as participle of *krı̄g̩n* by analogy of such verbs as *fardrı̄sn̩—fardrósn̩; gı̆šótn̩ = geschüttet; óngı̆tsundn̩ = angezündet*). The third person reflexive has been generalized for all persons and numbers (e.g. *ix zets mix = ich setze mich*)—this is undoubtedly due to Slavic influence. There are many other levellings and analogical developments that have taken place in Judeo-German.

Several interesting special developments that have taken place are: a gerund of adverbial force in -*dig*, which can be formed from any verb by suffixing this syllable to the infinitive (e.g. *er vent léfn̩dig* 'he cries while running'; these forms in -*ndig* are doubtless based on M.H.G. participial forms in -*ende*, perhaps influenced by *lëbendic* 'alive'); a monosyllabic abstract noun which can be formed from any verb and which is used in phrases like *er git a šmék* 'he gives a smell, he smells (momentaneously)'; the transfer of most neuter nuons to the feminine gender (e.g. *di hoiz* 'the house' <M.H.G. *daz hûs*; a similar development has taken place in Lithuanian, in which old neuters have generally become masculines, e.g. *árklas* m. 'plough' as contrasted with Latin *arātrum* and Greek ἄροτρον).

In phonology two great revolutions have taken place in Judeo-German. In the first place, the quantitative vocalic differences that are so important in modern German (contrast *siech* with *sich*, *schal* with *Schall*, *Sohn* with *Sonne*, *Musse* with *muss*) are not found in Judeo-German. All accented vowels are of practically uniform length—approximately midway in quantity between the German long and short vowels; the quality of *i* and *u* is that of the German long *i* and *u*, in other words close. Thus, the vowel of Judeo-German *zix* 'himself' is pronunced like that of German *siech*, as far as quality is concerned, but with a shorter quantity (yet not so short as in German *sich*); correspondingly with Judeo-German *u*. Judeo-German *o* is in quality identical with the German *o* in *voll*; there are two e-vowels, an open *e* (as in German *Mensch*) and a close *ẹ* (as in German *geben*, barring quantity); *a* does not differ in quality from the normal German *a*. We might put the matter thus: there are no long *i, u, o, a, e* in Judeo-German. This radical difference in phonetic basis between Judeo-German and modern standard German I am inclined to explain by Slavic influence (the same lack of quantitative differences in accented vowels obtains in Russian and Polish; thus, Russian accented *i* is medium in quantity between German *ī* and *i*).

The second phonetic revolution referred to is the rise of final voiced stops and spirants. In Middle High German and its modern representatives a voiced (lenis) stop or spirant becomes voiceless (fortis) when final (M.H.G. *tages, tac*; modern German *Todes, Tod*, i.e. *tōt*). In Judeo-German, however, a final sonant is not pronounced as surd, but preserves its sonant character; thus, *zógņ* 'to say': *ix zóg* 'I say'. I do not believe that sonants when final have really remained sonant. I prefer to explain the phenomenon by analogy. Original M.H.G. *tac* (= *tak*) *tages tage* was levelled to *tag tages tage*; when final -*e* later dropped, the *g* could no longer become surd, hence we have Judeo-German *tog* corresponding to Modern German *tak* (or *tax*)—*tā́gǝ* (or *tā́γǝ*). Similarly, *veg* 'road' <M.H.G. *wéc* by analogy with *wéges wége* (but modern German *vēx'*— *vḗgǝs* or *vḗjǝs*). That this explanation is correct is indicated by such words as *op* 'away' <M.H.G. *abe*, where no paradigmatic levelling could take place and where final *b* became *p*, according to regular German phonetic

law; cf. also *avék* 'away' (= German *weg*) as adverb with *veg* 'road' as noun (the adverb was not associated with the noun, hence suffered no levelling). In any event, the great frequency of final voiced stops and spirants in Judeo-German is a feature that is entirely foreign to the main body of German dialects but is paralleled within Germanic by English and Swedish.

In the following is given in brief the development in Judeo-German of the Middle High German vowels and consonants, no claim of absolute completeness of treatment being made. The main lines of change must suffice.

VOWELS

1. M.H.G. *a*.
   a. In closed syllables it remained unchanged: *gast*<M.H.G. *gast*; *vald*< M.H.G. *walt(wald-)*; *ganz* 'goose'<M.H.G. *gans*; *hart*<M.H.G. *hart*; *az*<M.H.G. *als*; *árbət*<M.H.G. *arbeit, arebeit*; *bald*<M.H.G. *balde*; *land*<M.H.G. *lant (land-)*; *halz*<M.H.G.*hals*; *gaŋg*<M.H.G. *ganc (gang-)*; *naxt*< M.H.G. *naht*. In open syllables followed by *x* (originally geminated, O.H.G.-*hh-*) it also remained, as in modern German: *máxṇ*<M.H.G. *machen*; *láxṇ*<M.H.G. *lachen*.
   b. In originally open syllables (in some cases now secondarily closed) it became lengthened to *ā* (cf. modern German *ā*<*a* in open syllables), which, falling in with original *ā*, developed to open *o*: *hóbṇ*<M.H.G.*haben*; *jógṇ*< M.H.G. *jagen*; *vógṇ* 'waggon'<M.H.G. *wagen*; *op*<M.H.G. *abe*; *nómṇ*< M.H.G. *name, namen*; *fótŗ*<M.H.G. *vater*. Many cases of *o*<*a* in originally closed syllables are readily explained by paradigmatic analogy: *tog*<*tac* (cf. *tage*). Original *tac tāge*, pl. *tāge* first developed to *tac táge, táge*, then, with consonantic levelling, to *tag tāge, táge*; when *ā*>*o*, this series became *tag tóge, tóge*; vocalic levelling gave *tog tóge, tóge*; dropping of final unaccented *-e* would have reduced these forms to *tog tog, tog*, to avoid which umlaut as characteristic of noun plurals came in by analogy; as final result we have to-day nom. *tog*, dat.-acc. *tog*, pl. *teg*. Other examples of analogical *o*<*a* in closed syllables are: *štot*<M.H.G. *stat*; *groz*<M.H.G. *gras*. In certain words *a* became lengthened before *r* to *ā* even in closed syllables; this *ā* also resulted in *o*: *gor*<M.H.G. *gar* (cf. modern German *gār*); *bort*< M.H.G. *bart*; *bórvəs* 'barefoot'<M.H.G. *barvuoz*; *tor, torst* '(he) dares, (you) dare'<M.H.G. *tar, tarst*. More difficult to explain are *dos*<M.H.G. *daz* and *vos*<M.H.G. *waz*; perhaps these forms arose in combinations like *daz ist* (originally syllabified, before 'fester Einsatz' developed before *ist*, as *dazist*)>*dāz ist*>*dos íz*.
   c. Cases of *e*<*a* are probably only apparent. *meg* (= modern German *mag*) is probably not directly developed from M.H.G. *mac*, but is due to analogy of 1st and 3rd person plural present indicative and infinitive *mégen* (upper German)>Judeo-German *mégṇ* (see 4. below). *ken* (= modern German *kann*) is similarly not directly developed from M.H.G. *kan* (> Judeo-German parallel form *kon*, see b above), but is due to analogy of *kénnen* 'to know' > Judeo-German *kénṇ*.

2. M.H.G. *â.*

   a. This sound regularly became *o*, which is in no respect phonetically different from *o*<M.H.G. *o* or M.H.G. *a* in open syllables: *on* 'without' < M.H.G. *âne; do* < M.H.G. *dâ; nox*< M.H.G. *nâch; hor* 'hair'<M.H.G. *hâr; jor*< M.H.G. *jâr; mol*<M.H.G. *mâl; hot* 'has', *host* 'hast', *hot* '(ye' have'< M.H.G. *hât, hâst, hât; blo* 'blue'<M.H.G. *blâ; gro* 'gray'<M.H.G. *grâ; lo* 'let!'<M.H.G. *lâ; g̑irótn̥*<M.H.G. *gerâten; nont* 'near'<M.H.G. *nâhent; mon*<M.H.G. *mân, mâhen* 'Mohn'. Note that Judeo-German sometimes preserves *o* as reflex of M.H.G. *â* where modern German has shortened *â* to *a* (contrast Judeo-German *nox* with modern German *nach; host, hot* with *hast, hat*).

   b. It is shortened to *a* (as in modern German) before *xt: g̑ĭdáxt*<M.H.G. *gedāht; g̑ĭbráxt*<M.H.G. *gebrāht.*

   c. In *vu* 'where', *â* of M.H.G. *wâ*, after being labialized to *ô* (cf. modern German *wo*), became still further labialized to *u.*

3. M.H.G. *ĕ.*

   a. This sound normally remained as open *e: erd*<M.H.G. *ĕrde; ber* 'bear'< M.H.G. *bĕr; velt*<M.H.G. *wĕrlt; šlext*<M.H.G. *slĕht; feld*<M.H.G. *vĕlt* (*vĕld-*); *hélfn̥*<M.H.G. *hĕlfen; zeks* < M.H.G. *sĕhs.* It is to be particularly noted that *ĕ* in open syllables did not, as in most dialects, lengthen to *ē* (> Judeo-German *ę*), but remained open *e: lébn̥*<M.H.G. *lĕben* (contrast modern German *leben*, i.e. *lébņ); bézm̥*<M.H.G. *bĕseme* 'Besen'; *némņ*< M.H.G. *nĕmen; lézņ* <M.H.G. *lĕsen; bétņ* 'to ask for' (= modern German *bitten*) < M.H.G. *bĕten* 'bitten (um Almosen)'; *gébņ*<M.H.G. *gĕben.*

   b. M.H.G. *-ĕhe-* regularly contracted to *e* (not, as in modern German, to *ē*> *ę*): *tsen* 'ten'<M.H.G. *zĕhen; zen* 'to see'<M.H.G. *sĕhen; šver* 'father-in-law'<M.H.G. *swĕher.*

   c. Before *r* plus consonant, *ĕ* regularly became broadened to *a* (cf. English *farm*<Middle English *ferm*): *barg* 'hill, mountain'<M.H.G. *bĕrc* (*bĕrg-*); *harts*<M.H.G. *hĕrze; fártsn̥* 'to break wind'<M.H.G. *vĕrzen; várfn̥*< M.H.G. *wĕrfen; štárbn̥*<M.H.G. *stĕrben; varg* (e.g. *grinvarg* 'green stuff, vegetation') <M.H.G. *wĕrch, wĕrc* (modern German *Werg* 'tow'). *e* remains, however, in *erd* 'earth'<M.H.G. *ĕrde.*

   d. *ĕ* appears as *i* in *bĭlņ* 'to bark'<M.H.G. *bĕllen.* This may be due to *i* of M.H.G. singular present indicative *bille, billest, billet*, though ordinarily *e* is generalized in Judeo-German (cf. *helft* = modern German *hilft*).

4. M.H.G. *ė* (*i*- umlaut of *a*).

   a. In originally closed syllables this sound fell in, as in modern German, with *e*<M.H.G. *ĕ.* Examples of *e*<*ė* are: *end*<M.H.G. *ende; bésŗ*<M.H.G. *béẕẕer; menš*<M.H.G. *mĕnsche; s vént zix* 'it depends' (= *es wendet sich*)< M.H.G. *wénden; epļ* 'apple'<M.H.G. *ĕpfel* (plural of *apfel*, but also used as singular; cf. Kluge's remark: 'in Schwaben, der Schweiz und der Oberpfalz ist das plurale *Äpfel* Singular-form geworden'); *šmékņ* 'to smell'<M.H.G. *smĕcken* 'to taste, to smell' (Kluge remarks: 'die Bedeutung "riechen" wahren das Alemannische und Baierische, auch das Hessische teilweise').

   b. M.H.G. *ĕhe*, like *ĕhe*, contracted to *e: trer* 'tear'<M.H.G. *trĕher* (singular-ized plural of *traher*; modern German *Thräne* is similarly originally plural, M.H.G. *trĕhene*, of M.H.G. *trahen*).

   c. *ė*, like *ĕ*, seems to have been broadened to *a* before *r* plus consonant in *árbəs* 'pea'<M.H.G. *érweiƶ* (modern German *Erbse*); parallel M.H.G. *arweiz* would probably have resulted in **órbəs* rather than *árbəs* (see 1. b above). Note *ferd* 'horse'<M.H.G. *pfärt* (*pfärd-*).

  d. *é* is preserved as *ę* (close quality as in French *été*) before *ŋg*, *ŋk*: *bręŋgṇ* 'to bring'<M.H.G. *bréngen* (Middle German dialectic form of *bringen*; cf. also Old Saxon *brengean*<**brangjan*); *déŋkṇ*<M.H.G.*dénken*; *zix bęŋkṇ* 'to long for', cf. M.H.G. *bénge* (alongside of *bange*) 'Angst, Sorge'. *ę*<*é* also appears in open syllables: *hębṇ* 'to lift'<M.H.G. *hében*, *héfen*; *kęt* (plural *kętṇ*)< M.H.G. *kéten* 'Kette'; *tsęlṇ*<M.H.G. *zéln*; *ęnïkļ* 'grandson'<M.H.G. *énikel*, *éninkel*; *ędļ*<M.H.G. *édel*; *hévṇ* 'yeast'<M.H.G. *héve*.

5. M.H.G. *ê*.
  a. This sound, while losing its length, retained its quality as close *ę*; *štęn* 'to stand'<M.H.G. *stên*; *gęn*<M.H.G. *gên*; *šnę*<M.H.G. *snê*; *vętəg* 'pain'< M.H.G. *wêtac* 'leiblicher Schmerz, Leiden, Krankheit' (literally 'woe-day'); *ędr̦* 'rather, sooner' (with inorganic -*d*-)<M.H.G. *êr*. Before final *r*, *ę* is followed by glide *ə*: *zę̦ər* 'very'<M.H.G. *sêre*.
  b. It becomes broadened to open *e* before *r* in: *mer* 'more'<M.H.G. *mêr*; *eršt*<M.H.G. *êrst*.

  . M.H.G. *æ* (*i*-umlaut of *â*).
  a. This sound fell in completely with *ë*. Examples of *e*<M.H.G. *æ* are: *šver*< M.H.G. *swære*; *ver*<M.H.G. *wære* (1st and 3rd person preterite subjunctive of *sîn*); *het*<M.H.G. *hæte* 'hätte'; *gǐrétṇnis* 'capable person, wohlgeratene Person' (*ret-*<M.H.G. *ræt-*, cf. *geræte* 'Rat, Überlegung').
  b. *æ* has become *i* in: *gix* 'quick'<M.H.G. *gæhe* (*gex*, which would be normally expected, is also found).

7. M.H.G. *i*.
  a. As in modern German, M.H.G. *i* has normally remained: *zix*<M.H.G. *sich*; *gǐfinṇ*<M.H.G. (ge)*finden*; *iz* < M.H.G. *ist*; *blind*<M.H.G. *blint* (*blind-*); *fiš*<M.H.G. *visch*.
  b. In *bárnə* 'pear'<M.H.G. *bir*(genitive *birn*) and *karš* 'cherry'<M.H.G. *kirse*, this sound seems, like *ë*, to have become *a* before *r* plus consonant (see 3 c). Is *a* in these words due to parallel dialectic *ë* (cf. Anglo-Saxon *peru*: O.H.G. *bira*; Lat. *cerasum*: O.H.G. *kirsa*)?
  c. *em* 'him' <M.H.G. *im*(e) is probably developed from parallel Middle German dialectic *em*(e).

8. M.H.G. *î*.
  a. As in modern German, M.H.G. *î* regularly became diphthongized to *ai*: *taix* 'lake, creek'<M.H.G. *tîch* 'pond'; *zait* 'side'<M.H.G. *sîte*; *tsait*< M.H.G. *zît*; *drai*<M.H.G. *drî*; *váilə* '(short) while'<M.H.G. *wîle*; *main*< M.H.G. *mîn*.
  b. In *git* 'gives', *gist* 'givest', *i* is shortened from *î* (M.H.G. *gît*, *gîst*), rather than directly derived from *i* of *gibet*, *gibest*.

9. M.H.G. *o*.
  a. In closed syllables *o* remained: *dort*<M.H.G. *dort*; *oks*<M.H.G. *ohse*; *fol*< M.H.G. *vol* (*voll-*); *mórgṇ*<M.H.G. *morgen*; *ort*<M.H.G. *ort*.
  b. It has become *u* in *fun*<*von*. *u* of *zun* 'Sohn', *zun* 'Sonne', and *kúmṇ* 'kommen' is not derived from original *o*, but goes back to *u* (see 11 a).
  c. In orginally open syllables *o* became lengthened, as in modern German, to *ō*, which then, falling in with original long *ō*, developed to *ę* (see 10 a):

ẹb 'ob'<M.H.G. *obe*; *ẹvṇ* 'stove'<M.H.G. *oven*; *ẹbṇ*<M.H.G. *oben*; *fẹgl*<
M.H.G. *vogel*; *hẹzṇ* 'trousers'<M.H.G. *hosen*. In words where *o* of close and
o of open syllables varied paradigmatically, older *o*: *ẹ*(*o*: *ō*) was levelled out
to *ẹ* (*ō*) *hẹf*<M.H.G. *hof* (*hoves*). It is not clear why we have *ẹ*, instead of *o*,
in *hẹkṛ* 'hunchback'<M.H.G. *hocker* (perhaps<parallel *hoker with ungeminated *k*; cf. parallel *hoger*).

10. M.H.G. *ô*.
    a. This sound regularly became *ẹ*, probably through transitional stages *oi*>
       öi>*ei*. Examples are: *grẹs*<M.H.G. *grôz*; *šẹn* 'already'<M.H.G. *schôn*(*e*);
       hẹx<M.H.G. *hôch*; *brẹt*<M.H.G. *brôt*; *rẹt*<M.H.G. *rôt*; *azẹ́*<M.H.G. *alsô*;
       lẹz<M.H.G. *lôs*; *rẹ*<M.H.G. *rô*. Before final *r* glide *ə* intervenes: *ẹ́ər* 'ear'<
       M.H.G. *ôre*.
11. M.H.G. *u*.
    a. It normally remains as *u*: *un* 'and'<M.H.G. *unde*; *štub*<M.H.G. *stube*;
       tsuŋg<M.H.G. *zunge*; *šnur* 'daughter-in-law'<M.H.G. *snur*; *zun* 'son'<
       M.H.G. *sun* (modern German *Sohn* is specifically Middle German, M.H.G.
       son); *zun* 'sun'<M.H.G. *sunne* (modern German *Sonne* is specifically
       Middle German); *kúmṇ* < M.H.G. *kumen* (variant of *komen*, probably ex-
       tended by analogy from singular of present indicative *kume, kumest, kumet*);
       zúmṛ 'summer'<M.H.G. *sumer*; *trúkṇ* 'dry'<M.H.G. *trucken*; *rúkṇ* 'to
       shove'<M.H.G. *rucken* (parallel to *rücken*); *hunt*<M.H.G. *hunt* (*hund*-).
    b. M.H.G. *u* seems to have become *i*, probably via *ü*, in *um zist* 'um sonst'<
       M.H.G. *umbe sust*.
    c. Before *r* plus consonant *u* is broadened to *o* in *vórtsḷ* 'root'<M.H.G. *wurzel*
       (cf. Middle German *worz* for *wurz* 'plant, root'), also before final *r* in *nor*
       'only'<M.H.G. *nur*.
12. M.H.G. *û*.
    a. Diphthongization has taken place, as in modern German, but to *oi* (prob-
       ably through *ui*, which seems to be found in some Judeo-German dialects),
       not *au*. Examples are: *oif*<M.H.G. *ûf*; *hoiz*<M.H.G. *hûs*; *moiz*<M.H.G.
       mûs; *moil*<M.H.G. *mûl* 'Maul'; *kloiz* 'Talmudic school'<M.H.G. *klûse*
       'abgeschlossene Wohnung'; *hoit*<M.H.G. *hût*; *toizṇd*<M.H.G. *tûsent*
       (*tûsend*-); *boiən*<M.H.G. *bûwen*. Glide *ə* appears after *oi* before final *r*;
       zoiər<M.H.G. *sûr*; *poiər* 'peasant'<M.H.G. *bûr*.
    b. Before *x* plus consonant it is shortened to *u* in *mir dúxt* 'it seems to me'<
       M.H.G. *dûhte* (preterite of *dunken, dünken*); cf. *â*>*a* before *x* plus consonant
       (see 2 b above).
    c. M.H.G. *û* has become *a* in *farzámṇ* 'to miss, neglect'<M.H.G. *versûmen*.
       No reason that is apparent can be given for this singular change.
    d. M.H.G. *û* has apparently become *ai* in: *klaibṇ* 'to gather'<M.H.G. *klûben*
       'pflücken, stückweise ablesen, auflesen' (>Modern German *klauben*). This
       is hard to understand phonologically. With its strong participle *gĭklĭbṇ*, it
       looks remarkably as though developed from M.H.G. *klĭben*, past participle
       gekliben 'anhangen, Wurzel fassen und gedeihen', though there are semantic
       difficulties here. Perhaps *kloibṇ<*klûben* and *klaibṇ*<*klĭben* became con-
       fused in one form.
13. M.H.G. *ü*.
    a. Ordinarily *ü* was unrounded and thus fell in completely with original *i*:
       mil<M.H.G. *mül* 'mill'; *ĭbṛ*<M.H.G. *über*; *zin* 'sons'<M.H.G. *süne*; *kinig*

<M.H.G. *künic* (*künig*-); *únmiglǝx*<M.H.G. *unmügelich*; *hintḷ*, diminutive of *hunt* 'dog'<M.H.G. *hunt* (*hund*-); *lígṇ* 'lie' (subst.)<M.H.G. *lügen, lügene.*

b. It became velarized to *u* in: *fúlǝ* 'fulness'<M.H.G. *vülle*; *kúšṇ* 'to kiss'< M.H.G. *küssen* (perhaps by analogy of *kuš* 'kiss'); *fúftsṇ* 'fifteen'<M.H.G. *vünfzёhen*; *fúftsig* 'fifty'<M.H.G. *fünfzic* (*fünfzig*-) (cf. M.H.G. *vunf, vumf* as parallel forms of *vünf, vümf*).

c. Before final *r* and before *rr* it became broadened to *a* (cf. 3 c, 4 c, 7 b) in: *far*<M.H.G. *vür*; *dar* 'thin'<M.H.G. *dürre.*

14. M.H.G. *iu*.
This sound (pronounced *ǖ*) represents older diphthongal *iu* and *ū* as *i*-umlaut of *û*. In Judeo-German it became unrounded to *ī*, which, falling in with original *ī*, became diphthongized to *ai*. Examples are: *háizṛ* 'houses'< M.H.G. *hiuser*; *maiz* 'mice'<M.H.G. *miuse*; *nai* 'new'<M.H.G. *niuwe*; *aix*<M.H.G. *iuch*; *áiǝr*<M.H.G. *iuwer*; *bá. xḷ*<M.H.G. *biuchel*, diminutive of *bûch* 'Bauch'; *lait*<M.H.G. *liute.*

15. M.H.G. *ö*.
a. As with other umlaut vowels, *ö* was unrounded to *e*, thus falling together with original *ё*. Examples of *e*<M.H.G. *ö* are: *rёkḷ*<M.H.G. *röckel*, diminutive of *roc* (*rock*-) 'coat'; *hérnṛ*<M.H.G. *hörner*, plural of *horn*; *gĭkёxts* 'something cooked'<*geköchtes* (such forms seem to be based on substantivized neuter past participles in *-tes*, e.g. gekochtes, influenced by neuter collectives in *ge-* . . . *-e* with umlaut, e.g. *gehörne*).

b. In *ęl* 'oil'<M.H.G. *öl, öle* it seems that M.H.G. *ö* resulted in *ę* instead of expected *e*. However, *ęl* may go back to parallel M.H.G. *ol, ole* according to 9 c.

16. M.H.G. *œ* (*ō̆*).
a. This sound became unrounded to *ē*, thus falling together with original *ê*, whence Judeo-German *ę:* *šęn*<M.H.G. *schœne*; *flḗtsṇ*<M.H.G. *vlœtzen* (causative of *vliezen*); *lḗzṇ* 'to take in money' (<'to release value'?)< M.H.G. *lœsen*; *trḗstṇ*<M.H.G. *trœsten..*

b. It is broadened to *e* before *r*(cf. 5 b): *hḗrṇ*<M.H.G. *hœren.*

c. In certain comparatives *ē*<M.H.G. *œ* developed to *e* instead of *ę* without apparent phonetic reason: *grḗsṛ* 'larger'<M.H.G. *grœzer*; *šḗnṛ*<M.H.G. *schœner*; *héxṛ* 'higher'<M.H.G. *hœher*. In *héxṛ* open *e* may be phonetically explained as due to shortening of *ō̄* to *ö* before *x* (which had been introduced into comparative from positive *hôch*; **hœcher*, instead of *hœher*,>**höcher*> *héxṛ*); cf. 1 a (last sentence), 2 b, 12 b. The combined influence of *héxṛ* and such *e*-comparatives as *léŋgṛ* 'longer' (in which *e* regularly developed from *ê*, *i*-umlaut of *a*) may have served to establish a category of *e*-comparatives, which analogically displaced the phonetically justified comparatives **grḗsṛ*, **šḗnṛ*. The change thus effected is functionally useful, inasmuch as a difference of form is established between the comparative and the inflected positive (nominative masculine singular): *a grḗsṛ man* 'ein grosser Mann', but *er iz grḗsṛ* 'er ist grösser' (modern German *schöner* corresponds to both *šḗnṛ* and *šḗnṛ*). That this change of *œ* to *e* is not phonetic, but analogic in character, is further indicated by the parallel *klḗnṛ*<*kleiner* (but positive *klęn*<*klein*).

17. M.H.G. *uo*.
a. This diphthong was monophthongized to *u* and, there being no quantitative differences in Judeo-German accented vowels, fell together with

original *u*: *šux*<M.H.G. *schuoh*; *mútr̩*<M.H.G. *muoter*; *bux*<M.H.G. *buoch*; *štul*<M.H.G. *stuol*; *ku*<M.H.G. *kuo*; *brúdr̩*<M.H.G. *bruoder*; *tsu*<M.H.G. *zuo*; *fus*<M.H.G. *vuoz*.

b. In *ton* 'to do'<M.H.G. *tuon* it appears as *o*. This is probably due to the analogy of the participle *gιtón*<M.H.G. *getân* (the ablaut *uo–â*, Judeo-German *u–o*, is isolated and therefore easily levelled out).

18. M.H.G. *üe*.

This diphthong, which serves as *i*-umlaut of *uo*, became unrounded to *ie* and, falling together with original *ie*, became monophthongized to *i* (it is also possible that *üe* first became monophthongized to *ü* and then unrounded to *i*): *grin*<M.H.G. *grüene*; *ki*<M.H.G. *küeje* 'cows'; *mid*<M.H.G. *müede*; *kil*<M.H.G. *küele, küel*; *bιxl̩*<M.H.G. *büechel*, diminutive of *buoch*.

19. M.H.G. *ie*.

a. As *uo*, when monophthongized, fell together with *u*, so *ie*, after being monophthongized, fell together with original *i*: *lιxt*<M.H.G. *lieht*; *tif*<M.H.G. *tief*; *flīgn̩*<M.H.G. *fliegen*; *bīgn̩*<M.H.G. *biegen*; *hir* M.H.G. *hier*; *fιr*<M.H.G. *vier*.

b. It became broadened to *e* before *r* plus consonant in *êrgəts* 'somewhere' <M.H.G. *iergen(t)*, *nérgəts* 'nowhere'<M.H.G. *niergen(t)*. Contrast *i-*<M.H.G. *ie-* in *ιmr̩*<M.H.G. *iemer* and *ιtst(r̩)* 'now'<M.H.G. *iezent*.

c. *zẹ* 'they'<M.H.G. *sie* (but *zi* 'she'<M.H.G. *sie*) is perhaps best explained as secondarily lengthened from M.H.G. *se*, proclitic form of *sie*.

20. M.H.G. *ei*.

a. This was not preserved as diphthong *ai*, as in modern German, but was monophthongized to *ẹ* (probably via *ē*):*hẹsn̩*<M.H.G. *heizen*; *ẹn*<M.H.G. *ein*; *brẹt*<M.H.G. *breit*; *hẹm*<M.H.G. *heim* (note also Judeo-German adverb *ahẹm* 'nach Hause'); *ẹ* 'egg'<M.H.G. *ei*; *ẹdm̩* 'son-in-law'<M.H.G *eidem*; *klẹn*<M.H.G. *kleine, klein*; *mẹnn̩*<M.H.G. *meinen*; *hẹln̩*<M.H.G *heilen*; *rẹn*<M.H.G. *rein*.

b. It appears as *e* in *ệmr̩* 'pail'<M.H.G. *eimer, eimber* (cf. M.H.G. parallel form *ember*). *e* of *klénr̩* 'smaller' is best explained as due to analogy (see explanation of *grésr̩* and *šénr̩* in 16 c).

21. M.H.G. *ou*.

This diphthong early became monophthongized to *ō* (cf. *ei>ē*, see 20 a) and was further developed, together with original *ō*, to *ẹ* (probably via *oi>öi>ei*): *bẹm*<M.H.G. *boum*; *ẹg*<M.H.G. *ouge*; *kệfn̩*<M.H.G. *koufen*; *štẹb* <M.H.G. *stoup (stoub-)*; *rẹx*<M.H.G. *rouch*.

22. M.H.G. *eu, öu*.

This diphthong also became Judeo-German *ẹ* (perhaps via *ō̄>ē*; or via *öi>ei*, cf. M.H.G. *vröide* as variant of *vröude*): *frẹd* 'joy', *Frẹdə* 'Joy' (girl's name) <M.H.G. *vröude, vreude*; *hẹ* 'hay'<M.H.G. *höuwe, höu*: *lẹb* 'lion'<M.H.G. *löuwe* (parallel to *lëwe*, which would have developed to **leb*).

We thus see that the original rich vocalism of Middle High German has been greatly simplified in Judeo-German by unrounding rounded vowels (*ü>i,ü>ī>i,üe>ie>i,ö>e,ȫ>ē>ẹ*), by obliterating quantitative vocalic differences (*ī<ie* and *i* both give *i*; *ū<uo* and *u* both give *u*; these secondary *ī* and *ū* are of course to be carefully kept apart from original M.H.G. *î* and *û*, which did not fall together with them because they had already become diphthongized when *ie* became *ī* and

uo became *ū*), and by monophthongizing of diphthongs (*ei* > *ē* > *ę̄*, *ou* > *ō* > *oi* > *öi* > *ei* > *ę̄*). In particular *ę̄* is, at least in the Lithuanian dialect, the reflex of no less than eight distinct vowels and diphthongs: *ė* (in open syllables), *ê*, *ei*, *eu* (*öu*), *œ*, *ô*, *ou*, and *o* (in open syllables). Similarly, *i* goes back to *i*, *ü*, *ie*, and *üe*; *o* to *o* (in closed syllables), *â*, and *a* (in open syllables). Many words that in Middle High German are phonetically distinct have, in Judeo-German, fallen together owing to the operation of the phonetic laws we have sketched. Thus, *brę̄t* corresponds to modern German *breit* and *Brot*; *šę̄n* to *schön* and *schon*; *štę̄n* to *stehen* and *Stein*; *nox* to *noch* and *nach*; *ę̄gṇ* to *eigen* and *Augen*.

Unaccented M.H.G. *e* has generally dropped in absolute finality; examples of this have incidentally occurred in the discussion of the accented vowels. Where unaccented -*e* is preserved (as 'Murmelvokal' -*ə*), it is generally due to a functional, not a phonetic, reason (e.g. *gútə lait* 'good people' and *a gútə tóxtr̥* 'a good daughter', in which -*ə* as adjectival ending, indicates respectively plurality and feminine gender. Unaccented M.H.G. *e* unites with following tautosyllabic *l*, *m*, *n*, and *r* to form sonantic (syllabic) *l̥*, *m̥*, *n̥*, and *r̥*. In unaccented syllables and when after vowels or when followed by one or more stop or spirant consonants M.H.G. *e* appears as *ə* (e.g. *ę̄rgəts* < M.H.G. *iergent*; *áiər* < M.H.G. *iuwer* 'your'). Unaccented M.H.G. *e* sometimes disappears in other than final position. Thus, regularly in participial -*et* after all consonants, including *d* and *t*, -*det* and -*tet* contracting to -*t* (e.g. *gĭvárt* < M.H.G. *gewartet*; *gĭhít* < M.H.G. *gehüetet*; *gĭrét* < M.H.G. *gerédet*); similarly, -*est* of second person singular and -*et* of third person singular and second person plural present indicative (and imperative) regularly become -*st* and -*t*, -*det* and -*tet* contracting to -*t* (e.g. *du vártst* < M.H.G. *du wartest*; *er rét*, *gĭfínt* < M.H.G. *ĕr rédet*, *gefindet*: *ir hít* < M.H.G. *ir hüetet*; second person plural imperative *ret* < M.H.G. *rédet*). Such syncopated forms go back in part to M.H.G. originals (e.g. M.H.G. *vint* 'finds' alongside of *vindet*; *getraht* alongside of *getrahtet*).

Other unaccented vowels than *ə* are also found, though rather less frequently than in modern German. They occur chiefly in secondarily accented syllables. Examples of suffixed elements with vowel not dulled to *ə* are: -*ik* (e.g *kínik* < M.H.G. *künic*); -*iš* < M.H.G. -*isch* (e.g. *mĭíš* 'ugly'); -*nis* < M.H.G. -*nisse* (e.g. *gĭrétṇnis*); -*uŋg* (e.g. *mę̄nuŋg* < M.H.G. *meinunge*); -*kęt* < M.H.G. -*keit* (e.g. *gútskęt* 'goodness', *gré̄skęt* 'greatness'). Diminutive -*lîn* appears in Judeo-German as secondarily accented -*le*, preceding M.H.G. -*e*- being developed to -*a*- (e.g. *kíndalè* < M.H.G. *kindelîn*; these diminutives in -*alè* imply a loving or caressing attitude, whereas forms in *-əl, -l̥* are simply diminutive). M.H.G. *-lich* regularly appears as *-ləx* (e.g. *frę̇ləx* <M.H.G. *vrœlich*). Full vowels of unaccented syllables which have no definite significance as word-forming elements tend more frequently than in modern German to be dulled to *ə* (e.g. *árbəs* 'pea' <M.H.G. *érweiż, arweiż, árbət* 'work' <M.H.G. *arbeit*). This is true even in cases where the unaccented vowel is the stem vowel of the second member of a compound, provided the analysis of the compound is not felt as obvious (e.g. *bórvəs* 'barefoot' <M.H.G. *barvuoż: kímpət* 'confinement after childbirth' <M.H.G. *kintbétte*). An example of extreme reduction, in which not only an unaccented diphthong but also the consonant following it is lost, is *knóbl̥* 'garlic' <M.H.G. *knobelouch.*

M.H.G. *e* standing in a syllable immediately preceding the accent seems regularly to develop to *a*: *ba-* <M.H.G. *be-* (e.g. *baklógn̥* <M.H.G. *beklagen*); *far-* <M.H.G. *ver-* (e.g. *farbrénn̥* <M.H.G. *verbrénnen*); *ar-* <M.H.G. *hër* (e.g. *ar-* in local adverbs—*arúnṭr, aríbr, aroís*, and others); *ant-* <M.H.G. *en(t)-* (e.g. *antkégn̥* <M.H.G. *engègen(e)*; *antlę́fn̥* <M.H.G. *entloufen*); *a-* <M.H.G. *en-* in adverbs (e.g. *avék* <M.H.G. *en-wёc* 'away'; *ahér* <M.H.G. *ёn-hёr* 'hither'; *ahín* 'thither'; *ahę́m* 'towards home'). Accented *ent-*, however, remains: *entfərn̥* 'to answer' <M.H.G. *entwürten* (parallel to *antwürten*). Unaccented M.H.G. *bî* also developed to *ba* (e.g. *ba mír* 'bei mir' <M.H.G. *bî mir*); unaccented M.H.G. *ûf* became *af* (e.g. *af a báŋk* 'on a bench'); M.H.G. unaccented *vor* developed to *far*, thus falling together with M.H.G. *ver-* and *vür* (see 13c; *far* < *vür* very likely also developed in unaccented position) (e.g. *farbái* 'vorbei'; *far jórn̥* 'years ago' <M.H.G. *vor jâren; far tóg* 'before daybreak'; *fartsáitn̥s* 'long ago'). M.H.G. *ein* as article, which always stands in proclitic position, has become *a* (before consonants), *an* (before vowels); as numeral 'one', however, it develops to *ęn* (see 20 a). M.H.G. *zer-, ze-* appears as *tsu-* (e.g. *tsurísn̥* <M.H.G. *zerrissen*); this correspondence, however, is undoubtedly not purely phonetic in character, as parallel M.H.G. *zur-, zu-* is found in Middle German dialects. M.H.G. verb prefix *er-* appears in Judeo-German as *dr-*; cf. parallel M.H.G. *der-*. M.H.G. *ge-* appears as *gĭ-* with short open *i* (e.g. *gĭmáxt* <M.H.G. *gemacht: gĭzúnt* <M.H.G. *gesunt*); it is barely possible that this *gĭ-* goes back to O.H.G. *gi-*. Proclitic *man*, in its indefinite sense, becomes reduced to *mn̥* (e.g. *mn̥ mę́nt* 'man meint').

The whole Judeo-German vowel scheme thus reduces itself to six full vowels: *a, o, i, u, e, ę*; a 'Murmelvokal' *ə* (also *ĭ*); and two diphthongs: *ai, oi*.

The Middle High German consonants have undergone less sweeping changes than the vowels. The most important innovation has already been mentioned: the generalization of a paradigmatic final stem sonant, the otherwise constant interchange in German dialects between final surd and medial sonant being thus obliterated in Judeo-German. The comparatively few consonant changes that it has suffered will be noted under the various consonants. The chief points of general application are these:—The stops exist in two strictly differentiated series as surds and sonants; there is no amalgamation of the two into one group of 'voiceless mediae', as in many Middle German dialects, nor has the sonant lost any of its resonant quality; the surds and sonants are as clearly set against each other as in English. The distinction that obtains in modern German between guttural x (after back vowels) and palatal x' (after palatal vowels, r, and l) is absent in Judeo-German; the guttural x (as in German *Bach*) is used in all positions (thus, to German *schlecht* corresponds Judeo-German *šlext* with x as in Dutch *slecht* and as in Swiss dialects). The pronunciation of r differs in different parts of the Judeo-German area. While the trilled tongue-tip r, which may be due to Slavic influence, is found in Southern Russia, the uvular r (r grasseyé) prevails in the Lithuanian dialect; it is pronounced with considerable vigour, but is not markedly trilled, hence is probably better defined as voiced velar spirant (γ). This uvular r and the frequency of guttural x serve to give Judeo-German a characteristic guttural acoustic effect. In our consideration of the consonants we begin with the semivowels.

1. M.H.G. *j*.
   a. It is generally preserved as *j* (*y* of English *young*): *juŋg*<M.H.G. *junc* (*jung-*); *jor*<M.H.G. *jâr*; *jógn̥*<M.H.G. *jagen*.
   b. Where it served as glide consonant in M.H.G. between preceding palatal vowel and following unaccented *e* (as in *küeje, müeje, sæjen*) it has dropped in Judeo-German (together with final *-e*): *ki* 'cows'<M.H.G. *küeje*.
   c. It has dropped initially before Judeo-German *i* (M.H.G. *ü*): *iŋgl*<M.H.G. *jüngel(în)*; *id* 'Jew'<M.H.G. *jüde* (parallel to *jude*). It is interesting to note that *i-*<*ji-* requires *a* as preceding article: *a id* 'ein Jude' (not *an id*).
2. M.H.G. *w*.
   a. This sound, where preserved, became dento-labial *v*: *vald*<M.H.G. *walt* (*wald-*); *tsve̦*<M.H.G. *zwei*; *šver* 'heavy'<M.H.G. *swære*; *švax*<M.H.G. *swach; kvéln̥* 'to well up, swell (with joy)'<M.H.G. *quëllen* (i.e. *kwëllen*); *vort*<M.H.G. *wort*.
   b. It appears as *f* after *t* in *éntfərn̥* 'to answer'<M.H.G. *antwürten*.
   c. After *l* and *r* it became stopped to *b*, as in modern German: *árbəs* 'pea'< M.H.G. *ärwî; farbʒ* 'colour'<M.H.G. *varwe*.
   d. Between vowels (but not after *u*-vowels) *w* seems, as in Swabian dialects

(cf. also German *hieben*<M.H.G. *hiewen*), to have become *b*: *lẹb* 'lion'<
M.H.G. *lëwe, löuwe*; *ębig*<M.H.G. *ëwic (ëwig-)*; *ɩŋbr̩* 'ginger'<M.H.G.
ingewër (cf. M.H.G. variants *ingebër, imbër*).

  e. It is syncopated between *u*-vowel and following vowel: *bóiən* 'to build'<
M.H.G. *bûwen*; *atər*<M.H.G. *iuwer*.

3. M.H.G. *l*.

  a. Normally it remains: *land*<M.H.G. *lant (land-)*; *laŋg*<M.H.G. *lanc
(lang-)*; *laixt*<M.H.G. *licht*; *als* 'all'<M.H.G. *allez*; *fáln̩*<M.H.G. *vallen*;
gold<M.H.G. *golt (gold-)*.

  b. It has been syncopated before an accented syllable in: *az* 'that, when'
<M.H.G. *als*; *azę́* 'so'<M.H.G. *alsô*.

4. M.H.G. *r*.

  a. As we have seen, it became uvular in pronunciation: *rẹt*<M.H.G. *rôt*; *régn̩*
<M.H.G. *rëgen*; *rẹx*<M.H.G. *rouch*; *ber* 'bear'<M.H.G. *bër*; *gor*<M.H.G.
gâr; *hérn̩*<M.H.G. *hæren*.

  b. In *mátr̩n* 'to torment'<M.H.G. *martern r* has been syncopated by dissimilation from *r* of *-ern*. In forms of *vérn̩*<M.H.G. *wërden r* is syncopated before
final *-t* and *-st*: *du vest*<*du wirst*, *er vet*<*er wrlt* (*e* of *vest* and *vet* is analogical), *ir vet*<*ir wërdet*.

5. M.H.G. *n*.

  a. This sound normally remains, also in infinitive ending *-en*: *nai*<M.H.G.
niuwe; *nit* 'not'<M.H.G. *niet* (variant of *nieht, niht*); *noz*<M.H.G. *nase*;
nas<M.H.G. *naz*; *ken*<M.H.G. *kan* and *kënne*; *hélfn̩*<M.H.G. *hëlfen*;
zint<M.H.G. *sint* 'since'.

  b. In *ein* as indefinite article *n* has remained only before vowels, otherwise it
is syncopated: *a mán* 'ein Mann' but *an óks* 'ein Ochs' (cf. English *a, an*).
Wrong division has produced, e.g., *nam* 'nurse' (M.H.G. *ein' amme*>*an
am*>*a nam*); *nol* 'awl' (M.H.G. *ein' âle*>*an ol*>*a nol*). *n* has been syncopated also in: *lébədik* 'alive'<M.H.G. *lëbendic*; *fúftsn̩*<M.H.G. *vünf-
zëhen*, *fúftsig*<M.H.G. *vünfzic*. It is barely possible that *fúftsn̩* and
fúftsig have been remodelled, by analogy of *finf* 'five', from etymologically
justified **fux-*<**fūx-*<**fuŋx-*<Indogermanic **pŋkw-*(cf. Swabian *fuchzē*
'fifteen'; see W. Streitberg, *Urgermanische Grammᶦtik*, 1900, p. 111).

  c. In M.H.G. *nëben* 'near' *n-* has become dissimilated to *l*: *lébn̩*.

  d. It is assimilated before *p* to *m* in *kimpət*<M.H.G. *kintbëtte*; *vaimpr̩ləx*
diminutive plural<M.H.G. *win-bër*.

6. M.H.G. *m*.

This consonant seems to have remained in all cases: *mę́dl̩* 'girl'<M.H.G.
meidel; *man*<M.H.G. *man (mann-)*; *mos*<M.H.G. *mâz*; *mir*<M.H.G.*mir*;
kúmn̩<M.H.G. *kumen*; *hẹm*<M.H.G. *heim*. It is particularly noteworthy
that unaccented *-em* has not been weakened to *-n̩* as in modern German:
bézm̩ 'switch used in rubbing down in sweat-bath'<M.H.G. *bëseme* (cf.
German *Besen*); *fódm̩*<M.H.G. *vadem* (cf. German *Faden*); *bę́dm̩* 'loft,
attic'<M.H.G. *bodem* (cf. German *Boden*). In *zamd* 'sand' *m*, as we have
seen, is more archaic than *n* (M.H.G. *sant, sand-*).

7. M.H.G. *ŋ* (written *n*).

This sound, which occurs only before *g* and *k*, has been preserved in all cases:
gɩgáŋgn̩<M.H.G. *gegangen*; *juŋg*<M.H.G. *junc (jung-)*; *ɩŋgl̩*<M.H.G.
jüngel(în); *dáŋkn̩*<M.H.G. *danken*; *dę́ŋkn̩*<M.H.G. *dënken*.

8. M.H.G. *v, f* (Urgermanisch *f*) and *-ff-, -f-* (Urgermanisch *p*).

   a. As in other modern German dialects, these two etymologically distinct sounds fell together in Judeo-German, except for intervocalic *-v-* (see b): *fóṭ*<M.H.G. *vater*; *fil*<M.H.G. *vil*; *fédṛ*<M.H.G. *vĕder*; *féṭṛ* 'uncle'< M.H.G. *vĕter* 'Vatersbruder'; *far-*<M.H.G. *ver-*; *šlófṇ*<M.H.G. *sláfen*; *tif* <M.H.G. *tief*; *hélfṇ*<M.H.G. *hĕlfen*; *šarf*<M.H.G. *scharf*; *dorf*<M.H.G. *dorf*; *ófṇ*<M.H.G. *offen*; *hef*<M.H.G. *hof*; *volf*<M.H.G. *wolf*.

   b. Medially before vowels M.H.G. *v* appears as *v* (voiced dento-labial identical with *v*<M.H.G. *w*, see 2 a): *évṇ* 'stove'<M.H.G. *oven*; *taivḷ* 'devil'<M.H.G. *tiuvel*; *hévṇ* 'yeast'<M.H.G. *hĕve*; *bórvəs* 'barefoot'<M.H.G. *barvuoẓ*. *hóbṛ* 'oats' goes back to M.H.G. *haber*, not *haver* (see 10 a).

9. M.H.G. *pf* (*ph*).

   a. Initially *pf* has become simplified to *f*: *funt*<M.H.G. *pfunt*; *ferd*<M.H.G. *pférd* (*pférd-*); *ix flég* 'I was wont to' (present in form, but imperfect in meaning)<M.H.G. *pflĕge*; *fan* 'pan'<M.H.G. *pfanne* (*fainkuxṇ* 'Pfann- kuchen' is probably made over by analogy of *fain*<*fín*).

   b. Medially and finally it lost its spirantal element and became *p*: *kop*< M.H.G. *kopf*; *klópṇ*<M.H.G. *klopfen*; *épḷ*<M.H.G. *épfel, apfel*; *štúpṇ* 'to shove' (*er štupt úntṛ* 'he eggs on')<M.H.G. *stupfen* 'stechend stossen, antreiben'.

10. M.H.G. *b*.

    a. Normally *b* is preserved (as voiced lenis); it occurs also finally(< M.H.G. *-p*), probably by analogy of medial *-b-*: *breṭ*<M.H.G. *breit*; *breṭ*<M.H.G. *brôt*; *bai, ba*<M.H.G. *bî*; *barg*<M.H.G. *bĕrc* (*bĕrg-*); *lébṇ*<M.H.G. *lĕben*; *lébṇ*<M.H.G. *nĕben*; *hóbṛ* 'oats'<M.H.G. *haber* (of which *haver*>modern German *Hafer* is variant); *tsíbḷ* 'onion'<M.H.G. *zibolle* (variant of *zwibolle, zweibel*); *štub*<M.H.G. *stube*; *štẹb*<M.H.G. *stoup* (*stoub-*).

    b. In *óvṇt* 'evening'<M.H.G. *âbent*, M.H.G. *b* has become spirantized to *v*; also in *hórəvṇ*, see 18 c. For M.H.G. medial bilabial spirant *b*, from older *-b-*, in Middle German dialects see V. Michels, *Mittelhochdeutsches Elemen- tarbuch*, 1900, § 159.

    c. M.H.G. *-mb-* has, as in modern German, become assimilated to *-mm->-m-*: *kam* < M.H.G. *kamp* (*kamb-*); *um* < M.H.G. *umbe*; *lam*, diminutive *lémale* < M.H.G. *lamp* (*lamb-*), diminutive *lémbelîn*.

    d. In a number of words M.H.G. *b* appears as *p*. This is intelligible where final *-b* developed to *-p* and was not levelled out by analogy of medial *-b-*: *zip* 'sieve' < M.H.G. *sip* (*sib-*); *op* < M.H.G. *abe, ab* (*aróp* 'herab'; as verb pre- fix before participial *gî-*, *op-* appears as *ó-*: *ógîton* 'abgetan'). Less easily explained are certain examples of initial and medial *p*: *poiər* 'peasant' M.H.G. *bûr*; *púṭṛ* 'butter' < M.H.G. *buter*; *gópḷ* 'fork' < M.H.G. *gabel*; *klépṇ* 'to be stuck to' < M.H.G. *klĕben*; *vaimpṛ-*(*ləx*) < M.H G. *wînber*. In estimating these and similar developments (*t*<*d*, *k*<*g*) it must be remem- bered that Judeo-German knows no 'voiceless lenis' stops, but only fully voiced lenis stops (corresponding to Upper German voiceless lenis) and unaspirated voiceless fortis stops (corresponding to Upper German voice- less fortis).

11. M.H.G. *p*.

    This sound regularly remains: *paršẹn* < M.H.G. *pĕršôn* (for *a*<*ĕ* see 3 c); *špílṇ* < M.H.G. *spilen*; *šprung* < M.H.G. *sprunc* (*sprung-*).

12. M.H.G. *s*, *-ss-* and *-ʒ-*, *-ʒʒ-*.
   a. Initial and medial *s* (except before voiceless consonants) became voiced to
   z (this includes also final *-s* when alternating with medial *-s-*); *zun* < M.H.G.
   sun 'son' and *sunne* 'sun'; *zógṇ* < M.H.G. *sagen*; *zégṛ* 'clock' < M.H.G.
   seiger; *zúxṇ* < M.H.G. *suochen*; *az* < M.H.G. *als, alse*; *azé* < M.H.G. *alsó*;
   únzṛ < M.H.G. *unser*; *kez* 'cheese' < M.H.G. *kæse*; *blózṇ* < M.H.G. *blâsen*;
   bloz 'breath' < M.H.G. *blâs (blâs-)* 'Hauch'; *groz* < M.H.G. *gras (gras-)*.
   Medial ungeminated *-ʒ-* has also developed to *z* in: *lózṇ* 'to let' < M.H.G.
   lâzen. Judeo-German *ʒ* in *muz* 'must' may be similarly developed from medial ungeminated *-ʒ-* (M.H.G. *muoʒ : müeʒen* > *muz* : *múzṇ* with generalized
   vocalism of *muoʒ* and medial *-z-* of *mueʒen*) or, perhaps less likely, from
   medial *-s-* of preterite *muose* (later superseded by analogical *muoste*).
   More often, however, *-ʒ-* is treated like *-ʒʒ-* (see b).
   b. Final *-ʒ*, medial *-ʒʒ-* and (generally) *-ʒ-*, and medial *-s-* before voiceless
   consonants appear in Judeo-German, as in modern German, as voiceless
   s: *ois* 'out' < M.H.G. *ûʒ*; *fus* < M.H.G. *vuoʒ*; *vais* < M.H.G. *wîʒ*; *dos* <
   M.H.G. *daʒ*; *ésṇ* < M.H.G. *ëʒʒen*; *bésṛ* < M.H.G. *bëʒʒer*; *baisṇ* < M.H.G.
   bîʒen; *hésṇ* < M.H.G. *heizen*; *nest* < M.H.G. *nëst*; *um zist* < M.H.G. *umbe
   sust*; *host* < M.H.G. *hâst*. Judeo-German *méstṇ* 'to measure' (with analogic
   participle *gĭmóstṇ*) has perhaps resulted from confusion of M.H.G. *mëʒʒen*
   'messen' and *mëstern* 'den Inhalt messen'. M.H.G. *ist* > Judeo-German *iz*
   is due to loss of *-t* and voicing of *s* because of its frequent use as proclitic
   (*iz* probably generalized from antevocalic use, e.g. *iz a mán*<M.H.G.*is(t)
   ein man*).
   c. For some not evident reason medial M.H.G. *-s-* appears as Judeo-German
   -s- instead of *-z-* in: *késṛ* < M.H.G. *keiser*; *nísṇ* 'to seeeze' < M.H.G. *niesen*.
   d. M.H.G. *-ss-* seems to have regularly developed to *š*, i.e. modern German
   sch (it has thus not, as in modern German, fallen together with M.H.G.*-ʒʒ-*
   -ʒ-): *kuš* < M.H.G. *kus (kuss-)*; *kúšṇ* (with vocalism of *kuš*) <M.H.G.
   küssen 'to kiss;' *kíšṇ* < M.H.G. *küssen* 'pillow'; *píšṇ* 'to urinate' < *pissen*.
   e. After *r* both *s* and *ʒ* appear as *š*; *karš* < M.H.G. *kirse*; *paršén* 'beautiful
   woman' < M.H.G. *përsôn*; *eršt* < M.H.G. *erst*; *hirš* < M.H.G. *hirʒ*.
   f. Before *l, m, n, w, p*, and *t* initial M.H.G. *s* developed, as in modern German,
   to *š*: *šlext* < M.H.G. *slëht*; *šmaisṇ* 'to beat' < M.H.G. *smîzen* 'streichen,
   schlagen'; *šnė* < M.H.G. *snê*; *šver* < M.H.G. *swære*; *špet* < M.H.G. *spæte*;
   štęn < M.H.G. *stein*.
13. M.H.G. *sch*.
   This sound is regularly preserved as *š*: *šépṇ* < M.H.G. *schëpfen*; *šaínṇ* <
   M.H.G. *schînen*; *šétļ* 'perruque with evenly parted hair worn by orthodox
   Jewish women' < M.H.G. *scheitel* 'crown of the head, parting of the hair';
   míšṇ < M.H.G. *mischen*; *ídiš* < M.H.G. *jüdisch*.
14. M.H.G. *z* and *-tz-*.
   These affricatives are everywhere preserved as *ts*: *tsen* < M.H.G. *zëhen*; *tson*
   < M.H.G. *zan*; *tsvė* < M.H.G. *zwei*; *harts* < M.H.G. *hërze*; *kats* < M.H.G.
   katze.
15. M.H.G. *d*.
   a. Normally *d* is preserved (as voiced lenis); it occurs also finally (< M.H.G.
   -t), probably by analogy of medial *-d- dax*<M.H.G. *dach*; *dar* 'thin<M.H.G.
   dürre; *drai* < M.H.G. *drî*; *moid* <M.H.G. *maget (maged-)*; *bod* <M.H.G. *bat*

(*bad-*); *feld* < M.H.G. *vĕlt* (*vĕld-*); *ferd* < M.H.G. *pfĕrt* (*pfĕrd-*); *ódṛ* 'vein' < M.H.G. *áder*. Examples of *nd* < M.H.G. *nd* (including cases of *-nt* alternating with *-nd-*) < O.H.G. *nt* are: *bíndṇ* < M.H.G. *binden*; *óntsindṇ* < M.H.G. *anzünden*; *vúndṛn* < M.H.G. *wundern*; *blind* < M.H.G. *blint* (*blind-*); *land* < M.H.G. *lant* (*land-*); *rund* < M.H.G. *runt* (*rund-*); *kind* < M.H.G. *kint* (*kind-*); *end* < M.H.G. *ĕnde*. For examples of *nt* < M.H.G. *-nt* (*-nd-*) see 15 d below.

b. M.H.G. *rd* appears as *r* in: *vérṇ* < *wĕrden* (similarly *ix ver* < M.H.G. *ich wĕrde, gĭvórṇ* < M.H.G. *geworden; -rst* and *-rt* of this verb develop to *-st*, *-t*, see 4 b). This development is not strictly normal, but is probably due to frequently proclitic character of *wĕrden* owing to its use as auxiliary verb; contrast *ferd* < M.H.G. *pfĕrd-*. Quite parallel to this is *l* < M.H.G. *ld* in: *mánzbil* 'man' < M.H.G. *mannes bilde* (e.g. *zwei mannes bilde er dâ gesach* 'da sah er zwei Männer', *Der Wartburgkrieg*, herausgegeben von Karl Simrock, 1858, p. 65, l. 4 of no 37), in which *bilde* has lost its accent (*-z-* of *mánzbil* due to voiced surroundings of M.H.G. *-s-*); contrast accented *bild* 'picture' < M.H.G. *bilde*. In certain cases *nd* is assimilated to *nn* > *n* (cf. *m* < M.H.G. *mb*, see 10 c): *un* 'and' < M.H.G. *unde*; *fránṇ* 'in existence, to be found' < *vorhanden*; *gĭfínṇ* 'to find' (simplex *fínṇ* not in use) < M.H.G. *gevinden*; *gĭštánṇ* < M.H.G. *gestanden*; *tson* < M.H.G. *zant* (*zand-*), but also *zan*. In *un* we can readily explain *n* < *nd* as due to lack of accent (cf. *r* < *rd* and *l* < *ld* above); in *fránṇ* and *gĭštánṇ* it seems very likely that original *-ndṇ* regularly developed to *-nṇ*, internasal *-d-* becoming completely assimilated (in such forms as *bíndṇ, gĭbúndṇ* it is clear that *-ndṇ* was restored by analogy of forms like *ix bind, er bint*; note that in *fránṇ*, whose connexion with M.H.G. *hant* (*hand-*) was lost, and *gĭštánṇ*, with its infinitive and present *štēn, ix štē*, no disturbance by analogical levelling could take place). As for *gĭfínṇ* (also *gĭfunṇ, ix gĭfín*) and *tson* (also plural *tsēnṛ*; diminutive *tsēndḷ* has not original *-nd-* but intrusive *-d-*, see 15 c below), I would suggest that M.H.G. *nd* of *zand-* and *vinden* (which goes back to O.H.G. *nd—zand, findan—* < Urgermanisch *nþ*—cf. Gothic *tunþus, finþan*) was, at least in some dialects, phonetically distinct from M.H.G. *nd* < O.H.G. *nt* (thus, O.H.G. *findan* > M.H.G. *vinden* > Judeo-German *-fínṇ;* O.H.G. *bintan* > M.H.G. *binden* > Judeo-German *bíndṇ*); in *ándṛ* < M.H.G *ander* < O.H.G. *ander*, *-nd-* may have been protected from becoming *-n-* because of following *-r-* (cf. M.H.G. *winter* < O.H.G. *wintar* as contrasted with *winden* < *wintan*).

c. Between *n* as stem ending and *-ḷ*(*-l-*) as diminutive ending *d* develops as glide consonant (cf. Gothic *timrjan*: O.H.G. *zimbarôn*): *bėndḷ* 'little bone' < M.H.G. *beinel; fėndḷ* 'little pan', diminutive of *fan* < M.H.G. *pfanne; hėndḷ* 'little cock' < M.H.G. *hėnel; hindḷ* 'little hen' < M.H.G. *hüenel;* diminutive plural of nouns in *-n-* is *-ndlǝx* (e.g. *bėndlǝx* 'little bones, fruit pits').

d. In certain cases, as we have seen in 15 a, M.H.G. *-nt* (*-nd-*) and *-lt* (*-ld-*) developed to *-nd* and *-ld*, as would be normally expected for Judeo-German. In a large number of examples, however, *-t* is generalized, replacing *-d-* also medially: *gĭzúnt* (also e.g., in *a gĭzúnṛ* 'ein gesunder') < M.H.G. *gesunt* (*gesund-*); *hunt* (also, e.g., diminutive *hintḷ*; contrast *hindḷ* as diminutive of *hun* 'hen') < M.H.G. *hunt* (*hund-*); *hant* (also, e.g., diminutive *hėntḷ*; contrast *hėndḷ* as diminutive of *hon* 'cock') < M.H.G. *hant* (*hand-*); *vint* (also, e.g., diminutive *vintļ*) < M.H.G. *wint* (*wind-*); *funt* < M.H.G. *pfunt* (*pfund-*); *fraint* < M.H.G. *vriunt* (*vriund-*); *faint* < M.H.G. *vîant* (*vîand-*); *bunt* (also, e.g., diminutive *bintļ*) < M.H.G. *bunt* (*bund-*); *óvņt* < M.H.G. *âbent* (*âbend-*); *g̑idúlt* < M.H.G. *gedult*, *gedulde* (but also *gedultec*); *gelt* < M.H.G. *gëlt* (*gëld-* but also *gëlt-*). I can suggest no definite rule for such differences of treatment as *blind* < M.H.G. *blint* (*blind-*) < O.H.G. *blint* (*blint-*) and *vint* < M.H.G. *wint* (*wind-*) < O.H.G. *wint* (*wint-*). Possibly *-nd* forms are generalized in words where medial *-nd-* occurs often (e.g. *blind* because supported by inflected *blîndə* and *blîndŗ*), but *-nt* forms where medial *-nd-* either occurs infrequently (thus, M.H.G. *bündel* would not be of frequent enough occurrence to influence *bunt*, hence itself suffers analogical levelling to *bintļ*, which can hardly be directly traced to O.H.G. *buntil*) or has become obsolete in Judeo-German (thus M.H.G. *hénde* had to develop, with loss of *-e*, to Judeo-German *hend*, which could not maintain its *-d* against singular *hant*, hence itself suffers analogical levelling to *hent*, which can hardly be directly traced to O.H.G. *hénti*); *bunt* and *bîndņ* appear contradictory, but can be readily explained, as they would not be felt to be connected closely enough to influence each other. In *úntŗ* < M.H.G. *under* < O.H.G. *untar*, *-nd-* has, as in modern German, again become hardened to *-nt-*, probably because of following *-r* (cf. M.H.G. *winter* < *wintar*); similarly *hîntŗ* < M.H.G. *hinder*. As for Judeo-German *gelt* as contrasted with *feld*, it should be noted that O.H.G. has correspondingly *gëlt* but *fëld*.

e. Different from these examples of *-nt* and *-lt* from M.H.G. *-nd-* and *-ld-* are certain cases of initial *t* < normal M.H.G. *d* (cf. *p* < *b*, 10 d): *taitš* < M.H.G. *diutsch*, *tiutsch* (also *fartaitšņ* 'to translate' < M.H.G. *diutschen*, *tiutschen* 'auf deutsch sagen, erklären'); *túŋkļ* < M.H.G. *dunkel*, *tunkel* (M.H.G. *tunkel* is normal, hence this example belongs rather under M.H.G. *t*); *tẹtļ* 'date' < M.H.G. *datel* (*tẹtļ* may be assimilated from *dẹtļ; why *ẹ* instead of expected *o*?).

16. M.H.G. *t*.

a. This sound, aside from cases of M.H.G. *-t*: *-d-*, has been kept in all positions: *ton* < M.H.G. *tuon*; *túmļ* < M.H.G. *tumel* 'betäubender Schall, Lärm'; *tẹl* < M.H.G. *teil*; *kótŗ* 'tomcat' < M.H.G. *kater*; *vîntŗ* < M.H.G. *winter*; *zint* 'since' < M.H.G. *sint*; *bet* < M.H.G. *bëtte*; *rẹt* < M.H.G. *rôt*; *g̑ivált* < M.H.G. *gewalt*; *nont* 'near' < M.H.G. *nâhent* (note also Judeo-German comparative *néntŗ*).

b. It is not easy to see why *-tļ* has become *-dļ* in *bẹrdļ*, diminutive of *bort* 'beard' < M.H.G. *bart*. Perhaps original *bẹrtļ was transformed by analogy of diminutives in *-ndļ* (see 15 c).

Initial *tw-*, as in modern German, has developed to *tsv-*: *tsvîŋgņ* < M.H.G. *twingen*; *tsvógņ* 'to wash one's head' < M.H.G. *twahen*, past participle *getwagen*; *tsvórəx* < M.H.G. *twarc* (*twarg-*) 'Quarkkäse' (this word may have been directly derived from Slavic, e.g. Polish *tvarog*, from which it was borrowed by M.H.G., in which case Judeo-German *tsv-* < *tv-* < *tw-* would have taken place after Judeo-German had become isolated from other German dialects; this, however, is rendered very improbable by parallel form *zwarc* in late M.H.G.).

d. Medial *-tw-* has become *-p-* in: *épəs* 'something' < M.H.G. *ët(e)waz* (cf. Latin *b* < *dw* in *bis*, *p* < *tw* in *postis*).—How explain *rátvņ* 'to save'? It is undoubtedly connected with M.H.G. and O.H.G. *rétten* < West Germanic **hraddjan* < Urgermanisch **hradjan*, but cannot be directly derived from it. Perhaps parallel to **hrad-jan* with *j*-suffix was **hrad-wan* with *w*-suffix > O.H.G. **(h)ratwan* > M.H.G. **ratwen*, dialectically preserved in Judeo-German as *rátvn̥*. In that case *-tw-* > *-p-* may hold only in normally unaccented words.

 e. *-st* has become *-s* > *-z*, because of lack of accent, in: *iz* < M.H.G. *ist*. Similarly, *-rtn̥* has become *-rn̥* in: *éntfərn̥* 'to answer' < M.H.G. *entwürten*.

17. **M.H.G. *h* (as spirant), *ch*.**
As was noted above, no distinction is made in Judeo-German between guttural *x* and palatal *x'* (as in modern German *ich*), but both are represented by guttural *x*. This feature may be archaic rather than due to levelling.

 a. It is kept in all positions except before *s*: *laixt* < M.H.G. *líhte*; *nox* < M.H.G. *noch*; *nox* < M.H.G. *nâch*; *zix* < M.H.G. *sich*; *kalx* < M.H.G. *kalch* (parallel to normal *kalk*) < O.H.G. *kalch*; *marx* 'marrow' < M.H.G. *march* (parallel to *mark*); *gix* 'quick' < M.H.G. *gâch*; *šux* 'shoe' < M.H.G. *schuoch* (note analogical plural *šix* < M.H.G. *schuohe*); *hex* < M.H.G. *hôch* (note analogical comparative *hexr̥*: < M.H.G. *hœher*); *bilxr̥* 'more proper' < M.H.G. *billich* 'gemäss, geziemend' (*g* of modern German *billig* is secondary in origin).

 b. Before *s*, as in modern German, it has become *k*: *oks* < M.H.G. *ohse*; *vakst* grows < M.H.G. *wähset*.

 c. Before diminutive *-l̥* nouns ending in *l* insert *x*: *špilxl̥*, 'plaything', diminutive of *špil* M.H.G. *spil*; *mailxl̥*, diminutive of *moil* 'mouth' < M.H.G. *mûl*; *kêlxl̥* 'little throat, voice' < M.H.G. *kël*. I doubt if this *-xl̥* is in any way connected with modern German diminutive *-chen*.

18. **M.H.G. *h* (as aspirate).**
 a. It is preserved initially: *halz* < M.H.G. *hals*; *hon* < M.H.G. *hane* 'cock'; *hot* < M.H.G. *hât*; *ahin* < M.H.G. *hin*.

 b. Between vowels, as in modern German, it disappears: *laiən* 'to lend' < M.H.G. *líhen*; *nont* 'near' < M.H.G. *nâhent*. For M.H.G. *-ëhe-* and *-êhe-* > *-e-* see 3 b and 4 b of Vowels. *h* has also disappeared in *fránn̥* 'present' < *vorhanden*.

 c. In a few words *h* is inorganic: *hailn̥* 'to hurry' < M.H.G. *îlen*; *hórəvn̥* 'to work hard' < *arben, areben* (Swiss *arbən*, Nassau *erwə*; see Kluge, *Deutsches Etymologisches Wörterbuch*, s.v. Arbeit) with *v* < *b*, see 10 b.

19. **M.H.G. *g*.**
 a. Normally *g* is preserved (as voiced lenis); it occurs also finally (< M.H.G. *-c*), probably by analogy of medial *-g-*; it has nowhere undergone spirantization to *γ* (as in modern German *tấγə*) or *j* (as in modern German *vêjə*). Examples are: *gut* < M.H.G. *guot*; *gel* 'yellow' < M.H.G. *gël*; *zógn̥* < M.H.G. *sagen*; *négl̥* 'nails' < M.H.G. *négele*; *veg* < M.H.G. *wëc* (*wëg-*); *karg* < M.H.G. *karc* (*karg-*). It is preserved also after *ŋ*: *ziŋgn̥* < M.H.G. *singen* (contrast modern German *ziŋn̥*); *juŋg* < M.H.G. *junc* (*jung-*) (contrast modern German *juŋ*).

 b. In certain words with M.H.G. *-c*: *-g-* Judeo-German has generalized *-k*: *tsvaŋk* 'tongs, pincers' < M.H.G. *zwange* (note retention of *w* as *v* in Judeo-German); *sok* 'juice' < M.H.G. *soc, sog-* (parallel to more normal *suc, sug-*), which, however, is more likely borrowed, as indicated by its *o*-vocalism, from Russian *sok* 'juice' (Germanic loan-word) than directly derived from M.H.G. In nouns and adjectives ending in M.H.G. *-ic* (*-ig-*) Judeo-German has regularly *-ik*: *kinik* < M.H.G. *künic* (*künig-*); *hónik* < M.H.G. *honic* (*honig-*); *lēbədik* 'alive' < M.H.G. *lēbendic* (*lēbendig-*).

   c. In a few cases Judeo-German has *k* < M.H.G. *g* not alternating with *-c*: *bēŋkṇ* 'to long for' < M.H.G. *bangen* 'bange werden', *bénge* 'Angst, Sorge'; *kúkṇ* 'to look' < M.H.G. *gucken* (here *g—k* may have become assimilated to *k—k*). Compare *t* < M.H.G. *d* (15 e) and *p* < M.H.G. *b* (10 d).

   d. In *art* (e.g. *es árt mir nit* 'it does not concern me, I don't care') *g* seems to have been syncopated between *r* and *t*; cf. M.H.G. *arget* 'macht besorgt, *arg*'.

   e. *g* has developed as hiatus-filler in *gĭšrĭgṇ*, past participle of *šraiən* 'to yell'. Possibly *r—g* as dissimilated product of *r—r* of M.H.G. *geschrirn*.

20. M.H.G. *k*.

This sound is everywhere preserved: *korn* < M.H.G. *korn*; *kez* 'cheese' < M.H.G. *kœse*; *klęn* < M.H.G. *klein(e)*; *krĭxṇ* < M.H.G. *kriechen*; *knẹdĺ* 'dumpling' < M.H.G. *knödel*; *hákṇ* < M.H.G. *hacken*; *zak* < M.H.G. *sac* (*sack-*); *avék* 'away' < M.H.G. *enwëc* (not levelled out to *avég* because no longer felt to be connected with *veg* 'way'). M.H.G. *qu* (i.e. *kw*) appears as *kv*: *kvélṇ* 'to bubble with joy' < M.H.G. *quëllen*.

Such, in brief, is the history of the Middle High German vowels and consonants in Judeo-German. It will have been noticed that the changes in the Judeo-German consonant system, when compared with its Middle High German prototype, are not as radical as in the case of the vowels and that many of the important consonantal developments are common to modern German. As in the vowel system, so also in the consonant system, simplification, though to a less degree, has taken place (e.g. M.H.G. *pf* is represented by *p* or *f*, according to its position).

ACCENT

In stress accent no changes have taken place, the stem (normally the first) syllable, according to the well-known Germanic law of accent, regularly receiving the stress. In *lébədik* 'alive' <M.H.G. *lēbendic* the accent falls on the first syllable, not, as in modern German *lebendig*, on the second; the lack of stress in the second syllable is probably responsible for the syncope of the *n*. With the Judeo-German accent of this word cf. the following from the epic of 'Kûdrûn' (I, 29):

'Si sprach: "so rîche nieman ist lébendic erkant".'

Exceptions to the general law of Germanic accent are exceedingly rare. A case in point is *švestṛkĭnd* 'cousin' (literally 'sister's (or brother's) child').

Hebrew loan-words (Hebrew words are either ultimate or, far less frequently, penultimate in accent) accommodate themselves so far to the German rule that, if ultimate in accent, they throw their stress back to the penultimate syllable; words of more than two syllables, however, cannot be accented back of the penult. This sweeping and simple law of penultimate accentuation of Hebrew words holds, it should be noticed, not merely for such as have been incorporated into Judeo-German, but for the present pronunciation of Hebrew in general. In the case of naturalized words a final vowel (whether followed by a consonant or not) has, in accordance with the genius of the German language, been weakened to the dull *ə*. Thus Hebrew *xᵃzî̆r* 'pig' > Judeo-German *xáʐ; lāšón* 'language' > *lóšṇ; gannáβ* 'thief' > *gánəf; mišpāχá̆* 'family' > *mišpóxə*. In reading Hebrew as such, however, these final vowels are not reduced; the words given above are then pronounced: *xázir, lóšẹn, gánov, mišpóxo*. These examples show incidentally that the Hebrew *ā* and *ō* developed, together with the Middle High German *â* and *ô*, into *o* and *ẹ* respectively.

As regards the accentuation of the Slavic (Russian and Polish) loanwords, the rule is, on the whole, to keep the native accent. It should be noted that such words hold relatively the same position in Judeo-German that, e.g., French words with un-German accent (such as *Position, raffiniert*) hold in modern German.

Besides stress accent, a very important factor in the pronunciation of Judeo-German is the musical intonation of the sentence. In the normal pronunciation of sentences there is a very considerable variation of musical cadence. Simple statements, interrogation, surprise, indignation, emphatic insistence, irony, and many other moods are differentiated by these differences of cadence; it would be possible, indeed, to construct a rather long series of types of sentence-cadence for the pronunciation of word groups in various emotional keys, some of which would show excessively violent rises and falls in pitch. This mobility of musical expression gives Judeo-German much of its characteristic acoustic effect. The rhetorical effectiveness of Judeo-German speech is increased by the use of a large number of modal particles (cf. German *doch ja, schon, wohl, mal*), which are partly Middle High German, partly Slavic, and partly Hebrew in origin. Altogether, they neatly hit off many nuances of mental attitude and despair in many cases of adequate translation.

I trust that I have shown that a thorough investigation of the phonology, morphology, and vocabulary of Judeo-German will prove abundantly fruitful to students of German dialectology.

TIBETAN INFLUENCES ON TOCHARIAN. I*

As FAR BACK as 1922, in an article[1] which in many respects remains the most significant contribution yet made to the larger understanding of the status of Tocharian, Eduard Hermann pointed out the importance of Tibetan because of its far-reaching morphological influence on Tocharian. Little attention, however, seems to have been paid to this aspect of the Tocharian problem, yet it is safe to say that one can not take a step in interpreting the forms of Tocharian, syntax and morphology both, unless one bears in mind the moulding influence exerted on Tocharian, both A and B, by this non-Indo-European language. In brief, Tocharian is a Tibetanized Indo-European idiom. Once this is understood, the much discussed problem of whether both A and B were spoken in Chinese Turkestan or B ('Kuchean') alone, the A manuscripts appearing in the eastern part of the area merely because they were brought there by speakers of B from a real or supposed western home in Tokharestan (Bactria), falls by the wayside as an utterly pointless question. If dialect A has specifically Tibetan features in its structure—and it has—how could these have developed except through actual contact between speakers of Tocharian A and speakers of Tibetan, and where could such contact be had except in Chinese Turkestan itself, at a point not far removed from linguistically Tibetan territory?

In the present paper we shall take up a number of specific points which seem to argue for a measure of Tibetan influence on Tocharian.

1. TOCHARIAN 'HEART FATHER'

In §373a the authors of the *Tocharische Grammatik*[2] give us an example of a tatpuruṣa compound with substantive as first element: *āriñc-pācar* 'heart-father'. The form occurs in the phrase *kāpñe āriñc-pācar* 'dear heart-father' in two passages of the *Tocharische Sprachreste* (356 b 3; 407 a 3). This curious turn of phrase can also be expressed in adjectival form, i.e., by means of an adjectival derivative of *āriñc* in *-i* or *-ṣi* (SSS §§42; 44a). As it happens, these adjectives occur with 'son' and 'sister', not with 'father', but the total number of examples of both types of usage is not large enough to justify the inference that there is a specific difference of idiom in the use of 'heart' with 'father' (and 'mother') on the one hand and with 'child' and 'brother' or 'sister' on the other. It

---

* Language, 12 (1936) : 259–271.
[1] A review of Sieg und Siegling, *Tocharische Sprachreste*, I. Band: *Die Texte*, in *Zeitschrift für vergleichende Sprachforschung*, 50 (1922): 296–314, particularly pp. 309–311.
[2] Referred to as SSS, i.e., E. Sieg, W. Siegling, and W. Schulze.

is far more likely that one might say either *āriñc-pācar* or **āriñci pācar*, **āriñcṣi pācar*.³ The adjectival examples are:

āriñcim se- (338 b 7; 'heart son'. *se-* broken off but presumably to be restored to instrumental *seyo*, requiring oblique m. form in *-ṃ* of preceding adjective, and pairing with preceding *märkampalṣiṃ tuṅkyo*)

āriñcṣinäṃ se (Frgm.: 'heart son'; obl. m. sing.)

kāpñe āriñcṣinäs sewās (356 b 1: 'dear heart sons'; obl. m. plur.)

āriñcṣinäṃ ṣar (451 a 4: 'heart sister'; obl. f. sing.)

Parallel to such a Tocharian form as *āriñcṣinäs sewās* 'heart sons', which could presumably alternate with compounded **āriñc-sewās* (ob. m. plur.) 'heart-sons', would seem to be Tibetan *t'ugs-kyi sras* 'heart's son' or *t'ugs-sras* 'heart-son'.⁴ The actual meaning of the term, according to Jäschke, is 'spiritual son, an appellation given to the most distinguished scholars or saints'. *Sras* is the 'respectful' word for 'son' in Tibetan, *bu* the ordinary word. Similarly, *t'ugs* is the respectful word corresponding to *sñiṅ* 'heart, breast, mind', *yid* 'soul, mind', *sems* 'soul', and other words of mental or psychological connotation.⁵ The Tibetan *t'ugs-kyi sras*, a genitive construction, seems to correspond to the adjectival Tocharian *āriñcṣi se*, the Tibetan *t'ugs-sras*, a compound, to a Tocharian compounded **āriñc-se*.

The use of Tocharian *āriñcṣi* 'heart' (adj.) in other cases seems to correspond rather closely to that of Tibetan *t'ugs-* in comparable compounds. Thus, *āriñcṣi ākāl* 'heart wish' (nom. m. sing.)⁶ parallels such Tibetan compounds as *t'ugs-dam*⁷ (the respectful analogue of *yi(d)-dam*) 'a prayer, a wish in the form of a prayer' (= *smon-lam* 'wish-road'; cf. *yid-smon* 'soul-wish, wish') and *t'ugs-dgoṅs* (= *dgoṅs-pa* 'wish') 'heart-wish, will'. Another such Tocharian collocation is *āriñcṣinäṃ yärṣlune* 'heart homage' (obl. m. sing.),⁸ for which I have not found an exact Tibetan parallel.

All these Tocharian-Tibetan parallels may be merely due to literary transcriptions, in which case one may be tempted to argue back to

---

³ Inasmuch as *c* represents a palatal affricative, roughly *tś*, the two forms *āriñci* and *āriñcṣi* are likely to be merely orthographic variants of a single form in *-ṣi*, the most common Tocharian adjectival suffix. If this is correct, *āriñci* (occurring only as an oblique sing., *āriñcim*) would not be formally parallel to such adjectives in palatalizing *-i* as *ñäkci* : *ñkät* 'god' and *mañi* : *mañ* 'moon, month', as is assumed by SSS.

⁴ See H. Jäschke, *A Tibetan-English Dictionary* (London, 1881) s.v. *t'ugs*, p. 233.

⁵ For 'respectful' terms in Tibetan see H. Jäschke, *Tibetan Grammar*, Addenda, by A. H. Francke assisted by W. Simon (Berlin, W. de Gruyter, 1929), pp. 35–36, 131–136.

⁶ SSS §44a; *Tocharische Sprachreste*, 58 b 2.

⁷ Jäschke, *A Tibetan-English Dictionary*, p. 233.

⁸ *Tocharische Sprachreste*, 6 b 2.

Tibetan originals for at least certain of the Tocharian A texts. It is difficult, however, to see nothing but a slavish imitation of a Tibetan model in such a compound as *āriñc-pācar*, an intimate term, the more so as there seems to be no specific parallel, say **t'ugs-p'a*, for this Tocharian word. (The respectful form for Tibetan *p'a* 'father' is another word, *yab*). The striking resemblances in vocabulary between Tocharian and Tibetan involving the word 'heart' (particularly *āriñcṣi se* 'heart son': Tib. *t'ugs-kyi sras* or *t'ugs-sras* and *āriñcṣi ākāl* 'heart wish': Tib. *t'ugs-dgoṅs*) coupled with stylistic resemblance even where there is difference of detail (e.g., *āriñc-pācar* 'heart-father', presumably modeled on such cases of Tocharian *āriñc-* or *āriñcṣi* as do correspond to Tibetan examples of *t'ugs-* or *t'ugs-kyi*) indicate rather that we are dealing with a general influence on Tocharian word formation, which could act creatively within Tocharian itself and which is therefore probably based on actual folk usage.

2. TOCHARIAN 'PITY'

The Tocharian term for 'pity', corresponding to Sanskrit *karuṇā*, is *kāryā lotklune*, in which *kāryā* can hardly be other than the old stem of *kri*, *kāry-*, translated by SSS as 'will'.[9] The word *lotklune* is a verbal substantive, 'turning', belonging to the verb *lotk-* 'to turn (to), to turn about, to become'.[10] Hence Tocharian 'pity' may be rendered 'a turning of one's will (toward one)'. This is only a first approximation to the precise meaning, as we shall see in a moment. The words *kāryā lotklune*, though written separately, should be thought of as a compound noun, 'will-turning', *kāryā-* being the stem form of *kri* (nom. sing.) very much as *wsā-* 'gold' (e.g., in such compounds as *wsā-yok* 'gold-colored' and in adjectival *wsāṣi* 'golden') is the old stem form of *wäs* 'gold'.[11] This seems to be indicated by the ablative form *kāryāṣ* (in *puk āṇmaṣ kāryāṣ* 'from [one's] whole soul [and] will'), not **kāryāṣ* (which would be expected if *kāry-* were the true stem),[12] and by the adjectival derivative *kāryastum* 'intending', which is better analyzed as *kārya-tsum* with *-ā-* shortened to *-a-* (such secondary *ā : a* ablaut is common in Tocharian) than, more mechanically, as *kāry-atsum*.[13]

---

[9] SSS §388 b. The occurrences in *Tocharische Sprachreste* are: 426 b 2 (*kāryā lot(klu)ne*, apparently translating Sanskrit *k[aruṇa]yā*); 399 a 5 (*tām kₐleyam kāryā lotklune* 'pity for that woman'); 399 b 1 (*wākmats kāryā l..ku-*, broken off, apparently 'a special compassion', with *l(ot)ku(ne)* miswritten for *lotklune?*); and 465 a 2 (*kāryā lot [klu]-*, broken off).
[10] SSS, p. 467.
[11] SSS §363 c.
[12] SSS §208. *-āṣ* is here referred to as 'die vollere Endung', while *kāryā* above is interpreted as the *ā*-case of *kri* (§200 b) petrified into an adverb (§388 b).
[13] SSS §37.

The Tibetan terms for 'pity, compassion' are *t'ugs-rje* (respectful), *sñiṅ-rje*, *t'ugs-brtse-ba* (respectful), and *sñiṅ-brtse-ba*. The *t'ugs-* and *sñiṅ-* of these compounds are the respectful and normal forms for 'heart, mind' with which we are already familiar. *brtse-ba* is the verb 'to love' and its corresponding substantive 'love, affection, kindness'.[14] Hence *t'ugs-brtse-ba* and *sñiṅ-brtse-ba* merely intensify the meaning already given by the simplex by classifying it under the generic head of psychological experience ('heart'), a type of formative process which is very familiar in all Sinitic languages and which probably has reflexes in Tocharian.[15]

As for the *-rje-ba* (*-ba* is a substantivizing article making abstract nouns, adjectives, and 'infinitives', to adopt current terminology) of *t'ugs-rje-ba* and *sñin-rje-ba*, it is clearly not identifiable with the *rje* (*rje-ba*) that means 'lord, master', but with the verb *rje-ba* that means 'to barter, to give or take in exchange' or, in a more general sense, 'to change, to shift'.[16] Hence *t'ugs-rje-ba* and *sñiṅ-rje-ba* mean, in all probability, 'heart-shifting' (from oneself to another or, perhaps, from indifference to active pity). This fundamental meaning is clearly not far removed from the 'will-turning' of Tocharian and would be identical with it if we could be sure that the 'will' of SSS may be interpreted more properly as 'heart, mind'. 'Heart-turning' is better than 'will-turning' as a description of 'pity'. Perhaps the difference between *āriñc* and *kri* (stem *kāryā-*) is not so much that between 'heart' and 'will' as the similar but not identical, one between 'experiencing heart' and 'anticipatory heart'. At any rate it is precisely the parallelism in formation of Tocharian *kāryā lotklune* and Tibetan *t'ugs-rje-ba*, *sñin-rje-ba* that enables us to equate *kri, kāryā-* with *t'ugs* and *sñiṅ* and to give it its proper place in Indo-European. For it is, in all likelihood, a reflex of the Indo-European

---

[14] Jäschke, *A Tibetan-English Dictionary*, p. 442.

[15] E.g., under the category 'heart' comes 'thought': *āriñc pältsäk* 'heart thought'; under the category 'pain' come 'sorrow' and 'doubt': *klop śurām* 'pain sorrow', *klop sañce* 'pain doubt'; under the category 'love' come 'belovedness', 'homage', 'worship', 'friendliness' : *tuṅk kāpñune* 'love belovedness', *tuṅk poto* 'love homage', *tuṅk ynāñmune* 'love worship', *tuṅk ylārone* 'love friendliness'. Examples of this sort are not recognized by SSS as involving notions of classification but are interpreted, reasonably enough, as illustrating dvandva-like compounding, frequently with synonymous meaning of members, e.g., 'love (and) homage', cf. *śla tuṅk poto yo* 'together with [= one provided with] love and homage'. See SSS §358. They point out, however (§359), that such compounds are often treated as singulars, e.g., *klop sañce wikāluneyaṃ kälkām* 'pain doubt in-disappearance went (sing.)-for-her', which they translate as 'Schmerz (und) Zweifel verging [= vergingen] ihr' but which, on the analogy of such Tibetan forms as *sñiṅ-brtse-ba*, one is tempted to understand rather as '(that) pain (which is) doubt disappeared from her'. Naturally, there can be no sharp line of division between the 'classifying' compound and the synonym compound.

[16] Jäschke, *A Tibetan-English Dictionary*, p. 180.

stem (in -*yā*, f.) which gives us Greek καρδίᾱ, Ionic καρδίη 'heart'. The Tocharian word does not represent IE *k̑r̥d-yā́ (i.e., *k̑ᵢrd-yā́) but *k̑rᵢd-yā́ (reduced from the basic *k̑red- seen in Sanskrit *śrad-* and Latin *crēdō* < *kredᶻ-dō). The former would have given Tocharian A *kärci (-*d*- preserved as -*t*- after *r*, *l*, *n*; -*t*- palatalized to -*c*- before *e* or *y*; final -*yā* reduced to -*i*), while the latter develops to *kri*, *käryā*- (-*d*- disappears after IE vowels, cf. Toch. *pe* 'foot', dual *pe-ṃ*; -ᵢ*y*- > -*y*-, -*i*).[17] In other words, the present meanings of Tocharian *kri* (*käryā*-) are probably specialized from an archaic meaning 'heart', now rendered *āriñc*, a word of far from obvious etymology. It is likely that at the time of the influence exerted by Tibetan on Tocharian in the creation of the term *käryā lotklune* for 'pity', the stem (perhaps also word) *käryā*(-) still had its primary meaning of 'heart'. If this is true, that influence must have taken place long before the period of the writing down of our Tocharian A texts.

The syntactic use of Tocharian *käryā lotklune* is parallel to that of the Tibetan words to which it corresponds. An example cited in note 9, 'pity for that woman', has 'woman' (*kᵤli*, obl. *kᵤle*) in the locative (*kᵤley-aṃ*). With this are to be compared analogous Tibetan examples with locative (or 'dative') postposition -*la* 'in, at, to', e.g., *mi-la sñiṅ-rje sgompa* 'to pity a person', lit., 'person-to-heart-shift to-produce'.[18]

3. TOCHARIAN 'ELEPHANT'

The Tocharian A word for 'elephant', *oṅkaläm*, occurs in that form in the nominative singular, further in the genitive as *oṅkälme*. It also occurs in the plural: nom. *oṅkälmāñ*, oblique *oṅkälmās*, and secondary cases (gen., instrum., and *ā*-case) based on the oblique plural.[19] The -*a*- of the nominative, in spite of the fact that it is reduced to -*ä*- in the other cases, looks as though it might be the old thematic IE -*o*- of compounds still found in such cases as *atr-a-tampe* 'provided with hero-might' (: *aträ* 'hero') and *kāsw-a-pälskāñ* 'thoughts of good' (: *kāsu* 'good').[20] If we analyze as *oṅk-a-läm*, *oṅk-ä-lm*-, it becomes a transparent possibility that this strange word is compounded of *oṅk* 'man' and *läm*- 'to sit' (suppletive to *ṣäm*-; pret. *lyäm*, *lym-ā*, *lam-a*-, subj. *lam-a*-, verbal substantive *lm-ā-lune* and in derived causative forms[21]), whence *lam-e* 'position' < 'sitting-place'. *oṅk-a-läm* can be understood either as a simple ba-

---

[17] The treatment of IE *d* in Tocharian is a problem which I hope to consider at another time.
[18] Jäschke, *A Tibetan-English Dictionary*, p. 198.
[19] SSS §237.
[20] SSS §363a.
[21] SSS, pp. 475–6.

huvrīhi, 'having, holding a man's sitting-place' (with -*läm* referable to
the noun *lame*), or, perhaps more probably (pl. stem -*lmā*-: vb. stem
lmā-), as a more involved type of bahuvrīhi based on an underlying 'the
man sits', hence 'having a man sitting (on him)' (with -*läm* directly
referable to the verb stem).[22] The Tocharian material is too fragmentary
to allow of certainty in the formal analysis. The probability that *oṅkaläm*
is a compound is perhaps enhanced by the fact that its genitive is in -*e*;
cf. gen. *ptā-ñkt-e* 'Buddha-god', but *ñäkt-rs* 'god' (gen.).[23]

I can find no Sanskrit or Tibetan model for the Tocharian word.
Nevertheless, in an indirect way, Tibetan may be presumed to have influenced Tocharian—culturally rather than linguistically, in the strict
sense—in its description of an elephant as an animal used for riding. The
Tibetan word for 'elephant' is *glaṅ*, which, according to Jäschke,[24] means
also 'ox, bullock'. That the elephant is conceived of in Tibetan as functionally equivalent to a bullock is indicated by the words *glaṅ-po-č'e*,
glaṅ-č'en, literally 'big *glaṅ*', meaning 'elephant'. But an elephant is not
exactly a 'big ox', unless by 'ox' is meant 'beast of burden' or 'riding
animal'. That *glaṅ* properly meant this at one time is clinched by the
Tocharian A *klaṅk*, B *kleṅke* 'Reittier', obviously related by borrowing
to *glaṅ*. Tocharian allows of no final or intervocalic *ṅ* [ŋ], for this consonant, as in most Indo-European languages, is not a true phoneme but
merely an assimilated form of *n*. Hence Tibetan *glaṅ*, if Tibetan is the
source of the borrowing and not the borrower, was heard as *glaṅg
[or was this a more archaic Tibetan form at the time of the Tocharian
borrowing?], whence necessarily *klaṅka for Old Tocharian. IE -*os*
appears as Old Toch. -*a*, whence A zero, *B* -*e*; IE *o* > *a* > B *e* is regular.
SSS offer no proof that *klaṅk* is referable to verb stems *klāṅk*- and
kläṅk- (SSS 436), whose meanings they are unable to give.[24a] Should it
appear that Tocharian *klaṅk* is a native word derived, say, from a verb
'to ride', we would still probably have to assume a historical relation
between the Tocharian and Tibetan words. Inasmuch as Tibetan
possesses *kl*- as well as *gl*-, a Tibetan borrowing would prove the existence

---

[22] Somewhat comparable would seem to be such untypical Sanskrit examples as
putra-hata- 'whose son is killed', *a-danta-jāta*- 'whose teeth have not come to be'
(Wackernagel, *Altindische Grammatik* 2 .1.302), except that in these the second element is a verbal derivative (participle) instead of the underlying verb stem.

[23] SSS §123.

[24] Jäschke, *A Tibetan-English Dictionary*, p. 80.

[24a] *klāṅklye* (TS 264 a 2) is a nom. m. pl. of the verbal adjective *klāṅkäl, from a
verb *klāṅk*-. Inasmuch as the form is preceded by *yᵤkañ oṇkälmāñ w*. [read *wu* ?]
'horses (and) elephants two [?]', it seems reasonable to connect the word with *klaṅk*.
The passage may therefore read: 'Horses (and) elephants, two (sorts) to be used for
riding'. In that case *klaṅk*- would either be a denominative verb based on *klaṅk* or,
far less likely, *klaṅk* a noun derivative (with IE *o*-vocalism) based on the verb.

in Tocharian at one time of both *g* and *k*. This would not be suprising in view of the fact that IE *d* and *t* have different reflexes in Tocharian.

Incidentally, Tocharian *klaṅk* proves, if proof were still needed, that such Tibetan initial consonant clusters as *gl-*, *sr-*, and so on, must be taken seriously in spite of the testimony of most of the modern dialects. The classical Tibetan *gl-* is simplified to *l-* in Lahul, Spiti, Tsang-Ü, while in Khams and Balti it appears spirantized to *γl-*.[25] It will appear in the sequel that Tocharian is not without value for the earlier history of Tibetan.

4. Tocharian Absolutives

One of the most characteristic features of Tocharian syntax is the free use of what SSS call 'absolutives', better known as 'gerunds' or 'gerundials'. These are secondary case forms, chiefly ablatives (A, B), instrumentals (B) and *ā*-cases (A) of substantivized preterit participles in *-r*, the participles themselves (nom. m. sing.) ending in A in *-u* or *-o* (contracted from stem in *-ā-* + participial *-u*). In A the ablatives in *-äṣ* are far more common than the *ā*-case forms; in B the corresponding forms are ablatives in *-mem* and instrumentals in *-sa*. The actual forms of the absolutives are, therefore; A *-u-r-äṣ* (*-o-r-äṣ*), *-u-r-ā* (*-o-r-ā*), B *-o-r* (*-a-r*, *-e-r*)-*mem*, *-o-r-sa*. A literal etymological rendering of such an A form as *wawuräṣ* would be 'from having-given [*or* having-been-given]-ness', an ablative in *-äṣ* of an abstract noun in *-r* based on the preterit participle *wawu* of the reduplicated stem *waw-* corresponding to the indicative preterit stem *wäs-*, *ws-* 'to give', in suppletion to the verb stem *e-*, *āy-*, present *e-s-*.[26]

SSS point out, perhaps correctly, the etymological identity of the *-r-* of these absolutives with the well-known IE neuter *-r* (originally alternating with *-n-*), used to form verbal abstracts and of which a few survivals seem to remain in Tocharian, e.g., A (and B) *ok-a-r* 'growth, plant' (: *ok-* 'to grow'), A *kury-a-r*, B *kary-o-r* 'trade' (: B *käry-* 'to buy'), A *kärs-o-r* 'knowledge' (: *kärs-* 'to know'), *tärk-o-r* 'leave' (: *tärk-* 'to permit').[27] Such examples as A *kärsor* (: pret. part. *kärs-o*) and *tärkor* (: pret. part. *tärk-o*) and B *āyor* 'gift' (: pret. part. *āyo*) indicate that while the old IE stock of nouns in *-r* (such as Gk. πῖαρ 'fat', Lat. *iter*) had originally no connection whatever with the IE perfect participle (*-wṓns*, *-us-*) which may lie back of the Tocharian forms in *-u* and *-o*, there was in Old Tocharian (i.e., that form of speech from which A and B

[25] Jäschke, *A Tibetan-English Dictionary*, p. xviii, sub *glog*.
[26] SSS, p. 424. For absolutives see SSS §421 d.
[27] SSS §8.

diverged) a well-established tendency for an *r*-abstract to attach itself to this form, presumably to an old oblique neuter singular in *-u*, *-o* (cf. nom. m. sing. *-u*, *-o*, obl. *-unt*, *-ont*, nom. f. sing. *-us*, *-os*, obl. *-usām*, *-osāṃ*; SSS §257). It may be that the old distribution of oblique neuter forms of this type of verbal abstracts was: absolute *-u* (*-o*), with lost *-r*, but *-ur-* (*-or-*), with retained *-r*, before secondary case endings (e.g., *-uräṣ*, *-urā*). An old *-u*, *-o*: *-ur-*, *-or-* paradigm could level out to *-u*, *-o*: *-u(w)-*, *-o(w)-* or to *-ur*, *-or*: *-ur-*, *-or-*. The latter type of leveling seems to be represented by such words as *kärsor* and *tärkor*. SSS give two interesting examples in A of verbal nouns in *-u*, with inflected forms in *-ur-*: *lyalypu* 'what has been left over = *karman*' (substantivized pret. part. of causative of *lip-* 'to remain over'[28]), abl. *lyalypur-äṣ*; and *watku* 'command' (originally unreduplicated substantivized pret. part. of *wätk-* 'to command', cf. regular part. *wotku* < **wawtk-u* and its corresponding absolutive *wotkuräṣ*[29]), *ā*-case *watkur-ā*. These forms seem to be archaic and to represent an earlier stratum than *kärsor* and *tärkor*. It is interesting to note that B has an analogical form in *-r* to correspond to A *watku*, namely *yaitkor* (< **wewtka-u*[*-r*][30]).[31]

It seems, then, that we have in Tocharian three strata of verbal abstracts in *-r*: (1) a type perhaps directly derived from IE neuters in *-r*; (2) a type of *r*-nouns made over from old perfect participles (e.g., A *watku, watkur-*, B *yaitko-r*, A *kärso-r*); (3) absolutives, in various secondary case forms, based on type 2. Type 3 came to be attached mechanically to every verbal paradigm and so we have such discrepancies as *watku(r-)* : *wotku-r-äṣ*. The surprisingly small number, if any, of old *r*-nouns coupled with the creativeness of the *r*-forms in absolutives; the attachment of these formations to the perfect participle; the levelling out of an old *-u* : *-ur-* paradigm to a paradigm in *-ur* : *-ur-*, itself a formation that seems no longer productive in our recorded Tocharian; and the enormous spread of the absolutives in *-u-r-äṣ* and related forms conspire to indicate that a long period of time must have elapsed before the emergence of the Tocharian absolutives as we know them in the texts.

From the strictly Indo-European standpoint it is tempting to attach the Tocharian verbal abstracts in **-u-r*, *-o-r* and in *-u* : *-ur-* to IE verbal nouns in *-wr̥* (e.g., Hittite forms in *-war* : supines in *-wan*); in that case

---

[28] SSS §68 and p. 466.
[29] SSS §68 and p. 469.
[30] Original *-e-* of reduplicating syllables becomes palatalizing *-a-* in A and B. Palatalized *w*, say *wʸ* or *ẅ*, reverts to *w* in A but becomes *y* in B; another example is A *want* 'wind' : B *yente*.
[31] SSS §8.

such a B form as *yaitkor* might be supposed to stem directly from an IE type: pre-Toch. **wéwtk-wr̥*. We cannot prove this, however, and in any event it has to be shown why this old IE pattern, if it be such in Tocharian, was worked into the preterit system of the verb paradigm. The most plausible standpoint would be to assume that when the treatment of final syllables in Tocharian had reached the point at which IE **-wóns* had worn down to Toch. *-u*, the old perfect participle tended to become confused with the old *r*-neuter in *-u* (: *-ur-*) derived from IE **-wr̥*. We would still have to explain why such a fusion of forms was semantically possible.

I shall try to show that the Tocharian 'preteritizing' of IE verbal abstracts in **-wr̥*[32] and the form and syntax of Tocharian absolutives are all due to Tibetan influence. It will be well to give a few examples of these absolutives from the Tocharian texts:

A: *cesmäk puk śtwar śälkās pokeyo wawuräṣ poñcäs kosām tāpam*[33] *śkaṃ lo* 'eben-jene alle vier, Schläge (?) mit-der-Tatze ausgeteilthabend sämtlich ershlug-er-sie frass-sie und auf'[34]

wrasañ cam peke pälkoräṣ yneś pälskaṃ yāmuṣ '(die-) Menschen, dies Gemälde nachdem-(sie-)gesehen, für-Wirklichkeit im-Geiste die-(es-)-gehalten-haben [nom. m. pl. of part.]'[35]

käntantuyo wältsantuyo tmānantuyo korisyo waṣtäṣ lanturäṣ . . . kälpnānträ 'zu-Hunderten, Tausenden, Zehntausenden, Koṭi's aus-dem-Hause nachdem-(sie-)gegangen-waren . . . erlangen-sie'[36]

B: *mant eṅkor-meṃ weñāmeś* 'so (ihn-)ergriffen-habend, sprach-er-zu-ihnen'[37]

keklyauṣor-meṃ mrauskāte 'ayant-entendu il-prend-en-dégout-le-monde'[38]

In all these cases the absolutive (*wawur-äṣ* 'having given', *pälko-räṣ* 'having seen', *lantu-räṣ* 'having gone', B *eṅkor-meṃ* 'having got hold of',

---

[32] Alternatively, the direct attachment of verbal abstracts in *-r* to the reflex of the IE perfect participle (or other prototype of Toch. *-u*, *-o*).

[33] Corrected by SSS from *tāpap*.

[34] See E. Sieg, 'Die Geschichte von den Löwenmachern in tocharischer Version' in *Aufsätze zur Kultur- und Sprachgeschichte vornehmlich des Orients Ernst Kuhn gewidmet* (1916), pp. 149, 151. I have very slightly rearranged Sieg's translations so as to let the German version reflect the Tocharian original as literally as possible.

[35] *Tocharische Sprachreste*, 9 a 2; SSS, p. 271.

[36] *Tocharische Sprachreste*, 254 b 7; SSS, p. 198, Better, presumably, 'gegangen sind'.

[37] E. Sieg und W. Siegling, "Die Speisung des Bodhisattva vor der Erleuchtung," *Asia Major*, 2 (1935): 280, 283.

[38] S. Lévi, *Fragments de Textes Koutchéens* (1933), pp. 73–74. Better, presumably, 'il prit en dégout'; cf. A *mroskat* (pret. med., 3d pers. sing., of *mrosk-* '[der Welt] überdrüssig werden'), SSS, p. 457.

keklyauşor-meṃ 'having heard') indicates the priority of an event to the event expressed by the main verb or equivalent therefore, such as a participle (*kosām* 'he caused them to die', *yāmuş* '[they] who have made', *kälpnānträ* 'they attain', B *weñāmeś* 'he spoke to them', *mrauskāte* 'he became disgusted with the world'). The subjects of the two verb forms are the same but there is no true expression of person in the absolutive. It is a purely impersonal or generalized reference to an event which is set in prior relation to the main event by the use of an ablative case suffix.

If, now, we turn to Tibetan, we find that syntactically parallel forms, i.e., case-forms, among others ablatives, of the generalized or non-personal verb,[39] often in its perfect form, are found, and with identical function. Thus, to the five Tocharian absolutives illustrated above correspond the following Tibetan forms: *bskur-nas* 'after giving, having given' (*bskur*, perf. of *skur-ba* 'to give'; *-nas*, postposition with ablative force, 'from'), *mt'oṅ-nas* 'after seeing, having seen' (*mt'oṅ-ba* 'to see' has no separate perfect), *soṅ-nas* 'after going, having gone' (*soṅ*, perf. of ₒ*gro-ba* 'to go'), (*b)zuṅ-nas* 'after taking hold, having taken hold' ((*b)zuṅ*, perf. of ₒ*dzin-pa* 'to take hold'), *t'os-nas* 'after hearing, having heard' (*t'os-pa* 'to hear' has no separate perfect).

I shall give a few examples from Jäschke of Tibetan gerundial constructions in *-nas* 'from':

dei ts'ig-gis bskul-nas 'that-of word-by induced [perf. of *skul-ba* "to exhort, admonish"]-from' = 'induced by his words'[40]

rnam-śes las daṅ nyoṅ-moṅs-kyis bskul-nas 'part-know [= "vijñāna, soul"; *rnam-śes-pa* "to know fully"] work together-with misery-by induced-from' = 'the (departed) soul urged on, influenced, driven, by its former works and sins'[41]

lhuṅ-zed nam-mk'a-la bskyur-nas 'alms-bowl sky-to thrown [perf. of *skyur-ba* "to throw, cast", fut. *bskyur*]-from' = 'having thrown his mendicant's bowl up into the air'[42]

me-tog gtor-nas žus-pa 'flower strewn [perf. of *gtor-ba* "to strew, scatter"]-from spoken [perf. of *žu-ba* "to speak to a person of higher rank"]-the' = 'after having strewn flowers, they said humbly'[43]

---

[39] Properly speaking, the Tibetan verb has no inherent implication of person. All transitives, moreover, are best understood as inherently passive. It has never been made clear, so far as I can see, when the Tibetan verb is tenseless and when it has a set of tense-mode forms (present, perfect, future, imperative); thus, *mgu-ba* 'to rejoice' and *bgrod-pa* 'to walk' are used in all tenses and modes, whereas *slod-pa* 'to sit' has a specific perfect-future form *bsdad* and ₒ*god-pa* 'to design' ('present' or infinitive) has a perfect (*bgod*), a future (*dgod*), and an imperative (*k'od*).

[40] Jäschke, *A Tibetan-English Dictionary*, p. 23.

[41] *Ibid.*

[42] *Op. cit.*, p. 27.

[43] Jäschke, *Tibetan Grammar*, p. 157.

nam laṅs-nas soṅ 'night arisen [perf. of *laṅ-ba* "to rise", imperative *loṅ, loṅs*]-from went [perf. of ₒ*gro-ba* "to go", imperative *soṅ*]' = 'when the night had risen [= at daybreak] he went'[44]
laṅ-nas soṅ 'arise-from go' = 'after you will have risen, go!'[45]
de mt'oṅ-nas skad p'yuṅ-ste ṅus-so 'that seen-from noise caused-to-come-forth [perf. of ₒ*byin-pa*, fut. *dbyuṅ*, imperative *p'yuṅ*; caus. of *byuṅ-ba* "to come out"]-(gerund) wept-(period)' = 'when I saw that, raising clamor, I wept'[46]

The resemblance of the syntax of these sentences to that of the Tocharian examples is obvious. In both Tocharian and Tibetan the gerund precedes; has an implied, never expressed, subject (or agent) which is generally identical with the subject (or agent) of the main verb; is attached to the perfect participle of the verb (the Tibetan perfect is best interpreted as a participle and, when transitive, as a passive participle); and is a case form, often ablative, of the verbal noun. There can be little doubt that such Tibetan (or linguistically related) models as these are responsible for the essentially un-Indo-European absolutives of Tocharian. The Tibetan forms in *-nas* are only one type of gerund, of which Francke lists no less than eleven, most of them case forms[47]: *-de, -te, -ste* 'after, and'; *-čiṅ, -šiṅ, -žin* 'when, and'; *-kyin, -gin, -gyin, -'in, -yin* [gen. + *-n*] 'when, and'; *- kyi, -gi, -gyi, -'i, -yi* [gen.] 'but, though'; *-kyis, -gis, -gyis, -'is, -yis* [instrumental] 'because, as; but, though'; *-pa-s, -ba-s* [instr. of infinitive] 'because'; *-la* [dat.]; *-na* [loc.] 'when, if; as, because'; *-nas* [abl.] 'after'; *-las* [abl.] 'while' (added to inf.); *-pa-r* [terminal of inf.] 'that, and'. Until we know more about Tocharian syntax than we do, we shall not be able to state definitely what are the Tibetan prototypes of the A absolutives in *-ā* and the B absolutives in *-or-sa*. Formally, A forms in *-ur-ā, -or-ā* probably correspond to Tibetan gerunds in *-pa-r* (*-tu, -du, -ru, -r*: terminal or allative case suffix; Toch. *-ā* may be an old terminal [< IE **ad* 'to'?] which combines instrumental and modal uses), B forms in *-or-sa* (with instrumental *-sa*) to Tibetan instrumental gerunds in *-kyis* and *-pa-s* (note parallelism of Tib. *-pa-s*, nominalizing or 'infinitive' suffix + instrumental case suffix, to Toch. B *-or-sa*, verbal noun suffix of pret. + instrumental case suffix). A forms in *-ur-äṣ, -or-äṣ* and B forms in *-or-meṃ*, as we have seen, correspond closely, in form and function, to Tibetan gerunds in *-nas*.

In further numbers even more far-reaching Tibetan influences will be traced. These influences are by no means confined to general syntactic

---

[44] *Op. cit.*, p. 57.
[45] *Ibid.*
[46] *Ibid.*
[47] *Op. cit.*, pp. 155–158; see also, pp. 54–64.

procedures, as we shall see, but embrace a large number of lexical borrowings, some of them of grammatical importance, and morphological transfers. The phonology of Tocharian, a notoriously difficult field, receives abundant light from the treatment of Tibetan loan-words, and we shall see in the end that it is precisely the unanalyzed Tibetan element in Tocharian which has prevented us from arriving at a true notion of the placement of Tocharian in the Indo-European group of languages. We shall also find that it is quite possible to infer the dialectic zone within the vast Tibetan-speaking area to which the Tibetan influence on Tocharian is to be credited.

HEBREW "HELMET," A LOANWORD, AND ITS BEARING ON INDO-EUROPEAN PHONOLOGY*

AMONG THE Biblical Hebrew words which have long been suspected of being loanwords rather than derivable from Semitic roots is the word for "helmet," *kōḇáʿ*, construct state *kōḇaʿ*, plur. *kōḇāʿîm*; a parallel form is *qōḇáʿ*, construct state *qōḇaʿ*. The occurrences are:

1 Sam. 17 : 5 : *wᵉkōḇaʿ nᵉḥōšeṭ ʿal-rōšó* "and he [Goliath, the Philistine] had a helmet of copper upon his head"

1 Sam. 17 : 38 : *wᵉnāṭán qōḇaʿ nᵉḥōšeṭ ʿal-rōšó* "and he [Saul] put a helmet of copper upon his head" [var. lect. *kōḇaʿ*]

Is. 59 : 17 : *wᵉkōḇaʿ yᵉšúʿá bᵉrōšó* "and (he put on) a helmet of salvation upon his head"

Jer. 46 : 4 : *wᵉhiṯyaṣṣᵉḇú bᵉkōḇāʿîm* "and stand forth with (your) helmets"

Ezek. 23 : 24 : *ṣinná umāgén wᵉqōḇáʿ yāsîmū ʿāláyik sāḇîḇ* "buckler and shield and helmet shall they set up against thee round about"

Ezek. 27 : 10 : *māgén wᵉkōḇáʿ tillū-ḇák* "shield and helmet they hung up in thee"

Ezek. 38 : 5 : *kullám māgén wᵉkōḇáʿ* "all of them [Persia, Ethiopia, and Libya] with shield and helmet"

2 Chron. 26 : 14 : *wayyákεn lāhém ʿuzziyyáhū lᵉkol-haṣṣāḇá màginnîm urmāḥîm wᵉkōḇāʿîm wᵉširyōnóṭ uqšōṭóṭ* "and Uzziah prepared for them, for all the host, shields and spears and helmets and coats of mail and bows"

The word *kōḇáʿ* lingers on in post-biblical Hebrew with the meanings of "helmet" and "turban," also "thyroid cartilage, Adam's apple" (obviously a metaphorical transfer). It was doubtless in popular use in the Aramaic dialects, as we may judge from the occurrences of *kōḇᵉʿá* and *qōḇᵉʿá* in the Jewish Aramaic Targums, again in the two senses of "helmet" and "turban," more particularly "priest's turban," and from the Syriac *qūḇᵉʿá* (or *qubbᵉʿá?*[1]) "cowl, cape, hood" and, again in a transferred sense, "capital of a column." (The Syriac *kūḇāʿá* "helmet," on the other hand, is perhaps merely a bookish copy of the Biblical Hebrew *kōḇáʿ*.) Jewish Aramaic *kōḇᵉʿá*, *qōḇᵉʿá* and Syriac *qūḇᵉʿá* (*qubbᵉʿá*) do not agree on the basis of a common Semitic form and meaning (say *kaubaʿ-u* or *qaubaʿu* "helmet") but on the basis of a secondary borrowing of a West Aramaic *qōḇáʿ*, with suffixed article *qōḇᵉʿá*, "turban" (m.; cf. plural

---

* *Journal of the American Oriental Society*, 57 (1937): 73–77.
[1] According to Nöldeke. See Ges.-Buhl, sub *qōḇáʿ*.

qōḇeʿín, with article *qōḇeʿayyā́*) as *qūḇeʿā́* (*qubbeʿā́*). The older meaning of "helmet" was no longer strictly applicable in folk Aramaic, one may guess, and the Palestinian Aramaic -*ō*- was replaced in the borrowing Syriac by its nearest phoneme -*ū*- (with variant -*u*- followed by doubled consonant). Had the Syriac form been a true development of the *qauba'u which lies back of Hebrew *qōḇáʿ*, we should have expected a Syriac **qauḇeʿā́* (cf. Syriac *maut-ā́* "death": Jewish Aramaic *mōt-ā́*: Hebrew *mōt* < Sem. *maut-u). It is on the basis of a specifically Syriac *qūḇeʿā́* > *qubbeʿā́* that the Arabic culture loanwords *qubʿ-uⁿ*, f. *qubbaʿ-at-uⁿ*, "hood" are most easily understood; Ethiopic *qōḇĕʿ* too, with its -*ĕ*- (or zero) instead of original Sem. -*a*- is not directly traceable to *qauba'u but to some Aramaic prototype. The word seems to have no Accadian cognate. The actual Semitic occurrences are, therefore, limited, in effect, to Hebrew and Western Aramaic, with subsequent borrowings in Eastern Aramaic (Syriac), Arabic, and Ethiopic, and do not suggest a common Semitic word, but a specifically Hebrew word. This lingered on, mostly with the transferred meaning of "turban" rather than "helmet," in the Palestinian Aramaic dialects which superseded Hebrew and had borrowed the word from it. And, in turn, a lone Hebrew word for an object of such distinctive cultural connotations as "helmet" is likely to be of foreign origin.

The most likely guess would be that the word was borrowed from a language possessing a voiceless *k* that was unaspirated and was not strictly identifiable with either the normal Semitic *k* (ordinarily aspirated when non-emphatic : *k'*) or its emphatic correspondent (ordinarily velar and unaspirated when emphatic : *k̲*= *q*). Such a *k* would have to belong to a non-Semitic language; e.g., the Greek *κ* or, presumably, the Hittite fortis *k* (*k*- : -*kk*-) would be a case in point. Obviously, an original **kauba'*-, with unaspirated *k*, agrees with Semitic *k* (= *k'*) in position but with Semitic *q* in its lack of aspiration. It is well known that at a much later period a host of Greek words with *κ* were borrowed by Jewish Aramaic and Syriac with change of *κ* to *q*. The Hebrew variants *kōḇáʿ* and *qōḇáʿ* are suggestive internal evidence for the non-Semitic origin of the word and it was precisely this alternation that led Barth[2] to speak of the word as of doubtful origin. The formative type to which it would have to be referred as a native Semitic word (*qautal*) is very sparsely represented in Hebrew and the radical from which it might be derived (*kbʿ* or *qbʿ*) either non-existent in Hebrew or clearly irrelevant (*qāḇáʿ* "to rob one of something"). A variant *kbʿ* of the common radical *gbʿ* "hill" is most unlikely.

[2] Barth, *Die Nominalbildung in den semitischen Sprachen* § 38a2, n. 2.

Philistine, a non-Semitic language contiguous to Hebrew on the west but originally spoken in Asia Minor, is suggested by the first of our biblical citations as a possible source.[3] If this is correct, it would indicate the presence in Philistine of a voiced laryngeal or, more likely, velar spirant: γ (= Arabic gain) rather than ' (Arabic 'ain). The prototype of the Hebrew word would be something like *$kauba\gamma$-. The cultural evidence points to the helmet, in various forms, as originally more properly at home in Asia Minor than in Palestine.[4] We are, therefore, not unprepared for Hittite *$kupa\d{h}is$ (acc. $k\u{u}pa\d{h}in$, pl. $k\u{u}pa\d{h}ius$) "hat, cap?"[5] The -$\bar{u}$- or -u- of Hittite $k\bar{u}pa\d{h}i$- may go back to an IE au (cf. Hit. $\d{h}u\d{h}\d{h}as$ "grandfather," Latin $avus$ < IE *$xauxos$),[6] while the single -p- points to a lenis stop,[7] which would be heard by the Semitic ear as -b-. The word may have come to Hebrew directly from Philistine or it may have gradually worked its way south from some dialect (with -au- for Hit. -$\u{a}$-) of the Hittite-Luwian group through Syria, in which case the Western Aramaic forms quoted above represent a culture borrowing from the north rather than from Hebrew.

The most interesting phonologic point raised by the comparison of Hittite $k\u{u}pa\d{h}i$- with pre-Hebrew *$kauba$'- (*$kauba\gamma$-) is the correspondence of Hittite -$\d{h}$-, written single, with Hebrew -'-. As is well known, Hebrew and Aramaic ' represents a pool of Semitic ' (voiced laryngeal spirant) and γ (voiced velar spirant), kept apart in Arabic as ' and $\dot{g}$ respectively. The primary value of Hittite $\d{h}$ was probably that of a voiceless velar spirant (x), as in Accadian, and this value would normally be rendered in a Hebrew loanword as $\d{h}$, e.g. $\d{h}itt\hat{i}$ "Hittite": Hit. $\d{h}atti$. I have pointed out elsewhere, however, that in certain cases Hittite $\d{h}$ must, in all probability, be interpreted as the corresponding voiced (or lenis) velar spirant γ [this rather than '], e.g. $\d{h}apatis$ "vassal" [read $\gamma a\text{B}a\text{D}$ is[8]]: Canaanite *'$abad\bar{\imath}ma$ "slaves" (Hit. γ as nearest native phoneme to represent Semitic ');[9] $Tut\d{h}aliyas$: Hebrew $Tid\underline{}\hat{a}l$[10] (Hit. γ borrowed as γ > Can. ').

In the example before us a Hittite $\d{h}$ is found in intervocalic position. On general principles we should expect such a -$\d{h}$- to have the value of a

[3] See, e.g., A. S. Macalister, *The Philistines*, p. 80.
[4] See, e.g., Kurt Galling, *Biblisches Reallexikon*, sub "Helm"; M. Lidzbarski, *Ephemeris für semitische Epigraphik* II: 135 (Shardana warriors); P. Thomsen in Ebert, *Reallexikon der Vorgeschichte* V: 207.
[5] E. H. Sturtevant, *A Hittite Glossary*, 2nd ed., p. 83.
[6] E. H. Sturtevant, *A Comparative Grammar of the Hittite Language*, p. 101.
[7] *Ibid.*, pp. 73–83.
[8] B, D, G are here used for lenis voiceless stops.
[9] See *Language*, 10 (1934): 274–279.
[10] *Ibid.*, pp. 276–277.

voiced spirant, -γ-, in contrast to the voiceless value of -ḫḫ- (e.g. *paḫḫur* "fire" = *paxur*), for, as Sturtevant has shown, doubled stops in intervocalic position are voiceless (probably voiceless fortis), while single stops are voiced (more probably voiceless lenis). In other words, -*p*- (written -*pp*-) : -ʙ- (written -*p*-) as -*x*- or -*xx*- (written -ḫḫ-) : -γ- or lenis -*x*- (written -ḫ-). Very likely -*zz*-: the less common -*z*- represents a similar contrast between -*c*- (fortis voiceless affricate -*ts*-) and -*z*- (lenis voiceless affricate -ᴅ*z*-). The pair -*ss*-: -*s*- too may mean something more than a purely orthographic variation. The problem of the meaning of Hittite single and doubled consonants would seem to deserve further study. If we are right in reading Hit. *kŭpaḫi*- as *kŭʙaγi*- < **kauʙaγi-*, we are not far from discovering an actual example of the posited IE γ (Kuryłowicz's ə̑³) in a recorded Indo-European word of an Indo-European language, for it would be difficult to disconnect pre-Hittite **kauʙaγ-i*- (with derivative -*i*- : -*yo*- suffix?[11] -ʙ- softened from IE -*p*- after *w*?[12]) from the large group of IE words represented by Germ. **χauƀu-d-a*- "head" and Latin *capu-t* (dissimilated from **kaupu-?*). The intricate phonological problems that are further suggested by this (e.g., Latin *cappa* < **kapγ-ā* < **kaupγ*- because of analogy of *caput?*) are not our present concern.

Sturtevant's interpretation of Hittite -*eḫ*- before vowels (*seḫur* "urine"; *meḫur* "time"; *weḫ*- "to turn") as an orthographic method of representing an IE prevocalic **-e'-*[13] is not consistent with our theory, for it is difficult to believe that Hit. single -ḫ- between vowels could mean both -γ- and -'-. In another connection some evidence, of a different type from that here presented, will be given that makes it possible to interpret Hit. -*eḫ*- not as -*e'*- but as -*eγ*-. In other words, it will be suggested that while IE **-ax*- regularly remains in Hittite as -*aḫḫ*-, IE **-eγ*- (at least before vowels) similarly remains as -*eḫ*-; -*e*- of theoretical IE **-eγ*- does not undergo a change to pre-Hittite **-ǫγ*-[14] (in most IE dialects pre-consonantal **-eγ*- becomes **-ǫγ*- > heavy-base **-ō-*).

---

[11] Cf. Hittite *kesris* "glove" : *kessar* "hand."

[12] Cf. *Journal of the American Oriental Society*, 56 (1936): 281.

[13] *Language*: 12 (1936): 186–187.

[14] A number of other cases have been noted of Hittite -ḫ- : Canaanite -'-. These will be discussed at another time.

REVIEW OF JAMES A. MONTGOMERY AND ZELLIG S. HARRIS, "THE RAS SHAMRA MYTHOLOGICAL TEXTS"*

THIS IMPORTANT work contains the text of five of the ritualistic poems in cuneiform script recently discovered by French archaeologists at Ras Shamra, anciently Ugarit, on the coast of northern Syria. Two further poems are treated by Montgomery in the Journal of the American Oriental Society, 56.226-31, 440-5. The originals of these and other Ras Shamra texts, edited chiefly by C. Virolleaud, have appeared in 'Syria' since 1929 and a large literature of phonetic, grammatical, and lexical interpretation and of historical comment is already before us. It is destined to grow rapidly in volume and importance, for these West Semitic texts of the 14th century B.C. are of fundamental value both to the Semitic linguist and to the culture historian of the Near East. Besides the transliterated texts of Montgomery and Harris we now have a number of other editions, among which may be mentioned the Hebrew one of H. L. Ginsberg (Jerusalem, 1936) and the German one of H. Bauer (1937). Perhaps the best introduction to the fascinating story of the decipherment of the Ras Shamra tablets, in which both French and German scholars shared, is H. Bauer's little work, Das Alphabet von Ras Schamra (1932).

The present work contains, in addition to the first five mythological texts to appear, a valuable section on the location and discovery of the Ras Shamra tablets, preliminary contributions to the phonology and morphology of the Semitic dialect in which they are composed, material on the form and meaning of the texts as religious poems, a useful bibliography, and, most important of all, a glossary, with references, to all the Ras Shamra texts then known to the writers. Connected English translations have wisely been avoided, for the difficulties of interpretation are still numerous and there is great danger of a premature certainty induced by too great reliance on Hebrew parallels.

The transliteration in this and in Ginsberg's edition is into the familiar square Hebrew character. This is made possible by the fact that the Ras Shamra 'cuneiform' is not at all the standard ideographic and syllabic system of Accadian but a strictly alphabetic system of some thirty characters. Diacritical marks over the Hebrew characters serve to differentiate sounds peculiar to the Ras Shamra dialect; the non-committal X represents a sound whose phonetic placement is not clear

* *Language*, 13 (1937): 326–331.

(Ginsberg uses the Hebrew 'ayin with an added macron for this character). There is no doubt that this method of transliteration is a convenient one for the Semitist, particularly for the Semitist who approaches these materials with Hebrew as his preferred point of reference. The reviewer confesses to some dissatisfaction with the method, for he believes it is not as innocent as it seems to be. It unavoidably suggests phonetic identities or relationships which a closer study of the material may show to be illusory. It is to be hoped that scholarly usage will eventually agree on an adequate transliteration into Latin characters, such as is used in Bauer's edition. There is no reason why Ugaritic (Ras Shamra) should come to us with a Hebrew mask. It should be presented either with its own alphabet or in the type of transliterated form which the civilized world has agreed upon as conventionally acceptable. One suspects that Semitic linguistics has suffered not a little from 'litteritis' in the past. So far as possible, compared languages should be orthographically reduced to a common denominator. If some Semitists feel that the sequence *rkb* does not as unerringly suggest the root for 'ride' as does its equivalent in Hebrew or Arabic orthography, one can only say that they are making a needless virtue out of visual habits which are of no relevance for scientific linguistic research. Is it not reasonable to expect that scientific papers and monographs in the Semitic field, to the extent that they are not expressly devoted to scholarly purposes within a specific dialectic tradition (such as Rabbinics or Syriac literature or Islamic exegesis), should by common understanding content themselves with Latin transliterations? Tocharian is not presented to the scientific world in a Dēvanāgarī-like transfer from the original Brāhmi script; it is not obvious why Ugaritic should be presented in a Hebrew-like transfer from the original alphabetic cuneiform.

Perhaps the most interesting linguistic fact about the orthography of Ugaritic is the use it makes of three distinct signs for the Semitic phoneme ' (glottal stop or aleph). These are by no means used interchangeably but differ according to the vowel that follows or precedes. '$_1$ is used with an *a*-vowel, '$_2$with an *i*-vowel, '$_3$ with an *u*-vowel. Some have thought that the second sign could also be used when the glottal stop was not followed by a vowel, i.e. as final or when directly followed by another consonant, but it seems safest to assume that in such cases the choice of the aleph sign was determined by the preceding vowel and that the instances of final -*a*'$_2$ or of -*a*'$_2$- before consonants are due to a dialectic change of Semitic -*a*', -*a*'- to -*e*', -*e*'- (see Zellig S. Harris, A Conditioned Sound Change in Ras Shamra, JAOS 57.151–7), -'$_2$ (-'$_2$-) in these cases expressing an -*e*' (-*e*'-), a phonemic variant of -*a*' (-*a*'-) which is quasi-phonetically rendered '-*i*' (-*i*')'. Thus, *r'₂š* 'head' (Semitic **ra'šu*) is to be interpreted as *re'šu* (cf. later Aramaic *rēš-ā́*), not quite adequately rendered *r(i)'š*. Aside from these vocalic implications of the three alephs, vowels are not indicated in Ugaritic. As early Canaanite and Aramaic scripts represent only the consonants, it is obvious that if we can find Ugaritic test words with ', we are now in a position to make important inferences with reference to certain problems of West Semitic phonology and grammar in the 14th Cent. B.C. The most striking of these is the proof of the existence of nominative -*u*, genitive -*i*, and accusative -*a* in Ugaritic, exactly as in classical Arabic. The best test word is *ks'* 'throne', Hebrew *kissḗ*; < **kissi'u* Ugaritic has nom. *ks'₃* (= *kissi'u* or *kussu'u*), gen. *ks'₂* (= *kissi'i* or *kussu'i*), acc. *ks'₁* (= *kissi'a* or *kussu'a*). It is naturally important to show that the old Semitic case system survived in at least certain Northwest Semitic dialects of a later date than 1500 B.C. because our oldest Canaanite and Aramaic documents, mostly of a later age, give no clear evidence of this case system.

How are we to classify this new Semitic language? Opinions range all the way from accepting it as a Canaanite dialect peculiarly close to Hebrew-Moabite and Phoenician (in their Preface, Montgomery and Harris go so far as to speak of the Ras Shamra texts as 'cuneiform Hebraic texts', which is clearly claiming too much) to giving it an entirely independent position in the Semitic group, say midway between East Semitic (Accadian: Assyrian, Babylonian) and West Semitic (Canaanite, Aramaic, Arabic, South Arabic, Ethiopic). Goetze, if I understand him rightly, gives Ugaritic this middle position and suggests an identification with 'Amorite', an important Semitic language which we know only through place names and personal names recorded in Canaanite (Hebrew) and Accadian documents. A suggestive phonetic law tending to support this theory is the change of Semitic *đ* (interdental voiced spirant) to Ugaritic *d*. This superficially suggests an Aramaic correspondence but the suggestion is unsound, for in the earliest Aramaic documents the phoneme is represented by the Canaanite sign for *z* (in Canaanite, as in Accadian, Semitic *đ* early became *z*) and it is only later that Aramaic has *d*; Egyptian Aramaic of the fifth century B.C. writes both *d* and *z* for the phoneme in question, while Semitic *d* and *z* are consistently rendered *d* and *z* respectively in all Aramaic dialects of all periods. In other words, earlier Aramaic, having no sign for *đ*, which, like Arabic, it possessed as a distinctive phoneme perhaps as late as the fifth century B.C., merely used the Canaanite *z* as a second best orthography. It is therefore impossible to equate Ugaritic *d* < Sem. *đ* with late Aramaic *d* < Sem. *đ*. On the other hand, there seems some evidence for Amorite

d < Sem. *d̲*. A case in point would seem to be the Amorite place name
'ɛd̲rʹɛʻī occurring frequently in the Old Testament, which is probably
cognate with Semitic **dirāʻu* 'arm', metaphorically 'strength' (Hebrew
zᵉróaʻ, Aram. *dᵉrāʻ-á̄*; also with prothetic vowel: 'ɛzróaʻ, 'ɛdrāʻ-á̄).

It is difficult to make up one's mind about the placement of Ugaritic
in the present state of our knowledge because so many features of this
dialect, both positive and negative, may be due to its age rather than to
its dialectic affiliations. The lack of an article, for instance, as contrasted
with Hebrew *ha-*, Aram. *-ā*, and Arabic *al-* does not seem particularly
significant, for the partly prefixed, partly suffixed, articles of other
Semitic dialects have all the appearance of being comparatively late
dialectic developments, so that on this point Ugaritic is more likely to
be archaic Semitic than, say, un-Canaanite. Again, it has been claimed
that Ugaritic cannot be a Canaanite dialect because it does not share the
characteristically Canaanite change of Semitic *ā* to *ō*. Had it undergone
this change, we would have expected a preceding ' to be of type 'ₐ (as
in 'ₐ 'either, or' = 'ō < Sem. **ʻau*), whereas it is actually 'ₐ that is used
in such cases (e.g., fem. plur. of noun in -'- : -'ₐt = -'-āt-u, Arabic -āt-,
but Hebr. -ōt). But internal Canaanite evidence shows that this argument, like so many linguistic arguments that ignore chronology, is
unsound. When we say that Sem. *ā* becomes Canaanite *ō*, we should
not necessarily mean that at the earliest stage of Canaanite this sound
change had already taken place, but only that the actual Canaanite
documents we possess (Biblical Hebrew, Moabite, Phoenician and
Punic, Canaanite glosses in Tell el-Amarna tablets) show a darkening
of Sem. *ā* to *ō*, Punic *ū*. We have then to determine whether this phonetic
feature is a historically valid test for early inclusion of a given dialect
in the Canaanite group or represents a convergent development or diffusion within the dialectic area (cf., for instance, change of Germanic
hr-, *hl-* to *r-*, *l-* in all modern West Germanic dialects; it would be wrong
to infer an early West Germanic *r-*, *l-* in these cases, for documentary
evidence proves that all early West Germanic dialects—Old High German, Anglo-Saxon, Old Saxon—still possessed *hr-* and *hl-*). Now Hebrew
consonantal orthography indicates that we must suppose for the earliest
stage of Hebrew (a fortiori, for Canaanite in general) an *ā* (= Sem. *ā*)
for later *ō*. Thus, Hebrew *rōš* 'head' < older **rāš-u* < still older **ra'š-u*
is written *r'š*, with etymologically justified -'-. In other words, the
consonantal orthography of Hebrew goes clear back to a time when the
word was still pronounced **ra'š-u* (cf. Arabic *ra's-uⁿ*). It was only after
-*a'*- had 'quiesced' to -*ā*- that this vowel, falling in with the large group
of old Sem. *ā*-vowels, could become a 'Canaanite' *ō*. Hence, if *ā* > *ō* is

a test of Canaanite affiliation, consonantal Hebrew (e.g., *r'š*), as contrasted with later vocalized Massoretic Hebrew (e.g., *rōš*), must be non-Canaanite! This would be as reasonable as to say that English *ring*, like German *Ring*, is 'West Germanic', while Anglo-Saxon *hring* (cf. Old Icelandic *hringr*) belongs to a 'Gothic-Scandinavian' stage or group of Germanic. The fact of the matter probably is that Sem. *ā* first darkened to *ō* in some specific dialect of Canaanite, say Phoenician, that this tendency diffused to Hebrew-Moabite quite early (as early, say, as the Tell el-Amarna period) but long after Hebrew had received a fixed orthography, and that northern dialects, such as Ugaritic, were not affected by the tendency.

The reviewer does not feel that he is competent to express an opinion on the proper classification of Ugaritic. He feels rather strongly, however, that it has too many distinctive features, both in phonology and grammar, to be classified as a member of that group of Semitic dialects which is illustrated by Hebrew. Even Hebrew-Phoenician seems too narrow a unit to include Ugaritic. On the other hand it is difficult to escape the impression that its affiliations are rather with Canaanite than with South Semitic, Aramaic, or Accadian. This may turn out to be illusory, however. Perhaps the future will establish a Canaanite-Ugaritic (-Amorite) dialectic group, with features midway between those of Accadian and Aramaic-Arabic (specific Aramaic-Canaanite points of agreement being of later age and due to mutual borrowings). There is one important feature of noun morphology which Ugaritic seems to share with Canaanite and Aramaic and which may some day be thought to constitute crucial evidence for its dialectic classification. In both Hebrew and Aramaic 'segholate' nouns, i.e. nouns of stem form *qatl, qitl, qutl*, have an enlarged base, of type *qatal-*, in the plural (e.g., Canaanite-Aramaic sing., du. *malk-* 'king', pl. *malak-*; thus, Hebrew *malk-î* 'my king' but *mᵉlāk-îm* < *malak-īma 'kings'). Ugaritic has *r'₂š* 'head' (probably = *re'šu* < **ra'šu*) but pl. *r'₁š-m*. This latter form is probably to be read *ra'aš-īma* (or *ra'aš-ūma*), cf. Hebr. *rōš* 'head' (*r'š*) but *rāšîm* 'heads' (*r'š-ym*); the Hebrew singular points to early **ra'š-u*, as we have seen, while the plural points, in typical 'segholate' fashion, to early **ra'aš-īma*. It seems fair to assume that Ugaritic *mlk* 'king', pl. *mlk-m, are, in parallel fashion, to be read *malk-u*, *malak-īma (or *malak-ūma).

FROM SAPIR'S DESK*

INDO-EUROPEAN PREVOCALIC s IN MACEDONIAN

IF IT CAN BE SHOWN that IE prevocalic s, or rather initial s before vowels, and intervocalic s, became h in Macedonian, as it did in all Greek dialects, we would have one good reason to think that Macedonian was, if not a Greek dialect, as O. Hoffmann tried to show,[1] at least not merely an eastern Illyrian dialect that was somewhat hellenized, but a distinct IE branch that might be set midway between Greek and Illyrian.[2] It is therefore of interest that Schwyzer[3] quotes, apparently with approval, Hoffmann's equation of Macedonian ὁϝαν 'swine' with Lat. suem. He does not discuss Macedonian h- < IE s- but quotes the word to illustrate Macedonian interchange of o and u. However, if this equation is correct for o < IE u, it must also be correct for IE s- > h-. In fairness to the critical reader he might have added: first, that ὁϝαν is absolutely the only form that Hoffmann could muster for the alleged change of s- to h-; secondly, that in order to arrive at it, Hoffmann had to doubly emend the Hesychian gloss which he quotes. For what Hesychius (or rather our version of him) enters is not ὁϝαν but γοτάν. It seems proper to emend γ to ϝ in Hesychian glosses, when there is something to be gained, but for a theoretically archaic letter for h- (*hoϝαν in archetype) to show up as a corrupted γ- and a -ϝ- as a corrupted -τ- as well is beyond easy credence.

Schwyzer's use of this created word ὁϝαν is all the harder to understand as he quotes from Kretschmer what looks like rather satisfactory evidence that intervocalic IE -s- remained in Macedonian in its voiced form -z-, if -ζ- can be so interpreted in ἀλιζα 'Silberpappel : Span. aliso < Germanic, presumably Visigothic, *alisa (cf. German Erle, OHG elira < WGerm *alizō[4]). In other words, Schwyzer implies that IE s-

---

* Language, 15 (1939): 178–187. The original publication carried this notice: "The following notes were left by Sapir ready, or nearly ready, for publication. His colleague, E. H. Sturtevant, has seen them thru the press."

[1] See O. Hoffmann, Die Makedonen, ihre Sprache und ihr Volkstum, (1906).

[2] We know that intervocalic s remained in Illyrian from such names as Isarcus: Goth. eisarn (WP 1.4), Αὐσανκαλεί, Ausancalione, Anausaro (Hans Krahe, Die alten balkanillyrischen geographischen Namen, (1925) p. 82, and Vescleves-is < IE *klewes- (WP 1.310). Many Illyrian names with initial prevocalic s, such as Senta, Sextus, Sexticus, Sexto (these last are almost certainly not Latin in origin), Salvia, have every appearance of possessing IE s- (see lists in Krahe, op. cit. and Lexikon altillyrischer Personennamen, 1929).

[3] See Edward Schwyzer, Griechische Grammatik, allgemeiner Teil und Lautlehre (1934), digest of phonological evidence bearing on Macedonian, with literature, pp. 69–71.

[4] Schwyzer, p. 69, n. 3; and cf. WP 1. 151.

before vowels becomes Macedonian *h-*, but that intervocalic *-s-* appears as Macedonian *-z-*. There is no logical reason why such might not be the case, but it seems to be against general experience in IE. In Latin and Umbrian IE *s-* remains but intervocalic *-s-* is rhotacized to *-r-*, via *-z-*. Similarly, in West and North Germanic initial IE *s-* remains but intervocalic *-s-*, when the stress did not immediately precede (Verner's law), became voiced to *-z-* > *-r-*. Again, in Old Irish IE *s-* remains (aside from lenition in sentence sandhi) but intervocalic *-s-* becomes *-h-* > *-zero-*[5]. The last instance is particularly instructive because it exactly reverses the supposed treatment of IE *s* in Macedonian. Such parallel instances still further weaken the force of Hoffmann's evidence. The existence of other Macedonian glosses with intervocalic *-s-* naturally proves nothing unless we can show that *-s-* is referable to IE *-s-*. Thus, Macedonian καυσία 'broad-brimmed felt hat'[6] almost certainly derives from an earlier **kauts-* (or **kaudz-*), i.e. **kaut-* (or **kaud-*) with final dental assibilated by originally following *-y-*; cf. Tokharian A *koc*, B *kauc* 'high, upward'[7] < pre-Tokh. **kaut-y-* (original **kaud-y-* would level to **kaut-y-* before further developing to **kauc-*). (The point of this comparison is contained in Hoffmann's description: 'die καυσία, wie unsere Filzhüte, besass einen besonderen Kopfdeckel und eine nach oben gekrummten breiten Rand'.)

There is, further, a statistical argument which can be urged against Hoffmann. If we are to believe that IE prevocalic *s-* became Macedonian *h-*, there ought to be a fair sprinkling of initial '- in the some 140 Macedonian glosses we possess because of the great frequency of *s-* as an IE initial, regardless of whether we could etymologize such examples or not and allowing for textual corruption. Now, of the 36 Old Macedonian entries under *a-* in Hoffmann's monograph, not one has ἁ-, all have ἀ-; but of 77 'Macedonian' names (borrowed from Greek or, if genuinely Macedonian, given in our sources in Greek form), 7 have ʽΑ-. For New Macedonian[8] two cases in ἁ- are entered (ἁjάσμους and ἅλιος) out of 4 in *a-*, but these, needless to say, are merely due to the orthographic conservatism of the Koiné throughout its history. Of 4 Old Macedonian entries for ε-, one has ἑ, i.e. ἑταῖρος, almost obviously a

---

[5] See R. Thurneysen, *Handbuch des Altirischen* p. 79.

[6] Hoffmann, *op. cit.* pp. 55–58, particularly p. 56.

[7] These Tokh. words are not immediately referable to Germanic **hauha-* 'high', though perhaps ultimately related. See G. S. Lane, "Problems of Tocharian Phonology," *Language* 14 (1938): 26. [read **qou-q-* for **quo-q-*]. This is by no means an isolated example of special correspondence between Tokharian and Illyrian (including Macedonian), as I hope to show in detail at another time.

[8] Present-day Macedonian Greek is a development of the Koinē but has a number of interesting survivals of the old Macedonian language.

Greek loan-word; of 21 names, 5 have 'E-. Of 4 Old Macedonian entries for ι-, none has ἱ-; of 6 names, 4 have 'I-, all in 'Ιππο-. There is one Macedonian gloss in ἠ-, ἡμεροδρομας, again an obvious loanword, if only because of η instead of ā; of 6 names, 5 have 'H-. There is no Macedonian gloss in ὀ- and none in ὀ- unless we accept Hoffmann's emended ὀϝαν; of 7 names, 1 has 'O-. There is one gloss in ὐ-, none in ὑ-; and one name in Υ-. There is neither gloss nor name in ω-. In summary, there is not a single example of a genuine Macedonian word beginning with h-, quite aside from the problem of whether such words, if they existed, owed their h- to IE s- or not. All this looks badly for Macedonian 'ὀϝαν', which should obviously be restored to the original γοτάν of our source, even if we can do nothing with the IE placement of this word at present.

We have, then, no evidence whatever for a Macedonian treatment of IE s which is parallel to its treatment in Greek, but some slight positive evidence that IE s was preserved intervocalically as -z-. By analogical inference we shall have to assume that it was preserved initially, even though we cannot as yet give satisfactory etymologies of words with prevocalic initial s- in Macedonian.[9]

The Indo-European Words for 'Tear'

It has proved difficult to reconcile the Indo-European words for 'tear', no less than four apparently incompatible formations being found, illustrated by Skt. *áśru*, Lith. *ãśara*, OHG *trahan*, and Greek δάκρυ. The last is generally taken as the point of departure—a fatal error, as we shall see. The Hittite *'esḫaḫru*[1], which it seems impossible to disconnect from the better known IE forms, only adds a fifth incompatible form to the confusion. Yet it is precisely this Hittite word which led me to an analysis of the whole family which I hope may seem as reasonable as it is unexpected.

Instead of first analyzing the various dialectic forms back to their respective prototypes I shall at once present the reconstructed complex of IE forms, interpret their formation and meaning, and then apply the schema to the material presented by the IE dialects. The reconstructed set of IE forms consists of a basic term (illustrated by Skt. *áśru*), an old collective of a peculiar type of reduplication (illustrated by Lith. *ašarà*), and two compounds in which the second element is the primary word for 'tear' or rather the old substantivized neuter adjective which had come to be used for 'tear' (illustrated by 1. OHG *trahan* and Gk. δάκρυ; 2. Hit. *'esḫaḫru*).

---

[9] See, e.g., genuine Macedonian personal names (*Sabattaras, Sippas, Sirras*) in Krahe's material.

[1] I interpret such Hittite orthographies as *e-eš-* as meaning *'es-*, i.e. glottal stop + vowel + consonant. My reasons for this I hope to develop in a later paper.

We shall assume:

1. $*x\acute{a}\hat{k}ru^2$ 'tear' (n.) < 'acrid'
2. $*xa\hat{k}xa(\hat{k})r$-$\acute{a}x$ 'tears' (reduplicated collective of 'feminine' form)
3. $*^w dr$-$x\acute{a}\hat{k}ru$ 'water' + 'acrid'
4. $*'esx\eta$-$x\hat{k}ru$ 'blood' (= 'effluvium') + 'acrid'

1. The word $*x\acute{a}\hat{k}ru$, which now looks like an ordinary neuter substantive u-stem, is best interpreted as an old dualized neuter in $-u$

[2] In this and subsequent papers on IE phonology I reconstruct in terms of the four IE 'laryngeal' consonants:' = glottal stop with fronted timbre ($*'e$- = usual $*e$-; tautosyllabic $*$-e' = usual -$\bar{e}$, not to be confused with $*'\bar{e}$ = usual $*\bar{e}$ when lengthened grade of e); $'$ = glottal stop with velar timbre ($*'a$- = usual $*a$-; tautosyllabic $*$-a' = usual -$\bar{a}$, not to be confused with $*'\bar{a}$ = usual $*\bar{a}$ when lengthened grade of $'a$); x = velar voiceless spirant ($*xa$ = usual $*a$-; tautosyllabic $*$-ax = usual $*$-$\bar{a}$, not to be confused with $*x\bar{a}$ = usual $*\bar{a}$ when lengthened grade of xa); γ- = velar voiced spirant ($*\varrho$ - = usual $*o$-[$*\bar{a}$-], not to be confused with $*'o$-, $*'o$-, $*xo$-, $*\gamma o$-, = usual $*o$-, respective o-grades of $*'e$-, $*'a$-, $*xa$-, $*\gamma \varrho$-, = usual $*e$-, $*a$-, $*a$-, $*o$- [$\bar{a}$-]; tautosyllabic $*$-$e\gamma$ = usual $*$-$\bar{o}$, not to be confused with $*\gamma \bar{o}$ = usual $*\bar{o}$ when lengthened grade of $\gamma \varrho$, nor with $*'\bar{o}$, $*'\bar{o}$, $*x\bar{o}$, $*\gamma \bar{o}$, = usual $*\bar{o}$ when lengthened o-grades of $*'e$, $'a$, xa, $\gamma \varrho$). Certain ambiguities of reconstruction make it necessary to use cover-symbols; A = any 'laryngeal'; A = $'$ or x, causing a-timbre. In this system there is no place for ϑ, $\bar{\imath}$, $\bar{u}$, $\bar{m}$, $\bar{n}$, l, $\bar{r}$. These correspond to $_eA$ (= $_e'$, $_e'$, $_ex$, $_e\gamma$), iA (or y_eA), uA (or w_eA), mA (or m_eA), nA (or n_eA), lA (or l_eA), rA (or r_eA). Properly speaking, i and u should be expressed as y and w. Better yet, all cases of 'i', 'u', 'm', 'n', 'l', and 'r' should be analyzed as $_ey$ or y_e, $_ew$ or w_e, $_em$ or m_e, $_en$ or n_e, $_el$ or l_e, $_er$ or r_e, according to whether they are reduction products of ey or ye, ew or we, em or me. en or ne, el or le, er or re, while i (or y), u (or w), m, n, l and r might be reserved as cover-symbols for those cases in which our evidence does not allow us to choose between type $_ey$ and type y_e. Much neater than such orthographies as $_ey$, y (or i) and y_e would be $_oy$, y, y_o, in which $_o$ is a symbol for schwa (murmur-vowel) and syllabification of semivowels, nasals, and liquids at one and the same time, an identification that seems phonemically sound for Indo-European. The true IE vowels, according to the proposed system, are therefore:

A. Full grade
  1. e-type: e, a, ϱ
  2. o-type: o
B. Lengthened grade
  1. $\bar{e}$, $\bar{a}$, $\bar{o}$
  2. o-type: $\bar{o}$
C. Reduced grade
  1. Syllabic: $_e$
  2. Non-syllabic: *zero*

Most Indo-Europeanists will find it awkward, at first, to think from such accepted entities as $*dh\bar{e}$- and $*w\bar{\imath}$- ($*\underset{.}{u}\bar{\imath}$-) to $*dhe'$- and $*w_ey A$- or $*wy_eA$- or $*wyA$-, but in the long run they will, I believe, be surprised to find how much more regular, simple, and phonologically satisfactory the new system is than the old. It may be added, by way of preliminary justification of the proposed reconstructive orthography, that IE x actually occurs in Hittite as $\hbar$ (= $\hbar_1$) and, under certain circumstances, in Phrygian-Armenian (e.g., as Phrygian -k in $\beta o\nu\acute{o}$-κ 'woman' < $*g^w_en\acute{a}$-x = $^xg^w_en$-$\acute{a}$; Arm. x in, e.g., $sxalem$ 'I go wrong, wander', Skr. $skhalat\bar{e}$ 'he stumbles, goes wrong' Gk. $\sigma\phi\acute{a}\lambda\lambda o\mu\alpha\iota$ 'I stumble, go wrong' < IE $*sk^wxal$-, at e-grade base) and that IE γ occurs in Hittite as $\hbar$ (= $\hbar_2$) and, after nasals, as -k- (I shall return to this at a later time), is preserved in Armenian under certain definable circumstances as -k- (IE γ and g, g^w probably leveled to g and shifted to k), and, when not initial, seems regularly preserved in Tokharian as -k-. The other two 'laryngeal' phonemes,' and $'$, are not so directly demonstrable but, in the long run, are just as inescapable. It was necessary to go into this long, and certainly not completely satisfying, preliminary statement because otherwise the schema of IE words for 'tear' can not be presented with due symmetry.

($= -_ew$), which is doubtless identical with the -w of masculine and neuter nom.-acc. duals in -ōu. Such petrified duals are not uncommon in Indo-European, e.g. *ĝón-u 'knee', Goth. *hand-u-* 'hand', Goth. *fōt-u-* 'foot'. The dualic -u of *xákr̥-u may refer to the two eyes. Whether the parallel form in *xakr̥-ó-m (e.g. Skt. *aśrá-m*) is the corresponding non-dualized thematic singular or is merely a relatively late transfer from the less common u-stem class to the more common -e/o- stem class is not clear. Either alternative is possible. The latter would seem to be the more acceptable one, but there is a similar parallelism in forms of group 3 (e.g. Gk. δάκρυ: OIr. *dér* and Goth. *tagr* < *dákrom and *dakróm) and in Lettish and Lithuanian, whose u-stems are particularly common, we nevertheless have a Balto-Slavic ā-stem, which is the normal feminine pendant to the masc.-neut. -e/o-stem. The word *xákru and perhaps *xakróm as well are best explained as neuter forms of the common IE adjective *xakré/o- 'sharp, acrid' (cf. Lat. *ācer, acer-bus*, Lith. *aštrùs*), as has been pointed out a number of times.[3] *wédr̥ (or *w₀dór, *wodór) xákru (or xakróm) 'water acrid' was the original IE term for 'tear'. Perhaps, when the noun was specifically named, it was *wedr̥ xakróm 'water acrid' (n.) but *xákru 'the dually acrid (n., sc. water)' when the noun was implicit. At any rate, *xákru must have been early petrified into the common word for 'tear', for it is presupposed by many of the compounds in groups 3 and 4.

2. The Balto-Slavic forms are obviously closely related to the Indo-Iranian and Tokharian ones, yet Lith. *ãšara* (*ašarà*, according to Kurschat[4]) and Lettish *asara* are not derivable from the base *xakr̥- of group 1. The second a-vowel of the Baltic forms is in no way a secondary

---

[3] See, e.g., A. Walde and J. Pokorny, *Vergleichendes Wörterbuch der indogermanischen Sprache* (Berlin, 1927), 1:769, sub *daḱru*. See also E. Sapir, "On the Etymology of Sanskrit *áśru*, Avestan *asru*, Greek *dákru*," in *Spiegel Memorial Volume* (Bombay, 1908), pp. 156–159. The present paper supplements and in large part corrects my earlier one. The interpretation there proposed of *dáḱru as 'biting (water)' (cf. Gk. δάκνω) is untenable because 'to bite' is IE *denḱ- (Gk. δάκ-νω < *dn̥ḱ-), to which dak- of dáḱru is unrelated. This was pointed out to me years ago by Professor R. G. Kent.

[4] See Trautmann, *Baltisch-Slavisches Wörterbuch*, s.v. *ašarā-* (14). *ašarà* is the more archaic form accentually and *āšara* is obviously due to leveling, in certain Lithuanian dialects, with those case forms e.g., dat. *āšarai*, in which the originally oxytone accent was transferred to the first syllable because of certain accent-shifting processes peculiar to Baltic in general or to Lithuanian in particular. The word is listed by Wiedemann, *Handbuch der litauischen Sprache*, p. 261, as a circumflected proparoxytone with invariable stress (his class 4, of circumflected sub-type); see also p. 47. For the original oxytonesis of feminine -ā-stems of three-syllabled words see T. Torbiörnsson, *Die litauischen Akzentverschiebungen und der litauische Verbalakzent*, Slavica 9, (Heidelberg, 1924), pp. 12 [type *ašakà*], 47–48, 53; H. Hirt, *Indogermanische Grammatik*: 5:257–60; J. Kurylowicz, "Le Problème des Intonations Balto-Slaves," *Rocznik Slawistyczny* 10 (1930):56–59.

element due to the consonant group *-šr- < *-k̂r-, for Lith. -šr- either remains or introduces a glide -t-, hence *ašrùs* or *aštrùs*.[5] Nor has -a- been established as a Baltic development of ₑ reduced from a in open syllables (our *xa, ˙a*); -ₑ- seems consistently to yield -i- before r or l + vowel.[6] -arà could be plausibly interpreted as a Baltic transfer of an old neuter to the feminine and the -ar- as a resulting assimilation of an older -er- to the new ending,[7] were it not that old neuters generally become Baltic masculines (e.g. Lith. *medùs* : Skt. *mádhu*; Lith. *árklas* : Gk. ἄροτρον),[8] that there is no *-ero-, *-erā formation for 'tear' quotable from any other IE dialect,[9] and that there are plenty of substantive u-stems, old and new, in Baltic. Neither an IE *xak̂or-' nor an IE *xak̂ər-' (our *xak̂ₑAr-') is thinkable; the former corresponds to no obvious ablaut pattern, the latter would have yielded a Lith. *ašrà, dat. *ášrai (cf. Lith. *galvà* 'head', dat. *gálvai* < IE *gholₑxw-áx, cf. Armenian *glux* < IE *ghlₑxw-ó-). There seems nothing left but to interpret the Baltic -a- as an IE -a-, i.e. -xa- (or -˙a-), and to reconstruct to *xak̂xar-áx, an example of 'broken' reduplication (for fully reduplicated *xak̂xak̂-rá-x, collective 'feminine' of *xak̂xak̂-ró-), the -ro- suffix favoring adaptation to such freely reduplicated models as Lat. *querquerus*, Gk. βάρβαρος, Gk. ὄλολυς. Possibly the loss of the second -k̂- (Baltic -š-) was a Baltic, not Indo-European, process: *xak̂xak̂ráx 'many-tears-collectivity, flow of tears' (cf. Gk. ὄλολυς 'howler, effeminate man') > Baltic *ašašrà > Lith. *ašarà*, Lettish *asara*.[10]

3. Our reconstruction for types 3 and 4 assumes that the underlying IE forms are compounds of *wédr 'water' (represented by Tokh. *wār*, Arm. *get* 'river', Phrygian βέδυ) or other ablauting form (e.g. Goth. *watō*, Hit. *watar, weten-as*, OChSl. *voda*; Gk. ὕδωρ), in its most reduced form *ʷdr-, and of *'ésxṇ- 'blood, effluvium' respectively with the *xák̂ru,

[5] See Brugmann, *Grundr.*² 1. §627.

[6] *Op. cit.* §522, 1; also Hirt, *Indogermanische Grammatik*, 2: 85, 86.

[7] For Baltic -aras, -ara for original *-eras, *era, see Brugmann, *op. cit.*, 2:1.357 and 1.238, also Wiedemann, *Handbuch der litauischen Sprache*, §59, 1, and Endzelin, *Lettische Grammatik*, §167.

[8] One might, of course, say that the expected Lith. *āš(t)rus could not hold its own because it would have conflicted with the nearly homonymous adjective *aš(t)rùs* 'sharp', hence a transfer to a fem. *aš(t)rà and subsequent assimilation in form to the common type -arà. All of which sounds a little made to order and far from plausible in view of the obvious antiquity of the word and the specific formal agreement of Lithuanian and Lettish.

[9] Note that in the apparently analogous Lith. *vākaras* 'evening' we deal with a genuine IE form in *-ero- (cf. OChSl. *večerъ*, Lat. *vesper, -er-is, -er-ī*, Gk. ἕσπερος; there can be no reasonable doubt, in spite of apparent difficulties, that these all belong together).

[10] For examples of such fully reduplicated and secondary broken forms in Indo-European see Brugmann, *op. cit.* 2: 1, §§70–74; Hirt, *op. cit.* 4. 6–9. There is, instead, a possibility of connecting the Baltic words and, less plausibly, the Slavic words for 'tear' with the Hittite form. See 4 below.

*xaḱrom discussed under 1. *ʷdr-xáḱru 'water-acrid' represents simply a more synthetic method of expressing *xáḱru, i.e. *wédṛ xaḱru, itself. *ʷdr-xáḱru 'the water-acrid' is, roughly speaking, to the analytic *wédṛ xaḱru 'water which is acrid' what such a Greek form as εὐ-πάτωρ 'the good-father' is to the analytic ἐὺς πατήρ 'a good father'. Ordinarily the reduced form of a syllable of type we- would be a syllabic w, i.e. wₑ-, u- (e.g. Gk. ὕδωρ, Skt. uda-ká-m) but we may suppose that in compounds in which the first element, 'water', was no longer felt in its literal meaning the phonetic groups *wdr-', possibly also *wdén-, *wdér-, would reduce to *dr-' (*dén-, *dér-).[11]

It would seem that there are several forms with dr-, reduced from *ʷdr- 'water', besides *dr-xáḱru 'tear.' Among them are:

(1) Gk. δροίτη 'wooden tub, bath-tub; coffin' < *dró-sitā < *ʷdr-ó-sitā 'water-tub, water-vat' (cf. Lat. dim. situla 'little tub', i.e. 'bucket, pail').[12]

(2) Gk. δρόσος 'dew; pure-water, tears' < *ʷdr-ó-kʷyos 'water-row', i.e. 'row of water-drops' (*-kʷyo-, thematized zero grade of *kʷey-, *kʷoy- 'to arrange in rows', W.-P., 1.509).

(3) Gk. δρίλακες· βδέλλαι [leeches]. Ἠλεῖοι (Hesych.). This extremely obscure Elean word receives a simple interpretation on our hypothesis. It is to be analyzed as *ʷdri-lak-es '(worms) stepped on in the water' (*ʷdri, an old consonant-stem locative; -lak- : Gk. λάξ, λάγ-δην 'with the heel', λαχ-μός < *lak-smó-s 'a kick'[13]).

(4) MIr. drochta 'vat, tub', dro-chat 'bridge'[14] < *ʷdro- 'water' + second element of compounds, of type 'container' and 'cross-pole, cross-

---

[11] There is no reason to think that reductions of etymologically nontransparent elements in compounds would be mechanically identical in form with reductions of morphologically parallel elements when uncompounded. Contrast, in English, board and -board of cupboard, wife and -y of hussy < hūs-wīf. It is, therefore, perfectly conceivable and even probable that w and y, and very likely still other consonant-phonemes, might disappear in Indo-European (or dialectically) when found in semantically obscure syllables immediately before other consonants. That no one has as yet formulated a phonetic law which would allow an old *wdr-' to simplify to *dr-' in certain cases and an old *wₒdr-, in apparently parallel instances, to maintain itself as *udr- merely means that the more intricate reduction processes of Indo-European are still in the main to be unraveled. A parallel case is probably that of IE *snusú-s 'daughter-in-law', in which many have felt that *snu- represents a hyper-reduced form of *sunu- 'son', in our terms an old *sʷnu-' which lost its -w- largely because in an untransparent compound of this type non-syllabic semivowels caught between consonants might be expected to drop out without a trace.

[12] This simple etymology seems preferable to those based on a supposed *drou- or *drow- 'wood, oak', with unlikely ablaut-form of first element. See Boisacq, Dict. étym. de la Langue Grecque, s.v. δροίτη; Walde-Pokorny, op. cit., 1:804.

[13] See Boisacq, op. cit., s.v. λάξ, for other words belonging to this group. The resemblance of δρίλακες to δρῖλος 'earth-worm' can hardly be other than fortuitous.

log' respectively. MIr. *-chta*, a depalatalized *-yo-* or *-yā-* stem[15], say
*-kat-yā-, is perhaps to be grouped with Lat. *catī-nu-s* 'basin'; *-chat*
(read — *add*) reconstructs to **-kant-o-*[16], cf. perhaps Gk. κοντός 'pole,
shaft of pike' (*-o-* of post-accentual syllables becomes OIr. *-a-*). These
analyses are necessarily uncertain, but 'water' seems a better mediating
term between 'tub' and 'bridge' than 'wood'. One cannot but suspect
that etymologists presuppose too great an emphasis on the wood of all
manner of artifacts that could never have been made of anything else.

(5) Germ. **troga-* 'trough' (OHG *trog* m., MHG *troc, trog-* m., German
Trog, AS *trog, troh* m., Eng. *trough,* Dutch *trog,* ON *trog* n.), **trugjō*
(LG *trügge*)[17] < **ʷdr-uĝh-yā́* 'water-conductor', originally perhaps, a
V-shaped construction—of wood— in which the water is run for the
animals; **-uĝh-*, reduced from **weĝh-*, as in Albanian *uδ-* (*uδ-ε* 'way';
urε 'bridge' < **uδ-rā* < **uĝh-rā́*).[18]

(6) Skt. *dróṇa* (m., n.) 'trough, tub', (m.) 'kind of cloud abounding
in water (like a trough)', *druṇī* 'water-bucket'[19] < **ʷdr-ó-wn-o-*, **ʷdr-un-ī* 'water-wood, water-trough', **-wn-* and **-un-* being reduced from
*wen- of Skt. *ván-a-m* 'tree; wood (RV.); wooden trough for Soma
(RV.)'.[20]

(7) Skt. *drapsá* (m.) 'drop' < **ʷdr-ops-ó-*, an archaic bahuvrihi
compound with oxytone thematic suffix (**-ó-*) and reduced grade of
second syllable of second element of compound (IE **ópos* 'work': **-ops-ó-*
like **wétos* 'year' : **tri-wets-ó-* '3-yeared', Skt. *tri-vats-á-*[21]), 'water-

---

[14] See Walde-Pokorny, *op. cit.*, 1: 805. There seems no warrant for the
'*hölzernes' in his rendering of *drochta* except a natural desire to connect the word
with the well-known IE set of words for 'tree, wood'.
[15] See Thurneysen, *Handbuch des Altirischen* §§165, 281, 282, 292. *-a* < OIr.
-(a)e.
[16] See Pedersen, *Vergleichende Grammatik der keltischen Sprachen,* 2: 47. Pedersen suggests an analysis into **druk-anto-* 'wood' (of aberrant form in *-k-*) +
formative element *-anto-* of unknown meaning = 'beam' > 'bridge'. A 'log'
(or 'pole') thrown over the water would seem to come a little nearer to yielding
the desired 'bridge'.
[17] See Walde-Pokorny, *op. cit.*, 1: 806 and, far more clearly, Kluge, *Etymologisches Wörterbuch der deutschen Sprache,* s.vv. *Trog* and *Truhe* ('chest'). Walde-
Pokorny throw together a whole group of words that cannot possibly have anything to do with each other: 'fest, kräftig, gesund; Trog; Kiste, Truhe; eine Art
Saum- odor Packsattel; eine Art Fischkorb; Hartriegel', all supposed derivatives
of IE **dru-* 'tree, wood'. This is purely verbal etymologizing, without regard to
cultural probability, at its worst. Even Kluge, who is more factual in such matters,
remarks, sub *Trog:* 'vorgerm. *dru-kó-,* das man mit Recht aus dem unter *Teer*
behandelten idg. Stamme *dru* (*dreu deru*) "Baum, Holz" ableitet; vgl. skr. *dru*
dáru "Holz": *Trog* also eigentlich "Hölzernes"?'
[18] See Walde-Pokorny, *op. cit.*, 1: 249.
[19] Referred by Walde-Pokorny, *op. cit.*, 1. 804, to **dru-* 'wood'.
[20] Cf. Grassmann, *Wörterbuch zum Rig-Veda,* s.v. *vána* n., 9.
[21] See Wackernagel, *Altindische Grammatik* 2.1: 109, 110.

worked, water-charactered, water-like'. The meaning of the element *-ops-* may have been rather that of 'property' (as in Skt. *ápnas* n., Lat. *ops*, *op-is*): 'water-propertied, having (some) water'.

No doubt other examples of IE **dr-* < **wdr-* 'water' can be found but these will suffice. There is some reason to think that the ablaut-type zero + *e* (**wder-*, **wden-*) might also lose the *w-* if this element was compounded with a following stressed element. Such a **den-* 'water' < **ʷden-* seems to be found in:

(8) Gk. (Epid.) δενδρύω 'to dive' < **ʷden-*.

[At this point Sapir's manuscript ends. Apparently he would have discussed the dissimilative loss of the first *r* in Gk δάκρυ, OHG *zahar*, etc., and a brief note suggests that in his opinion Lat. *lacrima* should be traced to **dlakru-*, no doubt with *l* for *r* by dissimilation

Then would have followed a justification of his derivation of Hitt. 'esḫaḫru (*e-eš-ḫa-aḫ-ru*) from IE **'ésxn̥-xĸ̂ru* 'blood acrid' or rather 'effluvium-acrid.' One sees clearly enough what the general course of the argument would have been; but it seems safer to leave its reconstruction to the reader. E. H. STURTEVANT.]

CULTURE

THE GENERAL VIEW
EDITOR'S PREFACE

T HESE ARE essays as much as they are studies: their concern is with the examination of concepts rather than the exploration of a particular set of data. Their influence has not been negligible, but it has been of a kind which is not easily made plain. They establish a mood of enquiry, a tenor of investigation within which some readers have found uncommon stimulation for their own thinking. Some also have found in them a turn of phrase, a felicitous passage, or novel light on a familiar concept, which sticks in imagination and is recalled from time to time, worked over, and elaborated with specific evidence, so that when it reappears in print the author is only half aware, if at all, of the provenience of his idea.

All but one of these pieces were written as a result of some specific request—to do a chapter for a compendium on the social sciences, to review a book, to give one lecture of a series on contemporary thought, to write up several topics for the Encyclopaedia of the Social Sciences. It was the more detailed and technical problems of linguistics and ethnology which tended to engross Sapir's attention, and hence when he did turn to such wider surveys as these it was usually in response to someone's special bidding.

The one article of the section which was not so done is the first, "Culture, Genuine and Spurious" (1924). At a period—which is by no means entirely over—when anthropologists generally eschewed any value judgments concerning cultures, Sapir ventured to give his idea of "what kind of a good thing culture is." While a good many of his colleagues were still exclusively concerned with primitive folk, Sapir was one of those who foreran the present trend by deploying the anthropologist's knowledge of culture—principally gained, to be sure, from the meticulous study of primitive cultures—toward an understanding of our own times.

If his judgments of American culture may now seem unduly tinged with the disparaging intellectual tone of the years following World War I, his comments on the behavior of nations are all the more telling for being read in the years following World War II. Thus the next paper of the section, "Anthropology and Sociology" (1927), notes that "the ideology which prevents a Haida clan from subordinating its petty pride to the general good of the village is precisely the same as that which to-day prevents a nation from allowing a transnational economic unit, say the silk industry, from functioning smoothly."

Despite its title, this paper is only incidentally concerned with the formal practice of the academic disciplines of anthropology and sociology. Its burden has rather to do with the nature of social organization in human aggregates, with the reciprocal influences of form and function in the groupings of mankind. Some aspects of the sociology of American life, only briefly mentioned in this article, were considered in two papers not included here, "Observations on the Sex Problem in America" (1928) and "What Is the Family Still Good For?" (1930).

Both religion and religions are brought under scrutiny in the next article, "The Meaning of Religion" (1928). It was originally presented as one of a lecture series given at Northwestern University; the series was later published in a set of volumes bearing the general title Man and His World, *edited by Baker Brownell. Sapir's treatment of the subject is of typically broad purview, in which both formal aspects and functional relations are considered. Those who find this essay, and the others of its kind, somewhat lacking in substance, may also discover that it points to, even if it may not thoroughly search through, fresh and important areas of ideas.*

The article entitled "Group" (1932), like the two which follow it in the section, was written for the Encyclopaedia of Social Sciences. *Its subject matter overlaps that of the earlier "Anthropology and Sociology" and reflects the development of Sapir's interests in the fifteen years between the publication of the two. There is, in this later paper, a greater cognizance of the psychological basis of group life, of the relevance of common personal experiences in affecting the shape and character of societal entities.*

"Custom" (1931) deals with the "totality of behavior patterns which are carried by tradition and lodged in the group." The tenure of custom, changes in customs, custom as symbolic affirmation of group loyalty—these considerations lead into an analysis of the relation of custom to law and ethics. Custom controlled by mundane sovereignty is seen as law; custom controlled by socially diffused or supernatural or impersonal sovereignty is seen as ethics.

"Fashion" (1931) discusses that aspect of custom which appears "in the guise of departure from custom." Among the motivations for fashion in our society is the need for self-affirmation because "it is precisely in functionally powerful societies that the individual's ego is constantly being convicted of helplessness." And when Sapir notes that a specific fashion is utterly unintelligible if lifted out of its place in a sequence of forms, he manifests the same holistic approach which characterizes all his work and which finds explicit expression in his linguistic studies in such a paper as "Sound Patterns in Language."

An ethnological analogue to Sapir's concept of linguistic drift is briefly noted in the first of the two excerpts from reviews appended to this section. The second excerpt, from a 1926 review of Lewisohn's Israel, *summarizes Sapir's views of Jewish matters, about which he thought a good deal, especially in his later years. This phase of Sapir's thinking, among others, has been discussed at some length by the editor of this volume in an obituary published in* Jewish Social Studies *(3 [1941]: 131–140). Also pertinent to this subject is a review, in 1925, of Paul Radin's* Monotheism among Primitive Peoples.

Several other book reviews, not included in this section for lack of space, merit special notice. His 1913 appraisal of von Hornbostel's use of acoustical data deals with the nature of apt evidence in historical reconstructions. His comments of 1916 on an article by John Dewey warns against the narrow explanations of human history which periodically come into vogue. "We must beware of being tricked by our inveterately monistic habits of mind." A related problem is treated in a review, in 1920, of Lowie's Primitive Society. *This review summarizes a major theoretical issue which Boas and his students fought through vigorously and won. It was the battle against certain oversimple and all-explaining schemata concerning culture which had gained wide following in various fields. Although Sapir's views diverged from those of Boas in some technical matters, and his spirit of enquiry was, on the whole, more free-ranging than any which Boas permitted himself, Sapir and his colleagues were entirely at one with their teacher on matters concerning the basic postulates and fundamental results of anthropological research.*

CULTURE, GENUINE AND SPURIOUS*

THERE ARE certain terms that have a peculiar property. Ostensibly, they mark off specific concepts, concepts that lay claim to a rigorously objective validity. In practice, they label vague terrains of thought that shift or narrow or widen with the point of view of whoso makes use of them, embracing within their gamut of significances conceptions that not only do not harmonize but are in part contradictory. An analysis of such terms soon discloses the fact that underneath the clash of varying contents there is unifying feeling-tone. What makes it possible for so discordant an array of conceptions to answer to the same call is, indeed, precisely this relatively constant halo that surrounds them. Thus, what is "crime" to one man is "nobility" to another, yet both are agreed that crime, whatever it is, is an undesirable category, that nobility, whatever it is, is an estimable one. In the same way, such a term as art may be made to mean divers things, but whatever it means, the term itself demands respectful attention and calls forth, normally, a pleasantly polished state of mind, an expectation of lofty satisfactions. If the particular conception of art that is advanced or that is implied in a work of art is distasteful to us, we do not express our dissatisfaction by saying, "Then I don't like art." We say this only when we are in a vandalic frame of mind. Ordinarily we get around the difficulty by saying, "But that's not art, it's only pretty-pretty conventionality," or "It's mere sentimentality," or "It's nothing but raw experience, material for art, but not art." We disagree on the value of things and the relations of things, but often enough we agree on the particular value of a label. It is only when the question arises of just where to put the label, that trouble begins. These labels—perhaps we had better call them empty thrones—are enemies of mankind, yet we have no recourse but to make peace with them. We do this by seating our favorite pretenders. The rival pretenders war to the death; the thrones to which they aspire remain serenely splendid in gold.

I desire to advance the claims of a pretender to the throne called "culture." Whatever culture is, we know that it is, or is considered to be, a good thing. I propose to give my idea of what kind of a good thing culture is.

THE VARYING CONCEPTIONS OF CULTURE

The word "culture" seems to be used in three main senses or groups of senses. First of all, culture is technically used by the ethnologist and

* *American Journal of Sociology*, 29 (1924): 401–429; parts of this article were also printed in *The Dalhousie Review*, 2 (1922): 165–178; and in *The Dial*, 67 (1919): 233–236.

culture-historian to embody any socially inherited element in the life of man, material and spiritual. Culture so defined is coterminous with man himself, for even the lowliest savages live in a social world characterized by a complex network of traditionally conserved habits, usages, and attitudes. The South African Bushman's method of hunting game, the belief of the North American Indian in "medicine," the Periclean Athenian's type of tragic drama, and the electric dynamo of modern industrialism are all, equally and indifferently, elements of culture, each being an outgrowth of the collective spiritual effort of man, each being retained for a given time not as the direct and automatic resultant of purely hereditary qualities but by means of the more or less consciously imitative processes summarized by the terms "tradition" and "social inheritance." From this standpoint all human beings or, at any rate, all human groups are cultured, though in vastly different manners and grades of complexity. For the ethnologist there are many types of culture and an infinite variety of elements of culture, but no values, in the ordinary sense of the word, attach to these. His "higher" and "lower," if he uses the terms at all, refer not to a moral scale of values but to stages, real or supposed, in a historic progression or in an evolutionary scheme. I do not intend to use the term "culture" in this technical sense. "Civilization" would be a convenient substitute for it, were it not by common usage limited rather to the more complex and sophisticated forms of the stream of culture. To avoid confusion with other uses of the word "culture," uses which emphatically involve the application of a scale of values, I shall, where necessary, use "civilization" in lieu of the ethnologist's "culture."

The second application of the term is more widely current. It refers to a rather conventional ideal of individual refinement, built up on a certain modicum of assimilated knowledge and experience but made up chiefly of a set of typical reactions that have the sanction of a class and of a tradition of long standing. Sophistication in the realm of intellectual goods is demanded of the applicant to the title of "cultured person," but only up to a certain point. Far more emphasis is placed upon manner, a certain preciousness of conduct which takes different colors according to the nature of the personality that has assimilated the "cultured" ideal. At its worst, the preciousness degenerates into a scornful aloofness from the manners and tastes of the crowd; this is the well-known cultural snobbishness. At its most subtle, it develops into a mild and whimsical vein of cynicism, an amused skepticism that would not for the world find itself betrayed into an unwonted enthusiasm; this type of cultured manner presents a more engaging countenance to the crowd, which only rarely gets hints of the discomfiting play of its irony, but it is an attitude of perhaps even more radical aloofness than snobbishness outright. Aloofness of some kind is generally a *sine qua non* of the second type of culture. Another of its indispensable requisites is intimate contact with the past. Present action and opinion are, first and foremost, seen in the illumination of a fixed past, a past of infinite richness and glory; only as an afterthought, if at all, are such action and opinion construed as instrumentalities for the building of a future. The ghosts of the past, preferably of the remote past, haunt the cultured man at every step. He is uncannily responsive to their slightest touch; he shrinks from the employment of his individuality as a creative agency. But perhaps the most extraordinary thing about the cultured ideal is its selection of the particular treasures of the past which it deems worthiest of worship. This selection, which might seem bizarre to a mere outsider, is generally justified by a number of reasons, sometimes endowed with a philosophic cast, but unsympathetic persons seem to incline to the view that these reasons are only rationalizations *ad hoc*, that the selection of treasures has proceeded chiefly according to the accidents of history.

In brief, this cultured ideal is a vesture and an air. The vesture may drape gracefully about one's person and the air has often much charm, but the vesture is a ready-made garment for all that and the air remains an air. In America the cultured ideal, in its quintessential classical form, is a more exotic plant than in the halls of Oxford and Cambridge, whence it was imported to these rugged shores, but fragments and derivatives of it meet us frequently enough. The cultured ideal embraces many forms, of which the classical Oxonian form is merely one of the most typical. There are also Chinese and talmudic parallels. Wherever we find it, it discloses itself to our eyes in the guise of a spiritual heirloom that must, at all cost, be preserved intact.

The third use made of the term is the least easy to define and to illustrate satisfactorily, perhaps because those who use it are so seldom able to give us a perfectly clear idea of just what they themselves mean by culture. Culture in this third sense shares with our first, technical, conception an emphasis on the spiritual possessions of the group rather than of the individual. With our second conception it shares a stressing of selected factors out of the vast whole of the ethnologist's stream of culture as intrinsically more valuable, more characteristic, more significant in a spiritual sense than the rest. To say that this culture embraces all the psychic, as contrasted with the purely material, elements of civilization would not be accurate, partly because the resulting conception would still harbor a vast number of relatively trivial elements, partly because certain of the material factors might well occupy a decisive place in the cultural ensemble. To limit the term, as is sometimes done, to art, religion, and science has again the disadvantage of a too rigid exclusiveness. We may perhaps come nearest the mark by saying that the cultural conception we are now trying to grasp aims to embrace in a single term those general attitudes, views of life, and specific manifestations of civilization that give a particular people its distinctive place in the world. Emphasis is put not so much on what is done and believed by a people as on how what is done and believed functions in the whole life of that people, on what significance it has for them. The very same element of civilization may be a vital strand in the culture of one people, and a well-nigh negligible factor in the culture of another. The present conception of culture is apt to crop up particularly in connection with problems of nationality, with attempts to find embodied in the character and civilization of a given people some peculiar excellence, some distinguishing force, that is strikingly its own. Culture thus becomes nearly synonymous with the "spirit" or "genius" of a people, yet not altogether, for whereas these loosely used terms refer rather to a psychological, or pseudo-psychological, background of national civilization, culture includes with this background a series of concrete manifestations which are believed to be peculiarly symptomatic of it. Culture, then, may be briefly defined as civilization in so far as it embodies the national genius.

Evidently we are on peculiarly dangerous ground here. The current assumption that the so-called "genius" of a people is ultimately reducible to certain inherent hereditary traits of a biological and psychological nature does not, for the most part, bear very serious examination. Frequently enough what is assumed to be an innate racial characteristic turns out on closer study to be the resultant of purely historical causes. A mode of thinking, a distinctive type of reaction, gets itself established, in the course of a complex historical development, as typical, as normal; it serves then as a model for the working over of new elements of civilization. From numerous examples of such distinctive modes of thinking or types of reaction a basic genius is abstracted. There need be no special quarrel with this conception of a national genius so long as it is not worshiped as an irreducible psychological fetich. Ethnologists fight shy of broad generalizations and hazily defined concepts. They are therefore rather timid about operating with national spirits and geniuses. The chauvinism of national apologists, which sees in the spirits of their own peoples peculiar excellences utterly denied to less blessed denizens of the globe, largely justifies this timidity of the scientific students of civilization. Yet here, as so often, the precise knowledge of the scientist lags somewhat behind the more naïve but more powerful insights of non-professional experience and impression. To deny to the genius of a poeple an ultimate psychological significance and to refer it to the specific historical development of that people is not, after all is said and done, to analyze it out of existence. It remains true that large groups of people everywhere tend to think and to act in accordance with established and all but instinctive forms, which are in large measure peculiar to it. The question as to whether these forms, that in their interrelations constitute the genius of a people, are primarily explainable in terms of native temperament, of historical development, or of both is of interest to the social psychologist, but need not cause us much concern. The relevance of this question is not always apparent. It is enough to know that in actual fact nationalities, using the word without political implication, have come to bear the impress in thought and action of a certain mold and that this mold is more clearly discernible in certain elements of civilization than in others. The specific culture of a nationality is that group of elements in its civilization which most emphatically exhibits the mold. In practice it is sometimes convenient to identify the national culture with its genius.

An example or two and we shall have done with these preliminary definitions. The whole terrain through which we are now struggling is a hotbed of subjectivism, a splendid field for the airing of national conceits. For all that, there are a large number of international agreements in opinion as to the salient cultural characteristics of various peoples. No one who has even superficially concerned himself with French culture can have failed to be impressed by the qualities of clarity, lucid systematization, balance, care in choice of means, and good taste, that permeate so many aspects of the national civilization. These qualities have their weaker side. We are familiar with the overmechanization, the emotional timidity or shallowness (quite a different thing from emotional restraint), the exaggeration of manner at the expense of content, that are revealed in some of the manifestations of the French spirit. Those elements of French civilization that give characteristic evidence of the qualities of its genius may be said, in our present limited sense, to constitute the culture of France; or, to put it somewhat differently, the cultural significance of any element in the civilization of France is in the light it sheds on the French genius. From this standpoint we can evaluate culturally such traits in French civilization as the formalism of the French classical drama, the insistence in French education of the study of the mother-tongue and of its classics, the prevalence of epigram in French life and letters, the intellectualist cast so often given to aesthetic movements in

France, the lack of turgidity in modern French music, the relative absence of the ecstatic note in religion, the strong tendency to bureaucracy in French administration. Each and all of these and hundreds of other traits could be readily paralleled from the civilization of England. Nevertheless, their relative cultural significance, I venture to think, is a lesser one in England than in France. In France they seem to lie more deeply in the grooves of the cultural mold of its civilization. Their study would yield something like a rapid bird's eye view of the spirit of French culture.

Let us turn to Russia, the culture of which has as definite a cast as that of France. I shall mention only one, but that perhaps the most significant, aspect of Russian culture, as I see it—the tendency of the Russian to see and think of human beings not as representatives of types, not as creatures that appear eternally clothed in the garments of civilization, but as stark human beings existing primarily in and for themselves, only secondarily for the sake of civilization. Russian democracy has as its fundamental aim less the creation of democratic institutions than the effective liberation of personality itself. The one thing that the Russian can take seriously is elemental humanity, and elemental humanity, in his view of the world, obtrudes itself at every step. He is therefore sublimely at home with himself and his neighbor and with God. Indeed, I have no doubt that the extremest of Russian atheists is on better speaking terms with God than are the devout of other lands, to whom God is always something of a mystery. For his environment, including in that term all the machinery of civilization, the Russian has generally not a little contempt. The subordination of the deeps of personality to an institution is not readily swallowed by him as a necessary price for the blessings of civilization. We can follow out this sweeping humanity, this almost impertinent prodding of the real self that lies swathed in civilization, in numberless forms. In personal relations we may note the curious readiness of the Russian to ignore all the institutional barriers which separate man from man; on its weaker side, this involves at times a personal irresponsibility that harbors no insincerity. The renunciation of Tolstoi was no isolated phenomenon, it was a symbol of the deep-seated Russian indifference to institutionalism, to the accreted values of civilization. In a spiritual sense, it is easy for the Russian to overthrow any embodiment of the spirit of institutionalism; his real loyalties are elsewhere. The Russian preoccupation with elemental humanity is naturally most in evidence in the realm of art, where self-expression has freest rein. In the pages of Tolstoi, Dostoyevski, Turgenev, Gorki, and Chekhov personality runs riot in its morbid moments of play with crime, in its depressions and apathies, in its generous enthusiasms and idealisms. So many of the

figures in Russian literature look out upon life with a puzzled and in-
credulous gaze. "This thing that you call civilization—is that all there
is to life?" we hear them ask a hundred times. In music too the Russian
spirit delights to unmask itself, to revel in the cries and gestures of man
as man. It speaks to us out of the rugged accents of a Moussorgski as
out of the well-nigh unendurable despair of a Tchaikovski. It is hard to
think of the main current of Russian art as anywhere infected by the dry
rot of formalism; we expect some human flash or cry to escape from behind the bars.

I have avoided all attempt to construct a parallel between the spirit of
French civilization and that of Russian civilization, between the culture
of France and the culture of Russia. Strict parallels force an emphasis on
contrasts. I have been content merely to suggest that underlying the
elements of civilization, the study of which is the province of the ethnologist and culture-historian, is a culture, the adequate interpretation of which
is beset with difficulties and which is often left to men of letters.

THE GENUINE CULTURE

The second and third conceptions of the term "culture" are what I
wish to make the basis of our genuine culture—the pretender to the
throne whose claims to recognition we are to consider. We may accept
culture as signifying the characteristic mold of a national civilization,
while from the second conception of culture, that of a traditional type
of individual refinement, we will borrow the notion of ideal form. Let
me say at once that nothing is farther from my mind than to plead the
cause of any specific type of culture. It would be idle to praise or blame
any fundamental condition of our civilization, to praise or blame any
strand in the warp and woof of its genius. These conditions and these
strands must be accepted as basic. They are slowly modifiable, to be
sure, like everything else in the history of man, but radical modification
of fundamentals does not seem necessary for the production of a genuine
culture, however much a readjustment of the relations may be. In other
words, a genuine culture is perfectly conceivable in any type or stage of
civilization, in the mold of any national genius. It can be conceived as
easily in terms of a Mohammedan polygamous society, or of an American
Indian "primitive" non-agricultural society, as in those of our familiar
occidental societies. On the other hand, what may by contrast be called
"spurious" cultures are just as easily conceivable in conditions of general
enlightenment as in those of relative ignorance and squalor.

The genuine culture is not of necessity either high or low; it is merely
inherently harmonious, balanced, self-satisfactory. It is the expression of

a richly varied and yet somehow unified and consistent attitude toward life, an attitude which sees the significance of any one element of civilization in its relation to all others. It is, ideally speaking, a culture in which nothing is spiritually meaningless, in which no important part of the general functioning brings with it a sense of frustration, of misdirected or unsympathetic effort. It is not a spiritual hybrid of contradictory patches, of water-tight compartments of consciousness that avoid participation in a harmonious synthesis. If the culture necessitates slavery, it frankly admits it; if it abhors slavery, it feels its way to an economic adjustment that obviates the necessity of its employment. It does not make a great show in its ethical ideals of an uncompromising opposition to slavery, only to introduce what amounts to a slave system into certain portions of its industrial mechanism. Or, if it builds itself magnificent houses of worship, it is because of the necessity it feels to symbolize in beautiful stone a religious impulse that is deep and vital; if it is ready to discard institutionalized religion, it is prepared also to dispense with the homes of institutionalized religion. It does not look sheepish when a direct appeal is made to its religious consciousness, then make amends by furtively donating a few dollars toward the maintenance of an African mission. Nor does it carefully instruct its children in what it knows to be of no use or vitality either to them or in its own mature life. Nor does it tolerate a thousand other spiritual maladjustments such as are patent enough in our American life of today. It would be too much to say that even the purest examples yet known of a genuine culture have been free of spiritual discords, of the dry rot of social habit, devitalized. But the great cultures, those that we instinctively feel to have been healthy spiritual organisms, such as the Athenian culture of the Age of Pericles and, to a less extent perhaps, the English culture of Elizabethan days, have at least tended to such harmony.

It should be clearly understood that this ideal of a genuine culture has no necessary connection with what we call efficiency. A society may be admirably efficient in the sense that all its activities are carefully planned with reference to ends of maximum utility to the society as a whole, it may tolerate no lost motion, yet it may well be an inferior organism as a culture-bearer. It is not enough that the ends of activities be socially satisfactory, that each member of the community feel is some dim way that he is doing his bit toward the attainment of a social benefit. This is all very well so far as it goes, but a genuine culture refuses to consider the individual as a mere cog, as an entity whose sole *raison d'être* lies in his subservience to a collective purpose that he is not conscious of or that has only a remote relevancy to his interests and strivings.

The major activities of the individual must directly satisfy his own creative and emotional impulses, must always be something more than means to an end. The great cultural fallacy of industrialism, as developed up to the present time, is that in harnessing machines to our uses it has not known how to avoid the harnessing of the majority of mankind to its machines. The telephone girl who lends her capacities, during the greater part of the living day, to the manipulation of a technical routine that has an eventually high efficiency value but that answers to no spiritual needs of her own is an appalling sacrifice to civilization. As a solution of the problem of culture she is a failure—the more dismal the greater her natural endowment. As with the telephone girl, so, it is to be feared, with the great majority of us, slave-stokers to fires that burn for demons we would destroy, were it not that they appear in the guise of our benefactors. The American Indian who solves the economic problem with salmon-spear and rabbit-snare operates on a relatively low level of civilization, but he represents an incomparably higher solution than our telephone girl of the questions that culture has to ask of economics. There is here no question of the immediate utility, of the effective directness, of economic effort, nor of any sentimentalizing regrets as to the passing of the "natural man." The Indian's salmon-spearing is a culturally higher type of activity than that of the telephone girl or mill hand simply because there is normally no sense of spiritual frustration during its prosecution, no feeling of subservience to tyrannous yet largely inchoate demands, because it works in naturally with all the rest of the Indian's activities instead of standing out as a desert patch of merely economic effort in the whole of life. A genuine culture cannot be defined as a sum of abstractly desirable ends, as a mechanism. It must be looked upon as a sturdy plant growth, each remotest leaf and twig of which is organically fed by the sap at the core. And this growth is not here meant as a metaphor for the group only; it is meant to apply as well to the individual. A culture that does not build itself out of the central interests and desires of its bearers, that works from general ends to the individual, is an external culture. The word "external," which is so often instinctively chosen to describe such a culture, is well chosen. The genuine culture is internal, it works from the individual to ends.

We have already seen that there is no necessary correlation between the development of civilization and the relative genuineness of the culture which forms its spiritual essence. This requires a word of further explanation. By the development of civilization is meant the ever increasing degree of sophistication of our society and of our individual lives. This progressive sophistication is the inevitable cumulative result of the sifting processes of social experience, of the ever increasing complications of our innumerable types of organization; most of all of our steadily growing knowledge of our natural environment and, as a consequence, our practical mastery, for economic ends, of the resources that nature at once grants us and hides from us. It is chiefly the cumulative force of this sophistication that gives us the sense of what we call "progress." Perched on the heights of an office building twenty or more stories taller than our fathers ever dreamed of, we feel that we are getting up in the world. Hurling our bodies through space with an ever accelerating velocity, we feel that we are getting on. Under sophistication I include not merely intellectual and technical advance, but most of the tendencies that make for a cleaner and healthier and, to a large extent, a more humanitarian existence. It is excellent to keep one's hands spotlessly clean, to eliminate smallpox, to administer anesthetics. Our growing sophistication, our ever increasing solicitude to obey the dictates of common sense, make these tendencies imperative. It would be sheer obscurantism to wish to stay their progress. But there can be no stranger illusion—and it is an illusion we nearly all share—than this, that because the tools of life are today more specialized and more refined than ever before, that because the technique brought by science is more perfect than anything the world has yet known, it necessarily follows that we are in like degree attaining to a profounder harmony of life, to a deeper and more satisfying culture. It is as though we believed that an elaborate mathematical computation which involved figures of seven and eight digits could not but result in a like figure. Yet we know that one million multiplied by zero gives us zero quite as effectively as one multiplied by zero. The truth is that sophistication, which is what we ordinarily mean by the progress of civilization, is, in the long run, a merely quantitative concept that defines the external conditions for the growth or decay of culture. We are right to have faith in the progress of civilization. We are wrong to assume that the maintenance or even advance of culture is a function of such progress. A reading of the facts of ethnology and culture history proves plainly that maxima of culture have frequently been reached in low levels of sophistication; that minima of culture have been plumbed in some of the highest. Civilization, as a whole, moves on; culture comes and goes.

Every profound change in the flow of civilization, particularly every change in its economic bases, tends to bring about an unsettling and readjustment of culture values. Old culture forms, habitual types of reaction, tend to persist through the force of inertia. The maladjustment of these habitual reactions to their new civilizational environment brings with it a measure of spiritual disharmony, which the more sensitive individuals feel eventually as a fundamental lack of culture. Sometimes the maladjustment corrects itself with great rapidity, at other times it may persist for generations, as in the case of America, where a chronic state of cultural maladjustment has for so long a period reduced much of our higher life to sterile externality. It is easier, generally speaking, for a genuine culture to subsist on a lower level of civilization; the differentiation of individuals as regards their social and economic functions is so much less than in the higher levels that there is less danger of the reduction of the individual to an unintelligible fragment of the social organism. How to reap the undeniable benefits of a great differentiation of functions, without at the same time losing sight of the individual as a nucleus of live cultural values, is the great and difficult problem of any rapidly complicating civilization. We are far from having solved it in America. Indeed, it may be doubted whether more than an insignificant minority are aware of the existence of the problem. Yet the present world wide labor unrest has as one of its deepest roots some sort of perception of the cultural fallacy of the present form of industrialism.

It is perhaps the sensitive ethnologist who has studied an aboriginal civilization at first hand who is most impressed by the frequent vitality of culture in less sophisticated levels. He cannot but admire the well-rounded life of the average participant in the civilization of a typical American Indian tribe; the firmness with which every part of that life—economic, social, religious, and aesthetic—is bound together into a significant whole in respect to which he is far from a passive pawn; above all, the molding rôle, oftentimes definitely creative, that he plays in the mechanism of his culture. When the political integrity of his tribe is destroyed by contact with the whites and the old cultural values cease to have the atmosphere needed for their continued vitality, the Indian finds himself in a state of bewildered vacuity. Even if he succeeds in making a fairly satisfactory compromise with his new environment, in making what his well-wishers consider great progress toward enlightenment, he is apt to retain an uneasy sense of the loss of some vague and great good, some state of mind that he would be hard put to it to define, but which gave him a courage and joy that latter-day prosperity never quite seems to have regained for him. What has happened is that he has slipped out of the warm embrace of a culture into the cold air of fragmentary existence. What is sad about the passing of the Indian is not the depletion of his numbers by disease nor even the contempt that is too often meted out to him in his life on the reservation, it is the fading away of genuine cultures, built though they were out of the materials of a low order of sophistication.

We have no right to demand of the higher levels of sophistication that they preserve to the individual his manifold functioning, but we may well ask whether, as a compensation, the individual may not reasonably demand an intensification in cultural value, a spiritual heightening, of such functions as are left him. Failing this, he must be admitted to have retrograded. The limitation in functioning works chiefly in the economic sphere. It is therefore imperative, if the individual is to preserve his value as a cultured being, that he compensate himself out of the non-economic, the non-utilitarian spheres—social, religious, scientific, aesthetic. This idea of compensation brings to view an important issue, that of the immediate and the remoter ends of human effort.

As a mere organism, man's only function is to exist; in other words, to keep himself alive and to propagate his kind. Hence the procuring of food, clothing, and shelter for himself and those dependent on him constitutes the immediate end of his effort. There are civilizations, like that of the Eskimo, in which by far the greater part of man's energy is consumed in the satisfaction of these immediate ends, in which most of his activities contribute directly or indirectly to the procuring and preparation of food and the materials for clothing and shelter. There are practically no civilizations, however, in which at least some of the available energy is not set free for the remoter ends, though, as a rule, these remoter ends are by a process of rationalization made to seem to contribute to the immediate ones. (A magical ritual, for instance, which, when considered psychologically, seems to liberate and give form to powerful emotional aesthetic elements of our nature, is nearly always put in harness to some humdrum utilitarian end—the catching of rabbits or the curing of disease.) As a matter of fact, there are very few "primitive" civilizations that do not consume an exceedingly large share of their energies in the pursuit of the remoter ends, though it remains true that these remoter ends are nearly always functionally or pseudo-functionally interwoven with the immediate ends. Art for art's sake may be a psychological fact on these less sophisticated levels; it is certainly not a cultural fact.

On our own level of civilization the remoter ends tend to split off altogether from the immediate ones and to assume the form of a spiritual escape or refuge from the pursuit of the latter. The separation of the two classes of ends is never absolute nor can it ever be; it is enough to note the presence of a powerful drift of the two away from each other. It is easy to demonstrate this drift by examples taken out of our daily experience. While in most primitive civilizations the dance is apt to be a ritual activity at least ostensibly associated with purposes of an economic nature, it is with us a merely and self-consciously pleasurable activity that not only splits off from the sphere of the pursuit of immediate ends but even tends to assume a position of hostility to that sphere. In a primitive civilization a great chief dances as a matter of course, oftentimes as a matter of exercising a peculiarly honored privilege. With us the captain of industry either refuses to dance at all or does so as a half-contemptuous concession to the tyranny of social custom. On the other hand, the artist of a Ballet Russe has sublimated the dance to an exquisite instrument of self-expression, has succeeded in providing himself with an adequate, or more than adequate, cultural recompense for his loss of mastery in the realm of direct ends. The captain of industry is one of the comparatively small class of individuals that has inherited, in vastly complicated form, something of the feeling of control over the attainment of direct ends that belongs by cultural right to primitive man; the ballet dancer has saved and intensified for himself the feeling of spontaneous participation and creativeness in the world of indirect ends that also belongs by cultural right to primitive man. Each has saved part of the wreckage of a submerged culture for himself.

The psychology of direct and indirect ends undergoes a gradual modification, only partly consummated as yet, in the higher levels of civilization. The immediate ends continue to exercise the same tyrannical sway in the ordering of our lives, but as our spiritual selves become enriched and develop a more and more inordinate craving for subtler forms of experience, there develops also an attitude of impatience with the solution of the more immediate problems of life. In other words, the immediate ends cease to be felt as chief ends and gradually become necessary means, but only means, toward the attainment of the more remote ends. These remoter ends, in turn, so far from being looked upon as purely incidental activities which result from the spilling over of an energy concentrated almost entirely on the pursuit of the immediate ends, become the chief ends of life. This change of attitude is implied in the statement that the art, science, and religion of a higher civilization best express its spirit or culture. The transformation of ends thus briefly outlined is far from an accomplished fact; it is rather an obscure drift in the history of values, an expression of the volition of the more sensitive participants in our culture. Certain temperaments feel themselves impelled far along the drift, others lag behind.

The transformation of ends is of the greatest cultural importance because it acts as a powerful force for the preservation of culture in levels in which a fragmentary economic functioning of the individual is inevitable. So long as the individual retains a sense of control over the major goods of life, he is able to take his place in the cultural patrimony of his people. Now that the major goods of life have shifted so largely from the realm of immediate to that of remote ends, it becomes a cultural necessity for all who would not be looked upon as disinherited to share in the pursuit of these remoter ends. No harmony and depth of life, no culture, is possible when activity is well-nigh circumscribed by the sphere of immediate ends and when functioning within that sphere is so fragmentary as to have no inherent intelligibility or interest. Here lies the grimmest joke of our present American civilization. The vast majority of us, deprived of any but an insignificant and culturally abortive share in the satisfaction of the immediate wants of mankind, are further deprived of both opportunity and stimulation to share in the production of non-utilitarian values. Part of the time we are dray horses; the rest of the time we are listless consumers of goods which have received no least impress of our personality. In other words, our spiritual selves go hungry, for the most part, pretty much all of the time.

THE CULTURED INDIVIDUAL AND THE CULTURAL GROUP

There is no real opposition, at last analysis, between the concept of a culture of the group and the concept of an individual culture. The two are interdependent. A healthy national culture is never a passively accepted heritage from the past, but implies the creative participation of the members of the community; implies, in other words, the presence of cultured individuals. An automatic perpetuation of standardized values, not subject to the constant remodeling of individuals willing to put some part of themselves into the forms they receive from their predecessors, leads to the dominance of impersonal formulas. The individual is left out in the cold; the culture becomes a manner rather than a way of life, it ceases to be genuine. It is just as true, however, that the individual is helpless without a cultural heritage to work on. He cannot, out of his unaided spiritual powers, weave a strong cultural fabric instinct with the flush of his own personality. Creation is a bending of form to one's will, not a manufacture of form *ex nihilo*. If the passive perpetuator of a cultural tradition gives us merely a manner, the shell of a life that once was, the creator from out of a cultural waste gives us hardly more than a gesture or a yawp, the strident promise of a vision raised by our desires.

There is a curious notion afloat that "new" countries are especially favorable soil for the formation of a virile culture. By new is meant something old that has been transplanted to a background devoid of historical associations. It would be remarkable if a plant, flourishing in heavy black loam, suddenly acquired a new virility on transplantation into a shallow sandy soil. Metaphors are dangerous things that prove nothing, but experience suggests the soundness of this particular metaphor. Indeed, there is nothing more tenuous, more shamelessly imitative and external, less virile and self-joyous, then the cultures of so-called "new countries." The environments of these transplanted cultures are new, the cultures themselves are old with the sickly age of arrested development. If signs of a genuine blossoming of culture are belatedly beginning to appear in America, it is not because America is still new; rather is America coming of age, beginning to feel a little old. In a genuinely new country, the preoccupation with the immediate ends of existence reduces creativeness in the sphere of the more remote ends to a minimum. The net result is a perceptible dwarfing of culture. The old stock of non-material cultural goods lingers on without being subjected to vital remodelings, becomes progressively impoverished, and ends by being so hopelessly ill adjusted to the economic and social environment that the more sensitive spirits tend to break with it altogether and to begin anew with a frank recognition of the new environmental conditions. Such new starts are invariably crude; they are long in bearing the fruits of a genuine culture.

It is only an apparent paradox that the subtlest and the most decisive cultural influences of personality, the most fruitful revolts, are discernible in those environments that have long and uninterruptedly supported a richly streaming culture. So far from being suffocated in an atmosphere of endless precedent, the creative spirit gains sustenance and vigor for its own unfolding and, if it is strong enough, it may swing free of that very atmosphere with a poise hardly dreamed of by the timid iconoclasts of unformed cultures. Not otherwise could we understand the cultural history of modern Europe. Only in a mature and richly differentiated soil could arise the iconoclasms and visions of an Anatole France, a Nietzsche, an Ibsen, a Tolstoi. In America, at least in the America of yesterday, these iconoclasms and these visions would either have been strangled in the cradle, or, had they found air to breathe, they would have half-developed into a crude and pathetic isolation. There is no sound and vigorous individual incorporation of a cultured ideal without the soil of a genuine communal culture; and no genuine communal culture without the transforming energies of personalities at once robust and saturated with the cultural values of their time and place. The highest type of culture is thus locked in the embrace of an endless chain, to the forging of which goes much labor, weary and protracted. Such a culture avoids the two extremes of "externality"—the externality of surfeit, which weighs down the individual, and the externality of barrenness. The former is the decay of Alexandrianism, in which the individual is no more; the latter, the combined immaturity and decay of an uprooted culture, in which the individual is not yet. Both types of externality may be combined in the same culture, frequently in the same person. Thus, it is not uncommon to find in America individuals who have had engrafted on a barren and purely utilitarian culture a cultural tradition that apes a grace already embalmed. One surmises that this juxtaposition of incongruous atmospheres is even typical in certain circles.

Let us look a little more closely at the place of the individual in a modern sophisticated culture. I have insisted throughout that a genuine culture is one that gives its bearers a sense of inner satisfaction, a feeling of spiritual mastery. In the higher levels of civilization this sense of mastery is all but withdrawn, as we have seen, from the economic sphere. It must, then, to an even greater extent than in more primitive civilizations, feed on the non-economic spheres of human activity. The individual is thus driven, or should be if he would be truly cultured, to the identification of himself with some portion of the wide range of non-economic interests. From the standpoint adopted in this study, this does not mean that the identification is a purely casual and acquisitive process; it is, indeed, made not so much for its own sake as in order to give the self the wherewithal to develop its powers. Concretely considered, this would mean, for instance, that a mediocre person moderately gifted with the ability to express his aesthetic instincts in plastic form and exercising the gift in his own sincere and humble way (to the neglect, it may be, of practically all other interests) is *ipso facto* a more cultured individual than a person of brilliant endowments who has acquainted himself in a general way with all the "best" that has been thought and felt and done, but who has never succeeded in bringing any portion of his range of interests into direct relation with his volitional self, with the innermost shrine of his personality. An individual of the latter type, for all his brilliance, we call "flat." A flat person cannot be truly cultured. He may, of course, be highly cultured in the conventional sense of the word "culture," but that is another story. I would not be understood as claiming that direct creativeness is essential, though it is highly desirable, for the development of individual culture. To a large extent it is possible to gain a sense of the required mastery by linking one's own personality with that of the great minds and hearts that society has recognized as its significant creators. Possible, that is, so long as such linking, such vicarious experience, is attended by some portion of the effort, the fluttering toward realization that is inseparable from all creative effort. It is to be feared, however, that the self-discipline that is here implied is none too often practiced. The linking, as I have called it, of self with master soul too often degenerates into a pleasurable servitude, into a facile abnegation of one's own individuality, the more insidious that it has the approval of current judgment. The pleasurable servitude may degenerate still further into a vice. Those of us who are not altogether blind can see in certain of our acquaintances, if not in ourselves, an indulgence in aesthetic or scientific goods that is strictly comparable to the abuse of alcoholic intoxicants. Both types of self-ignoring or self-submerging habit are signs of a debilitated personality; both are antithetical to the formation of culture.

The individual self, then, in aspiring to culture, fastens upon the accumulated cultural goods of its society, not so much for the sake of the passive pleasure of their acquirement, as for the sake of the stimulus given to the unfolding personality and of the orientation derived in the world (or better, a world) of cultural values. The orientation, conventional as it may be, is necessary if only to give the self a *modus vivendi* with society at large. The individual needs to assimilate much of the cultural background of his society, many of the current sentiments of his people, to prevent his self-expression from degenerating into social sterility. A spiritual hermit may be genuinely cultured, but he is hardly socially so. To say that individual culture must needs grow organically out of the rich soil of a communal culture is far from saying that it must be forever tied to that culture by the leading strings of its own childhood. Once the individual self has grown strong enough to travel in the path most clearly illuminated by its own light, it not only can but should discard much of the scaffolding by which it has made its ascent. Nothing is more pathetic than the persistence with which well-meaning applicants to culture attempt to keep up or revive cultural stimuli which have long outlived their significance for the growth of personality. To keep up or brush up one's Greek, for example, in those numerous cases in which a knowledge of Greek has ceased to bear a genuine relation to the needs of the spirit, is almost a spiritual crime. It is acting "the dog in the manger" with one's own soul. If the traveling in the path of the self's illumination leads to a position that is destructive of the very values the self was fed on, as happened, though in very different ways, with Nietzsche and with Tolstoi, it has not in the slightest lost touch with genuine culture. It may well, on the contrary, have arrived at its own highest possible point of culture development.

Nietzsche and Tolstoi, however, are extreme types of personality. There is no danger that the vast army of cultured humanity will ever come to occupy spiritual positions of such rigor and originality. The real danger, as is so abundantly attested by daily experience, is in submitting to the remorselessly leveling forces of a common cultural heritage and of the action of average mind on average mind. These forces will always tend to a general standardization of both the content and the spirit of culture, so powerfully, indeed, that the centrifugal effect of robust, self-sustaining personalities need not be feared. The caution to conformity with tradition, which the champions of culture so often feel themselves called upon to announce, is one that we can generally dispense with. It is rather the opposite caution, the caution to conformity with the essential nature of one's own personality, that needs urging. It needs to be urged as a possible counter-irritant to the flat and tedious sameness of spiritual outlook, the anemic make-believe, the smug intolerance of the challenging, that so imprison our American souls.

No greater test of the genuineness of both individual and communal culture can be applied than the attitude adopted toward the past, its institutions, its treasures of art and thought. The genuinely cultured individual or society does not contemptuously reject the past. They honor the works of the past, but not because they are gems of historical chance, not because, being out of our reach, they must needs be looked at through the enshrining glass of museum cases. These works of the past still excite our heartfelt interest and sympathy because, and only in so far as, they may be recognized as the expression of a human spirit warmly akin, despite all differences of outward garb, to our own. This is very nearly equivalent to saying that the past is of cultural interest only when it is still the present or may yet become the future. Paradoxical as it may seem, the historical spirit has always been something of an anticultural force, has always acted in some measure as an unwitting deterrent of the cultural utilization of the past. The historical spirit says, "Beware, those thoughts and those feelings that you so rashly think to embody in the warp and woof of your own spirit—they are of other time and of other place and they issue from alien motives. In bending over them you do but obscure them with the shadow of your own spirit." This cool reserve is an excellent mood for the making of historical science; its usefulness to the building of culture in the present is doubtful. We know immensely more about Hellenic antiquity in these days than did the scholars and artists of the Renaissance; it would be folly to pretend that our live utilization of the Hellenic spirit, accurately as we merely know it, is comparable to the inspiration, the creative stimulus, that those men of the Renaissance obtained from its fragmentary and garbled tradition. It is difficult to think of a renaissance of that type as thriving in the critical atmosphere of today. We should walk so gingerly in the paths of the past for fear of stepping on anachronisms, that, wearied with fatigue, we should finally sink into a heavy doze, to be awakened only by the insistent clatter of the present. It may be that in our present state of sophistication such a spirit of criticism, of detachment, is not only unavoidable but essential for the preservation of our own individualities. The past is now more of a past than ever before. Perhaps we should expect less of it than ever before. Or rather expect no more of it than it hold its portals wide open, that we may enter in and despoil it of what bits we choose for our pretty mosaics. Can it be that the critical sense of history, which galvanizes the past into scientific life, is destined to slay it for the life of culture? More probably, what is happening is that the spiritual currents of today are running so fast, so turbulently, that we find it difficult to get a culturally vital perspective of the past, which is thus, for the time being, left as a glorified mummy in the hands of the pundits. And, for the time being, those others of us who take their culture neither as knowledge nor as manner, but as life, will ask of the past not so much "what?" and "when?" and "where?" as "how?" and the accent of their "how" will be modulated in accordance with the needs of the spirit of each, a spirit that is free to glorify, to transform, and to reject.

To summarize the place of the individual in our theory of culture, we may say that the pursuit of genuine culture implies two types of reconciliation. The self seeks instinctively for mastery. In the process of acquiring a sense of mastery that is not crude but proportioned to the degree of sophistication proper to our time, the self is compelled to suffer an abridgment and to undergo a molding. The extreme differentiation of function which the progress of man has forced upon the individual menaces the spirit; we have no recourse but to submit with good grace to this abridgment of our activity, but it must not be allowed to clip the wings of the spirit unduly. This is the first and most important reconciliation—the finding of a full world of spiritual satisfactions within the straight limits of an unwontedly confined economic activity. The self must set itself at a point where it can, if not embrace the whole spiritual life of its group, at least catch enough of its rays to burst into light and flame. Moreover, the self must learn to reconcile its own strivings, its own imperious necessities, with the general spiritual life of the community. It must be content to borrow sustenance from the spiritual consciousness of that community and of its past, not merely that it may obtain the wherewithal to grow at all, but that it may grow where its power, great or little, will be brought to bear on a spiritual life that is of intimate concern to other wills. Yet, despite all reconciliations, the self has a right to feel that it grows as an integral, self-poised, spiritual growth, whose ultimate justifications rest in itself, whose sacrifices and compensations must be justified to itself. The conception of the self as a mere instrument toward the attainment of communal ends, whether of state or other social body, is to be discarded as leading in the long run to psychological absurdities and to spiritual slavery. It is the self that concedes, if there is to be any concession. Spiritual freedom, what there is of it, is not alms dispensed, now indifferently, now grudgingly, by the social body. That a different philosophy of the relation of the individual to his group is now so prevalent, makes it all the more necessary to insist on the spiritual primacy of the individual soul.

It is a noteworthy fact that wherever there is discussion of culture, emphasis is instinctively placed upon art. This applies as well to individual as to communal culture. We apply the term "cultured" only with reserve to an individual in whose life the aesthetic moment plays no part. So also, if we would catch something of the spirit, the genius, of a bygone period or of an exotic civilization, we turn first and foremost to its art. A thoughtless analysis would see in this nothing but the emphasis on the beautiful, the decorative, that comports with the conventional conception of culture as a life of traditionally molded refinement. A more penetrating analysis discards such an interpretation. For it the highest manifestations of culture, the very quintessence of the genius of a civilization, necessarily rest in art, for the reason that art is the authentic expression, in satisfying form, of experience; experience not as logically ordered by science, but as directly and intuitively presented to us in life. As culture rests, in essence, on the harmonious development of the sense of mastery instinctively sought by each individual soul, this can only mean that art, the form of consciousness in which the impress of the self is most direct, least hampered by outward necessity, is above all other undertakings of the human spirit bound to reflect culture. To relate *our* lives, *our* intuitions, *our* passing moods to forms of expression that carry conviction to others and make us live again in these others is the highest spiritual satisfaction we know of, the highest welding of one's individuality with the spirit of his civilization. Were art ever really perfect in expression, it would indeed be immortal. Even the greatest art, however, is full of the dross of conventionality, of the particular sophistications of its age. As these change, the directness of expression in any work of art tends to be increasingly felt as hampered by a something fixed and alien, until it gradually falls into oblivion. While art lives, it belongs to culture; in the degree that it takes on the frigidity of death, it becomes of interest only to the study of civilization. Thus all art appreciation (and production, for that matter) has two faces. It is unfortunate that the face directed to civilization is so often confounded with that which is fixed on culture.

The Geography of Culture

An oft-noted peculiarity of the development of culture is the fact that it reaches its greatest heights in comparatively small, autonomous groups. In fact, it is doubtful if a genuine culture ever properly belongs to more than such a restricted group, a group between the members of which there can be said to be something like direct intensive spiritual contact. This direct contact is enriched by the common cultural heritage on which the minds of all are fed; it is rendered swift and pregnant by the thousands of feelings and ideas that are tacitly assumed and that constantly glimmer in the background. Such small, culturally autonomous groups were the Athens of the Periclean Age, the Rome of Augustus, the independent city-states of Italy in late medieval times, the London of Elizabethan days, and the Paris of the last three centuries. It is customary to speak of certain of these groups and of their cultures as though they were identical with, or represented, widely extended groups and cultures. To a curiously large extent such usages are really figures of speech, substitutions of a part for the whole. It is astonishing, for instance, how much the so-called "history of French literature" is really the history of literary activity in the city of Paris. True enough, a narrowly localized culture may, and often does, spread its influence far beyond its properly restricted sphere. Sometimes it sets the pace for a whole nationality, for a far-flung empire. It can do so, however, only at the expense of diluting in spirit as it moves away from its home, of degenerating into an imitative attitudinizing. If we realized more keenly what the rapid spread or imposition of a culture entails, to what an extent it conquers by crushing the germs of healthier autonomous growths, we would be less eager to welcome uniformizing tendencies, less ready to think of them as progressive in character. A culture may well be quickened from without, but its supersession by another, whether superior or not, is no cultural gain. Whether or not it is attended by a political gain does not concern us here. That is why the deliberate attempt to impose a culture directly and speedily, no matter how backed by good will, is an affront to the human spirit. When such an attempt is backed, not by good will, but by military ruthlessness, it is the greatest conceivable crime against the human spirit, it is the very denial of culture.

Does this mean that we must turn our back on all internationalistic tendencies and vegetate forever in our nationalisms? Here we are confronted by the prevalent fallacy that internationalism is in spirit opposed to the intensive development of autonomous cultures. The fallacy proceeds from a failure to realize that internationalism, nationalism, and localism are forms that can be given various contents. We cannot intelligently discuss internationalism before we know what it is that we are to be internationalistic about. Unfortunately we are so obsessed by the idea of subordinating all forms of human association to the state and of regarding the range of all types of activity as contermiminous with political boundaries, that it is difficult for us to reconcile the idea of a local or restrictedly national autonomy of culture with a purely political state-sovereignty and with an economic-political international-ism.

No one can see clearly what is destined to be the larger outcome of the present world conflicts. They may exacerbate rather than allay national-political animosities and thus tend to strengthen the prestige of the state. But this deplorable result cannot well be other than a passing phase. Even now it is evident that the war has, in more ways than one, paved the way for an economic and, as a corollary, a semi-political internationalism. All those spheres of activity that relate to the satisfaction of immediate ends, which, from the vantage point that we have gained, are nothing but means, will tend to become international functions. However the internationalizing processes will shape themselves in detail, they will at bottom be but the reflection of that growing impatience of the human spirit with the preoccupation with direct ends, which I spoke of before. Such transnational problems as the distribution of economic goods, the transportation of commodities, the control of highways, the coinage, and numerous others, must eventually pass into the hands of international organizations for the simple reason that men will not eternally give their loyalty to the uselessly national administration of functions that are of inherently international scope. As this international scope gets to be thoroughly realized, our present infatuations with national prestige in the ecnomic sphere will show themselves for the spiritual imbecilities that they are.

All this has much to do with the eventual development of culture. As long as culture is looked upon as a decorative appanage of large political units, one can plausibly argue that its preservation is bound up with the maintenance of the prestige of these units. But genuine culture is inconceivable except on the basis of a highly individual spiritual consciousness, it rarely remains healthy and subtle when spread thin over an interminable area, and in its higher reaches it is in no mood to submit to economic and political bonds. Now a generalized international culture is hardly thinkable. The national-political unit tends to arrogate culture to itself and up to a certain point it succeeds in doing so, but only at the price of serious cultural impoverishment of vast portions of its terrain. If the economic and political integrity of these large state-controlled units becomes gradually undermined by the growth of international functions, their cultural *raison d'être* must also tend to weaken. Culture must then tend with ever increasing intensity to cling to relatively small social and to minor political units, units that are not too large to incorporate the individuality that is to culture as the very breath of life. Between these two processes, the integration of economic and political forces into a world sovereignty and the disintegration of our present unwieldy culture units into small units whose life is truly virile and individual, the fetich of the present state, with its uncontrolled sovereignty, may in the dim future be trusted to melt away. The political state of today has long been on trial and has been found wanting. Our national-political units are too small for peace, to large for safety. They are too small for the intelligent solution of the large problems in the sphere of direct ends; they are too large for the fruitful enrichment of the remoter ends, for culture.

It is in the New World, perhaps more than in any other part of the globe, that the unsatisfactory nature of a geographically widespread culture, of little depth or individuality to begin with, is manifest. To find substantially the same cultural manifestions, material and spiritual, often indeed to the minutest details, in New York and Chicago and San Francisco is saddening. It argues a shallowness in the culture itself and a readiness to imitation in its bearers that is not reassuring. Even if no definite way out of the flat cultural morass is clearly discernible for the present, there is no good in basking forever in self-sufficiency. It can only be of benefit to search out the depths of our hearts and to find wherein they are wanting. If we exaggerate our weakness, it does not matter; better chastening than self-glorification. We have been in the habit of giving ourselves credit for essentially quantitative results that are due rather to an unusually favoring nature and to a favoring set of economic conditions than to anything in ourselves. Our victories have been brilliant, but they have also too often been barren for culture. The habit of playing with loaded dice has given us a dangerous attitude of passivity—dangerous, that is, for culture. Stretching back opulently in our easy chairs, we expect great cultural things to happen to us. We have wound up the machinery, and admirable machinery it is; it is "up to " culture to come forth, in heavy panoply. The minute increment of individuality which alone makes culture in the self and eventually builds up a culture in the community seems somehow overlooked. Canned culture is so much easier to administer.

Just now we are expecting a great deal from the European war. No doubt the war and its aftermath will shake us out of some part of our smugness and let in a few invigorating air currents of cultural influence, but, if we are not careful, these influences may soon harden into new standardizations or become diluted into another stock of imitative attitudes and reactions. The war and its aftermath cannot be a sufficient cultural cause, they are at best but another set of favoring conditions. We need not be too much astonished if a Periclean culture does not somehow automatically burst into bloom. Sooner or later we shall have to get down to the humble task of exploring the depths of our consciousness and dragging to the light what sincere bits of reflected experience we can find. These bits will not always be beautiful, they will not always be pleasing, but they will be genuine. And then we can build. In time, in plenty of time—for we must have patience—a genuine culture—better yet, a series of linked autonomous cultures—will grace our lives. And New York and Chicago and San Francisco will live each in its own cultural strength, not squinting from one to another to see which gets ahead in a race for external values, but each serenely oblivious of its rivals because growing in a soil of genuine cultural values.

ANTHROPOLOGY AND SOCIOLOGY*

JUST AS unlettered and primitive peoples have an economic basis of life that, however simple in its operation, is strictly comparable to the economic machinery that so largely orders the life of a modern civilized society; and just as they have attained to a definite system of religious beliefs and practices, to traditionally conserved modes of artistic expression, to the adequate communication of thought and feeling in terms of linguistic symbols, so also they appear every'where as rather clearly articulated into various types of social grouping. No human assemblage living a life in common has ever been discovered that does not possess some form of social organization. Nowhere do we find a horde in which the relation between its individuals is completely anarchic.

The sexual promiscuity, for instance, that was such a favorite topic of discussion in the speculative writings of the earlier anthropologists seems to be confined to their books. Among no primitive people that has been adequately studied and that conforms to its own traditional patterns of conduct is there to be found such a thing as an unregulated sexual commerce. The "license" that has been so often reported is either condemned by the group itself as a transgression, as is the case on our own level, or is not license at all, but, as among the Todas of India and a great many Australian tribes that are organized into marriage classes, is an institutionally fixed mode of behavior that flows naturally from the division of the group into smaller units between only certain ones of which are marital relations allowed. Hence "group marriage," a none too frequent phenomenon at best, is nowhere an index of social anarchy. On the contrary, it is but a specialized example of the fixity of certain traditional modes of social classification and is psychologically not at all akin to the promiscuity of theory or of the underground life of civilized societies.

If it be objected that intermarrying sub-groups do, as a matter of fact, argue a certain social anarchy because they disregard the natural distinctiveness of the individual, we need but point out that there are many other intercrossing modes of social classification, the net result of which is to carve out for the biological individual a social individuality while securing him a varied social participation. Not all the members of the same marriage class, for instance, need have the same totemic affiliations; nor need their kinship relations, real or supposed, toward

* W. F. Ogburn and A. Goldenweiser, eds., *The Social Sciences and Their Interrelations* (Boston, Houghton Mifflin, 1927), chap. 9, pp. 97–113.

the other members of the tribe be quite the same; nor need they, whether as hunters or as votaries in ancestral cults, have the same territorial associations; nor need their social ranking, based perhaps on age and on generally recognized ability, be at all the same; the mere difference of sex, moreover, has important social consequences, such as economic specialization, general inferiority of social status of the women, and female exclusion from certain ceremonial activities. The details vary, naturally, from tribe to tribe and from one geographical province to another.

Primitive Society: The Evolutionary Bias

All this is merely to indicate that a large and an important share of anthropological study must concern itself with primitive types of social organization.[1] There is such a thing as primitive sociology, and the sociologist who desires a proper perspective for the understanding of social relations in our own life cannot well afford to ignore the primitive data. This is well understood by most sociologists, but what is not always so clearly understood is that we have not the right to consider primitive society as simply a bundle of suggestions for an inferred social pre-history of our own culture. Under the powerful ægis of the biological doctrine of evolution the earlier, classical anthropologists tacitly assumed that such characteristic features of primitive life as totemism or matrilineal kinship groups or group marriage might be assigned definite places in the gradual evolution of the society that we know to-day.

There is no direct historical evidence, for instance, that the early Teutonic tribes which give us the conventionally assumed starting point for Anglo-Saxon civilization had ever passed through a stage of group marriage, nor is the evidence for a totemistic period in the least convincing, nor can we honestly say that we are driven to infer an older organization into matrilineal clans for these peoples. Yet so convinced

---

[1] It is not the purpose of this article to give a systematic survey of the different kinds of primitive social units. A very convenient summary is given by Dr. A. Goldenweiser in his chapters on Society in *Early Civilization.* He points out that these units depend on locality; blood relationship (family, in its narrow sense; group of blood relations, as roughly defined by classificatory systems of kinship terms; clan, or matrilineal sib; gens, or patrilineal sib; hereditary moiety; maternal family, as defined by actual descent from a female progenitor; marriage class); age; generation; sex; and function (groups defined by industries; religious, military, and medical societies; units defined by hereditary privilege or wealth).

There are, of course, many other kinds of association that are not so easy to classify. In practice a good many overlappings occur. Thus, a clan or gens may at the same time be a territorial unit or it may exercise a predominant influence in a village in which other clans or gentes are represented; a religious society may at the same time be an age group or a sex group; a particular maternal family, as among the Iroquois, may be the social unit which has the privilege of giving the clan to which it belongs its chief; and so on.

were some of the most brilliant of the earlier anthropologists that just such social phenomena could be inferred on comparative evidence for the cruder peoples as a whole, and so clear was it to them that a parallel evolutionary sequence of social usages might be assumed for all mankind, that they did not hesitate to ascribe to the prehistoric period of Anglo-Saxon culture customs and social classifications that were familiar to them from aboriginal Australia or Africa or North America. They were in the habit of looking for "survivals" of primitive conditions in the more advanced levels, and they were rarely unsuccessful in finding them.

CRITIQUE OF CLASSICAL EVOLUTION

The more critical schools of anthropology that followed spent a great deal of time and effort in either weakening or demolishing the ingenious speculative sequences that their predecessors had constructed. It gradually appeared that the doctrine of social stages could not be made to fit the facts laboriously gathered by anthropological research. One of the favorite dogmas of the evolutionary anthropologists was the great antiquity of the sib (clan) or corporate kinship group. The earliest form of this type of organization was believed to be based on a matrilineal mode of reckoning descent. Now while it is true that a large number of fairly primitive tribes are organized into matrilineal sibs, such as many of the tribes of Australia, it proved to be equally true that other tribes no whit their superior in general cultural advance counted clan (gens) descent in the paternal line.

Thus, if we consider the distribution of sib institutions in aboriginal North America, it is not in the least obvious that the buffalo-hunting Omaha of the American Plains, organized into patrilineal sibs (gentes), were culturally superior to, or represented a more evolved type of social organization than, say, the Haida or Tlingit or Tsimshian of the west coast of British Columbia and southern Alaska, who possessed an exceedingly complex system of caste and privilege, had developed a very original and intricate art that was far beyond the modest advances made by any of the tribes of the Plains, and lived as fishermen in definitely localized villages, yet whose sibs (clans) were of the matrilineal type. Other American evidence could easily be adduced to prove that on the whole the matrilineally organized tribes represented a later period of cultural development than the patrilineal ones, whatever might be the facts in aboriginal Australia or Melanesia or other quarters of the primitive world. It was remarkable, for instance, that the confederated Iroquois tribes and the town-dwelling Creeks of the Gulf region and many of the Pueblos (for example, Zuñi and Hopi) of the Southwest, all three agricultural and all three obviously less primitive in mode of life and in social polity than our Omaha hunters, were classical examples of societies based on the matrilineal clan. Criticism could go farther and show that the most primitive North American tribes, like the Eskimo, the Athabaskan tribes of the Mackenzie Valley and the interior of Alaska, and the acorn-eating peoples of California, were not organized into sibs at all, whether of the matrilineal or the patrilineal type.

Countless other examples mght be enumerated, all tending to show that it was vain to set up unilinear schemes of social evolution, that supposedly typical forms of archaic society had probably never developed in certain parts of the globe at all, and that in any event the sequence of forms need not everywhere have been in the same sense. The older schematic evolution thus relapsed into the proverbial chaos of history. It became ever clearer that the culture of man was an exceedingly plastic process and that he had developed markedly distinct types of social organization in different parts of the world as well as interestingly convergent forms that could not, however, be explained by any formula of evolutionary theory.

At first blush critical anthropology seems to have demolished the usefulness of its own data for a broader sociology. If anthropology could not give the sociologist a clear perspective into social origins and the remoter social developments that were consummated before the dawn of history, of what serious consequence was its subject-matter for a general theory of society? Of what particular importance was it to study such social oddities, charming or picturesque though they might be, as the clan totemism or the clan exogamy of Australian blacks or American redskins? It is true that anthropology can no longer claim to give us a simple scaffolding for the building of the social history of man, but it does not follow that its data are a rubbish heap of oddments. It may be and probably is true that anthropology has more to tell us than ever before of the nature of man's social behavior; but we must first learn not to expect its teachings to satisfy any such arbitrary demands as were first made of it.

The primary error of the classical school of anthropology was (and of much anthropological theory still is) to look upon primitive man as a sort of prodromal type of cultured humanity. Thus, there was an irresistible tendency to see his significance not in terms of unfolding culture, with endless possibilities for intricate development along specialized lines, not in terms of place and of environing circumstance, but always in terms of inferred and necessarily distorted time. The present anthropological outlook is broader and far less formalized. What the sociologist may hope to get from the materials of social anthropology is not pre-digested history, or rather the pseudo-history that called itself social evolution, but insight into the essential patterns and mechanisms of social behavior. This means, among other things, that we are to be at least as much interested in the many points of accord between primitive and sophisticated types of social organization as in their sensational differences.

THE FAMILY AS PRIMARY SOCIAL UNIT

We can perhaps best illustrate the changing point of view by a brief reference to the family. The earlier anthropologists were greatly impressed by the importance and the stability of the family in modern life. On the principle that everything that is true of civilized society must have evolved from something very different or even opposed in primitive society, the theory was formulated that the family as we understand it to-day was late to arrive in the history of man, that the most primitive peoples of to-day have but a weak sense of the reality of the family, and that the precursor of this social institution was the more inclusive sib (clan). Thus the family appeared as a gradually evolved and somewhat idealized substitute of, or transfer from, a more cumbersome and tyrannically bound group of kinsfolk.

A more careful study of the facts seems to indicate that the family is a well-nigh universal social unit, that it is the nuclear type of social organization *par excellence*. So far from a study of clans, gentes, and other types of enlarged kinship group giving us the clue to the genesis of the family, the exact opposite is true. The family, with its maternal and paternal ties and its carefully elaborated kinship relations and kinship terminology, is the one social pattern into which man has ever been born. It is the pattern that is most likely to serve as nucleus for, or as model of, other social units. We can, then, understand the development of sib and kindred institutions as proliferations of the universal family image. The terminology of clan affiliation or non-affiliation is simply an extension of the terminology of specific familial and extra-familial relationships. The modern family represents the persistence of an old social pattern, not the emergence of a new one. Clan and gentile organizations blossomed here and there on a stem that is still living. What is distinctive of practically all primitive societies is not the clan or gens or moiety as such, but the tremendous emphasis on the principle of kinship. One of the indirect consequences of this emphasis may be the gradual overshadowing, for a certain period, of the family by one or more of its derivatives.

Diffusion and Inferred History

Such an example as this illustrates the value of anthropological data for the fixing of formal perspectives in social phenomena. Meanwhile, if anthropology no longer indulges in the grand panorama of generalized pre-history, it has by no means given up all attempts at reconstructing the history of primitive socieites. On the contrary, there is more inferential history being built out of the descriptive data of primitive life than ever before; but it is not a pan-human history, finely contemptuous of geography and local circumstance. Social institutions are no longer being studied by ethnologists as generalized phenomena in an ideal scheme, with the specific local details set down as incidental avatars of the spirit. The present tendency among students of primitive society is to work out the details of any given institution or social practice for a selected spot, then to study its geographical distribution or, if it is a composite of various elements, the distribution of each of these elements, and gradually to work out by inferences of one kind and another a bit of strictly localized social history. The greatest importance is attached to the discovery of continuities in these distributions, which are felt to be most intelligibly explained by the gradual diffusion of a given social feature from one starting point.

To-day we are not satisfied, for instance, to note the existence of maternal clans among the Haida, of Queen Charlotte Islands, and to compare them, say, with the maternal clans of the Zuñi and Hopi in the Southwest. Nothing can be done with these isolated facts. Should it appear that the clans of the two areas are strikingly similar in the details of their structure and functioning and that the areas are connected by a continuous series of intermediate tribes possessing maternal clans, there would be good reason to believe that the Haida and Zuñi-Hopi organizations are derivatives of a single historical process. But this is not the case. The clan organizations are very different and the clan areas are separated by a vast territory occupied by clanless tribes. The American ethnologist concludes that the general similarity in the social structures of the separated areas is not due to a commn history but to a formal convergence; he has no notion that the antecedents of clan development were necessarily the same in the two cases. On the other hand, the Haida clan system is strikingly similar in structure, type of localization, totemic associations, privileges, and functions to the clan systems of a large number of neighboring tribes (Tlingit, Nass River, Tsimshian, Bella Bella, Kitamat), so that one is irresistibly led to believe that the social system arose only once in this area and that it was gradually assimilated by peoples to whom it was originally foreign.

Analogous cases of the diffusion of social features over large and continuous but strictly limited areas can be cited without end (for example, Australian maternal clans; Australian marriage classes; men's clubs in Melanesia; age societies in the North American Plains; caste institutions in India), and in nearly all of these cases one may legitimately infer that their spread is owing chiefly to the imitation of a pattern that was restricted in the first place to a very small area.

The Reality of Parallel Social Developments

The recent tendency has been to emphasize diffusion and historical inferences from the facts of diffusion at the expense of convergences in social structure, certain extremists even going so far as to deny the possibility of the latter. It is important for students of the structural variations and the history of society to realize the important part that the borrowing of social patterns has played at all times and on all levels of culture; but the reality and the significance of formal parallelisms should never be lost sight of. At present anthropologists are timid about the intensive, non-historical study of typical social forms. The "evolutionary" fallacies are still fresh in their minds, and the danger of falling into any one of a variety of facile "psychological" modes of interpretation is too obvious. But anthropology cannot long continue to ignore such stupendous facts as the independent development of sibs in different parts of the world, the widespread tendency toward the rise of religious or ceremonial societies, the rise of occupational castes, the attachment of differentiating symbols to social units, and a host of others. Such classes of social phenomena are too persistent to be without deep significance. It is fair to surmise that in the long run it is from their consideration that the sociologist will have the most to learn.

Few anthropologists have probed deeply into these problems. Hasty correlations between various types of social phenomena have been made in plenty, such as Rivers's brilliant and unconvincing attempt to derive systems of kinship terminology from supposedly fundamental forms of social organization; but the true unraveling of the basic and largely unconscious concepts or images that underlie social forms has hardly been begun. Hence the anthropologist is in the curious position of dealing with impressive masses of material and with a great number of striking homologies, not necessarily due to historical contact, that he is quite certain have far-reaching significance, but the nature of whose significance he is not prepared to state. Interpretative anthropology is under a cloud, but the data of primitive society need interpretation none the less. The historical explanations now in vogue, often exceedingly dubious at best, are little more than a clearing of the ground toward a social interpretation; they are not the interpretation itself. We can only glance at a few of those formal convergences or underlying tendencies in primitive social organization which we believe to be of common interest to anthropology, to sociology, and to a social psychology of form which has hardly been more than adumbrated.

The Kinship "Image"

It has frequently been noted that the kinship principle tends to take precedence in primitive life over other principles of social classification. A good example of this is afforded by the West Coast tribes of Canada. Here the integrity of the local group, the village, with a recognized head chief, is pretty solidly established. Nevertheless we are constantly hearing in the legends of a particular family or clan, if feeling itself aggrieved for one reason or another, moving off with its house boards and canoes either to found a new village or to join its kinsmen in an old one. There is also direct historical evidence to show that the clan or family constitutions of the villages were being reassorted from time to time because of the great inner coherence and the relative mobility of the kinship groups Among the Nagas of Assam the villages as such had little of the spirit of community and mutual helpfulness, but were split up into potentially hostile clans which lived apart from one another and were constantly on guard against attack from fellow villagers Here the feeling of kinship solidarity, stimulated, it is true, by ceremonial ideas with regard to feuds and head-hunting, actually turned the village into a congeries of beleaguered camps. The significance of such facts is that they show with dramatic clarity how a potent social pattern may fly in the face of reason, of mutual advantage, and even of economic necessity.

The application to modern conditions is obvious enough. The ideology which prevents a Haida clan from subordinating its petty pride to the general good of the village is precisely the same as that which to-day prevents a nation from allowing a transnational economic unit, say the silk industry, from functioning smoothly. In each case a social group-pattern—or formal "image," in psychological terms (clan; nation)—so dominates feeling that services which would naturally flow in the grooves of quite other intercrossing or more inclusive group-patterns (mutual defense in the village; effective production and distribution of a class of goods by those actively engaged in handling it) must suffer appreciable damage.

Function and Form in Sociology

This brings us to the question of the functional nature of social groups. Our modern tendency is to see most associations of human beings in terms of function. Thus, it is obvious that boards of trade, labor unions, scientific societies, municipalities, political parties, and thousands of other types of social organization are most easily explained as resulting from the efforts of like-minded or similarly interested individuals to compass certain ends. As we go back to the types of organization which we know to be more deeply rooted in our historic past, such as the family, the nationality, and the political state, we find that their function is far less obvious. It is either all but absent from consciousness, as in the case of the family, or inextricably intertwined with sentiments and loyalties that are not explicable by the mere function, real or supposed, of the social unit. The state might be defined in purely territorial and functional terms, but political history is little more than an elaborate proof that the state as we have actually known it refuses either to "stay put" or to "stick to business." However, it is evident that the modern state has tended more and more in the direction of a clearer functional definition, by way both of restriction and of extension. The dynastic and religious entanglements, for instance, which were at one time considered inseparable from the notion of a state, have loosened or disappeared. Even the family, the most archaic and perhaps the most stubborn of all social units, is beginning to have its cohesiveness and its compulsions questioned by the intercrossing of functional units that lie outside of itself.

When we compare primitive society with our own, we are at once impressed by the lesser importance of function as a determinant of organization. Functional groupings there are, of course, but they are subsidiary, as a rule, to kinship, territorial, and status groups. There is a very definite tendency for communal activities of all sorts to socialize on the lines suggested by these groups. Thus, among the West Coast Indians, membership in the ceremonial or secret socities, while theoretically dependent upon the acquirement of power from the initiating guardian spirits, is in reality largely a matter of privilege inhering in certain lines of descent. The Kwakiutl Cannibal Society, for instance, is not a spontaneous association of such men and women as possess unusual psychic suggestibility, but is composed of individuals who have family traditions entitling them to dance the Cannibal dance and to perform the rituals of the Society. Among the Pueblo Indians there is a marked tendency for the priesthood of important religious fraternities to be recruited from particular clans. Among the Plains tribes the policing of the camp during the annual buffalo hunt was entrusted not to a group expressly constituted for the purpose but to a series of graded age societies, each serving in turn, as among the Arapaho, to the sibs, as among the Omaha, or to some other set of social units that had other grounds for existence.

We must be careful not to exaggerate the importance of facts such as these, for undoubtedly there is much intercrossing in primitive society of the various types of social organization; yet it remains true that, by and large, function tends to wait on alien principles, particularly kinship. In course of time, as numbers grow and pursuits become more specialized, the functional groups intercross more freely with what may be called the natural status groups. Finally, with the growing complexity of the mechanism of life the concept of the purpose of a given group forces itself upon the social consciousness, and if this purpose is felt to be compelling enough, the group that it unifies may reduce to a secondary position social units built on other principles. Thus, the clan tends to atrophy with the growth of political institutions, precisely as to-day state autonomy is beginning to weaken in the face of transnational functions.

Yet it is more than doubtful if the gradual unfolding of social patterning tends indefinitely to be controlled by function. The pragmatic temper of present-day thinking makes such as assumption seem natural. Both anthropology and history seem to show, however, that any kind of social grouping, once established, tends to persist, and that it has a life only partly conditioned by its function, which may be changed from age to age and from place to place. Certainly anthropology has few more impressive hints for sociological theory than the functional equivalence of different types of social units.

Among the Indians of the Plains, whether organized into sibs or merely into territorial bands, the decoration of articles of clothing, in so far as it does not involve a symbolic reference to a vision, in which case it becomes a matter of intimate personal concern, is neither vested in particular women nor differentiated according to sib or territorial units. The vast majority of decorative motives are at the free disposal of all the women of the tribe. There is evidence that in certain of the Plains tribes the women had developed industrial guilds or sororities for the learning of moccasin techniques and similar items, but if these sex-functional groups specialized in any way in the use of particular designs, it would only emphasize the point that the decoration of clothing had nothing to do with the basic organization of the tribe. The facts read quite differently for such West Coast tribes as the Haida and Tsimshian. Here, owing to the fact that the clans had mythological crests and to the further fact that these crests were often represented on articles of clothing in highly conventionalized form, artistic expression was necessarily intertwined with social organization. The representation of a conventionalized beaver or killer-whale on a hat or dancing apron thus actually becomes a clan privilege. It helps to define or objectify the clan by so much.

Another example of an identical or similar function applied to different social units is afforded by the ceremonial playing of lacrosse among several eastern tribes of the North American aborigines. Both the Iroquois and the Yuchi, of the Southeastern area, were organized into clans (matrilineal sibs), but while the Iroquois pitted their two phratries, or clan aggregations, against each other, among the Yuchi the game was not a clan or phratric function at all but was played by the two great status groups, "Chiefs" and "Warriors," membership in which depended on patrilineal, not matrilineal, descent.

The Transfer of Social Patterns

Such instances are not exceptions or oddities. They may be multiplied indefinitely. Any student who has worked through a considerable body of material of this kind is left with a very lively sense of the reality of types of organization to which no absolutely constant functions can be assigned. Moreover, the suspicion arises that many social units that now seem to be very clearly defined by their function may have had their origin in patterns which the lapse of time has reinterpreted beyond recognition. A very interesting problem arises—that of the possible transfer of a psychological attitude or mode of procedure which is proper to one type of social unit to another type of unit in which the attitude or procedure is not so clearly relevant. Undoubtedly such transfers have often taken place both on primitive and on sophisticated levels.

A striking example of the transfer of a "pattern of feeling" to a social function to which it is glaringly inapplicable is the following, again quoted from the West Coast Indians; The psychic peculiarity that leads certain men and women to become shamans ("medicine-men" and "medicine-women") is so individual that shamanism shows nearly everywhere a marked tendency to resist grooving in the social patterns of the tribe. Personal ability or susceptibility counts far more than conventional status. Nevertheless, so powerful is the concept of rank and of the family inheritance of privilege of every conceivable type among the West Coast people that certain tribes of this area, such as the Tlingit and Nootka, have actually made of shamanistic power an inheritable privilege. In actual practice, of course, theory has to yield to compromise. Among the Nootka, for instance, certain shamanistic offices are supposed to be performed by those who have an inherited right to them. Actually, however, these offices necessitate the possession of supernatural power that the incumbent may not happen to possess. He is therefore driven to the device of deputing the exercise of his office to a real shaman whom he pays for his services but who does not acquire the titular right to the office in question. The psychology of this procedure is of course very similar to the more sophisticated procedure of rubber-stamping documents in the name of a king who is profoundly ignorant of their contents.

A very instructive example of pattern transfer on a high level of culture is the complex organization of the Roman Catholic Church. Here we have a bureaucratic system that neither expresses the personal psychology of snobbery and place-hunting nor can be seriously explained as due to the exigencies of the religious spirit which the organization serves. There is, of course, reason to believe that this organization is to a great extent a carry-over of the complex structure of Roman civil administration. That the Jews and the evangelical Protestant sects have a far looser type of church organization does not prove that they are, as individuals, more immediately swayed by the demands of religion. All that one has a right to conclude is that in their case religion has socialized itself on a less tightly knit pattern, a pattern that was more nearly congruent with other habits of their social life.

Nor can there be a serious doubt that some of our current attitudes toward social units are better suited to earlier types of organization than to the social units as they actually function to-day. A dispassionate analysis of the contemporary state and full realization of the extent to which its well-being depends upon international understandings would probably show that the average individual views it with a more profound emotion than the facts warrant. To the state, in other words, are carried over feelings that seem far more appropriate for more nearly autonomous social bodies, such as the tribe or the self-supporting nationality. It is not unreasonable to maintain that a too passionate state loyalty may hinder the social functioning of her beloved son. It is difficult to view social and political problems of practical importance with a cool eye. One of the most subtle and enlightening of the fruits of anthropological research is an understanding of the very considerable degree to which the concepts of social pattern, function, and associated mental attitude are independently variable. In this thought lies the germ of a social philosophy of values and transfers that joins hands in a very suggestive way with such psychoanalytic concepts as the "image" and the transfer of emotion.

Rhythmic Configurations in Society

Modern psychology is destined to aid us in our understanding of social phenomena by its emphasis on the projection of formal or rhythmic configurations of the psyche and on the concrete symbolization of values and social relations. We can do no more than suggest here that both of these kinds of mental functioning are plentifully illustrated in primitive society, and that for this reason anthropology can do much to give their consideration an adequate place in sociological theory. They are just as truly operative in our more sophisticated culture, but they seem here to be prevented from a clear-cut expression along the lines of social organization by the interference of more conscious, rational processes and by the leveling and destructive influence of a growing consciousness of purpose.

The projection in social behavior of an innate sense of form is an intuitive process and is merely a special phase of that mental functioning that finds its clearest voice in mathematics and its most nearly pure aesthetic embodiment in plastic and musical design. Now it has often been observed how neatly and symmetrically many primitive societies arrange their social units and with how perfect, not to say pedantic, parallelism functions are distributed among these units. An Iroquois or Pueblo or Haida or Australian clan is closely patterned on the other clans, but its distinctive content of behavior is never identical with that of any of these. Then, too, we find significantly often a tendency to exteriorize the feeling for social design in space or time. The Omaha clans or Blackfoot bands, for instance, took up definite position in the camp circle; the septs of a Nootka or Kwakiutl tribe were ranked in a certain order and seated according to definite rule in ceremonial gatherings; each of the Hopi clans was referred to one of the four cardinal points; the Arapaho age societies were graded in a temporal series and took their turn from year to year in policing the camp: among some of the Western Bantu tribes of Africa the year was divided into segments correlated with territorial groupings. The significance of such social phenomena as these, which could easily be multiplied, is probably far greater than has generally been assumed. It is not claimed that the tendency to rhythmic expression is their only determinant, but it is certainly a powerful underlying factor in the development of all social parallelisms and symmetries.

Symbolic Associations

The importance of symbolical associations with social groupings is well known. Party slogans, national flags, and lodge emblems and regalia today can give only a diluted idea of what power is possessed by the social symbol in primitive life. The best-known example of the socialization of symbols among primitive people is of course that complicated, indefinitely varied, and enormously distributed class of phenomena that is conveniently termed totemism. The central importance of totemism lies not such much in a mystic identification of the individual or group with an animal, a plant, or other classes of objects held in religious regard (such identifications are be no means uncommon in primitive cultures, but are not necessary to, or even typical of, totemism) as in the clustering of all kinds of values that pertain to a social unit around a concrete symbol. This symbol becomes surcharged with emotional significance not because of what it merely is or is thought to be in rational terms, but because of all the vital experiences, inherited and personal, that it stands for. Totemism is, on the plane of primitive sociology, very much the same kind of psychological phenomenon as the identification in the mind of the devout Christian of the cross with a significant system of religious practices, beliefs, and emotions.

When a Haida Indian is a member of a clan that possesses, say, the Killer-whale crest, it is very difficult for him to function in any social way without being involved in an explicit or implicit reference to the Killer-whale crest or some other crest or crests with which it is associated. He cannot be born, become of age, be married, give feasts, be invited to a feast, take or give a name, decorate his belongings, or die as a mere individual, but always as one who shares in the traditions and usages that go with the Killer-whale or associated crests. Hence the social symbol is not in any sense a mere tag; it is a traditional index of the fullness of life and of the dignity of the human spirit which transcends the death of the individual. The symbol is operative in a great many types of social behavior, totemism being merely one of its most articulate group expressions. The symbol as unconscious evaluator of individual experience has been much discussed in recent years. It needs no labored argument to suggest how much light anthropology may throw on the social psychology of the symbol.

THE MEANING OF RELIGION*

A VERY USEFUL distinction can be made between "a religion" and "religion." The former appears only in a highly developed society in which religious behavior has been organized by tradition; the latter is universal.

The ordinary conception of a religion includes the notions of a self-conscious "church," of religious officers whose functions are clearly defined by custom and who typically engage in no other type of economic activity, and of carefully guarded rituals which are the symbolic expression of the life of the church. Generally, too, such a religion is invested with a certain authority by a canonical tradition which has grown up around a body of sacred texts, supposed to have been revealed by God or to have been faithfully set down by the founder of the religion or by followers of His who have heard the sacred words from His own lips.

If we leave the more sophisticated peoples and study the social habits of primitive and barbaric folk, we shall find that it is very difficult to discover religious institutions that are as highly formalized as those that go under the name of the Roman Catholic Church or of Judaism. Yet religion in some sense is everywhere present. It seems to be as universal as speech itself and the use of material tools. It is difficult to apply a single one of the criteria which are ordinarily used to define a religion to the religious behavior of primitive peoples, yet neither the absence of specific religious officers nor the lack of authoritative religious texts nor any other conventional lack can seriously mislead the student into denying them true religion. Ethnologists are unanimous in ascribing religious behavior to the very simplest of known societies. So much of a commonplace, indeed, is this assumption of the presence of religion in every known community—barring none, not even those that flaunt the banner of atheism—that one needs to reaffirm and justify the assumption.

How are we to define religion? Can we get behind priests and prayers and gods and rituals and discover a formula that is not too broad to be meaningless nor so specific as to raise futile questions of exclusion or inclusion? I believe it is possible to do this if we ignore for a moment the special forms of behavior deemed religious and attend to the essential meaning and function of such behavior. Religion is precisely one of those words that belong to the more intuitive portion of our vocabulary. We can often apply it safely and unexpectedly without the slightest concern for

* *The American Mercury*, 15 (1928): 72–79; published also under title "Religions and Religious Phenomena," in Baker Brownell, ed., *Religious Life* (New York, Van Nostrand, 1929), pp. 11–33.

whether the individual or group termed religious is priest-ridden or not, is addicted to prayer or not, or believes or does not believe in a god. Almost unconsciously the term has come to have for most of us a certain connotation of personality. Some individuals are religious and others are not, and all societies have religion in the sense that they provide the naturally religions person with certain ready-made symbols for the exercise of his religious need.

The formula that I would venture to suggest is simply this: Religion is man's never-ceasing attempt to discover a road to spiritual serenity across the perplexities and dangers of daily life. How this serenity is obtained is a matter of infinitely varied detail. Where the need for such serenity is passionately felt, we have religious yearning; where it is absent, religious behavior is no more than socially sanctioned form or an æsthetic blend of belief and gesture. In practice it is all but impossible to disconnect religious sentiment from formal religious conduct, but it is worth divorcing the two in order that we may insist all the more clearly on the reality of the sentiment.

What constitutes spiritual serenity must be answered afresh for every culture and for every community—in the last analysis, for every individual. Culture defines for every society the world in which it lives, hence we can expect no more of any religion than that it awaken and overcome the feeling of danger, of individual helplessness, that is proper to that particular world. The ultimate problems of an Ojibwa Indian are different as to content from those of the educated devotee of modern science, but with each of them religion means the haunting realization of ultimate powerlessness in an inscrutable world, and the unquestioning and thoroughly irrational conviction of the possibility of gaining mystic security by somehow identifying oneself with what can never be known. Religion is omnipresent fear and a vast humility paradoxically turned into bedrock security, for once the fear is imaginatively taken to one's heart and the humility confessed for good and all, the triumph of human consciousness is assured. There can be neither fear nor humiliation for deeply religious natures, for they have intuitively experienced both of these emotions in advance of the declared hostility of an overwhelming world, coldly indifferent to human desire.

Religion of such purity as I have defined it is hard to discover. That does not matter; it is the pursuit, conscious or unconscious, of ultimate serenity following total and necessary defeat that constitutes the core of religion. It has often allied itself with art and science, and art at least has gained from the alliance, but in crucial situations religion has always shown itself indifferent to both. Religion seeks neither the objective enlightenment of science nor the strange equilibrium, the sensuous harmony, of æsthetic experience. It aims at nothing more nor less than the impulsive conquest of reality, and it can use science and art as little more than stepping stones toward the attainment of its own serenity. The mind that is intellectualist through and through is necessarily baffled by religion, and in the attempt to explain it makes little more of it than a blind and chaotic science.

Whether or not the spirit of religion is reconcilable with that of art does not concern us. Human nature is infinitely complex and every type of reconciliation of opposites seems possible, but it must be insisted that the nucleus of religious feeling is by no means identical with æsthetic emotion. The serenity of art seems of an utterly different nature from that of religion. Art creates a feeling of wholeness precipitating the flux of things into tangible forms, beautiful and sufficient to themselves; religion gathers up all the threads and meaninglessnesses of life into a wholeness that is not manifest and can only be experienced in the form of a passionate desire. It is not useful and it is perhaps not wise to insist on fundamental antinomies, but if one were pressed to the wall one might perhaps be far from wrong in suspecting that the religious spirit is antithetical to that of art, for religion is essentially ultimate and irreconcilable. Art forgives because it values as an ultimate good the here and now; religion forgives because the here and now are somehow irrelevant to a desire that drives for ultimate solutions.

II

Religion does not presuppose a definite belief in God or in a number of gods or spirits, though in practice such beliefs are generally the rationalized background for religious behavior.

Belief, as a matter of fact, is not a properly religious concept at all, but a scientific one. The sum total of one's beliefs may be said to constitute one's science. Some of these beliefs can be sustained by an appeal to direct personal experience, others rest for their warrant on the authority of society or on the authority of such individuals as are known or believed to hold in their hands the keys of final demonstration. So far as the normal individual is concerned, a belief in the reality of molecules or atoms is of exactly the same nature as a belief in God or immortality. The true division here is not between science and religious belief, but between personally verifiable and personally unverifiable belief. A philosophy of life is not religion if the phrase connotes merely a cluster of rationalized beliefs. Only when one's philosophy of life is vitalized by emotion does it take on the character of religion.

Some writers have spoken of a specifically religious emotion, but it seems quite unnecessary to appeal to any such hypothetical concept. One may rest content to see in religious emotion nothing more nor less than a cluster of such typical emotional experiences as fear, awe, hope, love, the pleading attitude, and any others that may be experienced, in so far as these psychological experiences occur in a context of ultimate values. Fear as such, no matter how poignant or ecstatic, is not religion. A calm belief in a God who creates and rewards and punishes does not constitute religion if the believer fails to recognize the necessity of the application of this belief to his personal problems. Only when the emotion of fear and the belief in a God are somehow integrated into a value can either the emotion or the belief be said to be of a religious nature. This standpoint allows for no specific religious emotions nor does it recognize any specific forms of belief as necessary for religion. All that is asked is that intensity of feeling join with a philosophy of ultimate things into an unanalyzed conviction of the possibility of security in a world of values.

One can distinguish, in theory if not in practice, between individual religious experience and socialized religious behavior. Some writers on religion put the emphasis on the reality and intensity of the individual experience, others prefer to see in religion a purely social pattern, an institution on which the individual must draw in order to have religious experience at all. The contrast between these two points of view is probably more apparent than real. The suggestions for religious behavior will always be found to be of social origin; it is the validation of this behavior in individual or in social terms that may be thought to vary. This is equivalent to saying that some societies tend to seek the most intense expression of religious experience in individual behavior (including introspection under that term), while others tend toward a collective orthodoxy, reaching an equivalent intensity of life in forms of behavior in which the individual is subordinated to a collective symbol. Religions that conform to the first tendency may be called evangelistic, and those of the second type ritualistic.

The contrast invites criticism, as everyone who has handled religious data knows. One may object that it is precisely under the stimulation of collective activity, as in the sun dance of the Plains Indians or in the Roman Catholic mass, that the most intense forms of individual experience are created. Again, one may see in the most lonely and self-centered of religious practices, say the mystic ecstasies of a saint or the private prayer of one lost to society, little more than the religious behavior of society itself, disconnected, for the moment, from the visible church.

A theorist like Durkheim sees the church implicit in every prayer or act of ascetic piety. It is doubtful if the mere observation of religious behavior quite justifies the distinction that I have made. A finer psychological analysis would probably show that the distinction is none the less valid—that societies differ or tend to differ according to whether they find the last court of appeal in matters religious, in the social act, or in the private emotional experience.

Let one example do for many. The religion of the Plains Indians is different in many of its details from that of the Pueblo Indians of the Southwest. Nevertheless there are many external resemblances between them, such as the use of shrines with fetishistic objects gathered in them, the color symbolism of cardinal points, and the religious efficacy of communal dancing. It is not these and a host of other resemblances, however, that impress the student of native American religion; it is rather their profound psychological difference. The Plains Indians' religion is full of collective symbols; indeed, a typical ethnological account of the religion of a Plains tribe seems to be little more than a list of social stereotypes—dances and regalia and taboos and conventional religious tokens. The sun dance is an exceedingly elaborate ritual which lasts many days and in which each song and each step in the progress of the ceremonies is a social expression. For all that, the final validation of the sun dance, as of every other form of Plains religion, seems to rest with the individual in his introspective loneliness. The nuclear idea is the "blessing" or "manitou" experience, in which the individual puts himself in a relation of extreme intimacy with the world of supernatural power or "medicine."

Completely socialized rituals are not the primary fact in the structure of Plains religion; they are rather an extended form of the nuclear individual experience. The recipient of a blessing may and does invite others to participate in the private ritual which has grown up around the vision in which power and security have been vouchsafed to him; he may even transfer his interest in the vision to another individual; in the course of time the original ritual, complicated by many accretions, may become a communal form in which the whole tribe has the most lively and anxious interest, as is the case with the beaver bundle or medicine pipe ceremonies of the Blackfoot Indians. A non-religious individual may see little but show and outward circumstance in all this business of vision and bundle and ritual, but the religions consciousness of the Plains Indians never seems to lose sight of the inherently individual warrant of the vision and of all rituals which may eventually flow from it. It is highly significant that even in the sun dance, which is probably the least individualized kind of religious conduct among these Indians, the high-water mark of religious intensity is felt to reside, not in any collective ecstasy, but in the individual emotions of those who gaze at the center pole of the sun dance lodge and, still more, of the resolute few who are willing to experience the unspeakably painful ecstasy of self-torture.

The Pueblo religion seems to offer very much of a contrast to the religion of the Plains. The Pueblo religion is ritualized to an incredible degree. Ceremony follows relentlessly on ceremony, clan and religious fraternity go through their stately symbolism of dance and prayer and shrine construction with the regularity of the seasons. All is anxious care for the norm and detail of ritual. But is is not the mere bulk of this ritualism which truly characterizes the religion of the Hopi or Zuñi. It is the depersonalized, almost cosmic, quality of the rituals, which have all the air of pre-ordained things of nature which the individual is helpless either to assist or to thwart, and whose mystic intention he can only comprehend by resigning himself to the traditions of his tribe and clan and fraternity. No private intensity of religious experience will help the ritual. Whether the dancer is aroused to a strange ecstasy or remains as cold as an automaton is a matter of perfect indifference to the Pueblo consciousness. All taint of the orgiastic is repudiated by the Pueblo Indian, who is content with the calm constraint and power of things ordained, seeing in himself no discoverer of religious virtue, but only a correct and measured transmitter of things perfect in themselves. One might teach Protestant revivalism to a Blackfoot or a Sioux; a Zuñi would smile uncomprehendlingly.

III

Though religion cannot be defined in terms of belief, it is none the less true that the religions of primitive peoples tend to cluster around a number of typical beliefs or classes of belief. It will be quite impossible to give even a superficial account of the many types of religious belief that have been reported for primitive man, and I shall therefore be content with a brief mention of three of them: belief in spirits (animism), belief in gods, and belief in cosmic power (mana).

That primitive peoples are animistic—in other words, that they believe in the existence in the world and in themselves of a vast number of immaterial and potent essences—is a commonplace of anthropology. Tylor attempted to derive all forms of religious behavior from animistic beliefs, and while we can no longer attach as great an importance to animism as did Tylor and others of the classical anthropologists, it is still correct to say that few primitive religions do not at some point or other connect with the doctrine of spirits. Most peoples believe in a soul which animates the human body; some believe in a variety of souls (as when the principle of life is distinguished from what the psychologists would call consciousness of the psyche); and most peoples also believe in the survival of the soul after death in the form of a ghost.

The experiences of the soul or souls typically account for such phenomena as dreams, illness, and death. Frequently one or another type of soul is identified with such insubstantial things as the breath, or the shadow cast by a living being, or, more materially, with such parts of the human body as the heart or diaphragm; sometimes, too, the soul is symbolized by an imaginary being, such as a mannikin, who may leave the body and set out in pursuit of another soul. The mobile soul and the ghost tend to be identified, but this is not necessarily the case.

In all this variety of primitive belief we see little more than the dawn of psychology. The religious attitude enters in only when the soul or ghost is somehow connected with the great world of non-human spirits which animates the whole of nature and which is possessed of a power for good or ill which it is the constant aim of human beings to capture for their own purposes. These "spirits," which range all the way from disembodied human souls, through animals, to god-like creatures, are perhaps more often feared than directly worshipped. On the whole, it is perhaps correct to say that spirits touch humanity through the individual rather than through the group and that access is gained to them rather through the private, selfish ritual of magic than through religion. All such generalizations, however, are exceedingly dangerous. Almost any association of beliefs and attitudes is possible.

Tylor believed that the series: soul, ghost, spirit, god, was a necessary genetic chain. "God" would be no more than the individualized totality of all spirits, localized in earth or air or sea and specialized as to function or kind of power. The single "god" of a polytheistic pantheon would be the transition stage between the unindividualized spirit and the Supreme Being of the great historical religions. These simple and plausible connections are no longer lightly taken for granted by the anthropologists. There is a great deal of disturbing evidence which seems to show that the idea of a god or of God is not necessarily to be considered as the result of an evolution of the idea of soul or spirit. It would seem that some of the most primitive peoples we know of have arrived at the notion of an all powerful being who stands quite outside the world of spirits and who tends to be identified with such cosmic objects as the sun or the sky.

The Nootka Indians of British Columbia, for instance, believe in the existence of a Supreme Being whom they identify with daylight and who is sharply contrasted both with the horde of mysterious beings ("spirits") from whom they seek power for special ends and with the mythological beings of legend and ritual. Some form of primitive monotheism not infrequently co-exists with animism. Polytheism is not necessarily the forerunner of monotheism, but may, for certain culture, be looked upon as a complex, systematized product of several regional ideas of God.

The idea of "mana," or diffused, non-individualized power, seems to be exceedingly wide-spread among primitive peoples. The term has been borrowed from Melanesia, but it is as applicable to the Algonkian, Iroquois, Siouan, and numerous other tribes of aboriginal America as to the Melanesians and Polynesians. The whole world is believed to be pervaded by a mysterious potency that may be concentrated in particular objects or, in many cases, possessed by spirits or animals or gods. Man needs to capture some of this power in order to attain his desires. He is ever on the lookout for blessings from the unknown, which may be vouchsafed to him in unusual or uncanny experiences, in visions, and in dreams. The notion of immaterial power often takes curious forms. Thus the Hupa Indians of Northwestern California believe in the presence of radiations which stream to earth from mysterious realms beyond, inhabited by a supernatural and holy folk who once lived upon earth but vanished with the coming of the Indians. These radiations may give the medicine-woman her power or they may inspire one with the spirit of a ritual.

I can hardly do more than mention some of the typical forms of religious behavior, as distinguished from belief, which are of universal distribution. Prayer is common, but it is only in the higher reaches of culture that it attains its typically pure and altruistic form. On lower levels it tends to be limited to the voicing of selfish wants, which may even bring harm to those who are not members of one's own household. It is significant that prayers are frequently addressed to specific beings who may grant power or withhold ill rather than to the Supreme Being, even when such a being is believed to exist.

A second type of religious behavior is the pursuit of power or "medicine." The forms which this pursuit take are exceedingly varied. The individual "medicine" experience is perhaps illustrated in its greatest purity among the American aborigines, but it is of course plentifully illustrated in other parts of the world. Among some tribes the receipt of power, which generally takes place in the form of a dream or vision, establishes a very personal relation between the giver of the blessing and the suppliant.

This relation is frequently known as individual totemism. The term totemism, indeed, is derived from the Ojibwa Indians, among whom there is a tendency for the individual to be "blessed" by the same supernatural beings as have already blessed his paternal ancestors. Such an example as this shows how the purely individual relation may gradually become socialized into the institution typically known as totemism, which may be defined as a specific relation, manifested in a great variety of ways, which exists between a clan or other social group and a supernatural being, generally, but by no means exclusively, identified with an animal. In spite of the somewhat shadowy borderland which connects individual totemism with group totemism, it is inadvisable to think of the one institution as necessarily derived from the other, though the possibility of such a development need not be denied outright.

Closely connected with the pursuit of power is the handling of magical objects or assemblages of such objects which contained or symbolize the power that has been bestowed. Among some of the North American Indian tribes, as we have seen, the "medicine bundle," with its associated ritual and taboos, owes its potency entirely to the supernatural experience which lies back of it. Classical fetishism, however, as we find it in West Africa, seems not to be necessarily based on an individual vision. A fetish is an object which possesses power in its own right and which may be used to affect desired ends by appropriate handling, prayer, or other means. In many cases a supernatural being is believed to be actually resident in the fetish, though this conception, which most nearly corresponds to the popular notion of "idol," is probably not as common as might be expected. The main religious significance of medicine bundles, fetishes and other tokens of the supernatural is the reassuring power exerted on the primitive mind by a concrete symbol which is felt to be closely connected with the mysterious unknown and its limitless power. It is of course the persistence of the suggestibility of visual symbols which makes even the highest forms of religion tend to cluster about such objects as temples, churches, shrines, crucifixes, and the like.

The fourth and perhaps the most important of the forms of religious behavior is the carrying out of rituals. Rituals are typically symbolic actions which belong to the whole community, but among primitive peoples there is a tendency for many of them to be looked upon as the special function of a limited group within the whole tribe. Sometimes this group is a clan or gens or other division not based on religious concepts; at other times the group is a religious fraternity, a brotherhood of priests, which exists for the sole purpose of seeing to the correct performance of rituals which are believed to be of the utmost consequence for the safety of the tribe as a whole. It is difficult to generalize about primitive ritual, so varied are the forms which it assumes. Nearly everywhere the communal ritual whips the whole tribe into a state of great emotional tension, which is interpreted by the folk as a visitation from the supernatural world. The most powerful means known to bring about this feeling is the dance, which is nearly always accompanied by singing.

Some ethnologists have seen in primitive ritual little more than the counterpart of our own dramatic and pantomimic performances. Historically there is undoubtedly much truth in this but it would be very misleading to make of a psychology of primitive ritual a mere chapter in the psychology of æsthetic experience. The exaltation of the Sioux sun dancer or of a Northwest Coast Indian who impersonates the Cannibal Spirit is a very different thing from the excitement of the performing artist. It seems very much more akin to the intense revery of the mystic or ascetic. Externally, the ritual may be described as a sacred drama; subjectively, it may bring the participant to a realization of mystery and power for which the fetish or other religious object is but an external token. The psychological interpretation of ritual naturally differs with the temperament of the individual.

IV

The sharp distinction between religious and other modes of conduct to which we are accustomed in modern life is by no means possible on more primitive levels. Religion is neither ethics nor science nor art, but it tends to be inextricably bound up with all three. It also manifests itself in the social organization of the tribe, in ideas of higher or lower status, in the very form and technique of government itself. It is sometimes said that it is impossible to disentangle religious behavior among primitive peoples from the setting in which it is found. For many primitives, however, it seems almost more correct to say that religion is the one structural reality in the whole of their culture and that what we call art and ethics and science and social organization are hardly more than the application of the religious point of view to the functions of daily life.

In concluding, attention may be called to the wide distribution of certain sentiments or feelings which are of a peculiarly religious nature and which tend to persist even among the most sophisticated individuals, long after they have ceased to believe in the rationalized justification for these sentiments and feelings. They are by no means to be identified with simple emotions, though they obviously feed on the soil of all emotions. A religious sentiment is typically unconscious, intense, and bound up with a compulsive sense of values. It is possible that modern psychology may analyze them all away as socialized compulsion neuroses, but it is exceedingly doubtful if a healthy social life or a significant individual life is possible without these very sentiments. The first and most important of them is a "feeling of community with a necessary universe of values." In psychological terms, this feeling seems to be a blend of complete humility and a no less complete security. It is only when the fundamental serenity is as intense as fear and as necessary as any of the simpler sentiments that its possessor can be properly termed a mystic.

A second sentiment, which often grows out of the first, is a feeling for sacredness or holiness or divinity. That certain experiences or ideas or objects or personalities must be set apart as symbols of ultimate value is an idea which is repellent to the critical modern mind. It is none the less a necessary sentiment to many, perhaps to most, human beings. The consciously justified infraction of sentiments of holiness, which cannot be recognized by the thinking mind, leads frequently to an inexplicable personal unhappiness.

The taboos of primitive peoples strike us as very bizarre and it is a commonplace of psychoanalysis that many of them have a strange kinship with the apparently self-imposed taboos of neurotics. It is doubtful if many psychologists or students of culture realize the psychological significance of taboo, which seems nothing more nor less than an unconscious striving for the strength that comes from any form of sacrifice or deferment of immediate fulfillments. Certainly all religions have insisted on the importance of both taboo, in its narrower sense of specific interdiction, and sacrifice. It may be that the feeling of the necessity of sacrifice is no more than a translation into action of the sentiment of the holy.

Perhaps the most difficult of the religious sentiments to understand is that of sin, which is almost amusingly abhorrent to the modern mind. Every constellation of sentiments holds within itself its own opposites. The more intense a sentiment, the more certain is the potential presence of a feeling which results from the flouting or thwarting of it. The price for the reality and intensity of the positive sentiments that I have mentioned, any or all of which must of necessity be frequently violated in the course of daily life, is the sentiment of sin, which is a necessary shadow cast by all sincerely religious feeling.

It is, of course, no accident that religion in its most authentic moments has always been prepared to cancel a factual shortcoming in conduct if only it could assure itself that this shortcoming was accompanied by a lively sense of sin. Good works are not the equivalent of the sentiment of ultimate value which religion insists upon. The shadow cast by this sentiment, which is a sense of sin, may be intuitively felt as of more reassuring value than a benevolence which proceeds from mere social habit or from personal indifference. Religion has always been the enemy of self-satisfaction.

GROUP*

THERE IS a wide variety of meanings attached to the term group; different kinds of reality are imputed to the concept by psychologists and sociologists of different schools. To some the group is a primary concept in the study of human behavior; many sociologists say that the individual has no reality, aside from his biologically defined body, except as a carrier or crystallizer of meanings that are derivative of group action and interaction. To others, however, the individual remains as the sociologically primary entity and groups are the more or less artificial constructs which result when individuals, viewed as essentially complete physical and psychological entities, come into contact with each other. For the former sociologists a child can hardly be said to have social reality except in so far as there is in prior existence a supporting family or social agency substituting for the family and a fairly well defined set of rules of behavior defining the relation between the child and such a family. In much the same sense there would be no such individual as a musician except in so far as there are such groups as conservatories, historically determined lines of musicians and musical critics, dancing, singing and playing associations of varying degrees of formal organization and many other types of groups whose prior definition is needed to make the term musician actual. For the latter sociologists the child and the musician exist as given types of individuals, whether they are so born or so conditioned; and the groups which the sociologist discovers as operative in the behavior which actualizes such individual terms as child or musician are merely ad hoc constructions due to the specific experiences of individuals either within a given lifetime or over many generations. The difficulty of deciding whether the group or the individual is to be looked upon as the primary concept in a general theory of society is enhanced by fatal ambiguities in the meaning of the term group.

Any group is constituted by the fact that there is some interest which holds its members together. The community of interest may range from a passing event which assembles people into a momentary aggregate to a relatively permanent functional interest which creates and maintains a cohesive unit. The crowd which forms where there is an automobile accident, drawn together in the first place by a common curiosity, soon develops certain understandings. Its members may feel themselves to be informally delegated by society to observe and eventually report or to

* *Encyclopaedia of the Social Sciences* (New York, Macmillan, 1932), 7: 178–182.

help with advice or action or, if there has been an infraction of the traffic rules, to constitute a silent or audible image of criticism. Such a group cannot be despised by the sociologist for all its casualness of form and function. At the other extreme is such a body as the United States Senate, which is fixed as to numbers, principle of selection, time of meeting, function and symbolic importance in a representative capacity. The former consists of individuals who do not feel that they are assuming a known or imputed role when they become members of the group; the latter is constituted by political and legal theory and exists in a sense in advance of the appearance of specific members, so that those who actually take part in deliberations of the Senate are something other than or beyond themselves as individuals. There is in reality no definite line of division anywhere along the gamut of group forms which connect these extremes. If the automobile accident is serious and one of the members of the crowd is a doctor, the informal group may with comparatively little difficulty resolve itself into something like a medical squad with an implicitly elected leader. On the other hand, if the government is passing through a great political crisis, if there is little confidence in the representative character or honesty of the senators or if any enemy is besieging the capital and likely at any moment to substitute entirely new forms of corporate authority for those legally recognized by the citizens of the country, the Senate may easily become an unimportant aggregation of individuals who suddenly and with unexpected poignancy feel their helplessness as mere individuals.

Sociological theory can hardly analyze the group concept into its various forms unless it uses definable principles of classification. The primary principle of classification may rest on the distinction between physical proximity on the one hand and the adoption of a symbolic role on the other. Between the two extremes comes a large class of group forms in which the emphasis is on definite, realistic purpose rather than on symbolism. The three major classes of groups are therefore those physically defined, those defined by specific purposes and those symbolically defined. Examples of simple physical groups are a bread line, a little crowd milling in the lobby of a theater between the acts of a play, the totality of individuals who look on at a football game, a handful of people going up in an elevator and a Saturday afternoon crowd on Fifth Avenue. Groups possessed of a relatively firm organization and of a real or imputed specific purpose are, for example, the employees of a factory, the administrative personnel of a bank or stock company, a board of education, a society for the prevention of cruelty to animals, the taxpayers of a municipality, a trade union viewed as an agency for securing certain economic advantages to its members and a state legislature viewed simply as an agency of government. Groups of the third type differ from those of the second in that to external organization and one or more well defined functions there is added the general symbolic function of securing for the individual an integrated status in society. Examples of such symbolically defined groups are the family; the membership of a particular church or of a religious denomination; a political party in so far as it is not merely a mechanism for the election of political officers; a social club in so far as it means more than a convenience for luncheon or an occasional game of billiards; a university group looked at as something over and above an instrumentality for specific types of education; the United States Senate as a responsible spokesman of the American government; a state as the legalized representative of the nation; a nation as a large aggregate of human beings who feel themselves to be held together by many ties of sentiment and which believes itself, rightly or wrongly, to be a self-sufficient social entity in the world of physical necessity and of human relationships.

The examples have been purposely chosen to suggest doubts and multiple interpretations. Some degree of physical proximity is either required or fancied in order to make for group cohesiveness; some degree of purpose or function can be found in or rationalized for any conceivable group of human beings that has meaning at all; and there is no group which does not reach out symbolically beyond its actual composition and assigned function. Even so wide a group as a political party needs from time to time to give itself the face to face psychology of a mere physical gathering, lest the loyalty and enthusiasm which spring from handshakes, greetings, demonstrations, speeches and other tokens of immediate vitality seep away into a colorless feeling of merely belonging. The members of a church, standing obviously as a symbol of the relation between God and man, carry definite purposes of a practical sort, such as the securing of burial rights. Symbolisms of a potent sort may be illustrated in groups which are most readily classified under the first and second rubrics. Thus, a passer by may be attracted to the casual crowd brought together by an automobile accident not because he thinks he can be of any particular assistance nor because he is devoured by curiosity but merely because he wishes half unconsciously to register his membership in the human universe of potential suffering and mutual good will. For such an individual the nondescript group in question becomes the mystic symbol of humanity itself. Thus defined it may be more potent in a symbolic sense than the nation itself. So clearly defined a functional group as a board of education has or may have a symbolic significance for its community that far transcends its avowed purposes. Nevertheless, there are few groups of human beings that cannot be readily classified as coming primarily under one or the other of the three indicated heads. This tripartite classification is easiest to apply in the modern civilized world. In less sophisticated folk cultures and to an even greater extent in primitive societies the possibility of allocating groups to one rather than another of the three types becmes more difficult. Physical contact, a bundle of common purposes and heavy saturation with symbolism tend to be typical of all groups on these more primitive levels.

The suggested classification is based on an analysis of groups from an objective standpoint; that is, from the standpoint of an observing non-participant or the standpoint of humanity or the nation or any other large aggregate in which the significance of the individual as such tends to be lost. The interpretation of the various types of groups from the standpoint of individual participation offers new difficulties, and new principles of classification may be ventured. Individuals differ in the degree to which they can successfully identify themselves with the other members of the group in which they are included and in the nature of that identification. Such identification may be direct, selective or referential. Direct participation implies that the individual is or feels himself to be in a significant personal relation to all or most of the fellow members of the group with whom he comes in contact. For such an individual the reality of a committee, for instance, is not given by its external organization and assigned duties but rather by his ability to work with or fail to work with particular members of the committee and to get his own purposes accomplished with or in defiance of their help. A selective type of participation implies that the individual is able to identify himself with the group only in so far as he can identify himself with one or more selected members of the group who stand as its representatives and who tend to exhaust for the individual the psychological significance of the group itself. Or the selection may act negatively, so that the significance of the group is damaged for the individual because of feelings of hostility toward particular members of the group. This type of group identification is common in the workaday world. Referential participation implies that the individual makes no serious attempt to identify himself with some or all of the actual membership of a group but feels these fellow members to be the more or less impersonal carriers of an idea or purpose. This is essentially the legalistic type of approach.

The type of individual participation in the group and its purposes has something to do with its unconscious classification, so that the objective and subjective points of view are not in reality distinct. It is well to keep them apart, however, and to look upon them as intercrossing classifications. The least significant type of group psychologically would be the mere physical group with referential participation of the individual. The group so defined is little more than a statistical entity in the field of population. At the other extreme is the symbolically defined group with direct individual participation. Great art brings to the interpretation of symbolically defined groups, which tend to be somewhat colorless as human entities because of their indefinite membership, the touchstone of direct participation. In Hauptmann's *Die Weber* (Berlin 1892; tr. by M. Morison as *The Weavers*, London 1899), for instance, German labor, a symbolically defined group as conceived by the dramatist, is made doubly significant because of the illusion of direct participation in its membership.

The nature of the interest which lies at the basis of the formation of the group varies indefinitely. It may be economic, political, vocational, meliorative, propagandist, racial, territorial, religious or expressive of general attitudes or minor purposes, such as the use of leisure. To go into the details of the organization and purpose of such specifically defined groups would be tantamount to a description of the institutions of society. A popular classification of groups has been into primary or face to face groups and secondary groups. This is a convenient descriptive contrast but it does not take sufficient account of the nature of individual participation in the group. The distinction becomes of greater value if it is interpreted genetically as a contrast between those types of participation which are defined early in life and those which come later as symbolic amplifications or transfers of the earlier participations. From this point of view membership in a labor union with a dominant leader may have the value of an unconscious psychological recall of one's childhood participation in the family. Still another type of classification of groups which can readily be made is that based on the degree to which groups are self-consciously formed and group membership is voluntary. From this point of view the trade union or political party contrasts with the family or the state. The individual enters into the latter type of group through biological or social necessity, while he is believed to align himself with a trade union or political party without such necessity. This distinction is misleading, for the implicit social forces which lead to membership in a given political party, for instance, may for many individuals be quite as compulsive as those which identify him with the state or even the family. To make too much of the distinction is to confuse the psychological realities of various forms of participation with the roles which society imputes to the individual. The plurality of groupings for any one individual is a point that sociologists have emphasized. If one looks beyond the groups which are institutionally defined—in other words, beyond associations in the narrow sense of the word—any society, above all the complex society of modern times, has many more groups of more or less psychological significance than it possesses individuals who participate in these groups.

The changes in social groupings, studied partly through historical evidence, partly through the direct observation of contemporary trends, constitute a large part of the history of society. There are changes in the actual personnel of groups resulting from realignments brought about by such factors as economic change and changes in the means of communication, changes in the deepening or the impoverishment of the symbolic significance of the group and changes in the tendency to a more or to a less direct participation of the individual in his group. These types of change necessarily condition each other in a great variety of ways. An example of the first type is the gradual increase in the total potential membership of the political parties in England and the United States. The fact that individuals without property and women now share in the activities of the parties means that their present symbolic significance is different from what it originally was. Examples of the second type of change are provided by the universal tendency for groups which have a well defined function to lose their original function but to linger on as symbolically reinterpreted groups. Thus a political club may lose its significance in the realistic world of politics but may nevertheless survive significantly as a social club in which membership is eagerly sought by those who wish to acquire a valuable symbol of status. The third type of change is illustrated by the recent history of the American family, in which on account of many disintegrating influences direct and intense participation has become less pronounced. As far as the relation of brothers and sisters is concerned, for instance, the participation frequently amounts to hardly more than a colorless awareness of the fact of such kinship. Developments in the family illustrate the general tendency in modern life of secondary and voluntary groupings to assume the dominant role as against the primary and involuntary ones. Closely connected with this is the greater mobility of group membership due to a variety of factors, among which are increased facilities of transportation, the gradual breakdown of the earlier symbolic sanctions and an increasing tendency to conceive of a group as fundamentally defined by one or more specific purposes. Groups that are relatively permanent because they are needed to carry out important purposes tend to become more and more institutionalized. Hiking clubs, for instance, have replaced the more casual association of three or four men for the purpose of walking together in the country.

In the discussion of the fundamental psychology of the group such terms as gregariousness, consciousness of kind and group mind do little more than give names to problems to which they are in no sense a solution. The psychology of the group cannot be fruitfully discussed except on the basis of a profounder understanding of the way in which different sorts of personalities enter into significant relations with each other and on the basis of a more complete knowledge of the importance to be attached to directly purposive as contrasted with symbolic motives in human interaction. The psychological basis of the group must rest on the psychology of specific personal relations; no matter how impersonally one may conceive the behavior which is characteristic of a given group, it must either illustrate direct interaction or it must be a petrified "as if" of such interaction. The latter attribute is, however, not the peculiar property of group psychology but is also illustrated in the relations of single human beings toward one another. It is only an apparent contradiction of this point of view if the individual, as he so frequently does, allows himself to be controlled not by what this man or that man says or thinks, but by what he mystically imputes to the group as a whole. Group loyalty and group ethics do not mean that the direct relationship between individual and individual has been completely transcended. They mean only that what was in its origin a relation of individual dominance has been successively transferred until it is now attributed to the group as a whole.

The psychological realities of group participation will be understood only when theorizing about the general question of the relation of the individual to the group gives way to detailed studies of the actual kinds of understanding, explicit and implicit, that grow up between two or three or more human beings when they are brought into significant contact. It is important to know not only how one person feels with reference to another but how the former feels with reference to the latter when a third party is present. A latent hostility between two persons may be remedied by the presence of the third party, because for one reason or another he is an apt target for the conscious or unconscious hostility of both. His presence may serve to sharpen hostility between the persons because of his attractiveness for both and the consequent injection of a conscious or unconscious jealousy into the relations that obtain between them. Precise studies in the psychology of personal relations are by no means immaterial for the profounder psychological understanding of the group, for this psychology can hardly be other than the complex resultant of the pooling, heightening, canceling, transfer and symbolic reinterpretation of just such specific processes. As psychology recognizes more and more clearly the futility of studying the individual as a self-contained entity, the sociologist will be set free to study the rationale of group form, group function, group changes and group interrelationships from a formal or cultural point of view.

CUSTOM*

THE WORD custom is used to apply to the totality of behavior patterns which are carried by tradition and lodged in the group, as contrasted with the more random personal activities of the individual. It is not properly applicable to those aspects of communal activity which are obviously determined by biological considerations. The habit of eating fried chicken is a custom, but the biologically determined habit of eating is not.

Custom is a variable common sense concept which has served as the matrix for the development of the more refined and technical anthropological concept of culture. It is not as purely denotative and objective a term as culture and has a slightly affective quality indicated by the fact that one uses it more easily to refer to geographically remote, to primitive or to bygone societies than to one's own. When applied to the behavior of one's own group the term is usually limited to relatively unimportant and unformalized behavior patterns which lie between individual habits and social institutions. Cigarette smoking is more readily called a custom than is the trial of criminals in court. However, in dealing with contemporary Chinese civilization, with early Babylonian culture or with the life of a primitve Australian tribe the functional equivalent of such a cultural pattern as our court trial is designated as custom. The hesitation to describe as custom any type of behavior in one's own group that is not at once collective and devoid of major importance is perhaps due to the fact that one involuntarily prefers to put the emphasis either on significant individualism, in which case the word habit is used, or on a thoroughly rationalized and formalized collective intention, in which case the term institution seems in place.

Custom is often used interchangeably with convention, tradition and mores, but the connotations are not quite the same. Convention emphasizes the lack of inner necessity in the behavior pattern and often implies some measure of agreement, express or tacit, that a certain mode of behavior be accepted as proper. The more symbolic or indirect the function of a custom, the more readily is it referred to as a convention. It is a custom to write with pen and ink; it is a convention to use a certain kind of paper in formal correspondence. Tradition emphasizes the historic background of custom. No one accuses a community of being wanting in customs and conventions, but if these are not felt as possessed of considerable antiquity a community is said to have few if any tradi-

* *Encyclopaedia of the Social Sciences* (New York, Macmillan, 1931), 4: 658–662.

tions. The difference between custom and tradition is more subjective than objective, for there are few customs whose complete explanation in terms of history does not take one back to a remote antiquity. The term mores is best reserved for those customs which connote fairly strong feelings of the rightness or wrongness of modes of behavior. The mores of a people are its unformulated ethics as seen in action. Such terms as custom, institution, convention, tradition and mores are, however, hardly capable of a precise scientific definition. All of them are reducible to social habit or, if one prefers the anthropological to the psychological point of view, to cultural pattern. Habit and culture are terms which can be defined with some degree of precision and should always be substituted for custom in strictly scientific discourse, habit or habit system being used when the locus of behavior is thought of as residing in the individual, cultural pattern or culture when its locus is thought of as residing in society.

From a biological standpoint all customs are in origin individual habits which have become diffused in society through the interaction of individual upon individual. These diffused or socialized habits, however, tend to maintain themselves because of the unbroken continuity of the diffusion process from generation to generation. One more often sees custom helping to form individual habit than individual habit being made over into custom. In the main, group psychology takes precedence over individual psychology. In no society, however primitive or remote in time, are the interactions of its members not controlled by a complex network of custom. Even at an early stage of the palaeolithic period human beings must have been ruled by custom to a very considerable extent, as is shown by the rather sharply delimited types of artifacts that were made and the inferences that can be drawn from some of these as to beliefs and attitudes.

The crystallization of individual habit into custom is a process that can be followed out theoretically rather more easily than illustrated in practise. A distinction can be made between customs of long tenure and customs of short tenure generally known as fashions. Fashions are set by a specific individual or group of individuals. When they have had a long enough lease of life to make it seem unimportant to recall the source or original locality of the behavior pattern, they have become customs. The habit of wearing a hat is a custom, but the habit of wearing a particular style of hat is a fashion subject to fairly rapid change. In the sphere of language custom is generally referred to as usage. Uncrystallized usages of speech are linguistic fashions, of which slang forms a particular variety. Food habits too form a well recognized set of customs, within which arise human variations that may be called fashions of food and that tend to die out after a brief period. Fashions are not to be considered as additions to custom but rather as experimental variations of the fundamental themes of custom.

In course of time isolated behavior patterns of a customary nature tend to group themselves into larger configurations which have a formal cohesion and which tend to be rationalized as functional units whether they are such historically or not. The whole history of culture has been little more than a ceaseless effort to connect originally independent modes of behavior into larger systems and to justify the secondary culture complexes by an unconscious process of rationalization. An excellent example of such a culture complex, which derives its elements from thousands of disparate customs, is the modern musical system, which is undoubtedly felt by those who make use of it to be a well compacted functional whole with various elements that are functionally interdependent. Historically, however, it is very easy to prove that the system of musical notation, the rules of harmony, the instrumental techniques, the patterns of musical composition and the conventional uses of particular instruments for specific purposes are independently derivable from customs of very different provenience and of very different age, and that it is only by slow processes of transfer of use and progressive integration of all these socialized modes of behavior that they have come to help each other out in a complex system of unified meanings. Hundreds of parallel instances could be given from such diverse fields of social activity as language, architecture, political organization, industrial technique, religion, warfare and social etiquette.

The impermanence of custom is a truism. Belief in the rapidity of change of custom is exaggerated, however, because it is precisely the comparatively slight divergences from what is socially established that arouse attention. A comparison of American life today with the life of a mediaeval English town would in the larger perspective of cultural anthropology illustrate rather the relative permanence of culture than its tendency to change.

The disharmony which cumulatively results from the use of tools, insights or other manipulative types of behavior which had enriched the cultural stock in trade of society a little earlier results in change of custom. The introduction of the automobile, for instance, was not at first felt as necessarily disturbing custom, but in the long run all those customs appertaining to visiting and other modes of disposing of one's leisure time have come to be seriously modified by the automobile as a power contrivance. Amenities of social intercourse felt to be obstructive to the free utilization of this new source of power tend to be dismissed or abbreviated. Disharmony resulting from the rise of new values also makes for change in custom. For example, the greater freedom of manner of the modern woman as contrasted with the far more conventionally circumscribed conduct of women of generations ago has come about because of the rise of a new attitude toward woman and her relation to man. The influences exerted by foreign peoples, e.g. the introduction of tea and coffee in occidental society and the spread of parliamentary government from country to country, are stressed by anthropologists more than by the majority of historians and sociologists as determinants of change. Most popular examples of the imposition of fashions which proceed from strategic personalities are probably fanciful and due to a desire to dramatize the operation of the more impersonal factors, which are much more important in the aggregate than the specific personal ones. With the gradual spread of a custom that is largely symbolic and characteristic of a selected portion of the population, the fundamental reason for its continuance weakens, so that it either dies out or takes on an entirely new function. This mechanism is particularly noteworthy in the life of language. Locutions which are considered smart or chic because they are the property of privileged circles are soon taken up by the masses and then die because of their banality. A much more powerful and exact knowledge of the nature of individual interaction, particularly as regards the unconscious transfer of feeling, is needed before a really satisfying theory of cultural change can be formulated.

Those customs survive the longest which either correspond to so basic a human need that they cannot well be seriously changed or else are of such a nature that they can easily be functionally reinterpreted. An ex-example of the former type of persistence is the custom of having a mother suckle her child. There are numerous departures from this rule, yet both modern America and the more primitive tribes preserve as a custom a mode of behavior which obviously lies close to the life of man in nature. An example of the latter type of persistence, which may be called adaptive persistence, is language, which tends to remain fairly true to set form but which is constantly undergoing reinterpretation in accordance with the demands of the civilization which it serves. For example, the word robin refers in the United States to a very different bird from the English bird that was originally meant. The word could linger on with a modified meaning because it is a symbol and therefore capable of indefinite reinterpretation.

The word survival should not be used for a custom having a clearly defined function which can be shown to be different from its original place and significance in culture. When used in the latter, looser sense the word survival threatens to lose all useful meaning. There are few customs among us today which are not survivals in this sense. There are, however, certain customs which it is difficult to rationalize on any count and which may be looked upon as analogous to rudimentary organs in biology. The useless buttons in modern clothing are often cited as an example of such survivals. The use of Roman numerals alongside of Arabic numerals may also be considered a survival. On the whole, however, it seems safest not to use the word too freely, for it is difficult to prove that any custom, no matter how apparently lacking in utility or how far removed from its original application, is entirely devoid of at least symbolic meaning.

Custom is stronger and more persistent in primitive than in modern societies. The primitive group is smaller, so that a greater degree of conformity is psychologically necessary. In the more sophisticated community, which numbers a far larger total of individuals, departure from custom on the part of a few selected individuals, who may in turn prove instrumental for a change of culture in the community at large, does not matter so much for the solidarity of the group to begin with, because the chance individual of the group finds himself reinforced by the vast majority of his fellow men and can do without the further support of the deviants. The primitive community has also no written tradition to appeal to as an impersonal arbiter in matters of custom and therefore puts more energy into the conservation of what is transmitted through activity and oral tradition. The presence of documents relieves the individual from the necessity of taking personal responsibility for the perpetuation of custom. Far too great stress is usually laid on the actually conserving, as contrasted with the symbolically conserving, power of the written word. Custom among primitive peoples is apt to derive some measure of sacredness from its association with magical and religious procedures. When a certain type of activity is linked with a ritual which is in turn apt to be associated with a legend that to the native mind explains the activity in question, a radical departure from the traditionally conserved pattern of behavior is felt as blasphemous or perilous to the safety of the group. There is likewise a far lesser division of labor in primitive communities than in our own, which means that the forces making for experimentation in the solution of technical problems are proportionately diminished.

In the modern world custom tends to be much more conservative in the rural districts than in the city, and the reasons are similar to those given for the greater persistence of custom among primitive peoples.

The greater scatter of the rural population does not generally mean the more intensive individual cultivation of the forms of custom but rather a compensatory effort to correct the threats of distance by conformity.

Within a complex community, such as is found in modern cities, custom tends to be more persistent on the whole in the less sophisticated groups. Much depends on the symbolism of custom. There are certain types of custom, particularly such as are symbolic of status, which tend to be better conserved in the more sophisticated or wealthy groups than in the less sophisticated. The modern American custom, for instance, of having a married woman keep her maiden name is not likely soon to take root among the very wealthy, who here join hands with the unsophisticated majority, while the custom is being sparsely diffused among the intellectual middle class.

The varying degrees of conservatism in regard to custom can be illustrated in the behavior of a single individual because of the different types of social participation into which he enters. In England, for instance, the same individual may be in the vanguard of custom as a Londoner but insistent on the preservation of rural custom as a country squire. An American university man may be disdainful of customary opinion in his faculty club but be meekly observant of religious custom on Sunday at church. Loyalty or departure from custom is not a simple function of temperament or personality but part and parcel of the symbolism of multiple participation in society.

Custom is generally referred to as a constraining force. The conflict of individual will and social compulsion is familiar, but even the most forceful and self-assertive individual needs to yield to custom at most points in order that he may gain leverage, as it were, for the imposition of his personal will on society, which cannot be conquered without the implicit capture of social consent. The freedom gained by the denial of custom is essentially a subjective freedom of escape rather than an effective freedom of conquest. Custom makes for a powerful economy in the learning of the individual; it is a symbolic affirmation of the solidarity of the group. A by-product of these fundamental functions of custom is the more sentimental value which results from an ability to link the present and the past and thus to establish a larger ego in time, which supplements with its authority the larger ego represented by the community as it functions in the present.

The formulation of customs in the sphere of the rights and duties of individuals in their manifold relations leads to law. It is not useful to use the term law, as is often vaguely done in dealing with primitive societies, unless the enforcement of customary activity be made explicit, being vested in particular individuals or bodies of individuals. There are no societies that are wholly free from the binding force of implicit law, but as there are also many primitive societies which recognize some type of legal procedure it seems much better to speak of law only in the latter case. There are, for instance, few American Indian tribes in which customary obligations are recognized as a system of law that is capable of enforcement by the community. Psychologically law prevails, but not institutionally. This is in rather sharp contrast to the legal procedure which has been developed by the majority of African tribes. Here there is not merely the law of custom in an implicit sense but the perfectly explicit recognition of rules of conduct and of punishment for their infringement, with an elaborate method of discovering guilt and with the power of inflicting punishment vested in the king. The example of African law indicates that the essential difference between custom and law does not lie in the difference between oral tradition and the written formulation of custom. Law can emerge from custom long before the development of writing and has demonstrably done so in numerous cases. When custom has the psychological compulsion of law but is not controlled by society through the imposition of explicit penalties it may be called ethics or, more primitively, mores. It is difficult to distinguish law and ethics in the more simple forms of society. Both emerge from custom but in a somewhat divergent manner. Mundane or human sovereignty becomes progressively distinguished from socially diffused or supernatural or impersonal sovereignty. Custom controlled by the former is law; custom controlled by the latter is ethics.

The agencies instrumental in the formation of custom are for the most part quite impersonal in character and implicit in the mere fact of human interrelationships. There are also more self-conscious agencies for the perpetuation of custom. Among these the most important are law and religion, the latter particularly in the form of an organized church and priesthood. There are also organizations which are sentimentally interested in the conservation of customs which threaten to go out of use. In the modern world one often sees a rather weak nationalistic cause bolstered up by the somewhat artificial fostering of archaic custom. Much of the ritualism of the modern Scottish clans is secondarily rather than lineally conservative.

If complicated forms of conscious manipulation of ideas and techniques which rule the modern world are excluded from the range of the term custom, the force of custom may be said to be gradually lessening. The factors which favor this weakening of custom are: the growing division of labor with its tendency to make society less and less homogeneous; the growing spirit of rationalism, in the light of which much of the justification of custom fades away; the growing tendency to break away from local tradition; and, finally, the greater store set by individuality. The ideal which is latent in the modern mind would seem to be to break up custom into the two poles of individually determined habit on the one hand and of large scale institutional planning for the major enterprises of mankind on the other.

FASHION*

THE MEANING of the term fashion may be clarified by pointing out how it differs in connotation from a number of other terms whose meaning it approaches. A particular fashion differs from a given taste in suggesting some measure of compulsion on the part of the group as contrasted with individual choice from among a number of possibilities. A particular choice may of course be due to a blend of fashion and taste. Thus, if bright and simple colors are in fashion, one may select red as more pleasing to one's taste than yellow, although one's free taste unhampered by fashion might have decided in favor of a more subtle tone. To the discriminating person the demand of fashion constitutes a challenge to taste and suggests problems of reconciliation. But fashion is accepted by average people with little demur and is not so much reconciled with taste as substituted for it. For many people taste hardly arises at all except on the basis of a clash of an accepted fashion with a fashion that is out of date or current in some other group than one's own.

The term fashion may carry with it a tone of approval or disapproval. It is a fairly objective term whose emotional qualities depend on a context. A moralist may decry a certain type of behavior as a mere fashion but the ordinary person will not be displeased if he is accused of being in the fashion. It is different with fads, which are objectively similar to fashions but differ from them in being more personal in their application and in connoting a more or less definite social disapproval. Particular people or coteries have their fads, while fashions are the property of larger or more representative groups. A taste which asserts itself in spite of fashion and which may therefore be suspected of having something obsessive about it may be referred to as an individual fad. On the other hand, while a fad may be of very short duration, it always differs from a true fashion in having something unexpected, irresponsible or bizarre about it. Any fashion which sins against one's sense of style and one's feeling for the historical continuity of style is likely to be dismissed as a fad. There are changing fashions in tennis rackets, while the game of mah jong, once rather fashionable, takes on in retrospect more and more the character of a fad.

Just as the weakness of fashion leads to fads, so its strength comes from custom. Customs differ from fashions in being relatively permanent types of social behavior. They change, but with a less active and con-

* *Encyclopaedia of the Social Sciences* (New York, Macmillan, 1931), 6: 139–144.

scious participation of the individual in the change. Custom is the element of permanence which makes changes in fashion possible. Custom marks the highroad of human interrelationships, while fashion may be looked upon as the endless departure from the return to the highroad. The vast majority of fashions are relieved by other fashions, but occasionally a fashion crystallizes into permanent habit, taking on the character of custom.

It is not correct to think of fashion as merely a short lived innovation in custom, because many innovations in human history arise with the need for them and last as long as they are useful or convenient. If, for instance, there is a shortage of silk and it becomes customary to substitute cotton for silk in the manufacture of certain articles of dress in which silk has been the usual material, such an enforced change of material, however important economically or aesthetically, does not in itself constitute a true change of fashion. On the other hand, if cotton is substituted for silk out of free choice as a symbol perhaps of the simple life or because of a desire to see what novel effect can be produced in accepted types of dress with simpler materials, the change may be called one of fashion. There is nothing to prevent an innovation from eventually taking on the character of a new fashion. If, for example, people persist in using the cotton material even after silk has once more become available, a new fashion has arisen.

Fashion is a custom in the guise of departure from custom. Most normal individuals consciously or unconsciously have the itch to break away in some measure from a too literal loyalty to accepted custom. They are not fundamentally in revolt from custom but they wish somehow to legitimize their personal deviation without laying themselves open to the charge of insensitiveness to good taste or good manners. Fashion is the discreet solution of the subtle conflict. The slight changes from the established in dress or other forms of behavior seem for the moment to give the victory to the individual, while the fact that one's fellows revolt in the same direction gives one a feeling of adventurous safety. The personal note which is at the hidden core of fashion becomes superpersonalized.

Whether fashion is felt as a sort of socially legitimized caprice or is merely a new and unintelligible form of social tyranny depends on the individual or class. It is probable that those most concerned with the setting and testing of fashions are the individuals who realize most keenly the problem of reconciling individual freedom with social conformity which is implicit in the very fact of fashion. It is perhaps not too much to say that most people are at least partly sensitive to this aspect of fashion and are secretly grateful for it. A large minority of people, however, are insensitive to the psychological complexity of fashion and submit to it to the extent that they do merely because they realize that not to fall in with it would be to declare themselves members of a past generation or dull people who cannot keep up with their neighbors. These latter reasons for being fashionable are secondary; they are sullen surrenderers to bastard custom.

The fundamental drives leading to the creation and acceptance of fashion can be isolated. In the more sophisticated societies boredom, created by leisure and too highly specialized forms of activity, leads to restlessness and curiosity. This general desire to escape from the trammels of a too regularized existence is powerfully reenforced by a ceaseless desire to add to the attractiveness of the self and all other objects of love and friendship. It is precisely in functionally powerful societies that the individual's ego is constantly being convicted of helplessness. The individual tends to be unconsciously thrown back on himself and demands more and more novel affirmations of his effective reality. The endless rediscovery of the self in a series of petty truancies from the official socialized self becomes a mild obsession of the normal individual in any society in which the individual has ceased to be a measure of the society itself. There is, however, always the danger of too great a departure from the recognized symbols of the individual, because his identity is likely to be destroyed. That is why insensitive people, anxious to be literally in the fashion, so often overreach themselves and nullify the very purpose of fashion. Good hearted women of middle age generally fail in the art of being ravishing nymphs.

Somewhat different from the affirmation of the libidinal self is the more vulgar desire for prestige or notoriety, satisfied by changes in fashion. In this category belongs fashion as an outward emblem of personal distinction or of membership in some group to which distinction is ascribed. The imitation of fashion by people who belong to circles removed from those which set the fashion has the function of bridging the gap between a social class and the class next above it. The logical result of the acceptance of a fashion by all members of society is the disappearance of the kinds of satisfaction responsible for the change of fashion in the first place. A new fashion becomes psychologically necessary, and thus the cycle of fashion is endlessly repeated.

Fashion is emphatically a historical concept. A specific fashion is utterly unintelligible if lifted out of its place in a sequence of forms. It is exceedingly dangerous to rationalize or in any other way psychologize a particular fashion on the basis of general principles which might be considered applicable to the class of forms of which it seems to be an example. It is utterly vain, for instance, to explain particular forms of dress or types of cosmetics or methods of wearing the hair without a preliminary historical critique. Bare legs among modern women in summer do not psychologically or historically create at all the same fashion as bare legs and bare feet among primitives living in the tropics. The importance of understanding fashion historically should be obvious enough when it is recognized that the very essence of fashion is that it be valued as a variation in an understood sequence, as a departure from the immediately preceding mode.

Changes in fashion depend on the prevailing culture and on the social ideals which inform it. Under the apparently placid surface of culture there are always powerful psychological drifts of which fashion is quick to catch the direction. In a democratic society, for instance, if there is an unacknowledged drift toward class distinctions fashion will discover endless ways of giving it visible form. Criticism can always be met by the insincere defense that fashion is merely fashion and need not be taken seriously. If in a puritanic society there is a growing impatience with the outward forms of modesty, fashion finds it easy to minister to the demands of sex curiosity, while the old mores can be trusted to defend fashion with an affectation of unawareness of what fashion is driving at. A complete study of the history of fashion would undoubtedly throw much light on the ups and downs of sentiment and attitude at various periods of civilization. However, fashion never permanently outruns discretion and only those who are taken in by the superficial rationalizations of fashion are surprised by the frequent changes of face in its history. That there was destined to be a lengthening of women's skirts after they had become short enough was obvious from the outset to all except those who do not believe that sex symbolism is a real factor in human behavior.

The chief difficulty of understanding fashion in its apparent vagaries is the lack of exact knowledge of the unconscious symbolisms attaching to forms, colors, textures, postures and other expressive elements in a given culture. The difficulty is appreciably increased by the fact that the same expressive elements tend to have quite different symbolic references in different areas. Gothic type, for instance, is a nationalistic token in Germany, while in Anglo-Saxon culture the practically identical type known as Old English has entirely different connotations. In other words, the same style of lettering may symbolize either an undying hatred of France or a wistful look backward at madrigals and pewter.

An important principle in the history of fashion is that those features of fashion which do not configurate correctly with the unconscious system of meanings characteristic of the given culture are relatively insecure. Extremes of style, which too frankly symbolize the current of feeling of the moment, are likely to find themselves in exposed positions, as it were, where they can be outflanked by meanings which they do not wish to recognize. Thus, it may be conjectured that lipstick is less secure in American culture as an element of fashion than rouge discreetly applied to the cheek. This is assuredly not due to a superior sinfulness of lipstick as such, but to the fact that rosy cheeks resulting from a healthy natural life in the country are one of the characteristic fetishisms of the traditional ideal of feminine beauty, while lipstick has rather the character of certain exotic ardors and goes with flaming oriental stuffs. Rouge is likely to last for many decades or centuries because there is, and is likely to be for a long time to come, a definite strain of nature worship in our culture. If lipstick is to remain it can only be because our culture will have taken on certain violently new meanings which are not at all obvious at the present time. As a symbol it is episodic rather than a part of the underlying rhythm of the history of our fashions.

In custom bound cultures, such as are characteristic of the primitive world, there are slow non-reversible changes of style rather than the often reversible forms of fashion found in modern cultures. The emphasis in such societies is on the group and the sanctity of tradition rather than on individual expression, which tends to be entirely unconscious. In the great cultures of the Orient and in ancient and mediaeval Europe changes in fashion can be noted radiating from certain definite centers of sophisticated culture, but it is not until modern Europe is reached that the familiar merry-go-round of fashion with its rapid alternations of season occurs.

The typically modern acceleration of changes in fashion may be ascribed to the influence of the Renaissance, which awakened a desire for innovation and which powerfully extended for European society the total world of possible choices. During this period Italian culture came to be the arbiter of taste, to be followed by French culture, which may still be looked upon as the most powerful influence in the creation and distribution of fashions. But more important than the Renaissance in the history of fashion is the effect of the industrial revolution and the rise of the common people. The former increased the mechanical ease with which fashions could be diffused; the latter greatly increased the number of those willing and able to be fashionable.

Modern fashion tends to spread to all classes of society. As fashion has always tended to be a symbol of membership in a particular social class and as human beings have always felt the urge to edge a little closer to a class considered superior to their own, there must always have been the tendency for fashion to be adopted by circles which had a lower status than the group setting the fashions. But on the whole such adoption of fashion from above tended to be discreet because of the great importance attached to the maintenance of social classes. What has happened in the modern world, regardless of the official forms of government which prevail in the different nations, is that the tone giving power which lies back of fashion has largely slipped away from the aristocracy of rank to the aristocracy of wealth. This means a psychological if not an economic leveling of classes because of the feeling that wealth is an accidental or accreted quality of an individual as contrasted with blood. In an aristocracy of wealth everyone, even the poorest, is potentially wealthy both in legal theory and in private fancy. In such a society, therefore, all individuals are equally entitled, it is felt, so far as their pockets permit, to the insignia of fashion. This universalizing of fashion necessarily cheapens its value in the specific case and forces an abnormally rapid change of fashion. The only effective protection possessed by the wealthy in the world of fashion is the insistence on expensive materials in which fashion is to express itself. Too great an insistence on this factor, however, is the hall mark of wealthy vulgarity, for fashion is essentially a thing of forms and symbols, not of material values.

Perhaps the most important of the special factors which encourage the spread of fashion today is the increased facility for the production and transportation of goods and for communication either personally or by correspondence from the centers of fashion to the outmost periphery of the civilized world. These increased facilities necessarily lead to huge capital investments in the manufacture and distribution of fashionable wear. The extraordinarily high initial profits to be derived from fashion and the relatively rapid tapering off of profits make it inevitable that the natural tendency to change in fashion is helped along by commercial suggestion. The increasingly varied activities of modern life also give greater opportunity for the growth and change of fashion. Today the cut of a dress or the shape of a hat stands ready to symbolize anything from mountain climbing or military efficiency, through automobiling to interpretative dancing and veiled harlotry. No individual is merely what his social role indicates that he is to be or may vary only slightly from, but he may act as if he is anything else that individual phantasy may dictate. The greater leisure and spending power of the bourgeoisie, bringing them externally nearer the upper classes of former days, are other obvious stimuli to change in fashion, as are the gradual psychological and economic liberation of women and the greater opportunity given them for experimentation in dress and adornment.

Fashions for women show greater variability than fashions for men in contemporary civilization. Not only do women's fashions change more rapidly and completely but the total gamut of allowed forms is greater for women than for men. In times past and in other cultures, however, men's fashions show a greater exuberance than women's. Much that used to be ascribed to woman as female is really due to woman as a sociologically and economically defined class. Woman as a distinctive theme for fashion may be explained in terms of the social psychology of the present civilization. She is the one who pleases by being what she is and looking as she does rather than by doing what she does. Whether biology or history is primarily responsible for this need not be decided. Woman has been the kept partner in marriage and has had to prove her desirability by ceaselessly reaffirming her attractiveness as symbolized by novelty of fashion. Among the wealthier classes and by imitation also among the less wealthy, woman has come to be looked upon as an expensive luxury on whom one spends extravagantly. She is thus a symbol of the social and economic status of her husband. Whether with the increasingly marked change of woman's place in society the factors which emphasize extravagance in women's fashions will entirely fall away it is impossible to say at the present time.

There are powerful vested interests involved in changes of fashions, as has already been mentioned. The effect on the producer of fashions of a variability which he both encourages and dreads is the introduction of the element of risk. It is a popular error to assume that professional designers arbitrarily dictate fashion. They do so only in a very superficial sense. Actually they have to obey many masters. Their designs must above all things net the manufacturers a profit, so that behind the more strictly psychological determinants of fashion there lurks a very important element due to the sheer technology of the manufacturing process or the availability of a certain type of material. In addition to this the designer must have a sure feeling for the established in custom and the degree to which he can safely depart from it. He must intuitively divine what people want before they are quite aware of it themselves. His business is not so much to impose fashion as to coax people to accept what they have themselves unconsciously suggested. This causes the profits of fashion production to be out of all proportion to the actual cost of manufacturing fashionable goods. The producer and his designer assistant capitalize the curiosity and vanity of their customers but they must also be protected against the losses of a risky business. Those who are familiar with the history of fashion are emphatic in speaking of the inability of business to combat the fashion trends which have been set going by various psychological factors. A fashion may be aesthetically pleasing in the abstract, but if it runs counter to the trend or does not help to usher in a new trend which is struggling for a hearing it may be a flat failure.

The distribution of fashions is a comparatively simple and automatic process. The vogue of fashion plates and fashion magazines, the many lines of communication which connect fashion producers and fashion dispensers, and modern methods of marketing make it almost inevitable that a successful Parisian fashion should find its way within an incredibly short period of time to Chicago and San Francisco. If it were not for the necessity of exploiting accumulated stocks of goods these fashions would penetrate into the remotest corners of rural America even more rapidly than is the case. The average consumer is chronically distressed to discover how rapidly his accumulated property in wear depreciates by becoming outmoded. He complains bitterly and ridicules the new fashions when they appear. In the end he succumbs, a victim to symbolisms of behavior which he does not fully comprehend. What he will never admit is that he is more the creator than the victim of his difficulties.

Fashion has always had vain critics. It has been arraigned by the clergy and by social satirists because each new style of wear, calling attention as it does to the form of the human body, seems to the critics to be an attack on modesty. Some fashions there are, to be sure, whose very purpose it is to attack modesty, but over and above specific attacks there is felt to be a generalized one. The charge is well founded but useless. Human beings do not wish to be modest; they want to be as expressive—that is, as immodest—as fear allows; fashion helps them solve their paradoxical problem. The charge of economic waste which is often leveled against fashion has had little or no effect on the public mind. Waste sems to be of no concern where values are to be considered, particularly when these values are both egoistic and unconscious. The criticism that fashion imposes an unwanted uniformity is not as sound as it appears to be in the first instance. The individual in society is only rarely significantly expressive in his own right. For the vast majority of human beings the choice lies between unchanging custom and the legitimate caprice of custom, which is fashion.

Fashion concerns itself closely and intimately with the ego. Hence its proper field is dress and adornment. There are other symbols of the ego, however, which are not as close to the body as these but which are almost equally subject to the psychological laws of fashion. Among them are objects of utility, amusements and furniture. People differ in their sensitiveness to changing fashions in these more remote forms of human expressiveness. It is therefore impossible to say categorically just what the possible range of fashion is. However, in regard to both amusements and furniture there may be observed the same tendency to change, periodicity and unquestioning acceptance as in dress and ornament.

Many speak of fashions in thought, art, habits of living and morals. It is superficial to dismiss such locutions as metaphorical and unimportant. The usage shows a true intuition of the meaning of fashion, which while it is primarily applied to dress and the exhibition of the human body is not essentially concerned with the fact of dress or ornament but with its symbolism. There is nothing to prevent a thought, a type of morality or an art from being the psychological equivalent of a costuming of the ego. Certainly one may allow oneself to be converted to Catholicism or Christian Science in exactly the same spirit in which one invests in pewter or follows the latest Parisian models in dress. Beliefs and attitudes are not fashions in their character of mores but neither are dress and ornament. In contemporary society it is not a fashion that men wear trousers; it is the custom. Fashion merely dictates such variations as whether trousers are to be so or so long, what colors they are to have and whether they are to have cuffs or not. In the same way, while adherence to a religious faith is not in itself a fashion, as soon as the individual feels that he can pass easily, out of personal choice, from one belief to another, not because he is led to his choice by necessity but because of a desire to accrete to himself symbols of status, it becomes legitimate to speak of his change of attitude as a change of fashion. Functional irrelevance as contrasted with symbolic significance for the expressiveness of the ego is implicit in all fashion.

EXCERPTS FROM REVIEWS

FROM A REVIEW OF W. A. MASON,
"A HISTORY OF THE ART OF WRITING"*

WRITING at all times has constituted a plastic as well as a symbolic problem. The conveyance of thought has been only one of its uses; the delineation of pleasing contours, now severe and statuesque, now flowing in graceful meanderings, has always been something more than a by-product. As one passes from ideographic system to system and from alphabet to alphabet perhaps the thing that most forcibly strikes one is that each and every one of them has its individual style. In their earlier stages there is a certain randomness. This is corrected by the obscurely divining, converging hands of thousands of artists, until, at a given moment, the characters stand forth as a unique and unified work of art, as self-contained and as definitely stylized as any architectural tradition. The historian has no difficulty in showing how a starting-point gives a slant or drift to the future development of the system, how the particular forms, for instance, of the mediaeval black-letter are largely prefigured in the Phoenician alphabet. But he does not so clearly know just how and why the various styles develop, just how it is that the Arabic hand, the Roman type, the Armenian, the Hindu alphabets, all derived as they ultimately are from a single prototype, have so widely diverged, have their individualities so stamped upon them, that the proof of their common genesis is but the coldest of arracheological businesses.

Much can be said and has been said of the controlling power of the medium. Stone is different from papyrus and the pen is different from a camel's-hair brush. Yet when all this and more is indicated and worked out with laborious detail, we are really no nearer the central question of what psychological forces have hurried the national hand on to that aesthetic balance which is its ultimate style. We are not concerned to solve the baffling problem; we are merely concerned to state its actuality. It is not otherwise with language, with religion, with the forms of social organization. Wherever the human mind has worked collectively and un-consciously, it has striven for and often attained unique form. The important point is that the evolution of form has a drift in one direction, that it seeks poise, and that it rests, relatively speaking, when it has found this poise. It is customary to say that sooner or later a literary or sacerdotal tradition enjoins conservatism, but is it altogether an

* *The Freeman*, 4 (1921): 68–69.

accident that the injunction is stayed until the style is full-grown? I do not believe in this particular accident. To me it is no mere chance that the Chinese system of writing did not attain its resting-point until it had matured a style, until it had polished off each character, whether simple or compounded of "radical" and "phonetic" elements, into a design that satisfactorily filled its own field and harmonized with its thousands of fellows. A glance at the earlier forms of Chinese writing convinces one that it did not always possess true style, interesting and original as some of the early characters are.

From a Review of Ludwig Lewisohn, "Israel"*

Mr. Lewisohn is very bitter about the assimilationists. Assimilation, he thinks, has been tried and found wanting, in America no less than in Germany. But he seems to overlook some very simple facts and to refrain from certain very simple reflections. In the first place, when in the history of mankind has ethnic assimilation been a comfortable or an easy process? Had Mr. Lewisohn taken a bird's-eye view of human relations, instead of seeing the Jewish problem as the utterly unique thing which it is not, he would have realized the inevitability of conflict, now overt and sanguinary, now peaceful but insidious, between any two cultures or religions or peoples that offer as many points of difference as do the Jews and the traditions and peoples they have come into such close contact with. But instead of envisaging this conflict as a perpetually insoluble one, as a sort of fatal conundrum of history, he would, furthermore, have made the less dramatic but far more sober observation that the psychological distance which separates the Jew from the non-Jew today is, by and large, perceptibly less great than it has ever been. Ku Klux Klans and pogroms and the stiffening of Jewish disabilities here and there do not prove that assimilation is impossible, but they prove that it is a far less easily consummated process and a more tortuously winding one than some idealists would like to have it. They reiterate, in short, one of the annoying truisms of history. Mankind has never been unyielding, it has merely been stubbornly disposed not to yield.

Mr. Lewisohn is quite wrong, I believe, in ruling out assimilation as a solution of the Jewish problem. It is, patently, a very possible and a very excellent one in thousands of individual cases—in spite of the embarrassing fact that many highly educated Jews or very wealthy Jews are debarred from membership in clubs that are deemed desirable of entry. But he is perfectly correct in finding also another solution, for

* *The Menorah Journal*, 12 (1926): 214–218.

there is no reason whatever to believe that but one solution was pre-ordained. For one thing, it is altogether likely that large masses of Jews will continue to lead a somewhat distinctive life in the midst of other peoples. This too is a "solution," as such things go in that flux of human affairs which always refuses to reach the particular equilibrium desired by those who decide upon the course of events. For another, the Zionist experiment to which Mr. Lewisohn pins his hopes is an admirable solution insofar as it satisfied the aspirations of many thousands of courageous Jews, inspired by a number of distinct motives. One gains nothing by closing one's eyes to facts and by declaring, out of the rhetorical fervor of one's preference, this or that turn to be the right and only solution. For there is not one Jewish problem, there are many—keenly personal ones of all sorts, and varying group problems conditioned by local circumstances, economic and cultural. Mr. Lewisohn would not have hurt his plea for Zionistic support if he had frankly recognized the possibility of some measure of assimilation, for assimilation on a grand scale is obviously not possible in the immediate future.

Most books about the Jew have an unpleasant flavor of the apologetic about them. *Israel* is free from this taint. It presents the case for the Jew as a creator of cultural values with pride but not with partisanship. Mr. Lewisohn knows too much about the cultural history of Europe to indulge in a rhapsodical cataloguing of Jewish exploits in the arts and sciences. He puts most of his emphasis on the peculiar, narrow, over intellectualized, yet always intense and vital Jewish culture of eastern Europe and has it meet the more comfortable but also the more flabby and fragmentary culture of Anglo-Saxon America with outward deference and an inner awareness of a half useless superiority. In all this he is doing both Jew and non-Jew an immense service. No American, after reading Mr. Lewisohn's book, can continue to feel that the uncouth Jewish immigrant from Poland or Lithuania comes to this land as a spiritual mendicant. Most Americans, one fears, had rather taken for granted just that. A clearing of the atmosphere makes for health all around. . . .

It seems to me that if there is anything distinctive about the temper of Jewish thought today, it is that it has largely transcended the limits of any localism, however vast or powerful. This temper has been as often the subject of abuse as of favorable comment. Jewish "disloyalty" and "negativism," however, are but terms of disparagement for a spirit that is abroad in the world today and which it is the "mission" of the Jew— if the romantic philosopher of history must give him a mission—to foster as best he can. This spirit runs counter to the current nationalism which is perhaps more articulate than truly vital. It is not so much a destroyer of folk values as a solvent of them. It refuses to make a fetish of any localism or lineage but insists on utilizing the cultural goods of all localisms and of every lineage for a deeply personal synthesis. It is this spirit which Mr. Lewisohn has most truly at heart, unless I misread all the signs. But, baffled as he is by the difficulty of living such a life of personal values, unequal to the task and privilege of serenity in the face of injury to pride, he has sought to find this spirit in Zionism. Zionism has its own justification, but I cannot but think that Mr. Lewisohn is in error in identifying its philosophy with the critical, transnational philosophy that so many Jews have helped to create.

AMERICAN INDIANS
EDITOR'S PREFACE

T
HE FIRST *paper in this section, "Time Perspective," is Sapir's longest single monograph in ethnology. Essentially, it is a philosophical assay of anthropological method in historical reconstruction, and hence has been cited frequently in discussions of ethnological theory and closely studied by several academic generations of graduate students. The original edition has long been out of print; library copies in the main centers of anthropological teaching have become weary with decades of wear. One anthropologist tells the story of a winsome and intelligent young lady who used to do typing for him not many years ago when he was a graduate student. On his birthday she brought him a sheaf of typescript in gift wrappings. It was the whole of "Time Perspective," which she had meticulously copied. He married her.*

The opening paragraphs of this paper must be understood in the perspective of the time when they were written. Thus when Sapir decries "the emphasis on the general and schematic that has to so great an extent characterized the study of cultural anthropology," he is referring to works which loomed considerably larger in 1916 than they have in later years, although their influence still may be discerned. Several passages from the 1920 review of Lowie's Primitive Society *may be cited to indicate Sapir's reference more specifically.*

"Hence it has come about that the ready generalizers on social origins, the rapid readers of many monographic works on primitive societies in pursuit of the one unifying idea, have had it very largely their own way. This speculative school of anthropological theory was given its peculiar twist of evolutionary determinism by a number of Victorian writers—McLennan, Spencer, Maine. It received an authoritative, dogmatic formulation in the work of an American, Morgan, and a gracious literary embodiment in the books of such writers as Lang and Frazer. If we are now gradually recognizing what fallacies and illusions went to the building of the imposing structures of the classical school of anthropology, we owe it in no small measure to the new school of American anthropologists, dominated by the sympathetic yet acridly critical spirit of Professor F. Boas. . . . It has been all too lightly assumed that primitive society knows no complicating history, that its form and its cultural content alike are but the ordained reflexes of certain supposed traits of primitive mentality. This attitude is as persistent in the Freudian explanations of folk-belief and usage as in the social psychology of Wundt or the mechanical determinism of Spencer."

It should not be supposed from this that Sapir rejected bodily all the contributions of these writers. Indeed, in respect to the Freudian approaches especially, as several of the selections in the final section of this volume indicate, he was most alive to the value and importance of using them in a judicious manner. Similarly, he recognized that the just criticisms of Morgan's work did not negate the possibility of deriving a more cogent formulation of cultural evolution.

And it must be noted that Sapir's conception of the proper scope and methods of cultural anthropology became considerably broadened in his later years. Such a paper as "Cultural Anthropology and Psychiatry" (1932), for example, also stresses the historical, i.e., dynamic, method in analyzing cultural phenomena, but envisages that method as including a good deal more than the providing of chronological depth for the patterns of non-literate societies.

As its subtitle says, "Time Perspective" is a study in method. Specific problems and concrete data are alluded to and used for purposes of illustration, rather than intensively investigated for their own sake. In some places a casual sentence may foreshadow a conclusion which was later to become an accepted thesis. Kroeber makes mention of this in referring to the relatively recent development of the full-blown Plains culture in North America: "That there is nothing revolutionary in such a view is shown by the fact that as long ago as 1916 Sapir in a sentence analyzed the recent Plains culture into non-Plains origins. The reason why he did not follow the matter farther is that his essay was concerned with method rather than fact."[1]

Sapir did write a number of papers which were concerned with ethnographic fact. Two examples of his more descriptive work follow next in the section. The excerpts from "Song Recitative in Paiute Mythology" (1910) include the first and last parts of the paper, omitting the detailed linguistic and musical analyses. Last in this section is the 1915 paper which offers a succinct account of the rather complex social organization of the Northwest Coast peoples.

Among the other papers of this type which ethnologists have found especially useful are his "Religious Ideas of the Takelma Indians of Southwestern Oregon" (1907), "Terms of Relationship and the Levirate" (1916), and "The Life of a Nootka Indian" (1921), which was reprinted under the title "Sayach'apis, a Nootka Trader" (1922).

[1] A. L. Kroeber, *Cultural and Natural Areas of Native North America*, Univ. Calif. Publ. Am. Arch. and Ethn., 38 (1939): 76.

TIME PERSPECTIVE IN ABORIGINAL AMERICAN CULTURE: A STUDY IN METHOD*

CONTENTS

* Canada, Department of Mines, Geological Survey, Memoir 90 Anthropological Series No. 13 (Ottawa, Government Printing Bureau, 1916), 87 pp.

[389]

CULTURAL ANTHROPOLOGY is more and more rapidly getting to realize itself as a strictly historical science. Its data can not be understood, either in themselves or in their relation to one another, except as the end-points of specific sequences of events reaching back into the remote past. Some of us may be more interested in the psychological laws of human development that we believe ourselves capable of extracting from the raw material of ethnology and archæology, than in the establishment of definite historical facts and relationships that would tend to make this material intelligible, but it is not at all clear that the formulation of such laws is any more the business of the anthropologist than of the historian in the customarily narrow sense of the word. If the anthropologist, more often than the historian, has argued from descriptive data to folk psychology, we must hold responsible for this two factors. First, we must take account of the frequent, indeed typical, lack of direct chronological guides in the study of the culture of primitive peoples, whereby he is led to neglect or undervalue the importance of chronological insight and to seek, as a substitute, the unravelling of general laws operating regardless of specific time. In the second place, the cultures dealt with by the anthropologist exhibit, on the whole, less complexity than those made known to us by documentary evidence, whereby he is led to think of the former as less encumbered by secondary or untypical developments and better fit to serve as matter for psychological generalization. Something may also be credited to the fact that the data of the anthropologist give him a view of a greater diversity of cultures than the historian is accustomed to take in at one glance, whereby the former is provided with a truer perspective, or thinks he is, for the evaluation of the typical in the development of culture in general. These and possibly other factors render intelligible the emphasis on the general and schematic that has to so great a degree characterized the study of cultural anthropology. It cannot be held, however, that the actual data of our science are with more appropriateness to be turned over as a *corpus vile* to the folk-pyschologist than the data of the most advanced cultures of to-day. Granting that the labours of the folk-psychologist are justifiable in themselves, the main point remains that so-called primitive culture consists throughout of phenomena that, so far as the ethnologist is concerned, must be worked out historically, that is, in terms of actual happenings, however inferred, that are conceived to have a specific sequence, a specific localization, and specific relations among themselves. Few would be so bold as to maintain that the vast and ever growing mass of ethnological material will ever completely yield to such an historical interpretation, but it is highly important that an historical understanding of the facts be held up as the properly ethnological goal of the student.

Assuming, then, that we are desirous of adopting as thoroughly historical a method of interpretation of aboriginal American culture as circumstances permit, the question immediately suggests itself: how inject a
chronology into this confusing mass of purely descriptive fact? All that,
in the greatest number of cases, we know about a tribe, aside from
scattered information on its external history, covering a relatively short
span of time, is that such and such implements and processes were in use,
customs practised, and beliefs entertained at a point of time but little
antedating the present. Where, as in the case of the Aztec, Maya, and
Peruvian cultures, our knowledge is based on the recorded testimony of
earlier writers, we are still dealing, in the main, with facts pertaining to a
single point of time or, at best, to a brief span of time, too brief to throw
much light on the development of the whole culture. Our problem may
be metaphorically defined as the translation of a two-dimensional photo-
graphic picture of reality into the three-dimensional picture which lies
back of it. Is it possible to read time perspective into the flat surface of
American culture as we read space perspective into the flat surface of a
photograph?

Before being in a position to answer this question, we must be clear as
to just what we expect of our time perspective. It is evident at the outset
that the nature of our material imposes limitations not felt, or not felt
so keenly, by the historian. First of all, we shall to only a very limited
extent expect to construct an absolute chronology, that is, assign anything like definite dates. In some cases we shall be satisfied with an
approximate date, a margin of error being allowed that may vary from
a few years to several centuries, or, in the remoter past, even millennia.
In still other, perhaps the majority, of cases, we shall be content to
dispense with the assignment of dates altogether and shall aim merely to
establish a definite sequence of events. A second limitation is no less clear.
One of the characteristic traits of history is its emphasis on the individual and personal. While the importance of individual events and
personalities for the progress of human affairs is not to be underesti-
mated, the historical reconstructions of the cultural anthropologist can
only deal, with comparatively few exceptions, with generalized events
and individualities. Instead of speaking, for instance, of the specific
influence exerted by a particular shaman of a tribe at an inaccessible
period in the past, cultural anthropology will have to lump together a
number of such phenomena and generalize as to the influence exerted by
the class of shamans at a more or less well defined time and place. Or, if
it is a question of the social relations between two tribes, say the Haida

and Tsimshian, it may in a number of cases have to content itself with a broad definition of such relations, taking, for instance, the Haida and Tsimshian as such as the units directly involved, though perfectly aware that the actual mechanism of the relation is in every case borne by individuals, house-groups, or clans, that is, by subdivisions of the historical units ostensibly concerned. A great deal of such substitution of the whole for the part is unavoidable in ethnology. These two limitations must be frankly recognized, but they need not in the slightest obscure the application of historical methods to the field of cultural anthropology. They introduce a purely quantitative, not qualitative, correction into our initial ideal of historical treatment. Often enough, in dealing with an historical process not far removed from the present, the student will be enabled to follow out the precise course of events and the absolute time (within reasonable limits) of each; he will also be enabled to define clearly the nature of the social units, whether individual or collective, concerned in each stage of the process. Such opportunities to study the dynamics of primitive culture should never be missed; they are not only of specific value in the study of recent phases of the cultural development of a tribe, but afford valuable aid towards the formation of a technique in the historical interpretation of data far removed in time. In the main, however, the gaining of an historical perspective will mean the arrangement in as orderly temporal sequence as possible, within as definitely circumscribed absolute time limits as circumstances will allow, of the processes studied by our science, the carriers of these processes being generally defined more inclusively than in documentary history.

To turn to concrete illustrations. We may wish to ascertain, if possible, whether the movement of certain Siouan tribes (say the Omaha and Ponca) to the western plains was prior or subsequent to the development among them of a particular ritual (say the calumet adoption ritual). Neither the personalities or social units that took the lead in the western movement nor the agencies most immediately concerned in the development of the ritual need ever be successfully worked out; nor may we succeed in assigning a plausible date or range of time to either process. Nevertheless, it is quite clear that if we discover which of the two was first consummated, we shall have acquired a valuable clue (perhaps only a caution) towards the historical understanding of the ritual both in its relations to other cultural complexes within the tribes concerned and to the same or allied rituals in neighbouring tribes (say the Pawnee Hako ceremony). If the ritual can be shown to have developed after the arrival of the Siouan tribes on the plains, we at once begin to suspect the influence of the neighbouring tribes in the origination of the ritual among the former. Or, to take another example, we may wish to work out the relative chronology of origin of such a group of associated phenomena among the Nootka as the thunderbird type of origin myth, the use of the thunderbird in house paintings, the thunderbird dance, the references to the thunderbird in personal names, and the metaphorical use of the term "thundering" to apply to wealth. According to the relative ages determined for these cultural elements, we shall have to construct markedly different theories of their historical relations to one another, to similar phenomena among the Kwakiutl and other neighbouring tribes, and to still other cultural elements of a distinct but allied nature in the same and neighbouring tribes. The importance of setting the data of American ethnology into chronologic relations will no doubt be readily conceded. It is the aim of this paper to call attention to some of the methods that have been or may be employed to determine them.

The evidence at our disposal may be broadly classified into two main heads, direct and inferential evidence. By the former is meant such evidence as directly suggests temporal relations, by the latter such evidence as is inferred from data that do not in themselves present the form of a time sequence. The direct evidence available in American ethnology is, in the nature of the case, well understood and has been employed to a considerable extent. The inferential evidence, on the other hand, is apt to be rather felt than clearly understood and, while it has been not infrequently, sometimes only tacitly, utilized, it is undoubtedly capable of much greater service than generally recognized.

DIRECT EVIDENCE FOR TIME PERSPECTIVE

DOCUMENTARY EVIDENCE

The first type of direct evidence is that yielded by historical documents, such as the Jesuit Relations, Cook's Voyages, and a host of other works that will readily occur to everyone. During the more than four hundred years that have elapsed since the discovery of America, the native cultures have naturally not been static. Considerable movements of population in certain areas have also occurred. Comparison of statements made at different periods frequently enable us to give maximal and minimal dates to appearance of a cultural element or to assign the time limits to a movement of population. Evidence of this sort, for instance, has enabled Wissler to put the important cultural fact of the spread of the horse among the North American Indians on a chronological basis. Similar evidence, again, has enabled Mooney to follow the gradual movement of the Cheyenne from southern Minnesota to eastern Colorado and Wyoming. On the other hand, the mention of kayaks in one of the earliest Norse references to the Eskimo gives us a minimal date for the age of this type of boat. Similarly, a minimal date for the presence of age societies among several Plains tribes (*e.g.* the Mandan) is afforded by such writers as Maximilian and Catlin. The existence in museums of dated ethnological or archæological specimens belongs naturally to the same general type of evidence. Thus, a minimal age for the large split bird-shaped type of Nootka rattle is afforded by the existence in the British Museum of a Nootka specimen of this sort collected by Capt. Cook, one that in no way differs from specimens still in use among these Indians.

Use may also be made of negative documentary evidence, though great caution is, of course, required here. For example, the failure of the earlier writers to refer to the floral designs in beadwork, moose hair, or porcupine quills now thoroughly at home among certain eastern tribes (*e.g.* the Huron, Ojibwa, and Cree) leads to the suspicion that these are of relatively recent origin and due to European influence. The same suspicion in regard to the use of the sail among the West Coast Indians seems justified by its failure to appear in the illustrations of canoes found in the older writers.* In neither of these latter cases, however, does the negative evidence alone constitute a demonstration. Scores of other American examples of the significance for culture chronology of both positive and negative documentary evidence will occur to all.

Native Testimony

A second type of direct evidence is formed by statements, whether as formal legends or personal information, regarding the age or relative sequence of events in tribal history made by the natives themselves. Statements of this sort have been often recorded for earlier tribal movements, but are also forthcoming in considerable quantity for the origin and spread of cultural features. When they refer to the distant past, they must be handled with a good deal of reserve, for experience shows that the historical and mythical merge inextricably beyond a certain point. Nevertheless, I believe that there has been in certain quarters decidedly too much of a tendency to make light of all Indian accounts of migration and tribal or clan movements. The village to village movements of clans or septs recorded in various West Coast mythologies, for instance, certainly all have the ring of history or, better said, of legend based on historical events, for the motives and attendant circumstances of such

---

* I am indebted to Dr. C. F. Newcombe for this observation.

movements are frequently enough fanciful in character. Similarly, if we are told in Hopi clan legends that a particular pueblo received accessions from certain quarters, we need a more powerful argument than a general lofty scepticism to convince us of the total lack of historical value of such statements. The fact that the Tewa pueblo of Hano, situated in the Hopi country of Tusayan, demonstrably traces its origin to the Rio Grande valley should, among other facts of like nature, make us more receptive to the truth of similar movements in the past recorded in native legend. Again, there seems to be no good reason to doubt the substantial correctness of the northern provenience of the Nahuatl-speaking Aztec recorded for us in their legends. The fact that all the remoter linguistic relatives of Nahuatl (Cora-Huichol, Piman, Shoshonean) lie to the north of the historical home of the Aztecs is the best kind of confirmation of these legends.

Native testimony in regard to the provenience or origin of types of implements, social features, rituals, and other cultural elements is frequently of the greatest value in their historical interpretation, apart, of course, from the purely mythical narratives often introduced in connexion with such testimony. When, for instance, the Tsimshian claim to have derived their secret societies from the Northern Kwakiutl, this testimony, fully corroborated by other evidence, throws a flood of light on the relative chronology of the spread of the secret societies among the West Coast Indians. When, further, the Nootka Indians, while fully acknowledging the Kwakiutl origin of specific dances or songs secondarily woven into their Wolf Ritual, show no disposition whatever to credit the Wolf Ritual as such to the Kwakiutl, this fact does not, of course, disprove such origin, but it leads us to infer that the earliest Kwakiutl influence, if otherwise demonstrated, must reach back to a period considerably antedating the time at which the Tsimshian borrowed the whole complex from the Northern Kwakiutl, again a fact of great chronological value in the study of West Coast ceremonialism. To take another example, there seems to be little or no reason to doubt the accuracy of the Southern Paiute claim that the mourning ceremony, with its peculiar sets of songs, was due to the influence of Yuman tribes to the west, while the Bear dance was much more recently borrowed from the Utes to the north. Thus, native culture, directly studied from the point of view of its own data, does not, after all, present as completely static an aspect as we at first maintained. Certain trends in development are always discernible on closer study. To return to our metaphor, we may say that American culture is comparable not so much to the ordinary photograph as to the long-exposure star chart, in which the immensities of space are indeed reduced to a flat, but in which the extent and direction of movement of the nearer bodies, the planets, are betrayed by short lines.

Brief reference should be made to a special type of native testimony bearing on chronology, the dating of native monuments according to an aboriginal system of chronology. Evidence of this sort is at hand for the Aztec and Maya cultures. These monuments afford almost the only direct references to fixed dates in the remote past that are to be found in aboriginal America. The oldest of these dates, reaching back, for the Maya, to late classical times according to our reckoning, falls far short of the total span of time that we must allow for the development of aboriginal culture on this continent and gives us no appreciable help for the ultimate problem of the earliest occupation by man of America and of the origin of his culture. Nevertheless, the oldest Maya dates are invaluable as affording us some measure of the vast time perspectives lying back of American culture generally, for at the earliest datable period reached by direct evidence we already are confronted by a highly complex culture, far in advance of and further removed from what we must conceive the earliest American culture to have been than that of many northern tribes of to-day or yesterday. The certainty of a vast lapse of time in which American Indian culture developed on this continent or elsewhere is not impaired by the rejection of all the reputed finds of Tertiary man in America.

Stratified Archæological Testimony

The third type of direct chronological testimony is afforded by the stratified monuments studied by archæology. Properly speaking, such evidence, the rationale of which is based on the translation of successive deposition of artifacts and skeletal remains into a chronological cultural and racial sequence, is to be classed as inferential evidence, but the justifiability of the inferences as to time sequences is here so clear that it seems proper to consider it as direct. The method has yielded brilliant results in the study of prehistoric Europe and western Asia and is doubtless destined to teach us vastly more than has yet been disclosed to us about the earlier culture history of the rest of the world. For America, however, the results, while of distinct value as far as they go, have so far been rather more meagre than might have been expected. Whether this is primarily due to the nature of the culture history of America itself or to certain defects in the field methods of investigators, I would not venture to decide. Perhaps something is to be charged to both. In support of the former explanation we may point out that America is so vast a stretch of land in proportion to the relatively meagre aboriginal population and, as compared with the old world, of such recent occupancy that the chances of superimposition of cultures and races at a single spot are fairly slim. However, the stratigraphic type of reasoning is not necessarily restricted to cases where we have clearly distinct layers of archæological finds, but may with advantage also be applied to the study of developments within the same culture by noting the relative depth of occurrence of various artifacts. The fruitfulness of this type of research has been demonstrated by Nelson's discussion of the history of pottery in the Galisteo basin on the basis of the relative frequency of sherds of different types of ware at various levels. I am convinced that the stratigraphic method will in the future enable archæology to throw far more light on the history of American culture than it has done in the past. The results already obtained in this way by Dall's researches in the Aleutian shell-heaps, by Boas' recent study of the various strata of pottery finds in the valley of Mexico, and by Uhle's researches in the Peruvian site of Pachacamac, to mention only a few examples of the use of the method, argue well for its increased usefulness in the future. The correlation of the time sequences thus determined by archæology with those reconstructed from the data of ethnology presents a difficult theoretical problem, but in practice the difficulties are frequently less than might be supposed. That, in general, ethnologic and archæologic data form a cultural continuum, few would now venture to deny.

INFERENTIAL EVIDENCE FOR TIME PERSPECTIVE

So much for the direct evidence at our disposal for the establishment of time sequences in American culture. The inferential evidence for the same purpose may be yielded by physical anthropology, by the descriptive data of culture (ethnology and archæology which will henceforth be considered as two aspects of the same science), and by linguistics. It is customary to insist on the mutual independence of racial, cultural, and linguistic factors. This caution of method must, however, not be understood to mean that conclusions of direct value for the history of culture can not be derived from the data of physical anthropology and linguistics. In actual practice the units of distribution of these three sciences, while never coinciding throughout, do nevertheless show significant lines of accord. Thus, while the Plains physical type may not quite correspond in distribution to the Plains culture area, it is obvious that the typical Plains tribes, culturally speaking, are at the same time typical members of the Plains physical type. As we get away from both the culture and type, we simultaneously, though not necessarily in like degree, experience a shading off into other cultures and types. The dividing line between the Pueblo and Plains Indians is about the same culturally and racially. These homologies certainly represent a significant historical fact. Nor, again, is it without historical significance that the Eskimo linguistic stock, Eskimo culture, and Eskimo race coincide rather closely in distribution. To take still another example, the linguistic break between the Algonkian and neighbouring Iroquois tribes was undoubtedly accompanied by a considerable cleavage in culture also, though the cultural break was not as profound, ʹo be sure, as the linguistic one. That differences in culture ever neatly corresponded to differences of race and language can not be maintained, but I wish to point out that the numerous homologies are of at least as great historical importance as the discordances.

Evidence of Physical Anthropology

We shall first take up the inferential evidence yielded by physical anthropology. A racial peculiarity as such is, of course, of no cultural significance (bodily mutilations, *e.g.*, West Coast or Southeastern head deformations, are, properly speaking, cultural evidence that happens to be associated with racial material), but the simple fact that the bearers of a distinctive culture are often marked off from the bearers of other cultures by a distinctive physical type enables us not infrequently to employ the racial evidence for cultural purposes. The finding of Eskimo skeletal remains in regions no longer inhabited by the Eskimo is, if one prefers common sense to methodological tyranny, enough to establish the former spread of Eskimo culture in that region. Again, the fact that the Montagnais Indians of Lake St. John and the lower St. Lawrence show an admixture of Eskimo physical traits is somewhat indicative of the former occupancy of part of their present territory by the Eskimo, an inference which is confirmed by other testimony. This fact naturally has its importance in the working out of the sequence of Algonkian tribal movements.

A second type of cultural evidence of chronological value is yielded by a statistical side of physical anthropology. I refer to the relative thickness of population in any given area, whether this is inferred from the number of skeletal remains or directly gathered from the number of inhabitants known to occupy the area at a given time. If a large area is thinly peopled, we are inclined to infer that it has been occupied at a relatively recent period; while the presence of a large population in a restricted area generally argues long occupancy. From this point of view we shall have to conclude that the interior of Labrador was occupied by an Algonkian tribe (the Naskapi) at a time subsequent to the occupancy of the Maritime Provinces by other tribes of the same stock. Similarly, the great Plains area must have been practically unoccupied at a time when Yucatan and the valley of Mexico were already well peopled by a population considerably in advance of a primitive stage of culture; the comparatively late peopling of the Plains is an inference which can be reached also in other ways. The obvious caution to use in connexion with our present mode of reasoning is this, that geographical factors may limit the possibility of the increase of a primitive population beyond a certain point. Thus, the interior of Labrador would not be expected to support more than a sparse hunting population, even if peopled from time immemorial. With all due reservations, however, the value of density of population as an index of length of occupancy of a region cannot be gainsaid. A map, compiled from all the older sources available, showing approximately the relative density of the aboriginal population in different parts of the New World, before conditions were materially disturbed by contact with the whites, is a desideratum. Allowing for the geographical caution, it should throw not a little light on the currents of population in early America.

Though not strictly belonging here, we may also mention the evidence as to density of population supplied by the frequency of archæological remains in a given area. Thus, a comparison of the "thickness" of archæological remains of the Ohio valley with that of the remains of the middle Atlantic seaboard would seem to indicate a greater density of population and consequent priority of occupation for the former. We might conclude from this that the Algonkian tribes of the latter region (the Delaware) moved east to the Atlantic seaboard from the Ohio valley, an inference for which, as it happens, we have also other evidence.

EVIDENCE OF ETHNOLOGY

More important for our purpose than evidence derived from a consideration of the data of physical anthropology or the density of population is the inferential chronological evidence derived from a study of American culture itself. Several more or less distinct lines of argument suggest themselves; there are no doubt others, not mentioned here, that may be at least equally fruitful.

CULTURAL SERIATION

A method that has been often used to reconstruct historical sequences from the purely descriptive material of cultural anthropology is one that may be termed seriation of cultural elements in order of complexity. The tacit assumption involved in this method is that human development has normally proceeded from the simple or unelaborated to the complex. Hence the simpler forms of a cultural element, whether found in the same or several tribes, are often interpreted as of greater age than the more complex ones. Thus, the simple type of totem pole consisting of a single carved figure, found, for instance, among the Nootka Indians, is almost certainly an older type than the more elaborate poles of, say, the Haida and Tsimshian, in which several carved figures are superimposed upon one another; the two-piece fire-drill of so many western American tribes must go back to a remoter period of American or general culture history than either the bow-drill of the Eskimo or the pump-drill of the Iroquois; the unorganized shamanistic practices of the Eastern Cree and other relatively undeveloped Algonkian tribes may well represent an older stratum of religious activity than the more elaborate Medicine Lodge or Midewiwin of the Ojibwa and Menomini; the simple type of suitor myth is doubtless older than the more elaborate form of the same myth found in clan legends; the use of detached amulets certainly dates back to a remoter past than the employment of amulet assemblages in the form of medicine or war bundles with associated rituals; and so on indefinitely. The argument by seriation is utilized not only in proceeding from the simple to the complex but also in the alignment of cultural elements according to any other logical criterion, the sense in which such alignment is to be read being determined by theoretical motives. Here belong many series that have been constructed to show the development of geometric from realistic designs, the progress in these being not from the simple to the complex but from the logically prior to the logically secondary.

In the absence of outside chronological evidence, a different theoretical bias would make a chronological interpretation of the series in the opposite sense equally plausible; or one might feel constrained to break up the series altogether as determined by subjective considerations and, therefore, historically fortuitous. Evidence derived from seriation is, indeed, peculiarly apt to be controlled by a purely logical or concept-schematizing tendency. It fits in far better with the evolutionary than with the strictly historical method of interpreting culture. It can take little or no account of local or tribal differences or of mutual tribal influences, and thus substitutes for an historical construction a psuedo-historical one which may convince in the abstract but cannot easily be made to fit into an actual historical framework. The danger of the seriation method may be illustrated by an example. The Iroquois and Wyandot, as is well known, were organized into a number of exogamous clans bearing animal names, the members of each clan bearing individual names also characteristic of the clan. The clans, moreover, were grouped into two exogamous phratries. Now the neighbouring Mississauga, an Ojibwa tribe, were also divided into exogamous clans bearing animal or plant names, each of the clans being again characterized by sets of individual names. So far as we know, however, the Mississauga clans were not grouped into phratries. The seriation method of reconstructing culture history, proceeding from the simple to the complex, might well interpret these facts to mean that the Mississauga type of social organization was the older and that the phratric complication of the Iroquoian organization was a later development. Evidence derived from a study of Ojibwa social organization, however, would lead one to conclude that the Mississauga organization was, on the contrary, merely borrowed in simplified form from that of the Iroquois, so that, as far as the relation between the Iroquois and Mississauga is concerned, the more complex type of organization, the clan-phratric, must be considered the older.[1] In spite of its inherent weakness as an historical method, there is no doubt that seriation can yield very valuable historical results. It is probably at its best in the construction of culture sequences of the simple-to-complex type in the domain of the history of artifacts and industrial processes, particularly where the constructions are confined to a single tribe or to a geographically restricted area.

CULTURAL ASSOCIATIONS

I believe that a powerful method for the determination of the relative ages of cultural elements is the study of the associations that they form with one another, no matter whether these associations are of an organic (logically intelligible) or of a purely fortuitous character. There are several points to consider here. It is perfectly evident that the various elements and complexes that go to make up the whole of a culture are never isolated phenomena but that they enter into all sorts of relations. Some are necessary or demonstrable consequences of others, some are only different forms of a single underlying idea, still others are only externally connected.

PRINCIPLE OF NECESSARY PRESUPPOSITION

The first principle of chronologic reconstruction to observe is that elements which are presupposed by other elements or complexes are necessarily earlier in age than the latter. A very simple application of this principle is the determination of the relative ages of the art of dressing

[1] These remarks must not be misinterpreted to mean that the Iroquois phratry is necessarily an older social unit than the clan. The relative ages of the phratry and clan among the Iroquois themselves is, of course, another problem altogether.

skins and the buffalo-skin tipi of the Plains Indians. This type of dwelling was already firmly established among the Plains Indians when first met by the whites but it is clear that a well-developed technique of fleshing and dehairing the hide and of rendering it pliable (presumably by the application of deer brains soaked in water) was necessary before the buffalo hide could be utilized as tipi cover. Hence we conclude that the technique of skin dressing common to many American tribes belongs to an older stratum of Plains culture than the buffalo-skin tipi.[2] Two of the most widespread and probably among the oldest elements of North American culture are the woven rabbit-skin blanket and the throwing-stick used in hunting the rabbit. There are, of course, other methods of securing the rabbit than by means of the throwing-stick, *e.g.*, the snaring method, so that the inference as to the greater age of the throwing-stick is not absolutely required by the facts. Nevertheless, the throwing-stick is so simple and characteristic an instrument for the purpose that I would hazard the thesis that it carries us back farther into the past than the woven rabbit-skin blanket. This would receive strong confirmation if it could be shown that the technique was originally developed in the southern plateaus (say among the Shoshonean tribes) and gradually spread north and east. Of this, however, there is no proof. One of the most characteristic and widespread Eskimo designs is the circle and dot, with which the concentric circle design is probably closely connected. It is clear that practically the only method which the Eskimo could employ to produce these designs is the drill. Hence the Eskimo circle and dot and concentric circle designs, old as they probably are, are younger than the drill itself. The Blackfoot medicine-bundle rituals always centre around a manitou experience, hence they are doubtless of much more recent age than the development of the typical American manitou experience itself.

The caution that must be borne in mind in the use of this principle of necessary presupposition is this, that a cultural element may be borrowed by a tribe without its chronological antecedent. Thus, the use of a cultivated variety of tobacco as a religious offering may be adopted without the cultivation of the tobacco plant itself, though the latter is a necessary cultural antecedent, for the tobacco may be regularly purchased by the tribe adopting the custom. Or the chronological antecedent may be replaced in the borrowing tribe by an equivalent, so that the chronological sequence established does not hold for the entire area con-

---

[2] The question of whether the general type of conical tipi with pole foundation, of which the northern Algonkian conical birch-bark lodge is an example, is also of later origin than the skin-dressing technique, is, of course, not necessarily involved.

sidered, but only for a part of it. Thus, a decorative design which arises in one tribe as conditional to a certain technique may be freely adapted by the borrowing tribe to another technique.

REFLECTION OF CULTURAL ELEMENTS IN OTHERS

A second type of association of culture elements is similar to the first but differs in that the sequence determined is not a necessary one. I include here all cases in which one of the cultural elements forms the subject matter, as it were, of the other. If this "subject matter" forms an integral part of the new formation, if it is not a secondary or accessory feature, it must be assumed to have preceded the latter in origin. We may then speak of an older element of culture as being "reflected" in a later element or complex. Thus, the self-torture characteristic of the Sun Dance of the Plains is evidently an old practice which has become specialized in a definite setting; it is probably considerably older than the Sun Dance complex itself. Its age as an element of American culture seems further indicated by its occurrence in other connexions among the Kwakiutl and Nootka Indians, though independent origin for the two areas is not inconceivable.

Excellent examples of the "reflection" of older elements in later forms are afforded by references to implements, customs, or beliefs in myths. The more frequent and stereotyped such a reference, the more reason, gererally speaking, we have to assign the cultural element great age. Thus, the frequent references in Nootka family legends to whaling adventures is very good evidence of the antiquity of whaling among these Indians and show it to be older than a certain type of family legend itself. Conversely, the persistent failure of certain elements of culture to find mention in a representative set of myths is often good evidence, despite its negative character, for their comparatively recent origin. The fact that the Nootka Ts'ayeq or doctoring ceremony is never mentioned in the legends is good reason, despite its importance in the religious life of the people, for believing that it was introduced among these Indians at a later period than, say, the Wolf ritual or whaling rituals; this is confirmed by the fact that the more northern Nootka tribes lack the Ts'ayeq.

Place names and individual names are also sometimes useful as gauges for the relative ages of culture elements. To use the Nootka Indians once more, the fact that so many more of their individual names refer to whaling and whaling feasts than, say, to Wolf Ritual dances or potlatching, would seem to indicate a greater age for the former than for the latter. Similarly, one cannot but admit that agriculture must have been practised by the Hopi for a very great length of time indeed, for so large a proportion of their individual names to refer to corn culture. In general, any well defined style or traditional mode of treatment is apt to embody an old culture element.

RELATIVE FIRMNESS OF ASSOCIATION

A third method of utilizing the association of culture elements for chronological reconstruction is the relative degree of firmness or coherence with which they are attached to a complex. The firmer the association, the older the culture element; the looser the association, the more recent the culture element, at least in that particular connexion. In this way the obviously composite nature of many culture complexes, such as myths and rituals, can, under favourable circumstances, be resolved into a time sequence; in other words, the genesis and development of a culture complex may, to a certain extent, be read out of its own structure. That, *e.g.*, the Beaver bundle ritual of the Blackfoot, at least in its present form, is of later origin than the Sun Dance is suggested by its loose superimposition upon the Sun Dance complex itself. An instructive example is afforded by a comparison of the relative importance or constancy of different dances in the elaborate complex of dances constituting part of the Nootka Wolf Ritual. The great majority of these have properly nothing to do with the essential nucleus of the whole ceremony. Two of the dances are wolf dances and are probably the oldest of the set. A certain number of others, while not relating in any way to the wolf, are nevertheless typical dances of the whole ceremonial and are generally performed; these, while probably more recent than the wolf nucleus of the ritual, are no doubt of fairly considerable age. Finally, a large number of dances are so external in character to the ritual, that we must conclude them to be of late origin. Among these dances is to be included the Cannibal dance, which, indeed, we know from other evidence to be a recent acquisition from the Kwakiutl. Another example of an accessory and, therefore, late element of culture is to be seen in the vegetable foods of the Southern Paiute. Their main dependence for foods of this sort was on the large number of wild plant varieties (roots, seeds, cacti, pine-nuts) that they gathered and prepared in various ways. Nevertheless they were not entirely ignorant of agriculture even before the coming of the whites; they raised small patches of corn, beans, and sunflower seeds in a desultory way. The accessory character of Southern Paiute agriculture stamps it as a borrowing of no great antiquity from the Pueblo tribes to the south. An interesting type of accessory features is the explanatory (etiological) elements of many American myths. These are in doubtless every or nearly every case of later origin than the plots of the myths.

MALADJUSTMENT OF CULTURE TO ENVIRONMENT

In comparing a culture element or complex of one tribe with the related element or complex of a neighbouring tribe, we are sometimes struck by the fact that, despite its possible importance and elaboration in both, it seems somehow to be more at home in one than in the other. This is sometimes due to the fact that such a culture element or complex fits better into one geographical or cultural environment than the other. Thus, the sociological fact that the grizzly bear as crest is more in evidence among the Tlingit and Tsimshian than among the Haida, though it is well established among the latter too, is almost certainly to be connected with the geographical fact that the grizzly bear is not found in the Queen Charlotte islands, the home of the Haida. We may safely conclude that the Haida grizzly bear crest is a borrowing from the mainland tribes. Conversely, the killer-whale, though one of the most important crests of the Tsimshian, does not occupy anything like the place in social organization and beliefs that it does among the Haida, among whom it is the chief crest of one of the two phratries. Once more, it seems safe to conclude that the Tsimshian Indians borrowed the crest from the Haida and to connect the predominance of the killer-whale among the Haida with the fact that they are an island people, who would, therefore, be brought into closer contact with so characteristic a denizen of the deep as the killer than the mainland tribes. Similarly, the clumsy elm-bark canoe of the Iroquois seems less adapted to its cultural environment than the various types of birch-bark canoe of their Algonkian neighbours. We may risk the guess that the Iroquois bark canoe[3] is an imperfect copy in elm-bark, a characteristically Iroquois material, of the superior Algonkian types, and connect this further with the general cultural consideration that the Iroquois were rather more inclined to be cross-country walkers than the neighbouring Algonkian tribes, who were more adept river and sea folk. The type of chronological reasoning based on the transfer of a style or technique suitable to one material, to a material more easily accessible in a neighbouring region, is too well known to need comment.

The argument from geographical or cultural fitness may open up wide vistas of historical interest. I shall refer to only one speculative problem

[3] As contrasted with the shallow dug-out, probably an older type of Iroquois water craft.

of this type. One would imagine from the great importance of the thunderbird motive in West Coast culture, particularly in the southern part of the area, that the thunderstorm is a striking phenomenon in that part of the world. As a matter of fact, it is nothing of the kind. Only once in a great while, generally during the winter, one may hear a light rumble from the direction of the mountains. May we conclude from this that the thunderbird as a mythological motive gradually filtered into the West Coast, at a remote period in the past, the path of borrowing proceeding perhaps from the Eastern Woodlands and Plains, where the thunderbird motive is environmentally justified, across the western plateau, down the Columbia to the Pacific coast, and north to southern British Columbia?[4] Or would it seem more justifiable to consider the West Coast thunderbird motive as a heritage from a region of former occupancy in which its development could be more appropriately explained? In either case, we are impressed by the value of features of cultural maladjustment for inferences as to borrowing or tribal movement.[5]

FREQUENCY OF ASSOCIATION

A fifth method of studying culture associations for the purpose of reconstructing relative chronology is the noting, not, as in the preceding methods, of the character of the single associations, but of the frequency with which a particular culture element is associated with others. The more frequently an element is associated with others, the older, generally speaking, it will be felt to be. Our own feeling, for instance, that Christianity is an older historical development than, say, the locomotive, is not based altogether on the direct documentary evidence accessible to the inquirer, but, to a very considerable degree, on the far greater number of connexions (worship, ethical ideals, literature, plastic art, music, social prerogatives) into which the former enters in the whole of our culture. One feels that it takes considerable time for an element of culture to become so thoroughly ramified in the cultural whole as to meet us at every step. Such fundamental elements, as they are generally felt to be, are very frequently also the oldest, though not necessarily, of course, in all or even any of the forms in which they actually present themselves. A familiar example of such a fundamental, though not perhaps particularly striking, cultural trait is the emphasis among the Pueblo Indians on the four cardinal points. This emphasis is apparent in myth, ritual, and details of social organization, and is graphically expressed in

---

[4] This path of borrowing would explain the absence of the thunderbird motive in California.

[5] It should be carefully noted that the above remarks imply a relation of environment merely to the *content*, not the *forms* of culture.

sand paintings and otherwise. As a basic idea in Pueblo culture its extreme age can hardly be doubted. Similarly, the use of four as a ceremonial number in many American cultures; the notion of hereditary privileges in the male or female line among the West Coast Indians; the manitou dream or vision nearly everywhere in America; the grouping into moieties found in so many tribes, are all basic ideas which doubtless go back to a remote period, whether in American culture as a whole or, at least, in certain areas.

It is important to observe that a culture complex or element may take a prominent or even fundamental place in the life of a community and yet betray its relatively recent origin or introduction by its failure to enter into many associations with other elements or complexes. From this point of view, for instance, the decorative art of the Utes, despite its exuberance of development, does not impress one as being of great age. The Peyote cult of several Plains tribes is another such culture complex which, by its failure to enter into many culture combinations, leads to the supposition that it has been only recently introduced, a conclusion that is in this case directly given by documentary evidence. The cumulative-association method, as we may call it, is surely destined to play an important part in historical constructions, as it has already, more or less tacitly, done in the past.

CULTURAL ELABORATION AND SPECIALIZATION

Mere elaboration of detail is not itself sufficient to establish the age of a culture complex, as experience shows that an elaborate technique or ritual may be borrowed *in toto*. Favourable circumstances, moreover, such as the influence of a powerful personality, may greatly accelerate such elaboration; witness the rapid growth of the Ghost Dance ceremonial in recent times. However, quite aside from the question of cumulative associations, the more elaborately developed of two culture complexes of a tribe may generally lay claim to the greater age. Thus, the more complex medicine bundle rituals of the Blackfoot, such as the medicine-pipe, otter-bundle, and beaver-bundle rituals, are undoubtedly of greater age than many or all of the simpler ones. A useful distinction may be made between true or inner elaboration of detail and a superficial quantitative elaboration which often accompanies mushroom growth. As an example of such pseudo-elaboration may be cited the great number of versions of the origin legend of the Cannibal Dance current among the different Kwakiutl clans and tribes. It would be a mistake to lay much stress on the existence of these various versions as a proof of the age of the ceremonial (except from the point of view of geographical distribution, of which more anon), for they are evidently in large measure copied from one another. For this reason, among others, the clan legends of the Kwakiutl, which appear to show more variation, are doubtless older as a class than the ritualistic origin legends.

Considerable importance may often be attached to great specialization of form or technique as a sign of age, not so much of the specialized form as such as of the type of action or thought itself. The specialized weaving product known as the Chilcat blanket, for instance, while not necessarily of great age in its present form, undoubtedly presupposes a long period of development from simpler origins. Even without having recourse to a comparison of the Chilcat blanket weaving with the weaving of neighbouring tribes (*e.g.*, the Salish dog's hair blanket with geometrical designs), we shall have to conclude that the weaving of mountain-goat wool blankets among the Tlingit goes back to a respectable antiquity. It is particularly in the comparison of the same culture complex in different tribes that the argument from degree of elaboration finds useful application. As a rule, the complex is oldest in the tribe in which it has received the greatest elaboration. Thus, the peculiar association of myth and song so characteristic of the Mohave, Yuma, and doubtless other Yuman tribes of the Colorado, is also found, if apparently in rather different form, among the Southern Paiute tribes to the east. The elaboration, however, seems so much greater among the Yuman tribes that we may justly suspect the Paiute to have borrowed the idea of the sung myth (restricted among the Paiute to the dialogue portions of the myth) from the Yuman tribes. Again, the more intensive agriculture of the Iroquois as compared with that of their Algonkian neighbours implies that the latter learned the art at a later date than the Iroquois.

CULTURAL SURVIVALS

The seventh and last method of chronological reconstruction that makes use of the association of culture elements and complexes is the method of survivals, which has been so plentifully, one might almost say abusively, employed by evolutionary ethnologists. By a survival, I do not mean an element which is wilfully, or according to some general theory, construed to be the remnant of some more elaborate complex that is believed on general principles to have disintegrated in the tribe under consideration, but merely an obscure or isolated belief, custom, myth-episode, or other culture element that seems rather out of its context, as though its full content had been lost and it no longer stood in thoroughly intelligible relation to the rest of the culture. Survivals are particularly apt to be such customs or beliefs as are blindly accepted by the native without attempt at rationalization (reinterpretation). Taboos of various sorts, for instance, often belong here. The nucleus of the Nootka puberty rite for girls, to take another example, consists of a number of rigidly prescribed ceremonial acts whose meaning is no longer understood by the Indians and which they do not attempt to explain. This nucleus may be termed a survival complex and is undoubtedly older than the rest of the puberty ceremonial, much of which belongs to the rationalized stock in trade of the Indian. A survival may sometimes hark back to a practice of daily life superseded by a later one, as when, in a ceremonial, entry into the house must be made through the smoke-hole. Survivals, if we can only be sure we really have them, are of great historical interest, as they undoubtedly reach back far into the past. Survivals, may, however, be only apparent, so that great caution is needed in the utilization of them. An element of culture may be merely borrowed from another tribe in which its setting is perfectly plain; becoming detached from this setting, it may appear as an isolated survival-like element in the borrowing culture and deceptively suggest great age. Or the element may appear as a survival merely because all the descriptive data required for its elucidation have not been recorded.

GEOGRAPHICAL DISTRIBUTION OF CULTURE

So far the inferential evidence derived from ethnological data (by the seriation and association methods) has been gained from a consideration of the cultures, complexes, and elements themselves and in their mutual relations. There remains a third method, in many ways the most powerful of all. This is the method of inference from the geographical distribution of cultures and culture elements. We may either take the distribution of a single element or complex, determine the mode and extent of such distribution, and attempt to interpret the geographical evidence in terms of a time sequence; or we may take a so-called culture area as a whole, see what elements of resemblance and difference it has with other areas, and thus aim to get a glimpse of remoter time sequences. Needless to say, these two tasks are not clearly marked off from each other but, on the contrary, cross in various ways.

DIFFUSION OF CULTURE ELEMENTS

Continuous Distribution from a Cultural Centre

Generally speaking, the geographical distribution of a culture-element is continuous. It may stop abruptly at a prominent geographical barrier, such as a mountain range or desert tract, or send out spurs along favorable lines of communication, such as navigable streams or easily traversed coast lines, but, on the whole, the area distribution tends to be a compact land mass with a more or less clearly defined centre in which the culture element under consideration is most elaborately, or, better, most typically, developed. Cases of culture distribution of this type are perfectly familiar to American ethnologists. Two or three examples may be given to fix the attention. Agriculture in aboriginal America is spread over a perfectly continuous territory reaching from the heart of South America, north through Central America and Mexico, into the Pueblo country of Arizona and New Mexico, and east and north throughout the gulf region and Mississippi valley. The centre of distribution is probably to be assigned to the valley of Mexico. The quadrangular wooden house built up on a framework of corner posts and cross beams (with the level of the floor generally lower than the surface of the ground, with inclined roof, often with circular entrance) is a feature reaching from the Tlingit of southern Alaska south to the tribes of northwestern California. The centre of distribution may perhaps be fixed in the coast region of southern British Columbia. The Sun Dance is an elaborate but quite clearly defined ritualistic complex that is found represented among all the typical Plains tribes, but is also shared by a number of adjoining tribes on the east (*e.g.*, Ponca) and on the west (*e.g.*, Ute, Bannock, Flathead). The centre of distribution would seem to be in the heart of the Plains area, say among the Arapaho and Cheyenne.

In these and innumerable other cases the historical reasoning generally employed is easily understood. The cultural phenomenon whose distribution is studied must have originated but once in the area of distribution and have gained its present spread by a gradual process of borrowing from tribe to tribe. In this process the borrowed element is progressively subjected to various associative influences, so that it appears in its least typical form at the periphery of the area, in its most typical or historically oldest form at the cultural centre. This ideally simple mode of interpretation is, of course, seriously disturbed by several important factors. Thus, the spread of the culture element may, for environmental or resistant cultural reasons, be much more rapid in one direction than another, so that the culture centre is far removed from the actual geographical centre of distribution; the cultural centre may even conceivably lie at the periphery, especially if it happens to be near a powerful geographical barrier. Again, the historically oldest form of the culture element or complex may have undergone so much modification or elaboration at the centre as to appear in more typical form at a considerable distance from it; this factor may lead to the wrong determination of the cultural centre. Movements of population within the area of distribution, furthermore may bring about an easily misinterpreted type of culture distribution. Yet, in spite of these and other criticisms that may be urged, any or all of which would have to be considered in specific problems, the general value and validity of the theory of culture diffusion as a solution of the problem raised by the continuous distribution of a culture trait must be granted.

Sequence of diffusion.—For our purpose, that of chronological reconstruction, at least two important principles of method would result. In the first place, allowing for such corrections as various cautions make necessary, the tribe at the cultural centre must be inferred to have first developed the culture element or complex studied, while those geographically removed from the centre were later affected by it, those at the periphery receiving the new type of thought or action last of all. Thus, to use our former examples, the Carib and Arawak tribes of South America on one hand and the Pueblo Indians on the other have probably become agriculturists at a considerably later date than the more advanced peoples of Mexico; such still predominantly but not exclusively agricultural tribes as the Mandan and Iroquois have no doubt taken up agriculture later than the Pueblos; while such outlying tribes as the Southern Paiute and various southern bands of Ojibwa have evidently become desultory agriculturists at a relatively recent time. Again, the quadrangular house of the Hupa and Yurok of northwestern California undoubtedly represents a later period of diffusion, though not necessarily a later type of house, than the more elaborate structures of the Kwakiutl of British Columbia. And the Sun Dance has obviously come later to the Ponca on the one hand and the Ute on the other than to such typical Plains tribes as the Arapaho, Cheyenne, and Kiowa.

Relative ages of diffused culture elements.—The second mode of chronological inference from the facts of diffusion refers to the relative ages of two culture traits. We may say, roughly speaking, that the larger the territory covered by a culture trait, the older the trait itself. Thus, to return once more to our former examples, agriculture may be suspected to have developed earlier in America than the quadrangular type of wooden house, at least in its more massive form; while both features are certainly older than the Sun Dance complex. A host of other examples will occur to any one. The type of mythological plot known as the "magic flight," which is spread from Asia, through North America, down into South America, certainly possesses a hoarier antiquity than the incident of the diving for mud with which to fashion the earth, a motive which is found in an east and west zone of distribution from the Atlantic seaboard to California and the Columbia valley; the latter, in turn, is certainly an older product of myth invention than, say, the Loon Woman story, which is restricted to a number of tribes in California. The hand game, played with two or four cylindrical bone objects, is distributed over a tremendous area west of the Rockies, reaching from British Columbia south to northern Mexico; it need hardly be insisted that its age is greater than that, for instance, of the special type of stick game played by the northern tribes of the West Coast area. Similarly, the type of geometric designs, executed in twined or coiled basketry, that is found distributed among a vast number of western tribes (from the Tlingit and Chilcotin in the north to the Pima and beyond in the south) must be an immensely older cultural development than the peculiar semi-realistic designs of certain West Coast tribes (Kwakiutl, Bella Coola, Tsimshian, Haida, Tlingit).

Cautions in use of criterion of diffusion.—(1) Delimitation of Culture Concepts: This type of reasoning is often fascinating, it opens up interesting historical vistas, but it also has its peculiar dangers. A difficulty that often arises is the strict definition or delimitation of the culture elements whose distributions are compared. Properly speaking, no such element originates at a specific point of time, but is imperceptibly connected, by a process of gradual change, with another element or with other elements lying back of it. Thus, a specific type of house or a religious belief or practice is linked historically with other types of house or of religious belief or practice from which it has been modified or by which it has been influenced. Eventually, it is bound to be historically connected with (derived from) a cultural form with which it has little outward resemblance. Hence the logical necessity of delimiting by a specific characteristic or characteristics the particular elements of culture whose relative ages it is determined to ascertain. Such a procedure may seem arbitrary at times, but it is made unavoidable by the futility of the quest for true origins.[6] In comparing the ages of culture complexes (and most cultural "elements" are at last analysis complexes) the complexes themselves must be clearly defined as an assemblage (functionally unified, as a rule) of specific elements. The relative ages of culture complexes do not necessarily throw light on the ages of the elements themselves. Thus, it would be a great mistake to infer from the priority of American

[6] This is not the place to develop the thesis that the only conceivable kind of culture origin is the association into a functional unit of cultural elements already in existence in unassociated form. From this point of view any stage in the history of a culture element is fully as much an origin as the reconstructed or hypothetical starting point. Origins, as ordinarily understood, are set off from other points of a cultural sequence merely by more or less arbitrary relative evaluations of such points; to the "origin" is attached greater significance, for whatever reason you please, than to the immediately preceding and following points of the sequence. To use a geographical metaphor, an "origin" is the peak of a time-ridge.

agriculture to the Sun Dance complex also a necessary priority of agriculture to such elements of the Sun Dance complex as the ceremonial mock battle, the Sun Dance type of offerings, or the practice of self-torture; nor does the probable priority of the quadrangular wooden house to the Sun Dance complex involve its priority to the type of house which served as model for the Sun Dance lodge. The failure to distinguish between the age of a culture complex and that of one of its elements is largely responsible for much of the unhistorical character of cultural interpretation of the evolutionary type. Many a supposed "survival" is doubtless far older than the typical complex which is held to render it intelligible.[7] We cannot go into the question of how culture elements are to be marked off from one another and to what extent culture complexes are artificial abstractions or historically justifiable units. As speculative chronologists seeking to handle definite material, all we insist on is a clear-cut definition of the culture element and the assignment of a definite nucleus of associated traits to the culture complex.

2) Rate of Diffusion: A second factor in the historical ultilization of culture distributions is more difficult to control. This is the vast differences in rate of transmission that must be assumed for (or, to a considerable extent, may be observed in) the various types of culture traits. Thus, it is obvious that a humorous story travels faster than a religious ceremony, a device for trapping game than a system of relationship terms, a social dance than a system of property inheritance, the cultivation of a particular plant than the art of agriculture itself. Hence we cannot directly compare areas of distribution without full allowance for the nature of the distributed traits themselves and, where possible, of the factors involved in the processes of distribution. In other words, such areas must be weighted as well as measured. This weighting presents a difficult but not altogether hopeless problem. The different methods of inferring and comparing rates of culture transmission form a large problem in themselves and cannot be fully outlined here.

I would suggest, with all due reserve, that rate of culture transmission is due to three mutually independent factors or, better, types of factors: the relative ease or readiness with which a culture trait is communicated by one tribe to another, the readiness with which it is adopted by the borrowing tribe, and the external conditions which favour or militate against the adoption of the trait. Where all three groups of factors are

---

[7] These general considerations on the comparison of culture elements and complexes hold, of course, for the whole of this paper. They are introduced in connexion with the problem of distribution of culture traits because here the matter of definition of such traits is most imperative.

favourable towards the spread of the culture element, the rate of such spread is naturally at a maximum.

a) Conditions of culture lending: One of the most important conditions making for readiness of transmission is that a culture element be not hedged about with secrecy or taboo, that there be nothing esoteric about it. Thus, the spectacular part of a religious ceremony is much more readily borrowed by a neighbouring tribe than the esoteric elements known only to a few. Similarly, a myth or tale which is told for the mere fun of the telling travels faster than an origin or family legend that is owned by a specific society or clan. Again, a medicinal herb or other remedy whose use is widely known and openly practised in one tribe will be readily transmitted to a neighbouring tribe, while a method of treatment that is treasured as a secret by a particular family or religious society[8] tends to oppose itself to cultural transmission. In practice, of course, all cultural elements, no matter of how esoteric a nature, are capable of diffusion. It is a question here merely of relative rates of diffusion.

A still more important, if less easily grasped, condition of ready transmission is this, that the culture element in question be capable of detachment from its context and comprehensible as such. There is no doubt that different culture elements are thus detachable or, what amounts to the same thing, capable of conscious formulation by the native in quite different degrees. We have here a continuous gamut, ranging from the zero, or almost such, of a vocalic or consonantic change to indicate some subtle grammatical notion up to the maximum of what we may awkwardly term "conceptual detachability" of a type of implement of clear-cut form, material, and use. Obviously, culture elements are transmissible, roughly speaking, with an ease that is proportionate to their "conceptual detachability." Thus, we expect a ceremonial dance as such to be much more readily transmitted than any notions there may be as to its function; a myth plot more readily than, let us say, the cosmogonic ideas which serve as its frame; an element of decorative design than the precise mechanical technique in which it is executed or its style of artistic treatment in a particular tribe; a definite social custom, say the mother-in-law taboo, than the exact range of meaning covered by a relationship term.

b) Conditions of culture borrowing: The second group of factors involved in culture transmission, that referring to the receptivity of the

---

[8] Thus, the various lines of descent among the Nootka tribes all possess medicines which are guarded with jealous secrecy. Compare with this the secret knowledge of a remedy for rattlesnake bites possessed by the Rattlesnake fraternity of the Hopi Indians.

borrowing tribe, is probably even more important than the factors already considered. Only one of these factors need be mentioned here—the relative ease with which the borrowed culture element is assimilated to the culture of the borrowing tribe. Almost invariably we find that a new idea or activity borrowed from without falls in line with already existing ideas or activities; it does not so much constitute a new departure in cultural endeavour as fill out with a new richness of detail a pigeon-hole of culture ready to receive it. Frequently enough, in the process of borrowing, its primary significance is either lost or distorted; such loss or distortion is nearly always an expression of the assimilating power of the borrowing culture. In only a vast minority of cases, indeed, is an element of culture transplanted *in toto*, without undergoing assimilatory modifications. As far as the problem of rapidity of transmission is concerned, we are in the main safe in saying that the more perfectly an element fits into its new cultural environment, the more nearly, in other words, it answers to the immediate needs or interests of the borrowers, the more rapid will be the rate of transmission. Hence it is not difficult to understand why myth plots, spectacular dances, games, and certain decorative designs spread with tremendous rapidity and may, in many cases, cover larger areas of distribution than culture elements of greater age. These considerations make it peculiarly hazardous to infer greater age on the basis of geographical distribution when the elements compared belong to widely distinct categories of thought or activity, say social organization and methods of securing game.

c) External conditions of diffusion: The communicability of a culture element and the receptivity of the borrowing tribe, so far as already discussed, are conditioned by the nature of the element itself. External factors of various sorts, however, are generally highly important determinants of the course and rapidity of transmission. These form the third group referred to. Most or all of them may be summarized under the heading of degree of intimacy subsisting between the two tribes involved. Thus, tribes that are on a friendly footing for a long period of time interchange elements of culture more freely and rapidly than such as are continuously at war with one another A good example is afforded by the Mississauga, who, though an Algonkin tribe, assimilated in a relatively short time, because of their friendship with the Hurons and, in later times, Iroquois, a greater share of Iroquoian culture than such Algonkin tribes as the Malecite and Abenaki, who were never, at least until quite recently, on friendly terms with the Iroquois. Similarly, the culture of the Athabaskan Hupa is almost identical with that of their friendly non-

Athabaskan neighbours, the Yurok and Karok, while that of their Athabaskan neighbours immediately to the south was much less complex.

A particularly important aspect of our problem is the extent to which transmission of culture elements is encouraged by intermarriage. Intermarriage, involving, as it does, change of residence, is perhaps the most potent of the more intimate causes of the spread of a cultural feature. Where, as among certain of the West Coast tribes, the dowry system prevails and where, moreover, as among all these tribes, privileges are inherited by heirs even when identified with an alien tribe, it is evident that many elements of culture (personal names, legends, crests, dances, songs) travel with relatively little change for very considerable distances. Frequently, indeed, we may say more properly that a culture element follows the paths of family connexion than of geographical propinquity as such. Eventually, of course, the cumulative effect of several intermarriages within a given area, aided by the stimulation exercised by an alien culture element on the form of similar activities in the local cultural stock, will make perfectly continuous the distribution within this area of practically any borrowed element.

An important external aid to free cultural transmission is mutual intelligibility (or partial intelligibility) of speech between the tribes that are in cultural contact. Lack of this aid, as we have already seen in the case of the Hupa, Yurok, and Karok, does not by any means constitute an effective bar to the borrowing and spread of ideas and activities, but its presence is certainly a powerful reinforcer of them. It is not surprising, therefore, to find a host of cultural elements held in common by all the Iroquoian tribes, including the Hurons and Neuters, despite the hostility of these to the League; or to find the various tribes of Nootka Indians, speaking diverse but mutually intelligible dialects, sharing certain ethnological traits in contrast to their Kwakiutl and Salish neighbours. Such a case as that of the Hupa, Yurok, and Karok, or of the Tsimshian and Haida, is, properly speaking, only an apparent exception; for, where contact between tribes of radically distinct speech is close, there will practically always be found a number, sometimes even the majority of one of the tribes, who are bilingual. It is these bilingual individuals who undoubtedly serve, to a large extent, as the media of cultural interinfluences. Generally speaking, then, far-reaching cultural contact can hardly take place except as conditioned by some sort of mutual intelligibility of speech. It is often assumed off-hand that cultural resemblances between linguistically related tribes must go back to a time antedating the present linguistic differentiation. Yet it is evident from what we have said that the very fact of close linguistic affinity paves the way for a more than ordinarily rapid transmission within the geographical bounds of the larger linguistic unit. This in no way contradicts the statement made earlier in the paper that linguistic and cultural areas at least tend to be congruent. It merely points out that such congruence is not altogether necessitated by genetic factors (by a common historical heritage), but may, very largely, be shaped by the secondary process of borrowing under a favouring linguistic condition. This point of view may well cause hesitation in too free a use of the hypothesis of tremendous cultural conservatism in explaining the numerous and often startling resemblances in culture details between various Eskimo tribes. The hoary antiquity of at least some such features, when closely scrutinized, may resolve itself into a relatively recent spread of fashion.

We have already referred to geographical barriers as limiting the even spread of an element of culture. This opens up the question of accessibility of tribe to tribe, of aboriginal waterways and trade routes generally. Clearly, not only articles of trade, such as implements, foods, clothing, and ornament, but all manifestations of culture, whether material or not, travel easiest along such trade routes. Hence, in evaluating geographical distribution of culture elements for ethnological reconstruction, it makes all the difference whether the tribes observed to have a certain feature in common lie along a well established trade route or not; further, whether or not they are in the habit of meeting periodically, or at least frequently, for exchange of goods and participation in common activities (ceremonies, amusements). Considerations of this sort will sometimes force us to correct radically impressions derived from a mere bird's-eye view of geographical distribution. The distance, for example, between the Copper Eskimo and, say, the Eskimo of the east coast of Labrador is, even in a straight line, more than ten times as great as that which separates the Yurok, of the west coast of California, from the Pomo to the south. Nevertheless, the cultures of the two Eskimo groups mentioned doubtless present many more points of similarity than those of the Yurok and Pomo. Does this prove that the culture traits peculiar to the Eskimo are as a body older than those respectively characteristic of the Yurok and Pomo, or, to put it somewhat differently and perhaps more legitimately, that the Eskimo are, culturally speaking, a much more conservative people than either the Yurok or Pomo? Whether such inferences are correct or not, they do not necessarily follow from the facts of geographical distribution. We must remember that the Eskimo are in the habit of covering immense distances by umiak and sleigh, furthermore that neighbouring Eskimo tribes often meet for trade purposes and that in this way objects and ideas (stories, songs, dances), may, with no great lapse of time, travel far from their home. On the other hand, the Pomo were not marine travelers and, like most central Californian tribes, only desultory river travellers, while the Yurok, though good canoemen, were certainly not in the habit of venturing far out at sea; moreover, inland communication between the Yurok and Pomo would be rendered difficult by the coast range of mountains. In short, the culturally "weighted" distance between the Yurok and Pomo may even turn out to be greater than that between the Copper Eskimo and the remote East Labrador natives. I believe that one of the pressing needs for a study of the larger problems of American culture history is a careful mapping of the paths along which culture elements can be shown to have travelled with relative rapidity. Other things being equal, a culture element found distributed along lines of rapid transit must be considered as lesser in age than one distributed over the same geographical extent but largely along lines lying aside from trade routes.

Chronological inferences from geographical distribution.—Such considerations as general intimacy subsisting between tribes, intermarriage, linguistic kinship, and means of access constitute some of the external factors governing the rate of cultural diffusion. None of these can be considered as altogether independent of the others, but each may operate in quite different degree. We are now in a better position to make profitable use for chronology of the method of geographical distribution than if we interpret such distribution at its face value. Putting the various factors involved in the transmission of a culture element into the form of a formula, we may say that: a culture element is transmitted with a maximum ease when it is conceptually readily detachable from its cultural setting, is not hedged about in practice by religious or other restraints, is without difficulty assimilable to the borrowing culture, and travels from one tribe to another living in friendly, or at least intimate, relations with it, particularly when these tribes are bound to each other by ties of intermarriage and linguistic affinity and are situated on an important trade route. Geographical arguments as to the age of a culture element transmitted under all these conditions need to be most qualified. General statements, such as have been made by Rivers and others, as to the relative conservatism or ease of diffusion of broad categories of culture, such as religion, mythology, social organization, art, and technology, are of little practical service, as everything depends on the specific nature of the borrowed element, the degree of similarity between the two cultures brought into relation, and the favourable or unfavourable character of the external circumstances of borrowing. While one cannot disprove, for example, that social organization, as maintained by Rivers, is the most conservative of all cultural features, it seems clear to me that the various elements of social organization may behave quite differently from the point of view of diffusion. A tale, for instance, will normally travel much faster than a type of clan organization, to be sure, but it is perfectly conceivable, on the other hand, that an esoteric ritualistic myth may fail to be borrowed by a neighbouring tribe which has nevertheless adopted isolated features of social organization.

Convergent Developments Within Areas of Continuous Distribution

So far we have assumed that the geographical distribution of a culture element is continuous and that, this being, so, it may be represented as a single historical process of gradual diffusion. But two other possibilities present themselves. A culture trait may be continuous and yet not of single origin; in other words, it may have been independently evolved twice or even more often within its present area of distribution, so that the continuity of distribution represents a meeting and partial amalgamation of two or more distinct but similar streams of influence. Personally I do not believe that such types of diffusion, theoretically possible as they may be, are at all frequent. In probably the majority of supposed cases the two or more contiguous culture distributions are of elements that are of only superficial, not fundamental, similarity; where the similarity is undoubted and where, nevertheless, a single origin seems, for one reason or another, improbable, we are entitled to suspect that there has been an assimilation of two originally more clearly distinct elements into new forms. The criteria, formal and functional, of independent origin (convergence) versus historical relationship of similar cultural elements have been often discussed. The question is a large and puzzling one—puzzling, I venture to think, more in the abstract than as applied to specific cases. In any case, the determination of such independent origin or historical relationship must be assumed as made—how does not directly concern us here—before our methods of chronologic reconstruction can be applied.

Interrupted Distribution

Cautions in inferring historical connexion.—The second possibility is of more interest. A culture element may be not continuous but interrupted in its geographical distribution, that is, it may be found represented in two or more tribes or groups of tribes separated by a tribe or group of tribes which does not share this feature. Here, even more than in the preceding case, it must be clearly ascertained that the supposed similarity

in culture is fundamental or real before the problem of independent
origin versus historical relationship can be attacked at all. Where the
geographical distance is great, the resemblance limited to features of a
very general character, and, more important still, the historical trend of
the culture element which has been reconstructed for each area proves to
run in quite different senses, it would be extremely hazardous, in the
absence of other evidence, to infer historical connexion.

1) Danger of Conceptualizing Too Widely: The constant danger that
besets the investigator is to make historical or psychological actualities
out of merely conceptual abstractions—the more widely one defines the
terms of his abstractions the more easily will he be enabled to embrace
very distinct cultural phenomena within a single historical or psychological problem. Superficially the phratric organization of a number of
West Coast tribes (Haida, Tlingit, Tsimshian) bears points of resemblance to that of the Iroquois. Between the Iroquois and the West Coast
tribes lies a vast stretch of country inhabited almost entirely by tribes
without phratric organization. Have we here a case of convergent evolution or of an originally (or from time to time partly) continuous area of
phratry distribution which has become disrupted by the vicissitudes of
history? A closer study of the nature of the phratries in the two areas
soon convinces one that they are in essence more unlike than alike. While
the West Coast phratries are, at least in nucleus, enlarged kin groups
with specific crests, the Iroquois phratries are rather functional (quasi-
political) aggregations of clans.[9] What I have termed the "historical
trend" of the phratries seems different in the two regions. The West

[9] Two or three facts bearing on the complex problem of the nature of the two
phratic organizations will suffice here. While, among the West Coast Indians, the
phratry as such has its definite crest or crests, the relationship among its clans
being largely determined by ownership of this same crest, the Iroquois phratries
can hardly be said to be characterized by crests or totemic emblems. On the West
Coast the various clans, like those of the Iroquois, are characterized by distinctive
sets of personal names; unlike the Iroquois clans, however, a number of clans
belonging to the same phratry often possess certain names in common (I have in
in mind chiefly Mr. C. M. Barbeau's Tsimshian data), a fact that points to the
West Coast phratry (or phratric nucleus) as an old kin group that has become subdivided into a number of clans. Both these facts clearly emphasize the kin-group
nature of the West Coast phratry as contrasted with Iroquois phratry. Equally
instructive is the ceremonial relation subsisting between the phratries in the two
cases. Among the Iroquois the phratries act as such in their relations to each other
—in games, in mourning or commemoration ceremonies, in council deliberations.
Among the West Coast Indians reciprocal functions, it is true, have been reported
for the phratries (witness the phratric burial duties among the Tlingit) but where
a more complete analysis has been made (again I have in mind chiefly
Mr. Barbeau's Tsimshian data) it would seem that what is really involved in
such cases is not the (or an) opposite phratry as such but a group of paternal kinsmen which, in a society with matrilineal inheritance, must needs belong to the
(or an) opposite phratry. Here again the West Coast tribes emphasize the phratry
as a kin group, the Iroquois as a functional unit.

Coast phratry, aside from later accretions of originally disconnected clans, seems to have arisen as the result of its splitting up into a large number of clans, that have not altogether lost their sense of kinship. The Iroquois phratry, however, seems to be a secondary confederation of clans.[10] Thus we conclude that what threatened to be an interesting problem, opening up a wide historical perspective, is hardly more than a conceptualistic mirage.

2) Degree of Geographical Isolation: At this point I wish to urge that the degree of geographical isolation of the two areas involved must by no means be neglected in weighing the claims of a theory of independent origin against those of historical relationship. The greater the geographical distance, the stronger have we a right to demand the evidence to be of historical connexion, that is, the more rigidly do we apply our criteria. The reason for this is that, as the distance between two tribes possessing a feature in common increases, the greater becomes the difficulty of assuming that all the intervening tribes once also possessed the feature, but lost it, or that the tribes compared were once in geographical contact but were later severed by migration. Neither of these alternatives is at all impossible, though the former has undoubtedly been more often theoretically advanced than specifically demonstrated. The point to remember is that the probability of either decreases, other things being equal, with the increase of distance. The claim of Graebner and others of his school that the test of historical relationship between two culture elements is to be sought solely in certain formal and other characteristics of the elements themselves without any regard to the geographical difficulties involved must be rejected as naive. It tacitly assumes that we are able in every given case to decide whether a culture feature or group of features is or is not capable of more than one independent origin, that is, it affects to treat as mathematical certainties judgments which notoriously vary from individual to individual. Where there is in practice so much room for difference of interpretation of Graebner's criteria, we shall do well to cling humbly to the geographical caution. Hence, *e.g.*, a West Coast crutch paddle will not necessarily be heard to cry vigorously for its Melanesian mate.

Chronological value of interrupted cultural distribution.—A considerable number of valid cases, however, of historical relationship between culture elements found in geographically non-contiguous areas undoubtedly remains. How this validity is to be established it is not part of our task to

---

[10] There are several reasons for believing this to be true. One of the more important ones is the fact that while the clans correspond to a large extent in the Iroquoian tribes, their grouping into phraties does not. In other words, the Iroquoian clan tradition seems older, on the whole, than the phratric tradition.

define. Before similarity of geographically disconnected culture elements can be utilized for chronological purposes, it is obvious that their historical relationship must be assumed as demonstrated.[11] Such historical connexion, as already indicated, can be understood in two ways. We may either succeed in showing that the intervening tribes, who once possessed the culture element, have lost it; or we may show that one or more of the tribes of one of the areas formerly lived in geographical contact with the tribes of the other area and was, at a subsequent period, severed from them either by a peaceful migration or by the irruption of hostile tribes. In either case the problem is reduced to the normal one of the continuous diffusion of a culture element from a single centre.

For chronological purposes, cases of the interrupted distribution of a culture element are of particular importance. In a general way, a culture element whose area of distribution is a broken one must be considered as of older date, other things being equal, than a culture element diffused over an equivalent but continuous area. The reason for this is that in the former case we have to add to the lapse of time allowed for the diffusion of the element over its area of distribution the time taken to bring about the present isolation of the two areas, a time which may vary from a few years or a generation to a number of centuries. Thus, any culture traits which, *e.g.*, the Tuscarora may be shown to have in common with the non-contiguous tribes of the Iroquois League alone may well be suspected to be of greater antiquity than such as say the Neuters or Erie may be shown to share with the neighbouring League tribes alone.

More specifically, the interrupted distribution of a culture element gives us a minimum relative date for the origin of the culture element itself. The element must have arisen prior to the event or series of events that resulted in the geographical isolation of the two areas. Examples of this type of chronological reasoning will occur to every one; they are particularly easy to understand where there has been a tribal migration. Thus, the peculiar type of star myth (identification of mythological heroes with stars or constellations) found among both the Arikara of

[11] This does not mean that arguments based on time perspectives gained from a consideration of other data may not help to establish the independent origin or historical relationship of the similar culture elements investigated. Thus, to use our former example, if it could be shown on other evidence that the Iroquois phratries have necessarily originated subsequently to the rise of a culture element whose distribution is confined to the Eastern Woodlands tribes and whose former existence cannot be demonstrated among the West Coast or intervening tribes, it becomes increasingly difficult, impossible indeed, to historically connect the phratries of the two regions. On the other hand, if it could be shown on other evidence that the Iroquois phratries necessarily antedate the rise of a culture element of almost universal distribution in America, say the acquiring of power from manitous, the ground would be effectively cleared for the demonstration of the thesis that the phratries of the two regions are historically connected.

North Dakota and the Pawnee of Nebraska, but not among the intervening Siouan tribes, was doubtless developed before the northward drift of the Arikara away from their linguistic kinsmen. In a similar way, we may conclude that the family hunting territories, with tendency to paternal descent, of the Algonkin tribes of New England and the Maritime Provinces (Penobscot, Abenaki, Micmac), a feature found also among the Algonkin tribes of the Ottawa valley (Ojibwa, Algonquin) but not, as far as can be ascertained, among the intervening Iroquoian peoples, go back to a time preceding the irruption of the latter into what must formerly have been Algonkin territory.

More difficult of treatment are cases of interrupted distribution not due to movements of population. In only a small minority of these will the culture element in question turn out to have totally disappeared without trace in the intervening region. It is, indeed, almost inconceivable that the formerly existing cultural feature should have been so thoroughly wiped out or should have been so completely replaced by another element of equivalent function as to leave no trace. Generally we shall find that it either lingers on in modified form or that other cultural features (say mythological references) presuppose it. The more profoundly the element has become modified in the intervening region or the less evident traces it has left of its former existence, the older must we infer its formerly continuous distribution and its origin to be.[12] According to whether one emphasizes differences or similarities in analysing culture elements and complexes, the same problem may often be labelled one of either interrupted or continuous distribution. One application of the chronological thesis based on interrupted distribution will suffice here. The conical bark lodge with pole foundation is found distributed among many Algonkin tribes in Maine and Canada, also farther west among Athabaskan tribes. Among the Paiutes of the southern plateaus we find it again, except that instead of regular layers of birch bark we have cedar bark more loosely applied as a covering to the framework. Between the

[12] There is nothing to prevent our inferring its original centre of distribution to have been in the intervening territory itself in which the element is no longer found in characteristic form, if at all. Thus, Buddhism in Ceylon and in Tibet point, aside from such overwhelmingly corroborative documentary evidence as we possess, to its formerly continuous distribution via India, where, despite its lingering existence among Jain sectaries, it may be said to have disappeared as such. Now, we know that Buddhism arose neither in Ceylon nor in Tibet, but in India, whence it was diffused north, south, and east. Quite aside again from older documentary evidence, we could have inferred that Buddhism was diffused from India because several features connected with it point to Indian culture (*e.g.*, Buddhistic terms current in Tibet and elsewhere which are evidently of Sanskrit origin; certain philosophic ideas, such as continuous reincarnation and delivery from earthly existence attained by those of extraordinary religious merit, that are characteristic of Indian religion in general).

areas occupied by these two types of conical bark lodge are intruded the conical mat lodge (Interior Salish, Nez Percé) of the plateau and the buffalo-skin tipi of the plains. Obviously the mat and skin tipis are best considered as modifications of an older type of bark lodge. The point that chiefly interests us here is that the conical bark lodge must be assigned an age great enough to allow for the origin and development of its derivative forms. The older we deem the skin tipi to be, the greater the age we shall have to assign to the conical bark lodge itself. The comparison, with a view to determination of age, of culture elements with interrupted distributions among themselves and with such as have continuous distributions is naturally subject to all the cautions we have reviewed in dealing with continuously diffused elements.

Diffusion Versus Common Heritage

A contrast is often made between identity or similarity of culture due to diffusion and to independent retention of a common heritage. The alternative is, however, one of degree rather than of kind. Any culture element is practically certain to be diffused over more than a single community, indeed its currency in a single community is already an instance of diffusion that has radiated out, at last analysis, from a single individual. When, for one reason or another, the continuous area of distribution is broken up into two or more isolated ones, the element in question will normally continue to be diffused among the new neighbours of one or more of the geographically detached groups. Hence at no point in the history of the culture element has its gradual diffusion ceased. All that we mean when we say that two noncontiguous tribes have independently inherited a culture element is that its former diffusion among them antedated the events that brought about their isolation, not, as is sometimes loosely assumed, that there is no problem of diffusion involved as far as they are concerned. For us this raises no new problems. It is simply a matter of estimating the age of one historical process in terms of another.

CULTURE AREAS AND STRATA

The Concept of Culture Area from an Historical Standpoint

It is customary to group the tribes of North and South America, as of other parts of the globe, into a relatively small number of culture areas, that is, groups of geographically contiguous tribes that exhibit so many cultural traits in common as to contrast with other such groups. Despite the undoubted conveniences of this mode of classification, we should be under no illusions as to its character. The culture area is primarily a descriptive, not an historical, concept. The various culture elements that serve to define it are of very different ages and their grouping into a set of cultural differentia is applicable only to a particular, in our case generally a very recent, cross-section of history. This means that the different culture areas recognized in North America, say, are historically not necessarily comparable at all. If for instance, it could be shown, as seems not unlikely, that all or most of the cultural differentia constituting the Plains culture area arose at times subsequent to the development of most of the features characterizing the Eskimo and Eastern Woodland culture areas, we should be compelled to conclude that, from an historical standpoint, the Plains area is a sub-grouping of some kind when contrasted with the relatively primary groupings of the Eskimo and Eastern Woodland areas. Such a result necessarily follows from the quite different historical weightings given, let us say, to the skin tipi, buffalo hunting, the rawhide industry, the camp circle, and the Sun Dance, on the one hand, and to the kayak, the conical bark lodge, the two-pronged fish-spear, beaver hunting, the birch-bark industry, and "medicine" conjuring on the other.

As for the earlier cultural status of the tribes that constitute our "sub-grouping," two possibilities present themselves. We may find that the elimination of those historically secondary cultural elements that were responsible for the interpretation of the sub-grouping as a distinctive culture area either leaves the area possessed of primarily such features as are shared also by a single neighbouring culture area; or, on the contrary, discloses descriptively secondary (historically primary) lines of culture cleavage within the area, so that it breaks up into two or more sections that respectively belong to neighbouring culture areas. In the former case we may speak of a specialized cultural development originating within a larger culture area. Many, or at least some, of the features which at first seemed to constitute exclusive differentia will in this case prove to be merely specialized forms of elements whose presence may be demonstrated in the primary culture area. In the latter case, a number of superimposed cultural features, diffused over a continuous area, have proven strong enough to create a new culture area which breaks up and unites older ones.[13] It is not always easy in dealing with specific problems to determine whether a (secondary) culture area is the result of specialized development within a larger culture area or represents a "reassort-

---

[13] This process of "reassortment" of culture areas is taking place on a large scale to-day. Such modern features as the factory system, the organization of labour, steel armament, railways and numerous other technical advances, and the parlamentary form of government are simultaneously creating new geographical units of culture and breaking up old ones.

ment" of culture areas. Taking the Plains culture area, for example, we may either think of it as a specialized form of culture based on a more general Eastern Woodland culture; or we may prefer to see in it a culture blend in which participate tribes originally belonging to the Eastern Woodland, the Southeastern, the Plateau, and possibly the Southwestern culture areas. The latter view seems more tenable to me, though particular emphasis should, I believe, be placed on the historical relation between the Plains and Eastern Woodland areas.

The synthetic process by elimination that we have roughly indicated is, of course, a successive one. An historical analysis of North American culture would quite probably reduce the present culture areas to two or three fundamental ones, say a Mexican culture area, a Northwest Coast area, and a large Central area of which the Pueblo and Eskimo areas are the most specialized developments; the former as conditioned by profound Mexican influences, the latter as conditioned by a very peculiar environment. Whether or not the particular results here indicated prove correct, the method of chronologically weighting culture areas, or rather cultural differentia constituting such areas, is now more or less clear. These areas are not strictly comparable on a flat, but may represent quite distinct historic levels. The process of elimination is, as a matter of method, equivalent to the removal of an archæological stratum so as to enable us to penetrate to the culture lying disclosed just below.

The Concept of Culture Stratum and its Historical Difficulties

We are now face to face with the concept of a culture stratum. In the case of our own modern occidental civilization we distinctly feel that certain elements and complexes belong to a stratum that centres about the tremendous industrial advance characteristic of the nineteenth century, others to another stratum underlying this which is closely associated with the spread of Christianity, still others to a stratum of custom and belief which antedates the advent of Christianity. At first sight the concept of a culture stratum, that is, of a group of culture elements which go back in origin to a common period, differs from the concepts of a culture area and of a culture complex in that it is strictly chronological in character, whereas the latter are respectively culture-geographical and conceptual in nature. In actual practice, however—and here lies its weakness for chronological purposes—it is not possible to disentangle the culture stratum altogether from conceptual and geographical considerations.

As to the conceptual difficulty, consider for a moment the various vicissitudes that some element bound up with Christianity has undergone in the course of its history. Would such an element of modern English culture, for instance, as the inclusion of the Archbishop of Canterbury in the House of Lords have to be considered as belonging to a specifically Christian culture stratum or not? Much depends on the particular aspect of this institution that we choose to emphasize. If we treat it primarily as an anachronism in modern society, as a vestige symptomatic of a former status in England of church prerogative, we might well assign it to a Christian culture stratum, a stratum one of the ruling ideas of which was the supreme importance in daily life of a correct attitude towards certain religious dogmas and of the necessity of controlling such an attitude by means of a hierarchy of office. On the other hand, we may lay the emphasis rather on the parliamentary aspect, considering the Archbishop's seat as an element in the development of a parliamentary form of government. This development, however, is to be assigned to a culture stratum which is, in the main, subsequent to the Christian stratum. In this particular case we have a wealth of documentary evidence which enables us to analyse the institution into its various elements and to assign each of them to its proper chronological place. In the absence of such evidence, however, even the application of several of the criteria reviewed earlier in this paper might not throw enough light on the remoter history of the institution to prevent a certain blurring of perspective, with consequent more or less arbitrary assignment of the whole complex to a definite culture stratum in which it is grouped with conceptually associated complexes. The tendency, therefore, to lump culture elements and complexes that are pervaded by some central idea together as belonging to one culture stratum is strong and is seldom resisted by those who undertake to define such strata.

The geographical bias also may be elucidated by an example taken from our own culture. At the very time that the emphasis on industrial development was greatest there was plainly perceptible a stream of Oriental influence on art, literature, and philosophy (we have only to think, for instance, of the vogue of Chinese and Japanese porcelains and of Japanese prints and kimonos, of the direct influence exerted on our own painting and drawing by Japanese models, of Fitzgerald's Omar Khayyam, of the Vedantist societies that flourish in certain circles). To put it in terms of daily experience, the man who has just bought himself an automobile is likely to have also invested in a Japanese vase for the adornment of his parlor. Living in the present as we do, we feel keenly that the invention and use of the automobile and the popularity of Japanese vases are, as far as we are concerned, cultural elements of the same stratum, both first appearing in our culture at about the same period. Yet it is hardly likely that a culture-historian of the distant future, unpossessed of documentary evidence, would ascribe their appearance in our culture to the same time. It is more likely that he would class the automobile with the steamboat, railway, telegraph, telephone, and other inventions as having arisen in a certain period (call it the Age of Industrialism). The culture stratum going back to this period (and he migh be able to demonstrate that the strike, woman suffrage, and the Montessori method of education, among other elements, belong to the same stratum) he would probably succeed in diagnosing as being, on the whole, of indigenous origin. The Oriental influences we have spoken of (and let us even grant that he can show them to be largely contemporaneous in origin and to be quite distinct historically from the older stream of Oriental influence represented by the introduction of rice and tea) will impress him as constituting or belonging to a different stratum of exotic origin. There are likely to be but few, if any, indications of an associational character pointing to the fact that the indigenous elements are to be ascribed to the time when the later Oriental influences were coming in. If he succeeds in demonstrating, as he is quite likely to, that in China and Japan the porcelain vase, the silk, kimono, and the peculiarly Japanese art of delineation are very much older than the automobile and associated elements, he would be strongly tempted to conclude that the "Industrial" culture stratum is of later origin than the stratum associated with Oriental art also in occidental culture. And yet, as we happen to know, this would be doing very serious violence to the facts of history. In short, there will be the same tendency to unify and isolate as a culture stratum elements of demonstrably the same geographical provenience as to unify and isolate as a culture stratum elements of the same conceptual group.

The concept, then, of a culture stratum, as actually handled in the study of primitive culture, can hardly lay claim to being a clean-cut historical implement. It may be defined as a group of associated culture elements and complexes which in origin, if not always in their actual form as recorded, go back to the same general period, but which is apt to include elements of quite different date but related content and to exclude elements of like date but distinct geographical provenience. It is an historical concept in theory, in practice strongly biased by psychological and geographical considerations. What makes it possible for the ethnologist to speak of culture strata at all as of more than purely local application is the fact that many characteristic elements are so widely diffused that they are found grouped together within certain geographical limits. Thus, in the Plains area the camp circle and Sun Dance are correlated throughout the greater part of their area of distribution, not so much because they are an organically connected pair of elements as because, being, roughly speaking, of like provenience and age, they are distributed in largely parallel fashion. The different factors responsible for differences of rate of diffusion make themselves felt, however, at the rims of the distribution areas of these two elements, a point which shows conclusively that there can be no talk of organic connexion. Thus, the Sun Dance is found among the Utes and Bannocks to the west, who do not use the camp circle; the Sun Dance is absent among the Omaha to the east, who group their clans, when on the hunt, in the form of a camp circle; while the Nez Percé to the west, who have borrowed a number of Plains features (*e.g.*, the skin tipi and the rawhide parfleche) possess neither the Sun Dance nor camp circle. If two of the most characteristic features of Plains culture thus present what we might call a "ragged edge" of distribution, it is evident that the totality of such traits presents a far greater "raggedness of edge"; the distribution rim of some will fall well within the bounds of the typical Plains area, that of others will extend far beyond the bounds of this area into adjoining or distant culture areas. We are forced to conclude, then, that a culture stratum, unless it be to all intents and purposes identified with a coherent culture complex, cannot travel very far from its area of distribution without losing many or finally all of its characteristic elements. The notion of a culture stratum, composed of a large number of elements that are technically independent of each other, journeying without great loss of content, as though isolated in a hermetically sealed bottle, from one end of the world to the other is unthinkable and contradicts all historical experience. The phrase "kulturgeschichtliches Nonsens" might well be applied to such a Graebnerian conception of culture transmission, though its sponsor would fain have us think that it is the opposed notion that deserves it.[14]

Limitations to the Historical Usefulness of the Concepts of
Culture Area and Stratum

Our rapid review of the concepts of culture area and culture stratum may seem rather disappointing, but it should be remembered that our point of view is entirely historical, not descriptive or psychological. The culture area is a highly useful classificatory device for descriptive purposes, indeed it aids considerably also in the psychological interpretation of culture; its usefulness for historical purposes, however, depends entirely

[14] Father Schmidt's demonstration of the existence in South America of identically the same culture strata as Graebner had isolated in the South Seas is a welcome *reductio ad absurdum* of the latter's conception of culture diffusion.

on the extent to which its differentia can be interpreted as a culture stratum or a series of culture strata. The culture stratum itself is an intrinsically useful historical concept but, owing to reasons already advanced, it may be both unduly inclusive and exclusive; hence the erection of a sequence of culture strata, when unsupported by archæological evidence, must not be interpreted too rigidly but must allow for very extensive overlapping. And, most important of all, the culture stratum must not be freely handled as a universal counter, but needs to be restricted to the bounds set by at most a continent or parts of two adjacent continents. Some strata, indeed, must be considered as of hardly more than local application. As far as American culture is concerned, I think it would be more than advisable for the present to refrain from the attempt to establish a sequence of strata intended to hold for the whole of North and South America; further, to refrain from assigning such generalized elements as the crutch paddle, the simple bow, the exogamic clan, or the manitou concept to specific culture strata. A painstaking determination of the relative ages and directions of distribution of the single culture elements and complexes themselves must eventually yield a solid basis for their grouping into strata and for the extent and direction of distribution of these strata.

The main burden of affording us the historical depth that we seek to find in primitive culture must always be borne, I believe, by the analysis of the culture elements and complexes rather than by the culture strata that we build out of them. However, the determination of sequences of strata and of synchronous or chronologically parallel culture areas helps greatly in giving us a larger historical perspective. The greater the number of successive culture strata we are able to unravel, the more distant our vision into the past. The greater the number of culture areas whose differentia reach back to an equally remote past, the greater age can we claim for the fundamental culture that includes the culture of such areas.[15]

Thus, it makes a great difference in historical perspective whether our recognized North American culture areas as such can be shown to be of approximately equal age or to loosen up, as it were, into a smaller number that lie back of them, as previously suggested. In the former case we must allow for a far greater lapse of time for the formation of present-day culture areas than in the latter. A further value of the employment of culture areas and strata lies in the readiness with which we may by means of them handle groups of descriptive facts without the irksome necessity

[15] A culture, I hasten to add, that need by no manner of means be assigned to America itself.

of particularizing in every case. The economic value of such labels as
"Plains culture area" and "Plains culture stratum" (or, in Graebnerian
parlance, "camp-circle culture stratum") is by no means to be under-
rated, even by those to whom they seem of only secondary historical
value.

EVIDENCE OF LINGUISTICS

LANGUAGE AND CULTURE

We have, finally, to consider the manner in which linguistic data may be
employed to set culture elements in chronologic relation to one another.
There are two basic factors which make it possible for linguistic evidence
to serve such a purpose. In the first place, a language is not a disconnected
complex apart from culture but, on the contrary, is an important part of
the culture of a particular people living at a definite time and place. As
such it reflects in its subject matter, *i.e.*, chiefly vocabulary, many of the
non-linguistic elements of that culture. Its association with a definite
tribe or group of tribes often enables us to make valuable inferences as
to earlier distributions and movements of population, while its mirroring
of culture is obviously of great assistance in the securing of a perspective
for the culture itself. In the second place, language, like culture, is a
composite of elements of very different age, some of its features reaching
back into the mists of an impenetrable past, others being the product of
a development or need of yesterday. If now we succeed in putting the
changing face of culture into relation with the changing face of language,
we shall have obtained a measure, vague or precise according to specific
circumstances, of the relative ages of the culture elements. In this way
language gives us a sort of stratified matrix to work in for the purpose of
unravelling culture sequences; its relation to culture history may be
roughly compared—one should not press the analogy—to that of geology
to palæontology. How linguistic perspective is obtained, how linguistic
features or elements are assigned to a relatively late or early period, how
they may be reconstructed to earlier forms we can not undertake to
demonstrate here,[16] as these problems are far beyond the scope of the
present paper. We must here assume these results as possible of achievement and limit ourselves to a consideration of how they are to be utilized
for cultural reconstruction.

In three important respects language, as an instrument for reconstructing the past, has the advantage of culture. First of all, it forms a
far more compact and inherently unified conceptual and formal complex

[16] The general subject of time perspective in language, specifically in American
languages, I hope some day to take up in a separate paper.

than the totality of culture. This is due primarily to the fact that its function is far more limited in nature,[17] to some extent also to the fact that the disturbing force of rationalization that constantly shapes and distorts culture anew is largely absent in language. Any changes, then, that affect language are generally more consistently and regularly carried out than in culture; this means that there are, on the whole, fewer cautions to observe in the application of such chronological criteria as can be formulated. Secondly, linguistic changes proceed more slowly and, what is more important, at a generally more even rate than cultural ones. This means that, particularly where there is abundant comparative linguistic material available, we are enabled to penetrate farther back into the past and to obtain a more reliable feeling of relative durations of such linguistic time sequences as are available. Thirdly, and most important of all, a language is, of all historical products, at the same time the most perfectly self-contained and the least often apt to enter as such into the central field of consciousness. Its resourcefulness in meeting with, in other words adequately reflecting, new conditions is extreme, so that violent cultural changes are often accompanied by only moderate linguistic adjustments.[18] From all this it follows that a language, under normal circumstances, is relatively little affected by influences from without. Whereas in culture curiously little remains when the manifold streams of foreign influence have been eliminated, the elimination from a language of such linguistic features, whether as regards form or content, as are due to outside influences, nearly always leaves all but the whole of the formal framework and by far the greater part of its content standing intact as of native growth. That this greatly simplifies the chronologic problem is obvious. Moreover, where there has been foreign influence, it is very much easier to recognize it as such and see it in proper relief against the native ground-work than in the case of culture. Indeed, this very sharpness of contrast between the native and the foreign elements, a sharpness which naturally tends to become obliterated with age, is frequently helpful in the making of chronological inferences. However, we must be clear that the methodological advantages enjoyed by linguistics in inferred chronology are of direct benefit only to linguistics itself; they become of use also to culture only indirectly, that is, insofar as such advantages affect linguistic features that are closely associated with cultural considerations.

[17] The greater the specialization of function, the more neatly are the parts of a complex apt to be bound together and the finer the technique.
[18] Thus, it is amazing how little such languages as Iroquois or Chinese have been affected in their essentials by sweeping cultural changes in modern times. And yet they succeed perfectly in giving expression to all new needs in terms of traditional form and subject matter.

There are chiefly two ways in which linguistic data may yield results of chronologic interest to the history of culture. We may either take a single linguistic element (word, grammatical element, morphological peculiarity, phonetic characteristic) and study its cultural associations and geographical distribution; or we may take a language or linguistic group as such and work out its geographical distribution and, in most cases, differentiation into smaller units with a view to deducing from this certain historical facts. The method of association of culture elements corresponds to one aspect of the former of these linguistic problems, the method of distribution of culture elements to another aspect thereof and to the second linguistic problem. Roughly speaking, linguistic elements correspond to culture elements and complexes, linguistic groups to culture areas.

INFERENCES FROM ANALYSIS OF WORDS AND GRAMMATICAL ELEMENTS

DESCRIPTIVE AND NON-DESCRIPTIVE TERMS

Analysis of Culture Words

If we have any method of determining the relative age of a word[19] that has cultural significance, it is clear that we have at the same time a means of ascertaining something as to the relative age of the associated culture element itself. One of the most useful principles for the determination of the age of a word is a consideration of its form; that is, whether it can be analysed into simpler elements, its significance being made up of the sum of these, or is a simple irreducible term. In the former case we suspect, generally speaking, a secondary or relatively late formation, in the latter considerable antiquity. We assume here, of course, that we are able to eliminate borrowed words, which, however recently introduced, are naturally incapable of analysis from the point of view of the borrowing language.[20] We know, for instance, that the objects and offices denoted in English by the words *bow, arrow, spear, wheel, plough, king,* and *knight,* belong to a far more remote past than those indicated by such words as *railroad, insulator, battleship, submarine, percolator, capitalist,*

---

[19] In applying linguistic data to culture-historical uses in many Asiastic and European languages we are, of course, immensely aided by documentary evidence, inasmuch as the changing form and content of language are more or less adequately reflected in datable records. For aboriginal America, however, documentary linguistic evidence, while not altogether wanting, is relatively scanty. The methodology of linguistic reconstruction is, therefore, bound to restrict itself in the main to inferential evidence. Such evidence alone, indeed, is here considered.

[20] Thus, such a Wishram word as *it-stagin* "stockings" is incapable of Wishram analysis, but is naturally merely a recent loanword from English *stocking.*

and *attorney-general*, but we might have guessed this from the fact that the latter set, unlike the former, are clearly secondary formations, descriptive terms that seem to have been created out of older linguistic material to meet new cultural needs. This type of reasoning does not by any means imply that the older stock of non-descriptive words are necessarily in origin of a category distinct from the later descriptive ones. As a matter of fact, comparative, direct historical, or other evidence frequently enables us to show that what now appear to be non-descriptive terms are themselves originally descriptive in character, but, through the destructive agency of gradual phonetic change, have in time lost their morphological transparency.[21] It is this very obscuring, in course of time, of the analysis of a word, that gives the contrast between words of evident morphology and unanalysable words its chronological significance.

In aboriginal America there are undoubtedly countless examples that might be chosen of the operation of this method of inferring the relative ages of culture concepts, but linguistic data have as yet been so little employed by Americanists in the handling of ethnological problems[22] that we need not be surprised to find them only sparsely, if at all, represented in the literature. An example or two will, therefore, be of service. The Tsimshian word for crest, *dzabk*, offers a contrast, from the point of view of morphologic analysis, to that for phratry, *ptɛ·x*. While the latter is, so far as we can see at present, a morphologically irreducible term, the word *dzabk* is clearly a derivative of the verb *dzab* "to make," *-k* being a mediopassive suffix; *dzab-k* may thus be interpreted as "what is made" or "what is represented in visible form," referring probably to the carvings and other plastic representations of crests.[23] These linguistic facts may be deemed much too slender to justify the inference that the present phratric groupings, or better phratric groupings of some kind, antedated the development of clan and phratric emblems, though I should not be

---

[21] Thus, the word *king* (Anglo-Saxon *cyning*) can be shown to be a derivative of *kin* (Anglo-Saxon *cynn*); its significance at an earlier stage of its history was thus "one who belongs to (represents, leads) a kin-group." This example shows incidentally that linguistic analysis often helps to unravel the earlier history of a culture concept.

[22] Aside from the use of the concept of linguistic stock, particularly as expressed in Powell's linguistic map of aboriginal America north of Mexico. Many ethnologists indeed, have gone much further in the definitive and exclusive use of these stock groupings than the historical-minded linguist would concede as allowable.

[23] Similarly, the Kwakiutl word for crest, *ḵe·s'o·*, is doubtless a derivative of *ḵe·n* "to carve." According to Mr. Barbeau, the Tsimshian are quite aware of the relation of *dzabk* to the verb *dzab*, though another interpretation is sometimes offered. According to some, a *dzabk* is "what is made up, devised" and shown at a potlatch, referring rather to the invention of new ways of showing old crests or even the invention of new crests.

inclined to consider as improbable the fact of the inference. However, it seems that one may at least conclude that the extensive representation of the crest belongs to a later period of the history of Tsimshian social organization than the origin of phratry groupings. The present argument is corroborated by another linguistic criterion, that of the geographic distribution of a word, of which more anon. In the Nass River dialect, which is rather closely related to Tsimshian proper, the word for phratry, *ptɛ·q'*, is only dialectically different from the corresponding Tsimshian word, while an entirely different word, *'ayukᵘs*, is used to denote a crest.

This type of argument is frequently an alluring one when it is a question of comparing the relative antiquity of the same culture concept in two or more distinct tribes. Thus, the Nootka have a word for attendant at a feast, *yatsmi·ɬsi*, which can be readily analysed as "one-who (-*ḥsi*) walks (*yats-*) about-in-the-house (-*mi·ɬ-*)," whereas the corresponding Kwakiutl word, *'ɘlkᵘ*, is not capable of analysis. It hardly seems too far-fetched to surmise from this that the ceremonial aspect of feasting was earlier developed among the Kwakiutl than among the Nootka.

Analysis of Place Names

The analysis of place names is frequently a valuable means of ascertaining whether a people have been long settled in a particular region or not. The longer a country has been occupied, the more do the names of its topographical features and villages tend to become purely conventional and to lose what descriptive meaning they originally possessed.[24]

Thus, it is by no means an accident that a considerable number of village names among the Nootka are incapable of satisfactory analysis, whereas the names of topographical features among such less settled tribes as the Paiute and Ojibwa are in practically every case readily interpreted. It is sometimes instructive to compare the names for the same topographical feature among two or more tribes. Mt. Shasta, in northern California, is visible to a considerable number of distinct tribes. The Hupa call it *nɪn-nɪs-'an ɬak-gai*, a descriptive term meaning "white mountain"; while the Yana have a distinctive term for it, *wa'galu·*, which does not yield to analysis.[25] We may infer from this that the Hupa,

[24] Note, *e.g.*, the more or less transparent analysis of such names of cities in America as New York, Philadelphia, Washington, New Orleans, Indianapolis, St. Louis, San Francisco, Buffalo, as contrasted with such at present meaningless European names as London, Paris, York, Leeds, Rouen, Rheims, Rome, Naples.

[25] *wa-* may be identical with Yana *wa-* "to sit." Of how long standing the term *wa'galu'* must have been among the Yana is further evidenced by the fact that its diminutive, *wa'ganu·ba* "little-Mt. Shasta," is applied to Mt. Lassen, a volcanic peak within the confines of their own territory. Mt. Shasta is in neither Hupa nor Yana territory.

as an Athabaskan-speaking tribe, are newcomers in northern California as compared with the Yana, a conclusion that is certainly corroborated by other evidence.

Cautions in Use of Method

Danger in comparison of equivalent words in different languages.—In actual practice, however, it is apt to be dangerous to use the method we have considered when dealing with words for the same culture concept in different tribes. The chief reason for caution lies in the great differences exhibited by different languages in the relative freedom with which descriptive terms are formed. Some languages, such as Chinook and Takelma, have a relatively large number of radical elements and hence are not as apt to resort to descriptive formations as are languages, say Athabaskan, that have a smaller number of radical elements but greater powers of synthetic word-formation. Moreover, the rates of phonetic change undoubtedly differ very considerably in different languages, so that obscuration of an originally descriptive term may be brought about more readily in one than in another. How long a descriptive term for a culture concept of undoubted antiquity may linger on in a language which tends to keep its analysis of descriptive terms transparent is illustrated by the Athabaskan word for glove or mitten. Among the Athabaskan tribes of the Mackenzie valley we can hardly doubt that the mitten was an old element of their material culture; hence we would rather expect the term for mitten to be a non-descriptive term than a compound yielding readily to analysis. As a matter of fact these tribes use a word which simply means "hand-bag" (Chipewyan *la-djis*, Hare *lla-dji*, Loucheux *nle-djic*). We may put up with this when we recollect that Athabaskan shows a more than ordinary fondness for synthesis, but we are certainly given a jolt when we find that exactly the same transparent compound turns up in Navaho as the term for mitten (*la-djic*).

Changes in terminology.—Even when the method is in the main restricted to a comparison of culture words in the same language, a number of cautions are necessary. In the first place, a culture concept may prove to be old in spite of the fact that its designation is demonstrably of recent origin, for the older, perhaps non-descriptive, term may have become obsolete and given way to a later formation. One of the most potent sources of such changes in terminology is the widespread custom of tabooing words for a certain period after the death of a person whose name was identical with, compounded of, or even merely similar to such words. Normally the old word is reinstated after the taboo is lifted, but it must often have happened that the newer, generally descriptive, term lingered on out of habit alongside the older one and eventually even replaced it altogether. That the present term for an old culture concept is not necessarily the primary one in the particular tribe studied is demonstrated by the analogy of many evidently secondary terms for non-cultural concepts which must have been familiar to the natives from time immemorial. Thus, the crane must have been uninterruptedly known to the Hupa as far back as the time at which the hypothetical undifferentiated Athabaskan prototype of Hupa was spoken in the far north. Nevertheless, we find that the Hupa do not use the regular Athabaskan stem *del* for crane, but a descriptive term (*xas-lın tau*) meaning "he who frequents riffles." Very likely the old non-descriptive word for crane became obsolete because a name taboo enforced its temporary disuse. In general, then, it is safest to use the morphological criterion for the age of a culture word when comparative linguistic evidence does not show that it was preceded in use by a non-descriptive term of like meaning.

Changes in application of culture words.—There is, further, a reverse caution to be observed. The culture word may be of undoubtedly great antiquity but, owing to a change of meaning that it has undergone, the culture concept that it at present symbolizes need not, at least in its present form, be as old as the word itself. Thus, it goes without saying that the English word *needle*, which can be traced back to a very remote antiquity, did not always denote the delicately fashioned article of steel that we now know, but was originally applied to a more primitive prototype of bone and, later, of bronze. Still more striking is the history of our English word *Hell* which, in spite of its present characteristic significance, originally referred to a cold and cheerless domain presided over by a female deity. A striking instance of this sort from aboriginal America will further illustrate the necessity of caution. The Athabaskan non-descriptive noun stem *ŧeŧ* is found in both Chasta Costa and Navaho with exactly the same meaning, "matches." It is perfectly obvious from other considerations that this can not possibly be the primary meaning of the word and we learn, indeed, by comparison with other Athabaskan dialects (*e.g.*, Chipewyan) that *ŧeŧ* properly means "fire-drill" and was transferred to "matches" when these came in as a modern substitute for the former. I mention this example not because there is the slightest actual danger here of misinterpreting the evidence, but because the wrong inference (assuming that we had only Chasta Costa and Navaho to guide us) would be hard to controvert on purely formal linguistic grounds. We learn from this and other examples of transfer of meaning that without fairly complete comparative evidence it is often dangerous to argue as to the age of a specific form of culture element on the basis of the linguistic criterion we have been considering, though the relative age of a certain general type of culture element may be satisfactorily enough established by its means.

SPECIALIZED MEANINGS OF WORDS AND SPECIAL VOCABULARIES

While descriptive words are, in the main, apt to be of relatively recent age, they cannot all be put in the same class. Between complete lack of capability of analysis and absolute transparency of analysis there are naturally many stages. A type that is of particular interest to us is constituted by such words as are satisfactorily analysable from a purely linguistic standpoint but whose actual meaning does not correspond to that which is immediately suggested by analysis. Such words carry the history of their transfer of meaning with them. They are of value from our standpoint because a greater age may often be inferred for the culture concept implied in the linguistic analysis than for such culture concepts as are indicated by descriptive words of literal analysis. Contrast, for instance, the English words *carpet-sweeper* and *spinster*. The former is to be understood quite literally as "that which sweeps carpets," the latter does not now mean "one who spins" but "unmarried female of somewhat advanced age." *Spinster* clearly did at one time mean "one who spins," but, through association with a particular class of individuals, gradually took on a specialized meaning. From the length of time that it must have taken for so complete a transfer of meaning to become effective, a transfer including entire loss of the older meaning, we may reasonably infer the purely cultural fact that the art of spinning was known at an early time and that it was in the hands of the women; further, that it antedated by a long time the advent of the carpet-sweeper. These facts are, of course, well known to us from direct historical evidence, but it is methodologically important to show that it is possible to ascertain them, or at least to suggest them, on the basis of a purely linguistic criterion. The age of the word *spinster* is further assured by the relative rarity of the agentive suffix *ster* (compare *huckster, songster,* and stereotyped proper names like Baxter, *i.e.*, baker, and Webster, *i.e.*, weaver); this argument makes use of another linguistic criterion, of which more presently.

The application of the principle of specialization or other modification of meaning may yield interesting results as to the relative ages of two or more components of a ritual, say the Sun Dance of the Plains or the Night Chant of the Navaho. Names of rituals, dances, and other ceremonial activities are not always of clear application to the ceremonies as at present performed or understood; their analysis may not infrequently be expected to show either that one of the constituent elements, not necessarily the most prominent now, arose prior to certain others that perhaps at present give the ceremony most of its content or that a certain culture concept implied in the name is older than the ceremony as such. Thus, among the Nootka, the term *tutcḥa·* "buying a woman" is applied to a complex of ceremonial and economic procedure which corresponds to our own marriage ceremony. Properly speaking, the term should apply only to the distribution of property on the part of the bridegroom and his supporters to the bride's family as payment for her acquisition. As a matter of fact, however, it includes all the songs, dances, and speeches that precede the "wife-purchasing" potlatch and much of which has no necessary reference to the "purchase." Thus, there is a whole class of songs known as *tutcḥa·'yak* "for woman-purchase," whose connexion with marriage is merely conventional. Yet it is just the ceremonial procedure preceding the potlatch that is chiefly meant by the Indian when he speaks of *tutcḥa·*. Furthermore, the fact that the bride's family immediately distributes the gifts to their own villagers and, still more important, that they may in the near future return the gifts with a dowry of privileges and a potlatch distribution of as great value as or even greater value than the property received as "wife-purchase" frequently reduces the "buying of woman" as a type of marriage to little more than a form. Nevertheless, the cultural value of the term *tutcḥa·* lies precisely in the fact that it implies a purely economic wife-purchasing form of marriage as lying back of the present marriage complex with its secondary accretions of ceremonial procedure and weakening of economic significance.

Here we may say a word as to the inferential importance for cultural chronology of a specialized vocabulary defining a whole culture complex. We find on an analysis of the terminologies of the different complexes that go to make up a culture that they differ considerably in the completeness and precision with which the single elements constituting them are symbolized by words. Of two cultural complexes we naturally assign a greater antiquity to that possessing the more ramified vocabulary, particularly if the vocabulary consists largely of non-descriptive words. Contrast, for instance, the extensive and highly distinctive vocabulary concerned with the breeding and use of cattle (*cow, ox, bull, steer, heifer calf, cattle, beef, veal, butter, cheese, whey, curds, cream, to churn, to skim*— all unanalysable terms of evidently considerable age) with the more meagre and less distinctive vocabulary of such an industry as, say, the growing of oranges.[26] Linguistic evidence alone would make out a strong case for the greater age of cattle breeding and the dairy industry than of orange growing. Arguments of this type can frequently be applied with profit to the study of American culture. The great age of such complexes as sea-mammal hunting among the Nootka and Eskimo, canoeing among the West Coast tribes and Eastern Algonkin, agriculture among the Iroquois, and the gathering and preparation for food of wild roots and seeds among the Plateau tribes is in nearly every case attested by an appropriately rich vocabulary. On the other hand, the complexes of more recent age, say the decorative art of the Utes or the Ghost Dance religion, seem to make use of less extensive and distinctive vocabularies. I should go so far as to say that no study of a culture complex is historically complete without a thorough investigation of the range and nature of its vocabulary.

INFERENCES FROM GRAMMATICAL EVIDENCE

Grammatical Treatment of Culture Words

So far we have dealt only with words as such and with their analysis, where possible, into their constituent elements. Something of historical value may, further, be gleaned from the grammatical treatment of culture words. In every language there are a number of grammatical processes and elements that have ceased to be alive, as it were; that are no longer productive of new analogies, but that appear restricted in use to a limited number of stereotyped forms. Such grammatical features are clearly only survivals of features that were formerly more typical and more freely usable. They imply a considerable age for the words that they affect. This matter becomes of cultural interest when the words affected by irregular grammatical processes are of cultural reference. In this case we may infer a like antiquity for the culture concept itself. Thus, the antiquity that we have already demonstrated for cattle breeding in our own culture is further implied by such grammatical irregularities as the *-en* plural of *oxen*, the poetic plural *kine* for *cows*, and the change of *-f* to *-v-* in the plural *calves* and the verb *to calve*. Irregularities of this sort are not uncommon in American languages and are practically always indicative of the great age of the words that illustrate them and, generally speaking, of the associated concepts. Thus, in Nootka, three uncommon and evidently unproductive types of plural formation are the change

---

[26] In many modern industries quite extensive and explicit vocabularies have grown up, to be sure, but they are largely technical in character and of strictly limited appeal and thus lie rather apart from the main channel of linguistic history.

of final -ł to -ḥ, reduplication with a-vowel, and reduplication with inserted -t-. Now these irregular types are respectively illustrated in ḥa'wi·ḥ "chiefs" (singular ḥa'wił), qaqo·ł "slaves" (singular qo·ł), and ꞎa·tɛꞏntł "dogs" (singular ꞎɛni·tł; ꞎaiłc- is used as stem in all derivatives); from which we can with some degree of safety infer that a clearly defined chief's class, the institution of slavery, and the domestication of the dog belong to a remote antiquity in this area. Similarly, the singular and plural of the Tsimshian term for "chief" (sǝm'ɔ·gid: sǝmgigad) form a quite irregular and unparalleled set of forms in that language, though they are in this case not incapable of at least partial analysis sǝm- "very, real"; gad "man," gigad "men").

The criterion of morphologic irregularity, however, can be safely applied only positively, hardly negatively; that is, we may conclude with reasonable certainty that a culture concept associated with an archaic linguistic process is itself an old one, but we cannot be sure that a culture concept expressed by a word whose grammatical treatment is perfectly normal is of relatively recent origin. The reason for this is the ever present tendency for less well represented grammatical features to be ruled out by the analogy of other better represented ones of like function; not only do the forms of new words follow the most regular analogies present in the language but many of the old stock are remodelled in accordance with these analogies. This process is known to linguists as analogic levelling.[27] Thus, while such irregular plurals as *sheep* and *oxen* are of positive cultural value as indicating a great age for the domestication of sheep and cattle among the ancestors of the English (contrast such regular plurals as *elephants* and *tigers*, both of these animals becoming known at a much more recent period), it would be erroneous or at least unwarranted to infer from such regular forms as *horses* and *goats* that these animals were not domesticated at as early a date. The retention of a grammatical archaism is in almost every specific case governed by factors beyond our power of analysis; in other words, it is an accident. It must also be borne in mind that languages differ very much in the readiness with which they allow analogical levelling to operate. Some, like Takelma, seem to put up with a good deal of formal irregularity; others, like Yana or Paiute, while they may exhibit great complexity of structure, keep their formal machinery in well regulated grooves. This

---

[27] Analogic levelling and phonetic change are the two most important tendencies that make for linguistic variation. Analogic levelling is precisely the process that is illustrated by the child's *mans*, *runned*, and *brang*. These and similar examples merely lack the sanction of adult usage. Such a preterit as *worked* (for older *wrought*) was originally as gross a solecism as *brang* or *bringed* for *brought*.

difference in formal tendency is clearly based on psychological factors that we do not need to elucidate here.

Cultural Value of Grammatical Elements

In the cases that we have so far discussed the cultural content of the word has been borne by its radical portion, the stem. In some of the typically polysynthetic languages of America, however, non-radical elements, that is affixes, which are often possessed of very concrete significance, may imply a reference to some element of culture. As the process which turns an originally independent stem into a derivative affix is necessarily a slow one, the presence of such affixes, particularly when there is no longer an etymologic relation between them and any of the independent stems of the language, is generally good evidence of their age and, by inference, of that of the culture concept it embodies. Owing to the specialized character of the affix, as compared with the independent stem, the former has an even greater *a priori* claim to antiquity than the non-descriptive stem. Naturally the caution as to transfer of meaning, which we have already dealt with in the case of independent stems, is equally operative here; indeed, we may quite generally suspect the specific cultural application of an affix to be due to the turning over of an element of originally wider range of meaning to the exclusive use of a culture concept of growing importance (thus, we might easily conceive the gradual loss in the future of the wider agentive and instrumental function of English -*er* and its specialization into a cultural affix denoting "complex piece of machinery" on the basis of such forms as *typewriter, receiver, smelter, reaper,* and *developer*). Such a caution, however, would not seriously invalidate the use of our linguistic criterion, as a considerable period must be assumed to have elapsed before such specialization could be effected; it merely lessens somewhat the remoteness of cultural perspective implied by the existence of the affix.

One of the most interesting types of elements of this sort is constituted by such numeral classifiers as refer to objects of cultural interest. The presence in Yurok, *e.g.*, of numeral classifiers referring specifically to woodpecker-scalps and obsidian blades is in a high degree symptomatic of the great age of the custom of prizing these objects as valuable forms of property and further implies that the keen sense of property evinced by these Indians is by no means a recent development. Similarly, the occurrence in both Salish and Tsimshian of numeral classifiers defining canoes necessitates the conclusion that both groups of tribes have not only been acquainted with the canoe from time immemorial, but have long been dependent on it in the pursuit of their livelihood; this comes out even more strongly in the case of Tsimshian, which employes entirely distinct stems for "one" and "two" when these numbers refer to canoes. Further, the fact that Nootka has numeral classifiers specifically referring to such units of measurement as fathoms, spans, finger-widths, and board-lengths, is the best kind of evidence for the antiquity among these Indians of the use of units of measurement, a cultural trait, furthermore, that presupposes a well-developed property sense of long standing. It is, indeed, more than probable that the glimpses into the past afforded by the numeral classifiers of Yurok, Tsimshian, Salish, and Nootka reach back farther than the origin of many, if not most, of the social and ceremonial features of these tribes. Another interesting example of a group of affixes of cultural reference is afforded by several Nootka suffixes that refer to ceremonial procedure, *e.g.*, -'o·'il "to ask for something as a gift in a girl's puberty potlatch," -to·ta "to give a potlatch for someone," -'inl "to give a feast of some kind of food (in a potlatch)." Such elements clearly indicate that at least certain cultural concepts connected with the potlatch are of great age among the Nootka.

Negative evidence of the sort that we are considering can hardly be looked upon as significant in view of the fact that it is only exceptionally that grammatical affixes of cultural reference are found altogether. The weakness of such negative evidence would be at its greatest when used to compare the ages of the same culture element among different tribes, unless possibly the languages of these tribes were strictly comparable in structure. Thus, the complete structural dissimilarity of Hupa and Yurok robs of all its significance the fact that in the former the emphasis on woodpecker-scalps and obsidian blades finds no reflex in grammatical structure, though this emphasis is equally strong in the culture of both tribes.

GEOGRAPHICAL DISTRIBUTION OF CULTURE WORDS

DIFFUSION VERSUS COMMON HERITAGE

We now turn to the geographical distribution of linguistic data. The mode of argumentation is here essentially the same as that employed in studying the distribution of culture elements; in other words, the more extended the geographical distribution of a culture word, the older the word and, by inference, the older its associated concept. Owing to the ease with which borrowed culture elements are renamed, whether by means of a transfer of meaning of an old term or by means of a new descriptive term, the method must be used with great caution. There are, however, two factors in regard to which the evidence derived from linguistic data is generally less liable to misinterpretation than that which is directly derived from the distribution of culture.

In discussing the distribution of a culture element we found that it was in many cases practically impossible, or at least difficult, to distinguish between similarity due to diffusion from a certain centre and similarity due to retention of the element by tribes originally forming part of one and the same cultural community. For reasons which we cannot here take up fully it is, on the other hand, very frequently possible to distinguish between a word of native origin and one which has been borrowed from without. Applying this to the problem of distribution, we find that we are often able to distinguish between cultural terms that have been inherited in common by the languages forming a linguistic stock or subdivision thereof and cultural terms that have passed beyond the limits of such a group and been taken up by one or more languages of an alien group. Naturally, it is also very possible that a culture term travels from one language to others of the same linguistic group, so that the problem arises of how to keep apart primary stock words from such as have been diffused within the genetic group. Roughly speaking, we may say that the criteria for such distinction are the same as for the more fundamental distinction we have first mentioned; the criteria are merely more delicately applied, greater emphasis being placed on specifically dialectic linguistic features. Even when a doubt remains as to whether a culture term is to be looked upon as of indigenous or alien origin, a minimum date, in terms of one or more linguistic features, can be assigned to its introduction; this possibility is, of course, of great chronologic importance.

The second helpful linguistic factor that I have in mind is a corollary of the first. Owing to the very nature of linguistic evidence, we can not only in specific instances determine the negative fact that a word is of foreign origin (this is merely another way of stating that it is not of native origin), but proceed to the positive conclusion that it has of necessity been borrowed from a particular language. As soon as we are able to do this, we have a powerful argument for ascribing the origin of the culture element in question to one tribe rather than another and thus gain some idea of the sequence in which the element was assimilated by the different tribes of a region.

BORROWING OF CULTURE WORDS

Morphological Evidence

The evidence that stamps a word as of foreign origin, insofar as it is of a purely linguistic nature, is either morphological or phonetic. It may,

of course, involve both criteria at the same time. It is a pretty safe rule
for most languages that words of more than a certain length[28] must be
capable of at least partial analysis into elements (stem and formative
elements) characteristic of the language. If such an analysis is impossible,
there is very good reason to suspect the word to be of foreign provenience,
to have been borrowed from a language in which the standard radical
length is great enough to tolerate the word in question without analysis
or in which it is capable of morphological analysis. Thus, such thoroughly
assimilated English words as *hurricane, moccasin,* and *tomato* are incapable of analysis into English stems and formative elements; as their
length is well beyond the normal one for English stems, we conclude that
they are borrowed words and are confirmed in our conclusion by more
direct evidence. Incidentally this effectually clears the path for a study
of the culture-history of the moccasin as a style of footwear that has become popular in certain circles among the whites in America and of the
growing of the tomato for food purposes.

A good American Indian example of the morphological criterion of
borrowed words is the Nootka *tlo·kwa·na,* the term applied to the wolf
ritual, the chief ceremonial complex of these Indians. The normal
Nootka stem is monosyllabic, consisting generally of a consonant plus
a vowel plus a consonant; quite infrequently it is a sound group of two
syllables, while trisyllabic stems are entirely absent. The word *tlo·kwa·na*
looks as though it ought to be analysable into a stem *tlo·kw* plus a suffix
-a·na, but these elements have no meaning in Nootka. We therefore, suspect the word to be of foreign origin. Turing to Kwakiutl, we not only
learn that the similar word *dlo·gwala* is applied to a wolf dance performed
during the winter ceremonial but also—and this is more to the point here
—that it is readily analysable into a verb stem *dlo·gw-* "to be powerful"
plus a common durative suffix *-(a)la.* The important cultural inference
must be drawn that at least certain elements in the wolf ritual of the
Nootka have been assimilated from the neighbouring Kwakiutl. A similar
line of reasoning leads me strongly to suspect that the Nootka term
topa·ti, meaning any privilege that is obtained by inheritance, is of foreign
origin, and this in spite of the fact that it indicates one of the most fundamental aspects of Nootka culture. However, I have not as yet succeeded in connecting the word with any foreign linguistic elements.

---

[28] What might be termed the standard length of radical elements differs greatly
in different languages. In some it is a syllable (among such languages there are
some in which a consonant plus a vowel is the norm, others in which the normal
stem consists of a consonant plus a vowel plus a consonant), in others two or even
three syllables; a norm of three-syllabled radicals is certainly not common, however.

Should it eventually prove, after all, to be a native Nootka word, it would have to be considered as of great antiquity, as no descriptive meaning whatever now attaches to it. The most instructive instances of the borrowing of culture words are those which, like Nootka *tło·kwa·na*, can be definitely traced to a specific language, for in these the direction of diffusion is established.

But the morphological criterion sometimes fails us, notably in the case of short words which nowhere yield to analysis. We may be quite certain that the diffusion of a culture word is in part due to borrowing without our being in a position to say, from the linguistic evidence alone, in what direction the borrowing must be understood to have taken place. Considerations of another sort may often enable us to determine or surmise this direction, but even at the worst the linguistic evidence retains its value as immediately demonstrative of the fact of diffusion. A good instance of such ambiguity is the distribution of the word for "tobacco" among the Diegueño in southern California, the Shasta in northern California, and the Takelma in southwestern Oregon. There is no doubt that Diegueño *up*, Shasta *o·p*, and Takelma *o·"p*[29] are indicative of the gradual diffusion of the cultivated tobacco (very likely the name properly applies to only a particular species of native tobacco) over a large part of western North America, but it seems impossible, at least for the present, to ascribe the origin of the word to one rather than another of these languages. If a south to north spread of the culture plant is surmised, it is on other than purely linguistic evidence. The distribution of a widespread word for "dog" in western North America (*e.g.*, Nahuatl *chichi*, Yana *cucu*, Takelma *ísixi*)[30] presents a similar cultural problem.

Phonetic Evidence

Where the morphological criterion can not be employed, the phonetic one is sometimes of service. It rests on the fact that languages differ in their systems of phonetics, sounds or combinations of sounds that are usual in one being absent or at best rare in the other. Generally speaking, such phonetic features of a borrowed word as are strange to the borrowing language are replaced by their closest available equivalents, so that the word frequently assumes a deceptive appearance of being thoroughly at home. Thus, the English word *rum* appears in Lower Umpqua as

---

[29] Diegueño (a Yuman dialect) and Shasta are both Hokan languages and are thus remotely related, but it is highly improbable that this particular concordance rests on anything but culture diffusion. Takelma, so far as known, is not related to the Hokan languages.

[30] Which can be easily reconstructed, on both internal and comparative evidence, to *ísisi*.

lam, in Nootka as *naˑma*, neither of these languages possessing an *r*-sound, while Nootka also lacks *l*. Similarly, the Nootka word *tloˑkwaˑna* "wolf ritual," though no doubt borrowed from Kwakiutl *dloˑgwala*, presents no phonetic characteristics that are untypical of Nootka, the un-Nootka sounds *dl*, *gw*, and *l* of the Kwakiutl original being respectively replaced by *tl*, *kw*, and *n*, the nearest Nootka correspondents.

It does sometimes happen, however, that sounds otherwise foreign to a language are preserved in certain words of demonstrably foreign origin and that, generalizing from these, it is possible to establish the alien provenience of other words involving the same sound. Thus, it can be shown in English that the voiced sibilant *j* (as in French *jeu*, *âge*) is never found in words of native origin but is restricted in its occurrence to foreign, chiefly French, Latin, and Greek words, in which it either goes back to an original *j* (as in *rouge*) or, more often, to an original *zy* (as in *pleasure*, *erasure*, *aphasia*).[31] The value to English culture-history of these facts may be illustrated by reference to such a word as *garage*, in which both the *j*-sound and the place of the accent point to a foreign, specifically French, origin. The culture-historical inference that the automobile and garage are elements due to French influence can, of course, be made on more direct evidence, but it is none the less important from a methodological standpoint to realize that phonetic evidence alone strongly suggests it.

Not infrequently a sound, while of native origin in certain positions, occurs in certain other positions only in foreign words. Thus, while the sounds *z* and *dj* in medial and final position are common enough in native English words (*e.g.*, *as*, *fleas*, *chosen*; *edge*, *fledgling*), initially they occur only in foreign, more particularly French, Latin, and Greek words (*e.g.*, *zeal*, *zoology*; *Jew*, *just*, *John*). The culture-historical value of such distinctions comes out clearly in estimating the age of such words as *judge*, *jury*, and *general* and, to a certain extent, of the culture concepts connected with them. Frequently, also, the foreign provenience of a word is indicated by a combination of sounds each of which may be freely used in native words in all positions (*e.g.*, *-ps-* or *-ps* in Greek and Latin words, such as *rhapsody*, *apse*, *Cyclops*, *lapse;* such English forms as *lips* and *sips* are hardly comparable, as they can be readily resolved into *p*-stem plus *s*-suffix).

A couple of examples from American Indian languages will indicate

---

[31] In words like *erasure* and *closure*, *j* developed from *zy*, inasmuch as original Latin *-sūra*, via French *-sure*, *i.e.*, *-züre*, became *-zyure*, *-zyur*. In words like *aphasia* and *cohesion*, original intervocalic *-si-* became voiced non-syllabic *-zy-*. Native English *-zy-*, whence *-j-*, arises only optionally in sentence phonetics, *e.g.*, *äju* from *äz yu* (*i.e.*, *as you*).

the usefulness of the phonetic criterion in the recognition of loan words. In Haida *m* is a comparatively rare sound at best; initially it does not seem to occur in undoubtedly native words at all. The word *mat* "mountain goat," evidently related to the Tsimshian *mati*, is, therefore, clearly a loan-word from the latter language, not the reverse; the fact that the mountain goat is not found on Queen Charlotte islands, the home of the Haida, naturally strengthens the argument, but is not really necessary to it. If the word for "mountain goat" is borrowed in Haida from Tsimshian, there is good reason to believe that the mountain-goat crest, one of the less prominent crests of the Haida, was borrowed by them from the Tsimshian also, an inference which is confirmed by other testimony. In chronologic terms this means that the mountain-goat crest is of later origin among the Haida than among the Tsimshian. A similar problem is presented by the Upper Chinook word for "buffalo," *i-duiha* (also "bull"; *a-duiha* "buffalo-cow, cow") with its rather anomalous *h*, a sound occurring only rarely in Chinookan. Some of the Upper Chinook were in the habit of accompanying their Shahaptian neighbours on the annual buffalo hunt on the western plains, but this habit must have been of very recent origin, so that a non-descriptive word for "buffalo" is almost certain, on purely cultural evidence, to be of foreign origin. Thus the anomalous phonetics of *i-duiha* agrees well with the cultural evidence, though I have not been able to determine its prototype.[32]

COMMON HERITAGE OF CULTURE WORDS

Chronological Inferences

Of special interest are such culture-historical words as are distributed over a number of tribes speaking related languages or dialects, this distribution not being due to secondary diffusion but to dialectic retention of an old word that formed part of the vocabulary of the common prototype of the languages or dialects concerned. Allowing for the caution imposed by a possible change of meaning,[33] a consideration of such words throws much light on many of the older elements of culture possessed by the tribes to whom the languages belong. As is well known, interesting and valuable results have been obtained in this way in the culture-history of the Indo-germanic, Semitic, and other old world groups of

[32] Can it possibly be related to Cheyenne *hotwa* "bull" (see *American Anthropologist* n.s. vol. 8, 1906, p. 18)?

[33] Such caution, however, is far less frequently applicable to a word of identical or like meaning in a number of related languages than when our view is limited to a single language. Independent parallel development of meaning in two or more languages is not unknown (cf. Athabaskan *tɬcɬ* "fire-drill" as developed to "matches" above), but its probability rapidly lessens with the number of the languages compared.

peoples, but in aboriginal America the application of the method is hardly in its infancy. Its value to cultural chronology lies chiefly in this, that the culture concepts associated with the more widely distributed words of a dialectic group (linguistic stock) reach back to a more distant past, other things being equal, than those of more local distribution. Further, as between a culture word distributed over a certain area by dialectic differentiation and a culture word distributed over an equivalent area by borrowing, the greater antiquity must be accorded the former, the splitting up of a language into a number of dialects being a much less rapid process than the diffusion of a word.

A good example of the former type of inference is presented by some of the Athabaskan words for "house." That both the quadrangular plank house of the Hupa and the earth lodge (hogan) of the Navaho are, from the standpoint of older Athabaskan culture, chronologically secondary to the round bark tent is neatly indicated by linguistic evidence, the common Athabaskan word for "house," *ye, yĕx* (Kato *ye;* Anvik *yax;* Ten'a *yax;* Carrier *yax;* Chipewyan *ye';* Hare *yi;* Loucheux *je*) being respectively replaced by *xonta* and *hoγan* in these languages. Many more such examples could be adduced, but, as already remarked, the value of the method has hardly begun to be realized among Americanists.

Historical Value of Operation of Phonetic Laws

It must be acknowledged that in particular cases it is not always easy to distinguish between a word independently inherited by a number of languages from a common prototype and one which has spread by diffusion within the limits of a group of genetically related languages. Ordinarily the distinction is rendered comparatively easy by the fact that the borrowed words do not show the influence of such dialectic phonetic laws as operated before their adoption. However, a borrowed word may happen to have come into use at a period prior to the operation of all such phonetic laws as are capable of affecting it, in which case it exhibits all the phonetic characteristics of words belonging to the oldest ascertainable stratum of the language. The chronological value of such words remains great, for they give us a minimum age, in terms of often relatively datable phonetic laws, for their adoption and that of the concepts associated with them.[34]

A good example of such a culture word is the Nootka *ḥei'na,* which

[34] The phonologic criterion renders great service in the stratification of the borrowed culture words of a language. Countless examples could be given from the history of the culture languages of the old world. Thus, the minimum age for the origin of the probably borrowed hemp culture among the Germanic-speaking tribes is indicated by the phonetic form of the Germanic word for the plant (cf. Anglo-Saxon *hænep*); comparison with such forms of the word as Greek *kannabis* shows clearly that this culture, or at least the knowledge of the plant, was older

is identical in origin with the Kwakiutl $xwe\cdot'la$. This term designates the supernatural quartz which is capable of flying and which, among the Nootka, plays an important part in the conduct of and in the beliefs connected with the Wolf Ritual. Nootka possesses both x (velar voiceless spirant) and xw (labialized velar voiceless spirant), though these are not common sounds; original Wakashan (Kwakiutl-Nootka) x and xw have both regularly developed to h (velarized aspiration).[35] Moreover, Kwakiutl l regularly corresponds to Nootka n.[36] Hence the two words look somewhat as if they might be independent developments of a common Wakashan prototype. Could we be sure of this, we would have to assign a very great antiquity to the Wakashan belief in the supernatural power of flying quartz. At the very least, the word must have been borrowed by Nootka before the x-h shift, whence we may infer that it belongs to the oldest stratum of Kwakiutl ritualistic influence.

Another example of this type is afforded by the Uto-Aztekan word for "metate, grinding stone," $metla\text{-}(tli)$; this appears in Nahuatl as $metla\text{-}tl$, in Huichol as $mata$, in Luiseño as $mala\text{-}l$, in Southern Paiute as $mara\text{-}tsi\text{-}$. Linguistically there is nothing to show that these correspondences do not rest on dialectic development from a common Uto-Aztekan source; should this interpretation prove sound, we would be dealing with a very old culture element antedating the tremendous movements of population that have scattered the Uto-Aztekan peoples from Idaho to Central America. If, on the other hand, there should be other than linguistic evidence to show that the metate was gradually diffused from an Aztec centre of distribution to the Sonoran and Shoshonean tribes to the north, the linguistic evidence would still prove a great antiquity for this diffusion, as it must have been consummated before the operation of a number of distinctive phonetic laws of considerable geographical distribution and, therefore, age (assimilation in Sonoran and Shoshonean of e—a to a—a; spirantization of intervocalic $-t$- to Luiseño $-l$-[37] and Southern Paiute $-r$-[38]).[39]

---

than the characteristic Germanic changes of original k to h and of original b to p whence results an inference of very considerable antiquity, an antiquity exceeding that, *e.g.*, of the acquaintance of the West Germanic tribes with Christianity (cf. Anglo-Saxon *cyrice* "church," *i.e.*, *kürike*, from Greek *küriake*: note retained k in Anglo-Saxon, and West Germanic generally, because this word was borrowed subsequently to the time at which the shift from k to h operated).

[35] Nitinat and Makah, however, preserve Wakashan x and xw.

[36] Kwakiutl $'l$, when "hardened" from l, corresponds to Nootka $'y$, not $'n$. This consideration may ultimately prove Nootka *hei'na* to be borrowed from Kwakiutl $xwe\cdot'la$, not cognate with it. Nootka n would then have been substituted for Kwakiutl l as its nearest acoustic equivalent.

[37] This applies to all Luiseño-Cahuilla dialects, also to Tübatulabal.

[38] This applies to all Ute-Chemehuevi and Shoshoni-Comanche dialects.

[39] It would not be necessary to assume that Uto-Aztekan tl had not yet become t in Sonoran and Shoshonean, as tl of a borrowed Nahuatl word would in

GEOGRAPHICAL DISTRIBUTION OF LINGUISTIC STOCKS

CONCEPT OF LINGUISTIC STOCK

Probably the most valuable service that linguistics can render ethnology is the setting up of groups of languages into linguistic stocks. The concept of a linguistic stock is of particular interest to us because, while based on descriptive data, it is strictly historical in character. It implies the former existence of a comparatively undifferentiated language which, by gradual phonetic and morphologic changes, has diverged into distinct forms of speech. Each of these, of course, may in turn become ramified, and so on. Hence a proper classification of genetically related languages always tends to assume the form of a genealogical tree. While it may be possible to say with certainty that a given number of languages are genetically related, it is a much more embarrassing task to prove the corresponding negative, that certain languages, because offering few, if any, obvious traits of similarity, cannot be considered as going back to a common origin. It is not difficult to realize that the process of linguistic differentiation may, after a vast lapse of time, bring about such profound dissimilarity of phonetics, structure, and vocabulary that the positive proof of genetic relationship may be a difficult or even impossible task. Even the most inclusive classification of aboriginal American languages that could be made would, therefore, have positive validity as far as it went without justly allowing the necessity of the negative corollaries that might be drawn.

CHRONOLOGICAL INFERENCES FROM LINGUISTIC DIFFERENTIATION AS TO MOVEMENTS OF POPULATION

Comparison of Distinct Linguistic Stocks

The greater the degrees of linguistic differentiation within a stock, the greater is the period of time that must be assumed for the development of such differentiations. The greater the geographical extent covered by a linguistic stock, the greater is the period of time that must be allowed for the movements of the tribes speaking its languages. The latter criterion of relative age holds good, however, only insofar as geographical extent is proportionate to degree of linguistic differentiation. A tribe may overrun a large territory at a very much more rapid rate than a language splits up into two divergent dialects. Hence, while the extensive geographical spread of a language undoubtedly forms a favourable condition for dialectic differentiation, it is not necessarily directly proportionate to

---

these languages be replaced by its nearest phonetic equivalent, *t*. Compare such Castilianized words as *metate* and *ocote*.

the latter. Yet the chronological value of the facts of linguistic distribution, particularly when emphasis is placed on remoter time perspectives, depends on the linguistic differentiation implied in such distribution. Let us glance at a few American examples.

The Algonkin languages proper[40] are spoken over a vast territory reaching from the Atlantic to the Rockies and from Hudson bay to the Ohio valley. In this area are (or were) spoken a large number of distinct languages and dialects (*e.g.*, Naskapi, Montagnais, Cree, Micmac, Abenaki, Ojibwa, Menomini, Fox, Shawnee, Delaware, Natick, Miami, Arapaho, Cheyenne, Blackfoot). There can be no doubt that a very great lapse of time (probably several millennia) must be assumed to account for the geographical distribution and dialectic differentiation of the Algonkin languages proper. As compared with the Algonkin area, that of the Penutian languages of California (Yokuts, Miwok-Costanoan, Maidu, Wintun),[41] though large, is quite restricted. Are we justified in assuming from this that the movement of Algonkin peoples[42] from a relatively small area occupied by a people of homogeneous speech greatly antedated the analogous movement of Penutian peoples? Not unless we can show that the differentiation of the Algonkin languages is not less profound than that of the Penutian languages. As a matter of fact, the morphologic and lexical differences that obtain between even the most divergent Algonkin languages, say Cheyenne and Micmac, while by no means inconsiderable, are of comparatively little moment when set by the side of analogous differences obtaining between two such Penutian languages as Yokuts and Miwok. The fact that Cheyenne and Micmac were understood to be clearly related at a time when Yokuts, Costamoan, Miwok, Wintun, and Maidu[43] were looked upon as mutually independent

[40] That is, without the inclusion of the remotely related Yurok and Wiyot of California.

[41] This is the Penutian stock as defined by Dixon and Kroeber. I have collected evidence to show that it extends into Oregon, embracing Takelma, Coos, and Lower Umpqua, possibly certain other languages. For the sake of simplicity, however, I here use the term Penutian in its more restricted Californian sense.

[42] This and similar terms ("movement of people of such and such speech") do not by any means imply that all or even most of the present population speaking dialects of the stock have of necessity primarily descended from a relatively homogeneous group speaking the hypothetical prototype of the stock. A language may spread to neighbouring peoples without any great displacement of population. Linguistic displacement due to cultural contact is here included under "movement of tribes of related speech." In actual fact, to be sure, I believe it may be shown that far-reaching movements of population were quite frequent in aboriginal America. I doubt if linguistic displacement was as typical a process in America as in the old world, though it is by no means unknown (thus, the Tlingit-speaking Tagish were originally an Athabaskan tribe; the Nootka-speaking Ho·pat'cas'ath were originally a Salish tribe; the Tewa of Hano are adopting Hopi as their language).

[43] Gatschet's surmise of the genetic relationship of Costanoan and Miwok was the first step towards the recognition of the Penutian stock.

linguistic stocks, in itself indicates that the differentiation exhibited by the latter languages cuts deeper into the historic past than that found in the Algonkin languages. There can be no doubt, then, that the distribution of Penutian-speaking tribes antedates, as a whole, the scattering of Algonkin peoples from a comparatively restricted centre. If under the term "Algonkin" we include the remotely related Yurok and Wiyot of California, a comparison with the Californian Penutian group as to relative age of linguistic differentiation might well favour the former. However, too little is known of the details of either problem to enable us to answer such a question as yet.

Linguistic Differentiation of Earliest Man in America

One corollary of great historical interest follows from our argument as to the chronological significance of linguistic differentiation. If the apparently large number of linguistic stocks recognized in America[44] be assumed to be due merely to such extreme divergence on the soil of America as to make the proof of an original unity of speech impossible, then we must allow a tremendous lapse of time for the development of such divergences, a lapse of time undoubtedly several times as great as the period that the more conservative archæologists and palæontologists are willing to allow as necessary for the interpretation of the earliest remains of man in America.[45] We would then be driven to the alternative of assuming that the linguistic differentiation of aboriginal America developed only in small part (in its latest stages) in the new world, that the Asiatic (possibly also South Sea) immigrants who peopled the American continent were at the earliest period of occupation already differentiated into speakers of several genetically unrelated[46] stocks. This would make it practically imperative to assume that the peopling of America was not a single historical process but a series of movements of linguistically unrelated peoples, possibly from different directions and

[44] In spite of the reduction in American linguistic stocks which we have of late years been witnessing, there is no reasonable prospect, as far as I can see, of our ever getting beyond the assumption of a quite considerable number of isolated linguistic groups in North and South America.

[45] While it is absurd to juggle with specific figures, it may be interesting to note that at a recent scientific meeting a well known American palaeontologist, who is at the same time conversant with the problem of early man in America, expressed himself as believing ten thousand years an ample, indeed a maximum, period for the human occupation of this continent, as far as the geological evidence is concerned. This was only a somewhat reluctantly given personal opinion, but it very likely represents the general consensus of conservative opinion on the subject. Ten thousand years, however, seems a hopelessly inadequate span of time for the development from a homogeneous origin of such linguistic differentiation as is actually found in America.

[46] Or so remotely related at best that the fact of relationship could hardly be gathered from the descriptive evidence.

certainly at very different times. This view strikes me as intrinsically highly probable. As the latest linguistic arrivals in North America would probably have to be considered the Eskimo-Aleut[47] and the Na-dene (Haida, Tlingit, and Athabaskan).[48]

Differentiation of Linguistic Stocks into Distinct Languages

The criterion of linguistic differentiation has time value not only in relation to independent linguistic stocks but also, and indeed even more typically, in relation to the cognate languages of a single linguistic stock. The major divisions of a linguistic stock represent the oldest differentiations within it and the geographical distributions of each of these divisions as unit must be considered as of equal weight in an attempt to reconstruct the earliest ascertainable location and movements of the stock as a whole. In other words, the geographical centre of gravity, historically considered, of a linguistic stock is not determined directly on the basis of all the dialects of the stock but rather on the basis of its major divisions, regardless of whether they are greatly ramified into subdivisions or not.[49] The procedure in estimating the relative chronological significance of further linguistic ramifications is analogous to the above. To put it briefly, we must aim to weight the historical equivalence of languages at every step rather than to make historical inferences from their number.

To show how these considerations affect the reconstruction of earlier movements of linguistically related tribes we may briefly take up two or three actual problems. The geographical centre of distribution of the Algonkin tribes proper would seem to be the upper Great Lakes, but before we can attach an historical interpretation to this purely descriptive fact it is well to weight the linguistic evidence. As far as we can see at

[47] The Siberian Eskimo would, of course, still have to be considered as representing a regressive movement from America to Asia.

[48] From these considerations follows a highly important theoretical, if not at present practical, corollary. Should it ever be possible to prove a tangible genetic relationship between Asiatic and American languages, this would by no manner of means necessarily or even probably involve more than a small proportion of American languages. I do not consider it at all inconceivable that, *e.g.*, the Eskimo-Aleut and Na-dene languages may ultimately be shown to have respective Asiatic affinities but not American ones. I need hardly insist that these remarks have a merely theoretic validity.

[49] I am assuming here that it is possible to determine the linguistic divisions which are historically equivalent; further, that a distinction can be drawn between a historically fundamental divergence and a relatively secondary one, even though the latter is of greater descriptive magnitude (*e.g.*, English seems, on the whole, more distinct from German than does German from Danish, yet it can be shown very convincingly that the English-German divergence is historically secondary to the German-Danish, better West Germanic-Scandinavian, one). To justify these assumptions would lead us too far into the technique of comparative philology.

present, the Algonkin languages (aside from their more remote kinsmen, Yurok and Wiyot) fall into four equivalent groups—Blackfoot, Arapaho, Cheyenne, and Central-Eastern Algonkin,[50] the last including the greater number of Algonkin languages. In other words, the divergence between Arapaho and Blackfoot, despite the fact that their speakers are in both cases typical Plains tribes, reflects a linguistic (and tribal) differentiation of greater antiquity than that of two such distant tribes as the Naskapi and Shawnee. At best, therefore, the Great Lakes can be considered as the historical centre of distribution of only the Central-Eastern tribes; while the linguistic equivalence with this group of the Blackfoot, Arapaho, and Cheyenne, each of which lie to the west of the former, pushes the historical centre of distribution of the Algonkin tribes proper considerably to the west.[51] We can hardly avoid the inference that in the remoter past the general movement of Algonkin tribes was from west to east.[52]

A particularly neat instance of the ofttimes conclusive nature of linguistic evidence for the determination of the direction of a movement of population is that of the distribution of the Athabaskan languages. As is well known, these languages are spoken in three geographically isolated areas, a very large northern area (interior of Alaska to near Hudson bay), a Pacific area (southwestern Oregon and northwestern California), and a southern area (Arizona, New Mexico, and western Texas). As long as it is assumed, as is generally done on purely geographical grounds, that these three dialectic groups represent the equivalent major divisions of Athabaskan, there is no pressing reason of a linguistic nature for considering one rather than another as the historical centre of distribution. As a matter of fact, however, while the southern and Pacific dialectic groups are each of them clearly homogeneous and contrast with other groups of Athabaskan dialects,[53] I do not see that any evidence has been given to indicate that the northern dialects form a single group equiva-

[50] Since this was written, I have come to consider it highly probable that Cheyenne and Arapaho belong to a single group of Algonkin.

[51] This naturally has its significance in view of the presence of Yurok and Wiyot still farther west. It is hardly an accident that the greatest linguistic differentiation of Algonkin proper is found in the west, not in the Atlantic region.

[52] This in no way contradicts the fact that at a much later period there was clearly a westward drift of certain Algonkin tribes (Western Cree, Plains Ojibwa, Arapaho, Cheyenne). I am not inclined to believe that the western movement of the Cree is part of the same general movement of population that gave the Blackfoot their present home.

[53] Thus, Pacific Athabaskan as unit is characterized by *s* and *c* as reflexes of both original *s* and *z* and *c* and *j* respectively; in morphology we may note the frequent use of -*c* in "indefinite" tense forms of many verbs. Southern Athabaskan as unit is characterized by the development of original palatalized *k*-sounds to *ts*-sounds.

lent to these. Though these dialects have not yet been satisfactorily classified, it seems at least probable to me that they may ultimately be grouped into two or more major divisions, each equivalent in differential value to the southern group. Thus, I do not see that the divergence between, say, Carrier and Loucheux is less profound than that which obtains between, say, Chipewyan and Navaho. This being so, it would seem that the historical centre of gravity lies rather in the north than in either of the other two regions and that the occupation of these latter was due to a southward movement of Athabaskan-speaking tribes. It is important to observe that the argument is not in any way dependent on the fact that the northern tribes cover a much vaster territory than those of the other two groups or even directly on the fact that probably a larger number of distinct dialects are spoken in the north than elsewhere. The argument for the northern provenience of the Athabaskan tribes is clinched by a further linguistic fact, namely that the Athabaskan dialects form one of the three major divisions of the Na-dene stock, the other two being Haida and Tlingit. The fact that the latter are spoken in the northwest coast area so emphatically locates the historical centre of gravity of the stock in the north that it becomes completely impossible to think of the Athabaskan tribes as having spread north from California or the southwest.[54]

The value of the criterion of linguistic differentiation for a reconstruction of the relative ages of tribal movements, to a considerable extent also of the direction of such movements, has doubtless been made evident. If, as may sometimes happen, the linguistic evidence seems to run counter to other evidence or to a prevailing theory, it should not be lightly discarded as irrelevant to historical problems. While it may be forced to yield in the face of powerful testimony pointing to contrary conclusions, its claims always deserve serious consideration. Had the historical significance of linguistic differentiation been more generally appreciated, I doubt if the theory, for example, of the distribution of Eskimo tribes from the west coast of Hudson bay as a centre would have

[54] There is also specific linguistic evidence in both the Pacific and southern dialectic groups of Athabaskan tending to show that Athabaskan is intrusive in those areas. In another paper I have attempted to demonstrate that the Hokan languages (Shasta-Achomawi, Chimariko, Karok, Pomo, Yana, Esselen, Yuman, Seri, Chontal, probably also Chumash and Salinan) are related to the Coahuiltecan languages of the western Gulf coast (Coahuilteco, Comecrudo, Cotoname, Tonkawa, Karankawa, possibly also Atakapa); if this is correct, the Athabaskan tribes now separating Yuman from Karankawa and Tonkawa could hardly be other than intrusive. Similarly, in northern California, the territory lying between that of the Pomo and that of the linguistically related Shasta, Chimariko, and Karok is largely occupied by Athabaskan tribes. Finally, in Oregon, Coos and Lower Umpqua are cut off from the remotely related Takelma (the evidence for this I expect to produce in a future paper) by Athabaskan dialects.

received quite such ready acceptance. I do not wish expressly to oppose this theory, but merely to point out that it does not well agree with the linguistic evidence. The Eskimo linguistic stock is sharply divided into two dialectic groups, Eskimo proper and Aleut. Inasmuch as Aleut is confined to Alaska and as a considerable number of distinct Eskimo dialects are spoken in Alaska besides, it seems very probable to me that the earliest at present ascertainable centre of dispersion of the tribes of Eskimo stock lies in Alaska.

GEOGRAPHICAL DISTRIBUTION OF PHONETIC AND MORPHOLOGIC FEATURES

It is well known to students of language that striking phonetic and morphologic similarities are not infrequently found between neighbouring languages that, so far as can be ascertained, are in no way genetically related. Such resemblances, insofar as they are not merely fortuitous, must be due to the assimilatory influence exerted by one language over another. This may either mean that in the acquisition of an originally foreign language that gradually displaces the native one certain habits of speech (phonetic or structural peculiarities) are carried over by the speakers from the old into the new language[55] or that such peculiarities are, more or less unconsciously[56] and through the medium of bilingual individuals, created in one language on the model of analogous features in the other. Which of these factors is involved in any particular case it may often, or generally, be quite impossible to tell.

One of the most striking American examples of phonetic accord overriding fundamental linguistic independence is the occurrence in a considerable number of West Coast linguistic groups (Na-dene; Tsimshian; Kwakiutl-Nootka, Chemakum, Salish; Chinookan; Lower Umpqua, Coos) of velar consonants, voiceless laterals, and glottalized ("fortis") stops. These far-reaching resemblances in rather uncommon types of sounds are likely to be in part due to such assimilatory processes as we have mentioned. Examples of important morphological resemblances in unrelated, but geographically contiguous languages are the sex gender of Coast Salish and Chinookan; the occurrence of numeral classifiers and distributive (or plural) reduplication both in Tsimshian and in Kwakiutl-Nootka, Chemakum, and Salish;[57] the instrumental verb prefixes of

---

[55] Just as we, when a foreign language has been but imperfectly mastered, involuntarily substitute familiar for difficult and unfamiliar sounds and literally translate morphological and syntactic usages that are familiar to us into the new medium of communication.

[56] Sometimes no doubt also consciously. Fashions in speech, peculiar to one language, particularly if associated with ceremonial or literary values, may be directly imitated by the speakers of another.

[57] These three, as long ago pointed out by Boas, have several important morphological traits in common. They may well prove to be genetically related.

Maidu, Shoshonean, Washo, and Shasta-Achomawi;[58] and the local verb suffixes of Maidu, Washo, and of Shasta-Achomawi and Yana.[59] There seems no practical alternative in these and many other cases that might be mentioned to the hypothesis of morphological influence exerted by one language on another. The point of historical interest in such assimilatory phenomena is that they necessarily presuppose a very long period of tribal contact. They may, therefore, be employed as indications of the relative age of a tribal contact or even of the former existence of a contact now disrupted. While I do not think that too free a use should be made of this criterion for historical purposes, difficult as it generally is to isolate and apply, there is no doubt that in special cases it can yield interesting results.

An inference or two from some of the morphological facts listed above will be helpful towards the understanding of the method of application. Tsimshian, as far as we know, is genetically unrelated to either the Na-dene languages to the north or the group comprising Kwakiutl-Nootka, Salish, and Chemakum to the south. Culturally the Tsimshian Indians are more closely affiliated with the Na-dene tribes of the Pacific coast (Haida and Tlingit) than with even the northernmost of the latter tribes (Kitamat, Bella Bella; Bella Coola). Nevertheless, the morphologic resemblances noted above between Tsimshian and the languages south of it, when contrasted with the lack of correspondingly significant resemblances between Tsimshian and Na-dene, seems to be indicative of a much earlier contact of the Tsimshian with the Kwakiutl and Salish than with the Haida and Tlingit. Such contact need, of course, not have been in precisely the same territory as now occupied by the tribes nor need their geographical relation have been quite the same. Should our inference prove correct, it would probably mean that the great bulk of the cultural development exclusively peculiar to the Haida, Tlingit, and Tsimshian is of much more recent date than the earliest contact between the Tsimshian and the Kwakiutl and Salish.

A comparison of Maidu and Wintun seems to lead to a similar line of argument. Both of these languages are in contact with northern Hokan languages, Maidu with Shasta-Achomawi and Yana, Wintun with Yana, Shasta-Achomawi, Chimariko, and Pomo. Moreover, the Wintun ter-

---

[58] In this respect Maidu differs from the other Penutian languages (Yokuts, Miwok-Costanoan, Wintun, also Coos and Lower Umpqua; Takelma also, but quite independently of Maidu though perhaps again under Shasta-Achomawi influence, has developed a set of instrumental verb prefixes of a rather different type). On the other hand, instrumental verb prefixes seem characteristic of certain Hokan languages (Shasta-Achomawi, Chimariko, Pomo).

[59] Here again Maidu differs from all the other Penutian languages (including Takelma, Coos, and Lower Umpqua). Once again the peculiarity is characteristic of several Hokan languages (Yana, Shasta-Achomawi, Chimariko, Karok).

ritory extends considerably to the north of that of the Maidu. If anything, therefore, one would have expected Wintun to show more of a Hokan influence than, or at least as profound a Hokan influence as Maidu, instead of which we find that two of the most striking morphological features of Hokan, instrumental prefixes and local suffixes in verbs, are shared by Maidu but not by Wintun.[60] It hardly seems too rash to infer from this that the Maidu have been in longer contact with Hokan-speaking tribes than the Wintun. This can only mean that at an earlier date the Maidu were the northernmost of the Californian Penutian tribes and that the Wintun have only later gradually spread north from the lower Sacramento valley, where they were probably only in contact with other Penutian tribes and with the southern Yuki. Before this northward movement of the Wintun we may suppose the Pomo to have been in contact with their remote linguistic kinsmen, the Yana and Shasta-Achomawi.

CONCLUDING REMARKS ON METHOD

We have now completed our survey of the methods available for a reconstruction of time perspectives in aboriginal American culture-history. Anything like real completeness is, of course, entirely out of the question here, my chief aim having been rather to suggest some of the more important avenues of approach than to write a systematic methodology or to treat in exhaustive detail of the practical application of our methods to the more important problems of American ethnology.

A possible impression that may have been left in the mind of the reader is that I attach a exaggerated importance to the historical value of purely inferential evidence as contrasted with the more obvious direct evidence derived from a study of datable documents and from stratigraphic archæology. Such an impression is certainly not intended. I would not dispute for an instant the general superiority of direct to inferential evidence in the establishment of culture sequences, but have made it more particularly my aim to show in what way, in the absence or dearth of direct evidence, the inferential data may be made to yield historical perspectives. The methods to be pursued in the handling of historical documents are relatively obvious; moreover they may be found discussed in more than one manual of historical method. As for the historical methodology of archæological research, while I consider the

---

[60] It should be remembered that both Wintun and Maidu are Penutian languages and are, therefore, related. The linguistic psychology of the two languages seems, indeed, to be very much the same, so that, other things being equal, Wintun might be supposed to be as readily susceptible to Hokan influence as Maidu.

method of stratigraphy, where available, as probably the most fruitful of all, I have felt that it would be presumptuous for one as inexperienced in archæological technique as myself to do more than barely indicate the nature of this method. I earnestly hope that the present paper may stimulate some one better qualified than myself to prepare a systematic statement of the principles of such a methodology, with special reference to the reconstruction of time sequences in American culture.

In connexion with the treatment of inferential evidence, I feel myself open to a second criticism, that of a disproportionate insistence on purely linguistic criteria coupled with an undervaluation of the data of physical anthropology. This criticism also would be directed rather at the form than at the spirit of my contentions. I freely grant that incomparably the most significant of all inferential evidence bearing on the time perspective of culture is yielded by ethnological data. That I have treated the linguistic criteria at somewhat disproportionate length is due to two reasons, the one personal, the other pedagogical. My own interest in and relative familiarity with facts of a linguistic order have doubtless betrayed me into a tendency to make rather more of them than strict justice might allow. On the other hand, the actual historical value of linguistic criteria is so real and this value so little appreciated among Americanists generally, that it seemed pedagogically advisable, if not theoretically warranted, to somewhat overdo the emphasis on them. As for the claims of physical anthropology to more detailed consideration, I must here, too, confess that I feel too keenly my limitations in this regard to do more than briefly indicate a few possibilities. The incidental light thrown on culture history or on former movements of population by the data of physical anthropology is certainly worthy of a careful methodological treatment.

In answer to a third possible criticism, I must emphatically point out that I do not consider any single one of the inferential criteria that I have set up as necessarily valid in a specific case. An argument, *e.g.*, based on the associations formed by a culture element or on its geographical diffusion or on its linguistic representation may be entirely convincing in the handling of one problem, yet appear far-fetched or even totally inapplicable in the handling of another. Everything depends upon the specific conditions of a given problem. And, needless to say, any one criterion is never to be applied to the exclusion of or in opposition to all others. It is a comfortable procedure to attach oneself unreservedly or primarily to a single mode of historical inference and wilfully to neglect all others as of little moment, but the clean-cut constructions of the doctrinaire never coincide with the actualities of history.

If any general point should have come out more clearly than another in the course of our discussion, it is the danger of tearing a culture element loose from its psychological and geographical (*i.e.*, distributional) setting. No feeling of historical perspective can be gained for any culture element without careful reference to these settings. Another way of bringing out this point is to emphasize the necessity of historically evaluating or weighting a culture element or linguistic datum before it is employed for comparative purposes. The failure adequately to weight ethnological and linguistic data, but to rely largely on the counting of noses, is to an equal extent responsible for the historical vagaries of a Frazerian evolutionist and for those of his counterpart, the Graebnerian diffusionist.

SONG RECITATIVE IN PAIUTE MYTHOLOGY[*][1]

THE PROMINENT place occupied by song in the mental culture of the American Indians is well recognized by ethnologists, in spite of the relatively small bulk of aboriginal musical material that has heretofore been published. Generally Indian music is of greatest significance when combined with the dance in ritualistic or ceremonial performances. Nevertheless the importance of music in non-ceremonial acts—for instance, in the hand-game played by practically all tribes west of the Rockies—should not be minimized. It is the purpose of this paper to call attention to the part that song plays in one of these non-ceremonial cases, as illustrated by the southern Paiutes of southwestern Utah.[2] Not infrequently in America, particularly where song enters in, mythology is closely linked with ritual; but as Paiute myths have, as far as could be learned, no ritualistic aspect whatever, the term "non-ceremonial" as applied to them seems justified.

There is one type of myth-song that is evidently very common in America. This is the short song found inserted here and there in the body of a myth, generally intended to express some emotion or striking thought of a character. It is generally of very limited melodic range and very definite rhythmic structure. Sometimes it is quite different in character from the regular types of song in vogue, not infrequently being considered specifically appropriate to the character involved; while at other times it approximates in form such well-recognized types as the round-dance song or medicine song, according to the exigencies of the narrative. The text to such a song is very often obscure. Even where it does not consist either entirely or in part of mere burdens, the words are apt to be unusual in grammatical form, archaic, borrowed

* *Journal of American Folk-Lore*, 23 (1910): 455–472.

[1] Published with consent of the Museum of the University of Pennsylvania.

[2] Reference is here had to the Kaibab Paiutes of the neighborhood of Kanab, in southwestern Utah, and Moccasin Springs, in northwestern Arizona. They hunt deer on the well-timbered Kaibab Plateau south as far as the Colorado River. They now number about eighty or ninety individuals. Linguistically Kaibab Paiute belongs to the Ute-Chemehuevi group of Plateau Shoshonean, differing only dialectically from Ute, than which, it would seem, it is more archaic. The Paiute material made use of in this paper was obtained in four months' work for the University Museum of the University of Pennsylvania (February–June, 1910) with Tony Tillohash, a young man of the Kaibab Paiutes, then finishing a course of study at Carlisle. Despite his five years' absence from home, Tony's musical memory was quite remarkable. Besides the myth-songs spoken of here, over two hundred other songs of various kinds (three or four varieties of "cry" or mourning songs, bear-dance songs, round-dance songs, ghost-dance songs, medicine songs, gambling songs, scalp songs, and others less easy to classify) were obtained from him.

from a neighboring dialect, difficult to translate, or otherwise out of the ordinary. Ordinarily collectors of Indian myths have refrained from taking down music and words of such songs,[3] though there is small doubt in the mind of the writer that they occur in regions widely apart. From the point of view of style in native mythology, an aspect of the subject not generally given the attention it deserves, it would be highly desirable to record carefully all such myth-songs. A few such songs have been recorded by the writer in Uintah Ute and Kaibab Paiute myth-texts. As it is intended to publish them in their proper setting, it is not necessary to anticipate in this place. They do not differ in general character from songs of the type already published.

There is evidence of the existence of a second type of myth-song in America,—the song which itself narrates a myth. The most elaborate examples known of such myth-songs are the Homeric poems, which, as is well known, were sung by rhapsodists to the accompaniment of a stringed instrument. Dr. Kroeber refers to dream myths of the Mohave, that are sung by the person who has dreamt the myth. As he has as yet published no example of these songs, it is impossible at present to say whether the myths are sung entire or only in part, and whether the words are set by the dreamer once for all to a definitely recurring melody or set of melodies, or, as seems more probable, may vary in actual form so long as they fit the rhythm of the song and tell the story. It is not clear whether the Mohave myth-songs referred to are of the same general type as the Diegueño songs of which specimens have been recently published in text without music by Mr. Waterman.[4] These are set songs of no great length, that, in a more or less definitely determined series, relate, or perhaps more accurately refer, to a myth. It seems that also the Navaho and Pueblo Indians have such series of songs of mythical reference. In any case, however, such songs do not adequately reflect the mythology of the tribe, but seem rather to form an ancillary body of artistic material of ritual use, based on the mythology proper. As far as can be gathered, it seems more probable that the long Mohave myth-songs that Dr. Kroeber speaks of are in a class apart from these. Perhaps they resemble the Paiute recitatives to be spoken of presently.

So far as known, the Paiute do not have set songs referring to mythical incidents, though it does not seem unlikely that the texts of at least

[3] Published examples of this type of song are to be found in Boas, *Tsimshian Texts*, pp. 11, 63; Boas, *Kathlamet Texts*, pp. 24, 154; Boas, *Chinook Texts*, pp. 116, 117, 118, 144, 146, 150, 151, 192, 235; Sapir, *Wishram Texts*, pp. 58, 68, 90, 94, 96, 134, 142, 150; Sapir, *Takelma Texts*, pp. 14, 15, 46, 62, 102, 104, 106, 164.
[4] T. T. Waterman, *The Religious Practices of the Diegueño Indians*, Univ. Calif. Publ. Am. Arch. and Ethn., 8 (1910): 271–358.

some of the mourning and bear-dance songs did originally have such reference. On the other hand, what may be called "song recitative" is well developed in the mythology of this tribe. The narrative portions of a myth are always recited in a speaking voice. The conversational passages, however, are either spoken or sung, according to the mythical character who is supposed to be speaking. Some characters, such as Porcupine, Chipmunk, Skunk, and Badger, are represented as talking rather than singing; at any rate, the writer's informant did not know of any style of singing connected with them. Other characters, and among them are Wolf, Mountain-Bluejay, Gray-Hawk, Sparrow-Hawk, Eagle, Lizard, Rattlesnake, Red-Ant, Badger-Chief, and a mythical personage known as Iron-Clothes (literally, Stone-Clothes), regularly sing in speaking. Coyote regularly speaks, though, as often in other mythologies, character is sometimes given his words by a style of delivery meant to convey conceit, scorn, astonishment, or other state of mind appropriate to him. Once, however, on the death of his brother Wolf, he breaks out into an excitedly melancholy recitative. A Paiute song recitative is not peculiar to any particular myth, but always to a particular character, there being as many distinct styles of recitative as there are singing characters. Both Wolf and Gray-Hawk have been found in more than one myth, yet their recitative style remains the same in any myth that they are actors of. On the other hand, in one myth, that of Iron-Clothes, three styles of recitative are found exemplified, belonging to Rattlesnake, Red-Ant, and Iron-Clothes respectively. It is, then, theoretically possible, aside from rhythmic difficulties, to sing any given text to the tune of any recitative; and when so sung, the character in whose mouth the words are put is determined, as no two characters sing exactly alike.

The recitative consists of a melody of determined rhythm, there being a definite number of beats to the period, that recurs indefinitely. In some cases the recurring period is linked to the preceding period without a pause; in others there is a slight pause between the periods, which are thus given more evident unity of form. Owing to the varying words that go with the recurrent periods, and the consequent variations in number of syllables for each period, there must necessarily be slight changes in details of melody in passing from one period to another. Thus a quarter-note may, on its recurrence, be broken up into two eighths; two eighths may be resolved into a triplet of eighths; a triplet of eighths may be combined into a triplet consisting of a quarter and an eighth; and so on indefinitely, the fundamental rhythm and melody, however, always remaining the same. A few flaws of rhythm have been found here and there; but, on the whole, the rhythmical march of these recitatives is good, as indicated by the fact that for very considerable stretches the phonograph records have been found to go well with the beats of the metronome. The words that go with the recitatives are not fixed, except in one or two cases to be noted below, but are composed on the spur of the moment. Obviously the singer, in other words the narrator of the myth, has to be careful to choose words of appropriate syllabic structure, though he is helped out to a large extent by the freedom with which he can lengthen or break vowels and add padders. . . .

The existence of myth recitative in Paiute is interesting in connection with style and characterization in Indian mythology generally. It seems to be generally assumed that the only element of interest or importance in American mythology is the incident or complex of incidents, and myth comparison has been almost entirely confined to a comparison of such incidents. It seems, further, to be often thought that character plays little or no part except in so far as the identification of a mythological being with a given animal necessitates certain peculiarities of action. Had most or all of the many American myths now already published been collected as fully dictated texts, there is small doubt that Indian mythologies would be more clearly seen to have their peculiarities of style and character as well as incident. A myth obtained only in English may sometimes be more complete as a narrative than the same myth obtained in text, but will nearly always have much of the baldness and lack of color of a mere abstract. As a matter of fact, there is a very considerable tendency in American mythology to make characters interesting as such. One of the most common stylistic devices employed for the purpose is to set off the speech of the character by some peculiarity. Thus in Takelma we find that Coyote almost regularly begins his sentences or words with a meaningless *s-* or *c-*,[5] while Grizzly-Bear uses in parallel fashion an *l*, a sound not otherwise made use of in Takelma.[6] Similarly, in Ute mythology a meaningless *-áik·ᵛā* is sometimes added to words spoken by Coyote. When collecting material from the Wishram Indians of Yakima Reservation, the author heard of myths in which Bluejay, generally a humorous character, begins words with a meaningless *ts!-*. These myths were said to be characteristic rather of the down-river tribes, such as the Clackamas, than of the Wishram and Wasco themselves. Were pertinent material available to any considerable extent, it would probably be found that this simple quasi-humorous stylistic device could be illustrated by hundreds of examples from large regions

[5] Sapir, *Takelma Texts*, p. 56, note 2; p. 66, note 1; p. 87, notes 4 and 6.
[6] *Ibid.*, p. 118, note 2; p. 120, note 3.

in America.[7] Given such a general tendency to give color to the speech of a mythological character, we have a contributing factor towards the development of myth recitative.

It seems quite possible that the Paiute have borrowed the idea of myth recitative rather than developed it themselves. The closely related Utes seem to possess no such device. On the other hand, the Mohave to the west have been said, as we have seen, to possess long song-myths, though ignorance of the exact character of these makes it impossible at present to decide on their relation to the Paiute recitatives. It would not be surprising if it turned out, indeed, that these have been suggested by something similar among the Mohave, in which case the Muddy River Paiutes of southern Nevada will have served as intermediaries. In this connection we must not fail to note that practically all of the more than one hundred and twenty-five Paiute mourning-songs obtained are not in Paiute text, but in an unintelligible language said to be Mohave,—at any rate, some un-Shoshonean form of speech spoken to the west along the Colorado. There is thus reason for believing that the Mohave or other Yuman tribes have exerted a considerable influence on the musical stock in trade of the Paiute.

[7] Since this was written, the author has come across a rather interesting example of such phonetic play in the mythology of the Nootka of Alberni Canal. In the speech of Deer, every *s* or *c* becomes *ł*, *ts* or *tc* becomes ʟ, and *ts!* or *tc!* becomes ʟ!.

THE SOCIAL ORGANIZATION OF THE WEST COAST TRIBES*

As is well known, the aborigines of America had developed at the time of the discovery a number of more or less distinct types of social and political organization, ranging from the loosely organized hunting or root-gathering band, with little or no internal complexity and with no definite formal affiliations with other groups, to the complex state found, for instance, in Mexico or Peru, in which a large number of relatively small tribal units were united into a larger body politic, comparable in some measure to the states that we are familiar with in our own history. It is obvious that to a large extent the type of social organization developed by a particular group of people must be due to the economic status attained by it. A roving habit of life will not encourage the formation of social and political solidarity. Conversely, the conditions for social development are more favourable in a community occupying a relatively small territory, to certain parts of which it is bound for at least considerable periods. Typical of the most primitive type of social organization in America are the Eskimo. Among them the unfavourable climatic conditions and the consequent difficulty of maintaining life cause them to form small village groups which change their habitat according to the exigencies of the season, and every individual in which is obliged to procure means of subsistence for himself and his nearest kin. A sea-mammal hunting people like the Eskimo, that cannot find a continuous livelihood in a single spot, cannot be expected to evolve a complex social life, and we are therefore not surprised to find the individual as such more strongly emphasized among them than among most other people. Somewhat analogous, though vastly different in actual detail, is the condition of the roving bands of the Great Basin area of Utah, Nevada, and adjoining states. Here it is the semi-arid character of the soil that makes it impossible for a primitive community to develop a settled mode of life. The necessity of frequently changing camp in order to follow the game or visit the favourite root-gathering spots according to season, again militates against the formation of large and complexly organized social units.

The economic basis of a people is of course not in every case simply determined by the character of the country inhabited, for, with the increase of culture, means are evolved whereby the difficulties of an unfavourable environment are largely conquered. We need only point out

* *Transactions, Royal Society of Canada*, 2d series, 9 (1915): 355–374.

[468]

that the limitations enforced by the semi-arid country referred to on the present inhabitants of the region are vastly different from those enforced on the Shoshonean tribes who preceded them. There are, indeed, numerous analogous cases among the Indians themselves. Thus, the Pueblo tribes of New Mexico and Arizona, while occupying the same general region as their neighbours the Navaho, differ vastly in social organization from these. While the Navaho are a nomadic sheep-raising people forced by their manner of life to cover a vast territory and to split up into a large number of small groups, which form into larger bodies only at the ritual performances that bring the people together from time to time, the Pueblos are enabled by their intensive system of agriculture to form into perfectly coherent well-knit communities that are housed in permanent villages comparable in many ways to our own towns. Here the conditions are evidently favourable for the development of authority vested in certain individuals and of a number of complex social inter-relations. Similarly, it seems not improbable that the more intensive pursuit of agriculture by the Iroquoian tribes than by their Algonkian neighbours, among whom hunting occupied a relatively more important place economically, was fundamentally responsible for the greater social and political elaboration characteristic of the former.

I do not, of course, mean to urge that a type of social organization is directly dependent on economic factors to the exclusion of everything else. As a matter of fact, it is perfectly clear that many historic causes may bring about social developments in no way connected with the economic status of the community. For one thing, no group of people is ever entirely isolated and free to develop entirely from within and as influenced by purely environmental causes. The influence exerted by neighbouring peoples must always be borne in mind, and frequently enough in America we find that much in the social constitution of certain tribes remains unintelligible until we take into consideration the stimulus of contact with neighbouring tribes. Thus, there is no doubt that the so-called Wabanaki Confederacy of certain Eastern Algonkian tribes was brought into being largely by the suggestive influence of the powerful Iroquois Confederacy that harassed these tribes. Similarly, there is no doubt that the relatively greater degree of social complexity obtaining among certain Athabaskan hunting tribes of British Columbia, such as the Carrier and Chilcotin, when contrasted with their more simply organized kinsmen to the north and east, was more or less directly due to imitation of social features found among the Coast tribes that neighboured them to the west.

This note of warning is here sounded because it is too often assumed by facile system-makers that the social organization of a people can be more or less directly inferred from its economic conditions. With all reservations, however, I believe it is fairly clear that the peculiar environment of the West Coast tribes of British Columbia had much to do with the development of their rather complex social life. Not so much that these conditions explain in every case the actual forms of organization that we find to prevail among these tribes, as that they seem to furnish a general stimulus for the growth of relatively settled communities with intricate social ramifications. In the first place, the Indians of the West Coast had abundant means for subsistence at their disposal. The streams teemed with various kinds of salmon throughout the year, and the sea offered a great variety of edible sea-mammals and invertebrates. It was thus possible for a rather large group of people to make a comfortable living in a quite restricted bit of coast territory. Access to the sea at a few points and the control of a few streams up which the community could follow the salmon at their spawning periods were all that was needed to insure ample means of subsistence for all. Furthermore, the unusually great rainfall of the coast country made it necessary for the Indians to house themselves in substantial shelters, and at the same time gave them the ready means wherewith to fill this want. I refer to the heavily wooded character of the coast. The inexhaustible supply of readily worked wood, particularly the red cedar, gave the Indians all that was necessary for the building of large houses. In a word, the West Coast Indians were fishermen and sea-mammal hunters who, unlike the Eskimo, were able to thrive within relatively restricted territories, and who dwelt for the greater part of the year in permanent villages consisting of a long row of large wooden houses strung along the beach. Most of these houses were large enough to provide not merely for a family in the narrower sense of the word, but for a large house group forming a family in a larger sense and dominated by one man who, on grounds of descent, took precedence of all others in the house group. The village community with its definite number of house groups may, then, be expected to be the most fundamental social unit in this area and, indeed, in spite of all complications that have been brought about among some of the tribes, the legends of the Indians themselves and the study of the facts involved seem, in practically every case, to argue back to the village community as the primary social unit.

The social groupings that prevail among the West Coast Indians may be classified under four heads: groupings according to rank, groupings based on kinship, local groupings, and ceremonial or ritualistic groupings. The last of these may hardly be considered as coming within the scope of social organization; but among certain of the West Coast tribes, more particularly the Kwakiutl, they have become so intimately connected with the social structure that it is difficult to exclude entirely a reference to ceremonial groups. These four types of social units naturally intercross in a great many different ways, so much so that it becomes no easy matter to present a thoroughly intelligible picture of the social structure of a typical West Coast tribe.

Before examining each of these types of organization somewhat more closely, it will be well to acquaint ourselves briefly with the distribution of the tribes we are considering. The northernmost of the tribes generally included under the term of West Coast Indians, are the Tlingit, who occupy the long strip of coast forming the panhandle of southern Alaska. They are subdivided into a large number of distinct tribes, among the better known of which are the Yakutat, Chilcat, and Sitka Indians. These speak a number of mutually intelligible dialects forming a linguistic unit that is only very remotely related to certain other American languages. The Haida Indians occupy the Queen Charlotte Islands and part of the Prince of Wales archipelago north of these. These Indians formerly inhabited a large number of villages distributed along the coasts of the Islands; but are now almost entirely reduced to the two villages of Skidgate and Massett in the Queen Charlottes, and a number of villages in the Prince of Wales archipelago, occupied by the Kaigani. South of the Tlingit, on the mainland, are the Tsimshian, who inhabit the region of Nass and Skeena rivers. They are divided into three closely connected dialectic groups which form one of the isolated linguistic stocks of America, at least so far as is at present known. The Haida and Tlingit languages, on the other hand, can be shown to be distantly related. South of the Tsimshian are the Bella Coola, in many respects a peculiar tribe, that form an isolated offshoot of the great Salish family which has representatives as far south as Columbia river. The northwestern, northern, and northeastern shores of Vancouver Island and the mainland opposite are occupied by a large number of tribes that are closely connected linguistically and may be embraced under the general term of Kwakiutl, which term, however, applies strictly speaking only to the Indians of Fòrt Rupert in northern Vancouver Island. The more northern of the Kwakiutl tribes, such as the Bella Bella and Kitamat, offer a contrast in social organization to their southern neighbours, being more closely allied in several important respects to the linguistically unrelated Tsimshian. The western coast of Vancouver Island is inhabited by a number of tribes grouped together under the term Nootka. The Nootka language is genetically related to

Kwakiutl, though only fairly distantly so. Finally, in the southeastern part of Vancouver Island and on the mainland opposite, there are a considerable number of linguistically quite divergent but related tribes making up the bulk of the Coast Salish, as far as they are represented in Canada. From our present point of view the Tlingit, Haida, Tsimshian, Bella Coola, and northern Kwakiutl, are to be grouped together in contrast to the southern Kwakiutl, Nootka, and Coast Salish. The former of these may be considered as the more typical in regard to social organization. It is interesting to observe that the broad line of division runs through a linguistic group, an example of the failure of linguistic and cultural classifications to coincide such as we have numerous parallels of in America, and indeed all over the world.

All these tribes are characterized by a clear development of the idea of rank; indeed, it may be said that nowhere north of Mexico is the distinction between those of high and those of low birth so sharply drawn as in the West Coast tribes. Three classes of society may be recognized —the nobility, the commoners, and the slaves. It is not practicable to distinguish between chiefs and nobles, as has been done for instance by Hill-Tout for the Coast Salish, as the lesser chiefs or nobles grade right in continuously with the head chiefs. Intermarriages between nobles and commoners or slaves, and between commoners and slaves, were in theory quite impossible, and in earlier days could at best have been but rare. We learn here and there from their legends that individuals of low rank were sometimes raised to a higher rank by marriage into a chief's family; but the very point made in such case serves to emphasize the essential differences of rank. High rank is determined primarily by descent—whether in the male or female line depends on the tribe. A very important factor, furthermore, in determining rank is wealth, as illustrated more particularly by the distribution of great quantities of property at ceremonial feasts generally known as potlatches. It is not enough for one of high birth to rest in his hereditary glory. If he wishes to preserve the respect of his fellow tribesmen, he must at frequent intervals reassert his rank by displays of wealth, otherwise he incurs the risk of gradually losing the place that properly belongs to him on the score of inheritance. We read, indeed, of cases in which men of lower rank have by dint of reckless potlatching gained the ascendency over their betters, gradually displacing them in one or more of the privileges belonging to their rank. Among the West Coast Indians, as in Europe, there is, then, opportunity for the unsettling activities of the parvenu.

A necessary consequence of the division of the village community into a number of large house-groups is that, associated with each chief, there is, besides the immediate members of his own family, a group of commoners and slaves, who form his retainers. The slaves are immediately subject to his authority and may be disposed of in any manner that he sees fit. The commoners also, however, while possessing a much greater measure of independence, cannot be considered as unattached. Everything clustered about a number of house-groups headed by titled individuals, and in West Coast society, as in that of mediaeval feudalism, there was no place for the social free-lance. If the number of commoners and slaves connected with a chief's family grew too large for adequate housing under a single roof, one or more supplementary houses could be added on to the first; but they always remained under its sphere of influence. In this way we can understand how even a group of houses forming an outlying village might be inhabited entirely by people of low birth, who were directly subject to one or more chiefs occupying houses in the mother village. From this point of view the whole tribe divides into as many social groups as there are independent chiefs.

The rank of chief or noble is connected in most cases with a certain degree of personal power, but real communal authority is naturally vested in only the highest chief or chiefs of the village, and then not always as absolutely as we might be inclined to imagine. Even the highest chief is primarily always associated with a particular family and house, and if he exercises general authority, it is not so much because of his individual rank as such, as because the house group that he represents is, for one reason or another, the highest in rank in the community. In legendary terms this might be expressed by saying that the other groups branched off from or attached themselves to that of the head chief.

Fully as characteristic of high rank as the exercise of authority is the use of a large variety of privileges. The subject of privileges among the West Coast Indians is an exceedingly complex one and cannot be adequately disposed of here. Privileges include not only practical rights of economic value, such as the exclusive or main right to a particular fishing ground or the right to receive a certain part of a whale which has drifted on to the tribal shore; but also, and indeed more characteristically, many purely ceremonial or other non-material rights. It is these which form the most important outward expression of high rank, and their unlawful use by those not entitled to them was certain in every case to bring about violent friction and not infrequently actual bloodshed. One of the most important of these privileges is the right to use certain carvings or paintings, nearly always connected with the legendary history of the family which the chief represents. We shall have somewhat more to say of these crests later; here I wish to point out that from our present point of view the crests are but one of the many privileges that are associated with high rank. A further indication of such rank is the right to use certain names. The right to the use of any name is, properly speaking, determined by descent, and the names which have come to be looked upon as higher in rank than others naturally descend only to those that are of high birth. These names comprise not only such as are applied to individuals and of which a large number, some of higher, others of lower rank, are at the disposal of the nobleman; but also names that he has the exclusive right to apply to his slaves, to his house, very often to particular features of his house, such as carved posts and beams, and in some cases even names applied to movable objects such as canoes or particularly prized harpoon-heads or other implements. Further indicative of rank is the right to perform particular dances both in secular feasts or potlatches and, though perhaps to a somewhat less extent, also at ritualistic performances.

Perhaps the clearest outward manifestation of rank is in the place given a chief whenever it is necessary to arrange in some order the various participants in a public function. Thus, in a public feast or potlatch, those of high rank are seated in certain parts of the house that are preserved exclusively for the nobility. These are the rear of the house and the halves of the sides which are nearest the rear. These seats are graded as to rank, and it is perhaps not too much to surmise that the obvious grading made visible to the eye by a definite manner of seating at feasts was in a large measure responsible for the extension of the idea of grading of ranks and privileges generally. The exact seat of honor differed somewhat with the different tribes. In some it was the centre of the rear; in others that seat on the right side of the house, as one faces the door, which was nearest the corner. Other arrangements into series which could give a concrete idea of the ranking enjoyed by an individual are the order in which gifts are distributed to the chiefs at a potlatch; furthermore, the order in which they are called out when invited by a representative of another tribe to attend a feast which is to be given some time in the near future by the latter. The ranking orders thus arrived at by seating, distribution of gifts, invitations to feasts, and in various other ways that it is not necessary to enter upon here, might be expected to coincide. To a certain extent they do tend to approximate, and the highest in rank in a community will nearly always be found to head any such list that might be constructed. In practice, however, one finds that the various orders do not necessarily strictly correspond, in other words, that a person might individually be of lesser rank than another from the point of view of seating, but would have a prior claim to be invited, say. This curious state of affairs shows clearly enough that at last analysis rank is not a permanent status which is expressed in a number of absolutely fixed ways, but is rather the resultant standing attained by the inheritance of a considerable number of theoretically independent privileges which do, indeed, tend in most cases to be associated in certain ways, but may nevertheless be independently transmitted from generation to generation.

Nowhere in America is the idea of the grading of individuals carried to such an extent as among the West Coast Indians. It applies, however, only to the nobility, the commoners and the slaves not being differentiated among themselves with regard to rank. It has already been indicated how the ceremonial seating, for instance, of the nobility is expressive of their higher or lower status relatively to each other. In those tribes, like the Haida and Tlingit, that are subdivided into phratries and clans, a matter that we shall take up presently, this grading of chiefs represents something of a political or administrative basis, inasmuch as subsidiary to the town chief we have a number of clan heads. Subordinate to these, in turn, are the heads of the various house groups. Here again, however, it is important to notice that the town chief is always at the same time the chief of the particular clan that is dominant in that village and that the clan chief is at the same time the head of the particular house group that forms the nucleus of, or is the highest in rank in, the clan. In other words, ranking is not so much of a political or administrative character as it is determined by the handing down of status and privilege from holder to heir. It follows that the political organization, such as it is, impresses one as superimposed on the house group or family organization by inner growth of the latter. So strong a hold has the idea of ranking taken upon the Indians that we find it operative even in cases where it would naturally not be expected to find application. Thus, it is often customary for a number of invited tribes as such, as represented of course by certain chiefs, to be assigned definite ceremonial seats and thereby by implication to be ranked relatively to each other—at times a somewhat risky proceeding. Furthermore, in some tribes it is even customary for medicine men to be organized on the basis of rank, such ranking not necessarily depending entirely on the individual supernatural powers displayed by the medicine men as on the fact that they are entitled by inheritance of medical lore to such and such honours.

As already indicated, the subject of privileges is a vast one, and a complete enumeration of all the economic, ceremonial, and other privileges of one high in rank would take a long time. To a certain extent a man has the right to split his inheritance, in other words, to hand down to one of his sons or nephews, as the case might be, certain privileges, to another certain others. Very often such a division is reducible to the association of privileges with definite localities, a point which is of primary importance in connection with the village community as the fundamental unit in West Coast organization. Thus, if one by the accidents of descent has inherited according to one line of descent a number of privileges associated with village A, in which he is no longer resident, and a number of other privileges according to another line of descent originally associated with village B, in which he is resident, it would be a quite typical proceeding for him to bring up one of his heirs, say the one naturally highest in rank, to assume control of one set of privileges, a younger heir of the other. If the privileges originally connected with village B, let us say, tend to give one a higher place in the tribe than those connected with village A, the chances are that the first heir will be induced to take up his permanent residence in that village, while the transmitter may take the younger heir down to the more distant village and take up residence for a period in order to introduce his heir, as it were, to the privileges designed for him. In other words, there is a more or less definite tendency to connect honours with definite villages and, indeed, no matter how much rights of various sorts may become scattered by the division of inheritances, by the changes of residence due to intermarriage, and by other factors which tend to complicate their proper assignment, a West Coast Indian never forgets, at least in theory, where a particular privilege originated or with what tribe or clan a particular right, be it name, dance, carving, song, or what not, was in the first instance associated. In short, privileges are bound to the soil.

This brings us to what I believe to be one of the most fundamental ideas in the social structure of these Indians, that is, the idea of a definite patrimony of standing and associated rights which, if possible, should be kept intact or nearly so. Despite the emphasis placed on rank, I think it is clear that the individual as such is of very much less importance than the tradition that for the time being he happens to represent. The very fact that a man often bears the name of a remote ancestor, real or legendary, implies that the honours that he makes use of belong not so much to him individually as to his glorious ancestry, and there is no doubt that the shame of falling behind, in splendour and liberality, the standard set by a predecessor, does much to spur him on to ever greater efforts to increase his prestige and gain for himself new privileges. There is one interesting fact which clearly shows the importance of the family patrimony or of the standing of a particular line of descent as such, as distinct from the individual who happens to be its most honoured representative. This is the merging of various persons belonging to three or four generations into a single unit that need not be further differentiated. Among the Nootka Indians, for instance, an old man, his oldest son say, the oldest son of the son, and, finally, the infant child of the latter, say a daughter, form, to all intents and purposes, a single sociological personality. Titularly the highest rank is accorded, among the Nootka, to the little child, for it is always the last generation that in theory bears the highest honours. In practice, of course, the oldest members of the group get the real credit and do the business, as it were, of the inherited patrimony; but it would be difficult in such a case to say where the great-grandfather's privileges and standing are marked off against those of his son, or grandson, or great-granddaughter. In some cases even a younger son, who would ordinarily be considered as definitely lower in rank than his elder brother, might represent the standing of his father by the exercise of a privilege, say the singing of a particular song in a feast, that belongs to the patrimony of the family. "For men may come and men may go," says the line of descent with its distinctive privileges, "but I go on forever." This is the Indian theory as implied in their general attitude, though there is no doubt that tremendous changes have in many instances gradually evolved by the dying out of particular lines of descent and the taking over of their privileges by other groups only remotely perhaps connected with them by kin, by the introduction of a new privilege gained say as a dowry, and by numerous other factors. The best way to gain a concrete idea of such a structure of society is to think of the titled portion of the tribe as holding up a definite number, say 15 or more, honoured names, or occupying that number of seats, that have descended from the remote past. The classification of the tribe according to kin intercrosses with that based on rank, as by it individuals are brought together who, from the latter point of view, would have to be kept apart. It is clear that not all the members of a large family group can inherit the standing and all the privileges that belong to it. There must be a large number, particularly the younger sons and daughters and those descended from them, who are less favoured than their elders and who will inherit only some, probably the lesser, privileges. In the course of time, as their relationship to the heads of the family or clan becomes more and more remote, they must be expected to sink lower and lower in the general social scale, and there is no doubt that a large proportion of the commoners are to be considered as the unprivileged kinsmen of the nobles. This is no doubt the attitude of at least some of the Indian tribes, such as the Nootka, among whom such a notion of the relation between the classes of society as we find among the castes of India, say, is certainly not found. There is no doubt, however, that with the growth of power attained by the chiefs and with the increasing remoteness of the ties of kinship binding them with most of the commoners, the chasm between the two would gradually widen. The slaves must be left out of account in this connection. They do not enter into the genealogical framework of the tribe, but seem to a large extent to have been recruited from captives of war.

Indian legend, at least among the Nootka and Kwakiutl, generally conceives of the village community as having grown up out of the small family immediately connected in the remote past with a legendary ancestor. All the members of the village community are therefore looked upon as direct descendants of a common ancestor and must therefore, at least in theory, bear definite degrees of relationship to one another. Whether or not the members of a village are actually so connected is immaterial, the essential point being that even in those tribes where there is no clan organization properly so-called, there is, nevertheless, a distinct feeling of kinship among all or most of the members of each of its village communities. This is borne out by the fact that individuals are taught to address each other by certain terms of relationship, even where the appropriateness of such terms is not obvious to them. Thus, a man well advanced in years might call a little child his older brother, for the reason that they are respectively descended from ancestors who stood to each other in that relation. Naturally intermarriages would bring about intercrossings of all sorts, and in course of time the more remote degrees of relationship would be forgotten and new ones, brought nearer home by more recent marriages, take their place.

Let us suppose that a village community is strictly homogeneous in structure, that is, contains no members that cannot count their descent in either the male or female line from the common ancestor. It is obvious that this state of affairs cannot last indefinitely. The accidents of war will doubtless bring it about that sooner or later some neighbouring village community, that has suffered considerably at the hands of an enemy and that finds itself subject to extermination at their hands, will seek protection from the first village community and, in order to gain this end, will receive permission to take up residence with it. It is immediately apparent that the new enlarged village community, provided it is permanent, will have increased in complexity of structure. Their adherence to their respective traditions will be such that neither of the former village communities will give up its peculiar set of privileges, so that a twofold division of the community, as accentuated by these privileges, will persist. If we imagine this process to have occurred several times, we will gradually arrive at a community which is subdivided into several smaller units which we may call septs or bands, or perhaps even clans, each of which has its distinct stock of legendary traditions and privileges exercised by its titled representatives and whose former connection with a definite locality is still remembered. The growth of the village community does not need, of course, to have taken place only in this fashion. Many other factors may be at work. The group added to the original community may be the survivors of a conquered village who are given a subordinate place. Furthermore, a member of another tribe or community that has married into the community may, if he (or she) has sufficient prestige, be able to assert the higher rank that he (she) brings with him (her) and found a new line of descent which will take its place side by side with those already represented. We see, then, a number of ways in which the typical division of a tribe into clans, such as we find among the Haida, may be expected to originate. Such a clan, from the point of view of West Coast conditions, may be defined as a group of kinsmen, real or supposed, who form one of the subdivisions of a village community and who inherit a common stock of traditions associated with a definite locality, the original home of the group.

Clans in this sense we have among the southern tribes that we have enumerated; but it is not until we reach the more northern tribes, such as the Tlingit, Haida, and Tsimshian, that the clan becomes a clearly defined and perfectly solidified unit. This is brought about primarily by the restriction of inheritance. Among the Nootka Indians, for instance, it is possible to inherit privileges in both the male and female lines, preference, where possible, being given to the former. This being the case, it is often hard to see exactly to which sept or clan a person properly belongs, and the decision is generally based on the character of the privileges that are transmitted to him, for, as we have seen, a privilege is always connected with a definite locality, sept, or original village community. In other words, a person steps into certain rights to which he has a claim by descent, and in the exercise of these becomes identified with the particular sept or clan with which they are associated. As the septs have their definite seating at feasts, it is easy to see how the identification of an individual with one sept rather than with another can be made visible. This will indicate also that there are certain natural limitations to the inheritance of all privileges that one has a theoretical claim to. This sort of clan division, however, for the reason that it is too ill-defined and vacillating, can hardly be considered as typical of what we ordinarily understand by clan organization. If, however, we once limit the inheritance of status and privileges to either the male or female line, to the absolute exclusion of the other, we obtain a series of septs or clans that are once and for all rigidly set off against each other. Among the more northern tribes, then, who inherit through the female line alone, there can never be the slightest doubt as to what clan a person is to be identified with.

Furthermore, among the more southern tribes intermarriage is prohibited only between such as are demonstrably related by blood, even if fairly remotely so. Owing to the structure of the village community, this would in many cases mean that there are few persons in a village that one is legally entitled to marry; but it is important to note that the village community as such need not be exogamous, that is, does not specifically prohibit intermarriage among its members. The clan of the northern tribes, which is more rigidly defined by descent and which therefore gains in solidarity, is further accentuated by strict exogamy. Whether such exogamy is a primary feature of the clan itself or is only a necessary consequence of the exogamy of certain larger groups known as phratries, which we shall take up in a moment, is a question which I would not venture to decide and which need not occupy us here. We spoke before of the fact that the original village communities, before amalgamating, each had its peculiar privileges. Certain of these privileges, particularly the crest paintings and carvings, are emblematic of the communities and may be said to give the septs or clans a totemic character. Among the southern tribes, however, it would seem that the crests, which are generally animals or supernatural beings, are employed exclusively by the nobles and that a commoner, even though identified with a particular sept, cannot be said to be in any sense associated with the crest. To what extent the crests are characteristic of the clan generally in the north and to what extent they are more especially in the nature of privileges enjoyed by the nobles, has not been made perfectly clear. It would seem that certain crests, whose origin is particularly remote, have lost such individual value as they may have had and have become clan emblems properly speaking, whereas others are more restricted in their use and would seem to be the peculiar privilege of certain titled individuals or families.

We shall now briefly review the main facts of clan organization among the Tlingit, Haida, Tsimshian, and Kwakiutl, concerning whom our published information is fullest. The Tlingit are divided into two main divisions, known respectively as Ravens and Wolves, the latter being in some of the villages referred to also as Eagles. In at least one of the southern Tlingit tribes, the Sanya, there is a division which stands outside of the grouping into two phratries, and the members of which may intermarry with either the Ravens or the Wolves. The Ravens and Wolves are respectively debarred from intermarriage within their own ranks. A Raven man must marry a Wolf woman, a Wolf man a Raven woman, while the children of the pair belong to the phratry of the mother. It is important to bear in mind that this dual division of the Tlingit Indians is not associated with particular villages or even tribes, but applies to all the Tlingit tribes. A Raven, for instance, from Tongas, the southernmost Tlingit village, is as strictly bebarred from marrying a Raven woman of Yakutat, in the extreme north, as a Raven woman of his own village. When we remember that he may never have been within miles of Yakutat and may know few or no Indians from that region, we see clearly that whether or not phratric exogamy is in origin an outgrowth of an interdict against marriage of those of close kin, an interdict which we find to be practically universal, it is certainly rather different from it psychologically. The leading crest or emblem of the Raven people is the raven, who is at the same time the most important mythological being in the beliefs of the Tlingit Indians. The main crest of the Wolf people is the wolf. The phratries stand to each other as opposites that do each other mutual services. Thus, the Wolves conduct the funeral ceremonies of the Ravens and, when they give a feast, distribute the property to the Ravens.

Each phratry is subdivided into a considerable number of clans, each with its own distinctive crest or crests, generally in addition to the general crest of the phratry to which it belongs. Unlike the two main phratries, the clans are not found in all the villages of the Tlingit, though many of them are found represented in more than one village. If we assume, as I believe to be the case, that the clans were originally nothing but village communities, it follows that the present distribution of clans is secondary and due to migrations or movements of part of the clansmen away from the main body of their kinsmen. Should a number of clansmen of the original clan village be induced for one reason or another to take up residence in another village, the home primarily of another clan, it is clear that they would, to begin with, be an intrusive element in their new home; but would in course of time be looked upon as forming an integral part of the village community, though of lesser importance than the dominant clan. The legends of the Indians themselves clearly indicate that such whole or partial clan movements have frequently taken place. Many of the names of the clans themselves plainly indicate their local origin. Thus, the Kiksadi are a Raven clan that are found represented in several Tlingit tribes, such as the Sanya, the Stikine people, and the Sitka Indians. The name means nothing more than People-of-the-Island-Kiks and clearly implies that the clan was, to begin with, at home in a particular locality and gradually became distributed over a large area by various movements of population. The force of tradition would always be strong enough to keep up the old clan crests and other clan privileges, wherever the clansmen moved. In course of time the appearance is attained of a clan distribution which has nothing to do with local communities as such.

Very similar conditions prevail among the Haida Indians. Here again we have two main phratries, subdivided into a large number of clans. As among the Tlingit, the Haida phratries are exogamous and descent in them is reckoned through the female line. One of them is termed Raven, though curiously enough, the main crest of this phratry is not the raven but the killer-whale. The opposite phratry is termed Eagle, this animal being the chief crest of the phratry. Among the Haida, as among the Tlingit, the native legends indicate that the clans were originally confined to certain definite localities, but that in course of time the clansmen moved about in various ways until now, when they are represented in a number of villages. One concrete instance will serve to illustrate the actual state of affairs. In the town of Skidegate there were represented in earlier times three distinct Eagle clans, and three distinct Raven clans, each of these six clans occupying its own houses. Of the six clans the dominant one was an Eagle clan known as People-of-the-great-house, claiming as their crests the Raven (this in spite of the fact that they do not belong to the Raven phratry), a supernatural being known as *wāsḡo*, the dog-fish, the weasel, the eagle, the sculpin, and the halibut. Presumably this clan formed the original nucleus of the present town of Skidegate about which the other clans in course of time clustered. The Haida clan names are generally either local in character, like most of the Tlingit names, or of an honorific character, like the one that we have just quoted.

The Tsimshian are organized similarly to the Tlingit and Haida, except that their clans are grouped into four phratries: the Raven, Eagle, Wolf and Grizzly Bear.

Among the southern Kwakiutl also the single tribes are subdivided into a number of clans, each of which, there is reason to believe on legendary and other evidence, originally formed a separate village community. These have chiefly honorific titles, such as "The-chiefs," "Those-who-receive-first," and "Having-a-great-name." Some of these names occur in more than one of the Kwakiutl tribes; but it seems more likely that these correspondences in name are due to imitations rather than to a genealogical connection between the clans of like name. The social structure of the Kwakiutl Indians differs from that of the Tlingit and Haida in that the clans are not grouped into phratries, and that they do not seem to be exogamous. As to descent, it seems that at least the most important privileges are regularly transmitted as a dowry to the son-in-law, who holds them in trust for his son. This method of inheritance has been explained as a peculiar Kwakiutl adaptation of an originally paternal system of inheritance to the maternal system in vogue among the more northern tribes, by whom the Kwakiutl were presumably influenced. There are, however, some difficulties in the way of this explanation, one of which is the fact that the Nootka Indians to the south are not organized on a purely paternal basis, but allow many privileges to descend through the female line. Among them also such privileges may be handed over as a dowry, though this system has not been standardized among them to the same· extent as among the Kwakiutl.

There are two important peculiarities of the West Coast crests which make them contrast with the totems of such typical totemic communities as the Iroquois Indians of the east or the Pueblos of the southwest. Among these latter, who, like the Haida and Tlingit, are organized into exogamous clans of maternal descent, a clan has a single crest or totem after which it is named. Moreover, no other clan can use this totem. The West Coast clans differ in both these respects. As we have already shown in the case of one of the Haida Eagle clans, a group of clansmen generally lay claim to more than one crest; further, only certain crests are confined to single clans, the more important ones being generally represented in several. Thus, the grizzly-bear is claimed as a crest by no less than twelve distinct Haida clans of the Raven phratry, the rainbow by eight, the sea-lion by five, the beaver by twelve Eagle clans, the whale by seven, the humming-bird by three, and so on. In some cases a clan even makes use of a crest which primarily belongs to the opposite phratry. Evidently there is not the same intimate and clear-cut association between totem and clan, as such, that is typical of the Iroquois and Pueblo Indians.

It is probable that the duplication of crests is to be explained chiefly on the theory that many clans arose as subdivisions of other clans. Such a clan offshoot would keep the old crest or crests, but might in time add one or more to its stock, without sharing them with the mother clan. The clan can, indeed, be arranged in the form of a genealogical tree and the crests stratified. The older the crest, the greater number of times is it found in the various clans; on the other hand, a crest found in only one clan may be suspected to be of recent origin, as it probably does not antedate the severance of its clan from the older group originally including it.

Whatever may have been its origin, the crest seems to have become, to a large extent, a symbol of greatness, and it became the desire of the chiefs to add to their prestige by the acquisition of new crests. They were not only obtained by inheritance, but could be secured as gifts, or even by forcible means in war. The fact that the name of the clan does not as a rule refer to a totem also seems to indicate that the clan may not, to begin with, be organically connected with a particular crest. That the clansmen are not conceived of as descended from one of their crest animals, and that there seem to be no taboos in force against the eating or killing of the crest animals, need not matter, for these are by no means constant features of even typical totemic societies.

There is another feature of the crests of the West Coast Indians which accentuates their difference from typical clan totems. This is the tendency they have to be thought of in very concrete terms, as carvings or paintings. It would in many cases, for instance, be more correct to say that a certain chief uses a ceremonial hat representing the Beaver, or that he has the right to paint the Thunder-bird on the outside of his house, than that he possesses the Beaver or Thunder-bird crest or totem. His justification for the use of these would be a legend, telling of how one of his ancestors gained the privilege by contact with the crest animals—a type of legend which is told to account for the use of nearly all crests. We see more clearly now why earlier in this paper I referred to crests as a particular type of an inheritable privilege. Incidentally, it is interesting to note that the Kwakiutl term for crest seems to denote primarily a carving.

Crests are shown or utilized in different ways. They may be painted on movable boards used as screens or otherwise, painted on the outside of the house or along the bed platform, carved on the house-posts or beams, or on memorial columns, or on the outside house-posts popularly known as totem poles, tattooed on the body, painted on the face during feasts, represented in dance-hats, masks, staffs, or other ceremonial paraphernalia, woven in ceremonial robes, referred to in clan legends, dramatically represented at potlatches in performances based on such legends, referred to in songs owned by the clan or clan-chiefs, and in individual or house names. Not all house names, however, refer to a crest. The village and clan names are also, as a rule, unconnected with crests. So accustomed have the West Coast Indians, particularly those of the north, become to the representation of crest animals in carving and painting, that they introduce them even in objects that are not as a rule connected with the exercise of privileges. Among such objects are the beautifully ornamented dishes, boxes, batons, spoons, rattles, clubbers, and gambling-sticks that are so often admired in ethnological museums. We see here how the elaboration of the crest system has fostered among these Indians the development of plastic art. It has also been suggested, and I believe with justice, that the tendency to artistic and dramatic representation in turn reacted upon the development of the crest system, a development that was strengthened by the ever-present desire for new privileges and for novel ways of exhibiting the old ones.

The origin of the crests need not have been the same in all cases. In some cases, for instance, it can be shown that they were obtained by marriage or as gifts in return for a service. These new crests would of course be handed down along with the old inherited ones. Such methods of obtaining crests, however, must be considered as purely secondary, and the real problem of accounting for their origin still remains. The most plausible explanation that has been offered is, on the whole, that which considers the clan crest as an extension of the personal manitou or tutelary being. Among practically all Indians we find the practice of seeking supernatural protection or power by fasting and dreaming of certain animals or objects that are believed to be endowed with such power. If we suppose that a personal guardian thus obtained is handed down by inheritance, we can readily understand how the manitou of an ancestor may gradually become transformed into a clan totem or crest. The main difficulty with this theory is that personal guardians or medicines do not normally seem to be inheritable. On the other hand, the legends related by the West Coast Indians to account for the origin of crests do bear an unmistaken resemblance to tales of the acquisition of supernatural guardians. It is not difficult to understand how the religious element, which must have been strongly emphasized in the manitou, gradually faded away as the manitou developed (or degenerated) into a crest. At any rate, the problem is far from being satisfactorily solved.

Even more fundamental than the clans are, among the northern tribes, the phratries which include them. Their origin also is far from clear. Whether they resulted from the amalgamation of a number of clans into larger units, or whether, on the contrary, the clans within the phratry are to be considered as local off-shoots from it, is often difficult to decide. On the whole, however, the latter alternative seems the more typical one. This is indicated, first of all, by the fact that each of the two main phratries is represented in every village, though, on the other hand, the necessary intermarriages between the phratries might soon bring about this state of affairs under any circumstances. More important is the fact that the phratric crest is shared by all or practically all the clans of the phratry; this seems to imply that the phratry with its crest is a fundamental unit antedating the rise of the separate clans. The fundamental importance of the two phratric divisions of the Haida is beautifully illustrated by their belief in the validity of this social arrangement in the supernatural world. Thus, every being of the sea was conceived of as belonging from the beginning of time to either the Raven or Eagle phratry. It is conceivable that the phratries are sociologically reinterpreted forms of originally distinct tribal units. Apropos of this possibility, it may be noted that in many tribal organizations certain clans, gentes, camp-circle units, or other social units are, either in fact or origin, a group of aliens incorporated into the main tribe. According to Tlingit legend, indeed, the Ravens were originally Coast people, the Wolves inland people. This may, however, be a mere rationalization of an obvious fact of zoological distribution, the raven being common on the coast while the wolf is chiefly confined to the woods.

So much for social organization according to rank and kinship. The third type of organization, the local, we have had to take up in connection with the other two. Local classifications as distinct from kin classifications arise only when the clan ceases to be confined to a single locality. When this happens, the kin and local groupings necessarily intercross and town administration arises, which provides for more than the needs of a clan or group of kinsmen.

The ritual organization which we have listed as a fourth type of social organization is best developed among the Kwakiutl Indians. Among these Indians the clan system which is operative during the greater part of the year, the so-called profane season, gives place during the winter to a ritualistic organization based on the right to the performance of religious dances. The dancers impersonate various supernatural beings from whom they are supposed to have received manitou power. In actual practice the performance of the dance is conditioned by the inherited right to them. Such rights are justified in legends accounting for the introduction of the dance by an ancestor, supposed to have come in contact with the supernatural being himself and to have been instructed by him. In a sense all those who perform the same dance form a secret society, though this term, which has been often used, does not seem particularly appropriate to me. The dances are graded into two series—a lower and a higher one. The dancers of the lower series are collectively known as Sparrows[1], those of the higher as Seals. One may pass in successive seasons from one so-called society to another, up to the point allowed by his or her particular inheritance. The most important of the dance-societies are the Ghosts, the Fool-dancers, the Grizzly-bears, and the Cannibals. While there are certain external resemblances between the ritual and clan organizations of the Kwakiutl, I believe it would be erroneous to consider the former as specialized forms of the latter. I consider it far more likely that the ritualistic activities were simply patterned on the normal clan organization, the ever-present tendency to ranking finding expression in both. The other tribes of this region have borrowed much of the Kwakiutl rituals, but do not seem to share their elaborate ritual organization.

The space at our disposal will not permit us to go more deeply into the intricacies of West Coast social organization. It is difficult to render clear in a few strokes what seems an essentially involved set of social phenomena and I am not at all certain that I have succeeded in my object. The main points that I have tried to bring out are the fundamental importance of inherited privileges as such, the growth of the village community into a clan, the peculiar character of the crest system of these Indians when compared with typical totemism elsewhere, and the almost exaggerated development of the idea of grading of individuals and privileges.

[1] Or some other small bird.

LITERATURE AND MUSIC
EDITOR'S PREFACE

THE SELECTIONS *in this section are but a token representation of Sapir's writing in musical and literary criticism. Sapir had studied composition with Edward MacDowell and his knowledge of musical history and technique was more than a layman's. As others have strong visual imagery, his sensory perceptions were particularly acute in the sphere of sound. In "Representative Music" (1918), the first article of the section, the capabilities and limitations of sound as used in music and as used in language are defined. A more detailed and technical analysis of the nexus between music and language is given in a study not reprinted here, "The Musical Foundations of Verse" (1921).*

Of his own verse, some hundred and eighty poems were published in magazines, and a slim volume called Dreams and Gibes *appeared in 1917. Most of his poems are brief pieces which—almost musically—evoke the mood raised by a passing incident or a slight episode. A few have more sustained themes, and these indicate what Sapir might have created in poetry had he chosen that as one of the principal avenues of his endeavor.*

In "The Heuristic Value of Rhyme" (1920) Sapir discusses, in the realm of aesthetics, the same problem of the interaction of form and feeling which also took his interest in the fields of culture and personality. His awareness of the values of formal tradition in poetry did not preclude his experimenting with poetic form or from being sympathetic to new directions in literary work. Hence he took great pleasure in the unorthodox rhythms and forms of the poems of Gerard Manley Hopkins, as is shown by the excerpts from the review written in 1921. All the more because—as he says—Hopkins' work should be "read with the ear, never with the eye."

The two final excerpts from reviews illustrate the manner in which Sapir brought ethnological insights to his literary criticism. Thus he says, in the 1922 review of American Indian Life, *that few literary travelers "have had the intensity to penetrate to those currents of life which make all backgrounds commonplace and acceptable. . . . perhaps the truest understanding would come from the donning of new and more tyrannous moralities." And in the 1923 comments on Housman, Sapir notes that Housman's earlier work was not the harbinger of a new outlook which it once seemed to be: "while Mr. Housman seems to anticipate and now to join with us in our despair, he is serene and bitter where we are bitter and distraught." The final paragraph of this review returns again to the question of form in aesthetics, and to the contemporary need for forms that "are at once more gracious and less discussible."*

REPRESENTATIVE MUSIC*

THE CONTEST between the absolutists and the supporters of "programme" in modern music has often been characterized by extreme and mutually irreconcilable attitudes. On the one hand we have the purists or formalists, who either explicitly deny or evade acknowledgment of any necessary relation between musical forms and states or functions of mind occurring in other than musical experience. To these a sonata or even a bare musical "theme" is aesthetically satisfying by virtue of its own inherent beauty of melody, rhythm, harmony, construction, or color, quite regardless of any non-musical "meaning" it may be thought to possess. Such people would be annoyed rather than helped by the interpretation of a certain Beethoven sonata as suffused by a spirit of moonlight pensiveness. Why mar the sheer beauty of a self-sufficing art-form by attaching to it a label of extraneous origin?

No less decided are some of the "programme" enthusiasts. While not denying to melody, rhythm, and the other means of musical expression an inherent sensuous beauty, and to musical construction the essential beauty of all design, they maintain that the enjoyment of such merely sensuous or structural beauty is an aesthetic one only in a more or less elementary phase. To a piece of music must, properly speaking, be denied the term art-form in its highest sense unless it does more than tickle our sense of rhythm or color or evoke our admiration by its skilful handling of the purely formal aspect of the musical problem. It must have vitality (to use a much abused word), that is, it must be associated in the mind of both creator and public, and this by virtue of its intrinsic quality, with some element or elements in their experience. It dare not stand coldly aloof, on pain of degenerating into clever trifling, from the more definitely articulated currents of life, but must seek to gain in significance, and therefore in aesthetic value, by embodying, in its own peculiar way, one or more of the incidents or phases of that life. The nature of such embodiment may vary indefinitely. In some cases the music may be content to picture a mood, in others to catch some aspect of nature, in others to define an idea, in still others to mark a succession of moods or ideas that in their totality comprise a "story."

The progress of musical art is thus toward ever increasing complexity and definiteness of emotional and conceptual expression. In other words, music must tend to be "representative" in character. Music has lagged far behind plastic art and poetry in this respect, but this is due primarily

* *The Musical Quarterly*, 4 (1918): 161–167.

to the great lapse of time which it has taken the art to develop a technique rich and flexible enough to fulfil its higher mission.

If the history of aesthetic criticism teaches us anything, it is the futility of trying to mark off the legitimate province of an art or an artform. Over and over again a critic has demonstrated, to the complete satisfaction of the discerning, certain inherent aesthetic limitations. He proved his point, but some genius has generally managed to override his formula and consign it to the dust-bin of things that were. My own aim is, therefore, not the presumptuous one of a definition of the proper sphere of music but rather an attempt to state what music seems to me best able to accomplish.

To begin with, can the absolutists really succeed in eliminating an emotional substratum, of varying vividness, from the appreciation of a musical composition? I do not refer to the emotional components of musical appreciation that are evident in the enjoyment of any of the elements of musical expression as such (such as pleasure in certain instrumental combinations or delight in the recurrence of a well-defined rhythmic figure or the more subtle pleasure derived from consideration of a certain balance of form), but only to a mood or attitude of mind induced by the composition as a whole and to which the former types of pleasure must normally be considered as subsidiary. As a matter of fact, it is difficult to listen to one of the greater compositions even of pre-programme days without finding ourselves put into a rather definite mood, a mood which to all intents and purposes defines the meaning of the music for us. And does not the verdict of the present in judging of the relative merit or appeal of musical works of the past often clearly imply just such an emphasis on the æsthetic importance of definite emotional quality? Thus, it is no exaggeration to say that most of the Mozart sonata movements, despite their spontaneous flow of melody and finish of external form, are of lesser æsthetic value to us than many of the simply constructed Bach preludes of the "Well-tempered Clavichord." These preludes belong to a remoter period of musical history, but their deep-felt, though restrained, quality of emotion, (think of the devotional spirit of the very first prelude manifest enough without the Gounod Ave Maria pendant; or of the mood of serene sadness that permeates the beautiful E flat minor prelude of the first set) keeps them alive where the Mozart sonatas, on the whole, must be regretfully admitted to have become a respectable and faded musical tradition. Craftsmanship, no matter how pleasing or ingenious, cannot secure a musical composition immortality; it is inevitably put in the shade by the technique of a later age. True, such craftsmanship may be admirable, as a dynamo or a well played game of billiards elicit admiration; yet admiration does not constitute æsthetic enjoyment.

Aside from the emotional substratum which we feel to be inseparable from a truly great and sincere work of musical art, are there not in the earlier supposedly absolutist art plenty of instances of direct realistic suggestion, sometimes intentional, no doubt, at other times a spontaneous product of association on the part of the listener? Is it possible, for instance, to listen to certain of the Beethoven scherzos without sensing the gamboling faun (or convention-freed ego) kicking his heels with a relish? But Beethoven, the idol of the absolutists, was no more an absolutist than Aristotle, the idol of the scholastics, was a scholastic. I do not think it would be going too far to say that all musical art worthy of the name has implicitly, if not avowedly, some of the fundamental qualities of so-called "programme" music; from a musical standpoint it should make little difference whether the emotional appeal is left to declare itself in the mind of the sympathetic listener or is trumpeted at him by means of a formidable printed analysis.

We have turned our backs on the uncompromising absolutist. Are we therefore to receive his most uncompromising opponent with open arms? I have already indicated in a general way the aims and procedure of representative music. It either uses all of its technical resources to define a mood or emotion, or it may, by the use of some special element of technique or combination of such elements, depict a selected feature of the external world (rapid passage work may be utilized to symbolize the flowing brook or the falling rain or the roaring wind, the high pitched piccolo tones may do service for the shrieking of the tempest or the chirping of birds, the loud discord of clashing harmonies may suggest a battle scene or the clangor of a foundry). Now there seems to me to be a profound psychological difference between those two types of procedure, intertwined as they necessarily often are in practice. That the former touches our emotional life while the latter plays upon our sense experience is obvious. The distinction I have in mind is more deep-seated. Realistic suggestion must make use of the principle of association, and the fact of such association becomes obvious to the listener on reflection. By the musical equivalent of a figure of speech, a feature common to two otherwise totally dissimilar phenomena (the thing symbolized and a certain mass of sound) is made to identify them. If, for some reason or other, the experience of the auditor has been such as not to make the association obvious, the suggestion loses all its force and the artist, insofar as he is writing merely representative music, has with that auditor failed of success. On the other hand, music is able to put us into more or less well defined emotional states without such associative intermediation, or, perhaps more accurately, the associative links are of so obscure and intimate a nature as never to rise into consciousness. In other words, the emotional effect of music is gained directly or, what amounts to essentially the same thing, gives the impression of being so gained. Once this point is clearly grasped, it becomes obvous that the function of music, insofar as it has æsthetic aims of other than a sensuous and formal nature, is primarily the expression of the emotional aspect of consciousness, only in a very secondary sense the expression of the conceptual aspect. This primary function is thus of poetic quality and may be briefly described as the interpretation of emotional quality in terms of sensuous and structural beauty. A still more concise way of putting the matter is to define music as an idealization of mood by means of tone.

It has often been instinctively felt that music which makes too free a use of realistic suggestion lays itself open to the charge of superficiality, of the abandonment of its own highest artistic capabilities. Even the greatest composers, in its employment, seem often to sail between the Scylla of triviality and the Charybdis of absurdity. And yet there is no doubt that it is capable of affording keen æsthetic pleasure. Probably the simplest and most fundamental element in such pleasure is the sheer delight that the mind seems to find in generalizing by analogy, in meeting familiar friends in new and unexpected guise; it is the tonal correspondent of the childish phantasy that interprets cloud shapes as battleships and monsters and human faces. More careful analysis, however, shows that this type of pleasure is, in the best examples of musical suggestion, powerfully reinforced by another though not always clearly distinct factor. The melodic, harmonic, rhythmic, or other musical idea which serves as the symbol of the concept represented has in such cases an independent sensuous beauty of its own, a beauty whose appeal transcends our normal interest in the concept itself. Hence such music amounts to an idealization of some aspect of the external world. To our greeting of a friend in disguise is added the much greater pleasure of finding him transported to a higher plane of being. And this brings us to a third and yet more significant phase in the use and appreciation of realistic suggestion, that in which the concept is not idealized for its own sake, is not merely represented as such, but is utilized as a symbol of the emotion simultaneously called forth by the music. Obviously this means a very considerable heightening of the quality of the emotion itself. The finest examples of realistic suggestion derive much of their charm from this very factor. In other words, realistic suggestion in music is most successful when it ceases to be merely what its name implies but contributes to the enrichment of the emotional aim of music. Thus even in so obviously suggestive a bit of music as the delightful "Jardins sous la pluie" of Debussy, the secret of the appeal, it seems to me, lies not so much in the clever devices of rhythm, melodic progression, and shading which symbolize the pitter-patter, the gustiness, the steady fall, and the tempestuous downpour of the rain as in the delicate and wistful line of emotion that runs through the composition; the rain but voices human feeling. And such humanizing of the external world *via* emotion is a significant indication of the primary function of musical art.

We have just seen that realistic suggestion may assist in the definition of the mood (thus, the suggestion of the shepherd's pipe may reinforce a mood or atmosphere of rustic peacefulness, a dancing rhythm of break-neck rapidity may accentuate a mood of reckless gaiety). In representative music, however, the emotion created by the music is conversely often employed to suggest an associated concept, concrete or abstract. When a certain harmonic progression, for instance, in one of Strauss's tone poems is used to symbolize a mountain, it is clear that the only associative link is furnished by the feeling of all-embracing massiveness suggested by the chords in relation to each other (I say "all-embracing," for a feeling of vast extension would seem to be implied in the sudden chromatic modulation at the close of the figure, the immediate juxtaposition of two harmonically remote keys being the musical equivalent of a bringing together of the widely removed in space; the feeling of "massiveness" is conveyed by the use of full compact chords in the bass). My claim here is that, considering the music itself as our starting point, the interpretation suggested by the composer is by no means the only justifiable one, psychologically speaking. Adopting the formula of "all-embracing massiveness" as expressing the quality of emotion conveyed by the passage in question, it seems clear that a quite unlimited number of alternative interpretations are possible (the vastness of the sea, Mother Earth, grim fate, eternal justice), each conditioned by considerations of personal interest and experience in the auditor. If the conceptual interpretation of a single musical passage of definite emotional quality is thus multiform without limit, how much more must this be the case with the conceptual interpretation of a series of such passages, in other words of an extended musical composition! The "story" which we are expected to read in a composition of the "programme" type must be considered as relevant only insofar as it conveniently summarizes in conceptual terms the emotional stream immediately expressed by the music. As such it may be highly welcome.

Whether the composer wills it or not, the particular story suggested by his title or analysis is only a more or less arbitrary selection out of an indefinitely large number of possible conceptualizations. We cannot refuse him the right to his own interpretation, to be sure; no more can he refuse each one of us the right to his. All he has done or can do, aside from the possibility of direct realistic suggestion, is to determine for us the character and sequence of our moods. He may modestly direct attention, by means of his programmatic apparatus, to the conceptual genesis in his own mind of this emotional stream or, probably more often than is generally thought, to his own merely secondary interpretation thereof, but he cannot *via* a non-conceptualizing medium, i. e. music, force any particular stream of thought on us except insofar as we surrender into his hands our own individuality of judgment and association. In short, the music does not "tell" the story but the story tells or rather guesses at the music. If the composer absolutely must appeal conceptually, as well as emotionally, to his hearers, he must have recourse to the conceptual implement which society has evolved, i. e. language. In other words, he must supplement his own expression of emotion by calling in the aid of the poet. His art then takes on the special forms of the song, music drama, oratorio.

I have said that all the composer can do is "to determine for us the character and sequence of our moods." It is not worth while for him to aim at a purely representative ideal; his highest success in this direction will fall miserably short of what is attained by the merest balderdash in literature. In the expression of the emotions, however, he has a field the unending fruitfulness of which is hardly realized by most people. We think it a field of narrow range because words, mere conceptual symbols, are lacking to indicate its infinite nuances. Select a half dozen musical examples of the expression of any typical emotion, say unbridled mirth or quiet sadness or poignant anguish, and compare them. The feelings they arouse in us are identical only when translated into the clumsy conceptual terminology of language. In actual fact they will be found to be quite distinct, quite uninterchangeable. It is literally true that the æsthetic expression of mood in tone is an exhaustless field of human endeavor. Does not the very potency of music reside in its precision and delicacy of expression of a range of mental life that is otherwise most difficult, most elusive of expression? Nay more, does not music ofttimes create nuances of feeling, nuances that add in profound measure to the more external enjoyment of its own sensuous and formal beauty?

THE HEURISTIC VALUE OF RHYME*

THE EMPLOYMENT of rhyme always presents a problem. We like to think that the poet, carried away by his vision and the passion of his theme, has his rhymes coming to him spontaneously, that there is in the creation of rhymed verses no too deliberate process of selection. We like to think that form and subject matter are wedded from the beginning in an indissoluble unity. But all art is largely technique, and technique involves experimentation, rejection, selection, modification of the originally envisaged theme. Undoubtedly the actual practice of poets differs widely as regards the discovery of their rhymes. We shall not go far wrong in assuming that it is only in the rare case that thought and form come to the creator as a God-given unit. Perhaps we may speak of "God-given" rhyme in some of the very best lyrics of such poets as Robert Burns and Heine. Normally rhyme must prove a taskmaster; not infrequently it must coerce the poet into dulling, if ever so slightly, the edge of his thought here or padding out a little its range there. It does not in the least follow that the compulsion he is under to satisfy the taskmaster renders his work any the less satisfying in the end. Indeed it is more than probable that the very feeling of compulsion often serves as a valuable stimulant in the shaping of his thought and imagination.

The strained image or the far-fetched phrase is a price paid all too frequently by the poet to the necessity of rhyming. Even the best of poets cannot always escape these sins, when he has set himself the task of squirming about in a difficult form pattern. Rhymes *ad hoc* are common in the work of our more facile poets. It would be possible to quote more than one passage from John Masefield's work in illustration of this melancholy truth. Thus, I find the following from "Truth," one of the poems published in "The Story of a Round House," to contain a weak, rhyme-compelled line:

> Stripped of all purple robes,
> Stripped of all golden lies,
> I will not be afraid.
> Truth will preserve through death;
> Perhaps the stars will rise,
> The stars like globes.
> The ship my striving made
> May see right fade.

Masefield here set himself a rather difficult verse pattern. He had to find a rhyme in his two-footed sixth line to match the "robes" of the first.

* *Queen's Quarterly*, 27 (1920): 309–312.

His solution of the difficulty, "the stars like globes," is hardly fortunate. A repetition of "the stars" is bad enough, "like globes" leaves the reader in sad wonder. It has pertinency neither as idea nor as imagery.

Another example of the made-to-order rhyme in Masefield's verse is to be found in "The Wanderer." We read:

> So, as though stepping to a funeral march,
> She passed defeated homeward whence she came,
> Ragged with tattered canvas white as starch,
> A wild bird that misfortune had made tame.

The "white as starch" seems dragged in by the heels.

It would be a far more difficult but also more thankful task to point out the heuristic value of rhyme, the stimulating, or even directly creative, effect that the necessity of finding a rhyming word may exercise on the fancy of the poet. There can be no doubt that imbedded in the smooth surface of great rhymed verse there lie concealed hundreds of evidences of technical struggles that have resulted in a triumph of the imagination, a triumph that could hardly have been attained except through travail. Many a felicitous fancy, many a gorgeous bit of imagery, would have forever remained undiscovered if not whipped into being by the rhyming slave-driver. One of the prettiest examples that occur to me I select from the work of Robert Frost, who of all poets will not readily be accused of an undue adherence to conventional patterns. In "Blueberries," one of the poems of "North of Boston," I find the lines:

> Blueberries as big as the end of your thumb,
> Real sky-blue, and heavy, and ready to drum
> In the cavernous pail of the first one to come.

It is impossible to prove anything about these lines without direct inquiry of the writer, who, moreover, may have forgotten the circumstances of composition. But I have always instinctively felt that the beautiful "drum" image was evoked in response to the rhyming necessity set by the preceding "thumb."

Nuances of feeling may receive an unexpected sharpening, a poignancy of contrast, by way of rhyme that its absence may have allowed to remain unrevealed. Turning the pages of "The Man against the Sky," I find this very characteristic bit of Edwin Arlington Robinson from "Lisette and Eileen":

> Because a word was never told,
> I'm going as a worn toy goes.
> And you are dead; and you'll be old;
> And I forgive you, I suppose.

Nothing could well be more casual, ostensibly, than the "I suppose" of the last line. Yet how better could all the poignant irony, the frenzy, the passionate resignation of Lisette have been expressed? One wonders if this superb fourth line could ever have fashioned itself in Robinson's brain if he had allowed himself to work in a freer medium.

Somewhat similar in its general effect is the following bit of humorous irony from "The Cake of Mithridates" (included in John Davidson's "Fleet Street and other Poems"):

> With that the baker, breathing spice,
>   Produced the cake hot from the fire,
> And every vizier ate a slice
>   Resolving to be less a liar.

There could be no more fittingly impertinent summary of the whole spirit of the poem than the unexpectedness of the final rhyme. The poem could not possibly have ended on a more appropriate note.

Both Robinson and Davidson are distinguished by a rare combination of intellect and passion. Perhaps it is precisely the passionate temperament cutting into itself with the cold steel of the intellect that is best adapted to the heuristic employment of rhyme. The temperament and the triumphant harnessing of form belong, both of them, to the psychology of sublimation following inhibition.

I may be pardoned if I once again quote Masefield. Masefield has passion, vigor, swiftness, a fine frenzy that stamps him a belated Elizabethan. He has caught in his verse the physical throb and external color of the present, his spirit belongs irredeemably to the past, to the romantic past at that. Few poets of his stature are so innocent of intellect. As luck would have it, shortly after I had noted the fire—liar rhyme in Davidson, I ran across the following instance of the identical rhyme in "The Daffodil Fields":

> But all my being is ablaze with her;
> There is no talk of giving up to-day.
> I will not give her up. You used to say
> Bodies are earth. I heard you say it. Liar!
> You never loved her, you. She turns the earth to fire.

Little comment is necessary. The external logic-chopping of these lines only serves to emphasize the unbridled, not to say unarticulated, passion. To the modern sensibility, is the last sentence felt as "in the drawing"? Have we not here again a facile rhyming technique seeking shelter and justification behind an all too uncritically evaluated rush of feeling? Tomorrow these lines will seem strangely cold. Robinson's cold lines will still burn.

It is not often that the artist can or cares to reveal much of the intimate processes of his work. Perhaps in most cases he is himself unable to analyze the process of creation with any degree of satisfaction. Where he can, however, it will certainly be of the greatest interest for a sound study of æsthetics to have him record something of this process. We have much too little material of the sort to work with. If æsthetics is ever to be more than a speculative play, of the genus philosophical, it will have to get down to the very arduous business of studying the concrete processes of artistic production and appreciation.

EXCERPTS FROM REVIEWS

FROM A REVIEW OF "POEMS OF GERARD MANLEY HOPKINS," EDITED BY ROBERT BRIDGES*

WHEN THE AUTHOR'S preface and the editor's notes are eliminated, we have here but a small volume of some eighty-five pages of poetry, and of these only a scant sixty-three consist of complete poems, the rest being fragments assembled from manuscripts in the Poet Laureate's possession. The majority of them date from the years 1876 to 1889; only three earlier poems are included. Hopkins is long in coming into his own; but it is not too much to say that his own will be secure, among the few that know, if not among the crowd, when many a Georgian name that completely overshadows him for the moment shall have become food for the curious.

For Hopkins' poetry is of the most precious. His voice is easily one of the half-dozen most individual voices in the whole course of English nineteenth-century poetry. One may be repelled by his mannerisms, but he cannot be denied that overwhelming authenticity, that almost terrible immediacy of utterance, that distinguishes the genius from the man of talents. I would compare him to D. H. Lawrence but for his far greater sensitiveness to the music of words, to the rhythms and ever-changing speeds of syllables. In a note published in *Poetry* in 1914, Joyce Kilmer speaks of his mysticism and of his gloriously original imagery. This mysticism of the Jesuit poet is not a poetic manner, it is the very breath of his soul. Hopkins simply could not help comparing the Holy Virgin to the air we breathe; he was magnificently in earnest about the Holy Ghost that

> over the bent
> World broods with warm breast and with ah! bright wings.

As for imagery, there is hardly a line in these eighty-odd pages that does not glow with some strange new flower, divinely picked from his imagination.

Undeniably this poet is difficult. He strives for no innocuous Victorian smoothness. I have referred to his mannerisms, which are numerous and not always readily assimilable. They have an obsessive, turbulent quality about them—these repeated and trebly repeated words, the

* *Poetry*, 18 (1921): 330–336.

poignantly or rapturously interrupting *oh's* and *ah's*, the headlong omission of articles and relatives, the sometimes violent word order, the strange yet how often so lovely compounds, the plays on words, and, most of all, his wild joy in the sheer sound of words. This phonetic passion of Hopkins rushes him into a perfect maze of rhymes, half-rhymes, assonances, alliterations:

> Tatter-tassel-tangled and dingle-a-dangled
> Dandy-hung dainty head.

These clangs are not like the nicely calculated jingling lovelinesses of Poe or Swinburne. They, no less than the impatient ruggednesses of his diction, are the foam-flakes and eddies of a passionate, swift-streaming expression. To a certain extent Hopkins undoubtedly loved difficulty, even obscurity, for its own sake. He may have found in it a symbolic reflection of the tumult that raged in his soul. Yet we must beware of exaggerating the external difficulties; they yield with unexpected ease to the modicum of good will that Hopkins has a right to expect of us.

Hopkins' prosody, concerning which he has something to say in his preface, is worthy of careful study. In his most distinctive pieces he abandons the "running" verse of traditional English poetry and substitutes for it his own "sprung" rhythms. This new verse of his is not based on the smooth flow of regularly recurring stresses. The stresses are carefully grouped into line and stanza patterns, but the movement of the verse is wholly free. The iambic or trochaic foot yields at any moment to a spondee or a dactyl or a foot of one stressed and three or more unstressed syllables. There is, however, no blind groping in this irregular movement. It is nicely adjusted to the constantly shifting speed of the verse. Hopkins' effects, with a few exceptions, are in the highest degree successful. Read with the ear, never with the eye, his verse flows with an entirely new vigor and lightness, while the stanzaic form gives it a powerful compactness and drive. It is doubtful if the freest verse of our day is more sensitive in its rhythmic pulsations than the "sprung" verse of Hopkins. . . .

Yet neither mannerisms of diction and style nor prosody define the essential Hopkins. The real Hopkins is a passionate soul unendingly in conflict. The consuming mysticism, the intense religious faith are unreconciled with a basic sensuality that leaves the poet no peace. He is longing to give up the loveliness of the world for that greater loveliness of the spirit that all but descends to envelop him like a mother; but he is too poignantly aware of all sensuous beauty, too insistently haunted by the allurements of the flesh. A Freudian psychologist might call him an imperfectly sex-sublimated mystic. Girlish tenderness is masked by ruggedness. And his fuming self-torment is exteriorized by a diction that strains, and by a rhythmic flow that leaps or runs or stamps but never walks. . . .

FROM A REVIEW OF A. E. HOUSMAN, "LAST POEMS"*

A Shropshire Lad had in much of its imagery something cold, sharp, precipitated, something of the momentaneous power that we attribute to an unexpected rustle in dead leaves. There is less of this quality in *Last Poems*, but it is present. The first poem is full of it:

> The sun is down and drinks away
> From air and land the lees of day,
>
> The long cloud and the single pine
> Sentinel the ending line,
>
> Oh lad, I fear that yon's the sea
> Where they fished for you and me.

These strangenesses are not awkward, not sought. They have more suddenness than ingenuity; they suggest omens, possibly, rather than pictures. Even the slightly euphuistic passages ring true, such as:

> And let not yet the swimmer leave
> His clothes upon the sands of eve.

It is ungracious and pedagogical to contrast, to mark off epochs. Yet a brief glance at our current exasperation, the better to fix Mr. Housman for our envy, a cordial good-bye to what is no longer strictly ours, and a vain question will not be thought too heavy a load of analysis. For, having laid down the *Last Poems* and mused of the lad, we find ourselves automatically closing the little book—and the manner of its closing is a symbol—not curtly, with a businesslike indifference, nor too lingeringly, with many browsings back and forth between the reluctantly closing covers, but slowly and decisively. We should like to feel ourselves more excitedly in the midst of Mr. Housman's work, but it will not go. A truth that we nearly hate whispers to us that there is no use pretending, that these lines lilt too doggedly and too sweetly to fall in quite with our more exigent, half-undiscovered harmonies, that many of the magic turns catch us cruelly absent-minded. And, most disappointing of all, for we are a little disappointed, and vexed at being so,

* *The Dial*, 75 (1923): 188–191.

we cannot seem to pool Mr. Housman's pessimism with our own. We seem to feel that our zero does not equate with his, that each has a different mathematical "sense" tendency.

We discover, as we probe into our puzzling disaccord, that we already love the Shropshire lad as we love our Coleridge and our Blake and begin to divine that we were a little hasty in dating our modern drift from Mr. Housman's first volume. Its flare and its protest were a psychological, a temperamental, phenomenon, not a strictly cultural one. Its disillusionment was rooted in personality, not largely in a sensing of the proximate age. Hence while Mr. Housman seems to anticipate and now to join with us in our despair, he is serene and bitter where we are bitter and distraught. His cultural world was an accepted one, though he chose to deny its conscious values; our own perturbations, could they penetrate into the marrow of his bone, would not find him a sympathetic sufferer. In the larger perspective his best work is seen to be a highly personal culmination point in a poetic tradition that is thoroughly alien to us of to-day, and nothing demonstrates this more forcibly than the apparent backwash in some of the *Last Poems*. There is no backwash in spirit or in style, there is simply the lessened intensity that allows general, underlying cultural traits to emerge. His zero and our zero do not equate for the reason that his is personal where ours is cultural.

Finally, the vain question. Such work as Mr. Housman's, admirably simple and clear, classical, as it is, once more raises the doubt as to whether we can truly be said to be expressing ourselves until our moods become less frenetic, our ideas less palpable and self-conscious, and, above all, our forms less hesitant. Our eccentricities have much interest and diagnostic value to ourselves, but should it not be possible to cabin their power in forms that are at once more gracious and less discussible? One wonders whether there is not in store for English poetry some tremendous simplification. One prays for a Heine who may give us all our mordancies, all our harmonies, and our stirrings of new life with simpler and subtler apparatus. There is room for a new *Shropshire Lad*.

From a Review of Elsie Clews Parsons (ed.), "American Indian Life"*

From the strictly literary standpoint, the volume would probably have to be rated a *succès d'estime*, but the volume neither desires nor demands a strictly literary rating. It poses an interesting question. To what extent can we penetrate into the vitals of primitive life and fashion for

* *The Dial*, 73 (1922): 568–571.

ourselves satisfying pictures on its own level of reality? Can the conscious knowledge of the ethnologist be fused with the intuitions of the artist? It is difficult to think oneself into the tacit assumptions of so alien a mode of life as was that of an American Indian tribe. It is not that its patterns are elusive or unintelligible, for they are not, but that the attempt to sink these visible patterns into an atmosphere which is as unobtrusive as it is colourful demands an imagination of a peculiarly tolerant kind. Few artists possess so impassioned an indifference to the external forms of conduct as to absorb an exotic *milieu* only to dim its high visibility and to make room for those tracks of the individual consciousness which are the only true concern of literary art. It is precisely because the exotic is easily mistaken for subject, where it should be worked as texture, that much agreeable writing on glamorous quarters of the globe so readily surfeits a reader who possesses not merely an eye, but what used to be called a soul. There is always something sentimental and unelemental about a tapestry. Many literary travellers have taken their eyes with them and stitched their impressions into skilful embroideries; few have had the intensity to penetrate to those currents of life which make all backgrounds commonplace and acceptable. A favourite method of approach is to leave one's domestic morality behind. This is helpful so far as it goes, but perhaps the truest understanding would come from the donning of new and more tyrannous moralities.

From such a volume as *American Indian Life*, disarming in its modesty, we cannot fairly expect samples of the perfection that I have counseled and to which not even the exotic elements in *Lord Jim* and *The Heart of Darkness* have attained. And yet out of its pages there comes more than a hint of how compelling an imaginative treatment of primitive life might be. It would almost seem that the bare recital of the details of any mode of life that human beings have actually lived has a hidden power that transcends the skill or the awkwardness of the teller. There are passages in the book that suggest that a great deal might be done to capture the spirit of the primitive by adhering, so far as possible, to its letter—in other words, by transcribing, either literally or in simple paraphrase, personal experiences and other texts that have been written down or dictated by natives. In any event, the accent of authentic documents always reveals a significant, if intangible, something about native mentality that is over and above their content....

Part Three

THE INTERPLAY OF CULTURE AND PERSONALITY

THE INTERPLAY OF CULTURE AND PERSONALITY

EDITOR'S PREFACE

THESE PAPERS, *among the pioneering attempts in the field, have given direction to a significant segment of recent anthropological writing. Kluckhohn and Murray's comment that an anthology of studies on "culture and personality" without Sapir is like* Hamlet *without* Hamlet *tells something of the impress of this aspect of Sapir's work.*

The lead article of the section, "Cultural Anthropology and Psychiatry" (1932), sets the themes of the articles which follow, both those of earlier and of later authorship. The final paper of the section, "The Emergence of the Concept of Personality in a Study of Culture" (1934), can serve as a summary of Sapir's views concerning problems and program in the field of culture-personality studies. The other articles are arranged chronologically, in order to give some hint of the development of Sapir's ideas and interests in this field.

Thus the excerpts from the four book reviews which appeared between 1917 and 1923 give Sapir's earlier reactions to the ideas propounded by Freud and Rivers and Jung and his estimates of them. With "Speech as a Personality Trait" (1927) there is an examination, within Sapir's chosen field of language, of the validity of the commonly made differentiation between social and individual phenomena. Similar problems, but set in a wider field, are considered in "The Unconscious Patterning of Behavior in Society" (1927), a paper which has been termed one of Sapir's best statements of the culture-personality nexus.

The two articles from the Encyclopaedia of the Social Sciences, *"Personality" and "Symbolism" (1934), present a further crystallization of his ideas concerning personality and the interplay of personality and culture. Sapir had participated in two colloquiums on personality investigation held under the auspices of the American Psychiatric Association in 1928 and in 1930. His remarks in the published proceedings of those meetings are preliminary statements of these ideas—ideas which were also elaborated in his seminar on culture and personality conducted at Yale in 1932–1933 for a specially selected group of foreign fellows of the Rockefeller Foundation.*

"Why Cultural Anthropology Needs the Psychiatrist" (1938) appeared in a psychiatric journal, and is addressed to psychiatrists as well as to anthropologists, for, as the last passage of the paper notes, the kind of psychiatry which anthropology so greatly needs has not yet been evolved.

Another paper, not reprinted here, which deals with the place of psychiatry and psychology among the social sciences is "The Contribution of Psychiatry to an Understanding of Behavior in Society" (1937).

The problems of social science, the valid degrees of independence and of interdependence of the respective social sciences, are considered in "Psychiatric and Cultural Pitfalls in the Business of Getting a Living" (1939). This paper was written for a Symposium on Mental Health at the 1938 meeting of the American Association for the Advancement of Science, but its scope has to do with the "character of a true science of man." The postulates and the program for such a science were among Sapir's chief interests during the last years of his life.

CULTURAL ANTHROPOLOGY AND PSYCHIATRY*

BEFORE we try to establish a more intimate relation between the problems of cultural anthropology and those of psychiatry than is generally recognized, it will be well to emphasize the apparent differences of subject matter and purpose which seem to separate them as disciplines concerned with human behavior. In the main, cultural anthropology has emphasized the group and its traditions in contradistinction to individual variations of behavior. It aims to discover the generalized forms of action, thought, and feeling which, in their complex interrelatedness, constitute the culture of a community. Whether the ultimate aim of such a study is to establish a typical sequence of institutional forms in the history of man, or to work out a complete distributional survey of patterns and cultural types over the globe, or to make an exhaustive descriptive analysis of as many cultures as possible in order that fundamental sociological laws may be arrived at, is important, indeed, for the spirit and method of actual research in the field of human culture. But all these approaches agree in thinking of the individual as a more or less passive carrier of tradition or, to speak more dynamically, as the infinitely variable actualizer of ideas and of modes of behavior which are implicit in the structure and tradition of a given society. It is what all the individuals of a society have in common in their mutual relations which is supposed to constitute the true subject matter of cultural anthropology and sociology. If the testimony of an individual is set down as such, as often happens in our anthropological monographs, it is not because of an interest in the individual himself as a matured and single organism of ideas but in his assumed typicality for the community as a whole.

It is true that there are many statements in our ethnological monographs which, for all that they are presented in general terms, really rest on the authority of a few individuals, or even of one individual, who have had to bear testimony for the group as a whole. Information on kinship systems or rituals or technological processes or details of social organization or linguistic forms is not ordinarily evaluated by the cultural anthropologist as a personal document. He always hopes that the individual informant is near enough to the understandings and intentions of his society to report them duly, thereby implicitly eliminating himself as a factor in the method of research. All realistic field workers in native custom and belief are more or less aware of the dangers of such an

* *Journal of Abnormal and Social Psychology*, 27 (1932): 229–242.

assumption and, naturally enough, efforts are generally made to "check up" statements received from single individuals. This is not always possible, however, and so our ethnological monographs present a kaleidoscopic picture of varying degrees of generality, often within the covers of a single volume. Thus, that the Haida Indians of Queen Charlotte Islands were divided into two exogamic phratries, the Eagles and the Ravens, is a statement which could, no doubt, be elicited from any normal Haida Indian. It has very nearly the same degree of impersonality about it that characterizes the statement that the United States is a republic governed by a President. It is true that these data about social and political organization might mean rather different things in the systems of ideas and fantasies of different individuals or might, as master ideas, be construed to lead to typically different forms of action according to whether we studied the behavior of one individual or of another. But that is another matter. The fundamental patterns are relatively clear and impersonal. Yet in many cases we are not so fortunate as in the case of fundamental outlines of political organization or of kinship terminology or of house structure. What shall we do, for instance, with the cosmogenic system of the Bella Coola Indians of British Columbia? The five superimposed worlds which we learn about in this system not only have no close parallels among the other tribes of the Northwest Coast area but have not been vouched for by any informant other than the one individual from whom Boas obtained his information. Is this cosmogenic system typical Bella Coola religious belief? Is it individual fantasy construction or is it a peculiar individual elaboration on the basis of a simpler cosmogenic system which belongs to the community as a whole? In this special instance the individual note obtrudes itself somewhat embarrassingly. In the main, however, the cultural anthropologist believes or hopes that such disquieting interruptions to the impersonality of his thinking do not occur frequently enough to spoil his science.

Psychiatry is an offshoot of the medical tradition and aims to diagnose, analyze, and, if possible, cure those behavior disturbances of individuals which show to observation as serious deviations from the normal attitude of the individual toward his physical and social environment. The psychiatrist specializes in "mental" diseases as the dermatologist specializes in the diseases of the skin or the gynecologist concerns himself with diseases peculiar to women. The great difference between psychiatry and the other biologically defined medical disciplines is that, while the latter have a definite bodily locus to work with and have been able to define and perfect their methods by diligent exploration of the limited and tangible area of observation assigned to them, psychiatry is apparently

doomed to have no more definite locus than the total field of human behavior in its more remote or less immediately organic sense. The conventional companionship of psychiatry and neurology seems to be little
more than a declaration of faith by the medical profession that all human
ills are, at last analysis, of organic origin and that they are, or should be,
localizable in some segment, however complexly defined, of the physiological machine. It is an open secret, however, that the neurologist's
science is one thing and the psychiatrist's practice another. Almost in
spite of themselves psychiatrists have been forced to be content with an
elaborate array of clinical pictures, with terminological problems of
diagnosis, and with such thumb rules of clinical procedure as seem to
offer some hope of success in the handling of actual cases. It is no wonder
that psychiatry tends to be distrusted by its sister disciplines within the
field of medicine and that the psychiatrists themselves, worried by a
largely useless medical training and secretly exasperated by their inability to apply the strictly biological part of their training to their
peculiar problems, tend to magnify the importance of the biological
approach in order that they may not feel that they have strayed away
from the companionship of their more illustrious brethren. No wonder
that the more honest and sensitive psychiatrists have come to feel that
the trouble lies not so much in psychiatry itself as in the role which
general medicine has wished psychiatry to play.

Those insurgent psychiatrists, among whom Freud must be reckoned
the most courageous and the most fertile in ideas, have come to feel
that many of the so-called nervous and mental disorders can be looked
upon as the logical development of systems of ideas and feelings which
have grown up in the experience of the individual and which have an
unconscious value for him as the symbolic solution of profound difficulties that arise in an effort to adjust to his human environment. The
morbidity, in other words, that the psychiatrist has to deal with seems,
for the most part, to be not a morbidity of organic segments or even of
organic functions but of experience itself. His attempts to explain a
morbid suspiciousness of one's companions or delusion as to one's status
in society by some organically definable weakness of the nervous system
or of the functioning of the endocrine glands may be no more to the
point than to explain the habit of swearing by the absence of a few teeth
or by a poorly shaped mouth. This is not the place to go into an explanation, however brief, of the new points of view which are to be credited
to Freud and his followers and which have invaded the thinking of even
the most conservative of psychiatrists to no inconsiderable extent. All
that interests us here is to note the fact that psychiatry is moving away

from its historic position of a medical discipline that is chronically unable to make good to that of a discipline that is medical only by tradition and courtesy and is compelled, with or without permission, to attack fundamental problems of psychology and sociology so far as they affect the well-being of the individual. The locus, then, of psychiatry turns out not to be the human organism at all in any fruitful sense of the word but the more intangible, and yet more intelligible, world of human relationships and ideas that such relationships bring forth. Those students of medicine who see in these trends little more than a return to the old mythology of the "soul" are utterly unrealistic, for they tacitly assume that all experience is but the mechanical sum of physiological processes lodged in isolated individuals. This is no more defensible a position than the naïvely metaphysical contention that a table or chair or hat or church can be intelligibly defined in terms of their molecular and atomic constitution. That A hates B or hopelessly loves B or is jealous of B or is mortally afraid of B or hates him in one respect and loves him in another can result only from the complications of experience. If we work out a gradually complicating structure of morbid relationships between A and B and, by successive transfers, between A or B and the rest of the human world, we discover behavior patterns that are none the less real and even tragic for not being fundamentally attributable to some weakness or malfunctioning of the nervous system or any other part of the organism. This does not mean that weakness or malfunctioning of a strictly organic character may not result from a morbidity of human relationships. Such an organic theory would be no more startling than to maintain that a chronic sneer may disfigure the shape of the mouth or that a secret fear may impair one's digestion. There are, indeed, signs that psychiatry, slowly and painfully delivering itself from the somatic superstitions of medicine, may take its revenge by attempts to "mentalize" large sections of medical theory and practice. The future alone can tell how much of these psychological interpretations of organic disease is sound doctrine or a new mythology.

There is reason, then, to think that while cultural anthropology and psychiatry have distinct problems to begin with, they must, at some point, join hands in a highly significant way. That culture is a superorganic, impersonal whole is a useful enough methodological principle to begin with but becomes a serious deterrent in the long run to the more dynamic study of the genesis and development of cultural patterns because these cannot be realistically disconnected from those organizations of ideas and feelings which constitute the individual. The ultimate methodological error of the student of personality is perhaps less obvious than the correlative error of the student of culture but is all the more insidious and dangerous for that reason. Mechanisms which are unconsciously evolved by the neurotic or psychotic are by no means closed systems imprisoned within the biological walls of isolated individuals. They are tacit commentaries on the validity or invalidity of some of the more intimate implications of culture for the adjustment processes of given individuals. We are not, therefore, to begin with a simple contrast between social patterns and individual behavior, whether normal or abnormal, but we are, rather, to ask what is the meaning of culture in terms of individual behavior and whether the individual can, in a sense, be looked upon as the effective carrier of the culture of his group. As we follow tangible problems of behavior rather than the selected problems set by recognized disciplines, we discover the field of social psychology, which is not a whit more social than it is individual and which is, or should be, the mother science from which stem both the abstracted impersonal problems as phrased by the cultural anthropologist and the almost impertinently realistic explorations into behavior which are the province of the psychiatrist. Be it remarked in passing that what passes for individual psychology is little more than an ill-assorted mélange of bits of physiology and of studies of highly fragmentary modes of behavior which have been artificially induced by the psychologist. This abortive discipline seems to be able to arrive at no integral conceptions of either individual or society and one can only hope that it will eventually surrender all its problems to physiology and social psychology.

Cultural anthropology has not been neglected by psychiatry. The psychoanalysts in particular have made very extensive use of the data of cultural anthropology in order to gather evidence in support of their theories of the supposed "racial inheritance of ideas" by the individual. Neurotic and psychotic, through the symbolic mechanisms which control their thinking, are believed to regress to a more primitive state of mental adjustment than is normal in modern society and which is supposed to be preserved for our observation in the institutions of primitive peoples. In some undefined way which it seems quite impossible to express in intelligible biological or psychological terms the cultural experiences which have been accumulated by primitive man are believed to be unconsciously handed on to his more civilized progeny. The resemblances between the content of primitive ritual—and symbolic behavior generally among primitive peoples—and the apparently private rituals and symbolisms developed by those who have greater than normal difficulty in adjusting to their social environment are said to be so numerous and far-reaching that the latter must be looked upon as an inherited survival of more archaic types of thought and feeling. Hence, we are told, it is very useful to study the culture of primitive man, for in this way an enormous amount of light is thrown upon the fundamental significance of modes of behavior in the neurotic which are otherwise inexplicable. The searching clinical investigation into the symbolisms of the neurotic recovers for us, on a modern and highly disguised level, what lies but a little beneath the surface among the primitives, who are still living under an archaic psychological régime.

Psychoanalysts welcome the contributions of cultural anthropology but it is exceedingly doubtful if many cultural anthropologists welcome the particular spirit in which the psychoanalysts appreciate their data. The cultural anthropologist can make nothing of the hypothesis of the racial unconscious nor is he disposed to allow an immediate psychological analysis of the behavior of primitive people in any other sense than that in which such an analysis is allowable for our own culture. He believes that it is as illegitimate to analyze totemism or primitive laws of inheritance or set rituals in terms of the peculiar symbolisms discovered or invented by the psychoanalyst as it would be to analyze the most complex forms of modern social behavior in these terms. And he is disposed to think that if the resemblances between the neurotic and the primitive which have so often been pointed out are more than fortuitous, it is not because of a cultural atavism which the neurotic exemplifies but simply because all human beings, whether primitive or sophisticated in the cultural sense, are, at rock bottom, psychologically primitive, and there is no reason why a significant unconscious symbolism which gives substitutive satisfaction to the individual may not become socialized on any level of human activity.

The service of cultural anthropology to psychiatry is not as mysterious or remote or clandestine as psychoanalytic mysticism would have us believe. It is of a much simpler and healthier sort. It lies very much nearer the surface of things than is generally believed. Cultural anthropology, if properly understood, has the healthiest of all scepticisms about the validity of the concept "normal behavior." It cannot deny the useful tyranny of the normal in a given society but it believes the external form of normal adjustment to be an exceedingly elastic thing. It is very doubtful if the normalities of any primitive society that lies open to inspection are nearer the hypothetical responses of an archaic type of man, untroubled by a burdensome historical past, than the normalities of a modern Chinese or Scotchman. In specific instances one may even wonder whether they are not tangibly less so. It would be more than a joke to turn the tables and to suggest that the psychoanalysis of an over-ritualized Pueblo Indian or Toda might denude him sufficiently to set him "regressing" to the psychologically primitive status of an American professor's child or a professor himself. The cultural anthropologist's quarrel with psychoanalysis can perhaps be put most significantly by pointing out that the psychoanalyst has confused the archaic in the conceptual or theoretical psychologic sense with the archaic in the literal chronological sense. Cultural anthropology is not valuable because it uncovers the archaic in the psychological sense. It is valuable because it is constantly rediscovering the normal. For the psychiatrist and for the student of personality in general this is of the greatest importance, for personalities are not conditioned by a generalized process of adjustment to "the normal" but by the necessity of adjusting to the greatest possible variety of idea patterns and action patterns according to the accidents of birth and biography.

The so-called culture of a group of human beings, as it is ordinarily treated by the cultural anthropologist, is essentially a systematic list of all the socially inherited patterns of behavior which may be illustrated in the actual behavior of all or most of the individuals of the group. The true locus, however, of these processes which, when abstracted into a totality, constitute culture is not in a theoretical community of human beings known as society, for the term "society" is itself a cultural construct which is employed by individuals who stand in significant relations to each other in order to help them in the interpretation of certain aspects of their behavior. The true locus of culture is in the interactions of specific individuals and, on the subjective side, in the world of meanings which each one of these individuals may unconsciously abstract for himself from his participation in these interactions. Every individual is, then, in a very real sense, a representative of at least one sub-culture which may be abstracted from the generalized culture of the group of which he is a member. Frequently, if not typically, he is a representative of more than one sub-culture, and the degree to which the socialized behavior of any given individual can be identified with or abstracted from the typical or generalized culture of a single group varies enormously from person to person.

It is impossible to think of any cultural pattern or set of cultural patterns which can, in the literal sense of the word, be referred to society as such. There are no facts of political organization or family life or religious belief or magical procedure or technology or aesthetic endeavor which are coterminous with society or with any mechanically or sociologically defined segment of society. The fact that John Doe is registered in some municipal office as a member of such and such a ward only vaguely defines him with reference to those cultural patterns which are conveniently assembled under some such term as "municipal administration." The psychological and, in the deepest sense of the word, the cultural realities of John Doe's registration may, and do, vary enormously. If John Doe is paying taxes on a house which is likely to keep him a resident of the ward for the rest of his life and if he also happens to be in personal contact with a number of municipal officers, ward classification may easily become a symbol of his orientation in his world of meanings which is comparable for clarity, if not for importance, to his definition as a father of a family or as a frequent participant in golf. Ward membership, for such an individual, may easily precipitate itself into many visible forms of behavior. The ward system and its functions, real or supposed, may for such a John Doe assume an impersonal and objective reality which is comparable to the objective reality of rain or sunshine.

But there is sure to be another John Doe, perhaps a neighbor of the first, who does not even know that the town is divided into wards and that he is, by definition, enrolled in one of them and that he has certain duties and privileges connected with such enrollment, whether he cares to exercise them or not. While the municipal office classifies these two John Does in exactly the same way and while there is a theory on foot that ward organization, with its associated functions, is an entirely impersonal matter to which all members of a given society must adjust, it is rather obvious that such a manner of speech is little more than a sociological metaphor. The cultures of these two individuals are, as a matter of fact, significantly different, as significantly different, on the given level and scale, as though one were the representative of Italian culture and the other of Turkish culture. Such differences of culture never seem as significant as they really are; partly because in the workaday world of experience they are not often given the opportunity to emerge into sharp consciousness, partly because the economy of interpersonal relations and the friendly ambiguities of language conspire to reinterpret for each individual all behavior which he has under observation in the terms of those meanings which are relevant to his own life. The concept of culture, as it is handled by the cultural anthropologist, is necessarily something of a statistical fiction and it is easy to see that the social psychologist and the psychiatrist must eventually induce him to carefully reconsider his terms. It is not the concept of culture which is subtly misleading but the metaphysical locus to which culture is generally assigned.

Clearly, not all cultural traits are of equal importance for the development of personality, for not all of them are equally diffused as integral elements in the idea-systems of different individuals. Some modes of behavior and attitude are pervasive and compelling beyond the power of even the most isolated individual to withstand or reject. Such patterns would be, for example, the symbolisms of affection or hostility; the overtones of emotionally significant words; certain fundamental implications and many details of the economic order; much, but by no means all, of those understandings and procedures which constitute the law of the land. Patterns of this kind are compulsive for the vast majority of human beings but the degree of compulsiveness is in no simple relation to the official, as contrasted with the inner or psychological, significance of these patterns. Thus, the use of an offensive word may be of negligible importance from a legal standpoint but may, psychologically considered, have an attracting or repelling potency that far transcends the significance of so serious a behavior pattern as, say, embezzlement or the nature of one's scientific thinking. A culture as a whole cannot be said to be adequately known for purposes of personality study until the varying degrees of compulsiveness which attach to its many aspects and implications are rather definitely understood. No doubt there are cultural patterns which tend to be universal, not only in form but in psychological significance, but it is very easy to be mistaken in those matters and to impute equivalences of meaning which do not truly exist.

There are still other cultural patterns which are real and compelling only for special individuals or groups of individuals and are as good as non-existent for the rest of the group. Such, for instance, are the ideas, attitudes, and modes of behavior which belong to specialized trades. We are all aware of the reality of such private or limited worlds of meaning. The dairy-man, the movie actress, the laboratory physicist, the party whip, have obviously built up worlds which are anonymous or opaque to each other or, at best, stand to each other in a relation of blanket acceptance. There is much tacit mythology in such hugely complex societies as our own which makes it possible for the personal significance of sub-cultures to be overlooked. For each individual, the commonly accepted fund of meanings and values tends to be powerfully specialized or emphasized or contradicted by types of experience and modes of interpretation that are far from being the property of all men. If we consider that these specialized cultural participations are partly the result of contact with limited traditions and techniques, partly the result of identification with such biologically and socially imposed groups as the family or the class in school or the club, we can begin to see how inevitable it is that the true psychological locus of a culture is *the indi-*

vidual or *a specifically enumerated list of individuals*, not an economically or politically or socially defined group of individuals. "Individual," however, here means not simply a biologically defined organism maintaining itself through physical impacts and symbolic substitutes of such impacts, but that total world of form, meaning, and implication of symbolic behavior which a given individual partly knows and directs, partly intuits and yields to, partly is ignorant of and is swayed by.

Still other cultural patterns have neither a generalized nor a specialized potency. They may be termed marginal or referential and while they may figure as conceptually important in the scheme of a cultural theorist, they may actually have little or no psychological importance for the normal human being. Thus, the force of linguistic analogy which creates the plural "unicorns" is a most important force for the linguistic analyst to be clear about, but it obvious that the psychological imminence of that force, while perfectly real, may be less than the avoidance, say, of certain obscene or impolite words, an avoidance which the linguist, in turn, may quite legitimately look upon as marginal to his sphere of interests. In the same way, while such municipal subdivisions as wards are, from the standpoint of political theory, of the same order as state lines and even national lines, they are not psychologically so. They are psychologically related to such saturated entities as New York or "the South" or Fifth Avenue or "the slums" as undeveloped property in the suburbs is economically related to real estate in the business heart of a great metropolis. Some of this marginal cultural property is held as marginal by the vast majority of participants in the total culture, if we may still speak in terms of a "total culture." Others of these marginal patterns are so only for certain individuals or groups of individuals. No doubt, to a movie actress the intense world of values which engages the participation of a physicist tends to be marginal in about the same sense as a legal fiction or unactualized linguistic possibility may be marginal cultural property. A "hard-headed business man" may consign the movie actress and the physicist to two adjoining sectors, "lively" and "sleepy" respectively, of a marginal tract of "triviality." Culture, then, varies infinitely, not only as to manifest content but as to the distribution of psychologic emphases on the elements and implications of this content. According to our scale of treatment, we have to deal with the cultures of groups and the cultures of individuals.

A personality is carved out by the subtle interaction of those systems of ideas which are characteristic of the culture as a whole, as well as of those systems of ideas which get established for the individual through more special types of participation, with the physical and psychological needs of the individual organism, which cannot take over any of the cultural material that is offered in its original form but works it over more or less completely, so that it integrates with those needs. The more closely we study this interaction, the more difficult it becomes to distinguish society as a cultural and psychological unit from the individual who is thought of as a member of the society to whose culture he is required to adjust. No problem of social psychology that is at all realistic can be phrased by starting with the conventional contrast of the individual and his society. Nearly every problem of social psychology needs to consider the exact nature and implication of an idea complex, which we may look upon as the psychological correlate of the anthropologist's cultural pattern, to work out its relation to other idea complexes and what modifications it necessarily undergoes as it accommodates itself to these, and, above all, to ascertain the precise locus of such a complex. This locus is rarely identifiable with society as a whole, except in a purely philosophical or conceptual sense, nor is it often lodged in the psyche of a single individual. In extreme cases such an idea complex or cultural pattern may be the dissociated segment of a single individual's mind or it may amount to no more than a potential revivification of ideas in the mind of a single individual through the aid of some such symbolic depositary as a book or museum. Ordinarily the locus will be a substantial portion of the members of a community, each of them feeling that he is touching common interests so far as this particular culture pattern is concerned. We have learned that the individual in isolation from society is a psychological fiction. We have not had the courage to face the fact that formally organized groups are equally fictitious in the psychological sense, for geographically contiguous groups are merely a first approximation to the infinitely variable groupings of human beings to whom culture in its various aspects is actually to be credited as a matter of realistic psychology.

"Adjustment," as the term is ordinarily understood, is a superficial concept because it regards only the end product of individual behavior as judged from the standpoint of the requirements, real or supposed, of a particular society. In reality "adjustment" consists of two distinct and even conflicting types of process. It includes, obviously, those accommodations to the behavior requirements of the group without which the individual would find himself isolated and ineffective, but it includes, just as significantly, the effort to retain and make felt in the opinions and attitudes of others that particular cosmos of ideas and values which has grown up more or less unconsciously in the experience of the individual. Ideally these two adjustment tendencies need to be compromised into behavior patterns which do justice to both requirements.

It is a dangerous thing for the individual to give up his identification with such cultural patterns as have come to symbolize for him his own personality integration. The task of external adjustment to social needs may require such abandonment on his part and consciously he may crave nothing more passionately, but if he does not wish to invite disharmony and inner weakness in his personality, he must see to it, consciously or unconsciously, that every abandonment is made good by the acquisition of a psychologically equivalent symbolism. External observations on the adjustment processes of individuals are often highly misleading as to their psychological significance. The usual treatment, for instance, of behavior tendencies known as radical and conservative must leave the genuine psychiatrist cold because he best realizes that the same types of behavior, judged externally, may have entirely distinct, even contradictory, meanings for different individuals. One may be a conservative out of fear or out of superb courage. A radical may be such because he is so secure in his fundamental psychic organization as to have no fear for the future, or, on the contrary, his courage may be merely the fantasied rebound from fear of the only too well known.

Strains which are due to this constant war of adjustment are by no means of equal intensity for all individuals. Systems of ideas grew up in endless ways, both within a so-called uniform culture and through the blending of various aspects of so-called distinct cultures, and very different symbolisms and value emphases necessarily arise in the endless subcultures or private symbol organizations of the different members of a group. This is tantamount to saying that certain systems of ideas are more perilously exposed to the danger of disintegration than others. Even if it be granted, as no one would seriously argue that it should not, that individual differences of an inherited sort are significantly responsible for mental breakdowns, it yet remains true that such a "failure" in the life of an individual cannot be completely understood by the study, however minute, of the individual's body and mind as such. Such a failure invites a study of his system of ideas as a more or less distinct cultural entity which has been vainly striving to maintain itself in a discouraging environment.

We may go so far as to suggest quite frankly that a psychosis, for instance, may be an index at one and the same time of the too great resistance of the individual to the forces that play upon him and, so far as *his* world of values is concerned, of the cultural poverty of his psychological environment. The more obvious conflicts of cultures with which we are familiar in the modern world create an uneasiness which forms a fruitful soil for the eventual development, in particular cases, of neurotic symptoms and mental breakdowns but they can hardly be considered sufficient to account for serious psychological derangements. These arise

not on the basis of a generalized cultural conflict but out of specific conflicts of a more intimate sort, in which systems of ideas get attached to
particular persons, or images of such persons, who play a decisive role in
the life of the individual as representative of cultural values.

The personal meanings of the symbolisms of an individual's sub-
culture are constantly being reaffirmed by society or, at the least, he
likes to think that they are. When they obviously cease to be, he loses his
orientation and that strange instinct, or whatever we call it, which in
the history of culture has always tended to preserve a system of ideas
from destruction, causes his alienation from an impossible world. Both
the psychosis and the development of an idea or institution through the
centuries manifest the stubbornness of idea complexes and their implications in the face of a material environment which is less demanding
psychologically than physically. The mere problem of biological adjustment, or even of ego adjustment as it is ordinarily handled by the
sociologist, is comparatively simple. It is literally true that "man wants
but little here below nor wants that little long." The trouble always is
that he wants that little on his own terms. It is not enough to satisfy
one's material wants, to have success in one's practical endeavors, to give
and receive affection, or to accomplish any of the purposes laid down by
psychologists and sociologists and moralists. Personality organizations,
which at last analysis are psychologically comparable with the greatest
cultures or idea systems, have as their first law of being their essential
self-preservation, and all conscious attempts to define their functions or
to manipulate their intention and direction are but the estimable rationalization of people who are wanting to "do things." Modern psychiatrists
should be tolerant not only of varying personalities but of the different
types of values which personality variations imply. Psychiatrists who are
tolerant only in the sense that they refrain from criticizing anybody
who is subjected to their care and who do their best to guide him back
to the renewed performance of society's rituals may be good practical
surgeons of the psyche. They are not necessarily the profoundly sympathetic students of the mind who respect the fundamental intent and
direction of every personality organization.

Perhaps it is not too much to expect that a number of gifted psychiatrists may take up the serious study of exotic and primitive cultures,
not in the spirit of meretricious voyaging in behalf of Greenwich Village
nor to collect an anthology of psychoanalytic fairy tales, but in order to
learn to understand, more fully than we can out of the resources of our
own cultures, the development of ideas and symbols and their relevance
for the problem of personality.

EXCERPTS FROM REVIEWS

From a Review of Oskar Pfister, "The Psychoanalytic Method"*

THE FREUDIAN psychology has traveled a course that might have been predicted with tolerable certainty. At first received with mingled derision and disgust, it has now attained a position not only of virtual security but, one is almost tempted to say unfortunately, of very genuine and widespread popularity. Whitmanesque poets sing paeans to Jung's libido, one of the metaphysical offshoots of the psychoanalytic movement, while half-baked doctors fearlessly disentangle homosexual "complexes" at the end of a first half-hour's consultation with hysterical patients. Those who are profoundly convinced of the epoch-making importance of the psychological mechanisms revealed by Freud and, even more, of the extraordinary suggestiveness of numerous lines of inquiry opened up by psychoanalysis, without, at the same time, being blind to criticisms that need to be made of certain psychoanalytic theory, can only hope and pray that this not altogether healthy overpopularity of the subject prove no hindrance to the study of the perplexing problems with which the Freudian psychology bristles. What is sorely needed at the present time, or will be before many years, is a thoroughly objective probing into the new psychology with a special view to seeking out the paths of reconciliation with the older orthodox psychology of conscious states and to the rigorous elimination of all aspects of Freudian theory that seem dispensable or ill-substantiated. The present militant attitude of the psychoanalysts toward their skeptical schoolmasters is naturally but a passing phase. The opposed schools of psychological interpretation will have to meet each other halfway and effect a common *modus vivendi*.

For the present it is obvious that the personal bias of the brilliant founder of psychoanalysis has given the Freudian psychology more than one twist that is not altogether necessitated by its invaluable kernel—the proof of the existence in the unconscious mind of emotionally toned "complexes," repressed trends that are directly elaborated out of the instinctive life and that leak out into consciousness in a large number of superficially dissimilar psychic phenomena, for example, dreams, automatic and compulsive reactions, neurotic symptoms. A firm belief in the validity of the main lines of psychological theory set forth by Freud by no means necessitates an unreserved adherence to such incidental con-

* *The Dial*, 63 (1917): 267–269.

comitants as his apparently one-sided interpretation of sexual perversions or his general conception of the compound nature of the sexual instinct. At the least, very radical shiftings of emphasis are certain to emerge. An analogous development has characterized the history of the theory of organic evolution. Only recently has the original Darwinian bias toward an overemphasis of the factor of natural selection yielded to the proper evaluation of other factors. The inertia of impetus given by the founder of a radical scientific departure is, indeed, one of the most humiliating, one of the most ironically human, things about the history of science. So far there seems to be a disposition on the part of psychoanalysts to accept the whole Freudian programme at practically its face value. What criticism there is within the ranks is chiefly on matters of relatively minor import. Even the Jung sedition, of which so much is made, consists of hardly more, it would seem, than a tendency to generalize and carry further some of the more doubtful elements of Freud's theoretical groundwork. I refer particularly to Jung's handling of symbolization as an interpretative principle and to his reckless application of the principles of individual psychoanalysis to cultural phenomena . . . .

Let us turn, now, to the theoretical structure reared by the psychoanalysts. We are entitled to ask: Leaving all questions of analytic detail and technique to one side, what are some of the basic contributions of the Freudian school to psychologic thinking? First and foremost, I should say, is the new spirit of attitude and method that psychoanalysis has introduced into the study of the mind. The orthodox psychology, for all its disavowal of the older faculty-mongering, has never really succeeded in grasping the vast network of individual mental phenomena as a single growth rooting in the most primitive type of mental life we know of, the instinctive life. It would be too much to say that psychoanalysis has succeeded in reconstructing the order of differentiation of mental phenomena, but it has taken a more patient attitude toward the actual dynamics of the individual mind and is thus in a better position to ferret out gradually the development of the fundamental instincts into the higher forms of mentality. Psychoanalysis takes hold of chunks of mental life as they present themselves in experience; it does not abstract driblets of mental experience for the purpose of classifying them and examining them under the microscope. In brief, the older psychology is an anatomy of mind, sometimes refined; psychoanalysis is an entering wedge toward a physiology of mind, generally quite crude for the present. From the clear recognition of this difference of method results the conviction that the two types of psychologic inquiry are not in any true sense opposed to each other. They merely attack their subject-matter from distinct viewpoints. They will, each of them, in the long run be found to be indispensable and mutually reconcilable.

The second point of capital importance that we must set down to the credit of psychoanalysis is the light it has thrown on the nature and functioning of the unconscious. To psychoanalysis the unconscious is not merely a negative *deus ex machina* which does convenient service in the explanation of memory and in the positing of a continuity of personality. It is a very real and active domain from which are worked the strings that move about the puppets of the conscious self. The naïve assumption of a self-contained consciousness whose motivation is safely interpretable in terms of conscious data alone has been exposed by the Freudian psychology as a huge fallacy.

One of the most interesting and promising vistas that have been opened up, though I find it but little stressed by the psychoanalysts themselves, is the quantitative consideration of emotion and will. I am not referring to the measuring of reactions under controlled experimental conditions. When psychoanalysis tells us that the emotion belonging to a certain trend is not always discharged in consciousness but may in part be inhibited in the unconscious or transferred to other reactions, we are evidently confronted by certain quantitative implications. It seems difficult to avoid the inference of a certain specific, theoretically measurable, sum of emotion or volitional impulse which can be divided up and distributed in a great variety of ways. The elaboration of the concepts that follow on the heels of this hypothesis has been but begun. It would not be surprising if this glimmer of a quantitative understanding of mental functioning blossomed out in time to an exactness of comprehension of psychological processes such as we have hardly an inkling of at present.

Among the more readily defined and generally recognized insights that we owe, directly or indirectly, to Freud are the genetic analysis and the treatment of the neuroses, to a much smaller extent also of the psychoses (forms of insanity); the frequency and radical importance of symbol-formation in the unconscious mind, understanding of which is sure to prove indispensable for an approach to the deeper problems of religion and art; the analysis and interpretation of dreams; the basic importance of the psychic sexual constitution, not merely in its proper functional sphere, but also in connections that seem unrelated; the far-reaching importance of infantile psychic experiences in adult life and the ever-present tendency to regression to them; and the general light thrown on the problem of mental determinism. Many other points might be enumerated, some clearly defined, others controversial. Indeed, there has scarcely ever been a new road opened in science that so spontaneously and fruitfully branched out into tributary trails. It is true that hardly anything is known of the psychoanalytic problems and solutions with absolutely satisfying clarity. Yet it takes no bold man to assert that enough has been glimpsed to promise perhaps the greatest fructification that the study of the mind has yet experienced.

From a Review of H. A. Alexander, "The Mythology of All Races, Vol. XI: Latin-American"*

The psychoanalysts latterly have pushed myth, primitive taboo, and other spiritual vagaries of the folk into the foreground of attention. This is therefore as good an opportunity as any of touching upon some of the fundamental points at issue. What shall we make of all these myths? Are these plumed serpents, swallowing monsters, virginal births, and deluges of no other than casual significance? Why do so many of these conceptions persist with an almost obsessive tenacity and why are so many of them world-wide in their distribution?

There are two methods of approach, the psychological and the historical. The psychologist takes a given myth pretty much for granted as a reasonably self-consistent psychic formation. It does not readily occur to him, for instance, to question whether character and incident have always been associated or whether the grouping of incidents is not a cumulative growth, a pastiche of elements that originally existed in independent form. If once he allowed himself to entertain destructive notions of this sort, he would gradually have his data slipping from under his hand. His psychological formulas of interpretation might be ever so relevant, but they would be helpless salt for the tails of mythic birds. Just as biblical mythology fitted into a neat exegetical frame until the advent of a higher criticism, so the successful application of these psychological formulas, Wundtian or Freudian, to any myth structure tacitly depends on the withholding of a preliminary historical critique. We can only begin to interpret when we have come to the end of our analysis.

The historical student of myth insists on destructive analysis. He is not content to take a myth as it is. He finds that it is generally a synthesis of several elements, each of which has its own historical antecedents, its independent affiliations. The same element may occur in the most diverse settings, pointing to mutually irreconcilable significances. Over and above, or rather beneath, the geographical distribution of myths as such he can work out the more pervasive distribution of the elements, the

* *The Nation*, 112 (1921): 88-890.

materials that are assembled into an endless variety of myth patterns. To the interpretative psychologist he can always put the question: How do you know that this myth or even this fragmentary episode is in any true sense a single psychic creation? How can you establish a psychic sequence underlying the myth when the association of its elements is historically fortuitous?

The crux is not sharp because historian and psychologist fall somewhat foul of each other. Obviously, history and psychology are not born enemies, they are such only in action. They could come to terms if they came truly to grips instead of scolding at each other over a barrier of misunderstanding. The historian too often believes that he has exhausted the significance of a phenomenon when he has established its place in a sequence, worked out its external relations, and indicated its lease of life. He dismisses the psychologist's fancies as irrelevant to the historical process, though he may enjoy them as projections of an imaginative mind. To the charge that his history gives no ultimate explanation of the rise and development of a myth or of any other socialized notion or institution, he is likely to answer that it is none of history's business to ferret out the buried psychological determinants of the significant elements of a culture, that these determinants are at last analysis highly variable phenomena of individual psychology, that it is hopeless to disentangle them at a remove of hundreds or thousands of years.

All this does not and should not silence the psychologist who looks for a specifically psychological motivation and content in mythology. Before he fastens upon these, however, he should more clearly apprehend the difficulties in his way. Two problems in particular must be faced. At what point in the analysis of a myth does the psychological mode of interpretation become possible or even hopeful? And, secondly, how can we advance from the known psychology of the individual to that diffused psychological content that inheres or seems to inhere in the myth as a socially transmitted entity? What, precisely, does it mean that certain myths, historical growths of the "folk mind," exhibit analogies to individual dreams or to the deranged fancies of abnormal minds? Have they —as history, as institutions—necessarily the same unconscious psychic significance that they may possess as dream or as psychotic symptom? Does the history of the cross as an art motif run strictly parallel to the history of the cross as a religious symbol? Does either history fully contain or explain the other, or are they not rather independent though intertwined? And is the psychic significance of the cross the same to all minds, even to all believing minds? To ask these parallel questions is, I believe, to see the psychology of myth in a fresher and more fruitful light.

The psychologist is right to seek psychology in myth, but his interpretations may be none the less misleading because of his historical naïveté. The truth would seem to be that there is not one psychology of mythology but that there are at least two such psychologies. One of these is concerned with the ultimate psychic determinants of cultural form. This is at bottom the same selective and creative psychology as operates in the history of art. Myths are not isolated formations. They differ characteristically for different times and places largely because they tend to conform to certain typical patterns. To assume that these characteristic differences are directly due to deep-seated differences of psychology of the myth-making folk is too naïve for serious consideration. The cumulative psychology of myth as a particular social pattern is the kind of psychology that the historian of myth would most need to know about, yet it is the one that the psychologist is least able to render an account of. It is the psychology which will some day underlie the study of all culture-history, for it manifests itself across the generations in a persistent striving for and perfecting of form, eventually in the disintegration and replacement of this form. To capture the very citadel of the psychoanalysts, we may say that the first requisite of a psychological understanding of mythology—of other phases of culture as well—is the discovery of a social psychology of "form-libido." Psychology is still too weak to know how to go about the task. In the beginning a science is qualitative, almost exclusively concerned with subject matter; only later does it envisage its problems mathematically and apprehend quantities, direction, form.

The second psychology of myth deals with the psychic significance, conscious or unconscious, of the single elements of mythology. Now if the history of culture teaches us anything, it is that while forms tend to persist, the psychic significance of these forms varies tremendously from age to age and from individual to individual. There is no permanence of psychic content. This content may diminish or increase in intensity or it may become completely transformed. It may be transferred from one form to another, and it is the psychoanalysts who should know this best of all. I believe that to reason from the "latent psychic content" of certain dreams or neurotic symptoms to the psychic motivation of formally analogous myths is loose thinking. Symbols, like other accepted forms, are ready to receive whatever psychic content the individual psychology or the social psychology of a given time and place is prepared to put into them. Myths may or may not have been motivated by certain unconscious psychic trends, but it is difficult to understand how they could indefinitely keep their significance as symbols of these trends. It seems much more reasonable to suppose that there is in myth no such constancy of symbolic significance as many of the psychoanalytic school assume but that the history of myth can be chiefly understood from the standpoint of the more general psychology of form-trends. Sexual or other symbolisms are likely, of course, to arise as secondary interpretations or unconscious contributory potencies in the mind of an individual, or by suggestion, of a society. Origin is not to be lightly inferred from the mere fact of unconscious association.

From a Review of W. H. R. Rivers, "Instinct and the Unconscious: A Contribution to a Biological Theory of the Psycho-Neuroses"*

Dr. Rivers worked exclusively with war-patients, in whom the psychic conflict underlying the neurosis was presumably connected with the instinctive activities that tend to preserve the organism in the presence of danger. Such typical neuroses as hysteria and Dr. Freud's "anxiety-neurosis" are here seen as morbid responses to danger which dodge the frank impulse to flight without leading to an acceptance by the organism of the effective aggression necessary to survival.

The neurotic symptoms dealt with by Dr. Rivers in his war-work were far too similar to those that Dr. Freud and other psycho-analysts had ascribed to a sexual origin to justify us in considering his neuroses as fundamentally distinct from theirs. We are thus driven to conclude that either Dr. Freud's or Dr. Rivers's interpretation needs correction or amplification at the hands of the other. One may perhaps suggest that too much attention has been bestowed on the causative value of particular types of "complexes," that the frustrated instincts that underlie these complexes are by no means the neatly sundered reaction-systems that they appear to be in psychological discussions, and that the ultimate physiological cause of the neurosis will be found to rest in the particular pattern of nervous activity implicit in the individual organism. This pattern may be conceived of as always in operation and as showing up in a morbid form when certain of its elements have been intensified under the stress of emotion.

All individuals have conflicts of the types that are held responsible for a neurosis, whence it seems to follow that the differentiating factor in a neurosis must be of a quantitative nature. Certain nervous patterns allow of a greater give than others, without essential loss of form. We can hardly hope to understand the rationale of suppression and neurosis until we have a theory of what actually happens to a nervous impulse in

* *The Freeman*, 5 (1921): 357–358.

terms of relative quantity, speed, acceleration, and diffusion, until, in other words, we can actually lay out the typical nervous rhythms of the individual organism.

Meanwhile, Dr. Rivers's book does undoubtedly indicate that Dr. Freud and his immediate followers have entirely overdone the necessity of sexual elements in conflicts powerful enough to bring on a neurosis, though it probably remains true that the sexual conflict is one of the most potent strains that the human organism can be made to bear. The really valuable contribution of the Freudian school seems to me to lie in the domain of pure psychology. Nearly everything that is specific in Freudian theory, such as the "Œdipus-complex" as a normative image or the definite interpretation of certain symbols or the distinctively sexual nature of certain infantile reactions, may well prove to be either ill-founded or seen in a distorted perspective, but there can be little doubt of the immense service that Dr. Freud has rendered psychology in his revelation of typical psychic mechanisms. Such relational ideas as the emotionally integrated complex, the tendency to suppression under the stress of a conflict, the symptomatic expression of a suppressed impulse, the transfer of emotion and the canalizing or pooling of impulses, the tendency to regression, are so many powerful clues to an understanding of how the "soul" of man sets to work. Psychology will not willingly let go of these and still other Freudian concepts, but will build upon them, gradually coming to see them in their wider significance. Dr. Rivers helps us in this appreciation not so much explicitly as implicitly. His new types of experience, his alternative hypotheses, and his general insistence on mechanism at the expense of typical content give us the invaluable touchstone of contrast.

FROM A REVIEW OF C. G. JUNG, "PSYCHOLOGICAL TYPES"*

Not until the last page is turned back does one fully realize how extraordinary a work one has been reading. It is often dry, it is sometimes impossible to follow, and it is never very closely reasoned, for Dr. Jung accepts intuitively as given, as elementary, concepts and psychological functions which others can get at only by the most painful of syntheses, if indeed they can find a way to some of them at all. But it is a fascinating book. Its one idea is like the intense stare of a man who has found something, and this something a little uncanny. Some of us are extraverts or tend to be so, and others of us are introverts or tend to be so: surely there is nothing strange or uncanny or new about this classification of

* *The Freeman*, 8 (1923): 211–212.

personalities. That some of us are interested in the accidents and particularities of the environment is a known fact; that others are more interested in general ideas and that they tend to turn inward, to reflect and introspect, is an equally well-known fact. Surely there are more basic distinctions than these; the emotional *v.* the intellectual type, for instance. But to reduce Dr. Jung's antithesis to a mere difference in the relative emphasis of interest or in the habitual direction of attention is not to have fully grasped his meaning. It is not a mere question of interest at all.

It is a question of the natural flow of the libido, to speak in the author's terms. The ego finds itself lost in an overwhelmingly potent and complex environment. Convulsively it seeks to save itself, to establish a set of relations and a network of presumptions which enable it to survive, to convince itself that it matters, to feel that it is ever victorious or about to become so. There are two ways of attaining this necessary understanding between the helplessness of the ego and the surrounding insistence of things, and these ways may not be chosen, aside from secondary compensations which obscure but do not efface the underlying psychology. They are dictated by the inherited mechanics of the libido. Whether these inherited differences in the impulse to adjustment are but psychic reinterpretations or summings-up of comparatively simple differences in the rhythmic form or intensity or rapidity or quality of nervous discharge, we do not at all know nor does it greatly matter.

The extravert saves himself by surrendering to the enemy. He refuses to be cowed by the object, to shrink back into a warm privacy of the mind. If he looks within, he is met by the cold cheer of blank walls and an untenanted room. Involuntarily he turns back to the object and becomes oblivious of all but the environment, material and spiritual. With this environment he identifies himself. To miss any of the substance or colour of the object is felt as a deprivation, for it is in the object that he realizes himself. All abstraction is more or less of an effort, if not actually painful, for it means being thrown back on a world, a system of evaluations, which is not prepared to receive him. To the genuine introvert, the extravert presents a spectacle at once amusing and baffling. He finds him feeding ravenously on the husks of reality, and he is a little piqued to discover that while the personality that he is contemplating has no "Pou sto" from which to become conscious of itself, it does nevertheless get about the universe in an alarmingly effective way. The introvert reflects that it pays to be naïve. To the introvert the object has always a shade of the inimical, the irrelevant, the unwarranted. It is not necessarily uninteresting, but it needs to be taken with a grain of salt.

The introvert has learned to adapt himself to reality by pruning it of its luxuriance, by seeing and by feeling no more in it than can be conveniently fitted into the richly chambered form of his ego. While he can not afford to ignore the object, he can translate or interpret it, minimize it, if need be, by some method of abstraction which takes most of the sting out of it, or he may entirely transfigure it. Where the extravert loses himself in the object, the introvert makes it over in such wise as to master it in terms of his psyche, leaving much of its individual quality to fall by the wayside—unsensed or unfelt or otherwise unvalued. It is just because the extravert is ever greedy for experience that he tends to lose the power to become greatly influenced by slight or fleeting stimuli. He believes that the introvert makes a mountain of a molehill, a self-important wealth of a mere driblet of substance, while the latter is prepared to find that his extravert friend labours over a mountain of the chaff of experience to bring forth a poor mouse of reflection, insight or feeling. The extravert is always asking, "Where did he get it?" The introvert wonders, "What will he do with it?"

It is easy to misunderstand the nature of these opposed types. One must be studiously careful not to water Dr. Jung's conception and dissolve it into current notions of successful and unsuccessful adjustment, of conduct right and wrong, of normal and relatively abnormal behaviour. Either type has its successes and its failures, its geniuses and its simpletons. Each has its characteristic pathology. But of one thing we may be certain. Neither type in its purity can do full justice to the other. The introvert can never wholly comprehend the extravert because he can not resign himself to what he inevitably feels to be a vicarious existence. To him the extravert must ever seem a little superficial, a chronic vagrant from the spirit's home. Nor can the extravert wholly convince himself that behind the introvert's reserve and apparent impoverishment of interest there may lie the greatest wealth of subjective experience, and such subtlety of feeling as he may hardly parallel in his own external responses. This lack of mutual comprehension may lead to an undercurrent of hostility, or it may fire the fancy and result in strange hero-worships and infatuations.

Those who have read Dr. Jung's "Collected Papers on Analytical Psychology" may remember that in an earlier tentative classification of types he was disposed to identify the introverted with the thinking, the extraverted with the feeling type. These very dubious identifications have now been abandoned. Dr. Jung is perfectly clear, and the reader will be with him, about the independence of a classification based on general attitude (extravert and introvert types) and one based on the specific functioning of the psyche. Whether Dr. Jung's theory of the existence of four distinct functional types of personality is correct it would be difficult to say. It may be that a given personality tends to find its way in the world chiefly by aid of the intellect, of emotion, of intuitive processes, or of sensation. It would be dangerous, however, to erect the eight neatly sundered types that result from a crossing of the two points of view into a psychological dogma. We may be quite certain that such a classification is too scholastic to prove entirely sound and workable. It is not easy to see, for instance, why a primary concept like that of sensation is paired with something as derivative as reason; nor does "intuition" readily allow itself to be accepted as a fundamental type of psychic functioning. Possibly Dr. Jung's vast clinical experience justifies his setting up these four functional types, but the evidence is not presented in his book.

Why is there something uncanny, something disquieting, about the main thesis of "Psychological Types"? It is because once again we are deprived of the serenity of an absolute system of values. If the orientation of the extravert is as different from that of the introvert as Dr. Jung says it is, it is obviously vain to expect them to pledge loyalty to the same truths. Must we resign ourselves to a new relativity of the psyche and expect no more of psychology than that it render clear to us the ways of a particular kind of mental attitude? It is impossible to believe that the spirit of man will rest content with a schism. It is certain that orthodoxies will be proclaimed to the end of mortal time.

SPEECH AS A PERSONALITY TRAIT*

IF ONE is at all given to analysis, one is impressed with the extreme complexity of the various types of human behavior, and it may be assumed
that the things that we take for granted in our ordinary, everyday life
are as strange and as unexplainable as anything one might find. Thus one
comes to feel that the matter of speech is very far from being the self-
evident or simple thing that we think it to be; that it is capable of a very
great deal of refined analysis from the standpoint of human behavior;
and that one might, in the process of making such an analysis, accumu-
late certain ideas for the research of personality problems.

There is one thing that strikes us as interesting about speech: on the
one hand, we find it difficult to analyze; on the other hand, we are very
much guided by it in our actual experience. That is perhaps something
of a paradox, yet both the simple mind and the keenest of scientists know
very well that we do not react to the suggestions of the environment in
accordance with our specific knowledge alone. Some of us are more
intuitive than others, it is true, but none is entirely lacking in the ability
to gather and be guided by speech impressions in the intuitive exploration
of personality. We are taught that when a man speaks he says something
that he wishes to communicate. That, of course, is not necessarily so.
He intends to say something, as a rule, yet what he actually communi-
cates may be measurably different from what he started out to convey.
We often form a judgment of what he is by what he does not say, and
we may be very wise to refuse to limit the evidence for judgment to the
overt content of speech. One must read between the lines, even when
they are not written on a sheet of paper.

In thinking over this matter of the analysis of speech from the point
of view of personality study, the writer has come to feel that we might
have two quite distinct approaches; two quite distinct analyses might be
undertaken that would intercross in a very intricate fashion. In the first
place, the analysis might differentiate the individual and society, in so
far as society speaks through the individual. The second kind of analysis
would take up the different levels of speech, starting from the lowest
level, which is the voice itself, clear up to the formation of complete
sentences. In ordinary life we say that a man conveys certain impressions by his speech, but we rarely stop to analyze this apparent unit of
behavior into its superimposed levels. We might give him credit for brilliant ideas when he merely possesses a smooth voice. We are often led

* *American Journal of Sociology*, 32 (1927): 892–905.

into misunderstandings of this sort, though we are not generally so easily fooled. We can go over the entire speech situation without being able to put our finger on the precise spot in the speech complex that leads to our making this or that personality judgment. Just as the dog knows whether to turn to the right or to the left, so we know that we must make certain judgments, but we might well be mistaken if we tried to give the reason for making them.

Let us look for a moment at the justification for the first kind of analysis, the differentiation between the social and the purely individual point of view. It requires no labored argument to prove that this distinction is a necessary one. We human beings do not exist out of society. If you put a man in a cell, he is still in society because he carries his thoughts with him and these thoughts, pathologic though they be, were formed with the help of society. On the other hand, we can never have experience of social patterns as such, however greatly we may be interested in them. Take so simple a social pattern as the word "horse." A horse is an animal with four legs, a mane and a neigh; but, as a matter of fact, the social pattern of reference to this animal does not exist in its purity. All that exists is my saying "horse" today, "horse" yesterday, "horse" tomorrow. Each of the events is different. There is something peculiar about each of them. The voice, for one thing, is never quite the same. There is a different quality of emotion in each articulation, and the intensity of the emotion too is different. It is not difficult to see why it is necessary to distinguish the social point of view from the individual, for society has its patterns, its set ways of doing things, its distinctive "theories" of behavior, while the individual has his method of handling those particular patterns of society, giving them just enough of a twist to make them "his" and no one else's. We are so interested in ourselves as individuals and in others who differ, however slightly, from us that we are always on the alert to mark the variations from the nuclear pattern of behavior. To one who is not accustomed to the pattern, these variations would appear so slight as to be all but unobserved. Yet they are of maximum importance to us as individuals; so much so that we are liable to forget that there is a general social pattern to vary from. We are often under the impression that we are original or otherwise aberrant when, as a matter of fact, we are merely repeating a social pattern with the very slightest accent of individuality.

To proceed to the second point of view, the analysis of speech on its different levels. If we were to make a critical survey of how people react to voice and what the voice carries, we would find them relatively naïve about the different elements involved in speech. A man talks and makes certain impressions, but, as we have seen, we are not clear as to whether it is his voice which most powerfully contributes to the impression or the ideas which are conveyed. There are several distinct levels in speech behavior, which to linguists and psychologists are, each of them, sets of real phenomena, and we must now look at these in order to obtain some idea of the complexity of normal human speech. I will take up these various levels in order, making a few remarks about each of them as I proceed.

The lowest or most fundamental speech level is the voice. It is closest to the hereditary endowment of the individual, considered out of relation to society, "low" in the sense of constituting a level that starts with the psychophysical organism given at birth. The voice is a complicated bundle of reactions and, so far as the writer knows, no one has succeeded in giving a comprehensive account of what the voice is and what changes it may undergo. There seems to be no book or essay that classifies the many different types of voice, nor is there a nomenclature that is capable of doing justice to the bewildering range of voice phenomena. And yet it is by delicate nuances of voice quality that we are so often confirmed in our judgment of people. From a more general point of view, voice may be considered a form of gesture. If we are swayed by a certain thought or emotion, we may express ourselves with our hands or some other type of gesturing and the voice takes part in the total play of gesture. From our present point of view, however, it is possible to isolate the voice as a functional unit.

Voice is generally thought of as a purely individual matter, yet is it quite correct to say that the voice is given us at birth and maintained unmodified throughout life? Or has the voice a social quality as well as an individual one? I think we all feel, as a matter of fact, that we imitate each other's voices to a not inconsiderable extent. We know very well that if, for some reason or other, the timbre of the voice that we are heir to has been criticized, we try to modify it, so that it may not be a socially unpleasant instrument of speech. There is always something about the voice that must be ascribed to the social background, precisely as in the case of gesture. Gestures are not the simple, individual things they seem to be. They are largely peculiar to this or that society. In the same way, in spite of the personal and relatively fixed character of the voice, we make involuntary adjustments in the larynx that bring about significant modifications in the voice. Therefore, in deducing fundamental traits of personality from the voice we must try to disentangle the social element from the purely personal one. If we are not careful to do this, we may make a serious error of judgment. A man has a strained or raucous voice, let us say, and we might infer that he is basically "coarse-grained." Such a judgment might be entirely wide of the mark if the particular society in which he lives is an out-of-doors society that indulges in a good deal of swearing and rather rough handling of the voice. He may have had a very soft voice to begin with, symptomatic of a delicate psychic organization, which gradually toughened under the influence of social suggestion. The personality which we are trying to disentangle lies hidden under its overt manifestations, and it is our task to develop scientific methods to get at the "natural," theoretically unmodified voice. In order to interpret the voice as to its personality value, one needs to have a good idea of how much of it is purely individual, due to the natural formation of the larynx, to peculiarities of breathing, to a thousand and one factors that biologists may be able to define for us. One might ask at this point:—Why attach importance to the quality of the voice? What has that to do with personality? After all is said and done, a man's voice is primarily formed by natural agencies, it is what God has blessed him with. Yes, but is that not essentially true of the whole of personality? Inasmuch as the psychophysical organism is very much of a unit, we can be quite sure on general principles that in looking for the thing we call personality we have the right to attach importance to the thing we call voice. Whether personality is expressed as adequately in the voice as in gesture or in carriage, we do not know. Perhaps it is even more adequately expressed in the voice than in these. In any event, it is clear that the nervous processes that control voice production must share in the individual traits of the nervous organization that condition the personality.

The essential quality of the voice is an amazingly interesting thing to puzzle over. Unfortunately we have no adequate vocabulary for its endless varieties. We speak of a high-pitched voice. We say a voice is "thick," or it is "thin"; we say it is "nasal," if there is something wrong with the nasal part of the breathing apparatus. If we were to make an inventory of voices, we would find that no two of them are quite alike. And all the time we feel that there is something about the individual's voice that is indicative of his personality. We may even go so far as to surmise that the voice is in some way a symbolic index of the total personality. Some day, when we know more about the physiology and psychology of the voice, it will be possible to line up our intuitive judgments as to voice quality with a scientific analysis of voice formation. We do not know what it is precisely that makes the voice sound "thick" or "vibrant" or "flat" or what not. What is it that arouses us in one man's voice, where another's stirs us not at all? I remember listening many years ago to an address by a college president and deciding on the spur of the moment that what he said could be of no interest to me. What I meant was that no matter how interesting or pertinent his remarks were in themselves, his personality could not touch mine because there was something about his voice that did not appeal to me, something revealing as to personality. There was indicated—so one gathered intuitively—a certain quality of personality, a certain force, that I knew could not easily integrate with my own apprehension of things. I did not listen to what he said, I listened only to the quality of his voice. One might object that that was a perfectly idiotic thing to do. Perhaps it was, but I believe that we are all in the habit of doing just such things and that we are essentially justified in so doing—not intellectually, but intuitively. It therefore becomes the task of an intellectual analysis to justify for us on reasoned grounds what we have knowledge of in pre-scientific fashion.

There is little purpose in trying to list the different types of voice. Suffice it to say that on the basis of his voice one might decide many things about a man. One might decide that he is sentimental; that he is extraordinarily sympathetic without being sentimental; that he is cruel— one hears voices that impress one as being intensely cruel. One might decide on the basis of his voice that a person who uses a very brusque vocabulary is nevertheless kind-hearted. This sort of comment is part of the practical experience of every man and woman. The point is that we are not in the habit of attaching scientific value to such judgments.

We have seen that the voice is a social as well as an individual phenomenon. If one were to make a profound enough analysis, one might, at least in theory, carve out the social part of the voice and discard it—a difficult thing to do. One finds people, for example, who have very pleasant voices, but it is society that has made them pleasant. One may then try to go back to what the voice would have been without its specific social development. This nuclear or primary quality of voice has in many, perhaps in all, cases a symbolic value. These unconscious symbolisms are of course not limited to the voice. If you wrinkle your brow, that is a symbol of a certain attitude. If you act expansively by stretching out your arms, that is a symbol of a changed attitude to your immediate environment. In the same manner the voice is to a large extent an unconscious symbolization of one's general attitude.

Now all sorts of accidents may happen to the voice and deprive it, apparently, of its "predestined form." In spite of such accidents, however, the voice will be there for our discovery. These factors that spoil the basic picture are found in all forms of human behavior and we must make allowances for them here as everywhere else in behavior. The

primary voice structure is something that we cannot get at right away
but must uncover by hacking away the various superimposed structures,
social and individual.

What is the next level of speech? What we ordinarily call voice is
voice proper plus a great many variations of behavior that are intertwined with voice and give it its dynamic quality. This is the level of
voice dynamics. Two speakers may have very much the same basic
quality of voice yet their "voices," as that term is ordinarily understood,
may be very different. In ordinary usage we are not always careful to
distinguish the voice proper from voice dynamics. One of the most important aspects of voice dynamics is intonation, a very interesting field
of investigation for both linguist and psychologist. Intonation is a much
more complicated matter than is generally believed. It may be divided
into three distinct levels, which intertwine into the unit pattern of behavior which we may call "individual intonation." In the first place,
there is a very important social element in intonation which has to be
kept apart from the individual variation; in the second place, this social
element of intonation has a twofold determination. We have certain
intonations which are a necessary part of our speech. If I say, for example, "Is he coming?" I raise the pitch of the voice on the last word.
There is no sufficient reason in nature why I should elevate the voice in
sentences of this type. We are apt to assume that this habit is natural,
even self-evident, but a comparative study of the dynamic habits of
many diverse languages convinces one that this assumption is on the
whole unwarranted. The interogative attitude may be expressed in other
ways, such as the use of particular interrogative words or specific grammatical forms. It is one of the significant patterns of our English language
to elevate the voice in interrogative sentences of a certain type, hence
such elevation is not expressive in the properly individual sense of the
word, though we sometimes feel it to be so.

But more than that, there is a second level of socially determined
variation in intonation,—the musical handling of the voice generally,
quite aside from the properly linguistic patterns of intonation. It is
understood in a given society that we are not to have too great an individual range of intonation. We are not to rise to too great a height in
our cadences; we are to pitch the voice at such and such an average
height. In other words, society tells us to limit ourselves to a certain
range of intonation and to certain characteristic cadences, that is, to
adopt certain melody patterns peculiar to itself. If we were to compare
the speech of an English country gentleman with that of a Kentucky
farmer, we would find the intonational habits of the two to be notably

different, though there are certain important resemblances due to the fact that the language they speak is essentially the same. Neither dares to depart too widely from his respective social standard of intonation. Yet we know no two individuals who speak exactly alike so far as intonation is concerned. We are interested in the individual as the representative of a social type when he comes from some far place. The Southerner, the New Englander, the Middle Westerner, each has a characteristic intonation. But we are interested in the individual as an individual when he is merged in, and is a representative of, our own group. If we are dealing with people who have the same social habits, we are interested in the slight intonational differences which the individuals exhibit, for we know enough of their common social background to evaluate these slight differences. We are wrong to make any inferences about personality on the basis of intonation without considering the intonational habit of one's speech community or that has been carried over from a foreign language. We do not really know what a man's speech is until we have evaluated his social background. If a Japanese talks in a monotonous voice, we have not the right to assume that he is illustrating the same type of personality that one of us would be if we talked with his sentence melody. Furthermore, if we hear an Italian running through his whole possible gamut of tone, we are apt to say that he is temperamental or that he has an interesting personality. Yet we do not know whether he is in the least temperamental until we know what are the normal Italian habits of speech, what Italian society allows its members in the way of melodic play. Hence a major intonation curve, objectively considered, may be of but minor importance from the standpoint of individual expressiveness.

Intonation is only one of the many phases of voice dynamics. Rhythm, too, has to be considered. Here again there are several layers that are to be distinguished. First of all, the primary rhythms of speech are furnished by the language one is brought up in and are not due to our individual personality. We have certain very definite peculiarities of rhythm in English. Thus, we tend to accent certain syllables strongly and to minimize others. That is not due to the fact that we wish to be emphatic. It is merely that our language is so constructed that we must follow its characteristic rhythm, accenting one syllable in a word or phrase at the expense of the others. There are languages that do not follow this habit. If a Frenchman accented his words in our English fashion, we might be justified in making certain inferences as to his nervous condition. Furthermore, there are rhythmic forms which are due to the socialized habits of particular groups—rhythms which are over and above the basic rhythms of the language. Some sections of our society will not allow emphatic stresses, others allow or demand a greater emphasis. Polite society will allow far less play in stress and intonation than a society that is constituted by attendance at a baseball or football game. We have, in brief, two sorts of socialized rhythm—the rhythms of language and the rhythms of social expressiveness. And, once more, we have individual rhythmic factors. Some of us tend to be more tense in our rhythms, to accent certain syllables more definitely, to lengthen more vowels, to shorten unaccented vowels more freely. There are, in other words, individual rhythmic variations in addition to the social ones.

There are still other dynamic factors than intonation and rhythm. There is the relative continuity of speech. A great many people speak brokenly, in uneasy splashes of word groups, others speak continuously, whether they have anything to say or not. With the latter type it is not a question of having the necessary words at one's disposal, it is a question of mere continuity of linguistic expression. There are social speeds and continuities and individual speeds and continuities. We can be said to be slow or rapid in our utterances only in the sense that we speak above or below certain socialized speeds. Here again, in the matter of speed, the individual habit and its diagnostic value for the study of personality can only be measured against accepted social norms.

To summarize the second level of language behavior, we have a number of factors, such as intonation, rhythm, relative continuity, and speed, which have to be analyzed, each of them, into two distinct levels, the social and the individual; the social level, moreover, has generally to be divided into two levels, the level of that social pattern which is language and the level of the linguistically irrelevant habits of speech manipulation that are characteristic of a particular group.

The third level of speech analysis is pronounciation. Here again one often speaks of the "voice" when what is really meant is an individually nuanced pronunciation. A man pronounces certain consonants or vowels, say, with a distinctive timbre or in an otherwise peculiar manner and we tend to ascribe such variations of pronunciation to his voice, yet they may have nothing at all to do with the quality of his voice. In pronunciation we again have to distinguish the social from the individual patterns. Society decrees that we pronounce certain selected consonants and vowels, which have been set aside as the bricks and mortar, as it were, for the construction of a given language. We cannot depart very widely from this decree. We know that the foreigner who learns our language does not at once take over the sounds that are peculiar to us. He uses the nearest pronunciation that he can find in his own language.

It would manifestly be wrong to make inferences of a personal nature from such mispronunciations. But all the time there are also *individual* variations of sound which are highly important and which in many cases have a symptomatic value for the study of personality.

One of the most interesting chapters in linguistic behavior, a chapter which has not yet been written, is the expressively symbolic character of sounds quite aside from what the words in which they occur mean in a referential sense. On the properly linguistic plane sounds have no meaning, yet if we are to interpret them psychologically we would find that there is a subtle, though fleeting, relation between the "real" value of words and the unconscious symbolic value of sounds as actually pronounced by individuals. Poets know this in their own intuitive way. But what the poets are doing rather consciously by means of artistic devices we are doing unconsciously all of the time on a vast, if humble, scale. It has been pointed out, for instance, that there are certain expressive tendencies toward diminutive forms of pronunciation. If you are talking to a child, you change your "level of pronunciation" without knowing it. The word "tiny" may become "teeny." There is no rule of English grammar that justifies the change of vowel, but the word "teeny" seems to have a more directly symbolic character than "tiny," and a glance at the symbolism of phonetics gives us the reason for this. When we pronounce the "ee" of "teeny," there is very little space between the tongue and the roof of the mouth; in the first part of the "i" of "tiny" there is a great deal of space. In other words the "ee" variation has the value of a gesture which emphasizes the notion, or rather feeling, of smallness. In this particular case the tendency to symbolize diminutiveness is striking because it has caused one word to pass over to an entirely new word, but we are constantly making similar symbolic adjustments in a less overt way without being aware of the process.

Some people are much more symbolic in their use of sounds than others. A man may lisp, for instance, because he is unconsciously symbolizing certain traits which lead those who know him to speak of him as a "sissy." His pronunciation is not due to the fact that he cannot pronounce the sound of "s" properly, it is due to the fact that he is driven to reveal himself. He has no speech defect, though there is of course also a type of lisping that is a speech defect and that has to be kept apart from the symbolic lisp. There are a great many other unconsciously symbolic habits of articulation for which we have no current terminology. But we cannot discuss such variation fruitfully until we have established the social norm of pronunciation and have a just notion of what are the allowable departures within this social norm. If one goes to England or France or any other foreign country and sets down impressions on the interpretative significance of the voices and pronunciation perceived, what one says is not likely to be of value unless one has first made a painstaking study of the social norms of which the individual phenomena are variants. The lisp that you note may be what a given society happens to require, hence it is no psychological lisp in our sense. You cannot draw up an absolute psychological scale for voice, intonation, rhythm, speed, or pronunciation of vowels and consonants without in every case ascertaining the social background of speech habit. It is always the variation that matters, never the objective behavior as such.

The fourth speech level, that of vocabulary, is a very important one. We do not all speak alike. There are certain words which some of us never use. There are other, favorite, words which we are always using. Personality is largely reflected in the choice of words, but here too we must distinguish carefully the social vocabulary norm from the more significantly personal choice of words. Certain words and locutions are not used in certain circles; others are the hall-mark of locale, status or occupation. We listen to a man who belongs to a particular social group and are intrigued, perhaps attracted, by his vocabulary. Unless we are keen analysts, we are likely to read personality out of what is merely the current diction of his society. Individual variation exists, but it can be properly appraised only with reference to the social norm. Sometimes we choose words because we like them; sometimes we slight words because they bore or annoy or terrify us. We are not going to be caught by them. All in all, there is room for much subtle analysis in the determination of the social and individual significance of words.

Finally, we have style as a fifth speech level. Many people have an illusion that style is something that belongs to literature. Style is an everyday facet of speech that characterizes both the social group and the individual. We all have our individual styles in conversation and considered address, and they are never the arbitrary and casual things we think them to be. There is always an individual method, however poorly developed, of arranging words into groups and of working these up into larger units. It would be a very complicated problem to disentangle the social and individual determinants of style, but it is a theoretically possible one.

To summarize, we have the following materials to deal with in our attempt to get at the personality of an individual, in so far as it can be gathered from his speech. We have his voice. We have the dynamics of his voice, exemplified by such factors as intonation, rhythm, continuity, and speed. We have pronunciation, vocabulary, and style. Let us look at these materials as constituting so and so many levels on which expressive patterns are built. One may get a sense of individual patterning on one of these levels and use this sense to interpret the other levels. Objectively, however, two or more levels of a given speech act may produce either a similarity of expressive effect or a contrast. We may illustrate from a theoretical case. We know that many of us, handicapped by nature or habit, work out compensatory reactions. In the case of the man with a lisp whom we termed a "sissy," the essentially feminine type of articulation is likely to remain, but other aspects of his speech, including his voice, may show something of his effort to compensate. He may affect a masculine type of intonation or, above all, consciously or unconsciously, he may choose words that are intended to show that he is really a man. In this case we have a very interesting conflict, objectified within the realm of speech behavior. It is here as in all other types of behavior. One may express on one level of patterning what one will not or cannot express on another. One may inhibit on one level what one does not know how to inhibit on another, whence results a "dissociation," which is probably, at last analysis, nothing but a notable divergence in expressive content of functionally related patterns.

Quite aside from specific inferences which we may make from speech phenomena on any one of its levels, there is a great deal of interesting work to be done with the psychology of speech woven out of its different levels. Perhaps certain elusive phenomena of voice are the result of the interweaving of distinct patterns of expression. We sometimes get the feeling that there are two things being communicated by the voice, which may then be felt as splitting itself into an "upper" and a "lower" level.

It should be fairly clear from our hasty review that, if we make a level-to-level analysis of the speech of an individual and if we carefully see each of these in its social perspective, we obtain a valuable lever for psychiatric work. It is possible that the kind of analysis which has here been suggested, if carried far enough, may enable us to arrive at certain very pertinent conclusions regarding personality. Intuitively we attach an enormous importance to the voice and to the speech behavior that is carried by the voice. We have not much to say about it as a rule, not much more than an "I like that man's voice" or "I do not like the way he talks." Individual speech analysis is difficult to make, partly because of the peculiarly fleeting character of speech, partly because it is especially difficult to eliminate the social determinants of speech. In view of these difficulties there is not as much significant speech analysis being made by students of behavior as we might wish, but they do not relieve us of the responsibility for making such researches.

THE UNCONSCIOUS PATTERNING OF BEHAVIOR IN SOCIETY*

WE MAY SEEM to be guilty of a paradox when we speak of the unconscious in reference to social activity. Doubtful as is the usefulness of this concept when we confine ourselves to the behavior of the individual, it may seem to be worse than doubtful when we leave the kinds of behavior that are strictly individual and deal with those more complex kinds of activity which, rightly or wrongly, are supposed to be carried on, not by individuals as such, but by the associations of human beings that constitute society. It may be argued that society has no more of an unconscious than it has hands or legs.

I propose to show, however, that the paradox is a real one only if the term "social behavior" is understood in the very literal sense of behavior referred to groups of human beings which act as such, regardless of the mentalities of the individuals which compose the groups. To such a mystical group alone can a mysterious "social unconsciousness" be ascribed. But as we are very far from believing that such groups really exist, we may be able to persuade ourselves that no more especial kind of unconsciousness need be imputed to social behavior than is needed to understand the behavior of the individual himself. We shall be on much safer ground if we take it for granted that all human behavior involves essentially the same types of mental functioning, as well conscious as unconscious, and that the term "social" is no more exclusive of the concept "unconscious" than is the term "individual," for the very simple reason that the terms "social" and "individual" are contrastive in only a limited sense. We will assume that any kind of psychology that explains the behavior of the individual also explains the behavior of society in so far as the psychological point of view is applicable to and sufficient for the study of social behavior. It is true that for certain purposes it is very useful to look away entirely from the individual and to think of socialized behavior as though it were carried on by certain larger entities which transcend the psycho-physical organism. But this viewpoint implicitly demands the abandonment of the psychological approach to the explanation of human conduct in society.

It will be clear from what we have said that we do not find the essential difference between individual and social behavior to lie in the psychology of the behavior itself. Strictly speaking, each kind of behavior is indi-

* E. S. Dummer, ed., *The Unconscious: A Symposium* (New York, Knopf, 1927), pp. 114–142.

vidual, the difference in terminology being entirely due to a difference in the point of view. If our attention is focused on the actual, theoretically measurable behavior of a given individual at a given time and place, we call it "individual behavior," no matter what the physiological or psychological nature of that behavior may be. If, on the other hand, we prefer to eliminate certain aspects of such individual behavior from our consideration and to hold on only to those respects in which it corresponds to certain norms of conduct which have been developed by human beings in association with one another and which tend to perpetuate themselves by tradition, we speak of "social behavior." In other words, social behavior is merely the sum or, better, arrangement of such aspects of individual behavior as are referred to culture patterns that have their proper context, not in the spatial and temporal continuities of biological behavior, but in historical sequences that are imputed to actual behavior by a principle of selection.

We have thus defined the difference between individual and social behavior, not in terms of kind or essence, but in terms of organization. To say that the human being behaves individually at one moment and socially at another is as absurd as to declare that matter follows the laws of chemistry at a certain time and succumbs to the supposedly different laws of atomic physics at another, for matter is always obeying certain mechanical laws which are at one and the same time both physical and chemical according to the manner in which we choose to define its organization. In dealing with human beings, we simply find it more convenient for certain purposes to refer a given act to the psycho-physical organism itself. In other cases the interest happens to lie in continuities that go beyond the individual organism and its functioning, so that a bit of conduct that is objectively no more and no less individual than the first is interpreted in terms of the non-individual patterns that constitute social behavior or cultural behavior.

It would be a useful exercise to force ourselves to see any given human act from both of these points of view and to try to convince ourselves in this way that it is futile to classify human acts as such as having an inherently individual or social significance. It is true that there are a great many organismal functions that it is difficult to think of in social terms, but I think that even here the social point of view may often be applied with success. Few social students are interested, for instance, in the exact manner in which a given individual breathes. Yet it is not to be doubted that our breathing habits are largely conditioned by factors conventionally classified as social. There are polite and impolite ways of breathing. There are special attitudes which seem to characterize whole societies that undoubtedly condition the breathing habits of the individuals who make up these societies. Ordinarily the characteristic rhythm of breathing of a given individual is looked upon as a matter for strictly individual definition. But if, for one reason or another, the emphasis shifts to the consideration of a certain manner of breathing as due to good form or social tradition or some other principle that is usually given a social context, then the whole subject of breathing at once ceases to be a merely individual concern and takes on the appearance of a social pattern. Thus, the regularized breathing of the Hindu Yogi, the subdued breathing of those who are in the presence of a recently deceased companion laid away in a coffin and surrounded by all the ritual of funeral observances, the style of breathing which one learns from an operatic singer who gives lessons on the proper control of the voice, are, each and every one of them, capable of isolation as socialized modes of conduct that have a definite place in the history of human culture, though they are obviously not a whit less facts of individual behavior than the most casual and normal style of breathing, such as one rarely imagines to have other than purely individual implications. Strange as it may seem at first blush, there is no hard and fast line of division as to class of behavior between a given style of breathing, *provided that it be socially interpreted*, and a religious doctrine or a form of political administration. This is not to say that it may not be infinitely more useful to apply the social mode of analysis of human conduct to certain cases and the individual mode of analysis to others. But we do maintain that such differences of analysis are merely imposed by the nature of the interest of the observer and are not inherent in the phenomena themselves.

All cultural behavior is patterned. This is merely a way of saying that many things that an individual does and thinks and feels may be looked upon not merely from the standpoint of the forms of behavior that are proper to himself as a biological organism but from the standpoint of a generalized mode of conduct that is imputed to society rather than to the individual, though the personal genesis of conduct is of precisely the same nature, whether we choose to call the conduct individual or social. It is impossible to say what an individual is doing unless we have tacitly accepted the essentially arbitrary modes of interpretation that social tradition is constantly suggesting to us from the very moment of our birth. Let anyone who doubts this try the experiment of making a painstaking report of the actions of a group of natives engaged in some form of activity, say religious, to which he has not the cultural key. If he is a skillful writer, he may succeed in giving a picturesque account of what he sees and hears, or thinks he sees and hears, but the chances of his being able to give a relation of what happens in terms that would be intelligible and acceptable to the natives themselves are practically nil. He will be guilty of all manner of distortion. His emphasis will be constantly askew. He will find interesting what the natives take for granted as a casual kind of behavior worthy of no particular comment, and he will utterly fail to observe the crucial turning points in the course of action that give formal significance to the whole in the minds of those who do possess the key to its understanding. This patterning or formal analysis of behavior is to a surprising degree dependent on the mode of apprehension which has been established by the tradition of the group. Forms and significances which seem obvious to an outsider will be denied outright by those who carry out the patterns; outlines and implications that are perfectly clear to these may be absent to the eye of the onlooker. It is the failure to understand the necessity of grasping the native patterning which is responsible for so much unimaginative and misconceiving description of procedures that we have not been brought up with. It becomes actually possible to interpret as base what is inspired by the noblest and even holiest of motives, and to see altruism or beauty where nothing of the kind is either felt or intended.

Ordinarily a cultural pattern is to be defined both in terms of function and of form, the two concepts being inseparably intertwined in practice, however convenient it may be to dissociate them in theory. Many functions of behavior are primary in the sense that an individual organic need, such as the satisfaction of hunger, is being fulfilled, but often the functional side of behavior is either entirely transformed or, at the least, takes on a new increment of significance. In this way new functional interpretations are constantly being developed for forms set by tradition. Often the true functions of behavior are unknown and a merely rationalized function may be imputed to it. Because of the readiness with which forms of human conduct lose or modify their original functions or take on entirely new ones, it becomes necessary to see social behavior from a formal as well as from a functional point of view, and we shall not consider any kind of human behavior as understood if we can merely give or think we can give, an answer to the question "For what purpose is this being done?" We shall have also to know what is the precise manner and articulation of the doing.

Now it is a commonplace of observation that the reasoning intelligence seeks to attach itself rather to the functions than to the forms of conduct. For every thousand individuals who can tell with some show of reason why they sing or use words in connected speech or handle money, there is barely one who can adequately define the essential outlines of these

modes of behavior. No doubt certain forms will be imputed to such behavior if attention is drawn to it, but experience shows that the forms
discovered may be very seriously at variance with those actually followed and discoverable on closer study. In other words, the patterns of
social behavior are not necessarily discovered by simple observation,
though they may be adhered to with tyrannical consistency in the actual
conduct of life. If we can show that normal human beings, both in con-
fessedly social behavior and often in supposedly individual behavior, are
reacting in accordance with deep-seated cultural patterns, and if, further,
we can show that these patterns are not so much known as felt, not so
much capable of conscious description as of naïve practice, then we have
the right to speak of the "unconscious patterning of behavior in society."
The unconscious nature of this patterning consists not in some mysterious function of a racial or social mind reflected in the minds of the
individual members of society, but merely in a typical unawareness on
the part of the individual of outlines and demarcations and significances
of conduct which he is all the time implicitly following. Jung's "racial
unconscious" is neither an intelligible nor a necessary concept. It introduces more difficulties than it solves, while we have all we need for the
psychological understanding of social behavior in the facts of individual
psychology.

Why are the forms of social behavior not adequately known by the
normal individual? How is it that we can speak, if only metaphorically,
of a social unconscious? I believe that the answer to this question rests
in the fact that the relations between the elements of experience which
serve to give them their form and significance are more powerfully "felt"
or "intuited" than consciously perceived. It is a matter of common
knowledge that it is relatively easy to fix the attention on some arbitrarily selected element of experience, such as a sensation or an emotion,
but that it is far from easy to become conscious of the exact place which
such an element holds in the total constellations of behavior. It is easy
for an Australian native, for instance, to say by what kinship term he
calls so and so or whether or not he may undertake such and such relations with a given individual. It is exceedingly difficult for him to give a
general rule of which these specific examples of behavior are but illustrations, though all the while he acts as though the rule were perfectly
well known to him. *In a sense it is well known to him.* But this knowledge
is not capable of conscious manipulation in terms of word symbols. It
is, rather, a very delicately nuanced feeling of subtle relations, both experienced and possible. To this kind of knowledge may be applied the
term "intuition," which, when so defined, need have no mystic connota-

tions whatever. It is strange how frequently one has the illusion of free knowledge, in the light of which one may manipulate conduct at will, only to discover in the test that one is being impelled by strict loyalty to forms of behavior that one can feel with the utmost nicety but can state only in the vaguest and most approximate fashion. It would seem that we act all the more securely for our unawareness of the patterns that control us. It may well be that, owing to the limitations of the conscious life, any attempt to subject even the higher forms of social behavior to purely conscious control must result in disaster. Perhaps there is a far-reaching moral in the fact that even a child may speak the most difficult language with idiomatic ease but that it takes an unusually analytical type of mind to define the mere elements of that incredibly subtle linguistic mechanism which is but a plaything of the child's unconscious. Is it not possible that the contemporary mind, in its restless attempt to drag all the forms of behavior into consciousness and to apply the results of its fragmentary or experimental analysis to the guidance of conduct, is really throwing away a greater wealth for the sake of a lesser and more dazzling one? It is almost as though a misguided enthusiast exchanged his thousands of dollars of accumulated credit at the bank for a few glittering coins of manifest, though little, worth.

We shall now give a number of examples of patterns of social behavior and show that they are very incompletely, if at all, known by the normal, naïve individual. We shall see that the penumbra of unconscious patterning of social behavior is an extraordinarily complex realm, in which one and the same type of overt behavior may have altogether distinct significances in accordance with its relation to other types of behavior. Owing to the compelling, but mainly unconscious, nature of the forms of social behavior, it becomes almost impossible for the normal individual to observe or to conceive of functionally similar types of behavior in other societies than his own, or in other cultural contexts than those he has experienced, without projecting into them the forms that he is familiar with. In other words, one is always unconsciously finding what one is in unconscious subjection to.

Our first example will be taken from the field of language. Language has the somewhat exceptional property that its forms are, for the most part, indirect rather than direct in their functional significance. The sounds, words, grammatical forms, syntactic constructions, and other linguistic forms that we assimilate in childhood have only value in so far as society has tacitly agreed to see them as symbols of reference. For this reason language is an unusually favorable domain for the study of the general tendency of cultural behavior to work out all sorts of formal elaborations that have only a secondary, and, as it were, "after the event" relevance to functional needs. Purely functional explanations of language, if valid, would lead us to expect either a far greater uniformity in linguistic expression than we actually find, or should lead us to discover strict relations of a functional nature between a particular form of language and the culture of the people using it. Neither of these expectations is fulfilled by the facts. Whatever may be true of other types of cultural behavior, we can safely say that the forms of speech developed in the different parts of the world are at once free and necessary, in the sense in which all artistic productions are free and necessary. Linguistic forms as we find them bear only the loosest relation to the cultural needs of a given society, but they have the very tightest consistency as aesthetic products.

A very simple example of the justice of these remarks is afforded by the English plural. To most of us who speak English the tangible expression of the plural idea in the noun seems to be a self-evident necessity. Careful observation of English usage, however, leads to the conviction that this self-evident necessity of expression is more of an illusion than a reality. If the plural were to be understood functionally alone, we should find it difficult to explain why we use plural forms with numerals and other words that in themselves imply plurality. "Five man" or "several house" would be just as adequate as "five men" or "several houses." Clearly, what has happened is that English, like all of the other Indo-European languages, has developed a feeling for the classification of all expressions which have a nominal form into singulars and plurals. So much is this the case that in the early period of the history of our linguistic family even the adjective, which is nominal in form, is unusable except in conjunction with the category of number. In many of the languages of the group this habit still persists. Such notions as "white" or "long" are incapable of expression in French or Russian without formal commitments on the score of whether the quality is predicated of one or several persons or objects. Now it is not denied that the expression of the concept of plurality is useful. Indeed, a language that is forever incapable of making the difference between the one and the many is obviously to that extent hampered in its technique of expression. But we must emphatically deny that this particular kind of expression need ever develop into the complex formal system of number definition that we are familiar with. In many other linguistic groups the concept of number belongs to the group of optionally expressible notions. In Chinese, for instance, the word "man" may be interpreted as the English equivalent of either "man" or "men," according to the particular context in which the word is used. It is to be carefully noted, however, that this formal ambiguity is never a functional one. Terms of inherent plurality, such as "five," "all," or "several," or of inherent singularity, such as "one" or "my" in the phrase "my wife," can always be counted upon to render factually clear what is formally left to the imagination. If the ambiguity persists, it is a useful one or one that does not matter. How little the expression of our concept of number is left to the practical exigencies of a particular case, how much it is a matter of consistency of aesthetic treatment, will be obvious from such examples as the editorial "we are in favor of prohibition," when what is really meant is "I, John Smith, am in favor of prohibition."

A complete survey of the methods of handling the category of number in the languages of the world would reveal an astonishing variety of treatment. In some languages number is a necessary and well developed category. In others it is an accessory or optional one. In still others, it can hardly be considered as a grammatical category at all but is left entirely to the implications of vocabulary and syntax. Now the interesting thing psychologically about this variety of forms is this, that while everyone may learn to see the need of distinguishing the one from the many and has some sort of notion that his language more or less adequately provides for this necessity, only a very competent philologist has any notion of the true formal outlines of the expression of plurality, of whether, for instance, it constitutes a category comparable to that of gender or case, whether or not it is separable from the expression of gender, whether it is a strictly nominal category or a verbal one or both, whether it is used as a lever for syntactic expression, and so on. Here are found determinations of a bewildering variety, concerning which few even among the sophisticated have any clarity, though the lowliest peasant or savage head-hunter may have control of them in his intuitive repertoire.

So great are the possibilities of linguistic patterning that the languages actually known seem to present the whole gamut of possible forms. We have extremely analytic types of speech, such as Chinese, in which the formal unit of discourse, the word, expresses nothing in itself but a single notion of thing or quality or activity or else some relational nuance. At the other extreme are the incredibly complex languages of many American Indian tribes, languages of so-called polysynthetic type, in which the same formal unit, the word, is a sentence microcosm full of delicate formal elaborations of the most specialized type. Let one example do for many. Anyone who is brought up in English, even if he has had the benefit of some familiarity with the classical languages, will take it for granted that in such a sentence as "Shall I have the people move across the river to the east?" there is rather little elbow room for varieties of formal expression. It would not easily occur to us, for instance, that the notion of "to the east" might be conveyed not by an independent word or phrase but by a mere suffix in complex verb.

There is a rather obscure Indian language in northern California, Yana, which not only can express this thought in a single word, but would find it difficult to express it in any other way. The form of expression which is peculiar to Yana may be roughly analyzed as follows. The first element in the verb complex indicates the notion of several people living together or moving as a group from place to place. This element, which we may call the "verb stem," can only occur at the beginning of the verb, never in any other position. The second element in the complete word indicates the notion of crossing a stream or of moving from one side of an area to the other. It is in no sense an independent word, but can only be used as an element attached to a verb stem or to other elements which have themselves been attached to the verb stem. The third element in the word is similarly suffixed and conveys the notion of movement toward the east. It is one of a set of eight elements which convey the respective notions of movement toward the east, south, west, and north, and of movement from the east, south, west, and north. None of these elements is an intelligible word in itself but receives meaning only in so far as it falls into its proper place in the complexly organized verb. The fourth element is a suffix that indicates the relation of causality, that is, of causing one to do or be something, bringing it about that one does or is in a certain way, treating one in such and such an indicated manner. At this point the language indulges in a rather pretty piece of formal play. The vowel of the verb stem which we spoke of as occupying the first position in the verb symbolized the intransitive or static mode of apprehension of the act. As soon as the causative notion is introduced, however, the verb stem is compelled to pass to the category of transitivized or active notions, which means that the causative suffix, in spite of the parenthetical inclusion of certain notions of direction of movement, has the retroactive effect of changing the vowel of the stem. Up to this point, therefore, we get a perfectly unified complex of notions which may be rendered "to cause a group to move across a stream in an easterly direction."

But this is not yet a word, at least not a word in the finished sense of the term, for the elements that are still to follow have just as little independent existence as those we have already referred to. Of the more formal elements that are needed to complete the word, the first is a tense suffix referring to the future. This is followed by a pronominal element which refers to the first person singular, is different in form from the suffixed pronoun used in other tenses and modalities. Finally, there is an element consisting of a single consonant which indicates that the whole word, which is a complete proposition in itself, is to be understood in an interrogative sense. Here again the language illustrates an interesting kind of specialization of form. Nearly all words of the language differ slightly in form according to whether the speaker is a man speaking to a man or, on the other hand, is a woman or a man speaking to a woman. The interrogative form that we have just discussed can only be used by a man speaking to a man. In the other three cases the suffix in question is not used, but the last vowel of the word, which in this particular case happens to be the final vowel of the pronominal suffix, is lengthened in order to express the interrogative modality.

We are not in the least interested in the details of this analysis, but some of its implications should interest us. In the first place, it is necessary to bear in mind that there is nothing arbitrary or accidental or even curious about the structure of this word. Every element falls into its proper place in accordance with definitely formulable rules which can be discovered by the investigator but of which the speakers themselves have no more conscious knowledge than of the inhabitants of the moon. It is possible to say, for instance, that the verb stem is a particular example of a large number of elements which belong to the same general class, such as "to sit," "to walk," "to run," "to jump," and so on; or that the element which expresses the idea crossing from one side to another is a particular example of a large class of local elements of parallel function, such as "to the next house," "up the hill," "into a hollow," "over the crest," "down hill," "under," "over," "in the middle of," "off," "hither," and so on. We may quite safely assume that no Yana Indian ever had the slightest knowledge of classifications such as these or ever possessed even an inkling of the fact that his language neatly symbolized classifications of this sort by means of its phonetic apparatus and by rigid rules of sequence and cohesion of formal elements. Yet all the while we may be perfectly certain that the relations which give the elements of the language their significance were somehow felt and adhered to. A mistake in the vowel of the first syllable, for instance, would undoubtedly feel to a native speaker like a self-contradictory form in English, for instance "five house" instead of "five houses" or "they runs" instead of "they run." Mistakes of this sort are resisted as any aesthetic transgression might be resisted—as being somehow incongruous, out of the picture, or, if one chooses to rationalize the resistance, as inherently illogical.

The unconscious patterning of linguistic conduct is discoverable not only in the significant forms of language but, just as surely, in the several materials out of which language is built, namely the vowels and consonants, the changes of stress and quantity, and the fleeting intonations of speech. It is quite an illusion to believe that the sounds and the sound dynamics of language can be sufficiently defined by more or less detailed statements of how the speech articulations are managed in a neurological or muscular sense. Every language has a phonetic scheme in which a given sound or a given dynamic treatment of a sound has a definite configurated place in reference to all the other sounds recognized by the language. The single sound, in other words, is in no sense identical with an articulation or with the perception of an articulation. It is, rather, a point in a pattern, precisely as a tone in a given musical tradition is a point in a pattern which includes the whole range of aesthetically possible tones. Two given tones may be physically distinguished but aesthetically identical because each is heard or understood as occupying the same formal position in the total set of recognized tones. In a musical tradition which does not recognize chromatic intervals "C sharp" would have to be identified with "C" and would be considered as a mere deviation, pleasant or unpleasant, from "C." In our own musical tradition the difference between "C" and "C sharp" is crucial to an understanding of all our music, and, by unconscious projection, to a certain way of misunderstanding all other music built on different principles. In still other musical traditions there are still finer intervalic differences recognized, none of which quite corresponds to our semitone interval. In these three cases it is obvious that nothing can be said as to the cultural and aesthetic status of a given tone in a song unless we know or feel against what sort of general tonal background it is to be interpreted.

It is precisely so with the sounds of speech. From a purely objective standpoint the difference between the k of "kill" and the k of "skill" is as easily definable as the, to us, major difference between the k of "kill" and the g of "gill" (of a fish). In some languages the g sound of "gill" would be looked upon, or rather would be intuitively interpreted, as a comparatively unimportant or individual divergence from a sound typically represented by the k of "skill," while the k of "kill," with its greater strength of articulation and its audible breath release, would constitute an utterly distinct phonetic entity. Obviously the two distinct k sounds of such a language and the two ways of pronouncing the k in English, while objectively comparable and even identical phenomena, are from the point of view of patterning utterly different. Hundreds of interesting and, at first blush, strangely paradoxical examples of this sort could be given, but the subject is perhaps too technical for treatment in this paper.

It is needless to say that no normal speaker has an adequate knowledge of these submerged sound configurations. He is the unconscious and magnificently loyal adherent of thoroughly socialized phonetic patterns, which are simple and self-evident in daily practice, but subtly involved and historically determined in actual fact. Owing to the necessity of thinking of speech habits not merely in overt terms but as involving the setting up of intuitively mastered relations in suitable contexts, we need not be surprised that an articulatory habit which is perfectly feasible in one set of relations becomes subjectively impossible when the pattern in which it is to be fitted is changed. Thus, an English-speaking person who is utterly unable to pronounce a French nasalized vowel may nevertheless be quite able to execute the necessary articulation in another context, such as the imitation of snoring or of the sound of some wild animal. Again, the Frenchman or German who cannot pronounce the "wh" of our American-English "why" can easily produce the same sound when he gently blows out a candle. It is obviously correct to say that the acts illustrated in these cases can only be understood as they are fitted into definite cultural patterns concerning the form and mechanics of which the normal individual has no adequate knowledge.

We may summarize our interpretation of these, and thousands of other, examples of language behavior by saying that in each case an unconscious control of very complicated configurations or formal sets is individually acquired by processes which it is the business of the psychologist to try to understand but that, in spite of the enormously varied psychological predispositions and types of conditioning which characterize different personalities, these patterns in their completed form differ only infinitesimally from individual to individual, in many cases from generation to generation. And yet these forms lie entirely outside the inherited biological tendencies of the race and can be explained only in strictly social terms. In the simple facts of language we have an excellent example of an important network of patterns of behavior, each of them with exceedingly complex and, to a large extent, only vaguely definable functions, which is preserved and transmitted with a minimum of consciousness. The forms of speech so transmitted seem as necessary as the simplest reflexes of the organism. So powerfully, indeed, are we in the grip of our phonetic habits that it becomes one of the most delicate and difficult tasks of the linguistic student to discover what is the true configuration of sounds in languages alien to his own. This means that the average person unconsciously interprets the phonetic material of other languages in terms imposed upon him by the habits of his own language. Thus, the naïve Frenchman confounds the two sounds "s" of "sick" and "th" of "thick" in a single pattern point—not because he is really unable to hear the difference, but because the setting up of such a difference disturbs his feeling for the necessary configuration of linguistic sounds. It is as though an observer from Mars, knowing nothing of the custom we call war, were intuitively led to confound a punishable murder with a thoroughly legal and noble act of killing in the course of battle. The mechanism of projection of patterns is as evident in the one case as in the other.

Not all forms of cultural behavior so well illustrate the mechanics of unconscious patterning as does linguistic behavior, but there are few, if any, types of cultural behavior which do not illustrate it. Functional considerations of all kinds, leading to a greater degree of conscious control, or apparent control, of the patterns of behavior, tend to obscure the unconscious nature of the patterns themselves, but the more carefully we study cultural behavior, the more thoroughly we become convinced that the differences are but differences of degree. A very good example of another field for the development of unconscious cultural patterns is that of gesture. Gestures are hard to classify and it is difficult to make a conscious separation between that in gesture which is of merely individual origin and that which is referable to the habits of the group as a whole. In spite of these difficulties of conscious analysis, we respond to gestures with an extreme alertness and, one might almost say, in accordance with an elaborate and secret code that is written nowhere, known by none, and understood by all. But this code is by no means referable to simple organic responses. On the contrary, it is as finely certain and artificial, as definitely a creation of social tradition, as language or religion or industrial technology. Like everything else in human conduct, gesture roots in the reactive necessities of the organism, but the laws of gesture, the unwritten code of gestured messages and responses, is the anonymous work of an elaborate social tradition. Whoever doubts this may soon become convinced when he penetrates into the significance of gesture patterns of other societies than his own. A Jewish or Italian shrug of the shoulders is no more the same pattern of behavior as the shrug of a typical American than the forms and significant evocations of the Yiddish or Italian sentence are identical with those of any thinkable English sentence. The differences are not to be referred to supposedly deep-seated racial differences of a biological sort. They lie in the unconsciously apprehended builds of the respective social patterns which include them and out of which they have been abstracted for an essentially artificial comparison. A certain immobility of countenance in New York or Chicago may be interpreted as a masterly example of the art of wearing a poker face, but when worn by a perfectly average inhabitant of Tokio, it may be explainable as nothing more interesting or important than the simplest and most obvious of good manners. It is the failure to understand the relativity of gesture and posture, the degree to which these classes of behavior are referable to social patterns which transcend merely individual psychological significances, which makes it so easy for us to find individual indices of personality where it is only the alien culture that speaks.

In the economic life of a people, too, we are constantly forced to recognize the pervasive influence of patterns which stand in no immediate relation to the needs of the organism and which are by no means to be taken for granted in a general philosophy of economic conduct but which must be fitted into the framework of social forms characteristic of a given society. There is not only an unconscious patterning of the types of endeavor that are classed as economic, there is even such a thing as a characteristic patterning of economic motive. Thus, the acquirement of wealth is not to be lightly taken for granted as one of the basic drives of human beings. One accumulates property, one defers the immediate enjoyment of wealth, only in so far as society sets the pace for these activities and inhibitions. Many primitive societies are quite innocent of an understanding of the accumulation of wealth in our sense of the phrase. Even where there is a definite feeling that wealth should be accumulated, the motives which are responsible for the practice and which give definite form to the methods of acquiring wealth are often signally different from such as we can readily understand.

The West Coast Indians of British Columbia have often been quoted as a primitive society that has developed a philosophy of wealth which is somewhat comparable to our own, with its emphasis on "conspicuous waste" and on the sacrosanct character of property. The comparison is not essentially sound. The West Coast Indian does not handle wealth in a manner which we can recognize as our own. We can find plenty of analogies, to be sure, but they are more likely to be misleading than helpful. No West Coast Indian, so far as we know, ever amassed wealth as an individual pure and simple, with the expectation of disposing of it in the fulness of time at his own sweet will. This is a dream of the modern European and American individualist, and it is a dream which not only brings no thrill to the heart of the West Coast Indian but is probably almost meaningless to him. The concepts of wealth and the display of honorific privileges, such as crests and dances and songs and names, which have been inherited from legendary ancestors are inseparable among these Indians. One cannot publicly exhibit such a privilege without expending wealth in connection with it. Nor is there much object in accumulating wealth except to reaffirm privileges already possessed, or, in the spirit of a parvenu, to imply the possession of privileges none too clearly recognized as legitimate by one's fellow tribesmen. In other words, wealth, beyond a certain point, is with these people much more a token of status than it is a tool for the fulfillment of personal desires. We may go so far as to say that among the West Coast Indians it is not the individual at all who possesses wealth. It is primarily the ceremonial patrimony of which he is the temporary custodian that demands the symbolism of wealth. Arrived at a certain age, the West Coast Indian turns his privileges over to those who are by kin or marriage connection entitled to manipulate them. Henceforth he may be as poor as a church mouse, without loss of prestige. I should not like to go so far as to say that the concepts of wealth among ourselves and among the West Coast Indians are utterly different things. Obviously they are nothing of the kind, but they are measurably distinct and the nature of the difference must be sought in the total patterning of life in the two communities from which the particular pattern of wealth and its acquirement has been extracted. It should be fairly clear that where the patterns of manipulation of wealth are as different as they are in these two cases, it would be a mere exercise of the academic imagination to interpret the economic activities of one society in terms of the general economy which has been abstracted from the mode of life of the other.

No matter where we turn in the field of social behavior, men and women do what they do, and cannot help but do, not merely because they are built thus and so, or possess such and such differences of personality, or must needs adapt to their immediate environment in such and such a way in order to survive at all, but very largely because they have found it easiest and aesthetically most satisfactory to pattern their conduct in accordance with more or less clearly organized forms of behavior which no one is individually responsible for, which are not clearly grasped in their true nature, and which one might almost say are as self-evidently imputed to the nature of things as the three dimensions are imputed to space. It is sometimes necessary to become conscious of the forms of social behavior in order to bring about a more serviceable adaptation to changed conditions, but I believe it can be laid down as a principle of far-reaching application that in the normal business of life it is useless and even mischievous for the individual to carry the conscious analysis of his cultural patterns around with him. That should be left to the student whose business it is to understand these patterns. A healthy unconsciousness of the forms of socialized behavior to which we are subject is as necessary to society as is the mind's ignorance, or better unawareness, of the workings of the viscera to the health of the body. In great works of the imagination form is significant only in so far as we feel ourselves to be in its grip. It is unimpressive when divulged in the explicit terms of this or that simple or complex arrangement of known elements. So, too, in social behavior, it is not the overt forms that rise readily to the surface of attention that are most worth our while. We must learn to take joy in the larger freedom of loyalty to thousands of subtle patterns of behavior that we can never hope to understand in explicit terms. Complete analysis and the conscious control that comes with a complete analysis are at best but the medicine of society, not its food. We must never allow ourselves to substitute the starveling calories of knowledge for the meat and bread of historical experience. This historic experience may be theoretically knowable, but it dare never be fully known in the conduct of daily life.

PERSONALITY*

THE TERM personality is too variable in usage to be serviceable in scientific discussion unless its meaning is very carefully defined for a given context. Among the various understandings which attach to the term there are five definitions which stand out as usefully distinct from one another, corresponding to the philosophical, the physiological, the psychophysical, the sociological and the psychiatric approaches to personality. As a philosophical concept, personality may be defined as the subjective awareness of the self as distinct from other objects of observation. As a purely physiological concept, personality may be considered as the individual human organism with emphasis on those aspects of behavior which differentiate it from other human organisms. The term may be used in a descriptive psychophysical sense as referring to the human being conceived as a given totality, at any one time, of physiological and psychological reaction systems, no vain attempt being made to draw a line between the physiological and the psychological. The most useful sociological connotation which can be given to the term is an essentially symbolic one; namely, the totality of those aspects of behavior which give meaning to an individual in society and differentiate him from other members in the community, each of whom embodies countless cultural patterns in a unique configuration. The psychiatric definition of personality may be regarded as equivalent to the individual abstracted from the actual psychophysical whole and conceived as a comparatively stable system of reactivity. The philosophical concept treats personality as an invariant point of experience; the physiological and psychophysical, as an indefinitely variable reactive system, the relation between the sequence of states being one of continuity, not identity; the sociological, as a gradually cumulative entity; and the psychiatric, as an essentially invariant reactive system.

The first four meanings add nothing new to such terms as self or ego, organism, individual and social role. It is the peculiarly psychiatric conception of personality as a reactive system which is in some sense stable or typologically defined for a long period of time, perhaps for life, which it is most difficult to assimilate but important to stress. The psychiatrist does not deny that the child who rebels against his father is in many significant ways different from the same individual as a middle aged adult who has a penchant for subversive theories, but he is interested primarily in noting that the same reactive ground plan, physical and psychic, can

* Encyclopaedia of the Social Sciences (New York, Macmillan, 1934), 12: 85–87.

be isolated from the behavior totalities of child and adult. He establishes his invariance of personality by a complex system of concepts of behavior equivalences, such as sublimation, affective transfer, rationalization, libido and ego relations. The stage in the history of the human organism at which it is most convenient to consider the personality as an achieved system, from which all subsequent cross sections of individual psychophysical history may be measured as minor or even irrelevant variations, is still undetermined. There is no way of telling how far back in the life of the individual the concept of an essentially invariant reactive system may usefully be pushed without too disturbing a clash with the manifest and apparently unlimited variability of individual behavior. If this conception of personality is to hold its own, it must in some way contradict effectively the notion of that cumulative growth of personality to which our practical intelligence must chiefly be directed. The psychiatrist's concept of personality is to all intents and purposes the reactive system exhibited by the precultural child, a total configuration of reactive tendencies determined by heredity, and by prenatal and postnatal conditioning up to the point where cultural patterns are constantly modifying the child's behavior. The personality may be conceived of as a latent system of reaction patterns and tendencies to reaction patterns finished shortly after birth or well into the second or third year of the life of the individual. With all the uncertainty that now prevails with regard to the relative permanence or modifiability of life patterns in the individual and in the race it is unwise, however, to force the notion of the fixation of personality in time.

The genesis of personality is in all probability determined largely by the anatomical and physiological make up of the individual but cannot be entirely so explained. Conditioning factors, which may roughly be lumped together as the social psychological determinants of childhood, must be considered as at least as important in the development of personality as innate biological factors. It is entirely vain in the present state of knowledge to argue as to the relative importance of these two sets of factors. No satisfactory technique has been developed for keeping them apart and it is perhaps safe to take for granted that there is no facet of personality, however minute, which is not from the genetic standpoint the result of the prolonged and subtle interplay of both.

It is unthinkable that the build and other physical characteristics of an individual should bear no relation to his personality. It is important to observe, however, that physical features may be of genetic significance in two distinct respects. They may be organically correlated with certain psychological features or tendencies or they may serve as consciously or unconsciously evaluated symbols of an individual's relation to others, belonging properly to the sphere of social determination. An example of the former class of physical determinants would be the association, according to Kretschmer, of the stocky, so-called pyknic, build, with the cyclothymic type of personality, which in its psychotic form shows as manic depressive insanity, the so-called asthenic and athletic builds being associated with the schizothymic type of personality, which, under the pressure of shock and conflict, may disintegrate into schizophrenia. An example of the latter type of determination, stressed by Alfred Adler and his school of individual psychology, would be the feeling of secret inferiority produced in a person who is of abnormally short stature, and the ceaseless effort to overcome this feeling of inferiority by developing such compensatory mechanisms as intelligent aggression or shrewdness, which would tend to give the individual a secondary ego satisfaction denied him by his sense of physical inferiority. It is highly probable that both of these genetic theories of personality have a substantial core of value although too much has doubtless been claimed for them.

The most elaborate and far reaching hypotheses on the development of personality which have yet been proposed are those of Freud and his school. The Freudian psychoanalysts analyze the personality topographically into a primary id, the sum of inherited impulses or cravings; the ego, which is thought of as being built upon the id through the progressive development of the sense of external reality; and the super-ego, the socially conditioned sum of forces which restrain the individual from the direct satisfaction of the id. The characteristic interplay of these personality zones, itself determined chiefly by the special pattern of family relationships into which the individual has had to fit himself in the earliest years of his life, is responsible for a variety of personality types. Freudians have not developed a systematic theory of personality types but have contented themselves with special hypotheses based on clinical evidence. There is no doubt that a large amount of valuable material and a number of powerfully suggestive mechanisms of personality formation have been advanced by the Freudian school. Even now it is abundantly clear that an unusual attachment to the mother or profound jealously of the older or younger brother may give the personality a slant which remains relatively fixed throughout life.

Various classifications of personality types have been advanced, some of them based on innate factors, others on experiential ones. Among the typological pictures the one worthy of special note is perhaps that of Jung. To him may be attributed the popular contrast between introverts and extraverts, the former abstracting more readily from reality and finding their sense of values and personal identification within themselves, while the latter evaluate experience in terms of what is immediately given by the environment. This contrast, it is true, means something substantial, but it is unfortunate that a host of superficial psychologists have attempted to fix Jung's meaning with the aid of shallow criteria of all sorts. Jung further divides personality into four main functional types—thinking, feeling, sensational and intuitive—the two former being called rational, the two latter irrational. For these somewhat misleading terms, organized and unorganized may fitly be substituted. The classification according to functional types is believed by Jung to intercross with the introvert extravert dichotomy. The validity and exact delimitation of these terms present many difficult problems of analysis. There is much that is suggestive in his classification of personality and it may be possible to integrate it with the dynamic theories of Freud and Adler. What is needed at the present time, however, is the ever more minute analysis and comparison of individual personality pictures.

There is an important relation between culture and personality. On the one hand, there can be little doubt that distinctive personality types may have a profound influence on the thought and action of the community as a whole. Furthermore, while cultural anthropologists and sociologists do not consider that the forms of social interaction are in themselves definitive of personality types, particular forms of behavior in society, however flexibly the individual may adapt himself to them, are preferentially adapted to specific personality types. Aggressive military patterns, for instance, cannot be equally congenial to all personalities; literary or scientific refinement can be developed only by individuals of highly differentiated personalities. The failure of social science as a whole to relate the patterns of culture to germinal personality patterns is intelligible in view of the complexity of social phenomena and the recency of serious speculation on the relation of the individual to society. But there is growing recognition of the fact that the intimate study of personality is of fundamental concern to the social scientist.

The socialization of personality traits may be expected to lead cumulatively to the development of specific psychological biases in the cultures of the world. Thus Eskimo culture, contrasted with most North American Indian cultures, is extraverted; Hindu culture on the whole corresponds to the world of the thinking introvert; the culture of the United States is definitely extraverted in character, with a greater emphasis on thinking and intuition than on feeling; and sensational evaluations are more clearly evident in the cultures of the Mediterranean area than in those of northern Europe. Social scientists have been hostile to such psychological characterizations of culture but in the long run they are inevitable and necessary.

SYMBOLISM*

The term symbolism covers a great variety of apparently dissimilar modes of behavior. In its original sense it was restricted to objects or marks intended to recall or to direct special attention to some person, object, idea, event or projected activity associated only vaguely or not at all with the symbol in any natural sense. By gradual extensions of meaning the terms symbol and symbolism have come to include not merely such trivial objects and marks as black balls, to indicate a negative attitude in voting, and stars and daggers, to remind the reader that supplementary information is to be found at the bottom of the page, but also more elaborate objects and devices, such as flags and signal lights, which are not ordinarily regarded as important in themselves but which point to ideas and actions of great consequence to society. Such complex systems of reference as speech, writing and mathematical notation should also be included under the term symbolism, for the sounds and marks used therein obviously have no meaning in themselves and can have significance only for those who know how to interpret them in terms of that to which they refer. A certain kind of poetry is called symbolic or symbolistic because its apparent content is only a suggestion for wider meanings. In personal relations too there is much behavior that may be called symbolic, as when a ceremonious bow is directed not so much to an actual person as to a status which that person happens to fill. The psychoanalysts have come to apply the term symbolic to almost any emotionally charged pattern of behavior which has the function of unconscious fulfilment of a repressed tendency, as when a person assumes a raised voice of protest to a perfectly indifferent stranger who unconsciously recalls his father and awakens the repressed attitude of hostility toward the father.

Amid the wide variety of senses in which the word is used there seem to emerge two constant characteristics. One of these is that the symbol is always a substitute for some more closely intermediating type of behavior, whence it follows that all symbolism implies meanings which cannot be derived directly from the contexts of experience. The second characteristic of the symbol is that it expresses a condensation of energy, its actual significance being out of all proportion to the apparent triviality of meaning suggested by its mere form. This can be seen at once when the mildly decorative function of a few scratches on paper is com-

* *Encyclopaedia of the Social Sciences* (New York, Macmillan, 1934), 14: 492–495.

pared with the alarming significance of apparently equally random scratches which are interpreted by a particular society as meaning "murder" or "God." This disconcerting transcendence of form comes out equally well in the contrast between the involuntary blink of the eye and the crudely similar wink which means "He does not know what an ass he is, but you and I do."

It seems useful to distinguish two main types of symbolism. The first of these, which may be called referential symbolism, embraces such forms as oral speech, writing, the telegraph code, national flags, flag signaling and other organizations of symbols which are agreed upon as economical devices for purposes of reference. The second type of symbolism is equally economical and may be termed condensation symbolism, for it is a highly condensed form of substitutive behavior for direct expression, allowing for the ready release of emotional tension in conscious or unconscious form. Telegraphic ticking is virtually a pure example of referential symbolism; the apparently meaningless washing ritual of an obsessive neurotic, as interpreted by the psychoanalysts, would be a pure example of condensation symbolism. In actual behavior both types are generally blended. Thus specific forms of writing, conventionalized spelling, peculiar pronunciations and verbal slogans, while ostensibly referential, easily take on the character of emotionalized rituals and become highly important to both individual and society as substitutive forms of emotional expression. Were writing merely referential symbolism, spelling reforms would not be so difficult to bring about.

Symbols of the referential type undoubtedly developed later as a class than condensation symbols. It is likely that most referential symbolisms go back to unconsciously evolved symbolisms saturated with emotional quality, which gradually took on a purely referential character as the linked emotion dropped out of the behavior in question. Thus shaking the fist at an imaginary enemy becomes a dissociated and finally a referential symbol for anger when no enemy, real or imaginary, is actually intended. When this emotional denudation takes place, the symbol becomes a comment, as it were, on anger itself and a preparation for something like language. What is ordinarily called language may have had its ultimate root in just such dissociated and emotionally denuded cries, which originally released emotional tension. Once referential symbolism had been established by a by-product of behavior, more conscious symbols of reference could be evolved by the copying in abbreviated or simplified form of the thing referred to, as in the case of pictographic writing. On still more sophisticated levels referential symbolism may be attained by mere social agreement, as when a numbered check is arbitrarily assigned to a man's hat. The less primary and associational the symbolism, the more dissociated from its original context, and the less emotionalized it becomes, the more it takes on the character of true reference. A further condition for the rich development of referential symbolism must not be overlooked—the increased complexity and homogeneity of the symbolic material. This is strikingly the case in language, in which all meanings are consistently expressed by formal patterns arising out of the apparently arbitrary sequences of unitary sounds. When the material of a symbolic system becomes sufficiently varied and yet homogeneous in kind, the symbolism becomes more and more richly patterned, creative and meaningful in its own terms, and referents tend to be supplied by a retrospective act of rationalization. Hence it results that such complex systems of meaning as a sentence form or a musical form mean so much more than they can ever be said to refer to. In highly evolved systems of reference the relation between symbol and referent becomes increasingly variable or inclusive.

In condensation symbolism also richness of meaning grows with increased dissociation. The chief developmental difference, however, between this type of symbolism and referential symbolism is that while the latter grows with formal elaboration in the conscious, the former strikes deeper and deeper roots in the unconscious and diffuses its emotional quality to types of behavior or situations apparently far removed from the original meaning of the symbol. Both types of symbols therefore begin with situations in which a sign is dissociated from its context. The conscious elaboration of form makes of such dissociation a system of reference, while the unconscious spread of emotional quality makes of it a condensation symbol. Where, as in the case of a national flag or a beautiful poem, a symbolic expression which is apparently one of mere reference is associated with repressed emotional material of great importance to the ego, the two theoretically distinct types of symbolic behavior merge into one. One then deals with symbols of peculiar potency and even danger, for unconscious meanings, full of emotional power, become rationalized as mere references.

It is customary to say that society is peculiarly subject to the influence of symbols in such emotionally charged fields as religion and politics. Flags and slogans are the type examples in the field of politics, crosses and ceremonial regalia in the field of religion. But all culture is in fact heavily charged with symbolism, as is all personal behavior. Even comparatively simple forms of behavior are far less directly functional than they seem to be, but include in their motivation unconscious and even unacknowledged impulses, for which the behavior must be looked upon as a symbol. Many, perhaps most reasons are little more than ex post facto rationalizations of behavior controlled by unconscious necessity. Even an elaborate, well documented scientific theory may from this standpoint be little more than a symbol of the unknown necessities of the ego. Scientists fight for their theories not because they believe them to be true but because they wish them to be so.

It will be useful to give examples of some of the less obvious symbolisms in socialized behavior. Etiquette has at least two layers of symbolism. On a relatively obvious plane of symbolism etiquette provides the members of society with a set of rules which, in condensed and thoroughly conventionalized form, express society's concern for its members and their relation to one another. There is another level of etiquette symbolism, however, which takes little or no account of such specific meanings but interprets etiquette as a whole as a powerful symbolism of status. From this standpoint to know the rules of etiquette is important, not because the feelings of friends and strangers are becomingly observed but because the manipulator of the rule proves that he is a member of an exclusive group. By reason of the richly developed meanings which inhere in etiquette, both positive and negative, a sensitive person can actually express a more bitter hostility through the frigid observance of etiquette than by flouting it on an obvious wave of hostility. Etiquette, then, is an unusually elaborate symbolic play in which individuals in their actual relationships are the players and society is the bogus referee.

Education is also a thoroughly symbolic field of behavior. Much of its rationale cannot be tested as to direction or value. No one knows or can discover just how much Latin, French, mathematics or history is good for any particular person to acquire. The tests of the attainment of such knowledge are themselves little more than symbolic gestures. For the social psychologist education, whatever else it may be or do, stands out as a peculiarly massive and well articulated set of symbols which express the needs of the individual in society and which help him to orient himself in his relations to his fellow men. That an individual possesses the bachelor's degree may or may not prove that he knows, or once knew, something about Roman history and trigonometry. The important thing about his degree is that it helps him to secure a position which is socially or economically more desirable than some other position which can be obtained without the aid of this degree. Society has misgivings about the function of specific items in the educational process and has to make symbolic atonement by inventing such notions as the cultivation of the mind.

It is important to observe that symbolic meanings can often be recognized clearly for the first time when the symbolic value, generally unconscious or conscious only in a marginal sense, drops out of a socialized pattern of behavior and the supposed function, which up to that time had been believed to be more than enough to explain it and keep it going, loses its significance and is seen to be little more than a paltry rationalization. Chairmanship of a committee, for instance, has symbolic value only in a society in which two things are believed: that administrative functions somehow stamp a person as superior to those who are being directed; and that the ideal society is a democratic one and that those who are naturally more able than others somehow automatically get into positions of administrative advantage. Should people come to feel that administrative functions are little more than symbolic automatisms, the chairmanship of a committee would be recognized as little more than a petrified symbol and the particular value that is now felt to inhere in it would tend to disappear.

An important field for investigation is that of personal symbolisms in the use of cultural patterns. Personal symbolisms are often the more valuable as they are hidden from consciousness and serve as the springs of effective behavior. Interest in a particular science may be an elaborately sublimated symbol of an unconscious emotional attachment to what a man who is significant in one's personal development is believed to be linked up with, such as the destruction of religion or the discovery of God, these grandiose preferences in turn serving as symbols of repressed hate or love. Much charitable endeavor is animated by an unconscious desire to peer into lives that one is glad to be unable to share. Society itself, perfecting its rigid mechanisms of charitable activity, cannot in every case or even in the vast majority of cases subject the charitable act to a pragmatic critique but must rest content for the most part with charity organization as its symbolic gesture toward alleviating suffering. Thus individual and society, in a never ending interplay of symbolic gestures, build up the pyramided structure called civilization. In this structure very few bricks touch the ground.

WHY CULTURAL ANTHROPOLOGY NEEDS THE PSYCHIATRIST*

UNTIL not so many years ago cultural anthropology and psychiatry seemed miles apart. Cultural anthropology was conceived of as a social science which concerned itself little, if at all, with the individual. Its province was rather to emphasize those aspects of behavior which belonged to society as such, more particularly societies of the dim past or exotic societies whose way of life seemed so different from that of our own people that one could hope to construct a generalized picture of the life of society at large, particularly in its more archaic stages of development. There was little need in the anthropology of a Tylor or Frazer to ask questions which demanded a more intimate knowledge of the individual than could be assumed on the basis of common experience. The important distinctions were felt to be distinctions of race, of geographical setting, of chronology, of cultural province. The whole temper of cultural anthropology was impersonal to a degree. In this earlier period of the development of the science it seemed almost indelicate, not to say indecent, to obtrude observations that smacked of the personal or anecdotal. The assumption was that in some way not in the least clearly defined as to observational method it was possible for the anthropologist to arrive at conclusive statements which would hold for a given society as such. One was rarely in a position to say whether such an inclusive statement was a tacit quotation from a primitive "John Doe" or a carefully tested generalization abstracted from hundreds of personal observations or hundreds of statements excerpted from conversations with many John Does.

Perhaps it is just as well that no strict methodology of field inquiry was perfected and that embarrassing questions as to the factual nature of the evidence which led to anthropological generalizations were courteously withheld by a sort of gentlemen's agreement. I remember being rather shocked than pleased when in my student days I came across such statements in J. O. Dorsey's "Omaha Sociology" as "Two Crows denies this." This looked a little as though the writer had not squarely met the challenge of assaying his source material and giving us the kind of data that we, as respectable anthropologists, could live on. It was as though he "passed the buck" to the reader, expecting him by some miracle of cultural insight to segregate truth from error. We see now that Dorsey was ahead of his age. Living as he did in close touch with the Omaha Indians, he knew that he was dealing, not with a society nor with a

* *Psychiatry*, 1 (1938): 7–12.

specimen of primitive man nor with a cross-section of the history of primitive culture, but with a finite, though indefinite, number of human beings, who gave themselves the privilege of differing from each other not only in matters generally considered as "one's own business" but even on questions which clearly transcended the private individual's concern and were, by the anthropologist's definition, implied in the conception of a definitely delimited society with a definitely discoverable culture. Apparently Two Crows, a perfectly good and authoritative Indian, could presume to rule out of court the very existence of a custom or attitude or belief vouched for by some other Indian, equally good and authoritative. Unless one wishes to dismiss the implicit problem raised by contradictory statements by assuming that Dorsey, the anthropologist, misunderstood one, or both, of his informants, one would have to pause for a while and ponder the meaning of the statement that "Two Crows denies this."

This is not the place to introduce anything like a complete analysis of the meaning of such contradictory statements, real or supposed. The only thing that we need to be clear about is whether a completely impersonal anthropological description and analysis of custom in terms which tacitly assume the unimportance of individual needs and preferences is, in the long run, truly possible for a social discipline. There has been so much talk of ideal objectivity in social science and such eager willingness to take the ideals of physical and chemical workmanship as translatable into the procedures of social research that we really ought not to blink this problem. Suppose we take a test case. John Doe and an Indian named Two Feathers agree that two and two make four. Someone reports that "Two Crows denies this." Inasmuch as we know that the testimony of the first two informants is the testimony of all human beings who are normally considered as entitled to a hearing, we do not attach much importance to Two Crows' denial. We do not even say that he is mistaken. We suspect that he is crazy. In the case of more abstruse problems in the world of natural science, we narrow the field of authority to those individuals who are known, or believed, to be in full command of techniques that enable them to interpret the impersonal testimony of the physical universe. Everyone knows that the history of science is full of corrective statements on errors of judgment but no value is attached to such errors beyond the necessity of ruling them out of the record. Though the mistaken scientist's hurt feelings may be of great interest to a psychologist or psychiatrist, they are nothing for the votaries of pure science to worry about.

Are correspondingly ruthless judgments possible in the field of social science? Hardly. Let us take a desperately extreme case. All the members of a given community agree in arranging the letters of the alphabet in a certain historically determined order, an order so fixed and so thoroughly ingrained in the minds of all normal children who go to school that the attempt to tamper with this order has, to the man in the street, the same ridiculous, one might almost say unholy, impossibility as an attempt to have the sun rise half an hour earlier or later than celestial mechanics decree to be proper. There is one member of this hypothetical society who takes the liberty of interchanging A and Z. If he keeps his strange departure from custom to himself, no one need ever know how queer he really is. If he contradicts his children's teacher and tries to tell them that they should put Z first and A last, he is almost certain to run foul of his fellow beings. His own children may desert him in spite of their natural tendency to recognize parental authority. Certainly we should agree that this very peculiar kind of a Two Crows is crazy, and we may even agree as psychiatrists that so far as an understanding of his aberrant phantasies and behavior is concerned, it really makes little difference whether what he is impelled to deny is that two and two are four or the order of the letters of the alphabet is a conventionally, or naturally, fixed order.

At this point we have misgivings. Is the parallel as accurate as it seems to be? There is an important difference, which we have perhaps overlooked in our joint condemnation. This difference may be expressed in terms of possibility. No matter how many Two Crows deny that two and two make four, the actual history of mathematics, however retarded by such perversity, cannot be seriously modified by it. But if we get enough Two Crows to agree on the interchange of A and Z, we have what we call a new tradition, or a new dogma, or a new theory, or a new procedure, in the handling of that particular pattern of culture which is known as the alphabet. What starts as a thoroughly irresponsible and perhaps psychotic aberration seems to have the power, by some kind of "social infection," to lose its purely personal quality and to take on something of that very impersonality of custom which, in the first instance, it seemed to contradict so flatly. The reason for this is very simple. Whatever the majority of the members of a given society may say, there is no inherent human impossibility in an alphabet which starts with a symbol for the sound or sounds represented by the letter Z and ends up with a symbol for the vocalic sound or sounds represented by the letter A. The consensus of history, anthropology, and common sense leads us to maintain that the actually accepted order of letters is "necessary" only in a very conditional sense and that this necessity can, under appropriate conditions of human interrelationship, yield to a conflict of possibilities, which may ultimately iron out into an entirely different "necessity."

The truth of the matter is that if we think long enough about Two Crows and his persistent denials, we shall have to admit that in some sense Two Crows is never wrong. It may not be a very useful sense for social science but in a strict methodology of science in general it dare not be completely ignored. The fact that this rebel, Two Crows, can in turn bend others to his own view of fact or theory or to his own preference in action shows that his divergence from custom had, from the very beginning, the essential possibility of culturalized behavior. It seems, therefore, that we must regretfully admit that the rebel who tampers with the truths of mathematics or physics or chemistry is not really the same kind of rebel as the one who plays nine-pins with custom, whether in theory or practice. The latter is likely to make more of a nuisance of himself than the former. No doubt he runs the risk of being condemned with far greater heat by his fellow men but he just cannot be proved to contradict some mysterious essence of things. He can only be said, at best, to disagree completely with everybody else in a matter in which opinion or preference, in however humble and useless a degree, is after all possible.

We have said nothing so far that is not utterly commonplace. What is strange is that the ultimate importance of these commonplaces seems not to be thoroughly grasped by social scientists at the present time. If the ultimate criterion of value interpretation, and even "existence," in the world of socialized behavior is nothing more than consensus of opinion, it is difficult to see how cultural anthropology can escape the ultimate necessity of testing out its analysis of patterns called "social" or "cultural" in terms of individual realities. If people tend to become illiterate, owing to a troubled political atmosphere, the "reality" of the alphabet weakens. It may still be true that the order of the letters is, in the minds of those relatively few people who know anything about the alphabet, precisely what it always was, but in a cultural atmosphere of unrest and growing illiteracy a Two Crows who interchanges A and Z is certainly not as crazy as he would have been at a more fortunate time in the past. We are quick to see the importance of the individual in those more flexible fields of cultural patterning that are referred to as ideals or tastes or personal preferences. A truly rigorous analysis of any arbitrarily selected phase of individualized "social behavior" or "culture" would show two things: First, that no matter how flexible, how individually variable, it may in the first instance be thought to be, it is as a matter of fact the complex resultant of an incredibly elaborate cultural history, in which many diverse strands intercross at that point in place and time at which the individual judgment or preference is expressed [this terminology is *cultural*]; second, that, conversely, no matter how rigorously necessary in practice the analyzed pattern may seem to be, it is always possible in principle, if not in experiential fact, for the lone individual to effect a transformation of form or meaning which is capable of communication to other individuals [this terminology is *psychiatric* or *personalistic*]. What this means is that problems of social science differ from problems of individual behavior in degree of specificity, not in kind. Every statement about behavior which throws the emphasis, explicitly or implicitly, on the actual, integral, experiences of defined personalities or types of personalities is a datum of psychology or psychiatry rather than of social science. Every statement about behavior which aims, not to be accurate about the behavior of an actual individual or individuals or about the expected behavior of a physically and psychologically defined type of individuals, but which abstracts from such behavior in order to bring out in clear relief certain expectancies with regard to those aspects of individual behavior which various people share, as an interpersonal or "social" pattern, is a datum, however crudely expressed, of social science.

If Dorsey tells us that "Two Crows denies this," surely there is a reason for his statement. We need not say that Two Crows is badly informed or that he is fooling the anthropologist. Is it not more reasonable to say that the totality of socialized habits, in short the "culture," that he was familiar with was not in all respects the same entity as the corresponding totality presented to the observation or introspection of some other Indian, or perhaps of all other Indians? If the question asked by the anthropologist involved a mere question of personal affirmation, we need have no difficulty in understanding his denial. But even if it involved the question of "objective fact," we need not be too greatly shocked by the denial. Let us suppose that the anthropologist asked the simple question, "Are there seven clans or eight clans in moiety A of your tribe?", or words to that effect. All other Indians that he has asked about this sheer question of "fact" have said eight, we will assume. Two Crows claims there are only seven. How can this be? If we look more closely to the facts, we should undoubtedly find that the contradiction is not as puzzling as it seems. It may turn out that one of the clans had been extinct for a long time, most of the informants, however, remembering some old man, now deceased, who had been said to be the last survivor of it. They might feel that while the clan no longer exists in a practical sense, it has a theoretical place in the ordered description of the tribe's social organization. Perhaps there is some ceremonial function or placement, properly belonging to the extinct clan, which is remembered as such and which makes it a little difficult to completely overlook its claims to "existence." Various things, on the other hand, may be true of Two Crows. He may have belonged to a clan which had good reason to detest the extinct clan, perhaps because it had humiliated a relative of his in the dim past. It is certainly conceivable that the factual non-existence of the clan coupled with his personal reason for thinking as little about it as possible might give him the perfectly honest conviction that one need speak of only seven clans in the tribe. There is no reason why the normal anthropological investigator should, in an inquiry of this kind, look much beneath the surface of a simple answer to a simple question. It almost looks as though either seven clans or eight clans might be the "correct" answer to an apparently unambiguous question. The problem is very simple here. By thinking a little about Two Crows himself, we are enabled to show that he was not wrong, though he seemed to disagree with all his fellow Indians. He had a special kind of rightness, which was partly factual, partly personal.

Have we not the right to go on from simple instances of this sort and advance to the position that any statement, no matter how general, which can be made about culture needs the supporting testimony of a tangible person or persons, to whom such a statement is of real value in his system of interrelationships with other human beings? If this is so, we shall, at last analysis, have to admit that any individual of a group has cultural definitions which do not apply to all the members of his group, which even, in specific instances, apply to him alone. Instead, therefore, of arguing from a supposed objectivity of culture to the problem of individual variation, we shall, for certain kinds of analysis, have to proceed in the opposite direction. We shall have to operate as though we knew nothing about culture but were interested in analyzing as well as we could what a given number of human beings accustomed to live with each other actually think and do in their day to day relationships. We shall then find that we are driven, willy-nilly, to the recognition of certain permanencies, in a relative sense, in these interrelationships, permanencies which can reasonably be counted on to perdure but which must also be recognized to be eternally subject to serious modification of form and meaning with the lapse of time and with those changes of personnel which are unavoidable in the history of any group of human beings.

This mode of thinking is, of course, essentially psychiatric. Psychiatrists may, or may not, believe in cultural patterns, in group minds, in historic tendencies, or even missions; they cannot avoid believing in particular people. Personalities may be dubbed fictions by sociologists, anthropologists, and even by certain psychologists, but they must be accepted as bread and butter realities by the psychiatrist. Nothing, in short, can be more real to a psychiatrist than a personality organization, its modification from infancy to death, its essential persistence in terms of consciousness and ego reference. From this point of view culture cannot be accepted as anything more than a convenient assemblage, or at best total theory, of real or possible modes of behavior abstracted from the experienced realities of communication, whether in the form of overt behavior or in the form of fantasy. Even the alphabet from this standpoint becomes a datum of personality research! As a matter of fact, the alphabet does mean different things to different people. It is loved by some, hated by others, an object of indifference to most. It is a purely instrumental thing to a few; it has varying kinds of overtones of meaning for most, ranging all the way from the weakly sentimental to the passionately poetic. No one in his senses would wish the alphabet studied from this highly personalistic point of view. In plain English, it would not be worth the trouble. The total meaning of the alphabet for X is so very nearly the same as that for any other individual, Y, that one does much better to analyze it and explain its relation to other cultural patterns in terms of an impersonal, or cultural, or anthropological mode of description. The fact, however, that X has had more difficulty in learning the alphabet than Y, or that in old age X may forget the alphabet or some part of it more readily than Y, shows clearly enough that there is a psychiatric side to even the coldest and most indifferent of cultural patterns. Even such cold and indifferent cultural patterns have locked in them psychiatric meanings which are ordinarily of no moment to the student of society but which may under peculiar circumstances come to the foreground of attention. When this happens, anthropological data need to be translated into psychiatric terms.

What we have tried to advance is little more than a plea for the assistance of the psychiatrist in the study of certain problems which come up in an analysis of socialized behavior. In spite of all that has been claimed to the contrary, we cannot thoroughly understand the dynamics of culture, of society, of history, without sooner or later taking account of the actual interrelationships of human beings. We can postpone this psychiatric analysis indefinitely but we cannot theoretically eliminate it. With the modern growth of interest in the study of personality and with the growing conviction of the enormous flexibility of personality adjust-

ment to one's fellow men, it is difficult to see how one's intellectual
curiosity about the problems of human intercourse can be forever satisfied
by schematic statements about society and its stock of cultural patterns.
The very variations and uncertainties which the earlier anthropologists
ignored seem to be the very aspects of human behavior that future
students of society will have to look to with a special concern, for it is
only through an analysis of variation that the reality and meaning of a
norm can be established at all, and it is only through a minute and sympathetic study of individual behavior in the state in which normal human
beings find themselves, namely in a state of society, that it will ultimately
be possible to say things about society itself and culture that are more
than fairly convenient abstractions. Surely, if the social scientist is interested in effective consistencies, in tendencies, and in values, he must not
dodge the task of studying the effects produced by individuals of varying
temperaments and backgrounds on each other. Anthropology, sociology,
indeed social science in general, is notoriously weak in the discovery of
effective consistencies. This weakness, it seems, is not unrelated to a
fatal fallacy with regard to the objective reality of social and cultural
patterns defined impersonally.

Causation implies continuity, as does personality itself. The social
scientist's world of reality is generally expressed in discontinuous terms.
An effective philosophy of causation in the realm of social phenomena
seems impossible so long as these phenomena are judged to have a valid
existence and sequence in their own right. It is only when they are translated into the underlying facts of behavior from which they have never
been divorced in reality that one can hope to advance to an understanding of causes. The test can be made easily enough. We have no difficulty in understanding how a given human being's experiences tend to
produce certain results in the further conduct of his life. Our knowledge
is far too fragmentary to allow us to understand fully, but there is never
a serious difficulty in principle in imputing to the stream of his experiences that causative quality which we take for granted in the physical
universe. To the extent that we can similarly speak of causative sequences
in social phenomena, what we are really doing is to pyramid, as skilfully
and as rapidly as possible, the sorts of cause and effect relations that
we are familiar with in individual experience, imputing these to a social
reality which has been constructed out of our need for a maximally economical expression of typically human events. It will be the future task
of the psychiatrist to read cause and effect in human history. He cannot
do it now because his theory of personality is too weak and because he
tends to accept with too little criticism the impersonal mode of social

and cultural analysis which anthropology has made fashionable. If, therefore, we answer our initial question, "Why cultural anthropology needs the psychiatrist," in a sense entirely favorable to the psychiatrist, that is, to the systematic student of human personality, we do not for a moment mean to assert that any psychiatry that has as yet been evolved is in a position to do much more than to ask intelligent questions.

PSYCHIATRIC AND CULTURAL PITFALLS IN THE BUSINESS OF GETTING A LIVING*

ALL SPECIAL sciences of man's physical and cultural nature tend to create a framework of tacit assumptions which enable their practitioners to work with maximum economy and generality. The classical example of this unavoidable tendency is the science of economics, which is too intent on working out a general theory of value, production, flow of commodities, demand, price, to take time to inquire seriously into the nature and variability of those fundamental biological and psychological determinants of behavior which make these economic terms meaningful in the first place. The sum total of the tacit assumptions of a biological and psychological nature which economics makes get petrified into a standardized conception of "economic man," who is endowed with just those motivations which make the known facts of economic behavior in our society seem natural and inevitable. In this way the economist gradually develops a peculiarly powerful insensitiveness to actual motivations, substituting life-like fictions for the troublesome contours of life itself.

The economist is not in the least exceptional in his unconscious procedure. Any one who deals habitually with what man makes and thinks, not because he is interested in man directly but because he wishes to find law and order in what man makes and thinks, slips, by insensible degrees, into the assumption that such regularities of form and process as he finds in selected categories of man's behavior are fundamentally due to a peculiar quality of self-determination in those categories rather than to the ceaseless, eternally shifting, balancing of concretely definable motivations of particular people at particular times and in particular places. The very terminology which is used by the many kinds of segmental scientists of man indicates how remote man himself has become as a necessary concept in the methodology of the respective sciences. Thus, in economics, one speaks of "the flow of commodities," without special concern for a close factual analysis of modifications of demand which, if studied in their full realism, might be shown to be due to such factors as hatred of an alien group, growth of superstition, increased interest in bawdy shows, or decline of prestige of hotel life, each of these motivational categories, in turn, opening up a series of inquiries into intricate problems of interpersonal relations, direct and symbolic. In aesthetics, one can speak of "necessary balances of lines or tone masses"

* *Mental Health*, Publication No. 9 (American Association for the Advancement of Science, 1939), pp. 237–244.

almost as though one were the Demiurge of the universe in whispered conversation with the law of gravitation, apparently without a suspicion that defects of eye and ear structure or highly indirect imputations of "meaning" due to the vacillations of fashion have anything to do with the "aesthetic" problem of how to create "satisfactory balances" of an "aesthetic order." In linguistics, abstracted speech sounds, words and the arrangement of words have come to have so authentic a vitality that one can speak of "regular sound changes" and "loss of genders" without knowing or caring who opened their mouths, at what time, to communicate what to whom.

Science vs. Man.—The purpose of these remarks is simply to indicate that science itself, when applied to the field of normal human interest, namely man and his daily concerns, creates a serious difficulty for those of us who find it profitable to envisage a true "psychiatric science" or "science of interpersonal relations."[1] The nature of this difficulty may be defined as follows. Inasmuch as science has greater prestige in our serious thinking than daily observation, however shrewd or accurate, or than those obscure convictions about human beings which result from a ceaseless experiencing of them, there tends to grow up in the minds of the vast majority of us a split between two kinds of "knowledge" about man. Every fragmentary science of man, such as economics or political

---

[1] As some of my readers have from time to time expressed their difficulty with my non-medical use of the terms "psychiatry" and "psychiatric," I must explain that I use these terms in lieu of a possible use of "psychology" and "psychological" with explicit stress on the total personality as the central point of reference in all problems of behavior and in all problems of "culture" (analysis of socialized patterns). Thus, a segmental behavior study, such as a statistical inquiry into the ability of children of the age group 7–11 to learn to read, is not in my sense a properly "psychiatric" study because the attention is focused on a fundamentally arbitrary objective, however important or interesting, one not directly suggested by the study of personality structure and the relations of defined personalities to each other. Such a study may be referred to "psychology" or "applied psychology" or "education" or "educational psychology." Equally marginal to "psychiatry" in my sense is such a study in the externalized patterning of "collective behavior" as the analysis of a ritual or handicraft, whether descriptively or historically. Studies of this type may be referred to "ethnology" or "culture history" or "sociology."

On the other hand, a systematic study of the acquirement of reading habits with reference to whether they help or hinder the development of fantasy in children of defined personality type is a properly "psychiatric" study because the concept of the total personality is necessarily utilized in it. A close study of the symbolisms of ritual or handicraft, provided these symbolisms are discussed as having immediate relevance for our understanding of personality types, is also a truly "psychiatric" study. "Personology" and "personalistic" would be adequate terms but are too uncouth for practical use. My excuse for extending the purely "medical" connotation of the terms "psychiatry" and "psychiatric" is that psychiatrists themselves, in trying to understand the wherefore of aberrant behavior, have had to look far more closely into basic problems of personality structure, of symbolism, and of fundamental human interrelationships than have either the "psychologists" or the various types of "social scientists."

science or aesthetics or linguistics, needs at least a minimum set of assumptions about the nature of man in order to house the particular propositions and records of events which belong to its selected domain. These fragmentary pictures of man are not in intelligible or relevant accord with each other nor do they, when wilfully integrated by a sort of philosophic fiat, give us anything remotely resembling the tightly organized and fatefully moving individuals that we cannot but know and understand up to a certain point, however much it may be to our advantage not to know and understand them at all. A student of aesthetics finds it very much to his advantage to make certain sweeping assumptions about the "aesthetic nature" of man in order to give himself maximum clearance for the development of those propositions and for the record and explanation of those events which professionally interest him, those that work with him and those that have preceded him in a prestige-laden tradition. Random observations about "beautiful" things or structures, such as arrangements of ideas, such observations as might be made by a child or by any naïve person who cannot define aesthetic terms and who has no conscious place for them in that personally useful vocabulary which defines his universe, tend to be dismissed as marginal to the proper concern of aesthetics, as untutored, as of impure conceptual manufacture. The aesthetician is amused or annoyed, as the case may be. He has to be almost a genius to be instructed. The less fateful is the split between his professional conception of man as a beauty-discerning and beauty-creating organism and his humble perceptions of man as a psychobiological organism, the less difficulty will he have to surrender the rigid outlines of his science to the fate of all historical constructs. Such a synthetist is secretly grateful for anything that jars him out of the certainties and necessities of his ghost-inhabited science and brings him back to the conditionalities of an experience that was too hastily and magnificently integrated ("cured," the psychiatrist might say) by his science in the first place.

It is not really difficult, then, to see why anyone brought up on the austerities of a well-defined science of man must, if he is to maintain his symbolic self-respect, become more and more estranged from man himself. Economic laws become more "real" than certain people who try to make a living; the necessities of the "State" get to outweigh in conceptual urgency the desire of the vast majority of human beings to be bothered as little as possible; the laws of syntax acquire a higher reality than the immediate reality of the stammerer who is trying to "get himself across"; the absolute beauty, or lack of it, of an isolated picture or isolated poem becomes a mere insistent item in the diary of the cosmos than the mere fact of whether there is anybody around who is moved by it or not.

Now fantasied universes of self-contained meaning are the very finest and noblest substitutes we can ever devise for that precise and loving insight into the nooks and crannies of the real that must be forever denied us. But we must not reverse the arrow of experience and claim for experience's imaginative condensations the primacy in an appeal to our loyalty, which properly belongs to our perceptions of men and women as the ultimate units of value in our day-to-day view of the world. If we do not thus value the nuclei of consciousness from which all science, all art, all history, all culture, have flowed as symbolic by-products in the humble but intensely urgent business of establishing meaningful relationships between actual human beings, we commit personal suicide. The theology of economics or aesthetics or of any other ordered science of man weighs just as heavily on us, whether we know it or not, as the outmoded theologies of gods and their worshippers. Not for one single moment can we allow ourselves to forget the experienced unity of the individual. No formulations about man and his place in society which do not prove strictly and literally accurate when tested by the experience of the individual can have more than a transitory or technical authority. Hence we need never fear to modify, prune, extend, redefine, rearrange, and reorient our sciences of man as social being, for these sciences cannot point to an order of nature that has meaning apart from the directly experienced perceptions and values of the individual.

"Economic Man."—Let us consider the meaning of the problem of "earning a living." It is not a simple problem, though it is relatively so for the economist. If the economist hears that A gets a salary of $1500.00 a year, his scientific curiosity does not go much beyond trying to ascertain if this income is a normal one for the services that A is said to be rendering. Should he discover that A is a "full professor" at a "university," he will note the fact that the salary is well below the average fee paid in America for the kind of work that "full professors" do. Beyond such observation he will have nothing to offer, though, if he is himself a professor or the son of a professor, he may allow himself a twinge of concern at the imperilment of the economic status of a peculiarly valuable class of person in the cultural scene of contemporary America. But, strictly speaking, A's salary of $1500.00 a year must be interpreted as an item in the strictly economic process of balancing the demand for such services as A is rendering, or is supposed to be rendering, with the supply of individuals capable of rendering them at as low a figure as A is willing to accept. It will not be important for the economist to try to find out

if A's salary is as low as it is because he is a member of a poor religious sect which is not in a position to pay more for the full professors of its sectarian university or universities (such curiosity is as unseemly for an economist as would be the desire of a physicist to know whether his falling body was blue or bright red, though the economist might allow his less austere colleague, the sociologist, to indulge in a few musings on the subject) or because A is, as a matter of fact, a millionaire with an educational hobby which he feels he ought to give his fellow citizens the benefit of at small cost to "society." You can't get any more of a personality sketch of A out of the economist than that A just does happen to illustrate a somewhat unusual equilibration of the law of supply and demand.

In fairness to the economist it must be stated that just as he fails to be seriously perturbed over the singularly low economic standard of A, *qua* full professor, so he fails to be greatly saddened by the spectacle of B's efforts to get along on $500.00 a year, even if it can be proved that B is married, has three or four children, and is not a millionaire in disguise. Should B also prove to be a full professor, the economist might be pardoned if there grows up in him a more serious uneasiness as to the imperilment of the economic status of a class in which, being a member of it, he has after all a little more than a merely mathematical interest. But no, B is not a full professor, he is merely a farmer and the economist is quickly reassured that all's well with B, or, if B really is having a desperately hard time of it, at least all's well with *B qua* farmer, for he finds that B's income is snugly within the normal limits of income earned by American agriculturists—among the most useful of our various classes of citizens, he is quite willing to add. Here too the economist is very skillful in placing B at any one of those strategic corners of space and time in which certain factors of supply and demand get properly equilibrated. Anyway, if his irrelevant "personalistic," not to say humanitarian, interests are too greatly aroused, he can take quick comfort in the fact that the average income of the American farmer is well above $500.00 a year, so that B, a member of the farmer class, ought not to be too greatly discouraged. Or, if B is not easily reassured, at least those who tend to be worried about B should cease to be so. Of course B may be a peculiarly shiftless person, but the economist will not press that point. It is better to be statistically magnanimous and to content oneself with reflecting that B just does happen to stand at one of the less rewarding corners of space and time. There is no need to develop an essentially "unscientific" interest in B's personality, in his "cultural" background, and in the nature of the value judgments and "symbolisms" of society re B that add up to so trifling an emolument for this particular farmer.

In still further fairness to the economist it should be said that not only is he prepared to accept as "normal" or "natural" incomes that an ordinary person or even a sociologist might describe as "subnormal" or "unnatural," from an angle of observation that subtends much more than the field of operation of "economic laws," but he is also prepared to accept as entirely "normal" or "natural" incomes that are fantastically beyond the ability of anyone to "handle" except by way of the most peculiar, remote, picturesque, symbolic, in short, dream-like or make-believe, extensions of the personalities of the recipients of such incomes. Should any impertinent, thoroughly unscientific, snooper whisper to the economist that, so far as he can see, C's $500,000.00 income (in virtue of his vice-presidency of the X bank plus shareholdership in the Y company plus investment in the Z oil-fields of Mexico plus a long list of other services rendered his fellowmen) seems to be strangely unaffected by the tissue of physical and psychological performances of the psychophysical entity or organism called C, it making apparently little difference whether C is on hand to instruct one of his secretaries to cut his coupons or is resting up in the Riviera, the economist loses patience. If he then speaks at all, it is to point out that, regardless of C's to him unknown and forever unknowable personality, C does, as a matter of fact, render just such services as society demands and receives just such emoluments as society is "agreed" naturally flow from the rendering of these services and that the supposed "facts" about C are of no more interest to him than are, to a professor of alphabetology, certain reports about bad boys scrawling obscene words on a brick wall instead of turning out Shakespearian plays.

In desperation, then, let us admit that the economist is right and reflect, once and for all, that the economist is no more interested in human beings than the alphabetologist is interested in literature, the numismatist in the morality of the kings of Bactria, or the theologian in the chemical rationalization of miracles; that is to say, respectively, *qua* economist, *qua* alphabetologist, *qua* numismatist, *qua* theologian. These various scientists have their "universes of discourse" that they are extremely proud of, through the instrumentality of which they secure valuable definitions of their egos and at least partially earn their living, and there's an end of it. The necessarily fragmentary, philosophically arbitrary "universe of discourse" gets provided with an excellent terminology, more or less self-contained and self-consistent principles, and some insight, however tangential, into a highly selective phase of human behavior (including human opinion about divine behavior).

There is no mischief in all this, once it is clearly understood that the scientist of man has chief concern for science, not for man, and that all science, partly for better and partly for worse, has the self-feeding voracity of an obsessive ritual. We must give up our naïve faith in the ability of the scientist to tell us anything about man that is not expressible in terms of the verbal definitions and operations that prevail in his "universe of discourse"—a beautiful, dream-like domain that has fitful reminiscences of man as an experiencing organism but is not, and cannot be, immersed in the wholeness of that experience. Hence, while economics can tell us much about the technical operations that prevail in the conceptually well-defined "economic field," a specific type of "universe of discourse" which has only fragmentary and, at many points, even a fictional relation to the universe of experienced behavior, it cannot give us a working conception of *man* even in his abstracted role of earning a living, for the experiential implications of earning a living are not seen by the economist as part of his scientific concern.

Man as Man.—But it is precisely these experiential implications that we non-economists are interested in. We want to know what making a living (just about making it or failing to make it or making it a hundred times over) does to A and B and C. To what extent is the specific economic functioning of A and B and C of importance, not only to themselves and those immediately dependent on them, but to all human beings who come in contact with them and, beyond these empirical kinds of importance, to the eye of science? Not, to be sure, to the eye of any safely ticketed science that has its conceptual vested interests to conserve but to an inclusive science of man, one that does the best it can to harbor the value judgments of experiencing human beings within its own catholic "universe of discourse." Such a science will perhaps be called a dangerous or treacherous congeries of opinions, ranging all the way from the feeble aspirations of theologically or classically tinctured humanism to the sentimental, direct-action interferences of mental hygiene. But we need not be so pessimistic. For centuries the only escape from fragmentarism was into the too ambitious dream-worlds of philosophy, worlds defined by the assumption that the human intelligence could behold the universe instead of twinkling within. Now that philosophy is being progressively redefined as a highly technical critique of the validity or conditionality of judgments, it is interesting to see two disciplines—each of them highly apologetic about its scientific credentials—which are taking on the character of inclusive perception of human events and personal relations in as powerfully conceptualized form as possible. These condensations of human experience are cultural anthropology and psychiatry—both of them poorly chosen terms, but we can do no better for the moment.

Cultural Anthropology and Psychiatry.—Each of these disciplines has its special "universe of discourse" but at least this universe is so broadly conceived that, under favorable circumstances, either of them can take on the character of a true science of man. Through the sheer weight of cultural detail and, more than that, through the far-reaching personality-conditioning implications of variations in the forms of socialized behavior, the cultural anthropologist may, if he chooses, advance from his relatively technical problems of cultural definition, distribution, organization, and history to more intimate problems of cultural meaning, both for individuals and for significantly definable groups of individuals. And the psychiatrist may, if he chooses, advance from theories of personality disorganization to theories of personality organization, which, in the long run, have little meaning unless they are buttressed by a comprehension of the cultural setting in which the individual ceaselessly struggles to express himself. The anthropologist, in other words, needs only to trespass a little on the untilled acres of psychology, the psychiatrist to poach a few of the uneaten apples of anthropology's Golden Bough.

So far the great majority of both kinds of scientists—if that proud classification be granted them—have feared to advance very far into the larger fields that lie open before them, and for a good reason. The fear of losing the insignia of standing in their respective disciplines, still dangerously insecure in the hierarchy of science, leads to an anxious snobbery which is easily misunderstood as modesty or self-restraint. But at least they have this great advantage, so far as the study of man is concerned: neither, in his heart of hearts, believes that the economist or the political scientist or the aesthetician or any other sort of technical expert in conceptually isolated realms or aspects of man's behavior is in a position to talk real sense about that behavior. An anthropologist knows that you can't talk economics without talking about religion or superstition at the same time; the psychiatrist knows that you can't talk economics without dropping some rather important hints about mental health and disease. On the whole, it seems safest to keep such knowledge in one's heart of hearts and to act as though one were content to carry on from where the economist left off. Therefore, as culturalists, let us not be too much concerned with what sorts of cultural universes A and B and C are living in; as psychiatrists, let us not be too much concerned with what the play of "economic forces" is doing to A and B and C and be satisfied to mumble, as occasion arises, something quite discreet about how an income of $500.00 a year would not seem to discourage B's paranoid trends or about how poor C's Don Juanism, with its secret unhappiness, might possibly have been mitigated if he had only had an income of $5000.00 a year to play with. It is so easy to be paranoid on $500.00 a year and it is so difficult to be a Don Juan—and C, by the way, is not an Apollo—on $500.00 a year.

Economic Factors in Personal Adjustment.—Everybody really knows a good deal about what economics has to do with the personal distribution of "cultural patterns" and with mental health. The facts are pitifully obvious. Professors who earn only $1500.00 a year cannot go to the opera very often and must therefore go in for plain living and high thinking. If they have good health, are happily married, and have more than average intelligence, they and their wives can manage to stave off envy of the banker and real-estate agent and their respective wives, mingle sturdy Puritanism with a subscription to "The Nation," and construct a pretty good cultural world for themselves. After all, $1500.00 is three times as much as $500.00. But if their health is not too good, if they are not too happily married, and if their intelligence, as generally proves to be the case, is about average, then it is to be feared that $1500.00 is not quite sufficient to buy themselves enough of cultural participation to stave off that corroding envy of the banker and real-estate agent and their respective wives which, psychiatrists tell us, is not very good for either the digestive tract or the personality organization. So, one surmises, a salary of $1500.00 a year for a full professor may have a good deal to do with the gradual cultural impoverishment of A's universe. A normal vitality will mask the degenerative cultural and psychiatric process from himself, his neighbors, the trustees of the university and, above all, the economist, who, having been unpleasantly jarred for a moment by his threat to the salary curve of full professors, need never think of him again.

At first A's difficulties find their solution in a slightly apologetic vein of irony, which cultivated visitors find rather charming. A certain school of social psychologists might at this point even prove that A was quite appreciably enriching culture both for himself and society. (Few would have the hardihood to suggest that he was enriching the cultural world of his wife, though his children might be robust enough to pick up a few crumbs of value or, perhaps, more accurately, a few ambivalently colored experiences which the softening retrospect of later years will transmute into crumbs of value—if not indeed into a philosophy, so strong is the the magic of Illusion.) But A's charm does not wear well, no better than the loveliness, once so fashionable, of the incipiently tubercular flush. Any competent novelist may step in at this point and tell us about the fascinating story of his growing sense of isolation, his growing morbidity, the growing concern of the trustees of the university for the mental health of his students, his inevitable, though regrettable, dismissal, and of how, in sheer desperation, he founded a new religion (it was a sectarian university after all), gave Robinson Jeffers a chance to write a masterpiece (which the economist's wife, if not the economist, can read with comfortable gusto), thereby again adding materially, though in a more passive sense, to America's store of cultural values, when, apparently out of a blue sky, his wife, unable to determine whether she loved him or hated him, committed suicide. Apparently the equilibrating power of $1500.00 a year was not enough to avert the tragedy. Dare either the culturalist or the psychiatrist say that a salary raise of $500.00 would have had no cultural or psychiatric importance? The feeble vein of irony might have grown into a sturdy fortress, for with an extra $500.00 he could have just managed to buy his wife a dress barely good enough to have them go to the annual tea given by the banker (we forgot to say that he was one of the trustees of the university) for the express purpose of having faculty and trustees get to know each other. As it is, he was morbidly isolated, she no less. And, if the truth were known, Robinson Jeffers had a lot of other things to write about.

All of this, the economist insists—and quite rightly—is neither here nor there. If sociologists want to worry about such things, let them. They don't have to be so scientific. But most sociologists dearly wish to be scientific. They collect case histories, to be sure, but it is generally seen to that they contain just enough data to make it possible to discover general truths (such as that full professors in southern universities are less amply rewarded for their services than in northern universities) but not enough data to make A intelligible. That would be invading the field of the novelist and no scientist, *qua* scientist, can afford to do that. So we must turn to the psychiatrist, it seems, and ask him to be so kind as to add the following law or observation or principle (the exact terminological placement of this truth to be decided on later): "Whoever is sophisticated enough, sensitive enough and representative enough of our country's higher culture to get himself appointed a full professor in one of the universities of said country, cannot, if he is married, be expected, in view of the known cost of many requisite symbols of status, to be either happy or comfortable at a salary which is less than a quarter (the figure is merely a random suggestion) of the income of the averagely prosperous banker or real-estate agent of the community in which he lives, it being presumed that the remaining three-quarters (or other suitable figure) be more or less adequately compensated for by such substitutive values as membership in scientific societies and the habit of reading difficult but not too expensive literature. It is suggested that

$1500.00 a year is well below the safe minimum for such a person. In the absence of powerful personality-preserving factors, such as unusually robust health or a far more than averagely happy marriage, so low a salary must be considered a definite factor in the possible deterioration of the professor's personality."

If the psychiatrist exclaims that this is mixing psychiatry and economics with a vengeance, we must gently remind him that personalities live in tangible environments and that the business of making a living is one of the bed-rock factors in their environmental adjustment. We are not in a position to distinguish sharply between innate or organismal strains, physical and psychological, and so-called external strains. They come to us fatally blended in practice and it is a wise man who can presume to say which is of more decisive importance. For all practical purposes a too low income is at least as significant a datum in the causation of mental ill-health as a buried Oedipus complex or sex trauma. Why should not the psychiatrist be frank enough to call attention to the great evils of unemployment or of lack of economic security? His recognized concern for the well-being of the individual gives him every right to be heard, where ordinary opinion or common sense is often dismissed as governed by sentimental prejudices.

Now as to the starveling farmer and his $500.00 income, he is too busy, from dawn to bed-time, to know whether his health is good or bad and he hasn't the faintest notion whether he is happily married or not. Imperious task follows task in an all-day grind, he barely manages, he cannot pay off his mortgage, he is thankful for reprieves. The notion of mental ill-health is a luxury to him, he'd rather suspect himself of laziness—there's so much to be done—just as he'd rather suspect the other fellow of being a little weak in the head than waste breath on the ill-effects of extreme poverty. His class comes in relatively little contact with the psychiatrist and the mental hygienist. You either somehow manage or you "bust." If you manage, there's little need to graduate the psychological quality of the performance. Happiness, soul-weariness, apathy, envy, petty greed, are just so many novelistic fancies, utterly dwarfed by the solid facts that the potatoes didn't do so well this year, that the cows must be milked as usual, that the market for hay is unexpectedly poor. It is only when the sober, inevitable, corroding impoverishment of the farmer's personality is lit up by some spectacular morbidity of sex or religion that the psychiatrist or novelist or poet is attracted to him. The far more important dullness of daily routine, of futile striving, of ceaseless mental thwarting, does not seem to clamor for the psychiatrist's analysis.

All this is known to be "uninteresting," hence we prettify the facts as best we can with shreds of folk-lore, survivals of a pioneering culture that had a self-containedness and satisfyingness of its own. That culture has rotted away and our farmer is little more than a disgruntled economic drudge and a cultural parasite. It is not only worth the psychiatrist's while to inquire into these conditions and report on them, it is his duty to do so. Perhaps we could better understand morbid religious frenzies, lynch law, and other devastating phenomena of contemporary American life if we looked more closely into the psychological tissue of our rural life. "North of Boston" and Faulkner's exhibits need to be supplemented by the sober case history and by the economico-psychiatric appraisal of the conditions of life in our rural sections.

As to C, the interest of the psychiatrist in his moods, conflicts, and aspirations is perennial. He has his troubles, it seems, his surfeits and futilities, and we are all glad to know that the psychiatrist is eager to put his technical skill at his disposal. All human life is sacred—to hark back to a nineteenth century prejudice—and C should, most certainly, be made a happier man, if C will only let the psychiatrist define happiness, which I take to be a synonym of mental health, for him. But is it wrong to remark that for every suffering C there are many thousands of suffering A's and many thousands of suffering B's? We shall not try to fantasy what ails C, there are many admirable textbooks of psychiatry which give us a fair notion of how to be miserable though wealthy. Perhaps C too inclines to suffer from an economic ill—that obscure, perverse, guilt feeling which, the psychiatrist tells us, so often festers in one's heart of hearts when one tries to balance one's usefulness to society with the size of one's income. Here too is a chance for psychiatrists to be reasonably vocal. Is it conceivable that good mental hygiene, even expert psychiatry, may find it proper to recommend some share of income reduction for the sake of the mental health of those who are too heavily burdened by a material prosperity that far outruns their needs or, if the truth were known, their secret desires? In this mysterious realm we need further light.

THE EMERGENCE OF THE CONCEPT OF PERSONALITY IN A STUDY OF CULTURES*

OUR NATURAL interest in human behavior seems always to vacillate between what is imputed to the culture of the group as a whole and what is imputed to the psychic organization of the individual himself. These two poles of our interest in behavior do not necessarily make use of different materials; it is merely that the locus of reference is different in the two cases. Under familiar circumstances and with familiar people, the locus of reference of our interest is likely to be the individual. In unfamiliar types of behavior, such as running a dynamo, or with individuals who do not readily fit into the normal contexts of social habit, say a visiting Chinese mandarin, the interest tends to discharge itself into formulations which are cultural rather than personal in character. If I see my little son playing marbles I do not, as a rule, wish to have light thrown on how the game is played. Nearly everything that I observe tends to be interpreted as a contribution to the understanding of the child's personality. He is bold or timid, alert or easily confused, a good sport or a bad sport when he loses, and so on. The game of marbles, in short, is merely an excuse, as it were, for the unfolding of various facts or theories about a particular individual's psychic constitution. But when I see a skilled laborer oiling a dynamo, or a polished mandarin seating himself at the dinner table in the capacity of academic guest, it is almost inevitable that my observations take the form of ethnographic field notes, the net result of which is likely to be facts or theories about such cultural patterns as the running of a dynamo or Chinese manners.

Ordinarily one's interest is not so sharply defined. It tingles with both personal and cultural implications. There is no awareness of the constantly shifting direction of interest. Moreover, there is much of that confusion which attends all experience in its initial stages in childhood, when the significant personality is interpreted as an institution and every cultural pattern is merely a memory of what this or that person has actually done. Now and then, it is true, there arises in the flow of adult experience a certain intuition of what would be the significant eventual formulation, personal or cultural, of a given fragment of behavior. "Yes, that is just like John," or "But we mustn't make too much of this trifle. Presumably all Chinamen do the same thing under the

* *Journal of Social Psychology*, 5 (1934): 408–415. Based on a paper presented to the National Research Council Conference on Studies in Child Development at Chicago on June 22, 1933.

circumstances"; are illustrative symbols for contrasting interpretations. Naturally the confusion of interests is one not merely of the mingling of directions but also of an actual transposition or inversion. A stubbornly individual variation may be misinterpreted as a cultural datum. This sort of thing is likely to happen when we learn a foreign language from a single individual and are not in a position to distinguish between what is characteristic of the language and what is peculiar to the teacher's speech. More often, perhaps, the cultural pattern, when significantly presented in experience, tends to allocate to itself a far too intimate meaning. Qualities of charm or quaintness, for instance, are notoriously dangerous in this regard and tend to be not so much personal as cultural data, which receive their especial contextual value from the inability of the observer to withhold a strictly personal interpretation.

What is the genesis of our duality of interest in the facts of behavior? Why is it necessary to discover the contrast, real or fictitious, between culture and personality, or, to speak more accurately, between a segment of behavior seen as cultural pattern and a segment of behavior interpreted as having a person-defining value? Why cannot our interest in behavior maintain the undifferentiated character which it possessed in early childhood? The answer, presumably, is that each type of interest is necessary for the psychic preservation of the individual in an environment which experience makes increasingly complex and unassimilable on its own simple terms. The interests connected by the terms culture and personality are necessary for intelligent and helpful growth because each is based on a distinctive kind of imaginative participation by the observer in the life around him. The observer may dramatize such behavior as he takes note of in terms of a set of values, a conscience which is beyond self and to which he must conform, actually or imaginatively, if he is to preserve his place in the world of authority or impersonal social necessity. Or, on the other hand, he may feel the behavior as self-expressive, as defining the reality of individual consciousness against the mass of environing social determinants. Observations coming within the framework of the former of these two kinds of participation constitute our knowledge of culture. Those which come within the framework of the latter constitute our knowledge of personality. One is as subjective or objective as the other, for both are essentially modes of projection of personal experience into the analysis of social phenomena. Culture may be psychoanalytically reinterpreted as the supposedly impersonal aspect of those values and definitions which come to the child with the irresistible authority of the father, mother, or other individuals of their class. The child does not feel itself to be contributing to culture through his

personal interaction but is the passive recipient of values which lie completely beyond his control and which have a necessity and excellence
that he dare not question. We may therefore venture to surmise that
one's earliest configurations of experience have more of the character of
what is later to be rationalized as culture than of what the psychologist
is likely to abstract as personality. We have all had the disillusioning
experience of revising our father and mother images down from the
institutional plane to the purely personal one. The discovery of the world
of personality is apparently dependent upon the ability of the individual
to become aware of and to attach value to his resistance to authority.
It could probably be shown that naturally conservative people find it
difficult to take personality valuations seriously, while temperamental
radicals tend to be impatient with a purely cultural analysis of human
behavior.

It may be questioned whether a dichotomy which seems to depend so
largely on the direction of one's interest in observed behavior can be an
altogether safe guide to the study of behavior in social situations. The
motivations of these contrasting directions of interest are unconscious,
to be sure, yet simple enough, as all profound motivations must be. The
study of culture as such, which may be called sociology or anthropology,
has a deep and unacknowledged root in the desire to lose oneself safely
in the historically determined patterns of behavior. The motive for the
study of personality, which we may term indifferently social psychology
or psychiatry, proceeds from the necessity which the ego feels to assert
itself significantly. Both the cultural disciplines and the psychological
disciplines are careful to maintain objective ideals, but it should not be
difficult to see that neither the cultural pattern as such nor the personality as such, abstracted as both of these are from the directly given facts
of experience, can, in the long run, escape from the peculiarly subtle
subjectivism which is implicit in the definitions of the disciplines themselves. As preliminary disciplines, whose main purpose is to amass and
critically sift data and help us to phrase significant problems of human
behavior, they are of course invaluable. But sooner or later their obscure
opposition of spirit must be transcended for an objectivity which is not
merely formal and non-evaluative but which boldly essays to bring every
cultural pattern back to the living context from which it has been abstracted in the first place and, in parallel fashion, to bring every fact of
personality formation back to its social matrix. The problems herewith
suggested are, of course, neither simple nor easy. The social psychology
into which the conventional cultural and psychological disciplines must
eventually be resolved is related to these paradigmatic studies as an

investigation into living speech is related to grammar. I think few cultural disciplines are as exact, as rigorously configurated, as self-contained as grammar, but if it is desired to have grammar contribute a significant share to our understanding of human behavior, its definitions, meanings, and classifications must be capable of a significant restatement in terms of a social psychology which transcends the best that we have yet been able to offer in this perilous field of investigation. What applies to grammar applies no less significantly, of course, to the study of social organization, religion, art, mythology, technology, or any segment, large or small, or groups of segments which convenience or tradition leads us to carve out of the actual contexts of human behavior.

There is a very real hurt done our understanding of culture when we systematically ignore the individual and his types of interrelationship with other individuals. It is no exaggeration to say that cultural analysis as ordinarily made is not a study of behavior at all but is essentially the orderly description, without evaluation, or, at best, with certain implicit evaluations, of a behavior to be hereinafter defined but which, in the normal case is not, perhaps cannot be, defined. Culture, as it is ordinarily constructed by the anthropologist, is a more or less mechanical sum of the more striking or picturesque generalized patterns of behavior which he has either abstracted for himself out of the sum total of his observations or has had abstracted for him by his informants in verbal communication. Such a "culture," because generally constructed of unfamiliar terms, has an almost unavoidable picturesqueness about it, which suggests a vitality which it does not, as a matter of scrupulous psychological fact, embody. The cultures so carefully described in our ethnological and sociological monographs are not, and cannot be, the truly objective entities they claim to be. No matter how accurate their individual itemization, their integrations into suggested structures are uniformly fallacious and unreal. This cannot be helped so long as we confine ourselves to the procedures recognized as sound by orthodox ethnology. If we make the test of imputing the contents of an ethnological monograph to a known individual in the community which it describes, we would inevitably be led to discover that, while every single statement in it may, in the favorable case, be recognized as holding true in some sense, the complex of patterns as described cannot, without considerable absurdity, be interpreted as a significant configuration of experience, both actual and potential, in the life of the person appealed to. Cultures, as ordinarily dealt with, are merely abstracted configurations of idea and action patterns, which have endlessly different meanings for the various individuals in the group and which, if they are to build up into any kind of significant psychic structure, whether for the individual or the small group or the larger group, must be set in relation to each other in a complex configuration of evaluations, inclusive and exclusive implications, priorities, and potentialities of realization which cannot be discovered from an inquiry into the described patterns.

The more fully one tries to understand a culture, the more it seems to take on the characteristics of a personality organization. Patterns first present themselves according to a purely formalized and logically developed scheme. More careful explorations invariably reveal the fact that numerous threads of symbolism or implication connect patterns or parts of patterns with others of an entirely different formal aspect. Behind the simple diagrammatic forms of culture is concealed a peculiar network of relationships, which, in their totality, carve out entirely new forms that stand in no simple relation to the obvious cultural table of contents. Thus, a word, a gesture, a genealogy, a type of religious belief may unexpectedly join hands in a common symbolism of status definition. If it were the aim of the study of culture merely to list and describe comprehensively the vast number of supposedly self-contained patterns of behavior which are handed on from generation to generation by social processes, such an inquiry as we have suggested into the more intimate structure of culture would hardly be necessary. Trouble arises only when the formulations of the culture student are requisitioned without revision or criticism for an understanding of the most significant aspects of human behavior. When this is done, insoluble difficulties necessarily appear, for behavior is not a recomposition of abstracted patterns, each of which can be more or less successfully studied as a historically continuous and geographically distributed entity in itself, but the very matrix out of which the abstractions have been made in the first place. All this means, of course, that if we are justified in speaking of the growth of culture at all, it must be in the spirit, not of a composite history made up of the private histories of particular patterns, but in the spirit of the development of a personality. The complete, impersonalized "culture" of the anthropologist can really be little more than an assembly or mass of loosely overlapping idea and action systems which, through verbal habit, can be made to assume the appearance of a closed system of behavior. What tends to be forgotten is that the functioning of such a system, if it can be said to have any ascertainable function at all, is due to the specific functioning and interplays of the idea and action systems which have actually grown up in the minds of given individuals. In spite of the often assorted impersonality of culture, the humble truth remains that vast reaches of culture, far from being in any real sense "carried" by a community or a group as such, are discoverable only as the peculiar property of certain individuals, who cannot but give these cultural goods the impress of their own personality. With the disappearance of such key individuals, the tight, "objectified" culture loosens up at once and is eventually seen to be a convenient fiction of thought.

When the cultural anthropologist has finished his necessary preliminary researches into the overt forms of culture and has gained from them an objectivity of reference by working out their forms, time sequences, and geographical distribution, there emerges for him the more difficult and significant task of interpreting the culture which he has isolated in terms of its relevance for the understanding of the personalities of the very individuals from whom he has obtained his information. As he changes his informant, his culture necessarily changes. There is no reason why the culturalist should be afraid of the concept of personality, which must not, however, be thought of, as one inevitably does at the beginning of his thinking, as a mysterious entity resisting the historically given culture but rather as a distinctive configuration of experience which tends always to form a psychologically significant unit and which, as it accretes more and more symbols to itself, creates finally that cultural microcosm of which official "culture" is little more than a metaphorically and mechanically expanded copy. The application of the point of view which is natural in the study of the genesis of personality to the problem of culture cannot but force a revaluation of the materials of culture itself. Many problems which are now in the forefront of investigation sink into a secondary position, and patterns of behavior which seem so obvious or universal as not to be worthy of the distinctive attention of the ethnologist leap into a new and unexpected importance. The ethnologist may some day have to face the uncomfortable predicament of inquiring into such humble facts as whether the father is in the habit of acting as indulgent guide or as disciplinarian to his son and of regarding the problem of the child's membership inside or outside of his father's clan as a relatively subsidiary question. In short, the application of the personality point of view tends to minimize the bizarre or exotic in alien cultures and to reveal to us more and more clearly the broad human base on which all culture has developed. The profound commonplace that all culture starts from the needs of a common humanity is believed in by all anthropologists, but it is not demonstrated by their writings.

An excellent test of the fruitfulness of the study of culture in close conjunction with a study of personality would be provided by studies in the field of child development. It is strange how little ethnology has concerned itself with the intimate genetic problem of the acquirement of culture by the child. In the current language of ethnology culture dynamics seems to be almost entirely a matter of adult definition and adult transmission from generation to generation and from group to group. The humble child, who is laboriously orienting himself in the world of his society, yet is not, in the normal case, sacrificing his fortright psychological status as a significant ego, is somehow left out of account. This strange omission is obviously due to the fact that anthropology has allowed itself to be victimized by a convenient but dangerous metaphor. This metaphor is always persuading us that culture is a neatly packed up assemblage of forms of behavior handed over piecemeal, but without serious breakage, to the passively inquiring child. I have come to feel that it is precisely the supposed "givenness" of culture that is the most serious obstacle to our real understanding of the nature of culture and cultural change and of their relationship to individual personality. Culture is not, as a matter of sober fact, a "given" at all. It is so only by a polite convention of speech. As soon as we set ourselves at the vantage point of the culture-acquiring child, the personality definitions and potentials that must never for a moment be lost sight of, and which are destined from the very beginning to interpret, evaluate, and modify every culture pattern, sub-pattern, or assemblage of patterns that it will ever be influenced by, everything changes. Culture is then not something given but something to be gradually and gropingly discovered. We then see at once that elements of culture that come well within the horizon of awareness of one individual are entirely absent in another individual's landscape. This is an important fact, systematically ignored by the cultural anthropologist. It may be proper for the systematic ethnologist to ignore such pattern differences as these, but for the theoretical anthropologist, who wishes to place culture in a general view of human behavior, such an oversight is inexcusable. Furthermore, it is obvious that the child will unconsciously accept the various elements of culture with entirely different meanings, according to the biographical conditions that attend their introduction to him. It may, and undoubtedly does, make a profound difference whether a religious ritual comes with the sternness of the father's authority or with the somewhat playful indulgence of the mother's brother. We have not the privilege of assuming that it is an irrelevant matter how musical stimuli are introduced to the child. The fact that the older brother is already an admired pianist in the little household may act as an effective barrier to the development of interest in any form of musical expression. Such a child may grow up curiously obtuse to musical values and may be persuaded to think that he was born with a naturally poor ear and is therefore debarred from sharing in the blessings of one important aspect of the cultural life of the community.

If we take the purely genetic point of view, all the problems which appear in the study of culture reappear with a startling freshness which cannot but mean much for the rephrasing of these problems. Problems of symbolism, of superordination and subordination of patterns, of relative strength of emotional character, of transformability and transmissibility, of the isolability of certain patterns into relatively closed systems, and numerous others of like dynamic nature, emerge at once. We cannot answer any of them in the abstract. All of them demand patient investigation and the answers are almost certain to be multiform. We may suggest as a difficult but crucial problem of investigation the following: Study the child minutely and carefully from birth until, say the age of ten with a view to seeing the order in which cultural patterns and parts of patterns appear in his psychic world; study the relevance of these patterns for the development of his personality; and, at the end of the suggested period, see how much of the total official culture of the group can be said to have a significant existence for him. Moreover, what degree of systematization, conscious or unconscious, in the complicating patterns and symbolisms of culture will have been reached by this child? This is a difficult problem, to be sure, but it is not an impossible one. Sooner or later it will have to be attacked by the genetic psychologists. I venture to predict that the concept of culture which will then emerge, fragmentary and confused as it will undoubtedly be, will turn out to have a tougher, more vital, importance for social thinking than the tidy tables of contents attached to this or that group which we have been in the habit of calling "cultures."

BIBLIOGRAPHY

BIBLIOGRAPHY

SCIENTIFIC PAPERS AND PROSE WRITINGS

1906

"The Rival Chiefs, a Kwakiutl Story Recorded by George Hunt" [edited, with synopsis, pp. 108–110, by Edward Sapir], in *Boas Anniversary Volume* (New York), pp. 108–136.

1907

"Religious Ideas of the Takelma Indians of Southwestern Oregon," *Journal of American Folk-Lore*, 20: 33–49.

"Notes on the Takelma Indians of Southwestern Oregon," *American Anthropologist*, n.s., 9: 251–275.

"Preliminary Report on the Language and Mythology of the Upper Chinook," *American Anthropologist*, n.s., 9: 533–544.

"Herder's *Ursprung der Sprache*," *Modern Philology*, 5: 109–142.

1908

"Luck-Stones among the Yana," *Journal of American Folk-Lore*, 21: 42.

"On the Etymology of Sanskrit áśru, Avestan asru, Greek dákru," in *Spiegel Memorial Volume*, J. J. Modi, ed. (Bombay), pp. 156–159.

1909

"Characteristic Features of Yana" [abstract], *Science*, n.s., 29: 613; *American Anthropologist*, n.s., 11: 110.

Review of Frank G. Speck, *Ethnology of the Yuchi Indians*, in *Old Penn Weekly Review* (Philadelphia), December 18, p. 183.

Wishram Texts, together with Wasco Tales and Myths, collected by Jeremiah Curtin and edited by Edward Sapir, American Ethnological Society Publications, Vol. II (Leyden). 314 pp.

Takelma Texts, University of Pennsylvania, Anthropological Publications, 2 (no. 1): 1–263.

1910

"An Apache Basket Jar," *University of Pennsylvania Museum Journal*, 1 (no. 1): 13–15.

"Some Fundamental Characteristics of the Ute Language" [abstract], *Science*, n.s., 31: 350–352; *American Anthropologist*, n.s., 12: 66–69.

"Two Paiute Myths," *University of Pennsylvania Museum Journal*, 1 (no. 1): 15–18.

"Takelma," in *Handbook of American Indians North of Mexico*, Bureau of American Ethnology, Bulletin 30, Pt. II, pp. 673–674.

"Wasco," in *Handbook of American Indians North of Mexico*, Bureau of American Ethnology, Bulletin 30, Pt. II, pp. 917–918.

Review of C. Hart Merriam, *The Dawn of the World*, in *Science*, n.s., 32: 557–558.

Yana Texts (together with *Yana Myths*, collected by Roland B. Dixon), University of California Publications in American Archaeology and Ethnology, 9: 1–235.
"Song Recitative in Paiute Mythology," *Journal of American Folk-Lore*, 23: 455–472.

1911

"Some Aspects of Nootka Language and Culture," *American Anthropologist*, n.s., 13: 15–28.
Review of R. B. Dixon, *The Chimariko Indians and Language*, in *American Anthropologist*, n.s., 13: 141–143.
"The Problem of Noun Incorporation in American Languages," *American Anthropologist*, n.s., 13: 250–282.
"An Anthropological Survey of Canada," *Science*, n.s., 34: 789–793.
"Chinook" (incorporated in Franz Boas, "Chinook"), in *Handbook of American Indian Languages*, Bureau of American Ethnology, Bulletin 40, Pt. I, pp. 578, 579, 625–627, 638–645, 650–654, 673–677.
"The History and Varieties of Human Speech," *Popular Science Monthly*, 79: 45–67; reprinted in *Annual Report*, Smithsonian Institution (1912), pp. 573–595; also in *Selected Readings in Anthropology*, University of California Syllabus Series, No. 101, pp. 202–224.

1912

"The Mourning Ceremony of the Southern Paiutes" [abstract], *Science*, n.s., 35: 673; *American Anthropologist*, n.s., 14: 168–169.
Review of A. A. Goldenweiser, *Totemism: An Analytical Study*, in *Psychological Bulletin*, 9: 454–461.
"The Work of the Division of Anthropology of the Dominion Government," *Queen's Quarterly*, 20: 60–69.
Summary Report, Geological Survey of Canada, for 1910 (Ottawa), pp. 3–4.
Summary Report, Geological Survey of Canada, for 1911 (Ottawa), pp. 5–7, 15–16.
Review of Franz Boas, *Kwakiutl Tales*, in *Current Anthropological Literature*, 1: 193–198.
"Language and Environment," *American Anthropologist*, n.s., 14: 226–242.
"The Indians of the Province" [of British Columbia], in *British Columbia: Its History, People, Commerce, Industries, and Resources* (London), pp. 135–140.
"The Indians of Alberta, Saskatchewan, and Manitoba," in *The Prairie Provinces* (London).
Review of Carl Stumpf, *Die Anfänge der Musik*, in *Current Anthropological Literature*, 1: 275–282.

1913

"A Note on Reciprocal Terms of Relationship in America," *American Anthropologist*, n.s., 15: 132–138.
"A Tutelo Vocabulary," *American Anthropologist*, n.s., 15: 295–297.
Review of Carl Meinhof, *Die Sprachen der Hamiten*, in *Current Anthropological Literature*, 2: 21–27.
"Southern Paiute and Nahuatl, a Study in Uto-Aztekan," Pt. I, *Journal, Société des Américanistes de Paris*, n.s., 10: 379–425.
"Algonkin *p* and *s* in Cheyenne," *American Anthropologist*, n.s., 15: 538–539.

"A Girls' Puberty Ceremony among the Nootka Indians," *Transactions, Royal Society of Canada*, 3d series, 7: 67–80.

Summary Report, Geological Survey of Canada, for 1912 (Ottawa), pp. 448–453, 505–506.

"Methods and Principles," review of Erich von Hornbostel, "Ueber ein akustisches Kriterium für Kulturzusammenhänge," in *Current Anthropological Literature*, 2: 69–72.

"Wiyot and Yurok, Algonkin Languages of California," *American Anthropologist*, n.s., 15: 617–646.

1914

"Indian Tribes of the Coast" [of British Columbia], in A. Shortt and A. G. Doughty, eds., *Canada and Its Provinces* (Toronto), 21: 313–346.

Notes on Chasta Costa Phonology and Morphology, University of Pennsylvania, Anthropological Publications, 2 (no. 2): 271–340.

Summary Report, Geological Survey of Canada, for 1913 (Ottawa), pp. 355–363, 389.

1915

Abnormal Types of Speech in Nootka, Canada Department of Mines, Geological Survey, Memoir 62, Anthropological Series, No. 5. 21 pp.

Noun Reduplication in Comox, a Salish Language of Vancouver Island, Canada Department of Mines, Geological Survey, Memoir 63, Anthropological Series, No. 6. 53 pp.

"The Social Organization of the West Coast Tribes," *Transactions, Royal Society of Canada*, 2d series, 9: 355–374.

Summary Report, Geological Survey of Canada, for 1914, (Ottawa), pp. 168–177.

A Sketch of the Social Organization of the Nass River Indians, Canada Department of Mines, Geological Survey, Museum Bulletin 19, Anthropological Series, No. 7. 30 pp.

"Notes on Judeo-German Phonology," *The Jewish Quarterly Review*, n.s., 6: 231–266.

"Algonkin Languages of California: a Reply," *American Anthropologist*, n.s., 17: 188–194.

"Southern Paiute and Nahuatl, a Study in Uto-Aztekan," Pt. II, *American Anthropologist*, n.s., 17: 98–120, 306–328; *Journal, Société des Américanistes de Paris*, n.s., 11 (1914): 443–488.

"The Na-dene Languages, a Preliminary Report," *American Anthropologist*, n.s., 17: 534–558.

"Corrigenda to Father Morice's *Chasta Costa and the Dene Languages of the North*," *American Anthropologist*, n.s., 17: 765–773.

1916

Summary Report, Geological Survey of Canada, for 1915 (Ottawa), pp. 265–274.

Review of Paul Abelson, ed., *English-Yiddish Encyclopedic Dictionary*, in *The Jewish Quarterly Review*, 7: 140–143.

"Phonetic Orthography and Notes to 'Nootka,' " in "Vocabularies from the Northwest Coast of America," Franz Boas, ed., *Proceedings, American Antiquarian Society*, 26: 4–18.

"Phonetic Orthography and Notes to 'Nootka,' " in *Phonetic Transcriptions of Indian Languages*, Smithsonian Miscellaneous Collections, 66: 1–15.
"Terms of Relationship and the Levirate," *American Anthropologist*, n.s., 18: 327–337.
"Percy Grainger and Primitive Music," *American Anthropologist*, n.s., 18: 592–597.
Time Perspective in Aboriginal American Culture: A Study in Method, Canada Department of Mines, Geological Survey, Memoir 90, Anthropological Series, No. 13. 87 pp.
"Culture in the Melting Pot," comments on John Dewey's article, "American Education and Culture." In *The Nation Supplement* (December 21), pp. 1–2.

1917

The Position of Yana in the Hokan Stock, University of California Publications in American Archaeology and Ethnology, 13: 1–34.
Summary Report, Geological Survey of Canada, for 1916, Anthropological Division, Part I, Ethnology and Linguistics, pp. 387–392, 394, 395.
"Do We Need a 'Superorganic'?" *American Anthropologist*, n.s., 19: 441–447.
"The Status of Washo," *American Anthropologist*, n.s., 19: 449–450.
"Linguistic Publications of the Bureau of American Ethnology, a General Review," *International Journal of American Linguistics*, 1: 76–81.
Review of C. C. Uhlenbeck, "Het Passieve Karakter van het Verbum Transitivum of van het Verbum Actionis in Talen van Noord-Amerika," in *International Journal of American Linguistics*, 1: 82–86.
Review of C. C. Uhlenbeck, "Het Identificeerend Karakter der Possessieve Flexie in Talen van Noord-Amerika," in *International Journal of American Linguistics*, 1: 86–90.
"A Freudian Half-Holiday," review of Sigmund Freud, *Delusion and Dream*, in *The Dial*, 63: 635–637.
" 'Jean-Christophe': An Epic of Humanity," review of Romain Rolland, *Jean-Christophe*, in *The Dial*, 62: 423–426.
"Realism in Prose Fiction," *The Dial*, 62: 503–506.
"A Frigid Introduction to Strauss," review of Henry T. Finck, *Richard Strauss, the Man and His Works*, in *The Dial*, 62: 584–586.
"The Twilight of Rhyme," *The Dial*, 63: 98–100.
Psychoanalysis as a Pathfinder," review of Oskar Pfister, *The Psychoanalytic Method*, in *The Dial*, 63: 267–269.

1918

Yana Terms of Relationship, University of California Publications in American Archaeology and Ethnology, 13: 153–173.
Review of Benigno Bibolotti, *Moseteno Vocabulary and Treatises*, in *International Journal of American Linguistics*, 1: 183–184.
"Representative Music," *The Musical Quarterly*, 4: 161–167.
"An Ethnological Note on the 'Whiskey-Jack'," *The Ottawa Naturalist*, 32: 116–117.
"Kinship Terms of the Kootenay Indians," *American Anthropologist*, n.s., 20: 414–418.

"Sancho Panza on His Island," review of G. K. Chesterton, *Utopias of Usurers and Other Essays*, in *The Dial*, 64: 25–27.

"God as Visible Personality," review of Samuel Butler, *God the Known and God the Unknown*, in *The Dial*, 64: 192–194.

"A University Survey of Religions," review of James A. Montgomery, ed., *Religions of the Past and Present* (Faculty Lectures, University of Pennsylvania), in *The Dial*, 65: 14–16.

"Tom," *Canadian Courier* (Dec. 7), p. 7.

1919

"Data on Washo and Hokan," in R. B. Dixon and A. L. Kroeber, *Linguistic Families of California*, University of California Publications in American Archaeology and Ethnology, 16: 108–112.

"A Flood Legend of the Nootka Indians of Vancouver Island," *Journal of American Folk-Lore*, 32: 351–355.

"Corrigenda and Addenda to W. D. Wallis' *Indogermanic Relationship Terms as Historical Evidence*," *American Anthropologist*, n.s., 21: 318–328.

"Corrigenda to 'Kinship Terms of the Kootenay Indians,' " *American Anthropologist*, n.s., 21: 98.

"Civilization and Culture," *The Dial*, 67: 233–236, Pt. 2 of "Culture, Genuine and Spurious," 1924, *q.v.*

Review (unsigned) of Cary F. Jacob, *The Foundations and Nature of Verse*, in *The Dial*, 66: 98, 100.

"The American Indian," review of C. Wissler, *The American Indian*, in *The New Republic*, 19: 189–191.

"The Poet Seer of Bengal," review of Tagore's *Lover's Gift, Crossing, Mashi and Other Stories*, in *The Canadian Magazine*, 54: 137–140.

"A Note on French Canadian Folk-Songs," *Poetry*, 20: 210–213.

1920

"The Hokan and Coahuiltecan Languages," *International Journal of American Linguistics*, 1: 280–290.

"A Note on the First Person Plural in Chimariko," *International Journal of American Linguistics*, 1: 291–294.

Review of J. Alden Mason, *The Language of the Salinan Indians*, in *International Journal of American Linguistics*, 1: 305–309.

"Nass River Terms of Relationship," *American Anthropologist*, n.s., 22: 261–271.

"The Heuristic Value of Rhyme," *Queen's Quarterly*, 27: 309–312.

"Primitive Society," review of R. H. Lowie, *Primitive Society*, in *The Nation*, 111: 46–47.

"Primitive Humanity and Anthropology," review of R. H. Lowie, *Primitive Society*, in *The Dial*, 69: 528–533.

"Primitive Society," review of R. H. Lowie, *Primitive Society*, in *The Freeman*, 1: 377–379.

"The Poetry Prize Contest," *The Canadian Magazine*, 54: 349–352.

1921

Language: An Introduction to the Study of Speech (New York, Harcourt, Brace. 258 pp.

Summary Report for Anthropological Division, Victoria Memorial Museum: Ethnology and Linguistics, 1920 (Ottawa), pp. 18–20.

"A Bird's-eye View of American Languages North of Mexico," *Science*, n.s., 54: 408.

"A Characteristic Penutian Form of Stem," *International Journal of American Linguistics*, 2: 58–67.

"A Supplementary Note on Salinan and Washo," *International Journal of American Linguistics*, 2: 68–72.

"A Haida Kinship Term among the Tsimshian," *American Anthropologist*, n.s., 23: 233–234.

"The Musical Foundations of Verse," *Journal of English and Germanic Philology*, 20: 213–228.

"The Life of a Nootka Indian," *Queen's Quarterly*, 28: 232–243, 351–367; reprinted under title of "Sayach'apis, a Nootka Trader," 1922, *q.v.*

"The Mythology of All Races," review of *The Mythology of All Races*, Vols. 3, 11, 12, in *The Dial*, 71: 107–111.

"Gerard Hopkins," review of Robert Bridges, ed., *Poems of Gerard Manley Hopkins*, in *Poetry*, 18: 330–336.

"Writing as History and as Style," review of W. A. Mason, *A History of the Art of Writing*, in *The Freeman*, 4: 68–69.

"Myth, Historian, and Psychologist," review of H. B. Alexander, *Latin-American* (Vol. XI, *The Mythology of All Races*), in *The Nation*, 112: 889–890.

"The Ends of Man," review of J. M. Tyler, *The New Stone Age in Northern Europe*; Stewart Paton, *Human Behavior*; E. G. Conklin, *The Direction of Human Evolution*. In *The Nation*, 113: 237–238.

"Maupassant and Anatole France," *The Canadian Magazine*, 57: 199–202.

"A Touchstone to Freud," review of W. H. R. Rivers, *Instinct and the Unconscious*, in *The Freeman*, 5: 357–358.

1922

"Culture, Genuine and Spurious," [Pt. 2], *The Dalhousie Review*, 2: 165–178; 358–368. Pts. 1 and 2 reprinted in *American Journal of Sociology* (1924), *q.v.*

The Fundamental Elements of Northern Yana, University of California Publications in American Archaeology and Ethnology, 13: 215–234.

"Athabaskan Tone," *American Anthropologist*, n.s., 24: 390–391.

"The Takelma Language of Southwestern Oregon," in *Handbook of American Indian Languages*, Bureau of American Ethnology, Bulletin 40, Part II, pp. 1–296.

"Vancouver Island Indians," in James Hastings, ed., *Encyclopaedia of Religion and Ethics* (New York), 12: 591–595.

"Sayach'apis, a Nootka Trader," in E. C. Parsons, ed., *American Indian Life* (New York), pp. 297–323.

"Language and Literature" (chap. 11 of *Language*, 1921), *The Canadian Magazine*, 59: 457–462.

"Practical Psychology," review of Frederick Pierce, *Our Unconscious Mind and How to Use It*, in *The Literary Review, New York Evening Post* (July 1), p. 772.

Review (unsigned) of Arthur Davison Ficke, *Mr. Faust*, in *The Dial*, 73: 235.

Review (unsigned) of George Saintsbury, *A Letter Book*, in *The Dial*, 73: 235.

Review of Gilbert Murray, *Tradition and Progress*, in *The Dial*, 73: 235.
Review (unsigned) of Selma Lagerlöf, *The Outcast*, in *The Dial*, 73: 354.
Review of Edgar Lee Masters, *Children of the Market Place*, in *The Dial*, 73: 457.
"A Symposium of the Exotic," review of E. C. Parsons, ed., *American Indian Life*, in *The Dial*, 73: 568–571.
"The Manner of Mr. Masefield," review of John Masefield, *King Cole*, in *The Freeman*, 5: 548–549.
"Mr. Masters's Later Work," review of Edgar Lee Masters, *The Open Sea*, in *The Freeman*, 5: 333–334.
"A Peep at the Hindu Spirit," review of *More Jataka Tales*, retold by Ellen C. Babbitt, in *The Freeman*, 5: 404.
Review of John Masefield, *Esther and Berenice*, in *The Freeman*, 5: 526.
"An Orthodox Psychology," review of R. S. Woodworth, *Psychology: A Study of Mental Life*, in *The Freeman*, 5: 619.
"Heavens," review of Louis Untermeyer, *Heavens*, in *The New Republic*, 30: 351.
"Introducing Irony," review of Maxwell Bodenheim, *Introducing Irony*, in *The New Republic*, 31: 341.
"Maxwell Bodenheim," review of Maxwell Bodenheim, *Introducing Irony*, in *The Nation*, 114: 751.
"Poems of Experience," review of Edwin Arlington Robinson, *Collected Poems*, in *The Freeman*, 5: 141–142; published also (under title, "Edwin Arlington Robinson") in *The Canadian Bookman* (August), pp. 210–211.
"Spoon River Muddies," review of Edgar Lee Masters, *The Open Sea*, in *The Canadian Bookman* (April), pp. 132, 140.
Review of Edward Thomas, *Collected Poems*, in *The New Republic*, 32: 226.
Summary Report for Anthropological Division, Vicotria Memorial Museum: Ethnology and Linguistics, fiscal year ending March 31, 1922 (Ottawa), pp. 22–25.

1923

Text Analyses of Three Yana Dialects, University of California Publications in American Archaeology and Ethnology, 20: 263–294.
"The Algonkin Affinity of Yurok and Wiyot Kinship Terms," *Journal, Société des Américanistes de Paris*, n.s., 15: 36–74.
"A Note on Sarcee Pottery," *American Anthropologist*, n.s., 25: 247–253.
"A Type of Athabaskan Relative," *International Journal of American Linguistics*, 2: 136–142.
"The Phonetics of Haida," *International Journal of American Linguistics*, 2: 143–159.
Review of Truman Michelson, "The Owl Sacred Pack of the Fox Indians," in *International Journal of American Linguistics*, 2: 182–184.
[With Hsü Tsan Hwa] "Two Chinese Folk-Tales," *Journal of American Folk-Lore*, 36: 23–30.
[With Hsü Tsan Hwa] "Humor of the Chinese Folk," *Journal of American Folk-Lore*, 36: 31–35.
"Archaeology and Ethnology" [bibliography], *Canadian Historical Review*, 4: 374–378.
Summary Report for Anthropological Division, Victoria Memorial Museum: Ethnology and Linguistics, fiscal year ending March 31, 1923 (Ottawa), pp. 28–31.

"The Two Kinds of Human Beings," review of C. G. Jung, *Psychological Types, or the Psychology of Individuation*, in *The Freeman*, 8: 211–212.

Review of Edwin Björkman, *The Soul of a Child*, in *The Double Dealer*, 51: 78–80.

"An Approach to Symbolism," review of C. K. Ogden and I. A. Richards, *The Meaning of Meaning*, in *The Freeman*, 7: 572–573.

"The Epos of Man," review of Johannes V. Jensen, *The Long Journey*, in *The World Tomorrow*, 6: 221.

"Mr. Housman's Last Poems," review of A. E. Housman, *Last Poems*, in *The Dial*, 75: 188–191.

1924

"Culture, Genuine and Spurious," *American Journal of Sociology*, 29: 401–429; Pt. 2, *The Dalhousie Review* (1922), *q.v.*; Pt. 1, (under title "Civilization and Culture") *The Dial* (1919), *q.v.*

"The Grammarian and His Language," *American Mercury*, 1: 149–155.

"Anthropology at the Toronto Meeting of the British Association for the Advancement of Science, 1924," *American Anthropologist*, n.s., 26: 563–565.

"Personal Names among the Sarcee Indians," *American Anthropologist*, n.s., 26: 108–119.

"The Rival Whalers, a Nitanat Story (Nootka Text with Translation and Grammatical Analysis)," *International Journal of American Linguistics*, 3: 76–102.

"Racial Superiority," *The Menorah Journal*, 10: 200–212.

"Twelve Novelists in Search of a Reason," review of *The Novel of Tomorrow and the Scope of Fiction*, by Twelve American Novelists. In *The Stratford Monthly* (May).

1925

"Memorandum on the Problem of an International Auxiliary Language," *The Romanic Review*, 16: 244–256.

"The Hokan Affinity of Subtiaba in Nicarague," *American Anthropologist*, n.s., 27: 402–435, 491–527.

"Pitch Accent in Sarcee, an Athabaskan Language," *Journal, Société des Américanistes de Paris*, n.s., 17: 185–205.

"Indian Legends from Vancouver Island," *Transactions, Women's Canadian Historical Society of Ottawa*, 9: 142–143.

"Sound Patterns in Language," *Language*, 1: 37–51.

"The Heuristic Value of Rhyme," *Queen's Quarterly*, 27: 309–312.

Summary Report for the Fiscal Year Ending March 31, 1924, Anthropological Division: Ethnology and Linguistics (Ottawa), pp. 36–40.

"Is Monotheism Jewish?" review of Paul Radin, *Monotheism among Primitive Peoples*, in *The Menorah Journal*, 11: 524–527.

"Are the Nordics a Superior Race?" *The Canadian Forum* (June), pp. 265–266.

Report of the Department of Mines, Dominion of Canada, for the Fiscal Year Ending March 31, 1925: Anthropological Division, Ethnology and Linguistics (Ottawa), pp. 37–41.

Review of A. Meillet and Marcel Cohen, eds., *Les Langues du monde*, in *Modern Language Notes*, 40: 373–375.

"Undesirables—Klanned or Banned," *The American Hebrew*, 116: 286.

"Let Race Alone," *The Nation*, 120: 211–213.

"The Race Problem," review of: F. G. Crookshank, *The Mongol in Our Midst;* H. W. Siemens, *Race Hygiene and Heredity;* Jean Finot, *Race Prejudice;* J. H. Oldham, *Christianity and the Race Problem.* In *The Nation*, 121: 40–42.

"An American Poet," review of H.D., *Collected Poems*, in *The Nation*, 121: 211.

"Emily Dickinson, a Primitive," review of *The Complete Poems of Emily Dickinson*, and M. D. Bianchi, *The Life and Letters of Emily Dickinson*, in *Poetry*, 26: 97–105.

"The Tragic Chuckle," review of Edwin Arlington Robinson, *Dionysus in Doubt*, in *Voices* (November), pp. 64–65.

1926

"Philology," in *The Encyclopaedia Britannica* (*Supplementary Volumes*, 13th ed.), 3: 112–115.

"Speech as a Personality Trait," abstract of a paper delivered before the Illinois Society for Mental Hygiene (Oct. 19) in *Health Bulletin*, Illinois Society for Mental Hygiene, December; also published in *American Journal of Sociology* (May, 1927), *q.v.*

"A Chinookan Phonetic Law," *International Journal of American Linguistics*, 4: 105–110.

Review of Knight Dunlap, *Old and New Viewpoints in Psychology*, in *American Journal of Sociology*, 31: 698–699.

Review of George A. Dorsey, *Why We Behave Like Human Beings*, in *American Journal of Sociology*, 32: 140.

Review of Otto Jespersen, *Mankind, Nation and Individual from a Linguistic Point of View*, in *American Journal of Sociology*, 32: 498–499.

Review of Father Berard Haile, *A Manual of Navaho Grammar*, in *American Journal of Sociology*, 32: 511.

"Leonie Adams," review of Leonie Adams, *Those Not Elect*, in *Poetry*, 27: 275–279.

Review of Ludwig Lewisohn, *Israel*, in *The Menorah Journal*, 12: 214–218.

1927

"Anthropology and Sociology," in W. F. Ogburn and A. Goldenweiser, eds., *The Social Sciences and Their Interrelations* (Boston), chap. 9, pp. 97–113.

"Language as a Form of Human Behavior," *The English Journal*, 16: 421–433.

"The Unconscious Patterning of Behavior in Society," in E. S. Dummer, ed., *The Unconscious: A Symposium* (New York), pp. 114–142.

"Speech as a Personality Trait," *American Journal of Sociology*, 32: 892–905; published also in *Health Bulletin*, (Illinois Society for Mental Hygiene, 1926), *q.v.*

"A Reasonable Eugenist," review of F. H. Hankins, *The Racial Basis of Civilization*, in *The New Republic*, 53: 146.

"Speech and Verbal Thought in Childhood," review of Jean Piaget, *The Language and Thought of the Child*, in *The New Republic*, 50: 350–351.

Review of Paul Radin, *Crashing Thunder: The Autobiograpyy of an American Indian*, in *American Journal of Sociology*, 33: 303–304.

Review of A. Hyatt Verrill, *The American Indian: North, South, and Central America*, in *American Journal of Sociology*, 33: 295–296.

"An Expedition to Ancient America: A Professor and a Chinese Student Rescue the Vanishing Language and Culture of the Hupas in Northern California," *The University of Chicago Magazine*, 20: 10–12.

1928

"A Summary Report of Field Work among the Hupa, Summer of 1927," *American Anthropologist*, n.s., 30: 359–361.

Review of James Weldon Johnson, ed., *The Book of American Negro Spirituals*, in *Journal of American Folk-Lore*, 41: 172–174.

"The Meaning of Religion," *The American Mercury*, 15: 72–79; published also under title "Religions and Religious Phenomena," (1929), *q.v.*

Review of Roland G. Kent, *Language and Philology*, in *The Classical Weekly*, 21: 85–86.

"When Words Are Not Enough," review of Clarence Day, *Thoughts without Words*, in *New York Herald Tribune Books*, 4: xii.

Proceedings, First Colloquium on Personality Investigation; Held under the Auspices of the American Psychiatric Association, Committee on Relations with the Social Sciences (New York), pp. 77–80.

"Observations on the Sex Problem in America," *American Journal of Psychiatry*, 8: 519–534.

Review of Knut Hamsun, *The Women at the Pump*, in *The New Republic*, 56: 335.

"Psychoanalysis as Prophet," review of Sigmund Freud, *The Future of an Illusion*, in *The New Republic*, 56: 356–357.

1929

"Central and North American Languages," *Encyclopaedia Britannica* (14th ed.), 5: 138–141.

"The Status of Linguistics as a Science," *Language*, 5: 207–214.

"Male and Female Forms of Speech in Yana," in St. W. J. Teeuwen, ed., *Donum Natalicium Schrijnen* (Nijmegen-Utrecht), pp. 79–85.

"Nootka Baby Words," *International Journal of American Linguistics*, 5: 118, 119.

[With Charles G. Blooah] "Some Gweabo Proverbs," *Africa*, 2: 183–185.

"Religions and Religious Phenomena," in Baker Brownell, ed., *Religious Life* (Man and His World, Vol. 11) (New York), pp. 11–33; printed also in *The American Mercury* (1928), *q.v.*

"A Study in Phonetic Symbolism," *Journal of Experimental Psychology*, 12: 225–239.

"The Discipline of Sex," *The American Mercury*, 16: 413–420; printed also in *Child Study* (1930), *q.v.*

"A Linguistic Trip among the Navaho Indians," *The Gallup Independent* (Ceremonial Ed., Aug. 23, 1929, Gallup, N.M.), pp. 1–2.

"What Is the Family Still Good For?" *Winnetka Conference on the Family* (Oct. 28), pp. 31–34; also published in *The American Mercury* (1930), *q.v.*

Review of M. E. DeWitt, *Our Oral Word as Social and Economic Factor*, in *American Journal of Sociology*, 34: 926–927.

Review of Waldo Frank, *The Rediscovery of America*, in *American Journal of Sociology*, 35: 335–336.

"The Skepticism of Bertrand Russell," review of Bertrand Russell, *Sceptical Essays*, in *The New Republic*, 57: 196.

"Franz Boas," review of Franz Boas, *Anthropology and Modern Life,* in *The New Republic,* 57: 278–279.

"Design in Pueblo Pottery," review of R. L. Bunzel, *The Pueblo Potter,* in *The New Republic,* 61: 115.

1930

[With Leslie Spier] *Wishram Ethnography,* University of Washington Publications in Anthropology, 3: 151–300.

Totality, Linguistic Society of America, Language Monographs, No. 6. 28 pp.

The Southern Paiute Language: Southern Paiute, a Shoshonean Language; Texts of the Kaibab Paiutes and Uintah Utes; Southern Paiute Dictionary, Proceedings, American Academy of Arts and Sciences, 65: (no. 1), pp. 1–296; (no. 2), pp. 297–536; (no. 3) (1931), pp. 537–730.

Proceedings, Second Colloquium on Personality Investigation; Held under the Joint Auspices of the American Psychiatric Association and of the Social Science Research Council (Baltimore, Md.), pp. 37–41, 122–125.

[With Albert G. Sandoval] "A Note on Navaho Pottery," *American Anthropologist,* n.s., 32: 575–576.

"Our Business Civilization," review of James Truslow Adams, *Our Business Civilization: Some Aspects of American Culture,* in *Current History,* 32: 426–428.

"The Discipline of Sex," *Child Study* (March), pp. 170–173, 187–188; printed also in *The American Mercury* (1929), *q.v.*

"What Is the Family Still Good For?" *American Mercury,* 19: 145–151; printed also in *Winnetka Conference on the Family* (1929), *q.v.*

1931

"Communication," *Encyclopaedia of the Social Sciences* (New York), 4: 78–81.

"Dialect," *Encyclopaedia of the Social Sciences* (New York), 5: 123–126.

"Fashion," *Encyclopaedia of the Social Sciences* (New York), 6: 139–144.

"Custom," *Encyclopaedia of the Social Sciences* (New York), 4: 658–662.

"Language, Race, and Culture," (chap. 10 of *Language,* New York, 1921, *q.v.*) in V. F. Calverton, ed., *The Making of Man* (New York), pp. 142–156.

Review of Ray Hoffman, *Nuer-English Dictionary,* in *American Anthropologist,* n.s., 33: 114–115.

"The Concept of Phonetic Law as Tested in Primitive Languages by Leonard Bloomfield," in Stuart A. Rice, ed., *Methods in Social Science: A Case Book* (Chicago), pp. 297–306.

"Notes on the Gweabo Language of Liberia," *Language,* 7: 30–41.

"The Case for a Constructed International Language" *Propositions, Deuxième Congrès International de Linguistes (Geneva, Aug. 25–29),* pp. 42–44.

"The Function of an International Auxiliary Language," *Psyche,* 11: 4–15; also published in *International Communication: A Symposium on the Language Problem,* by H. N. Shenton, E. Sapir, O. Jesperson (London, 1931), pp. 65–94.

"Wanted, a World Language," *The American Mercury,* 22: 202–209.

1932

"Group," *Encyclopaedia of the Social Sciences* (New York), 7: 178–182.

[With Morris Swadesh] *The Expression of the Ending-Point Relation in English, French, and German* (Alice V. Morris, ed.), Linguistic Society of America, Language Monographs, No. 10. 125 pp.

"Tw ، Navaho Puns," *Language*, 8: 217–219.
"Cultural Anthropology and Psychiatry," *Journal of Abnormal and Social Psychology*, 27: 229–242.
Review of James G. Leyburn, *Handbook of Ethnography*, in *American Journal of Science*, 5th series, 23: 186–189.

1933

"Language," *Encyclopaedia of the Social Sciences* (New York), 9: 155–169.
"La Réalité Psychologique des Phonèmes," *Journal de Psychologie Normale et Pathologique* (Paris), 30: 247–265.

1934

"Personality," *Encyclopaedia of the Social Sciences* (New York), 12: 85–87.
"Symbolism," *Encyclopaedia of the Social Sciences* (New York), 14: 492–495.
"The Emergence of the Concept of Personality in a Study of Cultures," *Journal of Social Psychology*, 5: 408–415.
"Hittite *hepatis* "Vassal" and Greek ὁ παδός," *Language*, 10: 274–279.
[With others] "Some Orthographic Recommendations," *American Anthropologist*, n.s., 36: 629–631.
"The Bush Negro of Dutch Guiana," review of Melville J. Herskovits and Frances S. Herskovits, *Rebel Destiny: Among the Bush Negroes of Dutch Guiana*, in *The Nation*, 139: 135.

1935

Review of A. G. Morice, *The Carrier Language (Déné Family): A Grammar and Dictionary Combined*, in *American Anthropologist*, n.s., 37: 500–501.
"A Navaho Sand Painting Blanket," *American Anthropologist*, n.s., 37: 609–616.

1936

"Kutchin Relationship Terms," in Cornelius Osgood, *Contributions to the Ethnography of the Kutchin*, Yale University Publications in Anthropology, No. 14, pp. 136–137.
"Hupa Tattooing," in R. H. Lowie, ed., *Essays in Anthropology Presented to Alfred Louis Kroeber* (Berkeley), pp. 273–277.
"Greek ἀτύζομαι, a Hittite Loanword, and Its Relatives," *Language*, 12: 175–180.
"Tibetan Influences on Tocharian. I," *Language*, 12: 259–271.
Review of D. Westermann and Ida C. Ward, *Practical Phonetics for Students of African Languages*, in *American Anthropologist*, n.s., 38: 121–122.
"Internal Linguistic Evidence Suggestive of the Northern Origin of the Navaho," *American Anthropologist*, n.s., 38: 224–235.
"Hebrew 'argắz, a Philistine Word," *Journal of the American Oriental Society*, 56: 272–281.
"κίμβδα, a Karian Gloss," *Journal of the American Oriental Society*, 56: 85.

1937

"The Contribution of Psychiatry to an Understanding of Behavior in Society," *American Journal of Sociology*, 42: 862–870.
"Hebrew 'Helmet,' a Loanword, and Its Bearing on Indo-European Phonology," *Journal of the American Oriental Society*, 57: 73–77.

"The Negroes of Haiti," review of Melville J. Herskovits, *Life in a Haitian Valley*, in *The Yale Review*, 26: 853–854.
Review of James A. Montgomery and Zellig S. Harris, *The Ras Shamra Mythological Texts*, in *Language*, 13: 326–331.

1938

"Hittite *siyanta* and Gen. 14: 3," *American Journal of Semitic Languages and Literatures*, 55: 86–88.
"Glottalized Continuants in Navaho, Nootka, and Kwakiutl (with a Note on Indo-European)," *Language*, 14: 248–274.
Foreword to Walter Dyk, *Son of Old Man Hat* (New York), pp. v–x.
"Why Cultural Anthropology Needs the Psychiatrist," *Psychiatry*, 1: 7–12.
Review of Thurman W. Arnold, *The Folklore of Capitalism*, in *Psychiatry*, 1: 145–147.
"Psychiatric and Cultural Pitfalls in the Business of Getting a Living," (advance contribution to Symposium on Mental Health, Section on Medical Sciences, American Association for the Advancement of Science, Winter Meeting, Richmond, Va.: Session IV, Physical and Cultural Environment, Thursday afternoon, December 29, 1938). Mimeographed. Published also in *Mental Health* (1939), *q.v.*

1939

[With Morris Swadesh] *Nootka Texts: Tales and Ethnological Narratives with Grammatical Notes and Lexical Materials*, William Dwight Whitney Linguistic Series, Linguistic Society of America (Philadelphia). 334 pp.
"Indo-European Prevocalic *s* in Macedonian," *American Journal of Philology*, 40: 463–465; published also in "From Sapir's Desk . . ." (1939), *q.v.*
"Songs for a Comox Dancing Mask" (edited by Leslie Spier), *Ethnos* (Stockholm), 4: 49–55.
Review of Zellig S. Harris, *A Grammar of the Phoenician Language*, in *Language*, 15: 60–65.
"From Sapir's Desk: Indo-European Prevocalic *s* in Macedonian; The Indo-European Words for 'Tear'" (edited by H. S. Sturtevant), *Language*, 13: 178–187.
"Psychiatric and Cultural Pitfalls in the Business of Getting a Living," *Mental Health*, Publication of the American Association for the Advancement of Science, No. 9, pp. 237–244; also mimeographed (1938).

1942

Navaho Texts, with Supplementary Texts by Harry Hoijer, edited by Harry Hoijer, Linguistic Society of America (Philadelphia). 543 pp.

1943

[With Leslie Spier] *Notes on the Culture of the Yana*, University of California Publications: Anthropological Records, 3: 239–298.

1944

"Grading, a Study in Semantics," *Philosophy of Science*, 11: 93–116.

1947

"The Relation of American Indian Linguistics to General Linguistics," *Southwestern Journal of Anthropology*, pp. 1–4.

POEMS

1917

"The Moth," *The Minaret*, June, p. 26; reprinted in *Dreams and Gibes* (1917).

"The Music of the Spheres," *The Minaret*, June, p. 28.

"Epitaph of a Philosopher," in *A Roycroft Anthology*, selected and edited by John T. Hoyle (East Aurora, N.Y.), p. 142; reprinted in *Dreams and Gibes* (1917).

Dreams and Gibes (Boston, The Poet Lore Company, Badger).

1918

"Reproof," *The Dial*, January 31, p. 102.

"Del Inferno," *The Pagan*, July, pp. 22–23; reprinted in *A Second Pagan Anthology*, pp. 57–59.

"In Days of Gloom—1918," *The Canadian Magazine*, August, p. 332.

"War," *The Pagan*, October, p. 13.

"In a Magic Wood of the Night," *The Stratford Journal*, October, pp. 164–165.

"Old Friends Meet Again," *The Pagan*, November, p. 35.

"Lines for an Unhappy Tragedian," *ibid.*, December, p. 42.

1919

"Prelude," *The Pagan.*, January, p. 31.

"The House-God," *ibid.*, p. 47.

"When the Greens of the Field Are Shot with Gold," *The University Magazine* (Montreal), February, p. 80.

"Snowstorm in the Dusk," *The Pagan*, February, p. 15; reprinted in *A Second Pagan Anthology*, p. 59.

"After the Rain," *The Pagan*, March, p. 24; reprinted in *A Second Pagan Anthology*, p. 60.

"An Evening Sky," *The Pagan*, April, p. 49.

"The Mirror (in the Manner of a Day-Dream)," *Youth*, April, pp. 78–79.

"The House of Virtues," *The Pagan*, May, p. 42.

"Twilight at the Beach," *ibid.*, June, p. 23.

"The Soul of Summer," *Poetry*, August, p. 248.

"Mary, Mary, My Love," *ibid.*, p. 249.

"Rain-Storm," *The Pagan*, July–August, pp. 48–49.

"A Song of the Fields and the Past," *The Canadian Magazine*, September, p. 380.

"The Chasm," *The Pagan*, September, p. 34.

"The Pool of Shadows," *ibid.*, October, pp. 33–34.

1920

"Your Voice," *The Pagan.*, February, p. 19.

"Helen of Troy," *The New Republic*, March 10, p. 58.

"God," *Contemporary Verse*, March, p. 34.

"Woven Silence," *The Pagan*, June, p. 41.

"The Harvest," *The Nation*, June 19, p. 825.

"French-Canadian Folk-Songs" (trans.), *Poetry*, July, pp. 175–185: "The Prince of Orange"; "The Dumb Shepherdess"; "The King of Spain's Daughter and the Diver"; "White as the Snow." (Note on French-Canadian Folk-Songs, *ibid.*, pp. 210–213.)

"The House of Tradition," *The Freeman*, September 22, p. 37.

"Gammer Collins," *ibid.*

"These River-Folk," *ibid.*, October 6, p. 88.

"Ballad of a Swan Maiden," *The Canadian Bookman*, December, p. 17; reprinted in *The Stratford Monthly*, July, 1924, pp. 46–48.

"Sullen Silence," *The Pagan*, April–May.

1921

"Backwater," *Poetry*, May, pp. 76–79: "A Childish Tale"; "The Old Town"; "Overlooked"; "She Sits Vacant-Eyed."

"Two Sonnets," *The Canadian Bookman*, June, p. 37: "The Tryst"; "A Sonnet of Rain."

"A Girl," *The Measure*, June, p. 14.

"Women Play Mandolines before Night," *The Measure*, August, p. 10.

"The Blind, Old Indian Tells His Names," *The Canadian Bookman*, September, pp. 38–40.

"The House to the Incoming Tenants," *The Nation*, September 7, p. 261.

"The Moon's Not Always Beautiful," *The Double Dealer*, October, p. 130.

"Upholding the World," *ibid.*, November, p. 221.

"Barker," *The Pagan*, October–November, p. 54.

1922

"Vestments," *The Double Dealer*, January, p. 41.

"Mist and Gleam," *The Pagan*, December, 1921—January, 1922, p. 51.

"Falling Asleep," *The Canadian Magazine*, February, p. 323.

"Ginger Spirits," *The International Interpreter*, April 8, p. 27.

"Three Folk-Songs of French Canada" (trans.), *Queen's Quarterly*, January–March, pp. 286–290: "The Return of the Soldier Husband"; "I Will Not Marry"; "The Trades."

"The King of Thule," *The Nation*, July 26, p. 96.

"A Walking Poem," *Poetry*, September, p. 317.

"Optimist" (from "Bubbles"), *The Double Dealer*, September, p. 131.

"Poems," *Queen's Quarterly*, July–September, pp. 20–25: "They Pity Her from Sunlight"; "Across the Years"; "To Joseph Conrad"; "The House of My Beloved"; "The Halt of Summer"; "No Miracle."

"Poems," *The Canadian Forum*, September, p. 753: "The Corn-Field"; "Sunset Verandah"; "To a Returned Soldier."

1923

"Three White Nuns," *The Canadian Magazine*, May, p. 18.

"Poems," *The Canadian Forum*, September, pp. 366–367: "The Measurer"; "Dreams"; "The Clock"; "This Age": "The Dispossessed"; "Philistine"; "Interlude": "Titans."

"Poetry," *Queen's Quarterly*, October–December, pp. 182–184: "The Jackal"; "A Pair of Tricksters"; "Gossip of the Gods."

1924

"This Age," *Voices*, December, 1923–January, 1924, p. 18.

"The Oil-Merchant," *The Canadian Forum*, January, pp. 111–112.

"Dawn," *The Stratford Monthly*, April, p. 62.

"The Squirrel," *ibid.*, June, p. 255.

"Promise of Summer," *The Double Dealer*, July, p. 160.

"Down to the Shore of the Thundering Sea," *The Canadian Forum*, September, p. 368.

"Warning"; "Distant Strumming of Strings"; "Vague Flutings"; "Drums": *The Canadian Forum*, November, p. 53.

"The Firmament Advises Man," *The Stratford Monthly*, November, p. 106.

"The Workshop," *The Double Dealer*, November–December, p. 55.

"Cogitatio Mystica"; "Poet's Coterie": *Voices*, December, p. 45.

1925

"Miriam Sings Three Hymns," *The Canadian Forum*, January, p. 110.

"Time's Wing," *The Nation*, January 21, p. 71.

"Music"; "For One a Little Awkward of Speech": *The Measure*, January, p. 11.

"The White Bird," *The Stratford Monthly*, January, pp. 17–18.

[With Marius Barbeau] *Folk Songs of French Canada* (New Haven; Yale University Press), 216 pp.

"Three Sonnets," *Voices*, March, pp. 135–136: "Ariel (to M.M.)"; "To the Silent Snow"; "Susquehanna Hills."

"Poems," *The Canadian Forum*, April, p. 210: "Christ Destroyer"; "Two Souls"; "Youth."

"Chronicle"; "Worms, Wind and Stone": *The Measure*, July, pp. 8–9.

"Her Reproach," *The Canadian Forum*, June, p. 270.

"Lovers of Happiness," *The Nation*, July 8, p. 72.

"The Siding," *The Canadian Forum*, July, p. 307.

"Be Not Afraid of Beauty"; "Quiescence"; "Lovers' Night"; "Where the Little Children Ride": *The Measure*, July, pp. 6–10.

"The Circus," *The Double Dealer*, June, p. 180.

"I Seek Returning Steps," *The Canadian Forum*, October, p. 13.

"Four Poems," *Voices*, October, pp. 16–18: "The Youth, Girolama Savonarola, Prophesies"; "The Hunt"; "The Window of His Soul"; "A Man Has Misgivings about a Stone Creature."

1926

"Foam Waves," *Poetry*, January, pp. 175–182: "Signal"; "Three Hags Come Visiting"; "Zuni"; "Messengers"; "Young Grief"; "Come with the Wind"; "Charon"; "She Went to Sleep Below."

"Dream of the Dead," *The Canadian Forum*, January, p. 118.

"For César Franck's Music"; "A Boy Plays Beethoven at the Piano": *The Forge* (Vol. 1, No. 1), p. 12.

"Three Poems," *Palms*, March, pp. 182–184: "By the Water"; "Star-Gazer"; "Revery Interrupts Time."

"Into the Sea," *The Canadian Forum*, March, p. 183.

"Six Poems," *Voices*, April, pp. 203–296: "Wind-Music"; "The Mother Loves and Fears"; "The Soul Stands Up"; "The Little Girl Reads Her First Story"; "My House is Sitting Eyeless on the Sea"; "Epistle."

"Poems," *The Canadian Forum*, May, p. 246: "Advice to a Girl"; "Memory."

"The Boy," *The Forge*, Spring number, p. 8.

"Music Brings Griefs," *The Nation*, July 28, p. 85.

"How You Were More Beautiful than Dusk," *The Canadian Forum*, October, p. 407.

1927

"Thoughts on the Soul," *Voices*, December, 1926–January, 1927, pp. 55–58.

"Poems," *The Canadian Forum*, February, p. 148: "The Fingers Are Not Flesh"; "Though You Have Set Up Hatred for a Sign"; "Dream Journey."

"Sing Bitter Song," *The Canadian Forum*, April, p. 210.

"Escape into the Night," *The Nation*, June 1, p. 612.

"Feathered Songs," *Poetry*, July, pp. 194–196: "Blowing Winds"; "He Implores His Beloved"; "The Tribune Tower"; "When Long in His Eye."

"Love Has Tears," *The Canadian Forum*, August, p. 340.

"Poetic-Philosophic Apostrophe," *The Forge*, Summer number, p. 14.

"Dirge," *The Dial*, September, p. 208.

1928

"Yet Water Runs Again," *The Dial*, June, p. 468.

"Involvement," *The Menorah Journal*, July, p. 50.

1929

"Rain on the Railroad Yards," *The Dial*, January, p. 42.

"About Love," *Palms*, January, pp. 104–106: "Body and Spirit"; "Somewhat Neglected"; "When Love Came."

1931

"Modern Sophisticate," *The Circle*, March, p. 28.

"Three Poems," *Poetry*, November, pp. 80–81: "Autumn Raindrops"; "Levels"; "God Blows a Message."